255744

158.65 DD

D0559276

THEATRICAL DESIGN IN
THE TWENTIETH CENTURY

Recent Titles in
Bibliographies and Indexes in the Performing Arts

THEATRICAL DESIGN IN THE TWENTIETH CENTURY

An Index to Photographic Reproductions of Scenic Designs

Compiled by

W. Patrick Atkinson

Bibliographies and Indexes in the Performing Arts,
Number 21

GREENWOOD PRESS
Westport, Connecticut • London

REF
PN
2091
.S8
T47
1996

Theatrical design in the twentieth century :
REF PN 2091 .S8 T47 1996

255744

Von Can

Southern Virginia University

Library of Congress Cataloging-in-Publication Data

Theatrical design in the twentieth century : an index to photographic
    reproductions of scenic designs / compiled by W. Patrick Atkinson.
        p.   cm.—(Bibliographies and indexes in the performing arts,
    ISSN 0742–6933 ; no. 21)
        Includes bibliographical references and index.
        ISBN 0–313–29701–0 (alk. paper)
        1. Theaters—Stage–setting and scenery—Indexes.   I. Atkinson, W.
    Patrick.   II. Series.
    PN2091.S8T47   1996
    016.792′025—dc20   96–4975

British Library Cataloguing in Publication Data is available.

Copyright © 1996 by W. Patrick Atkinson

All rights reserved. No portion of this book may be
reproduced, by any process or technique, without the
express written consent of the publisher.

Library of Congress Catalog Card Number: 96–4975
ISBN: 0–313–29701–0
ISSN: 0742–6933

First published in 1996

Greenwood Press, 88 Post Road West, Westport, CT 06881
An imprint of Greenwood Publishing Group, Inc.

Printed in the United States of America

The paper used in this book complies with the
Permanent Paper Standard issued by the National
Information Standards Organization (Z39.48–1984).

P

In order to keep this title in print and available to the academic community, this edition
was produced using digital reprint technology in a relatively short print run. This would
not have been attainable using traditional methods. Although the cover has been changed
from its original appearance, the text remains the same and all materials and methods
used still conform to the highest book-making standards.

Contents

Preface

No matter how much verbal discussion occurs concerning theatrical scene design over the past one hundred years, a complete description will of necessity involve graphics. Resources locating many collections of original scenic and costume designs are becoming available but may not provide a method to compare works of various designers. Since original designs may not easily be accessible to the casual researcher, photographic reproductions offer the only way most people can view these works. Many sources containing photographs are available, but comparing different productions of the same play may require arduous research. This index of one hundred and fourteen books and journals focuses on photographs of twentieth century sets, renderings, and models of theatre and opera productions. The selected publications consist of books about theatre history, scenic design, and stagecraft, as well as design exhibition catalogs and books about specific designers or types of productions. Most research libraries will hold many of these books, which should serve as a starting point for additional research.

In general, I have indexed only theatre and opera productions. Designs for dance or ballet are listed only if they are included in the output of a significant designer or if they are for commonly recognized and frequently produced works. The photos selected are those showing most if not all of the scenic design. Occasional photos show very little of a setting but have enough detail to establish a sense of the total visual picture.

Titles of productions found in photograph captions are sometimes abbreviated or written in the language of the country where the play was produced. I generally listed play titles as they are shown in the written text or in the photograph's caption, but made occasional changes to provide for easier reference. Commonly used abbreviated versions of a title may be cross-referenced with the complete title. Titles of well-known plays captioned in more than one language may be changed to the most commonly used translation so as to appear in a single location in the listing.

Designer's names may have different spellings, depending upon the origin of the text. When a name has more than one spelling, I chose the most common to reduce confusion in alphabetizing. Since published captions do not always indicate all of the participants, not all designers are identified along with their designs. Designer's names were included if other sources yielded the information.

The location of a production can sometimes be difficult to establish. When possible, the name of the theatre and its location will be listed. For multiple productions of the same play, the location of the production shown in the photograph is the one listed. If the production location is not established, the production company may be listed instead. The researcher may notice an occasional discrepancy between a production date or location shown in this index and the information listed in the caption of a particular photograph. In such cases, I made the change when reliable sources indicated the caption to be in error. The index generally provides the date and location of the illustrated production's premiere. Dates of subsequent productions may also be listed if their photographs are indexed. If a theatre has changed names over the years, the most recent name is the one used here. I have used the currently accepted names of cities and countries to avoid confusion about name changes since the beginning of the twentieth century. This is also true of productions in countries that have since split into two or more smaller states. I retained original names when the country's current name could not be determined. Occasionally, I retained the country as named in a caption when the caption listed the theatre and country without locating the city.

Although over seven thousand productions by more than two thousand designers are indexed in this volume, it is far from complete. Hundreds of books and periodicals published since 1900 offer thousands of additional photographic sources. The eventual catalog of twentieth century scenic design will document a vast amount of work by theatre artists around the world.

Using the Index

This publication consists of three sections. The first section is a bibliography alphabetized by the reference codes used in the index. These codes are generally based on an abbreviation of the book title. Although the entries in this section list bibliographic information needed to locate the source book, there really are only two parts to each entry, the code letters, shown in bold-face, and the bibliographic information. Two examples are shown here:

BTD   Goodwin, John. *British Theatre Design*. New York: St. Martin's, 1989.
TDT   *Theatre Design & Technology*. Journal of United States Institute for Theatre Technology.

The second section presents the production index. In this section, the play title is followed by the name of the designer, the production or company location, and production date. Descriptive information indicates the specific nature of the photograph: black & white, color, rendering, model, or setting. The description of the photograph is followed by bibliographic information including the three or four-letter source code noted in the previous paragraph. Each entry thus consists of a maximum of ten data fields. An example of a complete entry looks like this:

Follies[1].
   Aronson, Boris[2]. Winter Garden Theatre, NYC[3]: 1971[4]. B&W[5]. Set[6].
      TDT[7], vol. XXIV, n. 3 (Fall 1988)[8]. 17[9]. 2 photos[10].

1. Play title.

2. Scenic designer.

3. Production location or company.

4. Production date.

5. Photo type: Either black & white or color.

6. What the photograph depicts: Generally a rendering, model, or the actual setting.

7. Source code (refer to section 1).

8. Issue if the source is a magazine or journal.

9. Page number. If entries are listed as illustration numbers or plate numbers instead of by page number, that information will be noted.

10. Notes: This entry may list how many photos of the design are depicted for that entry, or perhaps a specific scene of the production if given in the caption.

An entry with more than one photo of the same play may look like this:

Siegfried.
> Svoboda, Josef. Royal Opera House, Covent Garden, London: 1975. B&W. Set. **JSS**, 68. Act III, sc. 1; B&W. Set. **JSS**, 68; B&W. Set. **JSS**, 70. Act II; Color. Set. **JSS**, between 54 & 55. Act I; B&W. Set. **STS**, 83; B&W. Model. **TDT**, vol. XII, n. 2 (Summer 1976). 30; B&W. Set. **TDT**, vol. XV, n. 1 (Spring 1979). 8; Grand Theater, Geneva: 1976. B&W. Set. **JSS**, 88. Act II; B&W. Set. **JSS**, 90. Act III, sc. 1; Color. Set. **JSS**, between 54 & 55. Act I; Color. Set. **TDT**, vol. XXVIII, n. 5 (Fall 1992). 9; Czechoslovakia: B&W. Model. **TDT**, vol. XVI, n. 1 (Spring 1980). 29.

Note that this entry indicates 7 photos of a 1975 production in London, 4 photos of a 1976 production in Geneva, and 1 photo of a production in Czechoslovakia.

The third section lists all photographic reproductions alphabetized by the scenic designer's name. For example:

Aronson, Boris[1]. *Follies*[2]. **TDT**[3], vol. XXIV, n. 3 (Fall 1988)[4]. 17[5].

1. Scenic designer.

2. Play title.

3. Source code (refer to section 1).

4. Issue if the source is a magazine or journal.

5. Page number.

Reference Codes

ALW Walsh, Michael. *Andrew Lloyd Webber: His Life and Works*. New York: Abrams, 1989.

ASC *Artists Sets and Costumes: Recent Collaborations between Painters and Sculptors and Dance, Opera, and Theater* (exhibition catalog). Philadelphia: Philadelphia College of Art, 1977.

ASD1 Aronson, Arnold. *American Set Design*. New York: TCG, 1985.

ASD2 Smith, Ronn. *American Set Design 2*. New York: TCG, 1991.

AST Rischbieter, Henning, ed. *Art and the Stage in the Twentieth Century*. Greenwich: New York Graphic Society, 1969.

BAT Waldemar, George. *Boris Aronson et l'Art du Théâtre*. Paris: Editions des Chroniques du jour. 1928.

BMF Jackson, Arthur. *The Best Musicals from Showboat to A Chorus Line*. New York: Crown, 1977.

BSE1 United States Institute for Theatre Technology. *The First Biennial Scenography Exposition* (exhibition catalog). New York: USITT, 1980.

BSE2 United States Institute for Theatre Technology. *The Second Biennial Scenography Exposition* (exhibition catalog). New York: USITT, 1982.

BSE3 United States Institute for Theatre Technology. *Third Biennial Scenography Exposition* (exhibition catalog). New York: USITT, 1984.

BSE4 United States Institute for Theatre Technology. *Fourth Biennial Scenography Exposition* (exhibition catalog). New York: USITT, 1986.

BSE5 United States Institute for Theatre Technology. *Design Exposition '88; Scenery, Costumes, and Lighting in the Performing Arts* (exhibition catalog). New York: USITT, 1988.

BTD Goodwin, John. *British Theatre Design*. New York: St. Martin's, 1989.

BWM Gottfried, Martin. *Broadway Musicals*. New York: Abrams, 1979.

CBM Willett, John. *Caspar Neher: Brecht's Designer*. London: Methuen, 1986.

CBS Spencer, Charles. *Cecil Beaton Stage and Film Designs*. New York: St. Martin's, 1975.

CGA Drogheda, Lord, Ken Davison, and Andrew Wheatcroft. *The Covent Garden Album*. London: Routledge & Kegan Paul, 1981.

COT Walton, J. Michael, ed. *Craig On Theatre*. London: Methuen, 1983.

CSC MacGowan, Kenneth and Robert Edmond Jones. *Continental Stagecraft*. New York: Harcourt, 1922.

CSD   Burdick, Elizabeth, ed. *Contemporary Stage Design U.S.A.* Middletown, Wesleyan UP, 1974.

DDT   Pecktal, Lynn. *Designing and Drawing for the Theatre.* New York: McGraw-Hill, 1995.

DFT   Jones, Robert Edmond. *Drawings for the Theatre.* New York: Theatre Arts, 1970.

DIT   Sheringham, George. *Design in the Theatre.* New York: Albert & Charles Boni, 1927.

DMS   Warre, Michael. *Designing and Making Stage Scenery.* New York: Reinhold, 1966.

DOT   Nicoll, Allardyce. *The Development of Theatre.* 5th ed. rev. New York: Harcourt, 1966.

DPT   Pecktal, Lynn. *Designing and Painting for the Theatre.* Holt, 1975.

DSL   Bellman, W.F. *Scene Design, Stage Lighting, Sound, Costume, and Makeup.* Harper, 1983.

DTT   Mielzinger, Jo. *Designing for the Theatre: A Memoir and a Portfolio.* New York: Bramhall, 1965.

EED   Elder, Eldon. *Eldon Elder: Designs for the Theatre.* New York: Drama Book Specialists, 1978.

EGC   Bablet, Denis. *Edward Gordon Craig.* New York: Theatre Arts, 1966.

EIF   Held, R.L. *Endless Innovations: Frederick Kiesler's Theory and Scenic Design.* Ann Arbor: UMI Research Press, 1982.

FCS   Oenslager, Donald. *Stage Design: Four Centuries of Scenic Invention.* New York: Viking. 1975.

FCT   Oenslager, Donald. *Four Centuries of Theater Design; Drawings from the Donald Oenslager Collection.* New Haven: Yale University Art Gallery, 1964.

HOB   Kislan, Richard. *Hoofing on Broadway.* New York: Prentice, 1987.

HPA   Hirsch, Foster. *Harold Prince and the American Musical Theatre.* Cambridge: Cambridge UP, 1989.

HPR   Ilson, Carol. *Harold Prince-From Pajama Game to Phantom of the Opera.* Ann Arbor: UMI Research Press, 1989.

HPS   Friedman, Martin L. *Hockney Paints the Stage.* New York: Abbeville, 1983.

JSS   Burian, Jarka. *Svoboda: Wagner-Josef Svoboda's Scenography for Richard Wagner's Operas.* Middletown: Wesleyan UP, 1983.

LBT   Schouvaloff, Alexander. *Leon Bakst: The Theatre Art.* London: Philip Wilson, 1991.

LST   Sainthill, Loudon. *Loudin Sainthill.* London: Hutchenson, 1973.

MAM   Altman, Richard. *The Making of a Musical: Fiddler on the Roof.* New York: Crown, 1971.

MBM   Gottfried, Martin. *More Broadway Musicals.* New York: Abrams, 1991.

MCD   Mander, Raymond and Joe Mitchenson. *Musical Comedy: A Story in Pictures.* New York: Taplinger, 1969.

MCN   Appelbaum, Stanley. *The New York Stage: Famous production Photographs.* New York: Dover, 1976.

MEM   Messel, Oliver. *Oliver Messel: An Exhibition Held at the Theatre Museum, Victoria and Albert Museum.* London: Robert Stockwell, 1983.

MOM   Jacobson, Robert. *Magnificence Onstage at the Met.* New York: Simon & Schuster, 1985.

MOR   Corey, Irene. *The Mask of Reality: An Approach to Design for Theatre.* Anchorage, KY: Anchorage, 1968.

MOT   Meyerhold, Vsevolod. *Meyerhold On Theatre.* New York: Hill & Wang, 1969.

MRH   Sayler, Oliver M., ed. *Max Reinhardt and His Theatre.* Benjamin Blom, 1968.

MRT   Fuhrich-Leisler, Edda. ed. *Max Reinhardt: "...ein Theater, das den Menschen wieder Freude gibt."* Vienna: Osterreichisches Theatermuseum. 1983.

NTO   Gorelik, Mordecai. *New Theatres for Old.* New York: Samuel French, 1940.

OAT   Craig, Edward Gordon. *On The Art Of The Theatre.* New York: Theatre Arts, 1956.

OMB   Castle, Charles. *Oliver Messel: a Biography.* London: Thames & Hudson, 1986.

OPE   Hartmann, Rudolf. ed. *Opera.* New York: William Morrow, 1976.

PLT   Simonson, Lee. *Part of a Lifetime.* New York: Duell, 1943.

PST   Russell, Douglas A. *Period Style for the Theatre.* Boston: Allyn & Bacon, 1987.

RAG   *Stage Designs and the Russian Avant-Garde.* Washington: International Exhibitions Foundation, 1976.

RBS   Green, Stanley. *Ring Bells! Sing Songs! Broadway Musicals of the 1930's.* New Rochelle: Arlington, 1983.

REJ   Pendleton, Ralph, ed. *The Theatre of Robert Edmond Jones.* Middletown: Wesleyan UP, 1958.

RSC   *Russian Stage and Costume Designs for the Ballet, Opera, and Theatre.* Washington: International Exhibitions Foundation, 1967.

RSD   Bablet, Denis. *The Revolutions of Stage Design in the 20th Century.* Paris: Leon Amiel, 1977.

RST   Rudnitsky, Konstantin. *Russian and Soviet Theatre 1905-1932.* New York: Abrams, 1988.

RWT   *Robert Wilson: The Theater of Images.* New York: Harper, 1984.

SCM   Komisarjevsky, Theodore and Lee Simonson. *Settings and Costumes of the Modern Stage.* New York: Benjamin Blom, 1966.

SCT   Arnold, Richard. *Scene Technology.* 2nd ed. Englewood Cliffs: Prentice, 1990.

SDA   Larson, Orville K. *Scene Design in the American Theatre from 1915 to 1960.* Fayetteville: Arkansas UP 1989.

SDB   Bay, Howard. *Stage Design.* New York: Drama Book, 1974.

SDC   Cheney, Sheldon. *Stage Decoration.* New York: Benjamin Blom, 1966. to 1928

SDD   Owen, Bobbi. *Scenic Design on Broadway: Designers and Their Credits, 1915-1990.* New York: Greenwood, 1991.

SDE   Frette, Guido. *Stage Design.* Milan: G. G. Görlich, 1955.

SDG   Rosenfeld, Sybil. *A Short History of Scenic Design in Great Britain.* Totowa, NJ: Rowman & Littlefield, 1973.

SDL   Parker, Wilford Oren and R. Craig Wolf. *Scene Design and Stage Lighting.* 6th ed. Fort Worth: Holt, 1990.

SDO   Oenslager, Donald. *Stage Design: Four Centuries of Scenic Invention.* New York: Viking, 1975.

SDR   Rowell, Kenneth. *Stage Design.* New York: Van Nostrand Reinhold, 1968.

SDT   Spoore, Dennis J. *Scene Design in the Theatre.* Englewood Cliffs: Prentice, 1990.

SDW1   Hainaux, René and Yves-Bonnat. *Stage Design Throughout the World Since 1935.* New York: Theatre Arts, 1956.

SDW2   Hainaux, René and Yves-Bonnat. *Stage Design Throughout the World Since 1950.* New York: Theatre Arts, 1964.

SDW3   Hainaux, René and Yves-Bonnat. *Stage Design Throughout the World Since 1960.* New York: Theatre Arts, 1973.

SDW4   Hainaux, Rene. *Stage Design Throughout the World, 1970-1975.* New York: Theatre Arts, 1976.

SFT   Burris-Meyer, Harold and Edward C. Cole. *Scenery for the Theatre.* Boston: Little, 1971.

SIO   Rebora, Roberto. *Scenografia in Italia oggi*. Milan: Görlich Editore, 1974.

SIP   Payne, Darwin. *The Scenographic Imagination*. 3rd ed.. Carbondale: Southern Illinois UP, 1993.

SJS   Burian, Jarka. *The Scenography of Josef Svoboda*. Middletown, CT : Wesleyan UP, 1971.

SON   Gottfried, Martin. *Sondheim*. New York: Abrams, 1993.

SOS   Speaght, Robert. *Shakespeare on the Stage*. Boston: Little, 1973.

SOW   *Stages of the World; a Pictorial Survey of the Theatre*. New York: Theatre Arts, 1949.

SST   Bellman, Willard. *Scenography and Stage Technology: An Introduction*. New York: Harper, 1977.

STN   Oenslager, Donald. *Scenery, Then and Now*. New York: W.W. Norton, 1966.

STS   Svoboda, Josef. *The Secret of Theatrical Space*. New York: Applause, 1993.

TAB   Rich, Frank. *The Theatre Art of Boris Aronson*. New York: Knopf, 1987.

TAS   Simonson, Lee. *The Art of Scenic Design*. New York: Harper, 1950.

TAT   Simonson, Lee, ed. *Theatre Art*. New York: Cooper Square, 1969.

TBB   Willett, John. *The Theatre of Bertolt Brecht*. London: Methuen, 1959.

TCI   *TCI* magazine. (formerly *Theatre Crafts*).

TCM   Payne, Darwin Reid. *Theory and Craft of the Scenographic Model*. Carbondale: Southern Illinois UP, 1985.

TCR   Sitarz, Paula Gaj. *The Curtain Rises*. Vol. II. Cincinnati: Betterway, 1993.

TCS1   Fuerst, Walter René and Samuel J. Hume. *Twentieth Century Stage Decorations*. Vol. 1. New York: Dover, 1967.

TCS2   Fuerst, Walter René and Samuel J. Hume. *Twentieth Century Stage Decorations*. Vol. 2. New York: Dover, 1967.

TCT   Glover, J. Garrett. *The Cubist Theatre*. Ann Arbor: UMI Research Press, 1983.

TDC   Binnie, Eric. *The Theatrical Designs of Charles Ricketts*. Ann Arbor, Michigan: UMI Research Press, 1985.

TDO   Oenslager, Donald. *The Theatre of Donald Oenslager*. Middletown: Wesleyan UP, 1978.

TDP   Gillette, J. Michael. *Theatrical Design and Production: An Introduction to Scene Design and Construction, Lighting, Sound, Costume, and Makeup*. Mountain View, CA: Mayfield, 1992.

TDT   *Theatre Design & Technology*. Journal of United States Institute for Theatre Technology.

TMI   Kislan, Richard. *The Musical*. New York: Prentice, 1980.

TMT   Lerner, Alan J. *The Musical Theatre: A Celebration*. New York: McGraw-Hill, 1986.

TNT   Craig, Edward Gordon. *Towards a New Theatre*. New York: Benjamin Blom, 1968.

TOP   Schouvaloff, Alexander. *Theatre on Paper*. London: Southeby's. 1990.

TPH   Altman, George. *Theater Pictorial: A History of World Theatre as Recorded in Drawings, Paintings, Engravings, and Photographs*. Berkeley and Los Angeles: University of California Press, 1953.

TSE   McNamara, Brooks, Jerry Rojo, and Richard Schechner. *Theatres, Spaces, Environments: 18 Projects*. New York: Drama Book, 1975.

TSS   Simonson, Lee. *The Stage is Set*. New York: Theatre Arts, 1963.

TSY   Russell, Douglas A. *Theatrical Style: A Visual Approach to the Theatre*. Palo Alto: Mayfield, 1976.

WLA   Appia, Adolphe. *The Work of Living Art*. Coral Gables: University of Miami Press, 1960.

WMC   Green, Stanley. *The World of Musical Comedy*. 4th ed. San Diego: A.S. Barnes, 1980.
WTP   Prideaux, Tom. *World Theatre in Pictures, from Ancient Times to Modern Broadway*. New York: Greenberg, 1953.

PRODUCTIONS

-A-

A quoi revent les jeunes filles.
    Moulaert, René. Théâtre du Marais, Brussels: 1923. B&W. Set. **TCS2**, plate 50.
A...My Name is Alice.
    Top of the Gate Cabaret, NYC: B&W. Set. **TCI**, vol. 19, n. 2 (Feb 1985). 30.
The Abduction from the Seraglio.
    Brown, Zack. Washington Opera, DC: 1982. B&W. Rendering. **TDT**, vol. XXVII, n. 3
        (Summer 1991). 11.
    Fielding, David. Scottish Opera, Edinburgh: B&W. Set. **TCI**, vol. 15, n. 5 (May 1981).
        15.
    Lynch, Thomas. San Francisco Opera: 1990. Color. Set. **TDT**, vol. XXVII, n. 3
        (Summer 1991). 9.
    Messel, Oliver. Glyndebourne Festival Opera, England: 1956. Color. Model. **OMB**,
        201.
    Oenslager, Donald. Central City Opera House, Colorado: 1946. B&W. Painter's
        elevations. **BSE2**, 54.
    Oenslager, Donald. Metropolitan Opera, NYC: 1946. B&W. Rendering. **TDO**, 115.
    _____. Oper Frankfurt at the Holland Festival: 1986. B&W. Set. **TCI**, vol. 24, n.
        5 (May 1990). 41.
Abe Lincoln in Illinois.
    Mielziner, Jo. Plymouth Theatre, NYC: 1938. B&W. Rendering. **DTT**, 112. Mrs.
        Lincoln's parlour; B&W. Set. **MCN**, 141; B&W. Rendering & set. **SDA**, 121. 2
        photos.
Abis's Action.
    Svoboda, Josef. Satire Theatre, Prague: 1946. B&W. Rendering. **SJS**, 134.
The Absurd Vice.
    Sbragia, Giancarlo. Teatro Verdi, Padova: 1974. B&W. Set. **SDW4**, illus. 265, 266.
Abundance.
    Salzer, Beeb. Gorki Theatre, Vladivostok: B&W. Model. **TDT**, vol. XXX, n. 2 (Spring
        1994). 18.
The Accidental Death of an Anarchist.
    Eigsti, Karl. Arena Stage, Washington, DC: 1984. B&W. Set. **ASD1**, 32.
    Eigsti, Karl. Belasco Theatre, NYC: 1984. B&W. Model. **DDT**, 167.
Accomplice.
    Jenkins, David. Richard Rodgers Theatre, NYC: 1990. B&W. Model. **DDT**, 435.

The Accomplish'd Maid.
    _____. Vineyard Theatre: Color. Set. **TCI**, vol. 25, n. 1 (Jan 1991). 38.
Achilles.
    Pronaszko, Andrzej & Zbigniew. Boguslawski Theater, Warsaw: 1925. B&W. Set.
    RSD, illus. 266.
Acis and Galatea.
    Craig, Edward Gordon. Great Queen Street Theatre, London: 1902. B&W. Rendering.
    EGC, plates 3a, 3b; B&W. Rendering. **SDG**, 149.
Acropolis.
    Grotowski, Jerzy. Teatr Laboratorium 13 Rzedow, Opole, Poland: 1962. B&W. Sketch
    & set. **SDW3**, 97. 2 photos.
    Hammond, Aubrey. B&W. Rendering. **DOT**, 222.
    Szajna, Josef. Teatr Laboratorium 13 Rzedow, Opole, Poland: 1962. B&W. Sketch &
    set. **SDW3**, 97. 2 photos.
The Actors of Good Faith.
    Voizot, Jacques. Théâtre du Lambrequin-Centre Dramatique du Nord, Tourcoing,
    France: 1973. B&W. Sketch. **SDW4**, illus. 87.
Actual Sho.
    Hunt, Jeff. B&W. Set. **TDT**, vol. XXVIII, n. 2 (Spring 1992). 6 of insert.
Adam and Eve.
    Oechslin, Ary. State Theatre, Bern: 1974. B&W. Set. **SDW4**, illus. 316.
The Adding Machine.
    Hoffman, Vlastislav. National Theatre, Prague: B&W. Set. **TCS2**, plate 243.
    Malolepsy, John F. University of New Mexico: 1987. Color. Set. **BSE5**, 20.
    Patel, Neil. Actors Theatre of Louisville: 1995. Color. Set. **TCI**, vol. 29, n. 4 (Apr
    1995). 6.
    Simonson, Lee. Garrick Theatre, NYC: 1923. B&W. Set. **TPH**, photo 463.
    _____. Color. Rendering. **SDL**, plates 8-13a.
The Admirable Crichton.
    Griffin, Hayden. Theatre Clwyd, Mold/Haymarket, London: 1988. B&W. Set. **TCI**,
    vol. 23, n. 2 (Feb 1989). 36.
Adobe Motel.
    Kellogg, Marjorie Bradley. Hartman Theatre Company, Stamford, Connecticut: 1981.
    B&W. Set. **ASD1**, 57.
Adrienne Lecouvreur.
    Malclés, Jean Dénis. La Scala, Milan: 1953. B&W. Rendering. **SDE**, 114. 2 photos.
    _____. Kamerny Theatre, Moscow: 1932. B&W. Set. **RST**, 84, 85. 3 photos.
Adrift.
    Justin, David. American Inside Theatre, Waukesha, Wisconsin: 1991. Color. Set. **TCI**,
    vol. 25, n. 8 (Oct 1991). 19.
The Adventures of a Poor Christian.
    Burri, Alberto. Teatro Stabile dell'Aquila, Italy: 1969. B&W. Set. **SDW3**, 118.
The Adventures of Chichikov.
    Kitaïev, Mark. USSR: Color. Model. **TDT**, vol. XII, n. 3 (Fall 1976). 35.
The Adventures of Mr. Broucek.
    Docherty, Peter. English National Opera, London Coliseum: B&W. Set. **TCI**, vol. 15,
    n. 5 (May 1981). 15.
The Affair.
    Akimov, Nikolai. Teatr Lensoveta, Leningrad: 1954. B&W. Rendering. **SDW2**, 177.
Une Affaire de Famille.
    Hoffman, Vlastislav. National Theatre, Prague: B&W. Set. **TCS2**, plate 99.

After the Fall.

Mielziner, Jo. ANTA Washington Square Theatre, NYC: 1964. B&W. Rendering.
DPT, 48; B&W. Rendering. **DTT**, 219. Touring set.

Mielziner, Jo. The Playhouse, Wilmington, Delaware: 1964. B&W. Rendering. **SDW3**,
131.

Schwab, Per. National Theatre, Oslo: 1965. B&W. Model. **SDR**, 54.

Agamemnon.

Gesek, Thaddeus. Yale School of Drama, New Haven, Connecticut: B&W. Set. **SFT**,
17.

Loquasto, Santo. Vivian Beaumont Theatre, Lincoln Center, NYC: Color. Set. **DSL**,
plate VII.

Ricketts, Charles. (unproduced): B&W. Rendering. **DIT**, plate 12; B&W. Sketch.
TPH, photo 354.

Strzelecki, Zenobiusz. National Theatre, Warsaw: 1963. B&W. Set. **RSD**, illus. 505.

Riddell, Richard. Stanford University, California: 1976. B&W. Set. **TCI**, vol. 11, n. 3
(May/Jun 1977). 24.

The Age of Night.

Stephanellis, John. Théâtron Technis, Athens: 1959. B&W. Rendering. **SDW2**, 106.

The Agents.

Chagall, Marc. State Jewish Theatre, Moscow: 1921. Color. Rendering. **RSD**, illus.
209.

Aglavaine et Sélysette.

Hoffmann, Ludwig von. Kammerspiele, Berlin: 1907. B&W. Set. **TCS2**, plates 15, 16.

Agnes of God.

Lee, Eugene. Music Box Theatre, NYC: 1982. B&W. Set. **TDT**, vol. XXII, n. 4
(Winter 1987). 11.

Agnes of Hohenstaufen.

Carboni, Erberto. Maggio Musicale Fiorentino, Florence: 1954. B&W. Rendering.
SDW2, 122.

Ah, Wilderness.

Dahlstrom, Robert A. Seattle Repertory Theatre: 1980. B&W. Rendering. **BSE2**, 8.

Glenn, David. Playmakers Repertory Company, Paul Green Theatre, Chapel Hill,
North Carolina: B&W. Set. **TCI**, vol. 13, n. 3 (May/Jun 1979). 31.

Jones, Robert Edmond. Guild Theatre, NYC: 1933. B&W. Set. **MCN**, 113.

Pecktal, Lynn. 1966. Color. Set. **DDT**, 440a.

Yeargan, Michael. Yale Repertory Theatre, New Haven: 1988. Color. Set. **ASD2**,
between 108, 109.

Aïda.

Montresor, Beni. Bavarian State Opera, Munich: 1979. B&W. Set. **TCI**, vol. 16, n. 5
(May 1982). 14.

Otto, Teo. Municipal Theatre, Frankfurt am Main: 1966. B&W. Rendering. **SDR**, 51.

Parravicini, Angelo. Metropolitan Opera, NYC: 1923. B&W. Rendering. **MOM**, 6.

Payne, Darwin Reid. B&W. Model. **TCM**, 133; B&W. Model. **SIP**, 12.

Pizzi, Pier Luigi. B&W. Rendering. **SIO**, 108.

Reinking, Wilhelm. Hamburg: 1939. B&W. Set. **SDB**, 19.

Schmidt, Douglas W. San Francisco Opera: 1981. Color. Set. **ASD1**, between 70 & 71.

Trapp, S. Von. B&W. Set. **TAS**, 92, 93. 3 photos.

Wagner, Wieland. Deutsches Staatsoper, Berlin: 1962. B&W. Set. **SDW3**, 182.

Wareing, John. (not produced): B&W. Model. **SDT**, 297.

_____. Basel: 1965. B&W. Set. **TCI**, vol. 4, n. 4 (Sep 1970). cover, 23.

_____. Olympic Stadium, Montreal: 1988. B&W. Set. **TCI**, vol. 24, n. 5 (May 1990). 14.

_____. B&W. Rendering. **SIP**, 243.

_____. Opera Colorado, Denver: Color. Set. **TCI**, vol. 25, n. 5 (May 1991). 36.

Aimer.

Dresa. 1922. B&W. Rendering. **DIT**, plate 85.

Ain't Misbehavin'.

Bardo, Dagmar. Pennsylvania Stage Company, Allentown: 1982. B&W. Set. **BSE4**, 71.

Beatty, John Lee. Longacre Theatre, NYC: 1978. Color. Set. **BWM**, 338; B&W. Set. **TCI**, vol. 12, n. 6 (Oct 1978). 15.

Faust, Vince. Kalamazoo Civic Players, Michigan: 1984. B&W. Set. **TCI**, vol. 20, n. 5 (May 1986). 25.

Ain't Supposed To Die a Natural Death.

Lundell, Kert. Ethel Barrymore Theatre, NYC: 1971. Color. Set. **BWM**, 336.

Ajax.

Tsypin, George. Arena Stage, Washington, DC: 1986. B&W. Set. **ASD2**, 173; Color. Set. **TCI**, vol. 20, n. 9 (Nov 1986). 20; Color. Set. **TCI**, vol. 25, n. 2 (Feb 1991). 35; B&W. Set. **TCI**, vol. 24, n. 5 (May 1990). 41; B&W. Set. **TDT**, vol. XXVII, n. 3 (Summer 1991). 12. 2 photos.

Akhnaten.

Roger, David. English National Opera, London: 1986. B&W. Set. **BTD**, 142, 143.

_____. Germany: B&W. Set. **TCI**, vol. 19, n. 2 (Feb 1985). 23.

Akropolis.

Wyspianski, Stanislaw. Laboratory Theater, Opole, Poland: 1962. B&W. Sketch. **RSD**, illus. 629, 630.

Aladdin.

Heythum, Antonín. Prague: 1933. B&W. Rendering. **TAS**, 98.

Okun, Alexander. Empire State Institute for the Performing Arts: 1987. B&W. Set. **TCI**, vol. 21, n. 9 (Nov 1987). 47.

Sainthill, Loudon. Coliseum, London: 1959. Color. Rendering. **LST**, 46, 47. Pantomime.

Aladin ou la Lampe Merveilleuse.

Bakst, Léon. Théâtre Marigny, Paris: 1919. B&W and color. Rendering. **LBT**, 196, 198, 199. 3 photos.

Albert Herring.

Gunter, John. Glyndebourne Festival Opera, England: 1985. Color. Set. **BTD**, 98.

Wexler, Peter. Savonlinna Opera Festival, Finland: B&W. Set. **SDT**, 285.

Alceste.

Butlin, Roger. Kentucky Opera Association: 1982. B&W. Set. **TCI**, vol. 17, n. 4 (Apr 1983). 8.

The Alcestiad.

Funicello, Ralph. Pacific Conservatory of the Performing Arts, Santa Maria, California: 1978. B&W. Set. **TCI**, vol. 13, n. 3 (May/Jun 1979). 37.

Alcestis.

Kamm, Tom & Robert Wilson. American Repertory Theatre, Cambridge, Massachusetts: 1986. B&W and color. Model & set. **TCI**, vol. 20, n. 9 (Nov 1986). 30, 31. 3 photos; Color. Set. **TCI**, vol. 24, n. 8 (Oct 1990). 41.

Perrottet-von Laban, André. Théâtre Municipal, Lucerne: 1952. B&W. Rendering. **SDW1**, 118.

Zuffi, Piero. La Scala, Milan: 1954. B&W. Rendering. **SDE**, 177-179. 5 photos.

The Alchemedians.

_____. Brooklyn Academy of Music, New York: 1985. B&W. Set. **TDT**, vol. XXII, n. 1 (Spring 1986). 8.

The Alchemist.

Hay, Richard L. Oregon Shakespeare Festival, Ashland: B&W. Set. **SDL**, 75.

Kestleman, Morris. New Theatre, London: 1946. B&W. Rendering. **SDW1**, 177.

Musika, Frantisek. State Theatre, Brno: 1932. B&W. Rendering. **TDT**, n. 42 (Fall 1975). 25.

Alcino.

'Hedeby - Pawlo, Kerstin. Kungliga Teatern, Stockholm: 1959. B&W. Set. **SDW2**, 209.

_____. New York City Opera, Lincoln Center: 1983. Color. Set. **TCI**, vol. 22, n. 2 (Feb 1988). 45.

Aleko.

Chagall, Marc. Palais des Beaux-Arts, Mexico: 1942. Color. Rendering. **RSD**, illus. 479, 480; B&W. Painting. **TPH**, photo 367.

Alexander Balus.

Heckroth, Heinrich. State Theatre, Münster: B&W. Set. **TCS2**, plate 217.

Alice in Wonder.

Maronek, James E. Goodman School of Drama, Chicago: 1980. B&W. Rendering. **BSE1**, 9.

Alice in Wonderland.

Beatty, John Lee. Virginia Theatre, NYC: 1982. B&W. Set. **TCI**, vol. 17, n. 4 (Apr 1983). 16, 17.

Ward, Anthony. Lyric Theatre, Hammersmith, London: 1986. B&W. Set. **BTD**, 161.

Alice Sit-by-the-Fire.

Bucks County, Pennsylvania: 1946. B&W. Set. **WTP**, 156, 157. 3 photos.

Alien Corn.

Throckmorton, Cleon. Belasco Theatre, NYC: 1933. B&W. Set. **MCN**, 111.

Alkmene.

Reinking, Wilhelm. Deutsches Staatsoper, Berlin: 1961. B&W. Set. **SDW2**, 68.

All God's Chillun Got Wings.

Godfrey, Peter. Gate Theatre, London: 1929. B&W. Set. **SCM**, 23.

Stenberg, Vladimir & Georgiy A. Kamerny Theatre, Moscow: 1929. B&W. Model. **RST**, 196; B&W. Model. **TAT**, plate 700.

All My Sons.

Gorelik, Mordecai. Coronet Theatre, NYC: 1947. B&W. Set. **TPH**, photo 469.

All Night Long.

Lobel, Adrianne. Second Stage, NYC: B&W. Set. **TDT**, vol. XXI, n. 2 (Summer 1985). 8.

All Over.

Ter-Arutunian, Rouben. Martin Beck Theatre, NYC: 1970. B&W. Sketch. **TCI**, vol. 5, n. 5 (Oct 1971). 6; B&W. Rendering. **CSD**, 135.

All the King's Men.

Dramatic Workshop of the New School for Social Research, NYC: B&W. Set. **TPH**, photo 378.

All the Way Home.

Hays, David. Belasco Theatre, NYC: 1960. B&W. Set. **SDR**, 57; B&W. Set. **SDW2**, 235.

Owen, Paul. Alley Theatre, Houston: B&W. Set. **TCI**, vol. 7, n. 3 (May/Jun 1973). 9.

All's Well that Ends Well.
> Eck, Marsha Louis. Stratford, Connecticut: B&W. Set. **TCI**, vol. 7, n. 2 (Mar/Apr 1973). 10.
> Gunter, John. Royal Shakespeare Company, GB: 1981. B&W. Set. **SDT**, 272; B&W. Model. **TDT**, vol. XIX, n. 1 (Spring 1983). 9.
> Laing, Stewart. Delacorte Theatre, NYC: 1993. Color. Set. **TCI**, vol. 27, n. 8 (Oct 1993). 6.
> Mahuke, Adolf. Städtische Bühnen, Dortmund: 1959. B&W. Rendering. **SOS**, 266.
> Moiseiwitsch, Tanya. Stratford Festival Theatre, Ontario, Canada: 1953. B&W. Set. **DMS**, plate 40; B&W. Set. **TCI**, vol. 20, n. 7 (Aug/Sep 1986). 22.
> _____. American Shakespeare Festival, Stratford, Connecticut: 1970. B&W. Set. **TCI**, vol. 19, n. 3 (Mar 1985). 25.
> _____. Color. Set. **TCI**, vol. 26, n. 1 (Jan 1992). 38.

Allegro.
> Mielziner, Jo. Majestic Theatre, NYC: 1947. B&W. Set. **BWM**, 191; B&W. Rendering. **DTT**, 137. Wedding drop; B&W. Set. **HOB**, 79.

Allez-Hop!
> Luzzati, Emanuele. Teatro Comunale, Bologna: 1968. B&W. Set. **SDW3**, 210.

Alpenkönig und Menschenfeind.
> Walser, Karl. Berliner Theater: 1909. B&W. Rendering. **AST**, 30.

Alphabetical Order.
> Kellogg, Marjorie Bradley. Long Wharf Theatre, New Haven, Connecticut: 1976. B&W. Sketch & set. **ASD1**, 58, 59; B&W. Rendering. **TDT**, vol. XXI, n. 2 (Summer 1985). 5.

Altona.
> Aeberli, Hans. Städtische Bühnen, Essen: 1959. B&W. Rendering. **SDW2**, 57.

Amabel.
> Mitchell, Poppy. Bush Theatre, London: 1979. B&W. Set. **BTD**, 86.

Amadeus.
> Bury, John. Broadhurst Theatre, NYC: 1979. B&W. Set. **TCI**, vol. 15, n. 3 (Mar 1981). 10, 11; Color. Set. **TCI**, vol. 26, n. 1 (Jan 1992). 47.
> _____. Dallas Theatre Center: 1984. Color. Set. **TCI**, vol. 23, n. 9 (Nov 1989). 59.
> _____. Missouri Repertory Theatre, Kansas City: 1990. B&W. Set. **TCR**, 119.

Amahl and the Night Visitors.
> Coltellacci, Giulio. Maggio Musicale Fiorentino, Florence: 1953. B&W. Rendering. **SDE**, 69; B&W. Set. **SDW2**, 124.
> Reaney, Mark. University of Kansas, Lawrence: B&W. Sketch & rendering. **TDT**, vol. XXV, n. 2 (Summer 1989). 26.

Les Amants Éternels.
> Constable, William. His Majesty's Theatre, Melbourne: 1951. B&W. Set. **SDW1**, 39.

Amazing Grace.
> Elder, Eldon. Mendelssohn Theatre, Ann Arbor, Michigan: 1967. Color. Rendering. **CSD**, 95; B&W. Rendering. **DDT**, 296; Color. Rendering. **EED**, (pages not numbered); B&W. Set. **TCI**, vol. 21, n. 5 (May 1987). 11.

L'Ambleto.
> Fercioni, Gian Maurizio. Salone Pier Lombardo, Milan: 1973. B&W. Set. **SDW4**, illus. 287.

Amelia Goes to the Ball.
> Oenslager, Donald. Central City Opera House, Colorado: 1941. B&W. Painter's elevations. **BSE2**, 52, 55.

Amen Corner.
    Eigsti, Karl. Nederlander Theatre, NYC: 1983. B&W. Show curtain. **DDT**, 395.
    Wittstein, Ed. Theater an der Wein, Vienna: 1965. B&W. Rendering. **CSD**, 142. Act II;
        Color. Rendering. **CSD**, 143. Act I.
America Hurrah.
    Leontov, Tania. Pocket Theatre, NYC: 1966. B&W. Set. **SDW3**, 165.
American Buffalo.
    Hicks, Grant. National Theatre (Cottesloe), London: 1978. Color. Set. **BTD**, 83.
    Kellogg, Marjorie Bradley. Long Wharf Theatre, New Haven, Connecticut: 1980.
        B&W. Rendering. **ASD1**, 54.
    Loquasto, Santo. Ethel Barrymore Theatre, NYC: 1977. Color. Set. **ASD1**, between 70
        & 71; B&W and color. Sketch & set. **TDT**, vol. XVII, n. 3 (Fall 1981). front cover.
        2 photos.
    Merritt, Michael. Goodman Theatre, Chicago: 1978. Color. Set. **ASD2**, between 108 &
        109.
The American Clock.
    O'Brien, Timothy. National Theatre (Cottesloe), England: 1986. Color. Set design
        collage. **BTD**, 35.
An American Comedy.
    Jackness, Andrew. Mark Taper Forum, Los Angeles: 1983. B&W. Set. **DDT**, 83.
American Notes.
    Arnone, John. New York Shakespeare Festival, NYC: 1988. B&W. Set. **ASD2**, 22.
The American Project.
    _____. Actors Theatre of Louisville: 1980. B&W. Set. **TCI**, vol. 15, n. 4 (Apr
        1981). 16, 17. 3 photos.
American Vaudeville.
    Stein, Douglas O. Alley Theatre, Houston: 1992. B&W. Set. **TCI**, vol. 26, n. 7 (Aug/
        Sep 1992). 11.
The American Way.
    Oenslager, Donald. Center Theatre, NYC: 1939. B&W. Rendering & set. **TDO**, 89-91.
        3 photos.
Amerika.
    Grzegorzewsky, Jerzy. Teatr Ateneum, Warsaw: 1973. B&W. Set. **SDW4**, illus. 214.
    Raffaëlli, Michel. Deutsches Staatsoper, Berlin: 1966. B&W. 18 set arrangements.
        RSD, illus. 544; B&W. Set. **SDW3**, 206. 3 photos.
Amnesia.
    _____. Olympic Arts Festival, Los Angeles: 1984. B&W. Set. **TCI**, vol. 20, n. 1
        (Jan 1986). 27.
Amor Brujo.
    Casorati, Felice. La Scala, Milan: 1949. B&W. Rendering. **SDE**, 59.
L'Amore dei Tre Re.
    Montresor, Beni. Washington Opera, DC: B&W. Set. **TCI**, vol. 16, n. 5 (May 1982).
        17.
L'Amore Stregone.
    Guttuso, Renato. La Scala, Milan: 1962-1963. B&W. Rendering. **SIO**, 148.
Amorina.
    Ljungberg. Dramatiska Teatern, Stockholm: 1951. B&W. Set. **SDW1**, 166.
The Amorous Devil.
    Svoboda, Josef. Fiesole, Italy: 1993. B&W. Set. **TDT**, vol. XXX, n. 5 (Fall 1994). 42.
        2 photos.

The Amorous Flea.
>   Beatty, John Lee. Queens Playhouse, Flushing, NY: 1974. Color. Rendering. **DPT**, between 124, 125.
>   Gilseth, Thom. Phoenix Little Theatre, Arizona: B&W. Set. **SDT**, 294.
>   Sporre, Dennis J. University of Iowa, Iowa City: B&W. Rendering. **SDT**, 85.
>   _____. B&W. Set. **TDT**, n. 40 (Spring 1975). 32.

L'Amour Médicin.
>   Moulaert, René. Théâtre du Marais, Brussels: 1923. B&W. Set. **TCS2**, plate 52.

Amphigorey:
>   The Musical. Gorey, Edward. Plays and Players Theatre, Philadelphia: 1992. B&W. Act curtain & rendering. **DDT**, 20, 187.

Amphiparnassus.
>   Severini, Gino. La Pergola, Florence: 1938. B&W. Rendering. **SDW1**, 131.

Amphitryon.
>   Bérard, Christian. Ziegfeld Theatre, NYC: 1952. B&W. Set. **WTP**, 45.

Amphitryon 38.
>   Benavente, Saulo. Instituto de Arte Moderno, Buenos Aires: 1950. B&W. Set. **SDW1**, 33.
>   Simonson, Lee. Theatre Guild, NYC: 1937. B&W. Set. **PLT**, illus. 54-56; B&W. Set. **SOW**, plate 36; B&W. Set. **TAS**, 153. 2 photos; B&W. Set. **TPH**, photo 464; B&W. Set. **WTP**, 46, 47.

The Anabaptists.
>   Allio, René. Théâtre National de Strasbourg: 1969. B&W. Model. **SDW3**, 143.
>   Svoboda, Josef. National Theatre, Prague: 1968. B&W. Set. **SDW3**, 143; B&W. Set. **SJS**, 128-130. 4 photos; B&W. Set. **STS**, 8.

Anarchie auf Silian.
>   Mahnke, Adolf. Schauspielhaus, Dresden: 1926. B&W. Model. **TCS2**, plate 160.

Anastasia.
>   Ezell, John. B&W. Show curtain. **SDL**, 475.
>   Kay, Barry. Covent Garden, London: 1971. B&W. Set. **CGA**, 176.

The Ancient Mariner.
>   Jones, Robert Edmond. Provincetown Playhouse, NYC: 1924. B&W. Sketch. **DFT**, plate 33; B&W. Rendering. **SDL**, 55; B&W. Rendering. **TDT**, vol. XXIV, n. 4 (Winter 1988). 10.

And a Nightingale Sang.
>   Dorsey, Kent. Color. Set. **TCI**, vol. 25, n. 8 (Oct 1991). 49.

And the Wind Blows.
>   Wagner, Robin. St. Mark's Playhouse, NYC: 1959. B&W. Rendering. **ASD1**, 157.

And the World Laughs With You.
>   Cochren, Felix E. Crossroads Theatre Company, New Brunswick, New Jersey: 1994. Color. Set. **TCI**, vol. 28, n. 4 (Apr 1994). 6.

The Andersonville Trial.
>   Williams, Jerry. Alley Theatre, Houston: B&W. Set. **TCI**, vol. 7, n. 3 (May/Jun 1973). 9.

Andorra.
>   Aronson, Boris. Biltmore Theatre, NYC: 1963. B&W. Set. **TAB**, 307.
>   Kerz, Leo. Center Stage, Baltimore: 1971. B&W. Set. **TCI**, vol. 7, n. 3 (May/Jun 1973). 12.
>   Otto, Teo. Schauspielehaus, Zürich: 1961. B&W. Model. **SDW2**, 111.
>   Schneider-Manns-Au, Rudolf. Volkstheater, Vienna. 1962. B&W. Rendering. **SDW3**, 128.

Andre Chenier.
>Sykora, Peter. Deutsche Oper, Berlin: B&W. Set. **TDT** vol. XXXI, n. 2 (Spring 1995). 13, 14. 4 photos.
>Benois, Alexander. La Scala, Milan: 1949. B&W. Rendering. **SDE**, 33.
>_____. Chicago Lyric Opera: 1916. B&W. Set pieces. **TDT**, vol. XXV, n. 2 (Summer 1989). 14.
>_____. Houston Grand Opera: 1977. B&W. Set. **TCI**, vol. 18, n. 7 (Aug/Sep 1984). 43.

Androcles and the Lion.
>Covarrubias, M. 1925. B&W. Set. **TSS**, 517.
>Musika, Frantisek. State Theatre, Brno: 1930. B&W. Set. **TDT**, n. 42 (Fall 1975). 25.
>Roth, Wolfgang. 1946. B&W. Set. **SDA**, 145. 2 photos.
>Rutherston, Albert Daniel. Savoy Theatre, London: B&W. Set. **TCS2**, plate 142.
>_____. Kammerspiele, Munich: 1913. B&W. Set. **MRH**, facing 21.

Andromaque.
>Simonini, Pierre. Tournée Georges Herbert: 1961. B&W. Set. **SDW2**, 101.

L'Anfiparnaso.
>Severini, Gino. Teatro della Pergola, Italy: 1938. B&W. Rendering. **AST**, 189.

Angel Street.
>Ayers, Lemuel. John Golden Theatre, NYC: 1941. B&W. Set. **SDA**, 204.
>Destefano, Scott. University of Puget Sound, Tacoma: 1978. B&W. Set. **TCI**, vol. 13, n. 3 (May/Jun 1979). 38.

Angelica.
>Scandella, Mischa, Teatro Stabile, Torino: 1959. B&W. Set. **SDW2**, 131.

Angelique.
>Kiesler, Frederick. NYC: 1948. B&W. Set. **EIF**, photo 37.

Angels Fall.
>Beatty, John Lee. Longacre Theatre, NYC: 1983. B&W. Rendering. **DDT**, 544.

Angels in America, Perestroika.
>Wagner, Robin. Walter Kerr Theatre, NYC: 1993. Color. Set. **TCI**, vol. 28, n. 7 (Aug/Sep 1994). 44.

Angels on Earth.
>Aronson, Boris. Yiddish Art Theatre (Second Avenue Theatre), NYC: 1929. B&W and color. Rendering & set. **TAB**, 34 , 294.

Aniara.
>Ericson, Sven. Kungliga Teatern, Stockholm: 1959. B&W. Set. **SDR**, 58; B&W. Rendering. **SDW2**, 208.
>Moulaert, René. Théâtre Royal de la Monnaie, Brussels: 1960. B&W. Rendering. **SDW2**, 30.

Animal Farm.
>Carey, Jennifer. National Theatre (Cottesloe), England: 1984. Color. Rendering. **BTD**, 39.

The Animal Kingdom.
>Bernstein, Aline. Broadhurst Theatre, NYC: 1932. B&W. Set. **MCN**, 109.

Ann Boleyn.
>Benois, Nicola. La Scala, Milan: 1957. B&W. Set. **SDW2**, 121.
>Lee, Ming Cho. New York City Opera, Lincoln Center: 1973. B&W. Set. **TCI**, vol. 18, n. 2 (Feb 1984). 21.

Anna Christie.
>Barber, David M. University of Texas, Austin: B&W. Rendering. **TDT**, vol. XXVI, n. 1 (Spring 1990). 18 of insert.

Beatty, John Lee. Roundabout Theatre, NYC: 1992. B&W. Set. **TCI**, vol. 27, n. 4 (Apr 1993). 7.
Roche, Emeline Clarke. City Center, NYC: 1952. B&W. Set. **WTP**, 170, 171. 4 photos.

Anna Karenina.
Koltai, Ralph. English National Opera, London: 1981. B&W. Set. **TDT**, vol. XIX, n. 3 (Fall 1983). 10.
Morgan, James. Circle in the Square Theatre, NYC: 1992. Color. Set. **TCI**, vol. 26, n. 9 (Nov 1992). 8.
_____. Los Angeles Opera: B&W. Set. **TCI**, vol. 17, n. 7 (Aug/Sep 1983). 33. 2 photos.

Anne of the Thousand Days.
Coltellacci, Giulio. Valle, Rome: 1952. B&W. Set. **SDW1**, 125.

Annie Get Your Gun.
Jenkins, George. Los Angeles: 1957. B&W. Painter's elevations. **SDB**, 122.
Mielziner, Jo. Imperial Theatre, NYC: 1946. B&W. Set. **BWM**, 242, 243. 4 photos; B&W. Set. **TMT**, 161; B&W. Set. **WMC**, 80; B&W. Set. **WTP**, 238, 239. 4 photos.
O'Hearn, Robert. Paper Mill Playhouse, Millburn, New Jersey: 1987. B&W. Show curtain. **DDT**, 395.

Annie.
Mitchell, David. Alvin Theatre, NYC: 1977. B&W. Backdrop. **ASD1**, 132; Color. Set. **BWM**, 152, 153, 156, 158-159. 5 photos; B&W. Model, rendering, & set. **DDT**, 101. 8 photos; B&W. Set. **TCI**, vol. 14, n. 1 (Jan/Feb 1980). 20; B&W. Model & set. **TCI**, vol. 11, n. 6 (Nov/Dec 1977). 28-31. 9 photos; B&W. Set. **WMC**, 310. 2 photos.

The Anonomous Work.
Kolodziej, Marian. Teatr Wybrzeze, Gdansk: 1968. B&W. Set. **SDW3**, 102.

Another Part of the Forest.
Funicello, Ralph. American Conservatory Theatre, San Francisco: 1981. B&W. Model. **ASD1**, 52.

Anteroom.
Lobel, Adrianne. Playwrights Horizons, NYC: 1985. B&W. Set. **ASD2**, 108.

Antigone.
Christiansen, Rolf. Städtische Bühnen, Freiburg: 1955. B&W. Rendering. **SDW2**, 58.
Cocteau, Jean. Opera Theatre, Paris: 1947. B&W. Set. **SDE**, 65.
Echarri, Isabel. France: 1981. B&W. Model. **TDT**, vol. XX, n. 1 (Spring 1984). 9.
Eichbauer, Helio. Teatro Opinião, Rio de Janeiro: 1969. B&W. Set. **SDW3**, 22.
Gamlin, Yngve. Studentteatern, Stockholm: 1951. B&W. Rendering. **SDW1**, 164.
Heinrich, Rudolf. Bavarian State Opera, Munich: 1976. B&W. Set. **TCI**, vol. 10, n. 6 (Nov/Dec 1976). 17; B&W. Set. **TDT**, vol. XII, n. 1 (Spring 1976). 27.
Malina, Jaroslav. Crafton-Preyer Theatre, University of Kansas, Lawrence: 1987. B&W. Multiple sketches. **TDT**, vol. XXIV, n. 2 (Summer 1988). 8-13, 18.
Martin, Karlheinz. Grosses Schauspielhaus, Berlin: B&W. Set. **TCS2**, plate 374.
Minks, Wilfried. Bremen: 1966. B&W. Set. **TCI**, vol. 12, n. 1 (Jan/Feb 1978). 29.
Neher, Caspar. Chur Stadttheater, Switzerland: 1948. B&W. Rendering & set. **CBM**, 24, 67. 3 photos; B&W. Set. **TBB**, 57.
Oenslager, Donald. American Shakespeare Festival, Stratford, Connecticut: 1967. Color. Rendering. **CSD**, 83; B&W. Rendering. **DPT**, 362; B&W. Rendering. **SDW3**, 123; B&W. Rendering. **TDO**, 139.

Olmstead, Richard. Carnegie-Mellon University, Pittsburgh: B&W. Set. **TDT**, vol. XXVIII, n. 2 (Spring 1992). 14 of insert.

Payne, Darwin Reid. B&W. Collage & model. **TCM**, 105, 106; B&W. Model. **SIP**, 167.

Röthlisberger, Max. State Theatre, Zurich: 1956. B&W. Rendering. **SDW2**, 112.

Schmidt, Douglas W. Repertory Theatre of Lincoln Center, NYC: 1971. B&W. Set. **DPT**, Facing 1; B&W. Set. **SIP**, 165.

Schultz, Rudolf. Landestheater, Hannover: 1946. B&W. Rendering. **SDW1**, 77.

Svoboda, Josef. Zurich: 1983. Color. Set. **TCI**, vol. 21, n. 8 (Oct 1987). 34.

Szajna, Josef. Teatr Ludowy, Nowa Huta, Poland: 1963. B&W. Set. **SDW3**, 23.

Winge, Sigurd. Trondelag Teater, Norway: 1970. B&W. Model. **SDW3**, 22.

Wotruba, Fritz. Burgtheater, Vienna. 1961. B&W. Sketch & model. **AST**, 229. 2 photos.

_____. Kamerny Theatre, Moscow: 1927. B&W. Set. **RST**, 197.

_____. B&W. Set. **SST**, 248.

_____. B&W. Set. **WTP**, 35-37.

Antony and Cleopatra.

Albert, Ernest (from drawings by Jules Guerin). New Theatre, NYC: 1909. B&W. Set. **MCN**, 34.

Aronson, Boris. Oregon Shakespeare Festival, Ashland: 1959. B&W. Set. **PST**, 211.

Hay, Richard. Oregon Shakespeare Festival, Ashland: 1977. B&W. Set. **TCI**, vol. 11, n. 6 (Nov/Dec 1977). 8.

Kerz, Leo. 1947. B&W. Set. **TPH**, photo 484. Lee, Ming Cho. New York Shakespeare Festival, NYC: 1963. Color. Model. **DMS**, plate 36.

Marillier, Jacques. Théâtre Sarah Bernhardt, Paris: 1964. B&W. Model. **SDW3**, 60. 3 photos.

Poncy, Eric. Grand Theater, Geneva: 1947. B&W. Rendering. **SDW1**, 118.

Schillingowsky, P. State Theatre, Leningrad: 1923. B&W. Sketch. **TPH**, photo 405.

Shchuko, Vladimir. State Theatre, Leningrad: 1923. B&W. Sketches & set. **RST**, 167. 3 photos; B&W. Rendering. **SOS**, 221.

Svoboda, Josef. Schiller Theatre, Berlin: 1969. B&W. Model. **STS**, 93.

Tilton, James. American Conservatory Theatre, San Francisco: 1971. B&W. Set. **TCI**, vol. 6, n. 5 (Oct 1972). 12.

Zeffirelli, Franco. Metropolitan Opera, NYC: 1966. B&W. Set. **TDT**, n. 7 (Dec 1966). 26, 27. 3 photos.

_____. London: 1951. B&W. Set. **WTP**, 145.

_____. B&W. Model. **TCI**, vol. 21, n. 8 (Oct 1987). 18.

Anyone Can Whistle.

Eckart, William & Jean. 46th Street Theatre, NYC: 1964. B&W. Set. **HPA**, 82; B&W. Set. **SON**, 67-70. 5 photos.

Anything Goes.

Keller, Ronald E. Virginia Commonwealth University Theatre: Color. Set. **TCI**, vol. 21, n. 3 (Mar 1987). 22.

Oenslager, Donald. Alvin Theatre, NYC: 1934. B&W. Set. **BWM**, 56, 207; B&W. Set. **SDA**, 247; B&W. Set. **TDO**, 59; B&W. Set. **TMT**, 127.

Seger, Richard. Pacific Conservatory of the Performing Arts, Santa Maria, California: Color. Set. **SCT**, between 152 & 153.

Walton, Tony. Vivian Beaumont Theatre, Lincoln Center, NYC: 1987. B&W and color. Model. **DDT**, 176, 177, 440d. 5 photos; Color. Set. **MBM**, 14, 15; B&W. Set. **TCI**, vol. 22, n. 7 (Aug/Sep 1988). 3.

Anzor.
>   Gamrekeli, Irakly. Rustaveli Theatre, Tbilisi: 1928. B&W. **RSD**, illus. 159; B&W.
>   Model & set. **RST**, 288, 289. 3 photos.

Aoi-No-Ue.
>   Shigeoka, Kan-ichi. Shimbashi Embujo, Tokyo: 1948. Color. Rendering & ground
>   plan. **SDW1**, 146. 2 photos.

Apocalypsis cum figuris.
>   _____. Polish Laboratory Theatre: B&W. Set. **TCR**, 124. 2 photos.

The Apollo of Bellac.
>   Mörner, Stellan. Dramatiska Teatern, Stockholm: 1949. B&W. Rendering. **SDW1**,
>   167.

The Apostle.
>   _____. Burgtheater, Vienna: 1901. B&W. Set. **TPH**, photo 295.

Apparitions.
>   Beaton, Cecil. Sadler's Wells Theatre, London: 1936. Color. Rendering. **CBS**, 53;
>   B&W. Rendering. **SDW1**, 170.

Appear and Show Cause.
>   Macie, Tom. Hillberry Repertory Theatre: B&W. Set. **SDT**, 277.

Applause.
>   Randolph, Robert. Palace Theatre, NYC: 1970. B&W. Sketches & models. **DPT**, 144;
>   B&W. Rendering. **TCI**, vol. 4, n. 3 (May/Jun 1970). 9-12. 4 photos.

The Apple Cart.
>   Schütte, Ernst. Deutsches Theater, Berlin: 1929. B&W. Set. **TPH**, photo 335.
>   Simonson, Lee. Theatre Guild, NYC: 1930. B&W. Set. **PLT**, illus. 25; B&W. Set.
>   **SCM**, 114. 2 photos.

The Apple Tree.
>   Walton, Tony. Shubert Theatre, NYC: 1966. Color. Set. **BWM**, 296.

The Apprenticeship of Duddy Kravitz.
>   Dunham, Clarke. Zellerbach Theatre, Philadelphia: 1987. B&W. Set. **DDT**, 163.

Approaching Zanzabar.
>   Hogland, Roy. University of Wisconsin, Oskosh: B&W and color. Rendering & set.
>   **TDT**, vol. XXX, n. 3 (Summer 1994). 6.
>   Landesman, Heidi. Second Stage, NYC: 1988. B&W. Set. **ASD2**, 74. 2 photos.

L'Apres-midi d'un Faune.
>   Bakst, Leon. B&W. Rendering. **DOT**, 217.

Arabella.
>   English National Opera, London: 1984. B&W. Set. **TCI**, vol. 19, n. 4 (Apr 1985). 21.

The Arcadians.
>   Hall, Stafford, Conrad Tritschler, R.C. McCleery, & W. Holmes. Shaftsbury Theatre,
>   London: 1909. B&W. Set. **MCD**, plate 80.

The Architect and the Emperor of Assyria.
>   Staheli, Paul. American Conservatory Theatre, San Francisco: B&W. Set. **TCI**, vol. 6,
>   n. 5 (Oct 1972). 17.

The Architecture of Catastrophic Change.
>   Sirlin, Jerome. Performance Works, San Francisco: 1990. Color. Set. **TCI**, vol. 25, n. 4
>   (Apr 1991). 21.

Ardéle.
>   Conklin, John. Hartford Stage, Connecticut: 1980. B&W. Set. **ASD1**, 24.
>   Malclés, Jean Dénis. Comédie des Champs-Élysées, Paris: 1948. B&W. Rendering.
>   **SDW1**, 100.

Ardelio e la Margherita.
  Barburini, Gilberto. Italy: 1953. B&W. Rendering. **SDE**, 30.
Arden of Faversham.
  Turina, Drago. Zagrebacko Dramsko Pozoriste: 1969. B&W. Sketch. **SDW3**, 34.
Are You Lonesome Tonight?
  Voytek. Phoenix Theatre, London: 1985. B&W. Set. **BTD**, 164, 165.
Ariadne auf Naxos.
  Heinrich, Rudolf. Bavarian State Theatre, Munich: B&W. Set. **TCI**, vol. 10, n. 6 (Nov/
    Dec 1976). 15.
  Kiesler, Frederick. NYC: 1934. B&W. Set. **EIF**, photo 14.
  Messel, Oliver. Edinburgh Festival: 1950. B&W. Set. **OMB**, 149.
  Pond, Helen & Herbert Senn. New York City Opera: 1973. B&W. Model. **DPT**, 132.
  Preetorius, Emil. State Opera, Berlin: 1932. B&W. Rendering. **SCM**, 68.
  Rice, Peter. Sadler's Wells Opera House, London: 1961. B&W. Rendering. **DMS**, plate
    50; B&W. Rendering. **SDB**, 91; B&W. Rendering. **SDW2**, 225.
  Rupnik, Kevin. Santa Fe Opera: 1990. Color. Rendering. **TCI**, vol. 24, n. 7 (Aug/Sep
    1990). 32. 2 photos.
  Stern, Ernst. Stuttgart: 1912. B&W. Sketches. **MRH**, facing 129. 2 photos.
  Svoboda, Josef. Deutsches Staatsoper, Berlin: 1970. B&W. Set. **SJS**, 154.
  Svoboda, Josef. National Arts Center, Ottawa: 1977. B&W. Set. **STS**, 68, 69.
  Yodice, Robert. Juilliard School, Lincoln Center, NYC: B&W. Set. **TCI**, vol. 10, n. 3
    (May/Jun 1976). 11. 2 photos.
Ariane and Bluebeard.
  Vanek, Joe. Opera North, Leeds, England: Color. Set. **TCI**, vol. 28, n. 1 (Jan 1994).
    39. 2 photos.
Arien.
  Borzik, Rolf. Brooklyn Academy of Music, New York: 1985. B&W. Set. **TCI**, vol. 20,
    n. 2 (Feb 1986). 14; B&W. Set. **TDT**, vol. XXII, n. 1 (Spring 1986). 10.
Ariodante.
  Baumeister, Willi. State Theatre, Stuttgart: B&W. Set. **SCM**, 65.
  Conklin, John. Santa Fe Opera: 1987. B&W. Set. **TCI**, vol. 21, n. 8 (Oct 1987). 19.
  MacNeil, Ian. Welsh National Opera: 1993. Color. Set. **TCI**, vol. 28, n. 4 (Apr 1994).
    31.
The Aristocrats.
  Knoblock, Boris. Realistic Theater, Moscow: 1934. B&W. Sketches. **RSD**, illus. 225,
    226.
  Rajkai, György. Jókai Szinház, Budapest. 1961. B&W. Rendering. **SDW2**, 140.
Arlechino.
  Domergue, J.G. B&W. Rendering. **DIT**, plate 88.
  Isler, Albert. State Theatre, Zurich: B&W. Set. **TCS2**, plate 88.
Armida.
  Clerici, Fabrizio. Teatro Comunale, Florence: 1950. B&W. Rendering. **SDE**, 65;
    B&W. Rendering. **SDW1**, 121.
  Savinio, Alberto. Maggio Musicale Fiorentino, Florence: 1952. B&W. Rendering.
    SDE, 149.
Armida's Pavilion.
  Benois, Alexander. 1907. B&W. Rendering. **SDE**, 31. 2 photos.
  Benois, Alexander. Ballets Russes, Paris Opera: 1909. B&W. Rendering. **RSD**, illus.
    42.

Armoured Train No. 14-69.
> Akimov, Nicolai. Leningrad Academic Theatre of Drama: 1927. B&W. Set. **RST**, 218;
> B&W. Model. **TAT**, plate 637.
> Hoffman, Vlastislav. National Theatre, Prague: 1954. B&W. Set. **SDW1**, 51.
> _____. Moscow Art Theatre: 1927. B&W. Set. **RST**, 218; B&W. Set. **SCM**, 86.

Arms and the Man.
> Goheen, Douglas-Scott. Yale School of Drama, New Haven, Connecticut: 1965. B&W.
> Set. **SFT**, 350.
> Macdermott, Norman. Everyman Theatre, Hampstead, London: 1922. B&W. Set.
> **TCS2**, plate 78.
> Parkman, Russell. New Mexico Repertory Theatre: 1993. Color. Set. **TCI**, vol. 27, n. 5
> (May 1993). 6.

Aroldo.
> Vagnetti, Gianni. Maggio Musicale Fiorentino, Florence: 1953. B&W. Rendering.
> **SDE**, 160, 161. 3 photos.

Around the World in 80 Days.
> Kula, Marie Liis. Teatr Iounogo Zritelia, Tallinn: 1965. B&W. Model. **SDW3**, 149.

Arsenic and Old Lace.
> Burroughs, Robert C. University of Arizona, Tucson: B&W. Rendering. **SDT**, 64.
> Payne, Darwin Reid. B&W. Model. **TCM**, 15.

The Art of Success.
> Ultz. Royal Shakespeare Company (The Other Place), London: 1986. B&W. Set.
> **BTD**, 64.

Artery.
> _____. Fort Mason Center, California: 1983. B&W. Set. **TCI**, vol. 20, n. 1 (Jan
> 1986). 27.

The Artful Widow.
> Majewski, Andrej. Teatr J. Slowacki, Crakow: 1959. B&W. Rendering. **SDW2**, 168.

Arthur Adamov.
> Aronson, Boris. Théâtre National Populaire, Villeurbanne, France: 1975. B&W. Set.
> **PST**, 440.

Artist Descending a Staircase.
> Straiges, Tony. Duke University, Durham, North Carolina: 1989. B&W. Set. **TCI**, vol.
> 24, n. 3 (Mar 1990). 23.

Artists and Admirers.
> Ward, Anthony. Royal Shakespeare Company, GB: 1993. Color. Set. **TCI**, vol. 27, n. 4
> (Apr 1993). 44.

As Mortal Men.
> MacKichan, Robert. Yale School of Drama, New Haven, Connecticut: B&W. Set.
> **SFT**, 76.

As Thousands Cheer.
> Johnson, Albert R. Music Box Theatre, NYC: 1933. B&W. Set. **BWM**, 238, 239;
> B&W. Set. **RBS**, 83-88; B&W. Set. **SDB**, 55. 2 photos.

As You Desire Me.
> Georgiadis, Nicholas. Lambetti Theatre, Athens: 1986. Color. Model. **BTD**, 75. Act II.

As You Like It.
> Arnone, John. La Jolla Playhouse, California: Color. Set. **TCI**, vol. 21, n. 8 (Oct
> 1987). 27.
> Bailey, James. Court Theatre, New York: 1950. B&W. Rendering. **SDW1**, 169.
> Coutaud, Lucien. Boboli Gardens, Florence: 1938. Color. Rendering. **SOS**, 187.

Crowley, Bob. Royal Shakespeare Company, GB: 1985. Color. Set. **BTD**, 54; B&W.
   Set. **SDT**, 274.
Dexel, W. Berlin: B&W. Rendering. **SCM**, 65.
Drabik, Vincent. Boguskawski Theater, Warsaw: 1925. B&W. Rendering. **RSD**, illus.
   144.
Farrah, Abd'Elkader. Royal Shakespeare Company, Stratford-upon-Avon: 1980. B&W.
   Set. **TCI**, vol. 15, n. 5 (May 1981). 12; B&W. Set. **TDT**, vol. XIX, n. 3 (Fall
   1983). 11.
Fraser, Claude Lovat. Shakespeare Memorial Theatre, Stratford-upon-Avon: 1919.
   B&W. Rendering. **TOP**, 137.
Griffin, Hayden. National Theatre, London: 1979. B&W. Set. **TCI**, vol. 19, n. 9 (Nov
   1985). 25.
Herrmann, Karl-Ernst. Schaubühne am Halleschen Ufer, Berlin: 1977. B&W. Set.
   TCI, vol. 13, n. 1 (Jan/Feb 1979). 18.
Howard, Pamela. Repertory Theatre, Birmingham (UK): 1967. Color. Rendering &
   set. **SDW3**, 46. 4 photos.
Iliska, Alexander Vladimir. National Theatre, Prague: 1923. B&W. Set. **TCS2**, plate
   91.
Kavelin, John. Carnegie-Mellon University, Pittsburgh: B&W. Set. **SDL**, 172.
Kissuer. Cologne, Germany: B&W. Set. **SST**, 258, 376.
Koltai, Ralph. National Theatre, London: 1967/1969. B&W. Set. **RSD**, illus. 519;
   B&W. Set. **SDW3**, 44; B&W. Set. **TCI**, vol. 11, n. 1 (Jan/Feb 1977). 15. 2 photos.
Koltai, Ralph. National Theatre, London: c.1968. B&W. Set. **SDG**, 196.
Miller, Michael. Syracuse Stage, New York: 1990. B&W. Set. **TCI**, vol. 25, n. 3 (Mar
   1991). 23.
Oenslager, Donald. (unproduced): 1941. B&W. Rendering. **TDO**, 109.
Payne, Darwin Reid. MacLeod Theatre, Southern Illinois University, Carbondale:
   B&W. Model & set. **TCM**, 38, 134, 136; B&W. Model. **TDP**, 124.
Seymour, Di. Royal Exchange Theatre, Manchester, England: 1986. B&W. Set. **BTD**,
   52.
Simonson, Lee. Theatre Guild, NYC: 1923. B&W. Set. **SDC**, plate 82. 2 photos;
   B&W. Sketches & set. **TAS**, 128, 129. 5 photos; B&W. Set. **TCS2**, plates 75, 76.
Svoboda, Josef. Tyl Theatre, Prague: 1970. B&W. Set. **SJS**, 156, 157. 3 photos; B&W.
   Set. **STS**, 7.
Thompson, Brian. Old Tote Theatre Company, Parade Theatre, Sydney: 1971. B&W.
   Set. **SDW4**, illus. 23.
Wittstein, Ed. American Shakespeare Festival, Stratford, Connecticut: 1968. B&W.
   Sketch & rendering. **DPT**, 112.
_____. Academy for Performing Arts, Hong Kong: B&W. Set. **TDT** vol. XXXI,
   n. 2 (Spring 1995). 28.
_____. California Institute of the Arts Modular Theatre: 1972. B&W. Set. **TCI**,
   vol. 7, n. 6 (Nov/Dec 1973). 12, 15.
_____. Color. Set. **SDL**, plates 14-4. 2 photos.
Ascent of Mt. Fuji.
Lee, Ming Cho. Arena Stage, Washington, DC: 1975. B&W. Set. **TCI**, vol. 18, n. 2
   (Feb 1984). 18.
Ashes.
Beatty, John Lee. Manhattan Theatre Club, NYC: 1976. B&W. Rendering. **ASD1**, 6;
   B&W. Set. **TDT**, vol. XVIII, n. 4 (Winter 1982). 8.

Aspects of Love.
   Björnson, Maria. Prince of Wales Theatre, London: 1989. Color. Set. **ALW**, 199, 200.
      5 photos; B&W. Model. **BTD**, 169. 4 photos; Color. Set. **TCI**, vol. 24, n. 4 (Apr
      1990). 44-46. 14 photos; Broadhurst Theatre, NYC: 1990. B&W and color. Set.
      MBM, 74, 76, 77.
The Aspern Papers.
   Edwards, Ben. Playhouse Theatre, NYC: 1962. B&W. Rendering. **DDT**, 367.
Ass and Shadow.
   Feuerstein, Bedrich. Liberated Theatre, Prague: 1933. B&W. Set. **TDT**, n. 41 (Summer
      1975). 21.
The Assassin.
   Aronson, Boris. Nederlander Theatre, NYC: 1945. B&W. Rendering. **TAB**, 299.
The Assassins.
   Egemar, Christian. Den Nationale Scene, Bergen, Norway: 1969. B&W. Set. **SDW3**,
      154.
   Eichbauer, Helio. Teatro Ipanema, Rio de Janeiro: 1969. B&W. Rendering. **SDW3**,
      154.
   Gubbels, Klaas. Stadsschouwburg, Nijmegen, Netherlands: 1968. B&W. Set. **SDW3**,
      155. 2 photos.
Assassins.
   Sherman, Loren. Playwrights Horizons, NYC: 1990. B&W. Set. **SON**, 182, 186;
      Color. Model. **TCI**, vol. 25, n. 3 (Mar 1991). 45. 2 photos.
   Ward, Anthony. Donmar Warehouse, Covent Garden, London: 1992. Color. Set. **TCI**,
      vol. 27, n. 4 (Apr 1993). 42. 2 photos.
      _____. London: B&W. Set. **SON**, 185.
L'Assommoir.
      _____. Thêátre de la Porte Saint-Martin, Paris: 1900. B&W. Set. **NTO**, facing
      148.
Astray.
   Svoboda, Josef. (project): 1942. B&W. Rendering. **TDT**, vol. XXVIII, n. 5 (Fall 1992).
      10.
   Svoboda, Josef. Municipal Theatre, Prague: 1944. B&W. Model. **STS**, 32.
At Home Abroad.
   Minelli, Vincent. Winter Garden Theatre, NYC: 1935. B&W. Rendering. **SDA**, 248.
At the Cafe au Gogo.
      _____. 1965. B&W. Set. **RSD**, illus. 611. Happening.
At the Gateway.
   Jones, Robert Edmond. Imperial Theatre, NYC: 1924. B&W. Sketch. **DFT**, plate 34;
      B&W. Rendering. **REJ**, 53.
At the South-East of Tokyo.
   Oda, Otoya. Shimbashi Embujo, Tokyo. 1952. Color. Rendering. **SDW2**, 148.
Atlantida.
   Vychodil, Ladislav. Bratislava: 1961. B&W. Rendering. **TDT**, vol. XV, n. 2 (Summer
      1979). 13; B&W. Set. **TDT**, n. 38 (Oct 1974). front cover; B&W. Set. **TDT**, n. 20
      (Feb 1970). 20. 2 photos.
ATLAS: an opera in three parts.
   Yabara, Yoshio. Houston Grand Opera: 1991. Color. Rendering. **TCI**, vol. 25, n. 3
      (Mar 1991). 13.
Atomic Death.
   Svoboda, Josef. Piccola Scala, Milan: 1965. B&W. Set. **SDW3**, 215. 5 photos.

An Attempt at Flying.
> Yeargan, Michael. Yale Repertory Theatre, New Haven: 1980. B&W. Set. **ASD2**, 177; B&W. Set. **DSL**, figure 2.6(b); B&W. Set. **TCI**, vol. 16, n. 5 (May 1982). 27.

Attila.
> Lee, Ming Cho. Chicago Lyric Opera: 1980. Color. Model. **DDT**, 24b; Color. Set. **TCI**, vol. 18, n. 2 (Feb 1984). 20.
> Varona, José. Deutsches Staatsoper, Berlin: 1971. B&W. Rendering. **DPT**, 18, 46; B&W. Set. **TCI**, vol. 14, n. 5 (Oct 1980). 30.

Attiorpheus.
> Nyvlt, Vladimir. Divadlo na Vinohradech, Prague: 1965. B&W. Model. **SDW3**, 146.

The Au Pair Man.
> Conklin, John. Vivian Beaumont Theatre, Lincoln Center, NYC: 1973. B&W. Set. **TCI**, vol. 14, n. 3 (May/Jun 1980). 22.

Aubade.
> Bignens, Max. State Theatre, Basel: 1949. B&W. Rendering. **SDW1**, 113.

The August Sunday.
> Svoboda, Josef. B&W. Set. **TDT**, n. 7 (Dec 1966). 25.

Aus der Fremde.
> Recalcati, Antonio. Theatertreffen, Berlin: 1980. B&W. Set. **TCI**, vol. 14, n. 6 (Nov/Dec 1980). 36.

Auschwitz, The Investigation.
> Palmstierna-Weiss, Gunilla. Royal Dramatic Theatre, Stockholm: 1966. B&W. Set. **TCI**, vol. 12, n. 7 (Nov/Dec 1978). 43. 2 photos.

The Automobile Graveyard.
> Florez, Modesto. Van Troi-Oriente, Cuba: 1968. B&W. Rendering. **SDW3**, 158.
> Garcia, Victor. Théâtre des Arts, Paris: 1967. B&W. Set. **SDW3**, 159. 2 photos.
> Lester, Lawrence. California State University, Northridge: Color. Set. **DSL**, plate IX; Color. Set. **SST**, plate XIII.

L'Autre Messie.
> Heythum, Antonín. National Theatre, Prague: B&W. Set. **TCS2**, plate 102.

The Autumn Garden.
> Bay, Howard. Coronet Theatre, NYC: 1950. B&W. Set. **TCI**, vol. 17, n. 2 (Feb 1983). 14.

Ave Eva.
> Vychodil, Ladislav. Bratislava: 1947. B&W. Set. **TDT**, vol. XV, n. 2 (Summer 1979). 10.

L'Aventure.
> Wahkévitch, Georges. 1951. B&W. Rendering. **SDE**, 168.

L'Avventura di un Povero Cristiano.
> Falleni, Silvano. 1971. B&W. Set. **SIO**, 53.

Awake and Sing.
> Aronson, Boris. Belasco Theatre, NYC: 1935. B&W. Set. **MCN**, 123; B&W. Set. **TAB**, 54, 55. 3 photos.

The Awakening of Spring.
> Walser, Karl. Kammerspiele, Munich: 1906. B&W. Set. **MRH**, facing 77.

Away.
> Thornley, David. New Zealand: B&W. Model. **TDT**, vol. XXVII, n. 4 (Fall 1991). 20.

The Awful Yet Unfinished Story of Norodom Sihanouk.
> Francois, Guy-Claude. Théâtre du Soleil, the Cartoucherie, France: 1985. B&W. Set. **TCI**, vol. 20, n. 3 (Mar 1986). 31.

Azabache.
> Vera, Gerardo. Seville, Spain: 1992. Color. Set. **TCI**, vol. 26, n. 9 (Nov 1992). 10.

Azouk.
> Benavente, Saulo. Teatro Versailles, Buenos Aires: 1955. Color. Rendering. **SDW1**, 35.

-B-

Baal.
> Herbert, Jocelyn. Phoenix Theatre, London: 1963. B&W. Rendering. **TDT**, vol. XXX, n. 5 (Fall 1994). 19, 20; B&W. Set. **TDT**, vol. XIX, n. 1 (Spring 1983). 8.
> Koltai, Ralph. Royal Shakespeare Company, GB: 1979. B&W and color. Set. **BTD**, 30.
> Maret, Jean-Claude. Belgium: 1972. B&W. Set. **SDW4**, illus. 228.
> Neher, Caspar. Deutsches Theater, Berlin: 1926. B&W. Set. **TBB**, 22; (unproduced): B&W. Rendering. **CBM**, 78; B&W. Rendering & set. **CBM**, 100.

Baba Goya.
> Eigsti, Karl. American Place Theatre, NYC: 1973. B&W. Set. **TCI**, vol. 8, n. 4 (Sep 1974). 21.

Babe's All-Nite Cafe.
> Rorke, Richard. Megaw Theatre, Northridge, California: B&W. Rendering. **SDT**, 115.

Babes in Arms.
> Sovey, Raymond. Shubert Theatre, NYC: 1937. B&W. Set. **BWM**, 181.

Babes in Toyland.
> Sicangco, Eduardo. 1991. Color. Model. **DDT**, 152d. 3 photos.
> Young, John. Majestic Theatre (Columbus Circle), NYC: 1903. B&W. Set. **WMC**, 13.
> _____. NYC: B&W. Set. **TMI**, 97.

Baby.
> Beatty, John Lee. Ethel Barrymore Theatre, NYC: 1983. Color. Set. **MBM**, 164; B&W. Set. **TCI**, vol. 19, n. 5 (May 1985). 23.
> _____. Dallas, Texas: B&W. Set. **TCI**, vol. 19, n. 5 (May 1985). 23.

The Bacchae.
> Guglielminetti, Eugenio. 1969. B&W. Set. **SIO**, 79. 2 photos.
> Polidori, Gianni. 1968. B&W. **SIO**, 118. 2 photos.
> Sporre, Dennis J. University of Illinois, Chicago: B&W. Rendering. **SDT**, 63, 102.

The Bacchantes.
> Casorati, Felice. La Scala, Milan: 1950. B&W. Rendering. **SDE**, 60.
> Hoffman, Vlastislav. National Theatre, Prague: B&W. Set. **TCS2**, plate 144.

Bacchus et Ariane.
> de Chirico, Georgio. Opéra de Paris: 1931. B&W. Rendering. **AST**, 182. 2 photos.

Back to Back.
> Gianfrancesco, Edward. WPA Theatre, NYC: 1983. Color. Set. **TCI**, vol. 20, n. 4 (Apr 1986). 34.

Back to Methuselah.
> Koltai, Ralph. National Theatre, London: 1969. B&W. Set. **RSD**, illus. 518; B&W. Set. **SDB**, 46; B&W. Set. **SDW3**, 88, 89. 7 photos; B&W. Set. **TCI**, vol. 11, n. 1 (Jan/Feb 1977). 14, 15. 4 photos.
> Shelving, Paul. Great Britain: 1925, B&W. Rendering & set. **DIT**, plates 29, 30.
> Simonson, Lee. Garrick Theatre, NYC: 1922. B&W. Set. **MCN**, 57; B&W. Set. **PLT**, illus. 22-24; B&W. Set. **TAS**, 124, 125. 4 photos; B&W. Set. **TCS2**, plate 363; B&W. Set. **TPH**, photo 369.

Le Baiser de la Fée.
  Rowell, Kenneth. Royal Ballet, Covent Garden, London: 1960. Color. Rendering.
    SDR, 75.
Baker Street.
  Smith, Oliver. Broadway Theatre, NYC: 1965. B&W. Rendering. **TCI**, vol. 16, n. 4
    (Apr 1982). 63.
The Baker's Wife.
  _____. B&W. Set. **BWM**, 346.
The Baker, the Baker's Wife and the Baker's Errand Boy.
  Malclés, Jean Dénis. Comédie des Champs-Élysées, Paris: 1968. B&W. Rendering.
    SDW3, 123.
Le Bal.
  de Chirico, Georgio. Opéra, Monte Carlo: 1929. B&W. Rendering. **AST**, 181; B&W.
    Rendering. **RSD**, illus. 311, 312. Ballet-Russes.
Balconville.
  Centaur Theatre, Montreal: B&W. Set. **TCI**, vol. 18, n. 2 (Feb 1984). 31.
The Balcony.
  Cardoso, W. Pereira & Victor Garcia. Ruth Escobar Theater, Sao Paulo: 1970. B&W.
    Set. **RSD**, illus. 622. 4 photos; B&W. Set. **SDB**, 200; B&W. Set. **SDW4**, illus.
    262-264.
  Eichbauer, Helio. Teatro João Caetano, Rio de Janeiro: 1970. B&W. Set. **SDW3**, 125.
  Farrah, Abd'Elkader. Royal Shakespeare Company, Barbican Centre, London: 1987.
    Color. Set. **BTD**, 66.
  Ostoja-Kotkowski, J.S. Adelaide University Theatre Guild, Australia: 1965. B&W. Set.
    SDW3, 125.
  Scheffler, John. Playhouse in the Park, Cincinnati: 1969. B&W. Set. **DPT**, 385.
The Ballad of Baby Doe.
  Oenslager, Donald. Central City Opera House, Colorado: 1956. B&W. Rendering.
    CSD, 40; B&W. Rendering. **DDT**, 334; B&W. Collages. **DPT**, 123; B&W. Render-
    ing. **SDA**, 267; B&W. Rendering. **SDB**, 70; B&W. Rendering. **TDO**, 128, 129.
  _____. Lincoln Center, NYC: 1976. B&W. Set. **TCI**, vol. 14, n. 6 (Nov/Dec
    1980). 13.
The Ballad of Soapy Smith.
  Lee, Eugene. New York Shakespeare Festival, NYC: 1984. B&W. Model. **ASD1**, 72.
Ballade.
  Aronson, Boris. New York City Center: 1952. B&W. Rendering & set. **TAB**, 18, 302.
Balladyna.
  Vychodil, Ladislav. Bratislava: 1960. B&W. Rendering. **TDT**, vol. XV, n. 2 (Summer
    1979). 13.
Ballerina.
  Whistler, Rex. London: 1933. B&W. Rendering. **SDB**, 105.
Ballet without Music.
  Scialoja, Toti. La Fenice, Venice: 1950. B&W. Set. **SDW1**, 130.
Balli Plastici.
  Depero, Fortunato. Teatro dei Piccoli di Palazzo Odescalchi, Rome: 1916/1918. B&W.
    Rendering. **AST**, 69; B&W. Rendering. **TCS2**, plate 162.
Un Ballo in Maschera.
  Conklin, John. San Francisco Opera: 1977. B&W. Set. **TCI**, vol. 14, n. 3 (May/Jun
    1980). 23.
  Doboujinsky, Mstislav. Metropolitan Opera, NYC: 1940. B&W. Rendering. **MOM**,
    10.

Wexler, Peter. Metropolitan Opera, NYC: 1979. B&W. Set. **TCI**, vol. 14, n. 6 (Nov/
Dec 1980). 15.

Ballroom.

Wagner, Robin. Majestic Theatre, NYC: 1978. Color. Set. **BWM**, 135; B&W. Set.
TCI, vol. 13, n. 2 (Mar/Apr 1979). 14. 3 photos; Color. Set. **TCI**, vol. 23, n. 8 (Oct
1989). 46.

Balm in Gilead.

Rigdon, Kevin. Steppenwolf Theatre, Chicago: 1981. B&W. Set. **TCI**, vol. 21, n. 2
(Feb 1987). 30.

_____. Emerson College, Boston: B&W. Set. **TCI**, vol. 23, n. 9 (Nov 1989). 52.

The Band Wagon.

Johnson, Albert R. New Amsterdam Theatre, NYC: 1931. B&W. Set. **BWM**, 63, 251,
252; B&W. Set. **MCN**, 104; B&W. Set. **RBS**, 47, 48; B&W. Set. **SCM**, 126;
B&W. Set. **SOW**, plate 95; B&W. Set. **WMC**, 165.

Bang!

Rigdon, Kevin. Steppenwolf Theatre, Chicago: 1986. Color. Set. **TCI**, vol. 21, n. 2
(Feb 1987). 30.

Bánk Bán.

Forray, Gabor. Erkel Theatre, National Opera, Budapest: B&W. Set. **TDT**, n. 38 (Oct
1974). 13.

Barabau.

Utrillo, Maurice. France: 1925. B&W. Rendering. **SCM**, 47.

Barabbas.

Martin, Denis. Théâtre National de Belgique, Brussels: 1954. B&W. Set. **SDW2**, 30.
Olson, Erik. Dramatiska Teatern, Stockholm: 1953. B&W. Set. **SDW1**, 168.
Pira, John. Nationaal Toneel, Antwerp: 1951. B&W. Set. **SDW1**, 47. 2 photos.

Barbarians.

Loquasto, Santo. Williamstown Theatre Festival, Massachusetts: 1986. B&W. Set.
TCI, vol. 20, n. 8 (Oct 1986). 18.

Das Barbecü.

Sicangco, Eduardo. Minetta Lane Theatre, NYC: Color. Set. **TCI**, vol. 29, n. 2 (Feb
1995). 35. 3 photos.

The Barber of Seville.

Butlin, Roger. Sydney Opera House: 1974. B&W. Model & set. **OPE**, 130, 133, 134.
Freyer, Achim. Deutsches Staatsoper, Berlin: 1968. B&W. Set. **SDW3**, 177. 6 photos.
Heeley, Desmond. New York City Opera, Lincoln Center: 1988. Color. Model. **TCI**,
vol. 22, n. 8 (Oct 1988). 58.

Iliprandi, Gian Carlo. 1953. B&W. Rendering. **SDE**, 92.
Jones, Robert Edmond. Central City Opera House, Colorado: 1941. B&W. Rendering.
REJ, 99.

Kouril, Miroslav. D37 Theatre, Prague: 1936. B&W. Set. **RSD**, illus. 283.
Lee, Ming Cho. Juilliard School of Music, NYC: B&W. Model. **TDT**, n. 24 (Feb
1971). 8.

Luzzati, Emanuele. 1952. B&W. Rendering. **SDE**, 102. 2 photos.
Marchi, Mario Vellani. Teatro Massimo, Palermo: 1953. B&W. Rendering. **SDE**, 118.
2 photos.

Ponnelle, Jean-Pierre. Kleines Festspielhaus, Salzburg: 1968. B&W and color. Set.
OPE, 128, 132, 135; B&W. Set. **TCI**, vol. 12, n. 3 (Mar/Apr 1978). 19.

Reinhardt, Andreas. Bavarian State Opera, Munich: 1974/1976. B&W. Set. **SDW4**,
illus. 124; B&W. Set. **TDT**, vol. XII, n. 1 (Spring 1976). 26; B&W. Set. **TCI**, vol.
11, n. 2 (Mar/Apr 1977). 10.

Roller, Alfred. Redoutensaal, Hofburg Palace, Vienna: B&W. Rendering. **CSC**, facing 190.

Sicangco, Eduardo. Texas Opera Theatre, Houston: 1984. B&W. Rendering & show portal. **BSE3**, 36, 37.

Wagner, Robin. Metropolitan Opera, NYC: 1982. B&W. Set. **ASD1**, 167; B&W. Set. **TDT**, vol. XIX, n. 4 (Winter 1983). 10. 2 photos.

Zelenka, Frantisek. Vinohrady Theatre, Prague: 1931. B&W. Rendering. **TDT**, n. 42 (Fall 1975). 26.

Zimmermann, Jörg. Stadttheater, Basle: 1973. B&W. Set. **OPE**, 130, 132, 134.

_____. Covent Garden, London: 1935. B&W. Set. **CGA**, 118.

_____. New York City Opera, Lincoln Center: B&W. Set. **TCI**, vol. 7, n. 1 (Jan/Feb 1973). 18.

Barchester Towers.

Mielziner, Jo. Martin Beck, Theatre, NYC: 1937. B&W. Rendering. **DTT**, 101.

Barefoot in Athens.

Aronson, Boris. Martin Beck Theatre, NYC: 1951. B&W. Rendering. **TAB**, 302.

Barefoot in the Park.

Smith, Oliver. Biltmore Theatre, NYC: 1963. B&W. Rendering. **TCI**, vol. 16, n. 4 (Apr 1982). 16.

Barnum.

Mitchell, David. St. James Theatre, NYC: 1980. B&W. Set. **ASD1**, 133; B&W. Model & rendering. **DDT**, 309, 312, 331. 3 photos; Color. Set. **DSL**, plate V; Color. Set. **MBM**, 140, 141; B&W. Set. **TCI**, vol. 14, n. 5 (Oct 1980). 16, 17. 6 photos; B&W. Set. **TCI**, vol. 21, n. 1 (Jan 1987). 30, 32; B&W. Set. **TDT**, vol. XVII, n. 1 (Spring 1981). 12, 13. 3 photos; B&W. Set. **WMC**, 7.

_____. S.S. Norway: B&W. Set. **TCI**, vol. 21, n. 1 (Jan 1987). 32.

_____. Theatre Memphis: B&W. Set. **TCI**, vol. 21, n. 1 (Jan 1987). 32.

_____. Omaha Community Playhouse, Nebraska: B&W. Set. **TCI**, vol. 21, n. 1 (Jan 1987). 33.

_____. Waterloo Community Playhouse, Iowa: Color. Set. **TCI**, vol. 21, n. 1 (Jan 1987). 31.

The Barrels.

Szinte, Gabor. Pesti Szinhaz, Budapest: 1968. B&W. Rendering. **SDW3**, 156.

The Barretts of Wimpole Street.

Mielziner, Jo. Empire Theatre, NYC: 1931. B&W. Set. **MCN**, 102; B&W. Set. **SCM**, 108.

The Bartered Bride.

Polakov, Lester. Opera Company of Boston: 1973. B&W. Sketches. **DPT**, 113; Color. Projection design. **DPT**, between 124 & 125.

Svoboda, Josef. Grand Opera of the Fifth of May, Prague: 1946. B&W. Set. **STS**, 42, 43; Stuttgart: 1990. B&W and color. Set. **TDT**, vol. XXX, n. 5 (Fall 1994). 38, 41.

Bartholomew Fair.

Dudley, William. National Theatre (Olivier), London: 1988. Color. Set. **BTD**, 43; B&W. Set. **TDT**, vol. XXV, n. 3 (Fall 1989). 20.

Le Baruffe Chiozzotte (Goldoni).

Damiani, Luciano. 1965. B&W. Rendering & set. **SIO**, 41-45. 6 photos.

The Basic Training of Pavlo Hummel.

Mitchell, David. New York Shakespeare Festival, NYC: 1971. B&W. Set. **ASD1**, 134.

The Bassarids.

Firth, Tazeena & Timothy O'Brien. Great Britain: Color. Model. **TDT**, vol. XII, n. 3 (Fall 1976). 35.

Ter-Arutunian, Rouben. Santa Fe Opera: 1968. B&W. Model. **DPT**, 110.
Vespignani, Renzo. La Scala, Milan: 1967-1968. B&W. Set. **SIO**, 157.
_____. Salzburg: B&W. Set. **TCI**, vol. 11, n. 2 (Mar/Apr 1977). 20.
Bassoon and Flute.
  Zelenka, Frantisek. National Theatre, Prague: 1929. B&W. Rendering. **TDT**, n. 42
  (Fall 1975). 26.
Bastien et Bastienne.
  Rava, Carlo E. Angelicum, Milan: 1950. B&W. Rendering. **SDE**, 142.
The Bath.
  _____. Russia: B&W. Model. **SCM**, 90.
The Bathhouse.
  Meyerhold, Vsevelod, plan; Sergei Vakhtangov, execution. Meyerhold Theatre, Mos-
  cow: 1930. B&W. Set. **MOT**, between 272 & 273; B&W. Set. **RST**, 260, 261.
  Szajna, Josef. Stary Teatr, Cracow: 1967. B&W. Set. **SDW3**, 221.
Battaglia Navale.
  Polidori, Gianni. 1964. B&W. Set. **SIO**, 113.
Battle of Angels.
  Beatty, John Lee. Circle Repertory Company, NYC: 1974. B&W. Rendering. **DPT**, 15.
The Battle of Carnival and Lent.
  _____. University of North Carolina, Chapel Hill: B&W. Set. **TCI**, vol. 5, n. 1
  (Jan/Feb 1971). 14.
Battleship Gertie.
  Aronson, Boris. Lyceum Theatre, NYC: 1935. B&W. Model. **TAB**, 295.
Bauer als Millionär.
  Crayon. Deutsches Schauspielhaus, Hamburg: B&W. Rendering. **TCS2**, plate 275.
Bauernzorn.
  Ockel, Reinhold. State Theatre, Aachen: 1926. B&W. Set. **TCS2**, plate 137.
Die Bauren (The Peasants).
  Hein, Peter. Volksbühne, Berlin: 1976. B&W. Model. **TDT**, vol. XVI, n. 1 (Spring
  1980). 16. 2 photos.
Bear Skin.
  Martin, Denis. Théâtre National de Belgique, Brussels: 1951. Color. Rendering.
  SDW2, 33.
The Beard.
  Jurkowitsch, Peter H. Theater Creativ im Savoy, Vienna: 1969. B&W. Set. **SDW3**,
  152.
Beatlemania.
  _____. Winter Garden Theatre, NYC: 1977. B&W. Set. **MBM**, 183.
Beatrix Cenci.
  Conklin, John. New York City Opera: 1973. B&W. Set. **DPT**, 310.
  _____. Washington Opera, DC: B&W. Set. **TCI**, vol. 17, n. 7 (Aug/Sep 1983).
  35.
Beautiful Aklunersta.
  Sheklashviki, Shmagi. USSR: B&W. Model. **TDT**, vol. XX, n. 1 (Spring 1984). 15.
The Beautiful Galatea.
  Oenslager, Donald. Central City Opera House, Colorado: 1951. B&W. Model. **TDO**,
  125.
The Beautiful People.
  Leve, Samuel. Lyceum Theatre, NYC: 1941. B&W. Rendering. **SDW1**, 199.

Beauty and the Beast.

Meyer, Stan. Palace Theatre, NYC: 1994. Color. Set. **TCI**, vol. 28, n. 7 (Aug/Sep 1994). 43.

Woolley, Reginald. Players Theatre, London: 1949. B&W. Rendering. **SDW1**, 188.

The Beaux' Stratagem.

_____. Carnegie-Mellon University, Pittsburgh: 1964. B&W. Set. **TCI**, vol. 7, n. 5 (Oct 1973). 24.

Elder, Eldon. Center Stage, Baltimore: 1971. B&W. Model. **EED**, (pages not numbered); B&W. Set. **TCI**, vol. 7, n. 3 (May/Jun 1973). 15. 3 photos.

Becket or the Honour of God.

Malclés, Jean Dénis. Théâtre Montparnasse, Paris: 1959. B&W. Set. **SDW2**, 94. 3 photos.

Becket.

Brown, Lewis. Tyrone Guthrie Theatre, Minneapolis: 1973. B&W. Set. **TCI**, vol. 9, n. 1 (Jan/Feb 1975). 11.

Hurry, Leslie. Royal Shakespeare Company, Aldwych Theatre, London: 1961. B&W. Sketches. **SDW2**, 216.

Becoming Memories.

Feiner, Harry. Pittsburgh Public Theatre: 1985. B&W. Set. **BSE4**, 20.

The Bed Before Yesterday.

Beatty, John Lee. Wilmington Playhouse: 1976. B&W. Sketch. **TDT**, vol. XVIII, n. 4 (Winter 1982). 7.

The Bed-bug, part 1.

Meyerhold, Vsevelod, plan; The. Kukriniksky, execution. Meyerhold Theatre, Moscow: 1929. B&W. Rendering & set. **RST**, 256, 257. 3 photos.

The Bed-bug, part 2.

Meyerhold, Vsevelod, plan; Alexander Rodchenko, execution. Meyerhold Theatre, Moscow: 1929. B&W. Set. **RST**, 258, 259.

Beethoven.

Ballif, Ariel. Yale School of Drama, New Haven, Connecticut: 1952. B&W. Set. **SFT**, 118. 6 photos.

Before I Got My Eye Put Out.

Faulkner, Cliff. South Coast Repertory Theatre, Costa Mesa, California: Color. Set. **TCI**, vol. 20, n. 9 (Nov 1986). 25.

Before the Dawn.

Itô, Kisaku. Tsukiji Shogekijo, Tokyo: 1934. B&W. Set & ground plan. **SDW1**, 148, 149.

Before the Sunset.

Deutsches Theater, Berlin: B&W. Set. **SCM**, 63.

Der Befreite Don Quichote.

Pillartz, T.C. State Theatre, Crefeld: B&W. Set. **TCS2**, plate 138.

The Beggar.

Stern, Ernst. Deutsches Theater, Berlin: 1917. B&W. Rendering. **MRT**, 29; B&W. Rendering. **RSD**, illus. 117.

The Beggar on Horseback.

Thompson, Woodman. Broadhurst Theatre, NYC: 1924. B&W. Set. **MCN**, 67; B&W. Rendering. **SCM**, 119. Design for the pantomime "A Kiss in Xanadu."

_____. Lincoln Center, NYC: 1970. B&W. Set. **TCI**, vol. 4, n. 4 (Sep 1970). 19.

Beggar's Holiday.

Smith, Oliver. Broadway Theatre, NYC: 1946. B&W. Set. **TCI**, vol. 16, n. 4 (Apr 1982). 13, 62.

The Beggar's Opera.
   Fraser, Claude Lovat. Lyric Theatre, Hammersmith, London: 1920. B&W. Rendering.
      SDG, 176.
   Gunter, John. National Theatre (Cottesloe), England: B&W. Set. **TCI,** vol. 18, n. 1
      (Jan 1984). 37; B&W. Model. **TDT,** vol. XX, n. 1 (Spring 1984). 19.
   Kiesler, Frederick. NYC: 1950. B&W. Sketch. **EIF,** photo 39.
   Steinberg, Paul. Santa Fe Opera: 1992. Color. Set. **TCI,** vol. 29, n. 4 (Apr 1995). 32.
   Straiges, Tony. Tyrone Guthrie Theatre, Minneapolis: 1979. B&W. Model. **ASD2,** 147;
      B&W. Model. **DDT,** 235; B&W. Set. **TCI,** vol. 16, n. 2 (Feb 1982). 15; B&W. Set.
      TCI, vol. 16, n. 2 (Feb 1982). 19; B&W. Set. **TCI,** vol. 17, n. 4 (Apr 1983). 23.
   Taylor, Robert U. Chelsea Theatre Center, Brooklyn, New York: 1972. B&W. Render-
      ing. **CSD,** 133; B&W. c **TCI,** vol. 11, n. 1 (Jan/Feb 1977). 25.
   Zimmerman, Reinhart. Berlin: 1963. B&W. Model & set. **SDB,** 75.
      _____. University of North Carolina, Chapel Hill: B&W. Set. **TCI,** vol. 5, n. 1
      (Jan/Feb 1971). 14.
The Beggars.
   Coltellacci, Giulio. Valle, Rome: 1951. B&W. Set. **SDW1,** 125.
Being a Father is Not Easy.
      _____. National Opera, Sofia, Bulgaria: B&W. Set. **SCM,** 83.
Le Bel Indifférent.
   de Nobili, Lila. 1953. B&W. Rendering. **SDE,** 127.
The Bell of Mayfair.
   Harford, W. Vaudeville Theatre, London. 1906. B&W. Set. **MCD,** plate 61.
La Belle au Bois Dormant.
   Korovin, Konstantin. 1915. B&W and color. Rendering. **FCS,** plate 171, color plate
      17.
La Belle Hélène.
   Vertès, Marcel. Opéra de Paris: 1955. B&W. Rendering. **SDW2,** 102.
La Belle Parée.
      _____. Winter Garden Theatre, NYC: 1911. B&W. Set. **WMC,** 53.
Bells Are Ringing.
   Du Bois, Raoul Pène. Shubert Theatre, NYC: 1956. Color. Set. **BWM,** 104.
Bent.
   Loquasto, Santo. New Apollo Theatre, NYC: 1979. B&W. Set. **ASD1,** 105; B&W. Set.
      TDT, vol. XVII, n. 3 (Fall 1981). 15, 17. 4 photos.
Benvenuto Cellini.
   Montresor, Beni. Covent Garden, London: 1976. B&W. Set. **CGA,** 189.
Bérénice.
   Allio, René. Théâtre de la Cité, Villeurbanne: 1969. B&W. Set. **SDW3,** 73, 219. 4
      photos.
The Best Little Whorehouse in Texas.
   Atkinson, Patrick. Missouri Summer Repertory Theatre, Columbia: 1985. B&W. Set.
      BSE4, 68.
   Kellogg, Marjorie Bradley. Entermedia Theatre, NYC: 1978. Color. Set. **MBM,** 101.
The Best Years of Our Lives.
   Jenkins, George. NYC: B&W. Rendering. **TCI,** vol. 14, n. 2 (Mar/Apr 1980). 25.
La Bête: A Comedy of Manners.
   Hudson, Richard. Eugene O'Neill Theatre, NYC: 1991. Color. Set. **TCI,** vol. 25, n. 4
      (Apr 1991). 46-49. 5 photos.
Bethlehem.
   Craig, Edward Gordon. 1902. B&W. Rendering & set. **EGC,** plates 4, 5.

Houseman, Laurence. Imperial Institute, London: 1902. B&W. Set. **DMS**, plate 23.

Betrayal.

Bury, John. National Theatre (Lyttleton), London: 1978. B&W. Set. **BTD**, 62. 4 photos; B&W. Set. **TCI**, vol. 14, n. 3 (May/Jun 1980). 6.

The Betrothal.

Ricketts, Charles. Gaiety Theatre, London: 1921. B&W. Rendering. **TDC**, 143.

Betty in Mayfair.

Harker, Joseph & Phil Harker. Adelphi Theatre, London: 1925. B&W. Set. **MCD**, plate 130.

Betty.

Ryan, E.H. & Alfred Terraine. Daly's Theatre, London: 1915. B&W. Set. **MCD**, plate 106.

Between East and West.

Jenkins, David. McCarter Theatre, Princeton, New Jersey: 1992. B&W. Set. **DDT**, 586.

Between the Fish and the Moon.

Chambers, Jan. Smith College, Massachusetts: Color. Set. **TDT**, vol. XXVI, n. 1 (Spring 1990). 7 of insert.

Beyond.

Jones, Robert Edmond. Provincetown Playhouse, NYC: 1924. B&W. Sketch. **DFT**, plate 18. Fireside; B&W. Set. **TCS2**, plates 96, 97.

Beyond the Horizon.

Hewlett & Charles Basing. Morosco Theatre, NYC: 1920. B&W. Set. **MCN**, 49.

Shoakang, Wang. Jiangsu Art Theatre, Nanjing, China: B&W. Set. **TDT**, vol. XXV, n. 1 (Spring 1989). 11, 12.

Beyond Therapy.

Jackness, Andrew. Brooks Atkinson Theatre, NYC: 1982. Color. Set. **TCI**, vol. 21, n. 4 (Apr 1987). 35.

Biedermann and the Firebugs.

Czclényi, Jósef. Némzeti Színház, Budapest: 1960. B&W. Rendering. **SDW2**, 139.

Fritzsche, Max. Schauspielehaus, Zürich: 1958. B&W. Set. **SDW2**, 110.

Svoboda, Josef. 1991. B&W. Set. **TDT**, vol. XXX, n. 5 (Fall 1994). 41.

The Big and the Small.

Herrmann, Karl-Ernst. Germany: B&W. Set. **TCI**, vol. 13, n. 6 (Nov/Dec 1979). 24.

Big Ben.

_____. Adelphi Theatre, London: 1946. B&W. Set. **BMF**, 97.

Big Deal.

Larkin, Peter. Broadway Theatre, NYC: 1986. Color. Set. **MBM**, 200, 201; Color. Set. **TCI**, vol. 20, n. 7 (Aug/Sep 1986). 25. 2 photos; B&W. Sketch. **TCI**, vol. 23, n. 1 (Jan 1989). 42.

The Big Enchilada.

_____. Mobius Theatre, University of Connecticut: 1975. B&W. Set. **TSE**, 54.

Big Hotel.

Beard, Mark. Ridiculous Theatre, NYC: 1989. B&W. Set. **TCI**, vol. 24, n. 1 (Jan 1990). 23.

The Big House.

_____. Yale Repertory Theatre, New Haven: B&W. Set. **TCI**, vol. 6, n. 3 (May/Jun 1972). 27.

The Big Love.

Mitchell, David. Coconut Grove Theatre, Miami: 1990. B&W. Set. **TCI**, vol. 25, n. 2 (Feb 1991). 10.

The Big People.
>   Aronson, Boris. Lyric Theatre, Bridgeport, Connecticut: 1947. B&W. Rendering.
>   **TAB**, 300.

Big River.
>   Landesman, Heidi. American Repertory Theatre, Cambridge, Massachusetts: 1984.
>   B&W. Set. **TCI**, vol. 20, n. 9 (Nov 1986). 21; Eugene O'Neill Theatre, NYC:
>   1985. B&W. Model. **ASD2**, 72; B&W. Set. **BSE4**, 88; B&W. Model. **DDT**, 171;
>   Color. Set. **MBM**, 24; B&W and color. Rendering & set. **TCI**, vol. 19, n. 7 (Aug/
>   Sep 1985). 31-36. 5 photos; B&W. Set. **TDT**, vol. XXI, n. 2 (Summer 1985). 6, 7;
>   La Jolla Playhouse, California: 1986. B&W. Set. **TCI**, vol. 21, n. 8 (Oct 1987). 28.

Bike Inquest.
>   Kavelin, John. Mark Taper Forum, Los Angeles: B&W. Set. **TCI**, vol. 14, n. 4 (Sep
>   1980). 46.

Billy Bishop Goes to War.
>   Donnelly, Mark. Old Globe Theatre, San Diego: B&W. Set. **SDT**, 105.
>   Schmidt, Robert N. Alley Theatre, Houston: B&W and color. Rendering & set. **TDT**,
>   vol. XXX, n. 3 (Summer 1994). 11.

Billy Budd.
>   Cairns, Tom & Antony McDonald. English National Opera, London: 1988. Color. Set.
>   **BTD**, 145.
>   Dudley, William. Metropolitan Opera, NYC: B&W. Set. **TCI**, vol. 16, n. 9 (Nov/Dec
>   1982). 30.
>   Dyer, Chris. Scottish Opera, Edinburgh: 1987. B&W. Set. **BTD**, 125.
>   Lee, Eugene. Trinity Square Theatre, Providence, Rhode Island: 1969. B&W. Set.
>   **TCI**, vol. 4, n. 2 (Mar/Apr 1970). 13; B&W. Set. **TDT**, vol. XVIII, n. 2 (Summer
>   1982). 9.
>   Piper, John. Royal Opera House, Covent Garden, London: 1951. B&W. Set. **CGA**,
>   140; B&W. Model. **SDW1**, 183.

Bingo.
>   Gropman, David. Yale Repertory Theatre, New Haven: 1976. B&W. Set. **ASD2**, 35. 4
>   photos.

The Bird Cage.
>   Aronson, Boris. Coronet Theatre (Eugene O'Neill Theatre), NYC: 1950. Color. Ren-
>   dering. **TAB**, 99.

The Bird of Paradise.
>   Gros, Ernest. Daly's Theatre, NYC: 1912. B&W. Set. **MCN**, 39.

The Birds.
>   Ganeau, François. Grand Theater, Geneva: 1964. B&W. Rendering. **SDW3**, 32.
>   Melena, Miroslav. B&W. Model. **TDT**, vol. XXVII, n. 2 (Spring 1991). 30.
>   Oenslager, Donald. (project): 1929. B&W. Rendering. **SCM**, 129; B&W. Rendering.
>   **STN**, 57-67. 6 photos.
>   Sadowski, Andrzej. Teatr Dramatyczny, Warsaw: 1960. B&W. Rendering. **SDW2**, 169.
>   _____. Camden Lock, GB: 1985. Color. Set. **BTD**, 201.
>   _____. Yale Dramatic Association, New Haven, Connecticut: B&W. Set. **WTP**,
>   42.

The Birth of a Poet.
>   Salle, David. Rotterdam: 1982. B&W. Set. **TCI**, vol. 19, n. 9 (Nov 1985). 36; Brook-
>   lyn Academy of Music, New York: 1985. B&W. Set. **TDT**, vol. XXII, n. 1 (Spring
>   1986). 14, 15.

Jones, Robert Edmond. Chicago Opera Association: 1920. B&W. Sketch. **DFT**, plate 10. Sc. 1: The courtyard of the palace; B&W. Sketch. **DFT**, plate 11. Sc. 2: The hall of mirrors; B&W. Rendering. **DIT**, plate 117.1; B&W. Rendering. **REJ**, 35; B&W. Rendering. **SDA**, 272. 2 photos.

The Birthday Party.
Gillette, J. Michael. B&W. Rendering. **TDP**, 80.

Bittersweet.
Calthrop, Gladys E. & Ernst Stern. His Majesty's Theatre, London: 1929. B&W. Set. **MCD**, plate 154.

Black and Blue.
Orezzoli, Hector & Claudio Segovia. Minskoff Theatre, NYC: 1989. Color. Set. **MBM**, 180, 181.

Black Comedy.
Beatty, John Lee. Roundabout Theatre, NYC: 1993. Color. Set. **TCI**, vol. 27, n. 9 (Nov 1993). 8.

Black Dragon Residence.
. University of Hawaii: 1972. B&W. Set. **TCI**, vol. 6, n. 5 (Oct 1972). 21; B&W. Set. **TCI**, vol. 6, n. 6 (Nov/Dec 1972). 26. 2 photos.

The Black Feast.
Raffaëlli. Michel. Landestheater, Darmstadt: 1963. B&W. Set. **SDW2**, 100.

The Black Pig.
Damiani, Luciano. Théâtre National Populaire, Villeurbanne, France: 1974. B&W. Set. **SDW4**, illus. 339-342.

The Black Rider.
Wilson, Robert. Brooklyn Academy of Music, New York: 1991/1993. Color. Set. **TCI**, vol. 28, n. 2 (Feb 1994). 8; Color. Set. **TCI**, vol. 25, n. 5 (May 1991). 20.

Black Snow.
McDonald, Anthony. American Repertory Theatre, Cambridge, Massachusetts: 1992. B&W. Set. **TCI**, vol. 27, n. 3 (Mar 1993). 9.

The Black Swan.
Constable, William. Empire Theatre, Sydney: 1951. Color. Set. **SDW1**, 41.

The Blacks.
Acquart, André. Théâtre de Lutece, Paris: 1959. B&W. Rendering. **RSD**, illus. 498; B&W. Set. **SDW2**, 83.
_____. Akademie der Künste, Berlin: 1964. B&W. Set. **TSY**, 213.

Blade to the Heat.
Hernandez, Riccardo. New York Shakespeare Festival, NYC: 1994. Color. Model. **TCI**, vol. 28, n. 9 (Nov 1994). 8.

Les Blancs.
Larkin, Peter. Longacre Theatre, NYC: 1970. B&W. Rendering. **TCI**, vol. 23, n. 1 (Jan 1989). 42.

Der Blaue Boll.
Barlach, Ernst. Berlin: 1930. B&W. Sketch. **AST**, 209. 4 photos.

Bless the Bride.
Moiseiwitsch, Tanya. Adelphi Theatre, London: 1947. B&W. Set. **MCD**, plate 193.

Blithe Spirit.
_____. Asolo State Theatre, Sarasota, Florida: 1989. B&W. Set. **TCR**, 89.
_____. B&W. Set. **WTP**, 160, 161. 4 photos.

Blitz.
Kenny, Sean. London: 1962. B&W. Set. **SDB**, 83. 2 photos; Color. Set. **TCI**, vol. 18, n. 4 (Apr 1984). 54.

Blockade.

_____. Moscow Art Theatre: 1929. B&W. Set. **RST**, 219.

Blond Eckbert.

Chitty, Alison. Santa Fe Opera: 1994. Color. Set. **TCI**, vol. 28, n. 8 (Oct 1994). 8.

Blood.

_____. Public Theatre, NYC: B&W. Set. **TCI**, vol. 5, n. 4 (Sep 1971). 11. 3 photos.

Blood Wedding.

Barcelo, Randy. 1979. Color. Set. **DDT**, 440a.

Barth, Ruodi. Hesse State Theatre, Wiesbaden: 1958. B&W. Rendering. **SDW2**, 109.

Borges, Jacobo. Teatro Nacional, Caracas: 1961. B&W. Set. **SDW2**, 243.

Dryden, Dan. University of California, San Diego: 1974. B&W. Set. **TCI**, vol. 8, n. 6 (Nov/Dec 1974). 2.

Falleni, Silvano. 1965. B&W. Set. **SIO**, 51.

Gonçalves, Martin. Teatro Ginastico, Rio de Janeiro: 1944. B&W. Set. **SDW1**, 49.

Gondolf, Walter. Grosses Haus, Cologne: 1957. B&W. Set. **SDW2**, 59.

Winkler, Robert. B&W. Model. **DMS**, plate 56.

The Bloodknot.

Woodbridge, Patricia. Manhattan Theatre Club, NYC: B&W. Set. **TCI**, vol. 15, n. 6 (Jun/Jul 1981). 16.

Bloomer Girl.

Ayers, Lemuel. Shubert Theatre, NYC: 1944. B&W. Set. **SDA**, 248; B&W. Set. **SDW1**, 191; B&W. Set. **WMC**, 181; B&W. Set. **SDB**, 56; B&W. Set. **TMT**, 157.

The Blue Bird.

Egorov, V.E. Moscow Art Theatre: 1908. B&W. Set. **RSD**, illus. 31; B&W. Rendering. **SDC**, plates 65, 66.

Groff, Robert A. (project): Color. Rendering. **TDT**, vol. XXVIII, n. 2 (Spring 1992). 6 of insert.

Robinson, Frederick Cayley. Haymarket Theatre, London: 1909. B&W. Rendering. **SDT**, 271.

Saverys, Albert. Théatre Royal Flamand, Gent: 1948. B&W. Set. **SDW1**, 48.

Unitt, Edward G. & Wickes. New Theatre, NYC: 1910. B&W. Set. **MCN**, 35.

_____. France: 1927. B&W. Projection. **TPH**, photo 374.

_____. Moscow Art Theatre: 1911. B&W. Sketch. **TPH**, photo 302.

Blue Vienna.

Bregenz Festival, Austria: B&W. Set. **TCI**, vol. 11, n. 2 (Mar/Apr 1977). 22.

Blue Window.

Arcenas, Loy. 1989. B&W. Set. **SDL**, 9.

Dorsey, Kent. Berkeley Repertory Theatre, California: 1987. Color. Set. **TCI**, vol. 21, n. 7 (Aug/Sep 1987). 14.

Faulkner, Cliff. South Coast Repertory Theatre, Costa Mesa, California: 1985. B&W. Set. **BSE4**, 75; B&W. Set. **TCI**, vol. 20, n. 4 (Apr 1986). 16.

Bluebeard.

Rowell, Kenneth. Sadler's Wells Opera House, London: 1966. B&W. Rendering. **SDR**, 43.

Werz, Wilfried. Comic Opera, Berlin: **TCI**, vol. 15, n. 1 (Jan 1981). 37.

Bluebeard's Castle.

Koltai, Ralph. English National Opera, London: B&W. Set. **TCI**, vol. 11, n. 1 (Jan/Feb 1977). 12. 2 photos.

Blues in the Night.

Falabella, John. Rialto Theatre, NYC: 1982. B&W. Rendering. **DDT**, 587.

Die Bluthochzeit.
>Masereel, Frans. Städtische Bühnen, Heidelberg: 1965. B&W. Rendering. **AST**, 212. 4 photos.

Bockegesang.
>Simonson, Lee. Theatre Guild, NYC: B&W. Set. **TCS2**, plates 100, 101.

The Body Beautiful.
>Aronson, Boris. Plymouth Theatre, NYC: 1935. B&W and color. Rendering. **TAB**, 14, 295.

Boesman and Lena.
>Eigsti, Karl. Circle in the Square Theatre, NYC: 1970. B&W. Rendering. **ASD1**, 35; B&W. Sketch. **DPT**, 121.

Le Boeuf sur le Toit.
>Dufy, Raoul. Comédie des Champs-Élysées, Paris: 1920. B&W. Rendering. **AST**, 110; B&W. Rendering. **TBB**, 128.

La Bohème.
>Bardon, Henry & David Walker. Glyndebourne Festival Opera, England: B&W. Set. **TCI**, vol. 13, n. 3 (May/Jun 1979). 20.

>Benois, Nicola. La Scala, Milan: 1949. B&W. Model. **SDE**, 34.

>Howland, Gerard. Los Angeles Music Center: 1993. Color. Set. **TCI**, vol. 27, n. 9 (Nov 1993). 9.

>Jampolis, Neil Peter. Netherlands Opera, Amsterdam: 1970. B&W. Model. **DPT**, 42.

>Keleher, Kate. University of Iowa/Hancher Auditorium: Color. Model. **SST**, plate IV.

>Montonati, Bruno. 1950. B&W. Rendering. **SDE**, 124.

>O'Hearn, Robert. Miami Opera Company, Florida: 1977. B&W. Rendering. **DDT**, 96.

>Oenslager, Donald. Central City Opera House, Colorado: 1952. B&W. Painter's elevations. **BSE2**, 53.

>Payne, Darwin Reid. B&W. Model. **TCM**, 19; B&W. Model. **SIP**, 9; B&W. Sketch & model. **TCM**, 42, 49, 65, 66. 4 photos.

>Ponnelle, Jean-Pierre. San Francisco Opera, Memorial Opera House, San Francisco: 1978. B&W. Set. **TCI**, vol. 13, n. 3 (May/Jun 1979). 50.

>Stevens, John Wright. Cincinnati Opera Company: B&W. Rendering. **SDT**, 296; Color. Rendering. **SDT**, between 152 & 153. Act II.

>Zeffirelli, Franco. 1962-1963. B&W. Set. **SIO**, 138; Metropolitan Opera, NYC: 1981. B&W and color. Rendering & set. **MOM**, 16-27. 14 photos.

>_____. Basel: 1963. B&W. Set. **TCI**, vol. 4, n. 4 (Sep 1970). 22, 23.

>_____. Brooklyn Academy of Music, New York: B&W. Set. **TCI**, vol. 1, n. 2 (May/Jun 1967). 15.

>_____. Juilliard School, Lincoln Center, NYC: B&W. Set. **TCI**, vol. 8, n. 4 (Sep 1974). 19. 2 photos.

>_____. Opera Theatre of St. Louis: Color. Set. **TCI**, vol. 26, n. 1 (Jan 1992). 35.

Boléro.
>Avetissian, Minas. Teatr Opery i Baleta, Erevan, Armenia: 1966. B&W. Rendering. **SDW3**, 188.

Bolivar.
>Léger, Fernand. Opéra de Paris: 1950. B&W. Rendering. **AST**, 96; B&W. Rendering. **SDW1**, 100; Teatro San Carlo, Naples: 1953. B&W. Rendering. **SDE**, 96, 97. 3 photos.

The Bolsheviks.
>Malinaouskaïte, Janina. Dramatitcheskij Teatr, Kaunas, Belarus: 1970. B&W. Rendering. **SDW3**, 160.

Bomarzo.
   Lee, Ming Cho. New York City Opera, Lincoln Center: 1968. B&W. Set. **TCI**, vol. 7,
      n. 1 (Jan/Feb 1973). 15. 2 photos; B&W. Set. **TCI**, vol. 18, n. 2 (Feb 1984). 21;
      B&W. Model. **TDT**, n. 24 (Feb 1971). 9.
Bonaparte.
   _____. Deutsches Theater, Berlin: B&W. Set. **TCS2**, plate 31.
The Bonds of Interest.
   Halty, Adolpho. Teatro Solis, Montevideo: 1958. B&W. Rendering. **SDW2**, 242.
Bonjour La Bonjour.
   Chichester, Malloy & John Puncan. B&W. model & rendering. **BSE3**, 91.
Bonus March.
   Morgan, Roger. Center Stage, Baltimore: B&W. Set. **TCI**, vol. 7, n. 3 (May/Jun 1973).
      14.
The Book of Job.
   Corey, Irene. Pineville, Kentucky: B&W. Set. **TCI**, vol. 6, n. 3 (May/Jun 1972). 15. 2
      photos.
Book of Splendors: Part II.
   Foreman, Richard. NYC: 1977. B&W. Set. **TCI**, vol. 12, n. 4 (May/Jun 1978). 33. 4
      photos.
Boom-Boom Land.
   Zimmerman, Reinhart. Comic Opera, Berlin: B&W. Set. **TCI**, vol. 15, n. 1 (Jan 1981).
      37.
The Boors.
   Dianjie, Xue. China: B&W. Model. **TDT** vol. XXXI, n. 2 (Spring 1995). 9.
   Padovani, Gianfranco. 1969-1970. B&W. Rendering. **SIO**, 99.
   Riechetoff, Nina. Théâtre de Bourgogne: 1960. B&W. Set. **SDW2**, 101.
Boots with Strawberry Jam.
   Robertson, Patrick. Nottingham Playhouse: B&W. Set. **SFT**, 122.
Border Warfare.
   Howard, Pamela. Tramway Theatre, Glasgow: 1988. B&W. Sketch & set. **BTD**, 199. 3
      photos.
Boris Godounov.
   Bakst, Léon. Théâtre des Champs-Elysées, Paris: 1913. B&W. Rendering. **TPH**, photo
      348.
   Benois, Nicola. La Scala, Milan: 1927. B&W. Rendering. **TCS2**, plate 232; Arena,
      Verona: 1952. B&W. Rendering. **SDE**, 35.
   Bilibine, Alexander. B&W. Rendering of proscenium curtain. **RSC**, 25.
   Cagnoli, G.F. Italy: B&W. Rendering. **SCM**, 79.
   Denic, Miomir. Opera Narodnog pozorista, Beograd: 1962. B&W. Set. **SDW3**, 184.
   Doboujinsky, Mstislav. 1952. B&W. Rendering. **RSC**, 28.
   Golovin, Alexander. Metropolitan Opera, NYC: B&W. Rendering. **TPH**, photo 349.
   Kochergin, Edward Stepanovich. Pskov Drama Theatre: 1973. B&W. Set. **SDW4**,
      illus. 126; B&W. Model. **TCI**, vol. 11, n. 5 (Oct 1977). 40; Color. Model. **TDT**,
      vol. XII, n. 3 (Fall 1976). 26.
   Lee, Ming Cho. Metropolitan Opera, NYC: 1974. B&W. Model. **ASD1**, 94; Color.
      Model. **CSD**, 93; B&W. Model. **DPT**, 32, 240; Color. Model. **DPT**, between 124 &
      125. Act III, sc. 1; B&W and color. Set. **MOM**, 28-39. 8 photos; B&W. Set. **TCI**,
      vol. 10, n. 5 (Oct 1976). 16.
   Liberts, Ludolf. B&W. Rendering. **RSC**, 46.
   Nagy, Elemer. B&W. Set. **TCI**, vol. 4, n. 1 (Jan/Feb 1970). 28.
   Pirchan, Emil. Opernhaus, Berlin: B&W. Set. **TCS2**, plates 90, 107.

Schneider-Siemssen, Günther. Grosses Festspielhaus, Salzburg: 1965. B&W. Set.
    TDT, n. 27 (Dec 1971). 15.
Svoboda, Josef. National Theatre, Prague: 1954. B&W. Set. **SDW1**, 53; State Opera,
    Hamburg: 1972. B&W. Set. **STS**, 98; B&W. Set. **TDT**, vol. XII, n. 2 (Summer
    1976). 13.
Wernicke, Herbert. Salzburg Festival: 1994. B&W. Set. **TCI**, vol. 29, n. 1 (Jan 1995).
    8. 2 photos.
Zolotariev, Nicolaï. Paliashvili Georgian Opera House, Tblissi: 1966. B&W and color.
    Rendering. **FCS**, plate 185, color plate 25. Act I, sc. 1; B&W and color. Rendering.
    SDO, 211, plate 25; B&W. Rendering. **SDW3**, 184.
Born Yesterday.
Oenslager, Donald. Lyceum Theatre, NYC: 1946. B&W. Set. **SDA**, 204; D&W. Set.
    SDW1, 204; B&W. Set. **TDO**, 113; B&W. Set. **WTP**, 192, 193. 3 photos.
Pfahnl, William. San Jose State University, California: 1980. B&W. Set. **BSE2**, 25.
Bosoms and Neglect.
Wulp, John. Goodman Theatre, Chicago: 1979. B&W. Model. **DDT**, 383.
The Boss.
Law, H. Robert. Astor Theatre, NYC: 1911. B&W. Set. **MCN**, 37.
Boston.
Syrkus, Szymon. Zeromski Theater, Warsaw: 1933. B&W. Set. **RSD**, illus. 262.
La Bottega di Caffé.
Herwig, Curt. Stadtbühnen, Magdeburg: 1925. B&W. Set. **TCS2**, plate 278.
Blvd de Paris (I've got the shakes).
Foreman, Richard. NYC: 1977. B&W. Set. **TCI**, vol. 12, n. 4 (May/Jun 1978). 30, 32.
    5 photos.
Le Bourgeois Gentilhomme.
Capek, Josef. National Theatre, Prague: 1926. B&W. Set. **TCS2**, plate 147; B&W. Set.
    TDT, n. 42 (Fall 1975). 24.
Fuerst, Walter René. Odéon Théâtre, Paris: B&W. Rendering. **TCS2**, plate 266.
Lalique, Susanne. Comédie Française, Paris: 1952. B&W. Set. **SIP**, 228; B&W. Set.
    SDW1, 99.
Martin, Denis. Théâtre National, Brussels: 1950. B&W. Rendering. **SDW1**, 46.
Oenslager, Donald. (project): B&W. Rendering. **STN**, 141.
Pòlidori, Gianni. Rome: 1953. B&W. Rendering. **SDE**, 134.
Quay, Stephen & Timothy. Royal National Theatre, London: 1992. B&W. Set. **TCI**,
    vol. 27, n. 1 (Jan 1993). 45. 2 photos.
Stern, Ernst. Deutsches Theater, Berlin: B&W. Set. **TCS2**, plates 28, 29.
La Boutique Fantasque.
Derain, André. 1920. B&W. Rendering. **TCS2**, plate 263.
Box Mao Box.
Neumann, Jörg R. Vienna: 1970. B&W. Set. **SDW3**, 150.
The Boy.
Howden, Philip, Alfred Terraine, Conrad Tritschler, & R.C. McCleery. Adelphi The-
    atre, London: 1917. B&W. Set. **MCD**, plate 113.
The Boy Friend.
Woolley, Reginald. Players Theatre, London: 1953. B&W. Set. **MCD**, plate 205;
    Royale Theatre, NYC: 1954. B&W. Set. **BWM**, 21.
    _____. B&W. Set. **SIP**, 13.
Boy Meets Girl.
Lundborg, Arne. Cort Theatre, NYC: 1935. B&W. Set. **MCN**, 127.

The Boys from Syracuse.
    Mielziner, Jo. Alvin Theatre, NYC: 1938. B&W. Set. **BWM**, 183, 184; B&W. Set.
        MCN, 143; B&W. Set. **SOW**, plate 97.
        _____. Tomlinson Theatre, Temple University, Philadelphia: B&W. Set. **TCI**,
        vol. 5, n. 5 (Oct 1971). 28.
The Boys in the Band.
    Harvey, Peter Theatre Four, NYC: 1968. B&W. Set. **SDB**, 194; B&W. Model. **SDW3**,
        164; B&W. Rendering. **CSD**, 86; B&W. Set. **DPT**, 89.
The Boys of Winter.
    Mitchell, David. Biltmore Theatre, NYC: 1985. B&W. Sketches. **DDT**, 114, 115. 6
        photos.
Brain.
    Blake, Warner. Boston University Theatre: 1972. B&W. Rendering. **CSD**, 63.
Brain Child.
    Lundell, Kurt. Forest Theatre, Philadelphia: 1974. B&W. Model. **CSD**, 101; B&W.
        Model. **DPT**, 133.
Brand.
    Egemar, Christian. Den Nationale Scene, Bergen, Norway: 1968. B&W. Set. **SDW3**,
        85. 2 photos.
    Hay, Richard L. B&W. Set. **SDL**, 60.
    Johansson-Cloffe, Carl. Dramatiska Teatern, Stockholm: 1950. B&W. Set. **SDW1**,
        160.
    Nichols, Gerald. Vasey Theatre, Villanova University, Pennsylvania: 1972. B&W. Set.
        ASC, 27.
    Oenslager, Donald. Yale School of Drama, New Haven, Connecticut: 1928. B&W.
        Rendering. **RSD**, illus. 443; B&W. Rendering. **STN**, 233-241. 5 photos; B&W.
        Rendering. **TDO**, 33.
    Pitoëff, Georges. Théâtre des Mathurins, Paris: 1928. B&W. Rendering. **RSD**, illus.
        420.
        _____. Moscow Art Theatre: 1906. B&W. Set. **TPH**, photo 299.
Brave Nazar.
    Saryan, Martiros. Teatr Opery i Baleta imeni Spendiarova, Erevan, Armenia: 1935.
        B&W. Rendering. **SDW2**, 193.
Bread.
    Lutze, V.V. State Dramatic Theatre, Leningrad: 1930. B&W. Set. **TAS**, 80; B&W.
        Model. **TAT**, plate 692.
        _____. Moscow Art Theatre: 1931. B&W. Set. **RST**, 273. 2 photos.
The Breadshop.
    Neher, Caspar. (unproduced): B&W. Rendering. **CBM**, 55.
The Break.
        _____. Vakhtangov Theatre, Moscow: 1927. B&W. Set. **RST**, 219.
Break of Noon.
    Svoboda, Josef. Louvain: 1984. Color. Set. **TCI**, vol. 21, n. 8 (Oct 1987). 35.
Breakfast with Les and Bess.
    Dorsey, Kent. Old Globe Theatre, San Diego: B&W. Set. **TCI**, vol. 19, n. 5 (May
        1985). 19.
    Tschetter, Dean. Lambs Theatre, NYC: 1983. B&W. Set. **TCI**, vol. 19, n. 5 (May
        1985). 19.
Breaking the Code.
    Asakura, Setsu. Japan: B&W. Model. **TDT**, vol. XXVII, n. 4 (Fall 1991). 25.

Da Costa, Liz. Theatre Royal, Haymarket, England: 1987. B&W. Set. **BTD**, 64; Eisenhower Theatre, Washington, DC: 1987. Color. Set. **TCI**, vol. 23, n. 9 (Nov 1989). 59.

Bremer Freiheit.

Minks, Wilfried. Theater der Freien Hansestadt, Bremen: 1972. B&W. Set. **SDW4**, illus. 406; B&W. Set. **TCI**, vol. 12, n. 1 (Jan/Feb 1978). 28.

The Bride of Messina.

Dietz, Wilhelm. Künstlertheater, Munich: Color. Rendering. **MRH**, facing 152

The Bridge of Fire.

Arapov, Anatoly. Maly Theatre, Moscow: 1929. B&W. Model & set. **RST**, 281. 2 photos

The Brig.

MacNamara, Brooks. Mitchell Hall, University of Delaware: B&W. Set. **SFT**, 129; B&W. Set. **TCI**, vol. 2, n. 6 (Nov/Dec 1968). 16, 17, 19, 20. 4 photos.

Brigadoon.

Hotopp, Michael J. Majestic Theatre, NYC: 1980. B&W. Model & set. **TCI**, vol. 15, n. 1 (Jan 1981). 30-33. 7 photos.

Smith, Oliver. Ziegfeld Theatre, NYC: 1947. B&W. Set. **BWM**, 280. 2 photos; B&W. Set. **CSD**, 17; B&W. Set. **HOB**, 78; B&W. Rendering. **SDT**, 41. Chapel scene; B&W. Set. **SOW**, plate 107; B&W. Set. **TCI**, vol. 16, n. 4 (Apr 1982). 13; B&W. Set. **TMT**, 167; B&W. Set. **WMC**, 240.

The Bright and Bold Design.

Metheny, Russell. Studio Theatre, Washington, DC: 1992. B&W. Elevation. **TCI**, vol. 27, n. 1 (Jan 1993). 7.

Brighton Beach Memoirs.

Eagan, Michael. Theatre Calgary: B&W and color. Set & elevation. **TCI**, vol. 21, n. 2 (Feb 1987). 24, 25. 3 photos.

Forrester, Bill. A Contemporary Theatre, Seattle: B&W. Set. **TCI**, vol. 21, n. 2 (Feb 1987). 24.

Gilseth, Thom. Phoenix Little Theatre, Arizona: B&W. Set. **SDT**, 290.

Mitchell, David. Alvin Theatre, NYC: 1983. B&W. Set. **TCI**, vol. 21, n. 2 (Feb 1987). 22.

Bring Back Birdie.

Mitchell, David. Martin Beck Theatre, NYC: 1981. B&W. Set. **TCI**, vol. 17, n. 8 (Oct 1983). 29.

Britannicus.

Dornes, Roger. Comédie Française, Paris: 1946. B&W. **SDW1**, 95.

The Broad Highway (The Great Highway).

Sievert, Ludwig. State Opera, Frankfurt, Germany: 1923. B&W. Rendering. **RSD**, illus. 120; B&W. Rendering. **TAS**, 73; B&W. Rendering. **TAT**, plate 396.

Broadway.

Beatty, John Lee. The Acting Company tour: 1979. B&W. Set. **TCI**, vol. 15, n. 5 (May 1981). 22.

Segal, Arthur P. Broadhurst Theatre, NYC: 1926. B&W. Set. **MCN**, 76.

Broadway Sings: The Music of Jule Styne.

Falabella, John. St. James Theatre, NYC: 1987. B&W. Set. **DDT**, 247.

The Broken Heart.

Piper, Tom. Royal Shakespeare Company, GB: 1995. B&W. Set. **TCI**, vol. 29, n. 3 (Mar 1995). 10.

The Broken Jug.
    Griffin, Hayden. Teatro Stabile di Genova: B&W. Rendering. **TCI**, vol. 19, n. 9 (Nov 1985). 21.
The Bronx Express.
    Aronson, Boris. Schildkraut Theatre, NYC: 1925. B&W and color. Rendering & set. **BAT**, plates 1, 12; B&W and color. Rendering & set. **TAB**, 36, 37, 293. 4 photos; B&W. Rendering. **TDT**, vol. XXV, n. 3 (Fall 1989). 14; Astor Theatre, NYC: 1925. B&W. Set. **TCS2**, plate 180.
Brooklyn, USA.
    Bay, Howard. Forrest Theatre, NYC: 1941. B&W. Rendering. **SDB**, 47; B&W. Rendering. **TCI**, vol. 17, n. 2 (Feb 1983). 54.
Brother Rat.
    Cirker & Robbins. Biltmore Theatre, NYC: 1936. B&W. Set. **MCN**, 135.
Brother to Dragons.
    Lee, Eugene. Trinity Square Theatre, Providence, Rhode Island: 1973. B&W. Set. **TDT**, vol. XVIII, n. 2 (Summer 1982). 9; Wilbur Theatre, Boston: 1974. B&W. Set. **DPT**, 151.
The Brothers Karamazov.
    Copeau, Jacques. Théâtre du Vieux Colombier, Paris: B&W. Rendering. **SDC**, plate 98. Drawing by Robert Edmond Jones.
    Dusek, Jan. Theatre On the Balustrade, Prague: B&W. Set. **TDT**, vol. XXIII, n. 1 (Spring 1987). 13.
    Jouvet, Louis. Théâtre du Vieux Colombier, Paris: 1913. B&W. Rendering. **CSC**, facing 174; B&W. Rendering. **SOW**, plate 62; Arsenal, Paris: 1920. B&W. Sketch. **RSD**, illus. 106.
    Kitaïev, Mark. Teatr Younogo Zritelia, Riga: 1973. B&W. Set. **SDW4**, illus. 146, 147.
    Masic, Slobodan. Atelje 212, Beograd: 1974. B&W. Set. **SDW4**, illus. 148-154.
    Wendland, Mark. Repertory Theatre of St. Louis: 1995. Color. Set. **TCI**, vol. 29, n. 5 (May 1995). 6.
The Browning Version.
    Toms, Carl. National Theatre, London: 1980. B&W. Set. **TCI**, vol. 15, n. 5 (May 1981). 13.
Brunhild.
    Daniel, Heinz. State Theatre, Altona: B&W. **TCS2**, plate 191.
Bubus, the Teacher.
    Meyerhold, Vsevelod, plan, Ilya Shlepyanov, execution. Meyerhold Theatre, Moscow: 1925. B&W. Set. **MOT**, between 200 & 201. 3 photos.
The Buccaneer.
    Jones, Robert Edmond. Plymouth Theatre, NYC: 1925. B&W. Rendering. **SDC**, plate 126.
Buddy.
    Walmsley, Andy. NYC: 1990. B&W and color. Set. **TCI**, vol. 24, n. 8 (Oct 1990). 34, 35.
The Bug.
    _____. Moscow: 1934. B&W. Set. **TPH**, photo 410.
The Bundle.
    Jackness, Andrew. Yale Repertory Theatre, New Haven: 1979. B&W. Set. **TCI**, vol. 13, n. 4 (Sep 1979). 8.
Die Bürgschaft.
    Neher, Caspar. State Opera, Berlin: 1932. B&W. Set. **CBM**, 36.

Buried Child.
>Kroschel, Michael. The Magic Theatre, San Francisco: B&W. Set. **TCI**, vol. 14, n. 4 (Sep 1980). 22.
>Landwehr, Hugh. Center Stage, Baltimore: 1985. B&W. Set. **ASD2**, 79; Color. Set. **TCI**, vol. 20, n. 9 (Nov 1986). 19.
>Straiges, Tony. Kreeger Theatre, Arena Stage, Washington, DC: 1983. B&W. Model. **DDT**, 234; B&W. Set. **TCI**, vol. 18, n. 3 (Mar 1984). 28.

Burn This.
>Beatty, John Lee. Mark Taper Forum, Los Angeles: 1987. B&W. Rendering. **DDT**, 540; B&W. Sketch & set. **TCI**, vol. 21, n. 5 (May 1987). 37.

A Burning Beach.
>Iacovelli, John. Los Angeles Theatre Center: B&W and color. Model & set. **TDT**, vol. XXVI, n. 1 (Spring 1990). 11 of insert. 2 photos.

Burning Bright.
>Mielziner, Jo. Broadhurst Theatre, NYC: 1950. B&W. Rendering. **DTT**, 160. Tent; B&W. Rendering; 161. Kitchen.

The Burning Flame.
>Manninen, Tanu. Vaasan Suomalainen Teatteri, Vaasa, Finland: 1952. B&W. Rendering. **SDW1**, 158.

Bus Stop.
>Aronson, Boris. Music Box Theatre, NYC: 1955. B&W and color. Rendering & set. **TAB**, 112, 113, 303. 3 photos.

The Business Man.
>Gamrekeli, Irakly. Rustaveli Theatre, Tbilisi: 1928. B&W. Rendering. **TAT**, plate 709.

Butterflies Are Free.
>Wareing, John. Playbox Theatre Company, Tucson: B&W. Set. **SDT**, 292.

By the Beautiful Sea.
>Mielziner, Jo. Majestic Theatre, NYC: 1954. B&W. Rendering. **DTT**, 188. Boardwalk curtain.

Bye Bye Birdie.
>Randolph, Robert. Martin Beck Theatre, NYC: 1960. B&W. Set. **DPT**, 209; B&W. Set. **BMF**, 62; Color. Set. **BWM**, 141.
>_____. 1966. B&W. Set. **HPA**, 36.

-C-

Cabal of Hypocrites.
>Mitchell, David. Actors Studio, NYC: 1984. B&W. Sketch. **ASD1**, 127.

Cabaret.
>Aronson, Boris. Broadhurst Theatre, NYC: 1966. Color. Set. **BMF**, 174; B&W. Set. **BWM**, 127; B&W. Set. **CSD**, 35; Color. Rendering. **DDT**, 24c; B&W. Set. **HPA**, 42 & 63; B&W and color. Sketch, rendering, model, & set. **TAB**, 19, 189-197, 307; B&W. Rendering. **TCI**, vol. 21, n. 5 (May 1987). 11; B&W. Set. **WMC**, 332; London: Color. Set. **SST**, plate VII.
>Benson, Tom. University of Arizona, Tucson: 1985. B&W. Rendering. **SDT**, between 152 & 153, 300; Color. Rendering & set. **TDP**, 108-110.
>Hird, Thomas C. California State University, Hayward: 1977. B&W. Set. **BSE1**, 15.
>Kritzler, Ilse. Brunswick Music Theatre, Brunswick, Maine: 1971. B&W. Rendering. **CSD**, 90.
>Leahy, Gerry. Florida State University, Tallahassee: Color. Set. **TCI**, vol. 26, n. 3 (Mar 1992). 40.

Maxwell, George. Pioneer Theatre Company, Salt Lake City: 1993. Color. Set. **TCI**,
   vol. 28, n. 1 (Jan 1994). 6.
Migid, Adel. Wright State University, Dayton, Ohio : 1978. B&W. Rendering. **BSE1**,
   26.
Reaney, Mark. University of Kansas, Lawrence: B&W. Rendering. **TDT**, vol. XXVI,
   n. 4 (Fall 1990). 43.
Stell, W. Joseph. University of Georgia Theatre: B&W. Set. **TDT**, vol. XIX, n. 3 (Fall
   1983). 15, 17.

Cabin in the Sky.
Aronson, Boris. Martin Beck Theatre, NYC: 1940. Color. Rendering, model, & set.
   TAB, 75-78, 297. 5 photos.

Caesar and Cleopatra.
Craig, Edward Gordon. Deutsches Theater, Berlin: 1906. B&W and color. Rendering.
   FCS, plate 167, color plate 16. Act I, sc. 3; B&W and color. Rendering. **SDO**, 189,
   plate 16; B&W. Rendering. **TNT**, facing 51, 53, 55.
Furse, Roger. St. James Theatre, London: 1951. B&W. Set. **SDW1**, 175; B&W. Set.
   WTP, 144.
Gauguin, Paul René. National Theatre, Oslo: 1951. B&W. Set. **SDW1**, 152.
Gérard, Rolf. National Theatre, NYC: 1950. B&W. Set. **WTP**, 146, 147. 5 photos.
Grosz, George. Deutsches Theater, Berlin: 1922. B&W. Rendering. **AST**, 176.
Jorgulesco, Jonel. Boston Repertory Theatre: B&W. Rendering. **TCS2**, plates 212,
   213.
Tilton, James. American Conservatory Theatre, San Francisco: 1971. B&W. Set. **TCI**,
   vol. 6, n. 5 (Oct 1972). 12.
Toms, Carl. B&W. Set. **TCI**, vol. 6, n. 1 (Jan/Feb 1972). 17.
Vakalo, Georges. Basilikon Théatron, Athens: 1952. B&W. Rendering. **SDW1**, 110.
Walser, Karl. B&W. Rendering. **TPH**, photo 331.

Café Crown.
Aronson, Boris. Cort Theatre, NYC: 1942. B&W. Rendering. **TAB**, 297.
Loquasto, Santo. Newman Theatre, NYC: 1988. B&W. Set. **DDT**, 384; Brooks
   Atkinson Theatre, NYC: 1989. Color. Set. **TCI**, vol. 23, n. 3 (Mar 1989). 8.

Cain.
   ˙Andreev, Nikolai. Moscow Art Theatre: 1920. B&W. Sketches. **RST**, 88. 3 photos.
Sievert, Ludwig. Theaterabt, Frankfurt: 1923. B&W. Set. **RSD**, illus. 140.

The Calamity.
Tofan, Mihai. Teatrul National, Bucharest: 1958. B&W. Set. **SDW2**, 176.

La Calandria.
Pizzi, Pier Luigi. 1967. B&W. Set. **SIO**, 106.

The Calendar that Lost Seven Days.
Vanerelli, Mario. Teatro Nacional Cervantes, Buenos Aires: 1949. B&W. Rendering.
   SDW1, 38.

Caliban.
Jones, Robert Edmond. Lewissohn Stadium of City College, NYC: 1916. B&W.
   Sketch. **DFT**, plate 2.

California Dog Fight.
Hicks, Grant. Bush Theatre, London: 1985. B&W. Set. **BTD**, 29.

Caligula.
Jankowska, Liliana & Antoni Tosta. Teatr S. Zeromski, Kielce, Poland: 1958. B&W.
   Rendering. **SDW2**, 171.
Klein, César. Deutsches Schauspielhaus, Hamburg: 1949. B&W. Rendering. **SDW1**,
   70.

Müller-Brockman, Josef. Riddersalen Theatre, Copenhagen: 1947. B&W. Rendering. **SDW1**, 116.

Polidori, Gianni. 1971. B&W. Set. **SIO**, 120.

_____. Yale Repertory Theatre, New Haven: B&W. Set. **TCI**, vol. 6, n. 3 (May/ Jun 1972). 26.

La Calisto.

Bury, John. Glyndebourne Festival Opera, England: B&W. Set. **TCI**, vol. 26, n. 1 (Jan 1992). 48.

Call Factory Committee!

_____. Theatre of Working Youth (TRAM), Moscow: B&W. Set. **RST**, 243.

Call Me Madam.

Du Bois, Raoul Pène. Imperial Theatre, NYC. 1950. B&W. Set. **BWM**, 246.

Call Me Mister.

Polakov, Lester. National Theatre, NYC: 1946. B&W. Set. **DDT**, 404.

The Call of Life.

Walser, Karl. Germany: 1906. B&W. Sketch. **TPH**, photo 293.

A Call on Kuprin.

Oenslager, Donald. Broadhurst Theatre, NYC: 1961. B&W. Rendering. **TDO**, 135.

Cambodia Agonistes.

Klingelhoffer, Robert. Pan-Asian Repertory Theatre, NYC: 1992. B&W. Model. **TCI**, vol. 27, n. 1 (Jan 1993). 6.

Camelot.

Smith, Oliver. Majestic Theatre, NYC: 1960. B&W and color. Set. **BWM**, 285, 286. 3 photos; B&W. Set. **DPT**, 155; B&W. Rendering & set. **SDA**, 256. 2 photos; B&W. Rendering. **TCI**, vol. 16, n. 4 (Apr 1982). 16; B&W. Model. **TMI**, 246; Color. Set. **TMT**, plate 10.

Stell, W. Joseph. Lakeview Theatre, Athens, Georgia: B&W and color. Sketch & rendering. **TDT**, vol. XXX, n. 3 (Summer 1994). 11 of insert.

Truscott, John. Theatre Royal, Drury Lane, London: 1964. B&W. Set. **MCD**, plate 220.

Camille.

Benois, Alexander. Odéon Theatre, Paris: B&W. Set. **SCM**, 42. Act V.

Bernstein, Aline. NYC: 1935. B&W. Set. **SCM**, 117. 2 photos.

Jones, Robert Edmond. Central City Opera House, Colorado: 1932. B&W. Rendering. **REJ**, 87, 89; B&W. Rendering. **SCM**, 101; B&W. Rendering. **SDB**, 40.

Lee, Ming Cho. B&W. Set. **SDL**, 60.

Maillart, Jean Dénis. Paris: B&W. Set. **SDE**, 112.

Meyerhold, Vsevelod, plan; Ivan Leistikov, execution. Meyerhold Theatre, Moscow: 1934. B&W. Set. **MOT**, between 304 & 305.

Pitoëff, Georges. Plainpalais Auditorium, Geneva: 1921. B&W. Set. **RSD**, illus. 421.

_____. Tyrone Guthrie Theatre, Minneapolis: 1980. B&W. Set. **TCI**, vol. 15, n. 8 (Oct 1981). 26.

Camino Real.

Conklin, John. Williamstown Theatre Festival, Massachusetts: 1968. Color. Model. **ASD1**, between 70 & 71; B&W. Model. **DDT**, 486; B&W. Set. **TCI**, vol. 14, n. 3 (May/Jun 1980). 16.

Hay, Richard L. Marion Theatre-Pacific Conservatory for the Performing Arts, Santa Maria, California: 1981. B&W. Rendering. **BSE3**, 28.

Lee, Eugene. Trinity Square Theatre, Providence, Rhode Island: 1988. Color. Set. **TCI**, vol. 22, n. 9 (Nov 1988). 58.

Mielziner, Jo. 1951. B&W. Rendering. **DTT**, 163. Don Quixote scene.

Schmidt, Douglas W. Playhouse in the Park, Cincinnati: 1968. B&W. Set. **CSD**, 26; B&W. Set. **DPT**, 96; B&W. Set. **TDT**, vol. XVII, n. 2 (Summer 1981). 16.

Wexler, Peter. Mark Taper Forum, Los Angeles: 1968. B&W. Set. **SDW3**, 130.

Williams, Jerry. Alley Theatre, Houston: B&W. Set. **TCI**, vol. 7, n. 3 (May/Jun 1973). 9.

Campaign Against Death.

Hoffman, Vlastislav. National Theatre, Prague: 1926. B&W. Set. **TDT**, n. 41 (Summer 1975). 17.

Il Campanello.

Boruzescu, Radu. The Acting Company tour: 1980. B&W. Set. **TCI**, vol. 15, n. 5 (May 1981). 24.

Sciltian, Gregorio. La Scala, Milan: 1971-1972. B&W. Rendering. **SIO**, 154.

Can Can.

Mielziner, Jo. Shubert Theatre, NYC: 1953. Color. Rendering. **SDL**, plates 8-12; Color. Rendering. **DTT**, 170. Dance hall; B&W. Rendering. **SDA**, 250; B&W. Rendering. **SDW2**, 236; B&W. Set. **TMT**, 180.

Mitchell, David. Minskoff Theatre, NYC: 1981. B&W. Model. **DDT**, 304.

Thor, Harald. Gärtnerplatz Theater, Munich: 1994. B&W. Set. **TCI**, vol. 29, n. 2 (Feb 1995). 8.

Candida.

_____. Madison Square Theatre, NYC: 1904. B&W. Set. **MCN**, 22.

Candide.

Baird, Campbell. Boston University: 1989. B&W. Set. **TCI**, vol. 23, n. 9 (Nov 1989). 51.

Beatty, John Lee. Goodman Theatre, Chicago: 1985. B&W. Set. **BSE4**, 97.

Berka, Tomás. Czechoslovakia: Color. Model. **TCI**, vol. 18, n. 1 (Jan 1984). 10; B&W. Model. **TDT**, vol. XX, n. 1 (Spring 1984). 8.

Brown, Zack. Arena Stage, Washington, DC: 1982. B&W. Set. **TCI**, vol. 18, n. 3 (Mar 1984). 28.

Dunham, Clarke. New York City Opera, Lincoln Center: 1982. B&W. Set. **HPA**, 155; Color. Set. **MBM**, 89; Color. Set. **TCI**, vol. 18, n. 8 (Oct 1984). 18.

Fuerst, Walter René. Odéon Théâtre, Paris: B&W. Set. **TCS2**, plate 265.

Funicello, Ralph. (project): 1968. B&W. Rendering. **CSD**, 81.

Ghiglia, Lorenzo. Teatro La Fenice, Venice: 1971. B&W. Set. **SDW4**, illus. 94-96.

Hudson, Richard. Old Vic Theatre, London: B&W. Set. **TCI**, vol. 23, n. 4 (Apr 1989). 20.

Landwehr, Hugh. CSC Repertory, New York: 1992. B&W. Set. **TCI**, vol. 26, n. 7 (Aug/Sep 1992). 9.

Lee, Eugene & Franne. Broadway Theatre, NYC: 1974. Color. Set. **BWM**, 291; B&W. Set. **CSD**, 23; B&W. Set. **DPT**, 57; B&W. Set. **HPA**, 152, 153; B&W. Set. **HPR**, 219.

Lynch, Thomas. Pennsylvania Opera Theatre: 1982. B&W. Set. **TCI**, vol. 18, n. 3 (Mar 1984). 26.

Miller, Bruce. Minnesota Opera: B&W. Set. **TCI**, vol. 12, n. 3 (Mar/Apr 1978). 28.

Smith, Oliver. Martin Beck Theatre, NYC: 1956. B&W. Rendering. **TCI**, vol. 16, n. 4 (Apr 1982). 62.

Candido, o dell' Ottimismo.

Ghiglia, Lorenzo. 1972. B&W. Set. **SIO**, 75. 2 photos.

Candle in the Wind.

Mielziner, Jo. Shubert Theatre, NYC: 1941. B&W. Rendering. **DTT**, 123. Power house scene.

Candleford.
Dudley, William. National Theatre (Cottesloe), England: B&W. Set. **TCI**, vol. 18, n. 1 (Jan 1984). 36.
Candy Kisses.
Byrne, John. Bush Theatre, London: 1984. B&W. Set. **BTD**, 58.
The Cannibals.
Roth, Wolfgang. 1969. B&W. Model. **TDT**, n. 42 (Fall 1975). 18.
Cantate Profane.
Hajdu, Etienne. Maison de la Culture, Amiens: B&W. Set. **RSD**, illus. 491.
The Canteen-Woman.
Vinogradov, Mily. Vakhtangov Theatre, Moscow: 1959. B&W. Rendering. **SDW2**, 200.
Canterbury Tales.
Cousins, Derek. Phoenix Theatre, London: 1968. B&W. Set. **MCD**, plate 228.
_____. Equity Library Theatre, NYC: B&W. Set. **TCI**, vol. 15, n. 6 (Jun/Jul 1981). 23.
Cantique des Cantiques.
Mitchell, Robert D. Les Grands Ballets Canadiens, Montreal: 1974. B&W. Model. **DPT**, 184 4 scenes.
Capitaine Schelle, ...
Cauchetier, Patrice. Théâtre de l'Espérance, Palais de Chaillot, Paris: 1971. B&W. Set. **SDW4**, illus. 317.
I Capricci di Callot.
Prampolini, Enrico. 1948. B&W. Rendering. **SDE**, 136.
Cappriccio.
Lennon, Dennis. Glyndebourne Festival Opera, England: B&W. Set. **TCI**, vol. 13, n. 3 (May/Jun 1979). 20.
The Caprices of Callot.
Prampolini, Enrico. Teatro Reale dell' Opera, Rome: 1942. B&W. Rendering. **SDW1**, 129.
Caprices of Marianne.
Owen, Paul. Actors Theatre of Louisville: 1987. Color. Set. **TCI**, vol. 23, n. 3 (Mar 1989). 39.
Captain Bada.
Minks, Wilfried. Städtische Bühnen, Ulm: 1959. B&W. Set. **SDW2**, 66.
Renard, Raymond. Théâtre de la Poche, Brussels: 1956. B&W. Set. **SDW2**, 31.
Captain Jinks of the Horse Marines.
Unitt, Edward G. Garrick Theatre, NYC: 1901. B&W. Set. **MCN**, 15.
Captain Kidd.
Harker, Joseph. Wyndham's Theatre, London: 1910. B&W. Set. **MCD**, plate 84.
Captains Courageous.
Barreca, Christopher. Ford's Theatre, Washington, DC: 1992. Color. Set. **TCI**, vol. 27, n. 1 (Jan 1993). 5.
The Capture of the Oresteia.
Deville, Roland. Théâtre National de Strasbourg: 1969. B&W. Set. **SDW3**, 18.
I Capuleti e i Montecchi.
Frigerio, Ezio. B&W. Rendering. **SIO**, 62. 2 photos.
Caravaggio.
Mielziner, Jo. Playhouse in the Park, Cincinnati: 1971. B&W. Set. **TDT**, n. 32 (Feb 1973). 24, 26, 27, 29. 4 photos.

48   *Card Index*

Card Index.
    Sadowski, Andrzej. Teatr Kameralny, Poland: B&W. Set. **TCI**, vol. 15, n. 4 (Apr
       1981). 14.
Cardillac.
    Siercke, Alfred. Hamburg Staatsoper: 1961. B&W. Rendering. **SDW2**, 72.
    Svoboda, Josef. La Scala, Milan: 1964. B&W. Rendering. **SJS**, 152.
Careless Rapture.
    Johnstone, Alick. Theatre Royal, Drury Lane, London: 1936. B&W. Set. **MCD**, plate
       181.
The Caretaker.
    Iacovelli, John. Los Angeles Theatre Center: B&W. Set. **TDT**, vol. XXVI, n. 1 (Spring
       1990). 11 of insert.
    Payne, Darwin Reid. B&W. Sketch, model & set. **SIP**, 42, 43, 69, 306, 307. 5 photos.
    _____. Asolo State Theatre, Sarasota, Florida: 1968. B&W. Set. **TCR**, 122.
Carib Song.
    Mielziner, Jo. Adelphi Theatre, NYC: 1945. Color. Rendering. **DTT**, 128. Act II,
       finale.
The Carmelites.
    Wahkévitch, Georges. La Scala, Milan: 1957. B&W. Set. **SDW2**, 102.
Carmen.
    Aravantinos, P. B&W. Rendering. **DIT**, plate 105.
    Armistead, Horace. Boston University Theatre: 1956. B&W. Rendering. **SDW2**, 229.
    Bay, Howard. Opera House, San Francisco: 1959. B&W. Painting & set. **SDB**, 71,
       108; Color. Rendering. **SDL**, plates 8-14a. Act III; B&W. Rendering. **SDT**, 44. Act
       II; Color. Rendering. **SDW2**, 231. Opera; B&W. Set. **TDT**, n. 3 (Dec 1965). inside
       back cover.
    Beavan, Jenny. Covent Garden, London: 1973. B&W. Set. **CGA**, 187.
    Bonnat, Yves (Yves-Bonnat). Théâtre Royal de la Monnaie, Brussels: 1961. Color.
       Rendering. **SDW2**, 97.
    Buffet, Bernard. Opéra de Marseille: 1962. B&W. Set. **SDW2**, 86.
    Clavé, Antoni. Théâtre Marigny, Paris: 1949. Color. Rendering. **RSD**, illus. 493;
       B&W. Rendering. **SDW1**, 90.
    Cytrynowski, Carlos. Grand Theater, Geneva: 1993. Color. Set. **TCI**, vol. 28, n. 1 (Jan
       1994). 12.
    Fioroni, Giosetta & Vittorio Gregotti. Teatro Communale, Bologna: 1967. B&W. Set.
       SDW3, 183.
    Gauchat, Pierre. Switzerland: B&W. Set. **SCM**, 80. Act III.
    Gregotti, Vittorio & Giosetta Fioroni. Teatro Communale, Bologna: 1967. B&W. Set.
       SDW3, 183.
    Hartman, Dominik. Opernhaus, Düsseldorf: 1955. B&W. Set. **SDW1**, 64.
    Jedrinsky, Wladimir. Opéra de Nice: 1958. B&W. Rendering. **SDW2**, 93.
    Jones, Robert Edmond. Radio City Music Hall, NYC: 1932. Color. Rendering. **SDA**,
       282, 283.
    Labò, Savino. 1953. B&W. Rendering. **SDE**, 94.
    Lazaridis, Stefanos. London: 1989. B&W. Set. **BTD**, 200.
    Loeffler, Edouard. Germany: B&W. Rendering. **TAT**, plate 360.
    Lowery, Nigel. Opera North, Leeds, England: 1987. Color. Set. **BTD**, 137. 2 photos.
    Malina, Jaroslav. University of Kansas, Lawrence: 1992. B&W. sketches, renderings,
       & set. **TDT**, vol. XXX, n. 2 (Spring 1994). 23-25. 16 photos.
    Messerer, Boris. Bolshoi Theatre, Moscow: 1967. B&W. Rendering. **SDW3**, 183.

Otto, Teo. Grosses Festspielhaus, Salzburg: 1966. B&W. Set. **TDT**, n. 27 (Dec 1971). 14.

Ponnelle, Jean-Pierre. San Francisco Opera: 1983. B&W. Set. **TCI**, vol. 17, n. 9 (Nov/ Dec 1983). 20.

Scheffler, John. Houston Grand Opera: 1974. B&W. Set. **DDT**, 441.

Svoboda, Josef. Goetheplatz Theatre, Bremen: 1965. B&W. Rendering. **SJS**, 153; B&W. Rendering. **STS**, 74; Metropolitan Opera, NYC: 1972. B&W. **STS**, 72, 73; B&W. Set. **TCI**, vol. 10, n. 5 (Oct 1976). 17; B&W. Set. **TDT**, vol. XII, n. 2 (Summer 1976). 23. 2 photos, Acts I & III.

Ulyanov, Nikolai. Operny Teatr Stanislavskovo, Moscow: 1935. B&W. Rendering. **SDW2**, 192. Watson, Lee. New Jersey State Opera, Newark: B&W. Set. **SDT**, 296.

Yamada, Shinkichi. Nippon Geteijo, Tokyo. 1951. B&W. Rendering. **SDW1**, 151.

_____. Chicago Lyric Opera: 1906. B&W. Model. **TDT**, vol. XXV, n. 2 (Summer 1989). 12.

_____. New York City Opera: Color. Set. **TCI**, vol. 28, n. 2 (Feb 1994). 40.

Carmen Jones.

Bay, Howard. Broadway Theatre, NYC: 1943. B&W. Set. **BWM**, 332; B&W. Rendering & set. **TCI**, vol. 17, n. 2 (Feb 1983). 12, 55; B&W. Rendering. **TDT**, n. 19 (Dec 1969). 22; B&W. Set. **TMT**, 153.

Carmencita and the Soldier.

_____. Musical Studio, Moscow Art Theater: 1924. B&W. Set. **TPH**, photo 303.

Carmina Burana.

Barth, Ruodi. Munich: B&W. Set. **TCI**, vol. 11, n. 2 (Mar/Apr 1977). 19. 2 photos.

Carnival.

Armstrong, Will Steven. Imperial Theatre, NYC: 1961. B&W. Set. **BWM**, 297. 2 photos.

Joy, James Leonard. Goodspeed Opera House, East Haddam, Connecticut: Color. Set. **TCI**, vol. 21, n. 9 (Nov 1987). 33.

Le Carnival des Enfants.

Dethomas, Maxime. Théâtre des Arts, Paris: 1910. B&W. Rendering. **RSD**, illus. 46, 47.

Carousel.

Butsch, Tom. Chanhassen Dinner Theatre, Minnesota: B&W. Set. **TCI**, vol. 14, n. 5 (Oct 1980). 24, 25. 3 photos.

Crowley, Bob. Royal National Theatre, London: 1993. Color. Set. **TCI**, vol. 27, n. 4 (Apr 1993). 38, 39. 4 photos.

Mielziner, Jo. Majestic Theatre, NYC: 1945. B&W. Set. **BWM**, 188. 2 photos; B&W. Set. **HOB**, 79; B&W. Set. **TMI**, 142, 145, 220; B&W. Set. **TMT**, 161; B&W. Set. **WMC**, 215. 2 photos; B&W. Set. **WTP**, 232.

_____. Drury Lane Theatre, London: 1950. B&W. Set. **BMF**, 46.

_____. Maine Township High School East, Park Ridge, Illinois: B&W. Set. **TCI**, vol. 13, n. 3 (May/Jun 1979). 26.

Le Carrosse du Saint-Sacrement.

Jouvet, Louis. Théâtre du Vieux-Colombier, Paris: B&W. Rendering. **CSC**, facing 180; B&W. Rendering. **SDC**, plate 98. Drawing by Robert Edmond Jones; B&W. Rendering. **SOW**, plate 63; B&W. Rendering. **TPH**, photo 355.

Casanova.

Colavecchia, Franco. New York City Opera: 1985. B&W and color. Model & rendering. **DDT**, 179, 312d.

Rosse, Herman. Belmont Theatre, NYC: 1923. B&W. Set. **TCS2**, plate 86.

Stern, Ernst. Coliseum, London: 1932. B&W. Set. **MCD**, plate 170.

Casey Jones.
> Bay, Howard. B&W. Show curtain. **SDB**, 110.
> Gorelik, Mordecai. Group Theatre, USA: 1938. B&W. Set. **NTO**, facing 68; B&W.
> Set. **SOW**, plate 90.

Casina.
> Oenslager, Donald. (project): B&W. Rendering. **STN**, 79.

Castle in Sweden.
> Dupont, Jacques. Théâtre de l'Atelier, France: 1960. B&W. Rendering. **SDW2**, 89.
> Hegle, Kaare. Det Nye Teater, Oslo: 1960. B&W. Rendering. **SDW2**, 152.

Castle Wetterstein.
> Minks, Wilfried. Wuppertaler Bühnen, Wuppertal: 1972. B&W. Set. **SDW4**, illus. 192.

Castor et Pollux.
> Pizzi, Pier Luigi. Les Arts Florissants, Aix-en-Provence: 1991. Color. Set. **TCI**, vol.
> 26, n. 4 (Apr 1992). 38.

The Cat and the Canary.
> Fulton, Larry. Impossible Ragtime Theatre, NYC: 1979. B&W. Set. **TCI**, vol. 14, n. 3
> (May/Jun 1980). 43.

The Cat and the Fiddle.
> Dreyfuss, Henry. Globe Theatre, NYC: 1931. B&W. Set. **BWM**, 170. 2 photos; B&W.
> Set. **MCN**, 106; B&W. Set. **RBS**, 55; B&W. Set. **SCM**, 118; B&W. Set. **SDA**,
> 245. 3 photos.

The Cat Bird.
> Simonson, Lee. Maxine Elliott's Theatre, NYC: 1920. B&W. Set. **PLT**, illus. 2, 3.

Cat on a Hot Tin Roof.
> Dudley, William. Eugene O'Neill Theatre, NYC: 1990. B&W. Set. **TCI**, vol. 24, n. 5
> (May 1990). 47.
> Lehto, Leo. Suomen Kansallisteatteri, Helsinki: 1956. B&W. Set. **SDW1**, 158.
> Mielziner, Jo. Morosco Theatre, NYC: 1955. B&W. Rendering. **DTT**, 184 Maggie and
> Brick disrobing; B&W. Rendering. **DTT**, 185. Children's party; B&W. Rendering.
> **DTT**, 186. Big Daddy; B&W. Rendering. **DTT**, 187. Brick and Maggie making up;
> B&W. Rendering. **SDW1**, 203.
> Darwin Reid. B&W. Model. **TCM**, 29; B&W. Model. **SIP**, 175.
> Pecktal, Lynn. Barter Theatre, Abington, Virginia: 1959. B&W. Set. **DPT**, 311.

Catch 22.
> Yoshimura, Akita. Hartman Theatre Company, Stamford, Connecticut: 1976. B&W.
> Set. **TCI**, vol. 10, n. 4 (Sep 1976). 6.

Catch Me If You Can.
> Karlin, Robert Lewis. Garland Dinner Theatre, Columbia, Maryland: c. 1969. B&W.
> Set. **TCI**, vol. 3, n. 4 (Sep 1969). 27.

Catch My Brother's Eye.
> Gordon, Pip. University of Iowa, Iowa City: 1988. B&W. Set. **TDT**, vol. XXV, n. 3
> (Fall 1989). 37.

*Catherine: Concerning the Fateful Origins of Her Grandeur with Diverse Musical Inter-
ludes, 3 Elephants, and No Ballet.*
> Labenz, Craig. Intiman Theatre, Seattle: 1992. Color. Set. **TCI**, vol. 26, n. 8 (Oct
> 1992). 6.

The Catherine Wheel.
> Loquasto, Santo. Winter Garden Theatre, NYC: 1981. B&W. Set. **ASD1**, 115. Twyla
> Tharp and dancers on Broadway/The Catherine Wheel.

Cats.
> Napier, John. London: 1981. B&W and color. Set. **ALW**, 129-131, 134-141. 14 photos; Color. Set. **BTD**, 148; B&W. Set. **DDT**, 3, 591; Color. Set. **MBM**, 2, 3, 64; B&W. Set. **SDL**, 1, 134, 135. 3 photos; B&W. Model & set. **TCI**, vol. 17, n. 1 (Jan 1983). 18-21. 6 photos; B&W. Model. **TDT**, vol. XIX, n. 1 (Spring 1983). 10; B&W. Set. **TDP**, 46.

The Caucasian Chalk Circle.
> Appen, Karl von. Theater am Schiffbauerdamm, Berlin: 1954. Color. Rendering. **RSD**, illus. 568, 570; B&W. Rendering & set. **SIP**, 168, 169; B&W. Rendering & set. **TBB**, 56, 123; B&W. Rendering & set. **TCM**, 23, 24; Sarah Bernhardt Theatre, Paris: 1955. B&W. Set. **SDW1**, 62.
> Funicello, Ralph. Seattle Repertory Theatre: 1987. B&W. Set. **TCI**, vol. 22, n. 1 (Jun 1988). 51. 3 photos.
> Marr, Scott. (project): B&W. Rendering. **TDT**, vol. XXVI, n. 1 (Spring 1990). 20 of insert.
> Oechslin, Ary. State Theatre, Bern: 1971. B&W. Model. **SDW3**, 117.
> Stell, W. Joseph. University of Georgia Theatre: c. 1968. B&W. Set. **TCI**, vol. 3, n. 1 (Jan/Feb 1969). 32-36. 7 photos.
> Taylor, Robert U. Colonnades Theatre Lab, NYC: B&W. Sketch. **TCI**, vol. 11, n. 1 (Jan/Feb 1977). 25.
> _____. Birmingham Southern College, Alabama: c. 1968. B&W. Set. **TCI**, vol. 3, n. 2 (Mar/Apr 1969). 9.
> _____. New York Shakespeare Festival, NYC: Color. Set. **TCI**, vol. 25, n. 9 (Nov 1991). 53.

Cavalcade.
> Porteous, Cameron. Shaw Festival Theatre, Niagara-on-the-Lake, Canada: 1986. Color. Set. **TCI**, vol. 22, n. 7 (Aug/Sep 1988). 62.

Cavalleria Rusticana.
> Colavecchia, Franco. Dorothy Chandler Pavilion, Los Angeles: 1988. B&W. Rendering. **DDT**, 151. 4 photos.
> Damiani, Luciano. Teatro alla Scala, Milan: 1966. B&W. Set. **SDW3**, 185.
> Landi, Angelo Maria. 1940. B&W. Rendering. **SDE**, 95.
> Steinberg, Paul. New Isreali Opera: 1992. Color. Set. **TCI**, vol. 29, n. 4 (Apr 1995). 32.
> Zeffirelli, Franco. Metropolitan Opera, NYC: 1970. B&W and color. Set. **MOM**, 40-55. 15 photos; B&W. Set. **TCI**, vol. 10, n. 5 (Oct 1976). 16.

The Cave.
> Arnone, John. 1993. Color. Set. **TCI**, vol. 27, n. 9 (Nov 1993). 9.

La Cecchina o la Buona Figliola.
> Zeffirelli, Franco. 1956-1957. B&W. Set. **SIO**, 137.

Celestials.
> _____. Sunnyside Garden Ball Room and Arena: 1965. B&W. Set. **RSD**, illus. 612. Happening.

La Celestina.
> Luzzati, Emanuele. Piccolo Teatro, Milan: 1952. B&W. Rendering. **SDE**, 99.
> Viudes, Vicente. Teatro Eslava, Madrid: 1958. B&W. Rendering & set. **SDW2**, 82. 2 photos.

Cement.
> Reinhardt, Andreas. Theater am Schiffbauerdamm, Berlin: 1973. B&W. Set. **SDW4**, illus. 324-328.

The Cenci.
>   Hurry, Leslie. Old Vic Theatre, London: 1959. Color. Rendering. **TOP**, 23.
>   Jones, Robert Edmond. (project): 1913. B&W. Sketch. **DFT**, plate 29. Act I, sc. 3: the banquet; B&W. Sketch. **DFT**, plate 30. Act IV, sc. 4: the arrest of Beatrice; B&W. Sketch. **DFT**, plate 31. Act V, sc. 3: a prison; B&W. Sketch. **DFT**, plate 32. Act V, sc. 4: the final scene; B&W. Rendering. **REJ**, 29; B&W. Rendering. **RSD**, illus. 428; B&W. Sketch. **TPH**, photo 459.

Cendrillion.
>   Bardon, Henry. New York City Opera, Lincoln Center: 1983. B&W. Set. **TCI**, vol. 18, n. 1 (Jan 1984). 8.

La Cenerentola.
>   Wong, Carey. Portland Opera, Oregon: 1977. B&W. Set. **TCI**, vol. 12, n. 5 (Sep 1978). 38. 4 photos.

Cerceau.
>   _____. Arena Stage, Washington, DC: Color. Set. **TCI**, vol. 25, n. 2 (Feb 1991). 48.

Ceremonies in Dark Old Men.
>   Jensen, John. Tyrone Guthrie Theatre, Minneapolis: B&W. Set. **TCI**, vol. 9, n. 1 (Jan/Feb 1975). 8.
>   McClennahan, Charles. Negro Ensemble Company: 1985. B&W. Sketch. **ASD2**, 114.

The Ceremony of Innocence.
>   Lundell, Kurt. American Place Theatre, NYC: 1967. B&W. Set. **DPT**, 25.

A Certain Joy.
>   Bay, Howard. 1952. B&W. Set. **SDB**, 116.

Le Chagrin dans le palais de Han.
>   Piot, René. Théâtre des Arts, Paris: 1912. B&W. Rendering. **RSD**, illus. 50.

The Chairs.
>   Herbert, Jocelyn. Royal Court Theatre, London: 1957. Color. Set. **TDT**, vol. XXX, n. 5 (Fall 1994). cover.
>   Noël, Jacques. Théâtre Gramont, Paris: 1956. B&W. Set. **DSL**, figure 1.2; B&W. Set. **RSD**, illus. 458; B&W. Set. **TCR**, 105.

The Chalk Circle.
>   Neher, Caspar. Deutsches Theater, Berlin: 1925. B&W. Rendering. **CBM**, 83.

Chandelier.
>   Marty, André. Comédie-Française, Paris: 1936. B&W. Set. **SOW**, plate 66.

Chang in a Moon Void.
>   Jesurun, John. Pyramid Lounge, NYC: 1982. B&W. Set. **TCI**, vol. 19, n. 7 (Aug/Sep 1985). 48, 49.

The Changeling.
>   Aronson, Boris. (project): 1947. B&W. Rendering. **TAB**, 300.
>   Dudley, William. National Theatre (Lyttleton), England: 1988. B&W and color. Set. **BTD**, 42, 43; B&W. Set. **TDT**, vol. XXV, n. 3 (Fall 1989). 20.
>   Yeargan, Michael. Yale Repertory Theatre, New Haven: 1985. B&W. Set. **ASD2**, 187.

The Changing Room.
>   Jenkins, David. Long Wharf Theatre, New Haven, Connecticut: 1972. B&W. Set. **CSD**, 25; B&W. Set. **TCI**, vol. 9, n. 6 (Nov/Dec 1975). 20; B&W. Set. **TCI**, vol. 7, n. 5 (Oct 1973). 6. 2 photos.
>   Jenkins, David. Morosco Theatre, NYC: 1973. B&W. Model. **CSD**, 87; B&W. Model. **DDT**, 433; B&W. Model. **DPT**, 126.

Le Chant du Rossignol.
>   Matisse, Henri. Ballets Russes, Paris Opera: 1920. B&W. Sketch of curtain. **AST**, 80.

Chantecler.

Amable, A. Petit. Théâtre de la Porte Saint-Martin, Paris: 1910. B&W. Set. **RSD**, illus. 4.

Gros, Ernest, J.M. Hewlett, A.T. Hewlett, & Charles Basing. Knickerbocker Theatre, NYC: 1911. B&W. Set. **MCN**, 36.

Scott, Robert. Yale School of Drama, New Haven, Connecticut: B&W. Show curtain. **SFT**, 287.

Delfau, André. 1961. B&W and color. Rendering. **FCS**, plate 187, color plate 26.

Chaplin.

Schmidt, Douglas W. Dorothy Chandler Pavilion, Los Angeles: 1983. B&W. Rendering. **ASD1**, 143; B&W. Drops. **DDT**, 398. 2 photos.

Charley's Aunt.

Brockman, C. Lance. Minnesota Centennial Showboat, Minneapolis: 1980. B&W. Rendering. **BSE3**, 12.

Koenig, John. Cort Theatre, NYC: 1940. B&W. Set. **WTP**, 152.

A Charmed Life.

Tröster, Frantisek. Estates Theatre, Prague: 1937. B&W. Rendering. **TDT**, n. 42 (Fall 1975). 29.

La Chatte.

Gabo, Naum & Antoine Pevsner. Ballets Russes, Monte Carlo: 1927. B&W. Set. **AST**, 136; B&W. Set. **RSD**, illus. 200; B&W. Set. **TCS2**, plate 165.

Chauve Souris.

Soudeikine, Serge. 49th Street Theatre, NYC: 1922. B&W. Rendering. **FCS**, plate 177; B&W. Rendering. **SDO**, 200.

The Cheat.

_____. Maly Theatre, Moscow: 1929. B&W. Set. **RST**, 246. 2 photos.

Chekov in Yalta.

Sherman, Loren. Walnut Street Theatre, Philadelphia: B&W. Model. **BSE4**, 98.

Chemin de Fer.

Burbridge, Edward. Phoenix Theatre, NYC: 1973. B&W. Set. **TCI**, vol. 8, n. 6 (Nov/Dec 1974). 17.

The Cherry Orchard.

Berka, Tomás. Bratislava: 1984. B&W. Model. **TDT**, vol. XXIII, n. 4 (Winter 1988). 28; B&W. Model. **TDT**, vol. XXVII, n. 4 (Fall 1991). 47.

Bernstein, Aline. Civic Repertory Theatre, NYC: 1928. B&W. Set. **MCN**, 92.

Berwoots, Jacques. Belgium: 1987. B&W. Model. **TDT**, vol. XXIII, n. 4 (Winter 1988). 29.

Blackman, Robert. American Conservatory Theatre, San Francisco: 1974. B&W. Set. **TSY**, 164.

Bliese, Thomas H. Mankato State University, Minnesota: 1980. B&W. Model. **BSE2**, 7.

Ciller, Josef. Uherské Hradiste, Czechoslovakia: 1979. B&W. Rendering. **TDT**, vol. XXVIII, n. 2 (Spring 1992). 34; B&W. Rendering. **TDT**, vol. XX, n. 1 (Spring 1984). 42.

Clarke, Bill. Playmakers Repertory Company, Paul Green Theatre, Chapel Hill, North Carolina: B&W. Set. **TCI**, vol. 25, n. 3 (Mar 1991). 48.

Fenes, Romulus. Romania: 1985. B&W. Model. **TDT**, vol. XXIII, n. 4 (Winter 1988). 29.

Hay, Richard L. Stanford Repertory Theatre, California: 1967. B&W. Set. **PST**, 362.

Hermann, Karl-Ernst. Berlin: 1969. B&W. Model. **TDT**, vol. XXIII, n. 4 (Winter 1988). 26.

Jordan, Hanna. Residenz Theater, Munich: 1970. B&W. Set. **TCI**, vol. 5, n. 3 (May/
    Jun 1971). 26, 28.
Kitaïev, Mark. Lensovet Theatre of Leningrad: 1987. B&W. Model. **TDT**, vol. XXIII,
    n. 4 (Winter 1988). 27; Color. Model. **TDT**, vol. XXIII, n. 4 (Winter 1988). front
    cover.
Landesman, Heidi. La Jolla Playhouse, California: 1990. B&W. Set. **ASD2**, 62; B&W.
    Set. **ASD2**, 65. Act III; B&W. Set. **ASD2**, 66. Act II; B&W. Set. **ASD2**, 67. Act IV.
Levental, Valery. USSR: 1984. Color. Model. **TDT**, vol. XII, n. 3 (Fall 1976). 26, 41;
    B&W. Model. **TDT**, vol. XXIII, n. 4 (Winter 1988). 27.
Loquasto, Santo. Vivian Beaumont Theatre, Lincoln Center, NYC: 1977. B&W. Set.
    ASD1, 119; B&W. Set. **TCI**, vol. 11, n. 4 (Sep 1977). 10; B&W. Set. **TCI**, vol. 14,
    n. 1 (Jan/Feb 1980). 18; B&W. Set. **TDT**, vol. XVII, n. 3 (Fall 1981). 20, 21. 5
    photos.
Motley (Margaret Harris, Sophia Harris, & Elizabeth Montgomery). National Theatre,
    NYC: 1944. B&W. Set. **WTP**, 98, 99. 6 photos.
Obolensky, Chloè. Majestic Theatre, Brooklyn Academy of Music, NY: 1988. B&W.
    Set. **TCI**, vol. 22, n. 4 (Apr 1988). 23.
Okun, Alexander. Williams College Theatre, Williamstown, Massachusetts: 1984.
    Color. Set. **TCI**, vol. 21, n. 9 (Nov 1987). 45.
Oustinov, Alexandre. Dramatitcheski Teatr imeni Chekhova, Taganrog: 1960. B&W.
    Set. **SDW2**, 189.
Rose, Jürgen. Deutsches Schauspielhaus, Hamburg: 1970. B&W. Set. **SDW3**, 92.
Scarfiotti, Ferdinando. Teatro Stabile di Roma: 1966. B&W. Rendering. **SDW3**, 92.
Silitch, Lioubiv. Moscow Art Theatre in Paris: 1958. B&W. Set. **SDW2**, 193.
Simov, Victor Andréiévich. Moscow Art Theatre: 1904. B&W. Set. **RSD**, illus. 18;
    B&W. Set. **SDC**, plate 42; B&W. Set. **TCS2**, plate 5; B&W. Set. **TSY**, 152; Mos-
    cow Art Theatre (tour): c.1904. B&W. Rendering. **CSC**, facing 10.
Stein, Douglas O. Denver Center, Colorado: 1986. B&W. Set. **DDT**, 240, 241. 3
    photos.
Tröster, Frantisek. Czechoslovakia: B&W. Set. **TDT**, vol. XXVII, n. 4 (Fall 1991). 46.
Tsypin, George. American Repertory Theatre, Cambridge, Massachusetts: 1994. B&W.
    Set. **TCI**, vol. 28, n. 4 (Apr 1994). 9.

Cherubin.
Perdziola, Robert. Manhattan School of Music, NYC: 1987. B&W. Rendering. **DDT**,
    19.

Chess.
Wagner, Robin. London: 1986. Color. Set. **TCI**, vol. 22, n. 8 (Oct 1988). 74; Color.
    Set. **ALW**, 197. 2 photos.
Wagner, Robin. Imperial Theatre, NYC: 1988. B&W. Model. **DDT**, 344; B&W. Set.
    MBM, 75, 211; B&W and color. Set. **TCI**, vol. 22, n. 8 (Oct 1988). 3, 70-73. 5
    photos.

Les Chevaliers de la Table Ronde.
Cocteau, Jean. Théâtre de l'Œuvre, Paris: 1937. B&W. Set. **TPH**, photo 363.

Chicago.
Walton, Tony. 46th Street Theatre, NYC: 1975. Color. Set. **BWM**, 121; B&W. Model.
    DDT, 285; Color. Set. **TCI**, vol. 28, n. 3 (Mar 1994). 33; B&W. Model & set. **TCI**,
    vol. 9, n. 5 (Oct 1975). 8. 4 photos.
Weaver, Arden. University of Minnesota, Duluth: B&W and color. Model & set. **TDT**,
    vol. XXX, n. 3 (Summer 1994). 12.

The Child Buyer.
Elder, Eldon. Garrick Theatre, NYC: 1964-1965. B&W. Rendering. **EED,** (pages not numbered).

Child's Play.
Mielziner, Jo. Royale Theatre, NYC: 1970. B&W. Rendering. **TCI,** vol. 4, n. 3 (May/Jun 1970). 19; B&W. Set. **TCI,** vol. 14, n. 1 (Jan/Feb 1980). 20.
Williams, Jerry. Alley Theatre, Houston: B&W. Set. **TCI,** vol. 7, n. 3 (May/Jun 1973). 9.

Childe Byron.
Potts, David. Circle Repertory Theatre, NYC: B&W. Set. **TCI,** vol. 15, n. 6 (Jun/Jul 1981). 16, 17.

Children of a Lesser God.
Walsh, Thomas. Mark Taper Forum, Los Angeles: 1980. B&W. Set. **TCI,** vol. 14, n. 4 (Sep 1980). 45.

The Children of Darkness (Gaoler's Wench).
Jones, Robert Edmond. Biltmore Theatre, NYC: 1930. B&W. Rendering. **SCM,** 102.

Children of the Sun.
Landwehr, Hugh. Williamstown Theatre Festival, Massachusetts: 1979. B&W. Set. **TCI,** vol. 14, n. 3 (May/Jun 1980). 16, 17.
Svoboda, Josef. National Theatre, Prague: 1973. B&W. Set. **SDW4,** illus. 199; B&W. Set. **STS,** 16; B&W. Set. **TDT,** vol. XII, n. 2 (Summer 1976). 31.

The Children's Hour.
Bay, Howard. Coronet Theatre, NYC: 1952. B&W. Set. **TCI,** vol. 17, n. 2 (Feb 1983). 15.
Bernstein, Aline & Sointu Syrjala. Maxine Elliott's Theatre, NYC: 1934. B&W. Set. **MCN,** 120.

Chinchilla.
Prowse, Philip. Phoenix Theatre, NYC: 1979. B&W. Set. **TCI,** vol. 15, n. 7 (Aug/Sep 1981). 20.

The Chinese Honeymoon.
Hann, Walter & Philip Howden. Royal Strand Theatre, London: 1901. B&W. Set. **MCD,** plate 35.

The Chinese Wall.
Schmid, Georg. Volkstheater, Vienna. 1956. B&W. Set. **SDW2,** 161.

Chipita Rodreguez.
Isackes, Richard M. University of Texas Opera, Austin: B&W and color. Sketch & set. **TDT,** vol. XXX, n. 3 (Summer 1994). 6.

The Chocolate Soldier.
_____. Theater an der Wien, Vienna: 1908. B&W. Set. **BMF,** 21.

A Chorus Line.
Harris, Jeff. Marriot Lincolnshire Theatre, Lincolnshire, Illinois: 1985. B&W. Set. **TCI,** vol. 19, n. 9 (Nov 1985). 10.
Wagner, Robin. Shubert Theatre, NYC: 1975. Color. Set. **BWM,** 34, 136; B&W. Set. **TCI,** vol. 14, n. 1 (Jan/Feb 1980). 21; B&W. Set. **TCI,** vol. 9, n. 6 (Nov/Dec 1975). 6, 11. 5 photos; B&W. Set. **TDT,** vol. XIX, n. 4 (Winter 1983). 5. 2 photos.
Wagner, Robin. Drury Lane Theatre, London: 1976. B&W. Set. **BMF,** 74, 75.
_____. Emerson College, Boston: B&W. Set. **TCI,** vol. 23, n. 9 (Nov 1989). 52.

A Chorus of Disapproval.
_____. South Coast Repertory Theatre, Costa Mesa, California: 1989. B&W. Set. **TCR,** 120.

Le Chout.
   Larionov, Michel. Gaiete-Lyrique, Paris: 1921. Color. Rendering. **AST**, 49; Color.
      Rendering. **RSD**, illus. 292. Ballet-Russes.
A Christmas Carol.
   Berliner, Charles. Cleveland Playhouse: 1987. Color. Set. **TCI**, vol. 21, n. 8 (Oct
      1987). 40.
   Dorsey, Kent. San Diego Repertory Theatre: B&W. Set. **SDL**, 373. 3 photos.
   Payne, Darwin Reid. B&W. Rendering. **SIP**, 17.
   Tiné, Hal. Landmark Theatre, Syracuse, NY: B&W. Set. **SDT**, 294.
   Walton, Tony. Paramount Theatre, NYC: 1994. B&W and color. Set. **TCI**, vol. 29, n. 1
      (Jan 1995). 66. 3 photos.
Christmas Eve.
   Blane, Sue. English National Opera, London: 1988. Color. Set. **BTD**, 108, 109.
Christophe Colomb.
   _____. 1930. B&W. Set. **TBB**, 115.
Christopher Columbus.
   Ingrand, Max. Théâtre Marigny, Paris: 1953. B&W. Set. **SDW1**, 99.
   _____. San Francisco Opera: 1968. B&W. Set. **TCI**, vol. 4, n. 1 (Jan/Feb 1970).
      10.
A Chronicle of Hitler's Life and Death.
   Chevalier, A. & Jo Tréhard Stade de Caen, France: 1971. B&W. Set. **SDW3**, 163;
      B&W. Set. **SDW4**, illus. 363.
Chu Chin Chow.
   Harker, Joseph & Phil Harker. His Majesty's Theatre, London: 1916. B&W. Set.
      MCD, plate 108.
La Chulapona.
   Kegler, Kathrin. Teatro Lirico Nacional de la Zarzuela, Madrid: 1992. Color. Set. **TCI**,
      vol. 26, n. 4 (Apr 1992). 36.
The Cid.
   Gischia, Léon. Festival of Avignon: 1951. B&W. Set. **RSD**, illus. 522.
   Nerom, Jacques van. Belgium: B&W. Model. **TDT**, vol. XVI, n. 1 (Spring 1980). 9.
   Oenslager, Donald. (project): B&W. Rendering. **STN**, 135.
La Cimice.
   Scandella, Mischa. B&W. Rendering. **SIO**, 125. 3 photos.
Cin-Ci-La.
   Bregni, Paolo. 1972. B&W. Rendering & set. **SIO**, 15.
Cinderella.
   Craig, Edward Gordon. 1904. B&W. Rendering. **TNT**, facing 25.
   Sainthill, Loudon. Coliseum, London: 1958. Color. Rendering. **LST**, 49. Pantomime.
   Varona, José. Deutsches Staatsoper, Berlin: 1976. B&W. Rendering. **DDT**, 28.
Cinna.
   Reymond, Suzanne. Comédie Française, Paris: 1951. B&W. Rendering. **SDW1**, 106.
   Sonrel, Pierre. Sarah Bernhardt Theatre, Paris: 1947. B&W. Set. **SDW1**, 106.
The Circle.
   Heeley, Desmond. NYC: 1989. B&W. Rendering. **SDD**, between 210 & 211.
A Circle in the Sun.
   Poklman, Donald. Children's Theatre Company, Minneapolis: B&W. Set. **TCI**, vol.
      17, n. 7 (Aug/Sep 1983). 31.
Circus 70.
   _____. Playhouse in the Park, Cincinnati: B&W. Set. **TCI**, vol. 5, n. 2 (Mar/Apr
      1971). 15.

Cirkus Dandin.
   Heythum, Antonín. Osvobozene Theatre, Prague: 1937. B&W. Set. **RSD**, illus. 279.
La Città Morta.
   Falleni, Silvano. 1964. B&W. Set. **SIO**, 50.
The City.
   Léger, Fernand. 1919. B&W. Rendering. **TCT**, plate 31.
City Junket.
   Grooms, Red. Color. Set. **TCI**, vol. 18, n. 4 (Apr 1984). 29.
City of Angels.
   Wagner, Robin. Virginia Theatre, NYC: 1989. B&W. Model. **DDT**, 16, 17, 340, 348. 8
   photos; B&W and color. Set. **MBM**, 144-146, 149-151. 6 photos; Color. Set. **TCI**, vol.
   24, n. 7 (Aug/Sep 1990). 14; Color. Set. **TCI**, vol. 24, n. 5 (May 1990). 46.
City of Voices.
   Malolepsy, John F. University of New Mexico, Albequerque: 1977. B&W. Model.
   BSE1, 17.
the CIVIL warS.
   Wilson, Robert. Schwouwburg, Rotterdam: 1982. B&W. Sketches, models, & set.
   RWT, 97, 110-112, 115-118. 27 photos; B&W. Set. **TCI**, vol. 19, n. 8 (Oct 1985).
   25; Germany: 1984. B&W. Set. **TCI**, vol. 20, n. 3 (Mar 1986). 27; Color. Set. **TCI**,
   vol. 19, n. 7 (Aug/Sep 1985). 45; B&W. Model. **TDT**, vol. XXVII, n. 2 (Spring
   1991). 14; American Repertory Theatre, Cambridge, Massachusetts: 1985. Color.
   Set. **TCI**, vol. 19, n. 8 (Oct 1985). 24, 25; Color. Set. **TCI**, vol. 24, n. 8 (Oct 1990).
   41.
A Civilization Misunderstood.
   Karakachev, Gueorgui. National Theater, Plevene, Bulgaria: 1959. B&W. Rendering.
   SDW2, 37.
Clarence Darrow.
   Mednikov, Vera. Cricket Theatre, Minneapolis: 1980. B&W. Set. **TCI**, vol. 17, n. 7
   (Aug/Sep 1983). 28.
   _____. Alaska Repertory Theatre, Anchorage: B&W. Set. **TCI**, vol. 13, n. 2
   (Mar/Apr 1979). 25.
Clash by Night.
   Aronson, Boris. Belasco Theatre, NYC: 1941. B&W and color. Rendering & set. **TAB**,
   17, 297. 3 photos.
Clavigo.
   Freyer, Achim. Kammerspiele, Berlin: 1971. B&W. Set. **TCI**, vol. 13, n. 5 (Oct 1979).
   19; Werkstaat des Schillertheater, Berlin: 1974. B&W. Set. **TCI**, vol. 13, n. 5 (Oct
   1979). 19.
   Svoboda, Josef. Zurich: 1993. B&W. Set. **TDT**, vol. XXX, n. 5 (Fall 1994). 41.
   _____. Redoutensaal, Hofburg Palace, Vienna: 1922. B&W. Set. **MRH**, facing
   163.
The Claw.
   Malina, Jaroslav. Cinoherní Studio, Ustí Nad Labem, Czech Republic: B&W. Render-
   ing & set. **TDT**, vol. XXX, n. 2 (Spring 1994). 19, 21, 22. 3 photos; B&W. Set.
   TDT, vol. XXVII, n. 2 (Spring 1991). 30, 34.
A Clearing in the Woods.
   Smith, Oliver. Belasco Theatre, NYC: 1957. B&W. Set. **SDA**, 156.
La Clemenza di Tito.
   Georgiadis, Nicholas. Aix-en-Provence: 1988. B&W. Model. **BTD**, 132, 133.

Ponnelle, Jean-Pierre. Flanders Festival: 1971. B&W. Set. **TCI**, vol. 12, n. 3 (Mar/Apr 1978). 19; Salzburg Festival: 1976. B&W. Set. **TCI**, vol. 12, n. 3 (Mar/Apr 1978). 16.

_____. Juilliard School, Lincoln Center, NYC: B&W. Set. **TCI**, vol. 8, n. 4 (Sep 1974). 19.

The Clever Little Vixen.
Heinrich, Rudolf. Komische Oper, Berlin: 1957. B&W. Set. **SDW2**, 50.

The Clever One.
Jürgens, Helmut. State Opera, Munich: 1948. Color. Rendering. **SDW1**, 67.
Pfeiffenberger, Heinz. Komische Oper, Berlin: 1948. B&W. Set. **SDW1**, 73. 2 photos.

The Climbers.
Physioc, Joseph & Ernest Albert. Bijou Theatre, NYC: 1901. B&W. Set. **MCN**, 14; B&W. Set. **SDA**, 27.

A Clinical case.
Altandag, Seza. Devlet Tiyatrosu, Ankara, Turkey: 1960. B&W. Rendering. **SDW2**, 213.

La Clizia (Machiavelli).
Ghiglia, Lorenzo. 1970. B&W. Set. **SIO**, 69-73. 4 photos.

The Cloak.
Bregni, Paolo. B&W. Set. **SIO**, 16.

Clochemerle.
Gauguin, Paul René. Folketertret, Oslo: 1954. B&W. Set. **SDW2**, 152.

Clock Symphony.
Bérard, Christian. Covent Garden, London: 1948. B&W. Rendering. **SDW1**, 82.

A Clockwork Orange.
Hudson, Richard. Royal Shakespeare Company, GB: 1990. B&W. Model. **TDT**, vol. XXVIII, n. 2 (Spring 1992). 21; Color. Model. **TDT**, vol. XXVII, n. 4 (Fall 1991). 7.

Close at Play.
Diss, Eileen. National Theatre, London: 1979. B&W. Set. **TCI**, vol. 15, n. 5 (May 1981). 12.

Close Ties.
Arnold, Richard. Northern Illinois University, DeKalb, Ilinois: B&W. Sketch & set. **SCT**, 18, 26.

_____. Coronet Theatre, Los Angeles: B&W. Set. **TCI**, vol. 16, n. 8 (Oct 1982). 28, 29.

Cloud Nine.
Malolepsy, John F. New Mexico Repertory Theatre: 1985. B&W. Rendering. **BSE5**, 16.

The Clouds.
Hadzikyriakos - Ghikas, Nicolas. Vassilikon Théâtron, Athens: 1951. B&W. Rendering. **SDW2**, 103.

The Clown of God.
Yunker, Don. Children's Theatre Company, Minneapolis: B&W. Set. **TCI**, vol. 17, n. 7 (Aug/Sep 1983). 16.

The Club.
_____. Circle in the Square Downtown, NYC: 1976. B&W. Set. **MBM**, 94, 98.

Coal Diamond.
_____. Actors Theatre of Louisville: 1980. B&W. Set. **TCI**, vol. 15, n. 4 (Apr 1981). 16.

Cock-a-Doodle-Dandy.
    Polakov, Lester. Carnegie Hall, NYC: 1958. B&W. Rendering. **DDT**, 169. 2 photos.
The Cocktail Party.
    _____. Indiana Repertory Theatre: Color. Set. **TCI**, vol. 25, n. 9 (Nov 1991). 55.
    _____. London: B&W. Set. **WTP**, 165. 3 photos.
Cocktail.
    Prampolini, Enrico. Théâtre de la Madeleine, Paris: 1927. B&W. Set. **RSD**, illus. 342.
Coco.
    Beaton, Cecil. Mark Hellinger Theatre, NYC: 1969. B&W. Set. **TCI**, vol. 14, n. 1 (Jan/
        Feb 1980). 20; Color. Set. **TMT**, plate 12.
The Cocoanuts.
    _____. Arena Stage, Washington, DC. B&W. Set. **TCI**, vol. 22, n. 9 (Nov 1988).
        27.
The Coffe Trade Foxes.
    Serroni, J.C. Alianca Francesa, Brazil: 1990. Color. Set. **TCI**, vol. 28, n. 4 (Apr 1994).
        36, 37.
The Coffee House.
    Minks, Wilfried. Theater der Freien Hansestadt, Bremen: 1969. B&W. Set. **SDW3**, 75.
        3 photos.
    _____. Corte del Teatro di San Luca, Italy: 1934. B&W. Set. **TPH**, photo 383.
A Cola Day in Hell.
    Brown, Michael. Brown University, Providence, Rhode Island: 1993. B&W. Set. **TDT**,
        vol. **XXX**, n. 5 (Fall 1994). 61.
Cold Harbor.
    _____. Mabou Mines, NYC: 1983. B&W. Set. **BSE4**, 91.
The Cold Wind and the Warm.
    Aronson, Boris. Morosco Theatre, NYC: 1958. B&W. Rendering. **TAB**, 305.
Colombe.
    Barsacq, André. Théâtre de l'Atelier, Paris: 1950. B&W. Rendering. **SDW1**, 84.
    Luzzati, Emanuele. Piccolo Teatro della Città di Genova: 1954. B&W. Rendering.
        SDE, 107.
    _____. Yale Dramatic Association, New Haven, Connecticut: B&W. Sketches.
        SDL, 77. 4 photos.
The Color Box.
    Karson, Nat. USA: 1933. B&W. Rendering. **TAT**, plate 576.
Columbus.
    Hoffman, Vlastislav. National Theatre, Prague: B&W. Set. **TCS2**, plate 145.
Come Back Little Sheba.
    Bay, Howard. Theatre Guild, NYC: 1950. B&W. Set. **SDA**, 228; B&W. Set. **TCI**, vol.
        17, n. 2 (Feb 1983). 15; B&W. Set. **TDT**, n. 19 (Dec 1969). 21; B&W. Set. **WTP**,
        205. 4 photos.
    Beatty, John Lee. Queens Playhouse, Flushing, NY: 1974. B&W. Sketch. **DPT**, 121.
Come Back to the Five and Dime, Jimmy Dean, Jimmy Dean.
    Gropman, David. Martin Beck Theatre, NYC: 1982. B&W. Model. **ASD2**, 32; B&W.
        Set. **DDT**, 40.
La Comédie non Divine.
    Jarocki, Stanislas. Teatr Polski, Poznan: B&W. Set. **TCS2**, plates 82-84. 4 photos.
The Comedy of Errors.
    Ballou, Bill. Shakespeare and Company: 1983. Color. Set. **TCI**, vol. 18, n. 5 (May
        1984). 12.
    Beyer, Rolf. Catholic University, Washington, DC: 1972. B&W. Set. **DDT**, 444.

Crowley, Bob. Royal Shakespeare Company, GB: 1983. B&W. Set. **SDT**, 274.

Faulkner, Cliff. San Diego National Shakespeare Festival: 1979. B&W. Set. **TCI**, vol. 14, n. 4 (Sep 1980). 38.

Krohg, Guy. Studioteatret, Oslo: 1947. B&W. Set. **DOT**, 244; B&W. Set. **SDW1**, 154.

Lee, Ming Cho. New York Shakespeare Festival, NYC: 1967. B&W. Model. **TDT**, n. 24 (Feb 1971). 6.

McCarry, Charles E. 1991. Color. Model. **DDT**, 24a.

Napier, John with Dermot Hayes. Royal Shakespeare Company, Aldwych Theatre, London: 1977. B&W. Set. **TCI**, vol. 12, n. 3 (Mar/Apr 1978). 10.

Sinkkonen, Eric. California Shakespeare Festival, Berkeley: 1994. Color. Model. **TCI**, vol. 28, n. 8 (Oct 1994). 7.

Vychodil, Ladislav. Montreal: 1984. B&W. Rendering. **TCI**, vol. 21, n. 8 (Oct 1987). 37.

Wijnberg, Nicolaas. De Rotterdamse Schouwburg, Rotterdam. 1960. B&W. Set. **SDW2**, 146.

_____. Kammerspiele, Munich: 1910. B&W. Set. **MRH**, facing 80.

_____. University of Michigan, Ann Arbor: B&W. Set. **TCI**, vol. 8, n. 5 (Oct 1974). 16.

Comedy of the End of Time.

Schneider-Siemssen, Günther. Salzburg Festival: 1973. B&W. Set. **TCI**, vol. 12, n. 6 (Oct 1978). 32. 3 photos; Salzburg Festival: 1976. B&W. Set. **TCI**, vol. 11, n. 2 (Mar/Apr 1977). 21. 3 photos; B&W. Set. **TCI**, vol. 27, n. 3 (Mar 1993). 28.

Comet Messinger-Siegfried.

_____. Brooklyn Academy of Music, New York: 1988. B&W. Set. **TCI**, vol. 22, n. 7 (Aug/Sep 1988). 27.

Coming Back to the Very Start.

Kochergin, Edward Stepanovich. Moscow: 1978. B&W. **TCI**, vol. 13, n. 6 (Nov/Dec 1979). 25; B&W. Model. **TDT**, vol. XVI, n. 1 (Spring 1980). 24.

Coming Through the Rye.

Cosler, Charles. Long Island Stage, Hempstead, New York: 1986. Color. Set. **TCI**, vol. 20, n. 5 (May 1986). 12.

Commander of the Second Army.

Meyerhold, Vsevelod, plan; Sergei Vakhtangov, execution. Meyerhold Theatre, Moscow: 1929. B&W. Set. **MOT**, between 256 & 257. 2 photos.

La Commedia degli Zanni.

Scandella, Mischa. 1965-1966. B&W. Set. **SIO**, 123.

The Commission.

Wonder, Erich. Bochum, Germany: 1982. B&W. Set. **TCI**, vol. 20, n. 8 (Oct 1986). 34.

Commune.

Rojo, Jerry N. Performance Garage, NYC: 1970. B&W. Set. **TCI**, vol. 5, n. 4 (Sep 1971). 15. 2 photos; B&W. Model & set. **TSE**, 121-127. 5 photos.

Communicating Doors.

_____. Chicago: Color. Set. **TCI**, vol. 29, n. 1 (Jan 1995). 45.

Company.

Aronson, Boris. Alvin Theatre, NYC: 1970. B&W and color. Set. **BMF**, 83, 191; B&W and color. Set. **BWM**, 320, 321; B&W. Set. **CSD**, 36; B&W. Rendering. **DPT**, 60; B&W. Set. **HPA**, 92; B&W. Set. **HPR**, 173; B&W. Set. **SDB**, 64; B&W. Set. **SDW3**, 212; B&W. Set. **SON**, 82; B&W and color. Sketches, model, & set. **TAB**, 20, 220, 222-227, 308. 15 photo; B&W. Model. **TAB**, 229. 3 photos of unused design; B&W. Set. **TCI**, vol. 18, n. 8 (Oct 1984). 15; B&W. Set. **TCI**, vol.

4, n. 5 (Oct 1970). 15; B&W. Set. **TCI**, vol. 14, n. 1 (Jan/Feb 1980). 20; B&W. Model. **TDT**, vol. XXV, n. 3 (Fall 1989). 11.
Le Compt Ory.
    Matteis, Maria de. Maggio Musicale Fiorentino, Florence: 1952. B&W. Rendering. **SDE**, 122.
    Messel, Oliver. King's Theatre, Edinburgh: 1954. Color. Model. **MEM**, 28, 29.
    Ponnelle, Jean-Pierre. State Opera, Berlin: 1957. B&W. Set. **SDW2**, 67.
Comus.
    Messel, Oliver. New Theatre, London: 1942. B&W. Set. **MEM**, 105. Masque.
The Concert.
    Gros, Ernest. USA: 1909. B&W. Set. **SDA**, 22. (see caption on pg. 22).
Concerto.
    Tchelitchew, Pavel. 1942. B&W. Sketches. **FCS**, plate 210. Ballet; B&W. Sketches. **FCT**, plate 13. 2 photos.
The Condemnation of Lucullus.
    Bregni, Paolo. 1973. B&W. Rendering & set. **SIO**, 20-23. 5 photos.
    Neher, Caspar. State Opera, Berlin: 1951. B&W. Set. **TDD**, 49.
The Condemned of Altoona.
    Wagner, Robin. Vivian Beaumont Theatre, Lincoln Center, NYC: 1966. B&W. Set. **TDT**, n. 5 (May 1966). 24. 2 photos.
The Consul.
    Armistead, Horace. Ethel Barrymore Theatre, NYC: 1950. B&W. Set. **WTP**, 214, 215. 5 photos.
    Brown, Zack. Eisenhower Theatre, Washington, DC: 1987. B&W. Rendering. **DDT**, 249.
The Contractor.
    Dancy, Virginia & Elmon Webb. Long Wharf Theatre, New Haven, Connecticut: B&W. Set. **TCI**, vol. 7, n. 5 (Oct 1973). 10.
The Contrast.
    _____. C.W. Post College, Long Island, New York: 1970. B&W. Set. **TCI**, vol. 6, n. 5 (Oct 1972). 24.
Conversations With My Father.
    Walton, Tony. Royale Theatre, NYC: 1992. B&W. Set. **DDT**, 14.
The Convoy.
    Borovsky, David. USSR: B&W. Model. **TDT**, vol. XII, n. 3 (Fall 1976). 41.
The Coot.
    Kantor, Tadeusz. Cricot 2, Cracow: 1963. B&W. Set. **AST**, 244.
Coppélia.
    Guthrie, David. Cleveland Ballet, Cleveland: B&W. Set. **SCT**, 122.
    Oháh, Gustave. Royal Opera, Budapest: B&W. Rendering & set. **SCM**, 72, 73.
    Straiges, Tony. American Ballet Theatre, NYC: 1990. B&W. Model. **ASD2**, 140; B&W. Model. **TCI**, vol. 25, n. 3 (Mar 1991). 10.
    Ter-Arutunian, Rouben. New York State Theatre, Lincoln Center, NYC: 1974. B&W. Set. **DPT**, 109.
    Varona, José. Pennsylvania Ballet: B&W. Rendering. **DDT**, 245; B&W. Rendering. **TCI**, vol. 14, n. 5 (Oct 1980). 28.
Copperfield.
    Straiges, Tony. ANTA Theatre, NYC: 1981. B&W. Model. **DDT**, 314; B&W. Model & set. **TCI**, vol. 16, n. 2 (Feb 1982). 16. 4 photos.

Le Coq D' Or.

> Goncharova, Natalia. Opéra de Paris: 1914. B&W. Rendering. **DIT**, plate 70; B&W
> and color. Rendering. **RSD**, illus. 286, 287; B&W. Rendering. **SDC**, plate 95;
> B&W. Rendering. **TCT**, plate 12.
>
> La Ferla, Sandro. Teatro Verdi, Trieste: 1974. Color. Set. **DPT**, between 284 & 285.
>
> Sainthill, Loudon. Royal Opera House, Covent Garden, London: 1954. B&W and
> color. Rendering. **LST**, 28-31. 3 photos.

Coriolanus.

> Alma-Tadema, Laurence. Lyceum Theatre, London. c. 1901 B&W. Set. **SDG**, 136.
>
> Appen, Karl von. Theater am Schiffbauerdamm, Berlin: 1964. B&W. Set. **SDW3**, 61.
> 6 photos.
>
> Aronson, Boris. Shakespeare Memorial Theatre, Stratford-upon-Avon: 1959. B&W
> and color. Rendering, model, & set. **TAB**, 132-134, 305. 5 photos.
>
> Bechtler, Hildegarde. Salzburg Festival: 1993. Color. Set. **TCI**, vol. 27, n. 8 (Oct
> 1993). 11.
>
> Boll, André. Théâtre romain de Fourviere, France: 1953. B&W. Rendering. **SDW2**, 85.
>
> Bury, John. National Theatre (Olivier), London: 1984. Color. Set. **BTD**, 63; Herodes
> Atticus, Athens: 1985. Color. Set. **BTD**, 15.
>
> Neher, Caspar. B&W. Rendering. **CBM**, 46, 47. 4 photos.
>
> Oenslager, Donald. Phoenix Theatre, NYC: 1954. B&W. Rendering. **SDA**, 216; B&W.
> Rendering. **TDO**, 127.
>
> Svoboda, Josef. National Theatre, Prague: 1974. B&W. Set. **TDT**, vol. XII, n. 2 (Sum-
> mer 1976). 24.
>
> Taylor, Robert U. Yale School of Drama, New Haven, Connecticut: 1967. B&W.
> Rendering. **DPT**, 101.
>
> Zuckermandel, Ludwig. B&W. Rendering. **SDC**, plate 110.
>
> _____. Royal Shakespeare Company, Stratford-upon-Avon: B&W. Set. **SIP**,
> 242.

The Coronation.

> Jones, Arne & Pierre Olofsson. Dramatiska Teatern, Stockholm: 1956. B&W. Set.
> **SDW2**, 209.

The Coronation of Poppea.

> Malolepsy, John F. Albuquerque Opera Theatre, New Mexico: 1984. B&W. Rendering.
> **BSE4**, 31.
>
> Maximowna, Ita. San Francisco Opera: 1975. B&W. Set. **PST**, 212.
>
> Ratto, Gianni. La Scala, Milan: 1953. B&W. Rendering. **SDE**, 141.

Corroboree.

> Constable, William. Empire Theatre, Sydney: 1950. B&W. Set. **SDW1**, 40.

Così fan tutte.

> Bardon, Henry & David Walker. Covent Garden, London: 1968. B&W. Set. **CGA**,
> 178.
>
> Bury, John. Glyndebourne Festival Opera, England: 1978. Color. Set. **BTD**, 114;
> B&W. Set. **TCI**, vol. 13, n. 3 (May/Jun 1979). 21.
>
> Craig, Russell. Great Britain: B&W. Model. **TDT**, vol. XX, n. 1 (Spring 1984). 18.
>
> Dahlstrom, Robert A. Seattle Opera: 1986. B&W. Set. **TDT**, vol. XXVII, n. 3 (Sum-
> mer 1991). 5.
>
> Gérard, Rolf. USA: 1952. B&W. Set. **SDA**, 270, 271. 6 photos.
>
> Griffin, Hayden. Metropolitan Opera, NYC: 1982. Color. Set. **BTD**, 107; B&W. Set.
> **TDT**, vol. XIX, n. 1 (Spring 1983). 7.
>
> Isackes, Richard M. Chicago Lyric Opera: 1983. B&W. Rendering. **TDT**, vol. XXVII,
> n. 3 (Summer 1991). 5 of insert.

Kelly, William A. North Carolina School of the Arts, Winston-Salem: Color. Set. **TDT**, vol. XXVI, n. 1 (Spring 1990). 20 of insert.

Lobel, Adrianne. PepsiCo Summerfare, Purchase, New York: 1986. B&W. Set. **ASD2**, 107; B&W. Set. **DDT**, 60; B&W and color. Model & set. **TDT**, vol. XXVII, n. 3 (Summer 1991). 15.

Luzzati, Emanuele. Munich: B&W. Set. **TCI**, vol. 11, n. 2 (Mar/Apr 1977). 19.

Osorovitz, Camillo. Théâtre Gérard Philipe, Saint-Denis, France: 1967. B&W. Rendering. **SDW3**, 176.

Ponnelle, Jean-Pierre. Salzburg Festival: 1969. B&W. Set. **TCI**, vol. 12, n. 3 (Mar/Apr 1978). 19.

Zelinske, Stephen. North Carolina School of the Arts, Winston-Salem: B&W. Set. **TCI**, vol. 12, n. 6 (Oct 1978). 37.

_____. 1989. Color. Set. **TCI**, vol. 27, n. 4 (Apr 1993). 30.

Count Dracula.

Boylen, Daniel P. Temple University, Philadelphia: B&W. Set. **TCI**, vol. 11, n. 5 (Oct 1977). 36, 37.

The Count of Clérambard.

Malclés, Jean Dénis. Comédie des Champs-Élysées, Paris: 1950. B&W. Rendering. **SDW1**, 101.

Perrottet-von Laban, André. Schauspielhaus, Zürich: 1951. B&W. Rendering. **SDW1**, 118.

Countess Dracula!

Thee, Christian. Studio Arena Theatre, Buffalo: 1979. Color. Set. **TCI**, vol. 22, n. 5 (May 1988). 38. 2 photos.

Country Fete.

Hofmann, Hans. Oskar Eberle, Schwyz, Switzerland: 1941. Color. Rendering. **SDW1**, 111.

The Country Girl.

Aronson, Boris. Lyceum Theatre, NYC: 1950. B&W and color. Rendering & set. **TAB**, 100, 101, 301. 5 photos; B&W. Set. **WTP**, 180. 2 photos.

Country People.

_____. Long Wharf Theatre, New Haven, Connecticut: B&W. Set. **TCI**, vol. 7, n. 5 (Oct 1973). 9.

The Country Wife.

Barkla, Jack. The Acting Company, NYC: B&W. Set. **TCI**, vol. 18, n. 4 (Apr 1984). 10; B&W. Set. **TCI**, vol. 16, n. 8 (Oct 1982). 24.

Duckwall, Ralph. California State University, Long Beach: Color. Set. **SST**, plate VI.

Messel, Oliver. Old Vic, London & Henry Miller's Theatre, NYC: 1936. B&W. Set. **MEM**, 92, 93; B&W. Set. **OMB**, 91; B&W. Set. **TPH**, photo 440; B&W. Set. **SOW**, plate 39.

Coyote Ugly.

Rigdon, Kevin. Steppenwolf Theatre, Chicago: 1985. Color. Set. **TCI**, vol. 21, n. 2 (Feb 1987). 31.

Cracovians and Mountaineers.

Daszewski, Wladislaw. Teatr Narodowy, Warsaw: 1950. B&W. Set. **SDW1**, 156.

The Cradle Song.

Calthrop, Gladys E. Civic Repertory Theatre, NYC: 1927. B&W. Set. **MCN**, 81.

Craig's Wife.

Viele, Sheldon K. Morosco Theatre, NYC: 1925. B&W. Set. **MCN**, 71.

Crazy For You.
>   Wagner, Robin. Shubert Theatre, NYC: 1992. Color. Set. **TCI**, vol. 26, n. 4 (Apr 1992). 28, 29. 4 photos.

The Crazy Locomotive.
>   Schmidt, Douglas W. Chelsea Theatre Center, Brooklyn, New York: 1977. B&W. Set. **ASD1**, 146; B&W. Set. **TCI**, vol. 11, n. 5 (Oct 1977). 15. 2 photos.

Crazy Quilt.
>   Mielziner, Jo. USA: 1931. B&W. Rendering. **SCM**, 122. "The Three Cabbies."

The Creation & Other Mysteries.
>   Othuse, James. Omaha Community Playhouse, Nebraska: 1988. Color. Set. **TCI**, vol. 24, n. 3 (Mar 1990). 33.

La Création du Monde.
>   Léger, Fernand. Théâtre des Champs-Elysées, Paris: 1923. B&W. Rendering & set. **AST**, 93 & 95; B&W and color. Rendering & set. **RSD**, illus. 325, 326; B&W. Set. **TCS2**, plate 261.

The Creation of the Sun.
>   Tománek, A. Czechoslovakia: B&W. Model. **TDT**, vol. XVI, n. 1 (Spring 1980). 27.

The Creation of the World and Other Business.
>   Aronson, Boris. Shubert Theatre, NYC: 1972. B&W and color. Rendering, model, & set. **TAB**, 167-169, 308. 10 photos.

The Crescendo.
>   Laurenti, Franco. Teatre Eliseo, Rome: 1960. B&W. Rendering. **SDW2**, 129.

Cri des coeurs.
>   Baty, Gaston. Théâtre Montparnasse, Paris: 1928. B&W. Set. **RSD**, illus. 416.

The Cricket on the Hearth.
>   _____. Moscow Art Theatre First Studio: 1913. B&W. Set. **RST**, 40. 2 photos; B&W. Set. **TPH**, photo 301.

Crime and Punishment.
>   Borovsky, David. Kreeger Theatre, Arena Stage, Washington, DC: 1987. B&W. Set. **TCI**, vol. 21, n. 4 (Apr 1987). 14.
>   Sheriff, Paul. New Theatre, London: 1946. B&W. Rendering. **SDW1**, 185; B&W. Set. **WTP**, 104, 105.
>   Vychodil, Ladislav. Czechoslovakia: 1982. B&W. Model. **TDT**, vol. XXIII, n. 4 (Winter 1988). 49; Stockholm: 1984. B&W. Rendering. **TCI**, vol. 21, n. 8 (Oct 1987). 36.

Crime on Goat Island.
>   Payne, Darwin Reid. B&W. Model, rendering, & set. **TCM**, 92, 93 , 96; B&W. Rendering, model & set. **SIP**, 96-98.

Crimes of the Heart.
>   Beatty, John Lee. Upstage at the Manhattan Theatre Club, NYC: 1980. B&W. Sketch. **TDT**, vol. XVIII, n. 4 (Winter 1982). 6; NYC: 1981. B&W. Set. **TCI**, vol. 16, n. 9 (Nov/Dec 1982). 26; National Company, USA: B&W. Sketch. **DDT**, 301.
>   Gardner, John. ACE-Charlotte Repertory Theatre, North Carolina: 1985. B&W. Set. **BSE4**, 54.

The Criminal at Large.
>   Throckmorton, Cleon. Belasco Theatre, NYC: 1932. B&W. Set. **SCM**, 131.

Crisis in Heaven.
>   Beaton, Cecil. Lyric Theatre, Hammersmith, London: 1944. B&W. Rendering. **CBS**, 33.

The Critic.
>   Sherman, Loren. (project): 1980. B&W. Model. **DDT**, 321.

_____. Old Vic Theatre, London: 1945-46. B&W. Set. **TPH**, photo 446.

_____. National Technical Institute for the Deaf: B&W. Set. **TCI**, vol. 3, n. 1 (Jan/Feb 1969). 11.

The Croatian Faustus.

Turina, Drago. Yugoslavia: Color. Model. **TCI**, vol. 18, n. 1 (Jan 1984). 11; B&W. Model. **TDT**, vol. XX, n. 1 (Spring 1984). 7.

The Crocodile.

Melena, Miroslav. Studio Y, Prague: B&W. Set. **TDT**, vol. XXVII, n. 2 (Spring 1991). 29, 30.

Croquignole.

Raban, Josef. Divadlo D 48, Prague: 1948. B&W. Set. **SDW1**, 51.

Cross Purpose.

Moniz Freire, Napoleão. O Tablado, Rio de Janeiro: 1961. B&W. Set. **SDW2**, 36.

The Crow.

Kanamori, Kaoru. Koseinenkin Hall, Tokyo: 1970. B&W. Set. **SDW4**, illus. 330.

The Crown Bride.

Svoboda, Josef. Prague: 1943. B&W. Rendering. **STS**, 35.

The Crucible.

Aronson, Boris. Martin Beck Theatre, NYC: 1952. B&W and color. Rendering & set. **TAB**, 105, 303. 5 photos.

Barreiro, Manuel. Teatro Mella, Havana: 1968. B&W. Rendering. **SDW3**, 131.

Hines, Thomas G. Barrington High School, Barrington, Illinois: B&W. Set. **SCT**, 4.

Payne, Darwin Reid. B&W. Model. **SIP**, 11.

Porteous, Cameron. Canada: B&W. Model. **TDT**, vol. XVI, n. 1 (Spring 1980). 12.

Rodriguez, John. Northwestern University: B&W. Model. **TCI**, vol. 12, n. 3 (Mar/Apr 1978). 34.

_____. Centenary College, Louisiana: 1961. B&W. Set. **MOR**, 23.

The Crucifer of Blood.

Wulp, John. Helen Hayes Theatre, NYC: 1978. B&W. Model & set. **DDT**, 162, 220. 5 photos; B&W. Set. **TCI**, vol. 13, n. 1 (Jan/Feb 1979). 20-23. 4 photos; B&W. Set. **TCI**, vol. 27, n. 8 (Oct 1993). 35; B&W. Set. **TCI**, vol. 22, n. 5 (May 1988). 42.

The Cry of the Peacock.

Beaton, Cecil. Mansfield Theatre, NYC: 1950. B&W. Set. **CBS**, 44, 45.

The Cry of the People for Meat.

_____. Bread and Puppet Theatre: 1969. B&W and color. Set. **RSD**, illus. 648, 650.

The Cuernicabra Fair.

Anchoriz, Leo. Teatro Goya, Madrid: 1959. B&W. Set. **SDW2**, 75.

Cul de Sac.

Koltai, Ralph. Sadler's Wells Theatre, London: 1965. B&W. Set. **SDR**, 25.

The Cunning Little Vixen.

Jampolis, Neil Peter/Maurice Sendak. New York State Theatre, Lincoln Center, NYC: 1981. B&W. Model. **DDT**, 189. 3 photos.

Robertson, Patrick. Glyndebourne Festival Opera, England: B&W. Set. **TCI**, vol. 13, n. 3 (May/Jun 1979). 20. 2 photos.

Sendak, Maurice/Neil PeterJampolis. New York State Theatre, Lincoln Center, NYC: 1981. B&W. Model. **DDT**, 189. 3 photos.

The Curious Women.

Kiesler, Frederick. NYC: 1940. B&W. Set. **EIF**, photo 21.

The Curse of the Starving Class.

Eigsti, Karl. Arena Stage, Washington, DC: 1979. B&W. Set. **ASD1**, 40.

Martin, Brian. INTAR Hispanic American Theatre, NYC: 1983. B&W. Set. **TCI**, vol. 20, n. 3 (Mar 1986). 10.

Merritt, Michael. Goodman Theatre II, Chicago: 1978. B&W. Set. **ASD2**, 133.

_____. Promenade Theatre, NYC: 1985. Color. Set. **TCI**, vol. 22, n. 2 (Feb 1988). 45.

The Cursed Crown.

Kokoschka, Oskar. Burgtheater, Vienna: 1961. B&W. Rendering. **AST**, 210. 2 photos; B&W. Set. **SDW2**, 158; Color. Rendering. **SDW2**, 159.

Cyclops.

Nomicos, Andréas. Vassilikon Théâtron, Athens: 1959. B&W. Set. **SDW2**, 105.

Cymbeline.

Ciller, Josef. Zagreb: 1986. B&W. **TDT**, vol. XXVIII, n. 2 (Spring 1992). 35.

Falabella, John. Huntington Theatre, Boston: 1991. Color. Set. **TCI**, vol. 26, n. 5 (May 1992). 12.

Hurry, Leslie. Shakespeare Memorial Theatre, Stratford-upon-Avon: 1949. B&W. Set. **SDW1**, 176.

Rutherston, Albert. Great Britain: 1923. B&W. Rendering. **DIT**, plate 54; B&W. Rendering. **SDC**, plate 81; B&W. Rendering. **SOW**, plate 44,.

Tsypin, George. New York Shakespeare Festival, NYC: 1989. B&W. Set. **ASD2**, 164; Color. Set. **TCI**, vol. 25, n. 2 (Feb 1991). 38.

Cyrano de Bergerac.

Ayers, Lemuel. Alvin Theatre, NYC: 1946. B&W. Rendering. **SDT**, 40.

Ball, Delbert & Marvin Carpentier. Theatre de la Jeune Lune, Minneapolis: 1989. B&W. Set. **TCI**, vol. 24, n. 3 (Mar 1990). 20.

Blackman, Robert. A.C.T., San Francisco: B&W. Set. **SST**, 377.

Bragdon, Claude. Hampden Theatre, NYC: 1925. B&W. Drawings. **SDA**, 218, 219. 4 photos; B&W. Set. **TCS2**, plate 136.

Carpentier, Marvin & Delbert Ball. Theatre de la Jeune Lune, Minneapolis: 1989. B&W. Set. **TCI**, vol. 24, n. 3 (Mar 1990). 20.

Donnelly, Mark. Denver Center, Colorado: B&W. Set. **SDT**, 279.

Elder, Eldon. Seattle Repertory Theatre: 1975. B&W. Set. **BSE4**, 74; B&W. Model & rendering. **EED**, (pages not numbered). 4 photos; B&W. Rendering. **TCI**, vol. 9, n. 6 (Nov/Dec 1975). 14.

Hays, David. Vivian Beaumont Theatre, Lincoln Center, NYC: 1967-1968. B&W. Set. **TCI**, vol. 2, n. 6 (Nov/Dec 1968). 31.

Jensen, John. Tyrone Guthrie Theatre, Minneapolis: 1973. B&W. Set. **SDL**, 209.

Kent, Carl. 1946. B&W. Rendering. **SDB**, 110.

Koltai, Ralph. Gershwin Theatre, NYC: 1984. B&W and color. Model & set. **TCI**, vol. 19, n. 1 (Jan 1985). 39, 40.

Palkovic, Tim. State University of New York, Plattsburgh: B&W. Sketch. **TDT**, vol. XX, n. 3 (Fall 1984). 11; B&W. Rendering. **TDT**, vol. XXX, n. 3 (Summer 1994). 45.

Payne, Darwin Reid. B&W. Model. **TCM**, 138-140. 3 photos.

Porteous, Cameron. Shaw Festival Theatre, Niagara-on-the-Lake, Canada: B&W. Set. **TCI**, vol. 18, n. 9 (Nov/Dec 1984). 40.

Svoboda, Josef. National Theatre, Prague: 1974. B&W. Set. **SDW4**, illus. 200; B&W. Set. **STS**, 24; B&W. Set. **TDT**, vol. XII, n. 2 (Summer 1976). 21.

Yeargan, Michael. Theatre Royal, Haymarket, London: 1993. Color. Set. **TCI**, vol. 27, n. 4 (Apr 1993). 12.

_____. Long Wharf Theatre, New Haven, Connecticut: B&W. Set. **TCI**, vol. 15, n. 9 (Nov/Dec 1981). 18. 2 photos.

_____. NYC: 1950. B&W. Set. **WTP**, 110, 111. 3 photos.

_____. Oregon Shakespeare Festival, Ashland: B&W. Set. **TCR**, 72.

Cyrano: The Musical.

Gallis, Paul. Neil Simon Theatre, NYC: 1993. Color. Set. **TCI**, vol. 28, n. 2 (Feb 1994). 42, 43. 4 photos.

-D-

D.E. (Give Us Europe).

Meyerhold, Vsevelod, plan; Ilia Shlepianov, execution. Meyerhold Theatre, Moscow: 1924. B&W. Set. **RST**, 140, 141. 6 photos; B&W. Set. **TBB**, 111; B&W. Set. **TCS2**, plate 184 .

DADADADADADA.

McGreevy, David. University of Kansas, Lawrence: 1983. B&W. Set. **TCI**, vol. 18, n. 7 (Aug/Sep 1984). 16.

The Dairymaids.

McCleery, R.C. & Conrad Tritschler. Apollo Theatre, London: 1906. B&W. Set. **MCD**, plate 57.

Dalibor.

Sladek, Jan. National Theatre, Prague: 1949. B&W. Set. **SDW1**, 52.

Svoboda, Josef. National Theatre, Prague: 1961. B&W. Rendering. **STS**, 45; King's Theatre, Edinburgh: 1964. B&W. Set. **SJS**, 58. 2 photos; National Theatre, Prague: 1964. B&W. Set. **TDT**, n. 7 (Dec 1966). 25.

Vychodil, Ladislav. Czechoslovakia: 1982. B&W. Model. **TDT**, vol. XXIII, n. 4 (Winter 1988). 49.

Dalliance.

Conklin, John. Long Wharf Theatre, New Haven, Connecticut: B&W. Set. **SDL**, 70.

La Dama Duende.

Exter, Alexandra. 1921. B&W. Rendering. **DOT**, 215.

Dame Kobold.

Mahnke, Adolf. Schauspielhaus, Dresden: B&W. Set. **TCS2**, plate 346.

Dames at Sea.

Harvey, Peter. Bouwerie Lane Theatre, NYC: 1968. B&W. Set. **TCI**, vol. 3, n. 5 (Oct 1969). 6-10. 6 photos; Lamb's Theatre, NYC: 1985. B&W. Set. **BSE4**, 26.

Damn Yankees.

Eckart, William & Jean. 46th Street Theatre, NYC: 1955. B&W. Set. **BWM**, 293. 2 photos; B&W. Rendering. **SDW2**, 233; B&W. Set. **TMT**, 189.

Schmidt, Douglas W. Marquis Theatre, NYC: 1994. Color. Set. **TCI**, vol. 28, n. 4 (Apr 1994). 47.

The Damnation of Faust.

Balo, Maurizio. Italy: B&W. Rendering. **TDT**, vol. XX, n. 1 (Spring 1984). 7.

_____. Orpheum Theatre, Boston: 1978. B&W. Set. **TDT**, vol. XIV, n. 3 (Fall 1978). 15.

Dance a Little Closer.

Mitchell, David. NYC: 1983. B&W. Set. **MBM**, 210.

The Dance of Death.

Echave, José. Teatro S.O.D.R.E. Montevideo: 1954. B&W. Rendering. **SDW2**, 241.

Loquasto, Santo. Vivian Beaumont Theatre, Lincoln Center, NYC: 1974. B&W. Set. **TDT**, vol. XVII, n. 3 (Fall 1981). 20.

Palmstierna-Weiss, Gunilla Dramatiska Teatern, Stockholm: 1967. B&W. Set. **SDW3**, 86.

Polidori, Gianni. 1963. B&W. Set. **SIO**, 113.
Vychodil, Ladislav. Malmo, Sweden: 1979. B&W. Rendering. **TDT**, vol. XVI, n. 4
   (Winter 1980). 23.
Dance With Your Gods.
Oenslager, Donald. Mansfield Theatre, NYC: 1934. B&W. Rendering. **TDO**, 53.
Dancin'.
Larkin, Peter. Broadhurst Theatre, NYC: 1978. B&W. Set. **DSL**, figure 2.8(b); B&W.
   Set. **TCI**, vol. 13, n. 1 (Jan/Feb 1979). 32. 2 photos.
Dancing at Lughnasa.
Vanek, Joe. Plymouth Theatre, NYC: 1991. Color. Set. **TCI**, vol. 25, n. 9 (Nov 1991).
   12; Color. Set. **TCI**, vol. 28, n. 1 (Jan 1994). 39; Great Britain: B&W. Model.
   TDT, vol. XXVII, n. 4 (Fall 1991). 36.
Dancing in the Chequered Shade.
Aronson, Boris. McCarter Theatre, Princeton, New Jersey: 1955. B&W. Rendering.
   TAB, 304.
The Dancing Years.
_____. Drury Lane Theatre, London: 1939. B&W. Set. **BMF**, 95.
Dandy Dick.
Blackman, Robert. American Conservatory Theatre, San Francisco: 1971. B&W. Set.
   TCI, vol. 6, n. 5 (Oct 1972). 16, 17.
Daniel Hjort.
Vasara, Eero. Jyväskylän Työväenteatteri, Jyväskylä, Finland: 1950. B&W. Model.
   SDW1, 159.
Danses Concertantes.
Berman, Eugene. New York City Center: 1944. B&W. Rendering. **SDR**, 32.
Dante.
Bel Geddes, Norman. B&W. Model. **SDC**, plate 103. 2 photos.
Szajna, Josef. Teatr Studio, Warsaw: 1972. B&W. Set. **SDW4**, illus. 13, 14; B&W. Set.
   TCI, vol. 15, n. 4 (Apr 1981). 12.
The Danton Case.
Darling, Jonathan. Northwestern University Theatre, Evanston, Illinois: Color. Set.
   TDT, vol. XXVIII, n. 2 (Spring 1992). 5 of insert.
Danton's Death.
Dusek, Jan. Czechoslovakia: B&W. Model. **TDT**, vol. XXVII, n. 4 (Fall 1991). 47.
Grund, Françoise. Marionetteatern-Dramaten, Stockholm: 1971. B&W. Set. **SDW4**,
   illus. 127-129.
Landwehr, Hugh. Center Stage, Baltimore: 1984-1985. Color. Set. **TCI**, vol. 20, n. 2
   (Feb 1986). 16.
Mielziner, Jo. Vivian Beaumont Theatre, Lincoln Center, NYC: 1965. B&W. Render-
   ing. **DPT**, 49; B&W. Rendering. **DTT**, 223. Tribunal scene.
Robertson, Patrick. National Theatre, London: 1971. B&W. Set. **TDT**, vol. XIX, n. 3
   (Fall 1983). 5.
Stern, Ernst. Deutsches Theater, Berlin: 1916. Color. Rendering. **MRH**, facing 216;
   B&W. Rendering. **MRT**, 27.
Strnad, Oskar. People's Theatre, Amsterdam: 1922. B&W. Rendering. **TAT**, plate 150;
   B&W. Rendering. **DIT**, plate 108; Vienna: 1929. B&W. Set. **MRT**, 81.
Danton.
Aronson, Boris. Grosses Schauspielhaus, Berlin: 1920. B&W. Sketch. **PST**, 410;
   B&W. Sketch. **TPH**, photo 337.

Stern, Ernst. Grosses Schauspielhaus, Berlin: 1920. B&W. Set. **MRH**, facing 144;
   B&W. Set. **MRT**, 70; B&W. Rendering. **RSD**, illus. 116; B&W. Set. **TCS2**, plate
   367.
Strnad, Oskar. Deutsches Volkstheater, Vienna: B&W. Rendering. **TCS2**, plate 192.
Daphnis et Chloé.
Chagall, Marc. Opéra de Paris: 1959. B&W. Set. **AST**, 64. 2 photos.
Dark Ages.
Fulton, Larry. Impossible Ragtime Theatre, NYC: 1979. B&W. Set. **TCI**, vol. 14, n. 3
   (May/Jun 1980). 43. 2 photos.
Dark at the Top of the Stairs.
Edwards, Ben, Music Box Theatre, NYC: 1957. B&W. Set. **TCI**, vol. 23, n. 7 (Aug/
   Sep 1989). 50.
Dark of the Moon.
Downing, Desmonde. Independent Theatre, Sydney: 1950. B&W. Rendering. **SDW1**,
   39.
Wagner, Robin. Arena Stage, Washington, DC: 1965. B&W. Sketch. **ASD1**, 159.
The Dark Years.
Ciulei, Liviu. Teatrul National, Bucharest: 1958. B&W. Rendering. **SDW2**, 173.
The Darling of the Gods.
Gros, Ernest. Belasco Theatre, NYC: 1902. B&W. Set. **MCN**, 21.
Daughter of Heaven.
_____. NYC: 1914. B&W. Rendering. **SDB**, 15.
The Daughter of Jorio.
de Chirico, Georgio. Pirandello's Theater, Rome: 1934. B&W. Set. **TPH**, photo 366.
Daughters.
Reaney, Mark. University of Kansas, Lawrence: B&W. Sketches. **TDT**, vol. XXV, n. 2
   (Summer 1989). 24.
David Triomphant.
Léger, Fernand. Opéra de Paris: 1937. B&W. Rendering. **AST**, 96.
David's Crown.
Habima Theater, Moscow: 1929. B&W. Set. **RSD**, illus. 216.
The Dawn.
Dmitriev, Vladimir. R.S.F.S.R. Theatre No. 1, Moscow: 1920. B&W. Set. **MOT**,
   between 144, 145; B&W. Sketch & set. **RSD**, illus. 168, 169; B&W. Model,
   rendering, & set. **RST**, 86, 87. 3 photos; B&W. Set. **TCT**, plates 15, 16.
The Dawns are Quiet Here.
Borovsky, David. Taganka Theatre, Moscow: 1972. B&W. Model. **SDW4**, illus. 288;
   B&W. Sketch, model & set. **TCI**, vol. 12, n. 7 (Nov/Dec 1978). 36, 37. 5 photos.
Day and Night.
Stenberg, Vladimir & Georgiy A. Kamerny Theatre, Moscow: 1926. B&W. Set. **RST**,
   238, 239. 3 photos.
Aronson, Boris. Unser Theatre, Bronx: 1924. B&W. Model & set. **BAT**, 15, 31. 4
   photos; B&W. Set. **TAB**, 33, 293. 4 photos.
A Day in Hollywood/A Night in the Ukraine.
Walton, Tony. John Golden Theatre, NYC: 1980. B&W. Set. **MBM**, 99; B&W. Model
   & set. **TCI**, vol. 14, n. 5 (Oct 1980). 18, 19. 9 photos; Color. Set. **TCI**, vol. 24, n. 8
   (Oct 1990). 53.
A Day in the Life of Joe Egg.
Frazer, Anne. Scott Theatre, Adelaide: 1969. B&W. Model. **SDW3**, 149.

The Day Room.
>   Arcenas, Loy. American Repertory Theatre, Cambridge, Massachusetts: 1986. B&W.
>   Sketch. **ASD2**, 14.

Day Trips.
>   Arcenas, Loy. Hartford Stage, Connecticut: 1990. B&W. Model. **ASD2**, 6; B&W.
>   Model. **DDT**, 34.

The Day's Dividing.
>   Labisse, Félix. Théâtre Marigny, Paris: 1948. B&W. Rendering. **SDW1**, 99.

The Days are Melting.
>   _____. Theatre of Working Youth (TRAM), Leningrad: B&W. Set. **RST**, 242.

The Days of the Commune.
>   Neher, Caspar. Theater am Schiffbauerdamm, Berlin: 1949. B&W. Rendering. **CBM**,
>   64; Municipal Theatre, Chemnitz, Germany: 1956. B&W. Set. **TBB**, 58.

The Days of the Turbins.
>   Ulyanov, Nikolai. Moscow Art Theatre: 1926. B&W. Rendering & set. **RST**, 214-217.
>   7 photos; Moscow Art Theatre: 1934. B&W. Set. **SOW**, plate 71.

Days on a Cloud.
>   Refn, Helge. Det kongelige Teater, Copenhagen: 1946. B&W. Rendering. **SDW1**, 61.

Days Without End.
>   Simonson, Lee. Henry Miller's Theatre, NYC: 1934. B&W. Set. **PLT**, illus. 53.

De temporum fine comoedia.
>   Schneider-Siemssen, Günther. Festspielhaus, Salzburg: 1973. B&W. Set. **OPE**, 54. 5
>   photos.

The Dead City.
>   Jürgens, Helmut. State Opera, Munich: 1955. B&W. Set. **SDW1**, 69.

Dead End.
>   Bel Geddes, Norman. Belasco Theatre, NYC: 1935. B&W. Set. **MCN**, 126; B&W.
>   Set. **SDA**, 103; B&W. Set. **SOW**, plate 80.
>   Gorelik, Mordecai. Belasco Theatre, NYC: 1934. B&W. Set. **NTO**, facing 68.
>   Younovitch, Sophia. Teatr Leninskovo Komsomola, Leningrad: 1959. B&W. Render-
>   ing. **SDW2**, 201.

Dead Souls.
>   Allio, René. Odéon Théâtre, Paris: 1960. B&W. Set. **RSD**, illus. 573; B&W. Set. **SDB**,
>   87; B&W. Set. **SDW2**, 84.
>   _____. Moscow Art Theatre: 1932. B&W. Set. **RST**, 302-304. 5 photos.

Deafman Glance.
>   Wilson, Robert. Stadsschouwburg, Amsterdam: 1971. B&W. Set. **RWT**, 16-19. 4
>   photos; B&W. Set. **TCI**, vol. 19, n. 8 (Oct 1985). 23. 3 photos.

Dear Antoine.
>   Funicello, Ralph. Loeb Drama Center, Harvard University: 1973. B&W. Set. **ASD1**,
>   49.

Dear Charles.
>   Scott, J. Hutchinson. New Theatre, London: 1952. B&W. Rendering. **TOP**, 73.

Death and Resurrection of a Puppet.
>   Fo, Dario. Teatro Circolo, Milan: 1971. B&W. Set. **SDW4**, illus. 307.

Death and the King's Horseman.
>   Gropman, David. Lincoln Center, NYC: 1987. B&W. Set. **ASD2**, 37.

Death and the Maiden.
>   Walton, Tony. Brooks Atkinson Theatre, NYC: 1992. B&W. Set. **DDT**, 331.

Death, Destruction and Detroit.
>   Wilson, Robert. Schaubühne am Halleschen, Berlin: 1979. B&W. Drawing & set.

RWT, 65, 66, 69-73, 151. 8 photos; B&W. Set. **TDT**, vol. XVI, n. 2 (Summer 1980). 11. 2 photos.

Death in a Pear Tree.
Szajna, Josef. Teatr Studio, Warsaw: 1978. B&W. Set. **TCI**, vol. 15, n. 4 (Apr 1981). 15.

Death in Venice.
Graham, Colin. Metropolitan Opera, NYC: 1994. Color. Set. **TCI**, vol. 28, n. 4 (Apr 1994). 6.

Maximowna, Ita. State Opera, Munich: 1975. B&W. Set. **OPE**, 68.

Tsypin, George. (project): 1984. B&W. Model. **DDT**, 43. 2 photos; B&W. Sculpture. **TDT**, vol. XXVII, n. 3 (Summer 1991). 11; Opera Company of Philadelphia: 1986. Color. Model. **ASD2**, between 108 & 109. 2 photos; Color. Model. **TCI**, vol. 25, n. 2 (Feb 1991). 36.

Death of a Salesman.
Edwards, Ben. Broadhurst Theatre, NYC: 1984. B&W. Model. **DDT**, 586.

Eigsti, Karl. Arena Stage, Washington, DC: 1974. B&W. Rendering. **ASD1**, 28.

Lee, Ming Cho. Avon Theatre, Stratford, Ontario, Canada: 1983. B&W. Rendering. **DDT**, 190.

Mielziner, Jo. Morosco Theatre, NYC: 1949. B&W. Rendering of backdrop. **DDT**, 162; Color. Rendering. **DTT**, 146. Opening set; Color. Rendering. **DTT**, 147. Leaf projection; B&W. Rendering. **RSD**, illus. 557; B&W. Rendering. **SDA**, 142. 2 photos; B&W. Rendering. **SDR**, 39; B&W. Rendering. **SDW1**, 200. 2 photos; B&W. Set. **SOW**, plate 109; B&W. Rendering & set. **TAS**, 99; B&W. Rendering. **TPH**, photos 481, 482.

The Death of Agrippina.
Pace. Studio des Champs-Élysées, Paris: 1960. B&W. Model. **SDW2**, 99.

The Death of Ivan the Terrible.
Soumbatashvili, Iossif. Tsentralnyj Teatr Sovietskoj Armii, Moscow: 1966. B&W. Rendering. **RSD**, illus. 503; B&W. Rendering. **SDW3**, 99.

The Death of Klinghoffer.
Tsypin, George. Théâtre de la Monnaie, Brussels: 1991. Color. Model. **TCI**, vol. 25, n. 2 (Feb 1991). 34; B&W and color. Set. **TDT**, vol. XXVII, n. 3 (Summer 1991). front cover & 10; Color. Set. **DDT**, 312d.

The Death of Tarelkin.
Stepanova, Varvara. G.I.T.I.S. Theater, Moscow: 1922. B&W. Set. **MOT**, between 184 & 185; B&W. Model. **RSD**, illus. 177; B&W. Set. **RST**, 126, 127; B&W. Set. **TCT**, plate 20.

The Death of the Kangaroo.
Grooms, Red. American Theatre for Poets, NYC: 1964. B&W. Set. **ASC**, 22.

The Death of Tintagiles.
Ricketts, Charles. St. James Theatre, London: 1912. B&W. Rendering. **TDC**, 45.

Sapunov, Nikolai Nikolaévich. Studio Theater, Moscow: 1905. B&W. Rendering. **RSD**, illus. 25.

The Death of Von Richthofen as Witnessed from the Earth.
Schmidt, Douglas W. Newman Theatre, NYC: 1982. B&W. Set. **ASD1**, 148; B&W. Set. **TCI**, vol. 16, n. 8 (Oct 1982). 8.

The Death of Wallenstein.
Stern, Ernst. Deutsches Theater, Berlin: 1914. Color. Rendering. **MRH**, facing 324.

Deathtrap.
Ritman, William. Music Box Theatre, NYC: 1978. B&W. Set. **TCI**, vol. 12, n. 6 (Oct 1978). 4; B&W. Set. **TCI**, vol. 22, n. 5 (May 1988). 32.

The Debutante Ball.
    McCarry, Charles E. New York Stage and Film: B&W. Set. **TDT**, vol. XXVIII, n. 2 (Spring 1992). 7 of insert.
The Deceiver.
    Marstboom, Antoon. Nationaal Toneel, Antwerp: 1948. B&W. Set. **SDW1**, 47.
Decor and Polovtsian Dances from Prince Igor.
    Roerich, Nicolas. Ballets Russes, Paris Opera: 1909. B&W. Rendering. **RSD**, illus. 45.
Deep Are the Roots.
    Bay, Howard. Fulton Theatre, NYC: 1945. B&W. Set. **SDB**, 42; B&W. Set. **TCI**, vol. 17, n. 2 (Feb 1983). 14.
The Defeat.
    Krohg, Guy. Folketertret, Oslo: 1959. B&W. Set. **SDW2**, 152.
Le Déjeuner de Soliel.
    _____. Comédie-Caumartin, Paris: 1925. B&W. Sketch. **TPH**, photo 358.
A Delicate Balance.
    Donnelly, Mark. Old Globe Theatre, San Diego: B&W. Set. **SDT**, 104.
    Jensen, John. Philadelphia Drama Guild: 1986. B&W. Set. **TCI**, vol. 20, n. 7 (Aug/Sep 1986). 8.
    Ritman, William. Martin Beck Theatre, NYC: 1966. B&W. Set. **TDT**, n. 6 (Oct 1966). 50.
Delightful Gardens of Existence.
    Aston, Tom & James Hayes. Oakland University, Rochester, Michigan: B&W. Set. **TCI**, vol. 4, n. 1 (Jan/Feb 1970). 34.
Demetrius.
    Wecus, Walter von. State Theatre, Bonn: B&W. Set. **TCS2**, plate 116.
Democracy.
    Rotch, Arthur. Perserverance Theatre, Alaska: B&W. Set. **TCI**, vol. 25, n. 9 (Nov 1991). 76. 2 photos.
The Deputy.
    Balthes, Heinz. Kammerspiele, Düsseldorf: 1964. B&W. Rendering. **RSD**, illus. 577.
El Desden, con el Desden.
    Bernedo, Mario. Compania Nacional de Teatro Clasico, Spain: 1992. Color. Set. **TCI**, vol. 26, n. 4 (Apr 1992). 35.
The Desert Song.
    Anania, Michael. New York City Opera: 1987. B&W. Set. **BSE5**, 10; Paper Mill Playhouse, Milburn, New Jersey: 1987. Color. Set. **TCI**, vol. 24, n. 2 (Feb 1990). 67.
    Aronson, Boris. Philharmonic Auditorium, Los Angeles: 1945. B&W. Rendering. **TAB**, 299.
Deserted Field.
    Szajna, Josef. Teatr Ludowy, Nowa Huta, Poland: 1965. B&W. Sketch & set. **SDW3**, 132, 133. 4 photos.
Deshima.
    Ueno, Watoku. La Mama Annex, NYC: 1993. B&W. Set. **TCI**, vol. 27, n. 4 (Apr 1993). 9.
Design for Living.
    Calthrop, Gladys E. Ethel Barrymore Theatre, NYC: 1933. B&W. Set. **MCN**, 110.
    Scheffler, John. Asolo State Theatre, Sarasota, Florida: B&W. Set. **TCI**, vol. 13, n. 5 (Oct 1979). 37.
Desire Under the Elms.
    Gonçalves, Martin. Teatro Ginastico, Rio de Janeiro: 1946. B&W. Set. **SDW1**, 49.

Gorelik, Mordecai. ANTA Theatre (Virginia Theatre), NYC: 1952. B&W. Rendering.
SDA, 228; B&W. Rendering. **SDW1**, 194; B&W. Set. **WTP**, 172, 173. 3 photos.

Heythum, Antonín. National Theatre, Prague: 1925. B&W. Rendering. **RSD**, illus.
281, 282; B&W. Rendering. **TAT**, plate 169; B&W. Rendering. **TDT**, n. 41 (Summer 1975). 22.

Jones, Robert Edmond. Greenwich Village Theatre, NYC: 1924. B&W. Sketch. **DFT**,
plate 26. The Cabot homestead; B&W. Set. **MCN**, 69; B&W. Rendering. **REJ**, 55;
B&W. Sketches & rendering. **TPH**, photos 460, 461.

Lee, Ming Cho. Indiana Repertory Theatre: 1983. B&W. Set. **TCI**, vol. 18, n. 2 (Feb
1984). 19.

Scheffler, John. Asolo State Theatre, Sarasota, Florida: B&W. Set. **TCI**, vol. 13, n. 5
(Oct 1979). 37.

Shelley, John. Gate Theatre, London: 1931. B&W. Set. **SCM**, 30.

Stenberg, Vladimir & Georgiy A. Kamerny Theatre, Moscow: 1926. B&W and color.
Rendering & set. **RST**, 237. 2 photos; B&W. Set. **SCM**, 88.

Vanek, Joe. Greenwich Theatre, London: 1987. Color. Set. **BTD**, 51.

The Desperate Hours.
Bay, Howard. Ethel Barrymore Theatre, NYC: 1955. B&W. Set. **SDA**, 229; B&W. Set.
TCI, vol. 17, n. 2 (Feb 1983). 15.

The Destiny of Me.
Beatty, John Lee. Lucille Lortel Theatre, NYC: 1992. B&W. Set. **TCI**, vol. 27, n. 1
(Jan 1993). 7.

Destry Rides Again.
Smith, Oliver. Imperial Theatre, NYC: 1959. B&W. Set. **WMC**, 195.

Detective Story.
Aronson, Boris. Hudson Theatre, NYC: 1949. B&W and color. Rendering & set. **TAB**,
96.

Deungsinbul (A Life Size Buddha).
Kim, Jakyoung. Silkroad Playhouse, La Mama's Annex Theatre, NYC: 1992. Color.
Set. **TCI**, vol. 27, n. 1 (Jan 1993). 7.

The Devil and Kate.
Jampolis, Neil Peter. Opera Theatre of St. Louis: 1990. B&W and color. Rendering &
set. **TCI**, vol. 24, n. 7 (Aug/Sep 1990). 34.

The Devil and the Good Lord (see *Lucifer and the Lord*).

Devil en 24 Heures.
Clavé, Antoni. Théâtre de l'Empire, Paris: 1953. B&W. Rendering. **SDR**, 33.

The Devil's Advocate.
Mielziner, Jo. Billy Rose Theatre, NYC: 1961. B&W. Rendering. **DTT**, 216. Dr.
Meyer's office.

The Devil's Disciple.
_____. Equity Library Theatre, NYC: B&W. Set. **TCI**, vol. 15, n. 6 (Jun/Jul
1981). 23.
_____. Seattle Opera: Color. Set. **TCI**, vol. 24, n. 8 (Oct 1990). 53.

The Devil's Garden.
Jones, Robert Edmond. NYC: 1915. B&W. Set. **SDC**, plate 48.

The Devil's General.
Neher, Caspar. Schauspielhaus, Zürich: 1946. B&W. Set. **CBM**, 91.

The Devil's Wall.
Svoboda, Josef. National Theatre, Prague: 1974. B&W. Set. **TDT**, vol. XII, n. 2 (Summer 1976). 14.

The Devils.
> Kenny, Sean. Royal Shakespeare Company, Aldwych Theatre, London: 1961. B&W.
>> Rendering. **SDW2**, 218.
> Mickley, William. Brandeis University, Waltham, Massachusetts: 1970. B&W. Set.
>> **SDB**, 46.
> Wexler, Peter. Mark Taper Forum, Los Angeles: B&W. Rendering. **SDT**, 299.

The Devils of Louden.
> Ter-Arutunian, Rouben. Santa Fe Opera: B&W. Set. **TCI**, vol. 4, n. 5 (Oct 1970). 11.

The Devotion of the Cross.
> Floriet, Bernard, Brigitte Tribouilloy, & William Underdown. Maison de la Culture,
>> Grenoble: 1969. B&W. Set. **SDW3**, 65. 2 photos.

DIA LOG/Curious.
> Wilson, Robert. Rotterdam: 1980. B&W. Set. **RWT**, 62, 63.

DIA LOG/Network.
> Wilson, Robert. Boston: 1978. B&W. Set. **RWT**, 61.

Dialogues of the Carmelites.
> Quinn, Jeff. (project): B&W. Rendering. **BSE5**, 19.
> Reppa, David. Metropolitan Opera, NYC: 1977. B&W. Set. **TCI**, vol. 16, n. 9 (Nov/
>> Dec 1982). 28.

Diamond Lil.
> Schmidt, Douglas W. American Conservatory Theatre, San Francisco: 1988. B&W.
>> Model. **DDT**, 170.

Diamond Studs.
> _____. Alaska Repertory Theatre, Anchorage: B&W. Set. **TCI**, vol. 13, n. 2
>> (Mar/Apr 1979). 25.

Diamonds.
> Straiges, Tony. Circle in the Square Theatre, NYC: 1984. Color. Set. **TCI**, vol. 19, n. 2
>> (Feb 1985). 10.

Diana a la Tuda.
> Guglielminetti, Eugenio. 1971. B&W. Set. **SIO**, 84, 85. 4 photos.
> Flores, Leonida. 1953. B&W. Rendering. **SDE**, 86.

Diary of a Scoundrel.
> _____. Dallas Theatre Center: 1988. Color. Set. **TCI**, vol. 23, n. 9 (Nov 1989).
>> 59.

The Diary of Anne Frank.
> Aronson, Boris. Cort Theatre, NYC: 1955. B&W and color. Rendering & set. **TAB**,
>> 122, 123, 125-127, 304. 7 photos; B&W. Drop. **TAB**, 128.
> _____. Milwaukee Repertory Theatre: Color. Set. **TCI**, vol. 24, n. 4 (Apr 1990).
>> 42.

La Diavolessa.
> Luzzati, Emanuele. Venezia Teatro, Venice: 1952. B&W. Rendering. **SDE**, 100. 3
>> photos.

The Dictator.
> Hoffman, Vlastislav. National Theatre, Prague: 1927. B&W. Rendering. **TAT**, plate
>> 188.

Dido and Aeneas.
> Craig, Edward Gordon. 1906. B&W. Rendering. **TNT**, facing 57.
> Oenslager, Donald. Yale School of Drama, New Haven, Connecticut: 1953. B&W.
>> Rendering. **DPT**, 359; B&W and color. Rendering. **FCS**, plate 215, color plate 31;
>> B&W. Rendering. **FCT**, plate 14; B&W and color. Rendering. **SDA**, 267, 291;

Color. Rendering. **SDL**, plates 8-14b; B&W and color. Rendering. **SDO**, 250, plate
31; B&W. Rendering. **TDT**, n. 39 (Dec 1974). 15; B&W. Rendering. **TDO**, 126;
Color. Rendering. **TDO**, facing 16.

Vossen, Frans. Kleine Komedie, Amsterdam: 1969. B&W. Set. **SDW3**, 201.

Vychodil, Ladislav. University of California, Santa Barbara: B&W. Set. **TDT**, n. 38
(Oct 1974). 25.

Le Dieu Blue.

Bakst, Léon. B&W. Rendering. **RSC**, 16.

The Dining Room.

Palkovic, Tim. State University of New York, Plattsburgh: B&W. Sketch. **TDT**, vol.
XX, n. 3 (Fall 1984). 11; B&W. Rendering. **TDT**, vol. XXX, n. 3 (Summer 1994).
45.

Sherman, Loren. Astor Place Theatre, NYC: 1982. B&W. Set. **DDT**, 257.

Dinner at Eight.

Platt, Livingston. Music Box Theatre, NYC: 1933. B&W. Set. **SCM**, 115.

Dinny and the Witches.

Burroughs, Robert C. University of Arizona, Tucson: B&W. Rendering. **SDT**, 295.

Diogenes.

Babic, Ljubo. National Theatre, Zagreb: B&W. Set. **TCS2**, plate 264.

Dionysus in '69.

Rojo, Jerry N. 1969. B&W. Set. **TCI**, vol. 5, n. 4 (Sep 1971). 6, 8, 14, 22.

Dirty Hands.

Cardile, Andrea. Italy: 1963. B&W. Rendering. **RSD**, illus. 501.

The Disguised Prince.

Girault. Comédie de Caen, France: 1970. B&W. Set. **SDW3**, 74.

Tréhard, Jo. Comédie de Caen, France: 1970. B&W. Set. **SDW3**, 74.

Dispatches.

Dudley, William. National Theatre (Cottesloe), England: B&W. Set. **TCI**, vol. 18, n. 1
(Jan 1984). 36.

The Displaced Person.

Lundell, Kurt. American Place Theatre, NYC: 1966. B&W. Set. **TCI**, vol. 6, n. 3
(May/Jun 1972). 21; B&W. Rendering & set. **TCI**, vol. 1, n. 1 (Mar/Apr 1967). 30,
31.

The Dispute.

Peduzzi, Richard. Théâtre National Populaire, Villeurbanne, France: 1973. B&W. Set.
SDW4, illus. 88-93.

Distant Fires.

_____. Circle in the Square Theatre, NYC: 1992. B&W. Set. **TCI**, vol. 26, n. 9
(Nov 1992). 9.

_____. Hartford Stage, Connecticut: B&W. Set. **SDL**, 68.

The Divine Comedy.

Bel Geddes, Norman. (not produced): 1921. B&W. Model. **CSD**, 11; B&W. Model.
DIT, plates 118.1-119.2; B&W. Model. **NTO**, facing 276; B&W. Model. **RSD**,
illus. 440, 442; B&W. Model. **SDA**, 69; B&W. Model. **SIP**, 6; B&W. Model.
SOW, plate 79; B&W. Model. **TCM**, xvii; B&W. Model. **TCS2**, plates 220, 221;
B&W. Rendering. **TDT**, vol. XVI, n. 1 (Spring 1980). 13.

The Diviners.

Beatty, John Lee. Circle Repertory Company, NYC: 1981. B&W. Rendering. **DDT**,
546.

Division Street.
> Funicello, Ralph. Mark Taper Forum, Los Angeles: 1979/1980. B&W. Set. **ASD1**, 46; B&W. Set. **TCI**, vol. 14, n. 4 (Sep 1980). 40; Ambassador Theatre, NYC: 1981. B&W. Model. **ASD1**, 42.
> Goodwin, Richard R. Center Stage, Baltimore: 1981-1982. B&W. Set. **TCI**, vol. 20, n. 2 (Feb 1986). 20.
> _____. Oakland Ensemble Theatre: 1986. B&W. Set. **TDT**, vol. XXIII, n. 1 (Spring 1987). 17.

Il Divorzio.
> Guglielminetti, Eugenio. B&W. Set. **SIO**, 81. 2 photos.

Do I Hear a Waltz?
> Montresor, Beni. 46th Street Theatre, NYC: 1965. B&W. Set. **BWM**, 199.

Do Re Mi.
> Aronson, Boris. St. James Theatre, NYC: 1960. Color. Show curtain. **TAB**, 148, 149. 6 photos; B&W and color. Rendering & set. **TAB**, 149-155, 306. 13 photos; B&W. Collage sketch. **TDT**, vol. XXV, n. 3 (Fall 1989). 12; B&W. Set. **WMC**, 257.

Do You Know the Milky Way?
> Lehto, Leo. Suomen Kansallisteatteri, Helsinki. 1958. B&W. Set. **SDW2**, 204.

The Doctor at the Emperor's Side.
> Zinan, Chen & Liu Yuxi. China: B&W. Model. **TDT** vol. XXXI, n. 2 (Spring 1995). 11.

Dr. Burke's Strange Afternoon.
> Hudak, Stefan. Mala Scéna, Bratislava: 1967. B&W. Rendering. **SDW3**, 161.

Doctor Faustus.
> Hume, Samuel J. Arts and Crafts Theatre, Detroit: 1917. B&W. Set. **TCS2**, plate 63; B&W. Set. **TDT**, vol. XX, n. 2 (Summer 1984). 15.
> Ledesma, A. L. Mexico City: 1966. B&W. Set. **SDB**, 176.
> McNamara, Brooks. Mitchell Hall, University of Delaware: B&W. Set. **TCI**, vol. 2, n. 6 (Nov/Dec 1968). 15, 18. 3 photos.
> Navon, Arieh. Hateatron Haleumi Habimah, Tel-Aviv: 1973. Color. Set. **SDW4**, illus. 70.
> Sinell, Ranier. State Theatre, Darmstadt: 1993. Color. Set. **TCI**, vol. 28, n. 1 (Jan 1994). 11.
> Sironi, Mario. Teatro Comunale, Florence: 1942. B&W. Rendering. **AST**, 192.
> _____. New York City Opera: 1993. Color. Set. **TCI**, vol. 27, n. 4 (Apr 1993). 5.
> _____. England: B&W. Set. **TPH**, photo 280.

Doctor Jazz.
> Du Bois, Raoul Pène. Winter Garden Theatre, NYC: 1975. B&W. Set. **DPT**, 288; B&W. Set. **DSL**, 206.

The Doctor's Dilemma.
> Oenslager, Donald. Shubert Theatre, NYC: 1941. B&W. Rendering. **TDO**, 99, 100.
> _____. Great Britain: B&W. Set. **WTP**, 138, 139. 4 photos.

Dog Beneath the Skin.
> Bay, Howard. (project): 1938. B&W. Sketch. **SDB**, 189; B&W. Rendering. **TCI**, vol. 17, n. 2 (Feb 1983). 10.

Dog Lady.
> Lee, Ming Cho. INTAR Theatre, NYC: 1984. B&W. Set. **ASD1**, 99.

Dog's Eye View.
> Jesurun, John. La Mama ETC, NYC: 1984. B&W and color. Set. **TCI**, vol. 19, n. 7 (Aug/Sep 1985). 47. 2 photos.

The Dog's Will.
    Wallbaum, Walter. Kammerspiele, Berlin: 1968. B&W. Rendering. **SDW3**, 139.
A Doll's House.
    _____. Birmingham Repertory Theatre, England: 1914. B&W. Set. **TCR**, 58.
    _____. Backstage Theatre, National Theatre, Norway: 1994. B&W. Set. **TCI**,
        vol. 28, n. 9 (Nov 1994). 36.
A Doll's Life.
    Firth, Tazeena & Timothy O'Brien. Mark Hellinger Theatre, NYC: 1982. B&W. Set.
        HPA, 137; Color. Set. **MBM**, 84, 85; B&W. Set. **TCI**, vol. 16, n. 9 (Nov/Dec
        1982). 22, 23. 5 photos.
The Dollar Princess.
    Harker, Joseph & Alfred Terraine. Daly's Theatre, London: 1909. B&W. Set. **MCD**,
        plate 82.
$ Value of Man.
    Wilson, Robert. Brooklyn Academy of Music, New York: 1975. B&W. Set. **RWT**, 42,
        43.
Dolores or the Miracle of the Plain Woman.
    Brayer, Yves. Opéra de Lyon: 1960. B&W. Rendering. **SDW2**, 86.
The Dolphins.
    Burman, Sigfrido. Teatro Calderon de la Barca, Barcelona: 1969. B&W. Set. **SDW3**,
        147.
Dominus Marlowe/A Play on Doctor Faustus.
    _____. Provisional Theatre, Los Angeles: B&W. Set. **TCI**, vol. 14, n. 4 (Sep
        1980). 33.
Don Carlos.
    Barth, Ruodi. Deutsche Oper am Rhein, Düsseldorf: 1972. B&W. Set. **OPE**, 150, 154,
        156, 159, 160, 162.
    Bubeník, Kvetoslav. Smetana Theater, Prague: 1960. B&W. Rendering. **SDW2**, 41.
    Forray, Gabor. National Opera, Budapest: B&W. Set. **TDT**, n. 38 (Oct 1974). 15.
    Gérard, Rolf. Metropolitan Opera, NYC: 1950. B&W. Rendering. **CSD**, 39; B&W.
        Rendering. **MOM**, 12.
    Gröning, Karl. Festspiele, Rechlinghausen, Germany: 1951. B&W. Rendering. **SDW1**,
        65.
    Heinrich, Rudolf. Bavarian State Opera, Munich: 1976. B&W. Set. **SCT**, 188; B&W.
        Set. **TCI**, vol. 10, n. 6 (Nov/Dec 1976). 16; B&W. Set. **TDT**, vol. XII, n. 1 (Spring
        1976). 27.
    Hlawa, Stefan. Burgtheater, Vienna: 1955. B&W. Set. **SDW2**, 156.
    Klein, César. State Theatre, Hamburg: 1934. B&W. Rendering. **SDW1**, 70.
    Oenslager, Donald. San Antonio, Texas: 1968. B&W. Rendering. **CSD**, 112; B&W.
        Rendering. **DDT**, 26, 326; B&W. Rendering. **DPT**, 363; B&W. Rendering. **TDO**,
        140.
    Payne, Darwin Reid. B&W. Model. **SIP**, 10.
    Polidori, Gianni. 1969. B&W. Model & set. **SIO**, 119.
    Ponnelle, Jean-Pierre. Teatro alla Scala, Milan: 1968. B&W. Set. **OPE**, 149, 154, 156,
        158, 161, 163.
    Rabinovitch, Isaac. Meyerhold Theatre, Moscow: 1922. B&W. Set. **TCS2**, plate 168.
    Refn, Helge. Royal Opera House, Stockholm. 1950. B&W. Set. **SDR**, 53.
    Rose, Jürgen. Staatsoper, Vienna: 1970. B&W. Set. **OPE**, 149, 155, 157, 159, 160,
        162.
    Schneider-Siemssen, Günther. Grosses Festspielhaus, Salzburg: 1975. B&W and color.
        Rendering & set. **OPE**, 152, 155, 157, 158, 161, 163; B&W. Set. **TCI**, vol. 27, n. 3

(Mar 1993). 29; B&W. Set. **TCI**, vol. 12, n. 6 (Oct 1978). 33; B&W. Set. **TDT**, vol. XII, n. 1 (Spring 1976). 28.

Shchuko, Vladimir. Bolshoi Theatre, Moscow: 1919. B&W. Rendering & set. **RST**, 75.

Sironi, Mario. Teatro Comunale, Florence: 1950. B&W. Rendering. **AST**, 192; B&W. Rendering. **SDE**, 152.

Stern, Ernst. Deutsches Theater, Berlin: 1909. B&W. Rendering. **FCS**, plate 191. Act II, sc. 1; B&W. Rendering. MRH, facing 326. 2 photos; B&W. Rendering. **SDO**, 217; Color. Rendering. **TCS2**, color plate 2; B&W. Set. **TCS2**, plates 22, 23.

Svoboda, Josef. Slovak National Theatre, Bratislava: 1956. B&W. Rendering. **SJS**, 149; Municipal Theatre, Cologne: 1974. B&W. Set. **SST**, 45. 2 photos; B&W. Set. **TDT**, vol. XII, n. 2 (Summer 1976). 26.

Visconti, Luchino. Covent Garden, London: 1958. B&W. Set. **CGA**, 160, 161.

_____. State Opera, Dresden: B&W. Set. **SCM**, 60.

Don Ciccio.

Angelini, Sandro. Teatro delle Novità, Bergamo: 1953. B&W. Rendering. **SDE**, 27.

Don Friolera's Horns.

Muñoz, Gori. Teatro Mayo, Buenos Aires: 1940. B&W. Rendering. **SDW1**, 37.

Don Gil with the Green Trousers.

Peetermans, Mimi. Nationaal Toneel, Antwerp: 1962. B&W. Set. **SDW2**, 31.

Don Giovanni.

Berman, Eugene. Metropolitan Opera, NYC: 1957. Color. Rendering. **MOM**, 13. 2 photos.

Bury, John. Glyndebourne Festival Opera, England: B&W. Set. **TCI**, vol. 13, n. 3 (May/Jun 1979). 21.

Conklin, John. Opera Theatre of St. Louis: 1983. B&W. Model. **TDT**, vol. XXVII, n. 3 (Summer 1991). 13.

Dahlstrom, Robert A. University of Washington, Seattle: 1978. B&W. Rendering. **TDT**, vol. XXVII, n. 3 (Summer 1991). 7.

Elson, Charles. Metropolitan Opera, NYC: 1955. B&W. Rendering. **SDW2**, 234.

Koltai, Ralph. Scottish Opera Company: 1964. Color. Model. **DMS**, plates 42, 43.

Moore, Henry. Festival of Two Worlds, Spoleto: 1967. B&W. Set. **AST**, 221. 2 photos.

Oberle, Karl Friedrich. Houston Grand Opera: 1986. B&W. Set. **TDT**, vol. XXVII, n. 3 (Summer 1991). 7.

Pascoe, John. Michigan Opera Theatre, Masonic Temple Theatre, Detroit: 1990. B&W. Rendering. **TCI**, vol. 24, n. 5 (May 1990). 15.

Payne, Darwin Reid. B&W. Computer aided perspective. **TDT**, vol. XXVIII, n. 3 (Summer 1992). 32.

Peduzzi, Richard. Salzburg Festival: 1994. B&W. Set. **TCI**, vol. 29, n. 1 (Jan 1995). 5.

Piper, John. King's Theatre, Edinburgh: 1951. B&W. Set. **SDE**, 132; B&W. Rendering. **SDR**, 44; Color. Rendering. **SDW1**, 171; B&W. Sketches. **TOP**, 207-209. 4 photos.

Ponnelle, Jean-Pierre. State Opera, Cologne: 1971. B&W. Set. **OPE**, 75, 82, 86, 89, 90; B&W. Set. **SST**, 379; Salzburg Festival: 1977. B&W. Set. **TCI**, vol. 12, n. 3 (Mar/Apr 1978). 19.

Roller, Alfred. Vienna: 1905. B&W. Rendering. **TCS2**, plates 55, 56.

Romero, Miguel. Santa Fe Opera: B&W and color. Rendering & set. **TDT**, vol. XXX, n. 3 (Summer 1994). 10.

Rose, Jürgen. Berlin: 1973. B&W. Set. **OPE**, 82, 85, 87, 88, 91.

Schmückle, Hans-Ulrich. Stadttheater, Augsburg: 1972. B&W. **OPE**, 77, 82, 85, 86, 88, 90.

Schneider-Siemssen, Günther. Grosses Festpielhaus, Salzburg: 1968. B&W and color.
Set. **OPE**, 75, 83, 85, 86, 89, 91; B&W. Set. **TCI**, vol. 12, n. 6 (Oct 1978). 33;
B&W. Set. **TDT**, n. 27 (Dec 1971). 14.
Slevogt, Max. Sächsische Staatsoper, Dresden: 1924. B&W. Rendering. **AST**, 34.
Smith, Oliver. Boston Opera: 1969. B&W. Rendering. **TCI**, vol. 16, n. 4 (Apr 1982).
63.
Svoboda, Josef. National Theatre, Prague: 1962. B&W. Set. **STS**, 76; B&W. Set. **TDT**,
n. 20 (Feb 1970). 18, 19. 3 photos; Goetheplatz Theatre, Bremen: 1966. B&W.
Model. **SJS**, 47; B&W. Model. **STS**, 77; Tyl Theatre, Prague: 1969. B&W. Set.
SJS, 140-142. 3 photos.
Tsypin, George. Pepsico Summerfare, Purchase, New York: 1987. B&W. Sketch & set.
ASD2, 166, 167. 3 photos, Color. Set. **TCI**, vol. 25, n. 2 (Feb 1991). 37; B&W.
Model, rendering, & set. **TDT**, vol. XXVII, n. 3 (Summer 1991). 15. 3 photos.
Zeffirelli, Franco. State Opera, Vienna: 1972. B&W and color. Set. **OPE**, 76, 83, 84,
87, 88, 90; B&W. Set. **SDW4**, illus. 113, 114.
_____ . Brno: B&W. Rendering. **TPH**, photo 388.
Don Juan.
Bérard, Christian. Theatre de l'Athénée, Paris: 1947. B&W. Set. **RSD**, illus. 410, 411;
B&W. Set. **SDW1**, 83. 2 photos.
Boutté, Jean-Luc. France: B&W. Set. **DSL**, figure 2.8(d).
Cassandre, A.M. Aix en Provence: 1949. B&W. Rendering. **SDE**, 60, 61. 3 photos.
Demangeat, Camille. Festival of Avignon: 1953. B&W. Set. **RSD**, illus. 531.
Exter, Alexandra. Paris: 1926. B&W. Rendering. **RAG**, 27.
Foreman, Richard. Tyrone Guthrie Theatre, Minneapolis: 1981. Color. Set. **TCI**, vol.
18, n. 7 (Aug/Sep 1984). 41.
Golovin, Alexander. Alexandrinsky Theatre, Moscow: 1910. B&W. Set. **MOT**, be-
tween 64 & 65.
Holzmeister, Clemens. Salzburg: 1950. B&W. Set. **SDE**, 89.
Ivanov, Kalina. B&W. Rendering. **BSE3**, 90.
Kautskj, Robert. La Scala, Milan: 1951. B&W. Rendering. **SDE**, 110. 2 photos.
Lee, Ming Cho. Arena Stage, Washington, DC: 1979. B&W. Set. **ASD1**, 90, 91; Color.
Set. **TCI**, vol. 20, n. 4 (Apr 1986). 21.
Marenic, Vladimir. Narodno Pozoriste, Beograd: 1966. B&W. Model. **SDW3**, 69.
Nesjar, Carl & Inger Sitter, National Theater, Oslo: 1960. B&W. Set. **SDW2**, 153.
Reinking, Wilhelm. La Scala, Milan: 1950. B&W. Rendering. **SDE**, 143, 144.
Roszkowska, Teresa. Teatr Polski, Warsaw: 1951. B&W. Rendering. **SDW2**, 168.
Sievert, Ludwig. Schauspielhaus, Frankfurt: B&W. Rendering. **TCS2**, plate 205.
Simonson, Lee. Garrick Theatre, NYC: 1921. B&W. Set. **PLT**, illus. 19.
Svoboda, Josef. National Theatre, Prague: 1972. B&W. Set. **TDT**, vol. XII, n. 2 (Sum-
mer 1976). 14.
Tröster, Frantisek. Tyl Theatre, Prague: 1957. B&W. Rendering. **SDW2**, 47.
Van Nerom, Jacques. Théâtre Royal des Galeries, Brussels: 1967. B&W. Set. **SDW3**,
70.
Vassiliou, Spyros. Basilikon Théatron, Athens: 1952. B&W. Rendering. **SDW1**, 110.
Wendel, Heinrich. Wuppertaler Bühnen, Wuppertal: 1959. B&W. Set. **SDW2**, 74.
Zídek, Ivo. Prague: 1989. B&W. Rendering. **TDT**, vol. XXVIII, n. 2 (Spring 1992).
37.
_____ . Carnegie-Mellon University, Pittsburgh: 1965. B&W. Set. **TCI**, vol. 7, n.
5 (Oct 1973). 25.
Don Juan and Death.
Exter, Alexandra. (project): B&W. Rendering. **RAG**, 29; B&W. Rendering. **RSC**, 35.

Don Juan Comes Back From the Wars.
> Lynch, Thomas. Oregon Contemporary Theatre, Portland: 1983. B&W. Rendering. **DDT**, 171.

Don Juan in Hell.
> Exter, Alexandra. (project): B&W. Rendering. **RAG**, 30; B&W. Rendering. **RSC**, 39.

Don Juan or The Love of Geometry.
> Echarri, Isabel. Théâtre Gérard Philipe, Saint-Denis, France: 1969. B&W. Set. **SDW3**, 203.
> Parker, W. Oren. Carnegie Institute of Technology, Pittsburgh: B&W. Set. **TDT**, n. 3 (Dec 1965). 2.

Don Juan Tenorio.
> Caballero, José. Teatro Oficial Español, Madrid: 1956. B&W. Set. **SDW2**, 76.
> Dali, Salvador. Teatro Maria Guerrero, Madrid: 1950. B&W. Set. **AST**, 198. 5 photos; B&W. Renderings & set. **SDW2**, 78. 4 photos; Color. Rendering. **SDW2**, 79.
> Lara, Carlos. Teatro Oficial Español, Madrid: 1956. B&W. Set. **SDW2**, 81.
> Mamposo, Manuel. Teatro Oficial Español, Madrid: 1956. B&W. Set. **SDW2**, 81.
> Palencia, Benjamín. Teatro Oficial Español, Madrid: 1956. B&W. Set. **SDW2**, 81.

Don Juan und Faust.
> _____. National Theatre, Weimar: B&W. Set. **TCS2**, plate 154.

Don Pasquale.
> Bauer-Ecsy, Leni. Württembergische Staatstheater, Grosses Haus, Stuttgart: 1972. B&W. Rendering & set. **OPE**, 137, 142, 145, 146.
> Heeley, Desmond. Metropolitan Opera, NYC: 1978. Color. Rendering. **TCI**, vol. 22, n. 8 (Oct 1988). 60.
> Pudlich, Robert. State Opera, Berlin: 1954. B&W. Rendering. **SDW2**, 68.
> Ratto, Gianni. La Scala, Milan: 1949. B&W. Rendering. **SDE**, 139.
> Schultz, Werner. Deutsche Staatsoper, Berlin: 1974. B&W. Set. **OPE**, 140, 142, 144, 146.
> Stros, Ladislav. Kleines Festspielhaus, Salzburg: 1971. B&W. Rendering & set. **OPE**, 136, 143, 147.
> Suchánek, Vladimír. Slovenské Národné Divadlo, Bratislava: 1973. B&W. Set. **OPE**, 138, 143, 145, 147.
> Van Norden, Hans. Stadsschouwburg, Amsterdam: 1954. B&W. Set. **SDW1**, 138.
> Vanek, Joe. English National Opera, London: Color. Set. **TCI**, vol. 28, n. 1 (Jan 1994). 41.
> Yodice, Robert. Juilliard School, Lincoln Center, NYC: B&W. Set. **TCI**, vol. 10, n. 3 (May/Jun 1976). 10. 2 photos.
> Zeffirelli, Franco. 1958-1959. B&W. Set. **SIO**, 138.

Don Quichotte.
> Conklin, John. Netherlands Opera, Amsterdam: 1981. B&W. Set. **ASD1**, 20.
> Burra, Edward. Royal Opera House, Covent Garden, London: 1950. B&W. Rendering. **SDW1**, 173.
> de Chirico, Georgio. Teatro Comunale, Florence: 1952. B&W. Rendering. **SDE**, 63, 64; B&W. Rendering. **SDW1**, 126.
> Dudley, William. National Theatre (Olivier), London: 1982. B&W. Set. **TDT**, vol. XIX, n. 1 (Spring 1983). 12.
> Urban, Joseph. Metropolitan Opera, NYC: B&W. Rendering. **DIT**, plate 120.
> Varona, José. Teatro Municipal, Rio de Janeiro: 1982. B&W. Rendering. **DDT**, 337.
> _____. American Ballet Theatre, NYC: 1978. B&W. Set. **TDT**, vol. XVII, n. 3 (Fall 1981). 20.

Don Rodrigo.

    Lee, Ming Cho. New York City Opera, Lincoln Center: 1966. B&W. Set. **CSD**, 42; B&W. Model. **DPT**, 245; B&W. Set. **TCI**, vol. 7, n. 1 (Jan/Feb 1973). 19.

Don't Be In Too Late.

    Kokkos, Yannis. Théâtre de la Ville, Paris: 1970. B&W. Set. **SDW3**, 149.

Don't Walk on the Clouds.

    Alley Friends, Architects. St. Clement's Church, NYC: 1971. B&W. Model. **ASC**, 35.

Doña Rosita.

    Ström, Carl-Johan. State Theatre, Göteborg, Sweden: 1951. B&W. Set. **SDW1**, 168.

Donna Giovanni.

    Parra, Carmen. Pepsico Summerfare, Purchase, New York: 1987. B&W. Set. **TCI**, vol. 21, n. 8 (Oct 1987). 20.

La Donna Sullo Scudo.

    Exter, Alexandra. Teatro Tatiana Pavlowa, Rome: 1927. B&W. Rendering. **FCS**, plate 181. Act I; B&W. Rendering. **FCT**, plate 12; B&W. Rendering. **RSC**, 30; B&W. Rendering. **SDO**, 206, 207.

Donnerstag aus Licht.

    Björnson, Maria. Royal Opera House, Covent Garden, London: 1985. B&W. Set. **BTD**, 110.

The Doom of Frankenstein.

    Wonsek, Paul. Studio Arena Theatre, Buffalo: 1984. B&W. Set. **TCI**, vol. 22, n. 5 (May 1988). 44.

The Doorway.

    Hume, Samuel J. Arts and Crafts Theatre, Detroit: B&W. Set. **TCS2**, plate 64.

The Dossier.

    Kosinski, Jan. Dramatyczny Theatre, Warsaw: 1960. B&W. Set. **RSD**, illus. 502.

Dostoevsky House.

    Barkhin, Sergei. USSR: B&W. Model. **TDT**, vol. XIX, n. 1 (Spring 1983). 21. (project).

Double Gothic.

    Kirby, Michael. Envelope at the Performing Garage, NYC: 1978. B&W. Set. **TDT**, vol. XV, n. 4 (Winter 1979). 21.

The Double Inconstancy.

    Ganeau, François. Comédie Française, Paris: 1950. B&W. Set. **SDW1**, 97.

    Peetermans, Mimi. Koninklijke Nederlandse Schouwburg, Antwerp: 1969. B&W. Set. **SDW3**, 74.

The Dove of Arden.

    Sharir, David. Teatron Machol Shel Margalit Oved, Isreal: 1971. B&W. Set. **SDW4**, illus. 346.

Down Side.

    _____. Long Wharf Theatre, New Haven, Connecticut: B&W. Set. **SDL**, 79.

Dracula.

    Gorey, Edward. Nantucket, Massachusetts: 1973. B&W. Show curtain. **DDT**, 438; Martin Beck Theatre, NYC: 1978. B&W. Set & show curtain. **DDT**, 222, 223, 420. 4 photos; B&W. Set. **DSL**, figures 2.8(c), 16.4; B&W. Set. **TCI**, vol. 13, n. 1 (Jan/Feb 1979). 32. 4 photos; B&W. Set & show curtain. **TCI**, vol. 22, n. 5 (May 1988). 39.

    Jackson, Bruce, Jr. Tacoma Actors Guild, Tacoma, Washington: 1985. B&W. Set. **BSE4**, 28.

    Scheffler, John. Brooklyn College, New York: 1985. B&W. Show curtain. **DDT**, 394.

The Dragon's Revenge.
_____. Sun Sing Playhouse, NYC: 1950. B&W. Set. **WTP**, 86, 87.
The Dragon.
Raffaëlli, Michel. Maison de la Culture de Grenoble: 1968. B&W. Set. **SDW3**, 105.
Sagert, Horst. Deutsches Theater, Berlin: 1965. Color. Rendering. **RSD**, illus. 587;
    B&W. Rendering & set. **SDW3**, 106, 107. 7 photos.
Drahomíra.
Svoboda, Josef. National Theatre, Prague: 1960. B&W. Set. **SJS**, 64; B&W. Set. **STS**,
    60.
The Drama of Life.
Egorov, V.E. Moscow Art Theatre: 1907. B&W. Model. **RSD**, illus. 30.
Dream of Peter Mann.
Negri, Richard. Lyceum Theatre, Edinburgh: 1960. B&W. Renderings. **SDW2**, 223.
A Dream of Reason.
Svoboda, Josef. Moscow Art Theatre: 1973. B&W. Set. **TDT**, vol. XII, n. 2 (Summer
    1976). 15.
The Dream on Monkey Mountain.
Burbridge, Edward. Mark Taper Forum, Los Angeles: 1970. B&W. Set. **SDL**, 7; B&W.
    Set. **SDW3**, 151; B&W. Set. **TCI**, vol. 8, n. 1 (Jan/Feb 1974). 17.
A Dream Play.
Ahlbom, Martin. State Theatre, Malmö, Sweden: 1947. B&W. Rendering. **SDW1**, 160.
Bignens, Max. State Theatre, Basel: 1957. B&W. Rendering. **SDW2**, 109.
Maronek, James E. Goodman Theatre, Chicago: 1967. B&W. Sketches. **TCI**, vol. 1, n.
    2 (May/Jun 1967). 34, 36-38. Multiple images.
Meyer, Hans. State Theatre, Bern: 1960. B&W. Set. **SDW2**, 110.
Monloup, Hubert. Comédie Française, Paris: 1970. B&W. Set. **SDW3**, 86.
Stegars, Rolf. Suomen Kansallisteatteri, Helsinki. 1959. B&W. Set. **SDW2**, 206.
Ström, Carl-Johan. State Theatre, Göteborg, Sweden: 1947. B&W. Set. **SDW1**, 168.
Svoboda, Josef. State University of New York, Albany: 1980. B&W. Set. **STS**, 68, 69;
    B&W. Set. **TDT**, vol. XVI, n. 4 (Winter 1980). 23.
_____. Sweden: B&W. Set. **TCR**, 73.
A Dreamer for the People.
Burgos, Emilio. Teatro Oficial Español, Madrid: 1958. B&W. Rendering. **SDW2**, 75.
Dreamgirls.
Wagner, Robin. Imperial Theatre, NYC: 1981. B&W. Set. **ASD1**, 152; B&W. Model.
    DDT, 343; B&W. Set. **SCT**, 246; B&W. Set. **TCI**, vol. 16, n. 5 (May 1982). 12,
    13. 5 photos.
Dreamland Burns.
Buchmuller, Eva. Squat Theatre, NYC: 1986. Color. Set. **TCI**, vol. 20, n. 7 (Aug/Sep
    1986). 10.
Dreams in an Empty City.
Livingstone, Alistair. Australia: B&W. Model. **TDT**, vol. XXVII, n. 4 (Fall 1991). 20.
Dress Rehearsal.
Navitskas, Felix. Kaunas Dramas Teatri, Belarus: 1958. B&W. Rendering. **SDW2**,
    189.
Dressed Like an Egg.
Akalaitis, Joanne. 1978. B&W. Set. **TCI**, vol. 13, n. 1 (Jan/Feb 1979). 33.
Morton, Ree. Public Theatre, NYC: 1977. B&W. Set. **ASC**, 30.
The Dresser.
Feiner, Harry. Missouri Repertory Theatre, Kansas City: 1983. B&W. Rendering.
    BSE3, 22.

Dreyfus in Rehearsal.
   Aronson, Boris. Ethel Barrymore Theatre, NYC: 1974. B&W. **TAB**, 309.
Drink.
   Lemeunier. Théâtre de la Porte Saint-Martin, Paris: 1900. B&W. Set. **RSD**, illus. 15.
Drinking Tea.
   Payot, Marc-Tom. Toneelstudio '50, Gent, Belgium: 1958. B&W. Sketch. **SDW2**, 30.
Drums and Trumpets.
   Appen, Karl von. Theater am Schiffbauerdamm, Berlin: 1955. B&W and color. Rendering & set. **RSD**, illus. 566, 567, 569.
Drums in the Night.
   Neher, Caspar. (unproduced): 1922. B&W. Rendering. **CBM**, 42.
   Reigbert, Otto. Kammerspiele, Munich: 1922. B&W. Set. **CBM**, 42; B&W. Rendering & set. **RSD**, illus. 124-127; B&W. Set. **TBB**, 23.
   Sievert, Ludwig. Schauspielhaus, Frankfurt: 1923. B&W. Rendering. **RSD**, illus. 119.
The Drunken Ship.
   Grosz, George & Edward Suhr. Volksbühne, Berlin: 1926. B&W. Rendering. **AST**, 176; B&W. Set. **RSD**, illus. 242; B&W. Set. **TPH**, photo 375.
DuBarry Was a Lady.
   Du Bois, Raoul Pène. 46th Street Theatre, NYC: 1939. B&W. Set. **BWM**, 210; B&W. Set. **MCN**, 148; B&W. Set. **RBS**, 188, 190.
The Duchess of Gerolstein.
   Stevens, John Wright. San Francisco Opera: B&W. Rendering. **SDT**, 293.
The Duchess of Malfi.
   Beaton, Cecil. (not produced): 1924. B&W. Rendering. **CBS**, 19.
   Furse, Roger. Haymarket Theatre, London: 1945. B&W. Rendering. **TPH**, photo 436; B&W. Set. **WTP**, 80, 81. 3 photos.
Duck Hunting.
   Dusek, Jan. Czechoslovakia: B&W. Rendering. **TDT**, vol. XXVI, n. 4 (Fall 1990). 26. 3 photos.
   Eigsti, Karl. Arena Stage, Washington, DC: 1978. B&W. Rendering. **ASD1**, 33.
Duck Song.
   Griffin, Hayden. Royal Shakespeare Company, Aldwych Theatre, London: 1974. B&W. Set. **TCI**, vol. 19, n. 9 (Nov 1985). 25.
The Duenna.
   Lanc, Émile. Théâtre Royal du Parc, Brussels: 1951. B&W. Set & ground plan. **SDW1**, 45. 3 photos.
   Sheringham, George. Great Britain: 1924. B&W. Model. **DIT**, plate 16; B&W. Model. **TPH**, photo 430.
   Vanek, Joe. Wexford Opera: B&W. Set. **TCI**, vol. 28, n. 1 (Jan 1994). 40.
Duet for One.
   Beatty, John Lee. Royale Theatre, NYC: 1981. B&W. Rendering. **DDT**, 382; B&W. Set. **DSL**, figure 2.7(a).
Duke Bluebeard's Castle.
   Forray, Gabor. National Opera, Budapest: B&W. Set. **TDT**, n. 38 (Oct 1974). 10.
Dutch Landscape.
   Landesman, Heidi. Mark Taper Forum, Los Angeles: 1988. B&W. Model. **ASD2**, 73.
The Dybbuk.
   Altman, Nathan. Habima Theater, Moscow: 1922. B&W. Set. **RSD**, illus. 217; B&W. Set. **SCM**, 92; B&W. Set. **TPH**, photo 413.
   Baty, Gaston. Studio des Champs-Elysees, Paris: 1928. B&W. Set. **RSD**, illus. 415.

Bernstein, Aline. Neighborhood Playhouse, NYC: 1925. B&W. Set. **MCN**, 72; B&W.
    Set. **SDC**, plate 62; B&W. Set. **SOW**, plate 75.
Conklin, John. Hartford Stage, Connecticut: 1995. Color. Set. **TCI**, vol. 29, n. 6 (Jun/
    Jul 1995). 7.
Leve, Samuel. NYC: 1982. B&W. Rendering. **SDD**, between 210 & 211. Act I, sc. 1.
Weiner, Wolle. Työväen Teatteri, Tampere, Finland: 1955. B&W. Rendering. **SDW2**,
    207.
_____. NYC: 1952. B&W. Set. **WTP**, 106, 107.
Dynamo.
Simonson, Lee. Martin Beck Theatre, NYC: 1929. B&W. Set. **CSD**, 12; B&W. Set.
    MCN, 94, 95; B&W. Set. **PLT**, illus. 52; B&W. Set. **RSD**, illus. 436, 437; B&W.
    Set. **SCM**, 110, 111; B&W. Model. **SDT**, 36; B&W. Set. **TDT**, n. 8 (Feb 1967). 35;
    B&W. Set. **TSS**, 521.

-E-

Each Man Helps His Country.
Nyvlt, Vladimir. Divadlo D 34, Prague: 1958. B&W. Rendering. **SDW2**, 43.
Early Girl.
McLane, Derek. Fringe Festival, Los Angeles: 1987. Color. Set. **TCI**, vol. 21, n. 10
    (Dec 1987). 10.
The Earth in Turmoil.
Popova, Lyubov. Meyerhold Theatre, Moscow: 1923. B&W. Set. **MOT**, between 184
    & 185; B&W and color. Rendering & set. **RST**, 138, 139. 3 photos.
The Earth is Round.
Masson, André. Sarah Bernhardt Theatre, Paris: 1946. B&W. Set. **SDW1**, 101.
Earth.
Menessier. Théâtre Antoine, Paris: 1902. B&W. Set. **RSD**, illus. 14.
The Easiest Way.
Gros, Ernest. Stuyvesant Theatre, NYC: 1909. B&W. Set. MCN, 33; B&W. Set. **SDA**,
    23.
The Eccentric.
_____. Second Moscow Art Theatre: 1929. B&W. Set. **RST**, 234.
L'Echange.
Hoffman, Vlastislav. National Theatre, Prague: B&W. Set. **TCS2**, plate 272.
Sliwinski, Stanislas. Teatr Maly, Warsaw: 1925. B&W. Set. **TCS2**, plate 238.
Echizen Bamboo Doll.
Asakura, Setsu. Kokuritsu Gekijo, Tokyo: 1973. B&W. Set. **SDW4**, illus. 282-285.
Echo.
Shestakov, Victor. Moscow Theatre of the Revolution: 1924. B&W. Set. **RST**, 134.
Echo and Narcissus (ballet-pantomime).
Appia, Adolphe. Jacques Delcroze Institute, Hellerau: 1919. B&W. Rendering. **RSD**,
    illus. 56; B&W. Rendering. **SDC**, plate 112; B&W. Rendering. **WLA**, 109.
Edison.
Wilson, Robert. Théâtre National Populaire, Lyon: 1979. B&W. Set. **RWT**, 74-76, 78,
    79. 5 photos.
The Education of H*Y*M*A*N K*A*P*L*A*N.
Eckart, William & Jean. Alvin Theatre, NYC: 1968. Color. Rendering. **CSD**, 123;
    Color. Rendering. **DDT**, 312c.
Edward II.
Allio, René. Théâtre de la Cité, Lyon: 1962. B&W. Set. **SDW2**, 84.

Feuerstein, Bedrich. National Theatre, Prague: 1922. B&W. Rendering. **RSD**, illus. 272, 273; B&W. Set. **TCS2**, plates 202, 203; B&W. Set. **TDT**, n. 41 (Summer 1975). 20.

Neher, Caspar. Kammerspiele, Munich: 1924. B&W. Rendering & set. **TBB**, 25, 95, 144.

Eel Beach.

Lanc, Émile. Rideau de Bruxelles: 1959. B&W. Rendering. **SDW2**, 29.

The Effect of Gamma Rays on Man-in-the-Moon Marigolds.

Payne, Darwin Reid. B&W. Rendering & model. **TCM**, xviii, xx, xxii. 4 photos.

Svoboda, Josef. National Theatre, Prague: 1972. B&W. Set. **TDT**, vol. XII, n. 2 (Summer 1976). 26.

The Egg.

Carlstedt, Birger. Svenska Teatern, Helsinki: 1958. B&W. Set. **SDW2**, 203.

Egmont.

Oenslager, Donald. (project): 1948. B&W. Rendering. **STN**, 189-197. 5 photos; B&W. Rendering. **TDO**, 142-145. 4 photos.

Egor Bulychov and Others.

Dmitriev, Vladimir. Vakhtangov Theatre, Moscow: 1932. B&W. Set. **RST**, 300, 301. 3 photos.

80 Days.

Schmidt, Douglas W. La Jolla Playhouse, California: 1988. B&W. Set. **TCI**, vol. 22, n. 9 (Nov 1988). 112.

Ein Fragment.

Cate, Donald. Julian Theatre, San Francisco: B&W. Set. **TCI**, vol. 14, n. 4 (Sep 1980). 24. 2 photos.

Einstein.

Reinhardt, Andreas. Deutsches Staatsoper, Berlin: 1974. B&W. Set. **SDW4**, illus. 225-227.

Einstein on the Beach.

Gianni, Christina A. & Robert Wilson. Metropolitan Opera, NYC: 1976. B&W. Drawings & set. **RWT**, 46-52, 139-148. 7 photos of set plus multiple drawings; B&W and color. Set. **TCI**, vol. 19, n. 8 (Oct 1985). 26, 27; B&W. Set. **TCI**, vol. 11, n. 2 (Mar/Apr 1977). 8, 9. 4 photos; B&W. Set. **TDT**, vol. XIV, n. 1 (Spring 1978). 16, 17, 19-21, 23, 24. 7 photos.

Eisdom.

Teschner, Richard. Austria: 1926. B&W. Rendering. **SCM**, 69.

The Elder Statesman.

Scott, J. Hutchinson. Cambridge Theatre, London: 1958. B&W. Set. **SDW2**, 227.

Electra.

Bechtler, Hildegard. Royal Shakespeare Company (The Pit), London: 1989. B&W. Set. **BTD**, 74.

Bubeník, Kvetoslav. National Theatre, Prague: 1956. B&W. Set. **SDR**, 58; B&W. Set. **SDR**, 83.

Buchholz, Gerhard T. Wiesbaden: 1925. B&W. Set. **TCS2**, plate 215.

Bury, John. Los Angeles Music Center Opera: 1991. Color. Set. **TCI**, vol. 26, n. 1 (Jan 1992). 46.

Craig, Edward Gordon. (unproduced) Theatersammlung, Vienna: 1905. B&W. Rendering. **EGC**, plates 10-11a; B&W. Rendering. **OAT**, xiv; B&W and color. Rendering. **RSD**, illus. 79, 84; B&W. Rendering. **TNT**, facing 35; B&W. Sketch. **TPH**, photo 321.

Gariano, Eliane. Festival d'Automne, Sainte Chapelle, France: 1973. B&W. Set. **SDW4**, illus. 11.

Georgiadis, Nicholas. Oxford Playhouse, England: 1956. Color. Rendering. **DMS**, plate 35.

Heinrich, Rudolf. Bavarian State Theatre, Munich: B&W. Set. **TCI**, vol. 10, n. 6 (Nov/ Dec 1976). 15.

Hepworth, Barbara. Old Vic Theatre, London: 1950. B&W. Set. **AST**, 220.

Hill, Hainer. Deutsches Staatsoper, Berlin: 1957. B&W. Set. **SDW2**, 54.

Jürgens, Helmut. USA: 1963. B&W. Rendering. **FCS**, plate 195; State Opera, Munich: 1963. B&W. Rendering. **SDO**, 223.

Karavan, Dani. Teatron Ha Cameri, Tel Aviv: 1964. B&W. Model. **RSD**, illus. 474.

Kokkos, Yannis. Théâtre des Quartiers d'Ivry-Théâtre des Amandiers, Nanterre, France: 1971. B&W. Sketch & set. **SDW4**, illus. 8-10; Théâtre National de Chaillot, Paris: 1985. B&W. Model. **TCI**, vol. 21, n. 8 (Oct 1987). 33; B&W. Set. **TDT**, vol. XXIII, n. 4 (Winter 1988). 22; Color. Set. **TDT**, vol. XXIII, n. 3 (Fall 1987). front cover (mislabelled as *Hernani*).

Lee, Ming Cho. Delacorte Theatre, NYC: 1964. B&W. Model. **ASD1**, 97; B&W. Model. **DDT**, 197; B&W. Model. **RSD**, illus. 542; B&W. Sketch & set. **SDW3**, 28; B&W. Model. **TDT**, n. 24 (Feb 1971). 4; B&W. Model. **TDT**, n. 1 (May 1965). back cover.

Mäkinen, Veikko. Tampereen Teatteri, Tampere, Finland: 1962. B&W. Set. **SDW2**, 205.

Monin, Guilliaume. Théâtre de l'Athénée, Paris: 1937. B&W. Set. **SDW1**, 102.

Svoboda, Josef. Rome (not performed): 1965. B&W. Sketches & model. **SJS**, 13, 54. 5 photos.

Urban, Joseph. Metropolitan Opera, NYC: 1931. B&W. Model. **SCM**, 100.

Wotruba, Fritz. Burgtheater, Vienna: 1963. B&W. Sketches & model. **AST**, 229. 3 photos.

_____. USA: 1946. B&W. Set. **WTP**, 33, 34.

_____. Centenary College, Louisiana: 1964. B&W and color. Set. **MOR**, 54, 55.

Electra in the Circus.

Paes Leme, Bellá. Movimento Brasileiro de Arte, Rio de Janeiro: 1956. B&W. Model. **SDW2**,36.

The Electrification of the Soviet Union.

Tsypin, George. Glyndebourne Festival Opera, England: 1987. B&W. Set. **DDT**, 168; B&W. Set. **TDT**, vol. XXVII, n. 3 (Summer 1991). 13. 3 photos.

Electronics.

Hays, David. New York City Ballet, Lincoln Center: 1961. B&W. Set. **SDW2**, 235.

The Elephant Man.

Jenkins, David. Booth Theatre, NYC: 1979. B&W. Model. **DDT**, 430; B&W. Set. **TCI**, vol. 14, n. 1 (Jan/Feb 1980). 26.

Nakamori, Kaoru. Japan: B&W. Model. **TDT**, vol. XX, n. 1 (Spring 1984). 12.

Elephant Memories.

_____. La Mama ETC, NYC: 1990. Color. Set. **TCI**, vol. 25, n. 1 (Jan 1991). 14.

Elephant Steps.

_____. Hunter College, NYC: B&W. Set. **TCI**, vol. 5, n. 3 (May/Jun 1971). 22.

Eleven Days of the Cruiser Potemkin.

Ciller, Josef. Provázek Theatre, Brno: 1972. B&W. Rendering. **TDT**, vol. XXVIII, n. 2 (Spring 1992). 34.

The Eleventh Commandment.
Svoboda, Josef. State Film Theatre, Prague: 1950. B&W. Set. **SJS**, 52.
Elisabeth.
Malureanu, F. Rumania: B&W. Set. **TDT**, vol. XII, n. 3 (Fall 1976). 39.
Schavernoch, Hans. Theater an der Wien, Vienna: 1992. Color. Set. **TCI**, vol. 27, n. 2 (Feb 1993). 42, 43. 4 photos.
L'Elisir D'Amore.
Don, Robin. Opera Northern Ireland: 1982. B&W. Set. **BTD**, 123.
Howland, Gerald. Städtische Bühnen Dortmund: 1983. B&W. Rendering. **BTD**, 116.
Marchi, Mario Vellani . La Scala, Milan: 1963-1964. B&W. Rendering. **SIO**, 155.
Montresor, Beni. Covent Garden, London: 1976. B&W. Set. **CGA**, 192.
O'Hearn, Robert. Metropolitan Opera, NYC: 1960. B&W. Rendering. **DPT**, 34. Act I, sc. 2; B&W. Rendering. **MOM**, 15; B&W. Rendering. **SDA**, 264.
Zeffirelli, Franco. 1954-1955. B&W. Rendering & set. **SIO**, 134, 135. 3 photos.
Elizabeth I.
Ciulei, Liviu. The Acting Company tour: B&W. Set. **TCI**, vol. 15, n. 5 (May 1981). 22.
Elizabeth of England.
Hoffman, Vlastislav. National Theatre, Prague: 1931. B&W. Rendering. **TDT**, n. 41 (Summer 1975). 18.
Elizabeth the Queen.
Simonson, Lee. Guild Theatre, NYC: 1930. B&W. Set. **PLT**, illus. 47.
Elmer Gantry.
Landesman, Heidi. La Jolla Playhouse, California: 1991. Color. Set. **TCI**, vol. 26, n. 1 (Jan 1992). 11.
The Embezzlers.
Rabinovitch, Isaac. Moscow Art Theatre: 1928. B&W and color. Rendering & set. **RST**, 254, 255. 3 photos.
The Emigrant from Briskane.
Kapezinskas, Augis. USSR: B&W. Rendering. **TDT**, vol. XX, n. 1 (Spring 1984). 16.
Emmeti.
Polidori, Gianni. Teatro Stabile, Genoa: 1966. B&W. Set. **SDW3**, 144.
Empedokles.
Recalcati, Antonio. Schaubühne am Halleschen, Berlin: 1976. B&W. Set. **TCI**, vol. 11, n. 2 (Mar/Apr 1977). 27.
Empedokles.
Svoboda, Josef. Smetana Theater, Prague: 1943. B&W. Rendering. **SJS**, 148; B&W. Rendering. **STS**, 35; B&W. Rendering. **TDT**, vol. XXVIII, n. 5 (Fall 1992). 10.
The Emperor Jones.
Damiani, Luciano. Bologna: 1950. B&W. Rendering & set. **SDE**, 76.
DeCamp, June. Color. Rendering. **SDL**, plates 8-13b.
Fuerst, Walter René. Odéon Théâtre, Paris: 1923. B&W. Model. **TCS2**, plate 219.
Kiesler, Frederick. Berlin: 1923. B&W. Sketch. **EIF**, photo 2.
Mielziner, Jo. 1933. B&W. Rendering. **DTT**, 78. (Jone's throne room); **DTT**, 79. (Snake eyes); **DTT**, 80. (Jungle terror); B&W. Rendering. **DTT**, 81. (Voodoo dance); B&W. Rendering. **MOM**, 8.
Oenslager, Donald. Yale School of Drama, New Haven, Connecticut: 1931. B&W. Set. **DOT**, 224; B&W. Rendering. **RSD**, illus. 444, 445; B&W. Rendering. **SCM**, 128; B&W. Set. **SFT**, 121; B&W. Rendering. **STN**, 257-263. 4 photos; B&W. Set. **TCI**, vol. 4, n. 4 (Sep 1970). 22; B&W. Rendering. **TDO**, 44, 45.
Throckmorton, Cleon. Provincetown Playhouse, NYC: 1920. B&W. Set. **MCN**, 50,

51; B&W. Rendering. **SDA**, 106. 2 photos; B&W. Set. **SOW**, plate 77; NYC: 1933.
B&W. Model. **TAT**, plate 621.

Vos, Marik. Dramatiska Teatern, Stockholm: 1958. B&W. Set. **SDW2**, 212.

Zhenguang, Wang. Jiangsu Art Theatre, Nanjing, China: 1988. B&W and color. Set.
TDT, vol. XXV, n. 1 (Spring 1989). 9-12, 18. 4 photos.

The Empire Builders.
Atlakson, Phil. State University of New York, Binghampton: B&W. Rendering. **TCI**,
vol. 19, n. 4 (Apr 1985). 115.

Empörung des Lucius.
Pirchan, Emil. State Theatre, Berlin: 1923. B&W. Rendering. **TCS2**, plate 124.

The Enchanted.
Caille, Pierre. Rideau de Bruxelles: 1946. B&W. Set. **SDW1**, 43.

The End of the Beginning.
Elder, Eldon. Syracuse Stage, New York: 1977-1978. B&W. Model. **EED**, (pages not
numbered).

End of the World.
Dunham, Clarke. Music Box Theatre, NYC: 1984. B&W. Set. **TCI**, vol. 18, n. 8 (Oct
1984). 19; B&W. Set. **TCI**, vol. 19, n. 8 (Oct 1985). 19.

Gould, Richard. Cleveland Playhouse: 1985. B&W. Set. **TCI**, vol. 19, n. 8 (Oct 1985).
19.

Endangered Species.
Israel, Robert. Music-Theatre Group/Brooklyn Academy of Music: 1990. B&W. Set.
ASD2, 59.

Endecott and the Red Cross.
Wulp, John. American Place Theatre, NYC: 1968. B&W. Set. **TCI**, vol. 13, n. 1 (Jan/
Feb 1979). 25.

Endgame.
Heiskanen, Pekka. Suomen Kansallisteatteri, Helsinki. 1957. B&W. Set. **SDW2**, 203.

Jacobs, Sally. Manhattan Theatre Club, NYC: B&W. Set. **TCI**, vol. 19, n. 5 (May
1985). 21.

Lee, Eugene. Manhattan Project: 1972. B&W. Set. **TDT**, vol. XVIII, n. 2 (Summer
1982). 9.

Robitschek, Roy. Neptune Theatre, Canada: B&W. Set. **TCI**, vol. 18, n. 9 (Nov/Dec
1984). 41.

Rojo, Jerry N. New York University: 1973. B&W. Set. **CSD**, 22; B&W. Rendering &
set. **TSE**, 18, 167.

Stein, Douglas O. American Repertory Theatre, Cambridge, Massachusetts: B&W. Set.
TCI, vol. 19, n. 5 (May 1985). 21; B&W. Set. **TDP**, 114.

_____. Germany: B&W. Set. **TCR**, 103.

Enemies.
Schmidt, Douglas W. Vivian Beaumont Theatre, Lincoln Center, NYC: 1971. B&W.
Set. **ASD1**, 145.

An Enemy of the People.
Hay, Richard L. Oregon Shakespeare Festival, Ashland: 1985. B&W. Set. **BSE5**, 11;
Color. Set. **SCT**, between 152 & 153. Act III, sc. 3.

L'Enfant et les Sortilèges.
Hockney, David. Metropolitan Opera, NYC: 1981. Color. Rendering & set. **HPS**, 150-
155, 169, 170, 172, 174, 175, 177. 22 photos.

Engaged.
Owen, Paul. Actors Theatre of Louisville: 1988. Color. Set. **TCI**, vol. 23, n. 3 (Mar
1989). 39.

The English Cat.
Hoffer, Hans. Alte Oper, Frankfurt: 1986. Color. Model, rendering & set. **TCI**, vol. 22, n. 3 (Mar 1988). 64, 65, 67. 14 photos.
Rubin, Steve. Santa Fe Opera: 1985. Color. Set. **TCI**, vol. 19, n. 10 (Dec 1985). 14.
L'Enlevement du Serail.
Dobujinsky, Rostislav. Chauve-Souris, Moscow: 1926. B&W. Rendering. **TCS2**, plate 268.
Enough Stupidity in Every Wise Man.
_____. Proletkult Theatre, Moscow: B&W. Set. **TCS2**, plate 182.
Enrico IV.
Gischia, Léon. Théâtre de l'Atelier, Paris: 1950. B&W. Rendering. **SDW1**, 98.
Taylor, Robert U. USA: B&W. Rendering. **TDT**, vol. XVI, n. 1 (Spring 1980). 13.
The Entertainer.
Lee, Ming Cho. Tyrone Guthrie Theatre, Minneapolis: 1983. Color. Set. **ASD1**, front cover; Color. Set. **TCI**, vol. 18, n. 2 (Feb 1984). 14.
Svoboda, Josef. National Theatre, Prague: 1957. B&W. Rendering & set. **SJS**, 122. 6 photos; B&W. Rendering. **STS**, 65.
Tagg, Alan. Royal Court Theatre, London: 1957. B&W. Rendering. **SDW2**, 227.
Die Entführung Aus Dem Serail (The Elopement from the Harem).
Messel, Oliver. Glyndebourne Festival Opera, England: 1956. Color. Model. **MEM**, 118.
Entreacto Barroco.
Arrocha, Eduardo. Teatro García Lorca, Havana: 1963. B&W. Rendering. **SDW2**, 48.
The Ephemeral is Eternal.
Mondrian, Piet. 1926. B&W. Model. **AST**, 148. 4 photos; B&W. Model. **RSD**, illus. 333-335.
Equus.
_____. Theatre Aquarius, Hamilton, Ontario: B&W. Set. **TCI**, vol. 18, n. 2 (Feb 1984). 30.
L'Erba della Stella dell'Alba.
Padovani, Gianfranco. 1971. B&W. Rendering. **SIO**, 101.
Erdgeist.
Kleines Theater, Berlin: 1902. B&W. Set. **SDB**, 16.
Ergo.
Lee, Ming Cho. Anspacher Theatre, Public Theatre, NYC: 1968. B&W. Rendering. **FCS**, plate 217; B&W. Rendering. **SDO**, 253.
Erik XIV
Mörner, Stellan. Dramatiska Teatern, Stockholm: 1950. B&W. Set. **DSL**, 4, 5; Color. Rendering. **SDW1**, 161; Color. Rendering. **SDW2**, 221.
Nivinsky, Ignati. Moscow: 1921. Color. Rendering. **RST**, 76, 77.
Ernani.
Aronson, Boris. San Francisco Opera: 1968. B&W. Set. **PST**, 333.
Eros from the Other World.
Belojanski, Stacha. Narodno Pozoriste, Beograd: 1949. B&W. **SDW1**, 133.
Erwartung.
Levine, Michael. Brooklyn Academy of Music, New York: 1993. B&W. Set. **TCI**, vol. 27, n. 4 (Apr 1993). 10.
Schneider-Siemssen, Günther. Royal Opera House, Covent Garden, London: 1957. B&W. Rendering. **OPE**, 53.
_____. Covent Garden, London: 1962. B&W. Set. **CGA**, 155.

Esclarmonde.
>   Montresor, Beni. San Francisco Opera: B&W. Rendering. **TCI**, vol. 16, n. 5 (May
>   1982). 16. 2 photos.

Les Esclaves.
>   Hoffman, Vlastislav. National Theatre, Prague: B&W. Set. **TCS2**, plate 241.

Escurial.
>   Burchette, Ginger Mae. B&W. Rendering. **BSE2**, 41.
>   Johnson, Gilbert V. B&W. Rendering. **BSE2**, 42.

L'Estasi.
>   de Chirico, Georgio. La Scala, Milan: 1968. B&W. Rendering & set. **SIO**, 146.

Esther.
>   _____. New York City Opera: Color. Set. **TCI**, vol. 28, n. 2 (Feb 1994). 38.

The Eternal City.
>   _____. Victoria Theatre, NYC: 1902. B&W. Set. **MCN**, 20.

The Eternal Fight.
>   Johansen, Svend. Det ny Teater, Copenhagen: 1950. B&W. Rendering. **SDW1**, 56.

Eternal Husband.
>   Greco, Ricardo. Club de Teatro de Lima: 1957. B&W. Set. **SDW2**, 164.

The Eternal Road.
>   Bel Geddes, Norman. Manhattan Opera House, NYC: 1937. B&W. Set. **RSD**, illus.
>   439; B&W. Set. **TPH**, photo 466.

Ethan Frome.
>   Gianfrancesco, Edward. 1978. Color. Set. **TCI**, vol. 20, n. 4 (Apr 1986). 36.
>   Mielziner, Jo. National Theatre, NYC: 1936. B&W. Rendering. **DTT**, 91; B&W. Set.
>   **MCN**, 129.

L'Etoile.
>   Steinberg, Paul. Opera Zuid: 1993. Color. Set. **TCI**, vol. 29, n. 4 (Apr 1995). 30.

Ettore Fieramosca.
>   Luzzati, Emanuele. 1972. B&W. Set. **SIO**, 95.

Eubie!
>   Eigsti, Karl. Ambassador Theatre, NYC: 1978. B&W. Rendering. **DDT**, 317.
>   _____. American Theatre Productions tour: B&W. Set. **TCI**, vol. 15, n. 5 (May
>   1981). 17.

Eugene Onegin.
>   Butlin, Roger. Scottish Opera, Edinburgh: 1979. B&W. Set. **TCI**, vol. 15, n. 5 (May
>   1981). 11, 14, 15. 3 photos.
>   Jampolis, Neil Peter. Eric Harvie Theatre, Banff, Alberta, Canada: 1986. B&W and
>   color. Set. **DDT**, 152a, 497.
>   Svoboda, Josef. Municipal Theatre, Frankfurt am Main: 1971. B&W. Set. **TDT**, vol.
>   XII, n. 2 (Summer 1976). 12.
>   Yeargan, Michael. Welsh National Opera: 1980. B&W. Set. **ASD2**, 190, 191. 5 photos;
>   B&W. Set. **TCI**, vol. 16, n. 5 (May 1982). 22. 2 photos.

Eugene the Unlucky.
>   Dmitriev, Vladimir. Petrograd Academic Theatre: 1923. B&W. Sketch. **RST**, 132.

The Eumenides.
>   Ricketts, Charles. 1922. B&W. Rendering. **SDT**, 33.
>   Riddell, Richard. Stanford University, California: 1976. B&W. Set. **TCI**, vol. 11, n. 3
>   (May/Jun 1977). 24.

Europa.
>   Martin, Karlheinz. Grosses Schauspielhaus, Berlin: B&W. Set. **TCS2**, plate 375.

Europeras 1 and 2.

_____. Pepsico Summerfare, Purchase, New York: 1988. B&W. Set. **TCI**, vol. 22, n. 7 (Aug/Sep 1988). 27.

Eurydice.

Chiari, Mario. La Pergola, Florence: 1947. B&W. Set. **SDW1**, 120.

Deering, Willem. Koninklijken Schouwburg, The Hague: 1948. B&W. Rendering. **SDW1**, 136.

Everyman.

Godefroid, Charlie. Théâtre National, Brussels: 1949. B&W. Set. **SDW1**, 44.

_____. B&W. Set. **WTP**, 56.

Everyone Goes Toward the Castle.

Humm, Ambrosius. Theater am Neumarkt, Zürich. 1972. B&W. Set. **SDW4**, illus. 203.

Evgraf.

Akimov, Nikolai. Second Moscow Art Theatre: 1926. B&W. Rendering. **RST**, 228, 229. 3 photos.

Evita.

Firth, Tazeena & Timothy O'Brien. Prince Edward Theatre, London: 1978. Color. Set. **ALW**, 89, 94; B&W and color. Set. **BTD**, 152, 153; B&W. Set. **TCI**, vol. 12, n. 6 (Oct 1978). 6; Broadway Theatre, NYC: 1979. Color. Set. **ALW**, 93, 94, 95. 5 photos; B&W. Set. **HPA**, 160, 161, 164, 168. 4 photos; B&W. Set. **HPR**, 273, 277; B&W and color. Set. **MBM**, 57, 59, 60, 61, 82. 3 photos; B&W. Set. **TCI**, vol. 13, n. 6 (Nov/Dec 1979). 14-19. 8 photos; Color. Set. **TCI**, vol. 18, n. 8 (Oct 1984). 15; B&W. Set. **TDT**, vol. XIX, n. 3 (Fall 1983). 16; B&W. Set. **TMT**, 229; (tour): B&W. Set. **TCI**, vol. 19, n. 5 (May 1985). 20.

The Exception and the Rule.

Montgomery, Richard. Little Theatre, Kingston, Jamaica: 1970. B&W. Set. **SDW3**, 111. 2 photos; B&W. Set. **SDW4**, illus. 239.

Piplits, Erwin. Gladsaxe Teater, Köbenhavn: 1970. B&W. Rendering. **SDW3**, 111. 2 photos.

Execution of Justice.

Landwehr, Hugh. Center Stage, Baltimore: 1984. B&W. Set. **TCI**, vol. 20, n. 2 (Feb 1986). 20.

Lee, Ming Cho. Arena Stage, Washington, DC: 1986. B&W. Set. **TCI**, vol. 20, n. 2 (Feb 1986). 12.

The Executioner of Peru.

Sima, Joseph. Art and Action, Paris: 1927. Color. Rendering. **RSD**, illus. 390.

Exit the Actor.

Szajna, Josef. Teatr 38, Crakow: 1960. B&W. Rendering. **SDW2**, 170.

Exit the King.

Bliese, Thomas H. University of Iowa, Iowa City: 1971. B&W. Set. **TCI**, vol. 6, n. 6 (Nov/Dec 1972). 12, 13. 3 photos.

Expropriete Propriety.

Iliprandi, Gian Carlo. 1953. B&W. Rendering. **SDE**, 92.

Extremities.

Kellogg, Marjorie Bradley. Cheryl Crawford Theatre, NYC: 1982. B&W and color. Model. **DDT**, 379, 440a.

Eyes on the Harem.

_____. INTAR Hispanic American Theatre, NYC: B&W. Set. **TCI**, vol. 13, n. 4 (Sep 1979). 52. 2 photos.

-F-

La Fable du Fils Changé.
   Iliprandi, Gian Carlo. 1952. B&W. Rendering. **SDE**, 90.
Fables for Adults.
   Navon, Arieh. Teatron Ironi Haifa, Israel: 1965. B&W. Model. **SDW3**, 164.
Fabriola.
   O'Connor, Charles. Ensemble Studio Theatre, Los Angeles: B&W. Rendering. **SDT**,
      298.
The Fabulous Invalid.
   Oenslager, Donald. Broadhurst Theatre, NYC: 1938. B&W and color. Rendering &
      set. **SDA**, 110-113, 288. 7 photos; B&W. Rendering. **SDB**, 34, 35; B&W and color.
      Rendering. **TDO**, 84-86, facing 152. 3 photos.
Face the Music.
   Johnson, Albert R. New Amsterdam Theatre, NYC: 1932. B&W. Set. **RBS**, 61; B&W.
      Set. SCM, 126, 127; B&W. Set. **WMC**, 75.
Les Facheux.
   Braque, Georges. Ballets Russes, Monte Carlo: 1924. B&W. Rendering of curtain.
      AST, 86, 88; Color. Rendering. **RSD**, illus. 310. Ballet-Russes.
Factory Work.
   Colin, Paul. Théâtre de l'Exposition de 1937, Paris: 1937. B&W. Rendering. **SDW1**,
      93.
Facundo in the Citadel.
   Benavente, Saulo. Teatro Nacional de Comedia, Buenos Aires: 1959. B&W. Set.
      SDW2, 25.
The Failures.
   Simonson, Lee. Theatre Guild, NYC: 1923. B&W. Set. **PLT**, illus. 20; B&W. Set.
      SDC, plate 115. 2 photos; B&W. Set. **TSS**, 515, 516.
The Fairground Booth.
   Sapunov, Nikolai Nikolaévich. Vera Komissarzhevskaya's Theatre, Petersburg: 1914.
      B&W. Rendering. **MOT**, between 96 & 97.
Fairy Lady.
   Hlawa, Stefan. Burgtheater, Vienna: 1955. B&W. Rendering. **SDW2**, 156.
The Fairy Queen.
   _____. Covent Garden, London: B&W. Set. **CGA**, 129.
The Faithful.
   Simonson, Lee. Theatre Guild, NYC: 1919. B&W. Set. **PLT**, illus. 6-9, 60; B&W. Set.
      SDC, plate 84. 2 photos; B&W. Set. **TAS**, 118, 119. 4 photos; B&W. Set. **TCS2**,
      plate 108; B&W. Set. **TSS**, 514.
The Faithful Shepherdess.
   Wilkinson, Norman. Great Britain: Color. Rendering. **DIT**, plate 18.
Falkensteyn.
   Hoffman, Vlastislav. National Theatre, Prague: B&W. Set. **TCS2**, plate 98.
Fall River Legend.
   Smith, Oliver. Metropolitan Opera, NYC: 1949. B&W. Rendering. **DOT**, 243; B&W.
      Rendering. **SDA**, 276; B&W. Rendering. **SDW1**, 205.
Fallen Angels.
   Ryan, Thomas M. Pegasus Players, Chicago: 1985. B&W. Rendering. **BSE4**, 95.
False Confidences.
   Brianchon, Maurice. Théâtre Marigny, Paris: 1946. B&W. Set. **SDW1**, 88.

Falsettoland.

_____. John Golden Theatre, NYC: Color. Set. **MBM**, 165.

_____. Washington, DC: Color. Set. **TCI**, vol. 25, n. 2 (Feb 1991). 48.

Falstaff.

Nagy, Elemer. Hartt College of Music: B&W. Set. **SFT**, 123.

Ponnelle, Jean-Pierre. Glyndebourne Festival Opera, England: 1976. B&W. Set. **TCI**, vol. 13, n. 3 (May/Jun 1979). 18; B&W. Set. **TCI**, vol. 10, n. 6 (Nov/Dec 1976). 4.

Schneider-Siemssen, Günther. Salzburg Festival: 1981. B&W. Set. **TCI**, vol. 27, n. 3 (Mar 1993). 28.

Zeffirelli, Franco. Metropolitan Opera, NYC: 1964. B&W and color. Rendering & set. **MOM**, 69-79. 11 photos.

Familiar Faces, Mixed Feelings.

Herrmann, Karl-Ernst. Wurttembergische Staatstheater, Stuttgart: 1976. B&W. Set. **TCI**, vol. 11, n. 2 (Mar/Apr 1977). 26.

The Family.

Aronson, Boris. Windsor Theatre, NYC: 1943. B&W. Set. **TAB**, 298.

Feiner, Harry. University of Missouri, Kansas City: 1982. B&W. Rendering. **BSE3**, 20.

Family Album.

Eichbauer, Helio. Teatro Ateneo, Caracas: 1968. B&W. Set. **SDW3**, 118. 2 photos.

A Family and a Fortune.

Beaton, Cecil. Yvonne Arnaud Theatre, Guildford: 1966. B&W. Set. **CBS**, 61.

Elder, Eldon. Seattle Repertory Theatre: 1974. B&W. Model & set. **DDT**, 214. 6 photos; B&W. Model. **EED**, (pages not numbered).

The Family of the Antiquary.

Ratto, Gianni. Piccolo Teatro, Genoa: 1953. Color. Rendering. **SDW1**, 123.

Famira Kifared.

Exter, Alexandra. Kamerny Theatre, Moscow: 1916. B&W. Set. **RST**, 30; B&W. Set. **TCT**, plates 24, 25.

The Fan.

Campo San Zaccaria, Italy: 1936. B&W. Set. **TPH**, photo 384.

Fancy Free.

Smith, Oliver. American Ballet Theatre, NYC: 1942. B&W. Rendering. **SDA**, 276; B&W. Rendering. **TPH**, photo 368.

La Fanfare d' un jour de printemps.

_____. Art and Action, Paris: 1930. B&W. Set. **RSD**, illus. 388.

Fantasio.

Pronaszko, Andrzej. Teatr imienia Slowack iego, Crakow: 1954. B&W. Set. **SDW1**, 157.

Stein, Douglas O. Tyrone Guthrie Theatre, Minneapolis: 1991. Color. Set. **TCI**, vol. 26, n. 2 (Feb 1992). 11.

Far Away Songs of Triumph.

Kôno, Kunio. Haiyuza, Tokyo: 1955. B&W. Set. **SDW2**, 150.

The Farce of the Harmless Murderer.

Van Hellem, Huib. Nationaal Toneel, Antwerp: 1949. B&W. Set. **SDW1**, 44.

Farewell Tokyo!

Kanamori, Kaoru. Gekidan-Shiki, Nissei Gekijo, Tokyo: 1970. Color. Set. **SDW3**, 214.

Farther West.

_____. Theatre Calgary: B&W. Set. **TCI**, vol. 18, n. 2 (Feb 1984). 31.

Fashion.
>Darling, Robert Edward. Yale School of Drama, New Haven, Connecticut: B&W. Set. **SFT**, 115.

Fashions of the Times.
>Kiesler, Frederick. NYC: 1944. B&W. Rendering. **EIF**, photo 27.

The Fateful Play of Love.
>Heythum, Antonín. National Theatre Studio, Prague: 1930. B&W. Set. **TDT**, n. 41 (Summer 1975). 23.

The Father.
>Easley, Holmes. Roundabout Theatre, NYC: B&W. Set. **TCI**, vol. 8, n. 2 (Mar/Apr 1974). 12.
>Oenslager, Donald. Cort Theatre, NYC: 1949. B&W. Set. **WTP**, 97.
>Reimer, Treva. Indiana University Theatre, Bloomington: 1983. B&W. Rendering. **BSE3**, 34.

Father Malachy's Miracle.
>Mielziner, Jo. Guild Theatre (Virginia Theatre), NYC: 1937. B&W. Rendering. **DTT**, 98. Exterior: street; B&W. Rendering. **DTT**, 99. Interior: sacristy.

Father Was a Peculiar Man. Chepulis, Kyle. NYC: Color. Set. **TCI**, vol. 29, n. 4 (Apr 1995). 42.

Il Fattaccio del Giugno.
>Polidori, Gianni. 1968. B&W. **SIO**, 117.

Les Fausses Confidences.
>Aronson, Boris. Comédie Française, Paris: 1977. B&W. Set. **PST**, 279.

Faust.
>Benedek, Kata. Budapest: c.1932. B&W. Rendering. **SCM**, 71.
>Corinth, Lovis. Lessing Theatre, Berlin: 1922. B&W and color. Rendering. **AST**, 32, 33. 3 photos.
>Csányi, Arpád. Hungary: B&W. Model. **TDT**, vol. XVI, n. 1 (Spring 1980). 7.
>Daniel, Heinz. Germany: 1931. B&W. Drawing. **TAT**, plate 327.
>Dupont, Jacques. Metropolitan Opera, NYC: 1965. B&W. Rendering. **MOM**, 15.
>Erler, Fritz. Künstlertheater, Munich: 1910. B&W. Rendering. **SDC**, plate 55; B&W. Rendering. **TCS2**, plates 57, 58, 60. 3 photos.
>Exter, Alexandra. B&W. Rendering. **RAG**, 28.
>Finke, Jochen. Mecklinburg State Theatre, Germany: 1979. B&W. Set. **TDT**, vol. XIX, n. 1 (Spring 1983). 20, 21. 4 photos.
>Fuerst, Walter René. Odéon Théâtre, Paris: B&W. Model. **TCS2**, plate 223.
>Geyling, Remigius. Burgtheater, Vienna: 1926. B&W. Projection. **TPH**, photo 372.
>Gunter, John. English National Opera, London: 1985. B&W. Set. **BTD**, 120, 121.
>Gutzeit, Kurt. B&W. Rendering. **TCS2**, plate 193.
>Holzmeister, Clemens. Felsenreitschule, Salzburg: 1933. B&W. Set. **MRT**, 77.
>Jones, Robert Edmond. Gallo Theatre, NYC: 1928. B&W. Rendering. **REJ**, 67.
>Jürgens, Helmut. Kammerspiele, Munich: 1949. B&W. Rendering. **SDW1**, 69.
>Klein, César. State Theatre, Berlin: B&W. Rendering. **TCS2**, plate 92.
>Lee, Ming Cho. New York City Opera, Lincoln Center: 1968. B&W. Rendering. **SDB**, 65.
>Mielziner, Jo. USA: B&W. Model. **SDC**, plate 105; B&W. Model. **TCS2**, plate 95.
>Otto, Teo. Deutsches Schauspielhaus, Hamburg: 1958. Color. Rendering. **RSD**, illus. 453.
>Payne, Darwin Reid. B&W. Model. **SIP**, 140.
>Reinhardt, Andreas. Deutsches Theater, Berlin: 1968. B&W. Rendering & set. **SDW3**, 79. 3 photos.

Remisoff, Nicolai. Pilgrimage Theatre, California: 1938. B&W. Set. **MRT**, 77.
Reufersward, Carl Frederik. Stockholm: 1969. B&W. Set. **SDB**, 142.
Roger, David. Lyric Theatre, Hammersmith, London: 1988. B&W. Set. **BTD**, 84, 85.
Roller, Alfred. Deutsches Theater, Berlin: 1909. B&W. Rendering & set. **TCS2**, plates
    19-21, 24, 25. 5 photos.
Simonson, Lee. USA: 1928. B&W. Set. **PLT**, illus. 38; B&W. Set. **SCM**, 109, 110;
    B&W. Set. **TAS**, 146, 147. 4 photos; B&W. Set. **TSS**, 527. 2 photos.
Singelis, James T. Cincinnati Opera Company: B&W. Set. **SDT**, 283.
Stern, Ernst. Color. Rendering. **CSC**, facing 108.
Stone, James Merrill. Cleveland Opera: 1986. Color. Set. **TCI**, vol. 20, n. 8 (Oct
    1986). 23.
Stromberg, Christine. Deutsches Theater, Berlin: 1968. B&W. Rendering & set.
    SDW3, 79. 3 photos.
Svoboda, Josef. Piccolo Teatro, Milan: 1988/1989. B&W. Set. **STS**, 102; B&W. Set.
    TDT, vol. XXVIII, n. 5 (Fall 1992). 18; B&W. Set. **TDT**, vol. XXX, n. 5 (Fall
    1994). 41. 2 photos.
Szajna, Josef. Cracow Opera: 1967. B&W. Rendering. **RSD**, illus. 482; Teatr Polski,
    Warsaw: 1974. B&W. Set. **SDW4**, illus. 103-105.
Urban, Joseph. Metropolitan Opera, NYC: 1917. Color. Rendering. **MOM**, 9.
Wonder, Erich. Cologne, Germany: 1983. B&W. Set. **TCI**, vol. 20, n. 8 (Oct 1986).
    33, 35.
Zelenka, Frantisek. National Theatre, Bratislava: 1932. B&W. Rendering. **TDT**, n. 42
    (Fall 1975). 26.
_____. Deutsches Theater, Berlin: 1909. B&W. Set. **MRH**, between 72 & 73. 3
    photos.
_____. Laboratory Theater, Opole, Poland: 1963. B&W. Sketch. **RSD**, illus.
    632.
_____. Yale School of Drama, New Haven, Connecticut: 1949. B&W. Set.
    WTP, 94, 95. 4 photos.
Faust, part II.
Heiliger, Bernhard. Schiller Theater, Berlin: 1966. B&W. Set. **SDW3**, 80.
Otto, Teo. Salzburg: B&W. Set. **TCI**, vol. 11, n. 2 (Mar/Apr 1977). 20.
Roller, Alfred. Deutsches Theater, Berlin: 1911. B&W and color. Rendering & set.
    B&W. Rendering. **FCS**, plate 190. Act V, sc. 17; **MRH**, between 72 & 73, facing
    74, 76. 6 photos; **SDO**, 216.
La Favorita.
Lee, Ming Cho. San Francisco Opera: 1973. B&W. Set. **DPT**, 244.
Fear.
_____. Moscow Art Theatre: 1931. B&W. Set. **RST**, 274. 2 photos.
Fear and Misery in the Third Reich.
Blane, Sue. Citizen's Theatre of Glasgow: B&W. Set. **TCI**, vol. 15, n. 7 (Aug/Sep
    1981). 26.
Neher, Caspar. Basel: 1947. B&W. Rendering. **CBM**, 58. 2 photos.
Feast of Youth.
Begovich, Patrice. University of California, Los Angeles: 1985. B&W. Set. **TCI**, vol.
    20, n. 8 (Oct 1986). 16.
Feathertop.
Gianfrancesco, Edward. 1984. Color. Set. **TCI**, vol. 20, n. 4 (Apr 1986). 36.
La Fedelta Premiata.
Perdziola, Robert. Manhattan School of Music, NYC: 1988. B&W and color. Render-
    ing. **DDT**, 152d, 399.

Fée de Sagasse.
 Benois, Alexander. 1949. B&W and color. Rendering. **FCS**, plate 173, color plate 18;
  Color. Rendering. **SDO**, plate 18.
Feedback.
 Svoboda, Josef. Moscow Art Theatre: 1977. B&W. Set. **STS**, 90.
Fen.
 Graves, Lynn. Empty Space Theatre, Seattle: B&W. Set. **TCI**, vol. 20, n. 3 (Mar
  1986). 18.
 Snider, Peggy. Eureka Theatre, San Francisco: Color. Set. **TCI**, vol. 20, n. 3 (Mar
  1986). 18.
Fences.
 Arcenas, Loy. Arena Stage, Washington, DC: 1990. B&W. Set. **ASD2**, 13.
 McClennahan, Charles. Stage West: 1990. B&W. Sketch & set. **ASD2**, 122.
 _____. Milwaukee Repertory Theatre: Color. Set. **TCI**, vol. 24, n. 4 (Apr 1990).
  40.
Fenisa's Bait.
 Muñoz, Gori. Teatro Liceo, Buenos Aires: 1958. B&W. Rendering. **SDW2**, 26.
Ferai.
 Barba, Eugenio, Iben Nagel Rasmussen, & Jacob Jensen. Odin Teatret, Holstebro,
  Denmark: 1969. B&W. Set. **SDW3**, 146.
The Fiancés of Harve.
 Dufy, Raoul. Comédie Française, Paris: 1944. Color. Rendering. **AST**, 111; B&W. Set.
  SDW1, 95.
Fiddle-Dee-Dee.
 _____. NYC: 1900. B&W. Set. **TMI**, 235.
Fiddler on the Roof.
 Aronson, Boris. Imperial Theatre, NYC: 1964. B&W. Rendering. **DPT**, 59; B&W. Set.
  TCI, vol. 4, n. 3 (May/Jun 1970). 32; B&W. Model. **CSD**, 34; B&W. Set. **HPR**,
  103; B&W. Set. **MAM**, 48, 49; B&W. Sketches. **TAB**, 172. Rejected sketches;
  Color. Drops. **TAB**, 176, 179, 180. 5 photos; B&W and color. Sketches, rendering,
  model, & set. **TAB**, 19, 173-175, 177, 178, 180, 181, 184-186, 307. 22 photos;
  B&W. Set. **TCI**, vol. 20, n. 5 (May 1986). 28; Color. Set. **TCI**, vol. 23, n. 7 (Aug/
  Sep 1989). 59; B&W. Rendering. **TMI**, 252; Alhambra Theatre, Tel Aviv: 1965.
  B&W. Set. **MAM**, 133; Amsterdam: 1966. B&W. Set. **MAM**, 136; London: 1967.
  B&W. Set. **MAM**, 143; Color. Drop. **TAB**, 181; B&W. Set. **TAB**, 182; Paris: 1969.
  B&W. Set. **MAM**, 150, 151; Color. Set. **TAB**, 182; NYC: 1990. Color. Set. **TCI**,
  vol. 28, n. 3 (Mar 1994). 32; Tokyo: Color. Model. **TAB**, 183. 4 photos.
 Bianchini, Henry. University of Hawaii, Hilo: 1983. Color. Set. **TCI**, vol. 20, n. 5
  (May 1986). 29.
 Butsch, Tom. Chanhassen Dinner Theatre, Minnesota: B&W. Set. **TCI**, vol. 14, n. 5
  (Oct 1980). 24.
 Hird, Thomas C. California State University, Hayward: 1979. B&W. Set. **BSE1**, 8. 2
  photos.
 Levental, Valery. Comic Opera, Berlin: B&W. Set. **TCI**, vol. 15, n. 1 (Jan 1981). 36.
 Williams, Jerry. Eugene Festival of Musical Theatre, Oregon: Color. Set. **TCI**, vol. 20,
  n. 5 (May 1986). 28.
 _____. Berlin: B&W. Set. **MAM**, 152-155. 2 photos.
Fidelio.
 Aronson, Boris. Metropolitan Opera, NYC: 1970. B&W. Rendering. **FCS**, plate 214.
  Act II, sc. 2; B&W and color. Rendering & set. **MOM**, 80-87. 6 photos; B&W.

Set. **SDB**, 78, 79; B&W. Rendering. **SDO**, 249; B&W. Rendering & set. TAB, 216, 308. 8 photos.

Broë, Roger. Palais des Beaux-Arts, Charleroi, Belgium: 1959. B&W. Rendering. **SDW2**, 27.

Casorati, Felice. La Scala, Milan: 1949. B&W. Rendering. **SDE**, 59.

Culshaw, Bernard. Kent Opera, GB: 1982. B&W. Set. **TCI**, vol. 19, n. 4 (Apr 1985). 18.

Dulberg, Ewald. Krolloper, Berlin: 1927. B&W. Rendering. **RSD**, illus. 71.

Elder, Eldon. Walt Whitman Hall, Brooklyn, New York: 1971-1972. B&W. Rendering. **EED**, (pages not numbered).

Freyer, Achim. Frankfurt Opera: 1976. B&W. Set. **TCI**, vol. 13, n. 5 (Oct 1979). 20.

Frigerio, Ezio. Teatro Comunale ente Autonomo, Florence. 1969. D&W. Rendering & set. **OPE**, 114, 123, 124, 127; B&W. Rendering. **SIO**, 56, 57. 9 photos.

Heinrich, Rudolf. Grosses Festspielhaus, Salzburg: 1968. B&W and color. Set. **OPE**, 113, 122, 125, 127; B&W. Set. **TCI**, vol. 10, n. 6 (Nov/Dec 1976). 12; Teatro alla Scala, Milan: 1974. B&W. Set. **OPE**, 121, 122, 124, 126.

Holzmeister, Clemens. Salzburg Musical Festival: B&W. Rendering. **DIT**, plate 109.

Jacobs, Sally. Royal Opera House, Covent Garden, London: 1986. B&W. Set. **BTD**, 121.

Jampolis, Neil Peter. Houston Grand Opera: 1984. B&W. Set. **DDT**, 454. 2 photos.

Lees, Allan. Her Majesty's Theatre, Sydney: 1970. B&W. Set. **SDW3**, 176.

Mumford, Peter. Opera North, Leeds, England: 1988. B&W. Set. **BTD**, 117.

Oenslager, Donald. Central City Opera House, Colorado: 1947. B&W. Rendering. **SDL**, 54; B&W. Rendering. **SDW1**, 204.

Peiran, Teng. (project): Color. Rendering. **TDT**, vol. XXVIII, n. 2 (Spring 1992). 14 of insert.

Reinking, Wilhelm. State Theatre, Wiesbaden: 1952. B&W. Set. **SDE**, 144.

Schneider-Siemssen, Günther. Staatsoper, Vienna: 1970. B&W. Rendering & set. **OPE**, 115, 122, 125, 126. 6 photos

Siercke, Alfred. State Opera, Hamburg: 1951. B&W. Set. **SDW1**, 79. 2 photos.

Soherr, Hermann. Deutsche Oper am Rhein, Düsseldorf: 1971. B&W. Set. **OPE**, 116, 123, 124, 127.

Tröster, Frantisek. National Theater, Bratislava: 1937. B&W. Rendering. **RSD**, illus. 275.

Uecker, Günther. Theater am Goetheplatz, Bremen: 1974. B&W. Model. **OPE**, 118, 119, 123, 126. 7 photos

The Field God.

Bromberg, Louis. Greenwich Village Theatre, NYC: 1927. B&W. Set. **MCN**, 84.

Fields of Ambrosia.

Jasien, Deborah. George Street Playhouse, New Brunswick, New Jersey: 1993. B&W. Set. **TCI**, vol. 27, n. 6 (Jun/Jul 1993). 10.

The Fiery Angel.

Israel, Robert. Los Angeles Music Center Opera: 1987. B&W. Set. **ASD2**, 60; Color. Set. **TCI**, vol. 22, n. 1 (Jan 1988). 10; Color. Set. **TCI**, vol. 24, n. 9 (Nov 1990). 35.

Svoboda, Josef. (not produced): 1970-1971. B&W. Model. **SJS**, 120. 4 photos; Milan: 1970. B&W. Model. **TDT**, n. 20 (Feb 1970). 11. 2 photos.

Fiesco.

Grünewald, Isaac. Royal Dramatic Theatre, Stockholm: B&W. Rendering. **TAT**, plate 442.

Fiesko of Genoa.
> Hausner, Xenia. Schiller Theater, Berlin: 1987. B&W. Set. **TCI**, vol. 22, n. 2 (Feb 1988). 8.

5th of July.
> Beatty, John Lee. Circle Repertory Company, NYC: 1978. B&W. Rendering. **ASD1**, 10; Color. Rendering. **DDT**, 440d. 2 photos; B&W. Rendering. **TDT**, vol. XVIII, n. 4 (Winter 1982). 10, 11.
> Camburn, Herbert L. California State University, Long Beach: 1983. B&W. Rendering. **BSE3**, 13.
> Kurtz, Kenneth. Players State Theatre, Miami, Florida: B&W. Set. **TCI**, vol. 17, n. 3 (Mar 1983). 19.

Fifty Million Frenchmen.
> Bel Geddes, Norman. Lyric Theatre, NYC: 1929. B&W. Set. **BMF**, 38.

Figaro/Figaro.
> McLane, Derek. Yale Repertory Theatre, New Haven: 1995. Color. Set. **TCI**, vol. 29, n. 3 (Mar 1995). 6.

La Figlia di Lorio (D'Annunzio).
> Polidori, Gianni. 1972. B&W. Model. **SIO**, 120.

La Fille mal gardée.
> Lancaster, Osbert. Covent Garden, London: B&W. Set. **CGA**, 170.

Filottete.
> Luzzati, Emanuele. 1970. B&W. Set. **SIO**, 92.

The Final Balance.
> Aronson, Boris. Unser Theatre, Bronx: 1925. B&W. Model & rendering. **BAT**, 3, 18. 4 photos; B&W. model, rendering, & set. **TAB**, 35, 293. 5 photos.

The Fine Art of Finesse.
> Schwartz, Robert Joel. Pearl Theatre Company: B&W and color. Rendering. **TDT**, vol. XXVIII, n. 2 (Spring 1992). 3, 8 of insert.

Finian's Rainbow.
> Mielziner, Jo. 46th Street Theatre, NYC: 1947. B&W. Set. **BWM**, 258. 2 photos; B&W. Rendering. **DTT**, 131. Senator's porch.

Finishing Touches.
> Edwards, Ben. Plymouth Theatre, NYC: 1973. B&W. White model. **DPT**, 127.

Fiorello!
> Eckart, William & Jean. Broadhurst Theatre, NYC: 1959. Color. Set. **BWM**, 97; Color. Rendering. **DDT**, 312b. 2 photos; B&W. Set. **HPA**, 30; B&W. Rendering. **SDD**, between 210 & 211. "The Marino Club."

The Fire Drum.
> Prampolini, Enrico. National Theatre, Prague: 1923. Color. Rendering. **RSD**, illus. 339.

The Firebird.
> Chagall, Marc. Metropolitan Opera, NYC: 1945. Color. Rendering. **RSD**, illus. 478, 481.
> Goncharova, Natalia. Ballets Russes, Paris Opera: 1926. B&W. Rendering. **AST**, 54. Act II; Lyceum Theatre, London: 1926. B&W. **DOT**, 219. Act II.
> Rose, Jürgen. Deutsches Staatsoper, Berlin: 1964. B&W. Set. **SDW3**, 189.
> Steger, Rod. University of Wyoming, Laramie: 1982. B&W. Rendering. **BSE3**, 38.
> Svoboda, Josef. Royal Theatre, Copenhagen: 1972. B&W. **STS**, 91; B&W. Set. **TDT**, vol. XII, n. 2 (Summer 1976). 16.

The Firebrand.

Thompson, Woodman. Morosco Theatre, NYC: 1924. B&W. Rendering. **SCM**, 121; B&W. Set. **TCS2**, plate 87.

Zelenka, Frantisek. Vinohrady Theatre, Prague: 1938. B&W. Rendering. **TDT**, n. 42 (Fall 1975). 26.

The Firebugs.

Svoboda, Josef. Raam Theatre, Antwerp, Belgium: 1991. B&W. Set. **TDT**, vol. XXVIII, n. 2 (Spring 1992). 40. 3 photos.

Fireworks.

Balla, Giacomo. Costanzi Theatre, Rome: 1917. B&W and color. model & rendering. **RSD**, illus. 351-354. Ballet-Russes.

Butz, Fritz. Schauspielehaus, Zürich: 1948. B&W. Rendering. **SDW1**, 114.

The Firstborn.

Aronson, Boris. Coronet Theatre (Eugene O'Neill Theatre), NYC: 1958. B&W. Rendering. **TDT**, vol. XXV, n. 3 (Fall 1989). 11.

The First Cavalry Army.

_____. Theatre of the Revolution, Moscow: 1930. B&W. Set. **RST**, 280.

First Class Passengers Only.

Beaton, Cecil. Arts Theatre, London: 1927. B&W. Rendering. **CBS**, 26.

The First Distiller.

Annekov, George. Hermitage Experimental Theatre, Petrograd: 1919. B&W. Rendering. **RAG**, 18; B&W. Rendering. **RSC**, 14; B&W. Rendering. **RSD**, illus. 171.

Williams, Christopher. Leeds Repertory Theatre, England: B&W. Rendering. **SCM**, 35.

First Lady.

Oenslager, Donald. Music Box Theatre, NYC: 1935. B&W. Rendering & set. **SFT**, 34, 41; 1961. B&W and color. Rendering. **TDO**, 136 and facing 136. 2 photos.

First Night.

Jampolis, Neil Peter. Westside Arts Theatre, NYC: 1994. Color. Set. **TCI**, vol. 28, n. 10 (Dec 1994). 11.

The Firstborn.

Aronson, Boris. Coronet Theatre (Eugene O'Neill Theatre), NYC: 1958. B&W and color. Rendering & set. **TAB**, 130, 305. 3 photos; B&W. Rendering. **TCI**, vol. 23, n. 8 (Oct 1989). 10.

The Fish with the Golden Sword.

Richter, Gerd. Württembergische Staatstheater, Stuttgart: 1958. B&W. **SDW2**, 69.

The Fisherwomen.

Oechslin, Ary. State Theatre, Bern: 1971. B&W. Set. **SDW4**, illus. 101.

The Fishing Port.

Yamazaki, Junnosuke. Shochiku-za, Tokyo: 1948. B&W. Rendering. **SDW1**, 150.

The 500 Hats of Bartholomew Cubbins.

Barkla, Jack. Children's Theatre Company, Minneapolis: B&W. Set. **TCI**, vol. 17, n. 7 (Aug/Sep 1983). 31.

Five Kings.

Morcom, James Stewart. Colonial Theatre, Boston: 1939. B&W. Rendering. **DDT**, 416. 2 photos.

Five Star Final.

Ackerman, P. Dodd. Cort Theatre, NYC: 1930. B&W. Set. **MCN**, 100; B&W. Set. **SDA**, 226.

Flash Gordon Conquers the Planet of Evil.
_____. Yale Cabaret, New Haven, Connecticut: B&W. Set. **TCI**, vol. 19, n. 2
(Feb 1985). 28.
Flavia e le Bambole.
Guglielminetti, Eugenio. 1971. B&W. Set. **SIO**, 83.
The Flea.
Kustodiev, Boris. Second Moscow Art Theatre: 1925. Color. Rendering. **RST**, 233. 2
photos.
A Flea in Her Ear.
Brown, Louis & Stuart Wurzel. American Conservatory Theatre, San Francisco: B&W.
Set. **TCI**, vol. 6, n. 5 (Oct 1972). 17.
Larkin, Grady. 1972. B&W. Set. **TCI**, vol. 9, n. 1 (Jan/Feb 1975). 17.
Quay, Stephen & Timothy. Old Vic Theatre, London: 1989. B&W. Set. **TCI**, vol. 27, n.
1 (Jan 1993). 44.
Warne, Park. Florida State University, Tallahassee: B&W. Set. **TDP**, 114.
Williams, Jerry. Alley Theatre, Houston: B&W. Set. **TCI**, vol. 7, n. 3 (May/Jun 1973).
9, 10.
Die Fledermaus.
Curtis, Ann & Christopher Morley. Covent Garden, London: 1976. B&W. Set. **CGA**,
196.
Rice, Peter. Opera Theatre of St. Louis: 1983. B&W. Sketches. **BTD**, 108. 3 photos.
_____. University of Washington, Seattle: B&W. Set. **TCI**, vol. 13, n. 6 (Nov/
Dec 1979). 30.
A Fleet Street Comedy.
Griffin, Hayden. National Theatre, London: 1985. B&W. Set. **TCI**, vol. 19, n. 9 (Nov
1985). 24.
The Flies.
Adam, H.G. Théâtre de la Cité, Lyon: 1943. B&W. Rendering. **RSD**, illus. 399.
Grate, Eric. Dramatiska Teatern, Stockholm: 1945. B&W. Set. **SDW1**, 165.
Flight Into Egypt.
Mielziner, Jo. Music Box Theatre, NYC: 1952. B&W. Rendering. **DTT**, 177. Sc. 1;
B&W. Rendering **DTT**, 178. Sc. 2.
Flight of Devils.
Singelis, James T. Long Island Stage, Hempstead, New York: B&W. Rendering. **SDT**,
289.
The Flood.
_____. Springfield College, Massachusetts: B&W. Rendering. **TCI**, vol. 9, n. 5
(Oct 1975). 17.
Flora, The Red Menace.
Eckart, William & Jean. Alvin Theatre, NYC: 1965. Color. Rendering. **DDT**, 24b.
Florian Geyer.
Slevogt, Max. Lessing Theatre, Berlin: 1904. B&W. Rendering. **AST**, 34.
Flower Drum Song.
Smith, Oliver. St. James Theatre, NYC: 1958. B&W. Set. **HOB**, 177; B&W. Set. **TCI**,
vol. 16, n. 4 (Apr 1982). 14; B&W. Set. **TMI**, 136, 170; B&W. Set. **WMC**, 222.
Flowering Cherry.
Aronson, Boris. Lyceum Theatre, NYC: 1959. B&W. Rendering. **TAB**, 306.
The Flowering Peach.
Recht, Raymond C. Lyceum Theatre, NYC: 1994. Color. Model. **TCI**, vol. 28, n. 6
(Jun/Jul 1994). 12, 13. 3 photos.

Wilcox, Richard. Yale School of Drama, New Haven, Connecticut: 1960. B&W. Set. **SDW2**, 240.

Flying Colors.

Bel Geddes, Norman. Imperial Theatre, NYC: 1932. B&W. Set. **RBS**, 69; B&W. Photomontage. **SCM**, 107.

The Flying Dutchman.

Balo, Maurizio. Opera de Paris Bastille: 1993. Color. Set. **TCI**, vol. 27, n. 10 (Dec 1993). 16.

Jampolis, Neil Peter. Tulsa Opera Company: 1982. B&W. Rendering. **DDT**, 455. 2 photos.

O'Brien, Timothy. Sadler's Wells Opera House, London: 1957. B&W. Rendering. **SDW2**, 223.

Oenslager, Donald. (project): 1932. B&W. Rendering. **SCM**, 128. Act I; B&W. Rendering. **TDO**, 48, 49.

Rodhe, Lennart. Kungliga Teatern, Stockholm: 1960. B&W. Set. **SDW2**, 212.

Svoboda, Josef. Smetana Theater, Prague: 1959. B&W. Set. **JSS**, 24. Act I; B&W. Set. **JSS**, 25 and between 54 & 55. Act III; B&W. Set. **JSS**, 25. Act II; B&W. Set. **STS**, 76; Beyreuth Festival Theatre: 1969. B&W. Set. **JSS**, 26, 28, 29; B&W. Set. **STS**, 82, 94; B&W. Set. **TCI**, vol. 14, n. 1 (Jan/Feb 1980). 22; B&W. Set. **TCI**, vol. 5, n. 1 (Jan/Feb 1971). 31. 3 photos; B&W. Set. **TDT**, n. 29 (May 1972). 11, 13.

Sykora, Peter. Beyreuth Festival Theatre: 1978. B&W. Set. **TCI**, vol. 14, n. 1 (Jan/Feb 1980). 22.

Vancura, Jan. Liberec Opera House: 1987. B&W. Set. **TDT**, vol. XXIX, n. 1 (Winter 1993). 23.

_____. Bregenz Festival, Austria: B&W. Set. **TCI**, vol. 11, n. 2 (Mar/Apr 1977). 22.

La Foire de Sorotchin.

Komisarjevsky, Theodore. France: 1930. B&W. Rendering. **SCM**, 46.

Foire Espagnole.

Goncharova, Natalia. B&W. Set. **TCS2**, plate 258.

Follies.

Aronson, Boris. Winter Garden Theatre, NYC: 1971. B&W and color Model. **CSD**, 36, 59, 126; B&W. Model. **DDT**, 15; B&W. Model. **DPT**, 8; B&W. Set. **HPA**, 99, 100, 102. 3 photos; B&W and color. Set. **SON**, 91, 93, 98, 99; B&W and color. Rendering, model, & set. **TAB**, 20, 235, 236, 238-242, 247, 249, 250, 253, 308. 17 photos; B&W. Set. **TCI**, vol. 14, n. 1 (Jan/Feb 1980). 21; B&W. Model. **TDT**, vol. XXV, n. 3 (Fall 1989). 12; B&W. Set. **TDT**, vol. XXIV, n. 3 (Fall 1988). 17. 2 photos.

Salzer, Beeb. B&W and color. Sketches & set. **SDL**, 364, plate 23-1. 3 photos.

Follow the Girls.

Bay, Howard. New Century Theatre, NYC: 1944. B&W. Rendering. **SDB**, 59; B&W. Rendering. **TCI**, vol. 17, n. 2 (Feb 1983). 12, 54.

Food From Trash.

Owen, Paul. Actors Theatre of Louisville: 1983. B&W. Set. **TCI**, vol. 17, n. 7 (Aug/Sep 1983). 10; Color. Set. **TCI**, vol. 23, n. 3 (Mar 1989). 37.

The Fool and the Nun.

Kantor, Tadeusz. Cricot 2, Cracow: 1963. B&W. Set. **AST**, 244.

Fool for Love.

Rose, Thomas. Cricket Theatre, Minneapolis: 1985. Color. Set. **TCI**, vol. 19, n. 7 (Aug/Sep 1985). 16.

Stacklin, Andy. Circle Repertory Theatre, NYC: 1983. B&W. Set. **TCI**, vol. 17, n. 8
   (Oct 1983). 12.
Fools.
   Beatty, John Lee. Eugene O'Neill Theatre, NYC: 1981. Color. Rendering. **ASD1**,
      between 70 & 71; B&W. Rendering. **TDT**, vol. XVIII, n. 4 (Winter 1982). 7.
   Rupnik, Kevin. Alaska Repertory Theatre tour: 1982. B&W. Set. **TCI**, vol. 17, n. 4
      (Apr 1983). 25.
For Lease or Sale.
   Coble, McKay. Playmakers Repertory Company, Paul Green Theatre, Chapel Hill,
      North Carolina: 1989. Color. Set. **TCI**, vol. 25, n. 3 (Mar 1991). 49.
For Lucrece.
   Cassandre, A.M. Théâtre Marigny, Paris: 1953. B&W. Set. **SDW1**, 89.
Les Forains.
   Bérard, Christian. Théâtre des Champs-Elysées, Paris: 1945. Color. Rendering. **SDW1**,
      85.
Forefather's Eve.
   Pronaszko, Andrzej. Polski Theater, Warsaw: 1934. B&W. Set. **RSD**, illus. 265.
   Zachwatowicz, Krystyna. Stary Teatr, Cracow: 1973. B&W. Set. **SDW4**, illus. 125.
The Foreigner.
   Gilseth, Thom. Phoenix Little Theatre, Arizona: B&W. Set. **SDT**, 286.
   Schultz, Karen. Astor Place Theatre, NYC: 1984. B&W. Model. **DDT**, 124; B&W. Set.
      TDP, 116.
The Forest.
   Meyerhold, Vsevelod, plan; Vasilii Federov, execution. Meyerhold Theatre, Moscow:
      1924. B&W. Set. **DOT**, 216; B&W. Set. **MOT**, between 184 & 185. 2 photos;
      B&W. Model & set. **RSD**, illus. 180, 181; B&W. Set. **RST**, 178, 179. 3 photos;
      B&W. Model. **SCM**, 92; B&W. Set. **TCT**, plate 21.
   Sherman, Loren. Seattle Repertory Theatre: 1986. B&W. Set. **TCI**, vol. 20, n. 4 (Apr
      1986). 12.
   Stohl, Phyllis. Yale School of Drama, New Haven, Connecticut: B&W. Set. **SFT**, 75.
   Wilson, Robert. Brooklyn Academy of Music, New York: 1988. Color. Model. **TCI**,
      vol. 23, n. 1 (Jan 1989). 46, 47. 3 photos.
Forgiving Typhoid Mary.
   _____. George Street Playhouse, New Brunswick, New Jersey: Color. Set. **TCI**,
      vol. 25, n. 9 (Nov 1991). 54.
Fortinbras.
   Brill, Robert. Mandell Weiss Forum, La Jolla Playhouse, California: 1991. Color. Set.
      TCI, vol. 25, n. 8 (Oct 1991). 22.
The Fortune Teller.
   Aronson, Boris. Philharmonic Auditorium, Los Angeles: 1946. B&W. Rendering.
      TAB, 300.
42nd Street.
   Wagner, Robin. Winter Garden Theatre, NYC: 1980. B&W. Set. **ASD1**, 155; Color.
      Drop elevation. **ASD1**, between 70 & 71; Color. Set. **MBM**, 20. Sleeping car;
      B&W. Set. **MBM**, 21; B&W. Set. **TCI**, vol. 14, n. 6 (Nov/Dec 1980). 28-30. 6
      photos; B&W. Set. **TDT**, vol. XIX, n. 4 (Winter 1983). 7. 2 photos; B&W. Set.
      WMC, II.
   _____. S.S. Norway: 1989. B&W. Set. **TCI**, vol. 23, n. 3 (Mar 1989). 41.
La Forza del Destino.
   Berman, Eugene. Metropolitan Opera, NYC: 1952. B&W. Sketch. **DPT**, 120. Act IV,
      sc. 2; B&W. Set. **SDA**, 262, 263. 4 photos.

Herbert, Jocelyn. Paris Opera House: 1975. B&W. Rendering. **TDT**, vol. XXX, n. 5 (Fall 1994). 21.

Jampolis, Neil Peter. Houston Grand Opera Company: 1973. B&W. Set. **DPT**, 292. 2 scenes.

Labò, Savino. Teatre dell'Arena, Verona: 1951. B&W. Rendering. **SDE**, 93, 94.

Svoboda, Josef. Vienna: 1989. B&W. Set. **TDT**, vol. XXX, n. 5 (Fall 1994). 41. 2 photos.

The Fountain.

Jones, Robert Edmond. Greenwich Village Theatre, NYC: 1925. B&W. Sketch. **DFT**, plate 27. The torture of Nano; B&W. Rendering. **REJ**, 57.

Four Baboons Adoring the Sun.

Walton, Tony. Vivian Beaumont Theatre, Lincoln Center, NYC: 1992. B&W and color. Set. **DDT**, 2, 440a.

Four Rough Fellows.

Sestina, L. Czechoslovakia: B&W. Model. **TDT**, vol. XVI, n. 1 (Spring 1980). 29.

Four Saints in Three Acts.

Lawson, Kate Drain & Florine Stettheimer. 44th Street Theatre, NYC: 1934. B&W. Set. **MCN**, 115; B&W. Set. **RBS**, 98.

Ter-Arutunian, Rouben. Lillie Blake School Theatre, NYC: 1986. Color. Set. **TCI**, vol. 21, n. 5 (May 1987). 14.

Les Fourberies de Scapin.

Bérard, Christian. Royal Opera House, Covent Garden, London: 1936. B&W. Rendering. **SDR**, 31.

Granval, Charles. Comédie Francaise, Paris: 1922. B&W. Set. **TCS2**, plate 250.

The Fourposter.

Maillart, Jean Dénis. Paris: 1952. B&W. Set. **SDE**, 113. 2 photos.

_____. Alaska Repertory Theatre, Anchorage: B&W. Set. **TCI**, vol. 13, n. 2 (Mar/Apr 1979). 25.

The Foursome.

Bjarnhof, Hannah. Aalborg Teater, Denmark: 1972. B&W. Set. **SDW4**, illus. 349.

Foxfire.

Mitchell, David. Ethel Barrymore Theatre, NYC: 1982. Color. Model. **DDT**, 24a.

Francesca.

Kiesler, Frederick. Vienna: 1923. B&W. Set. **EIF**, photo 5.

Francesca da Rimini.

Frigerio, Ezio. Metropolitan Opera, NYC: 1984. B&W and color. Rendering & set. **MOM**, 88-99. 12 photos.

Messel, Oliver. Royal Opera House, Covent Garden, London: 1937. B&W and color. Rendering & set. **MEM**, 95-97. 3 photos.

Frank Kruk.

Jankus, Yozak. Muzilalaja Teatr, S.S.S.R: 1959. B&W. Rendering. **SDW2**, 187.

Frank's Wild Years.

Rigdon, Kevin. Steppenwolf Theatre, Chicago: 1986. Color. Set. **TCI**, vol. 21, n. 2 (Feb 1987). 31.

Frankenstein.

Barkla, Jack. Children's Theatre Company, Minneapolis: 1984. Color. Set. **TCI**, vol. 22, n. 5 (May 1988). 45.

Beck, Julian. Teatro La Perla, Venice: 1965. B&W. Set. **RSD**, illus. 623, 624; Théatre 140, Brussels: 1966. B&W. Set. **SDW3**, 171.

Mercer, G.W. Indiana Repertory Theatre: 1987. B&W. Set. **TCI**, vol. 22, n. 5 (May 1988). 44.

Schmidt, Douglas W. Palace Theatre, NYC: 1981. B&W. Sketch & set. **ASD1**, 140, 141; B&W and color. Rendering. **DDT**, 142, 312c. 4 photos; Color. Set. **DSL**, plate IV; B&W. Renderings. **SDD**, between 210 & 211. Elizabeth's boudoir, The grave yard, & Victor's laboratory; B&W. Set. **TCI**, vol. 15, n. 6 (Jun/Jul 1981). 30, 31. 4 photos; B&W. Set. **TCI**, vol. 27, n. 8 (Oct 1993). 5, 35; B&W. Rendering. **TDT**, vol. XVII, n. 2 (Summer 1981). 21, 22. 5 photos.

Strachan, Kathy. Glasgow Citizens Theatre: 1988. B&W. Set. **BTD**, 68.

Frankenstein: Playing With Fire.

Arnone, John. Tyrone Guthrie Theatre, Minneapolis: 1987/1988. B&W. Set. **ASD2**, 24; B&W. Set. **DDT**, 205. 4 photos.

Franziska.

Martin, Karlheinz. Theater in der Königgrätzerstrasse, Berlin: 1925. B&W. Set. **TCS2**, plate 176.

_____. Raimund Theatre, Vienna: B&W. Set. **SDC**, plate 120.

Die Frau ohne Schatten.

Bauer-Ecsy, Leni. Württembergische Staatstheater, Grosses Haus, Stuttgart: 1970. B&W. Set. **OPE**, 234, 240, 242, 248.

O'Hearn, Robert. Metropolitan Opera, NYC: 1966. B&W. Rendering. **CSD**, 113; B&W. Set. **DPT**, 365; B&W. Rendering. **DPT**, 72. Emperor's terrace; B&W. Rendering. **DPT**, 73. Dyer's house; B&W. Rendering. **DPT**, 73. Empress' bed room; B&W and color. Rendering & set. **MOM**, 100-111. 11 photos; B&W. Rendering & set. **OPE**, 233, 240, 242, 247, 248; B&W. Set. **SDB**, 80, 81; B&W. Rendering. **SDR**, 61. 2 photos; B&W. Rendering. **TCI**, vol. 10, n. 5 (Oct 1976). 16. 2 photos.

Schneider-Siemssen, Günther. Staatsoper, Vienna: 1964. B&W. Rendering. **OPE**, 53. Act III; Grosses Festspielhaus, Salzburg: 1974. B&W and color. Rendering & set. **OPE**, 237, 241, 242, 245, 246, 249; B&W. Set. **TCI**, vol. 12, n. 6 (Oct 1978). 32; B&W. Set. **TDT**, vol. XII, n. 1 (Spring 1976). 26.

Svoboda, Josef. Royal Opera House, Covent Garden, London: 1967. B&W. Set. **CGA**, 171; Color. Rendering. **SDW3**, 186; B&W. Model, rendering, & set. **SJS**, 69-71. 5 photos; B&W. Rendering. **STS**, 29, 30; B&W. Rendering. **TDT**, n. 20 (Feb 1970). 8.

Zimmermann, Jörg. Deutsche Oper, Berlin: 1964. B&W. Set. **OPE**, 231, 240, 243, 244, 248; Kunigla Operan, Stockholm: 1975. B&W and color. Set. **OPE**, 236, 241, 242, 245, 246, 249.

Die Frau Vom Meer.

_____. B&W. Set. **SST**, 255.

The Fraud.

Debesa, Fernando. Teatro de Ensayo de la Universidad Catolica, Santiago: 1946. B&W. Set. **SDW1**, 54.

Touchagues. Théâtre de l'Atelier, Paris: 1936. B&W. Rendering. **SDW1**, 107.

Die Freier.

Wecus, Walter von. State Theatre, Bonn: B&W. Set. **TCS2**, plate 229.

Der Freischütz.

Kiesler, Frederick. NYC: 1946. B&W. Set. **EIF**, photo 28.

Meczies, Aliute & Günther Schneider-Siemssen. Covent Garden, London: 1977. B&W. Set. **CGA**, 197.

Vancura, Jan. Liberec Opera House: 1983. Color. Rendering. **TDT**, vol. XXIX, n. 1 (Winter 1993). 19.

Wendel, Heinrich. Deutsches Oper am Rhein, Düsseldorf-Duisburg: B&W. Set. **SDR**, 50.

Wong, Carey. Portland Opera, Oregon: 1974. B&W. Set. **TCI**, vol. 12, n. 5 (Sep 1978). 36. 2 photos.

Frida.

Jackness, Andrew. Majestic Theatre, Brooklyn Academy of Music, New York: 1992. Color. Set. **TCI**, vol. 27, n. 2 (Feb 1993). 52.

Friendly Hillock.

_____. Theatre of Working Youth (TRAM), Leningrad: B&W. Set. **RST**, 243.

The Frogs.

Yeargan, Michael. Yale Repertory Theatre, New Haven: 1974. B&W. Set. **ASD2**, 178.

_____. B&W. Set. **WTP**, 40, 41.

The Frogs of Spring.

Aronson, Boris. Broadhurst Theatre, NYC: 1953. B&W. Rendering. **TAB**, 303.

From Morn to Midnight.

Aronson, Boris. 1945. B&W. Set. **PST**, 389.

Klein, César. Lessing Theater, Berlin: 1921. B&W. Rendering. **RSD**, illus. 122.

Robbins, Kathleen M. & W.M. Schenk. University of Vermont: B&W. Rendering & set. **TCI**, vol. 12, n. 5 (Sep 1978). 48, 49. 4 photos.

Stern, Ernst. Deutsches Theater, Berlin: 1919. B&W. Rendering. **RSD**, illus. 121.

_____. Habben. State Theatre, Cologne: B&W. Set. **SST**, 259, 260.

_____. Lessing Theater, Berlin: 1917. B&W. Set. **TSY**, 187.

From Moses to Mao.

Chauveau, Patrick, Michel Lebois, Charles Marty, & Sabine. Théâtre National de Strasbourg: 1973. B&W. Set. **SDW4**, illus. 397-404. 8 photos.

From the House of the Dead.

Arroyo, Eduardo. Salzburg Festival: 1992. B&W. Set. **TCI**, vol. 27, n. 1 (Jan 1993). 25.

Björnson, Maria. Welsh National Opera. 1982. Color. Set. **BTD**, 111; B&W. Model. **TDT**, vol. XX, n. 1 (Spring 1984). 18.

Svoboda, Josef. Czechoslovakia: B&W. Set. **TDT**, vol. XXVI, n. 2 (Summer 1990). 35.

From the Journal of Hazard McCauley.

Clifton, Randy. CAST Theatre, Los Angeles: 1984. B&W. Set. **TCI**, vol. 19, n. 7 (Aug/Sep 1985). 41.

The Front Page.

Funicello, Ralph. Seattle Repertory Theatre: 1982. Color. Set. **ASD1**, between 70 & 71.

Sovey, Raymond. Times Square Theatre, NYC: 1928. B&W. Set. **MCN**, 91.

Walton, Tony. Vivian Beaumont Theatre, Lincoln Center, NYC: 1986. B&W and color. Set. **TCI**, vol. 21, n. 3 (Mar 1987). 16, 17, 20. 3 photos.

_____. B&W. Set. **SIP**, 8.

Frühlings Erwachen.

Minks, Wilfried. Breman: 1965. B&W. Sketch. **SDB**, 197.

_____. B&W. Set. **SST**, 117.

Fuente Ovejuna.

Edmunds, Kate. Berkeley Repertory Theatre, California: 1990. B&W. Set. **TCI**, vol. 25, n. 8 (Oct 1991). 50. 2 photos.

Ormerod, Nick. National Theatre (Cottesloe), England: 1989. B&W. Set. **BTD**, 41.

Rothgeb, John Reese. University of Texas, Austin: B&W. Set. **TDT**, n. 2 (Oct 1965). back cover.

Tröster, Frantisek. National Theatre, Prague: 1935. B&W. Set. **SOW**, plate 32; B&W. Set. **TDT**, n. 42 (Fall 1975). 28.

Vychodil, Ladislav. Bratislava: 1953. B&W. Set. **TDT**, vol. XV, n. 2 (Summer 1979).
11.

Funny Face.

Galitzine, Prince, Joseph Harker & Phil Harker. Princes Theatre, London: 1928. B&W.
Set. **MCD**, plates 157, 158.

A Funny Thing Happened on the Way to the Forum.

Walton, Tony. Alvin Theatre, NYC: 1962. B&W. Set. **BMF**, 71; B&W. Model. **DDT**,
46;B&W. Set. **HPA**, 81; B&W. Set. **HPR**, 77; B&W and color. Set. **SON**, 61,
64; B&W. Set. **WMC**, 287. 2 photos; Picadilly Theatre, London: B&W. Sketch.
DDT, 46.

_____. Equity Library Theatre, NYC: B&W. Set. **TCI**, vol. 15, n. 6 (Jun/Jul
1981). 23.

Fuochi d' Artificio.

Balla, Giacomo. Teatro Costanzi, Rome: 1917. Color. Rendering. **AST**, 70.

The Furies.

Vanerelli, Mario. Teatro Empire, Buenos Aires: 1950. B&W. Rendering. **SDW1**, 38.

Futurists.

Dudley, William. National Theatre (Cottesloe), England: 1986. Color. Set. **BTD**, 42.

-G-

The Gainsborough Girls.

Beaton, Cecil. Theatre Royal, Brighton: 1951. B&W. Sketch. **CBS**, 51; B&W. Rendering. **SDW1**, 169.

Gaité Parisienne.

Brown, Zack. 1987. Color. Rendering. **DDT**, 152d.

Galileo (see also *The Life of Galileo*).

Ciller, Josef. Martin, Czechoslovakia: 1979. Color. Model. **TCI**, vol. 18, n. 1 (Jan
1984). 10; B&W. Set. **TDT**, vol. XXVIII, n. 2 (Spring 1992). 35. 4 photos;B&W.
Model. **TDT**, vol. XX, n. 1 (Spring 1984). 8.

Conklin, John. Hartford Stage, Connecticut: 1979. B&W. Set. **TCI**, vol. 14, n. 3 (May/
Jun 1980). 20.

Laufer, Murray. St. Lawrence Center, Toronto: B&W. Set. **TCI**, vol. 18, n. 9 (Nov/Dec
1984). 41.

Lukala, Juha. Finland: Color. Model. **TDT**, vol. XII, n. 3 (Fall 1976). 35.

Otto, Teo. Schauspielehaus, Zürich: 1947. B&W. Set. **TBB**, 46, 80.

Prowse, Philip. Citizen's Theatre of Glasgow: 1971. B&W. Set. **TCI**, vol. 15, n. 7
(Aug/Sep 1981). 23.

Stenberg, Enar. G. Taganka Theatre, Moscow: 1966. B&W. Rendering. **SDW3**, 113. 3
photos; B&W. Rendering. **TDT**, n. 33 (May 1973). 16.

Straiges, Tony. Arena Stage, Washington, DC: 1980. B&W. Set. **TCI**, vol. 16, n. 2
(Feb 1982). 17.

Vychodil, Ladislav. Bratislava: 1958. B&W. Rendering. **TDT**, vol. XV, n. 2 (Summer
1979). 11.

_____. Maxine Elliott's Theatre, NYC: c.1947. B&W. Set. **WTP**, 122, 123. 4
photos.

Galileo Galilei.

Roth, Wolfgang. 1965. B&W. Rendering. **TDT**, n. 42 (Fall 1975). 22.

Schwab, Per. Den Nationale Scene, Bergen, Norway: 1960. B&W. Rendering. **SDW2**,
153.

The Gambler.
> Mielziner, Jo. Lyceum Theatre, NYC: 1952. B&W. Rendering. **DTT**, 182. Railway
> station.

The Game of Love and Chance.
> Wenig, Adolf. Divadlo Komedie, Prague: 1959. B&W. Rendering. **SDW2**, 47.

The Game of Love and Death.
> Bernstein, Aline. Theatre Guild, NYC: 1929. B&W. Set. **SCM**, 115.

The Gang on the Roof.
> Eastman, Donald. Capital Repertory Company, Albany, New York: 1993. Color. Set.
> **TCI**, vol. 28, n. 1 (Jan 1994). 10.

The Gang's All Here.
> Mielziner, Jo. Ambassador Theatre, NYC: 1959. B&W. Rendering. **DTT**, 201.
> President's hotel room; B&W. Rendering. **SDA**, 155.

The Garden.
> Ciller, Josef. Bratislava: 1990. B&W. Model. **TDT**, vol. XXVIII, n. 2 (Spring 1992).
> 35.

The Garden Girls.
> Rose, George. Bush Theatre, London: 1986. B&W. Set. **BTD**, 65.

The Garden of Ashes.
> Vanerelli, Mario. Odeon, Buenos Aires: 1955. Color. Rendering. **SDW1**, 35.

The Garden of Delights.
> Humm, Ambrosius. Theater am Neumarkt, Zürich: 1971. B&W. Set. **SDW4**, illus.
> 344.
> Raven, Frank. De Brakke Gronde, Amsterdam: 1969. B&W. Set. **SDW3**, 158.

The Garden of Paradise.
> Urban, Joseph. Park Theatre, NYC: 1914. B&W. Set. **SDA**, 56; B&W. Rendering.
> **SDB**, 51, 52. 3 photos.

The Garden of Sweets.
> Aronson, Boris. ANTA Theatre (Virginia Theatre), NYC: 1961. B&W. Rendering.
> **TAB**, 306.

Gardenia.
> Recht, Raymond C. Pittsburgh Public Theatre: B&W and color. Set. **TCI**, vol. 21, n. 7
> (Aug/Sep 1987). 34, 37.

Garrick.
> Kiesler, Frederick. 1937. B&W. Sketch. **EIF**, photo 47.

The Garrick Gaieties.
> Hancock, Carolyn. Garrick Theatre, NYC: 1926. B&W. Set. **MCN**, 75.

Gas.
> Annekov, George. Great Dramatic Theater, Petrograd: 1922. B&W. Rendering. **RSD**,
> illus. 189.
> Lozowick, Louis. Goodman Theatre, Chicago: B&W. Rendering. **SDC**, plate 121.
> Shelving, Paul. Birmingham Repertory Theatre, England: 1923. B&W. Set. **SDG**, 172.
> Täuber, Harry. Deutsches Volkstheater, Vienna: B&W. Set. **TCS2**, plate 161.
> _____. Berezil Theatre, Ukraine: 1923. B&W. Set. **RST**, 158.
> _____. Bolshoi Theatre, Moscow: 1922. B&W. Set. **RST**, 130, 131.

The Gas Heart.
> _____. Théâtre Michel, Paris: 1923. B&W. Set. **RSD**, illus. 327.

Gaspar Diaz.
> Noël, Jacques. Théâtre Hébertot, Paris: 1955. B&W. Set. **SDW1**, 105.

The Gates of Paradise.
> Olko, Wieslaw. Warsaw, Poland: 1988. B&W. Set. **TCI**, vol. 22, n. 9 (Nov 1988). 23.

The Gay Divorce.
    Joy, James Leonard. Goodspeed Opera House, East Haddam, Connecticut: Color. Set.
        TCI, vol. 21, n. 9 (Nov 1987). 33.
    Mielziner, Jo. Ethel Barrymore Theatre, NYC: 1932. B&W. Rendering. **SDT**, 38.
The Gay Gordons.
    McCleery, R.C. Aldwych Theatre, London: 1907. B&W. Set. **MCD**, plate 63.
Gemini.
    _____. Delaware Theatre Company, Wilmington: B&W. Set. **TCI**, vol. 17, n. 3
        (Mar 1983). 24.
General Gorgeous.
    Funicello, Ralph. American Conservatory Theatre, San Francisco: 1975. B&W. Set.
        TCI, vol. 14, n. 4 (Sep 1980). 21.
Geniuses.
    Jackness, Andrew. Playwrights Horizons & Douglas Fairbanks Theatre, NYC: 1982.
        B&W. Set. **DDT**, 587.
    Straiges, Tony. Arena Stage, Washington, DC: 1983. B&W and color. Model. **DDT**,
        152, 312d; B&W. Set. **TCI**, vol. 18, n. 3 (Mar 1984). 29.
The Gentle People.
    Aronson, Boris. Belasco Theatre, NYC: 1939. Color. Rendering. **DDT**, 24a; B&W.
        Set. **SDB**, 36; **SDW1**, 190; B&W. Sketch. **SOW**, plate 101; B&W and color.
        Rendering & set. **TAB**, 64, 65, 67, 296. 5 photos.
Gentlemen Prefer Blondes.
    Sicangco, Eduardo. Goodspeed Opera House, East Haddam, Connecticut: Color.
        Rendering & set. **TCI**, vol. 29, n. 2 (Feb 1995). 36, 37. 5 photos.
    Smith, Oliver. Ziegfeld Theatre, NYC: 1949. B&W. Set. **BWM**, 273, 347.
Geordie's March.
    Lawrence, Christopher. Shaw Theatre, London. 1973. B&W. Set. **SDW4**, illus. 347.
George M!
    John, Tom H. Palace Theatre, NYC: 1968. B&W. Set. **TCI**, vol. 2, n. 6 (Nov/Dec
        1968). 36; B&W. Set. **WMC**, 28.
George Washington, Jr.
    Young, John A. & Ernest Albert. Herald Square Theatre, NYC: 1906. B&W. Set.
        MCN, 29.
Georges Dandin.
    Stern, Ernst. Deutsches Theater, Berlin: B&W. Set. **TCS2**, plate 26.
    _____. Deutsches Theater, Berlin: 1912. B&W. Set. **MRH**, facing 54.
Ein Geschlecht.
    Babberger, Ludwig. Frankfurt, Germany: 1918. B&W. Rendering. **TPH**, photo 419.
Gethsemane Springs.
    Jacobs, Sally. Mark Taper Forum, Los Angeles: B&W. Set. **TCI**, vol. 14, n. 4 (Sep
        1980). 45.
Gewitter über Gothland.
    Müller, Traugott. 1927. B&W. Set. **TCS2**, plate 358.
Ghetto.
    Svoboda, Josef. Oslo: 1986. B&W. Set. **TCI**, vol. 21, n. 8 (Oct 1987). 35; Czechoslo-
        vakia: 1986. B&W. Model. **TDT**, vol. XXIII, n. 4 (Winter 1988). 49.
The Ghost Sonata.
    Beyer, Rolf. Dartmouth College, Hanover, New Hampshire: 1970. B&W. Set. **DDT**,
        444.
    Vos, Marik. Dramatiska Teatern, Stockholm: 1973. B&W. Set. **SDW4**, illus. 182.

Yeargan, Michael. Yale Repertory Theatre, New Haven: 1977. B&W. Set. **TCI**, vol.
    16, n. 5 (May 1982). 26.
_____. Northwestern University Theatre, Evanston, Illinois: 1981. B&W. Set.
    BSE4, 42.
Ghosts.
Chaney, Stewart. Empire Theatre, NYC: 1935. B&W. Set. **SDA**, 211; B&W. Set. **TDT**,
    n. 19 (Dec 1969). 3.
Herbert, Jocelyn. Royal Shakespeare Company, Aldwych Theatre, London: 1967.
    B&W. Set. **PST**, 360.
Martin, Harald. Det Nye Teater, Oslo: 1952. B&W. Set. **SDW2**, 153.
Munch, Edvard. Kammerspiele, Berlin: 1906. B&W and color. Rendering. **AST**, 22,
    23; B&W. Rendering. **MRH**, facing 16. 2 photos, B&W. Rendering. **MRT**, 63;
    B&W and color. Rendering. **RSD**, illus. 34-36.
Muntner. State Theatre, Cologne: B&W. Set. **SST**, 265.
Rojo, Jerry N. New York Public Theatre, NYC: 1975. B&W. Set. **TSE**, 174, 178, 179.
_____ 1930. B&W. Set. **WTP**, 96.
, National Theatre, Oslo: 1966. B&W. Set. **TSY**, 155.
_____. Burgtheater, Vienna: B&W. Set. **TPH**, photo 296.
Gianni Schicchi.
Neher, Caspar. Komische Oper, Berlin: 1950. B&W. Set. **SDW1**, 72.
The Giant.
Zelenka, Frantisek. Czechoslovakia: B&W. Rendering. **TDT** vol. XXXI, n. 2 (Spring
    1995). 41.
The Giants of the Mountain.
Frigerio, Ezio. 1967. B&W. Set. **SIO**, 55.
Otto, Teo. Schauspielehaus, Zürich: 1949. B&W. Model. **SDW1**, 117.
La Giara.
Sassu, Aligi. La Scala, Milan: 1961-1962. B&W. Rendering & set. **SIO**, 152, 153.
Gideon.
Hays, David. Plymouth Theatre, NYC: 1961. B&W. Set. **SDR**, 57.
A Gift of Time.
Aronson, Boris. Ethel Barrymore Theatre, NYC: 1962. B&W. Set. **TAB**, 158-160. 7
    photos.
Gijsbreght van Aemstel.
Vesseur, Wim. Stadsschouwburg, Amsterdam: 1960. B&W. Rendering. **SDW2**, 145.
Gilette.
Arcenas, Loy. American Repertory Theatre, Cambridge, Massachusetts: Color. Set.
    TCI, vol. 25, n. 3 (Mar 1991). 39.
Gilles de Rais.
Aronson, Boris. Théâtre National Populaire, Villeurbanne, France: 1976. B&W. Set.
    PST, 443.
Gilligan's Island.
Pardess, Yael. Organic Theatre, Chicago: 1992. Color. Set. **TCI**, vol. 27, n. 2 (Feb
    1993). 9.
Gimple the Fool.
Castrigno, Tony. Opera at the 92nd Street "Y", NYC: 1985. B&W. Set. **BSE4**, 101.
The Gin Game.
Mitchell, David. Long Wharf Theatre, New Haven, Connecticut: 1977. B&W. Set.
    ASD1, 124; John Golden Theatre, NYC: 1977. B&W. Set. **TCI**, vol. 12, n. 3 (Mar/
    Apr 1978). 12.
Tiné, Hal. Buffalo Arena Stage, New York: B&W. Set. **SDT**, 282.

Il Gioco dell'Epidemia.
    Rosso, Enrico Colombotto. 1970-1971. B&W. Set. **SIO**, 31, 32.
La Gioconda.
    Brown, Zack. San Francisco Opera: 1983. B&W. Set. **TCI**, vol. 17, n. 9 (Nov/Dec
        1983). 20.
    Jones, Robert Edmond. (project): 1927. B&W. Rendering. **REJ**, 65; B&W. Rendering.
        SCM, 100.
    Montresor, Beni. Metropolitan Opera, NYC: B&W. Set. **TCI**, vol. 10, n. 5 (Oct 1976).
        16, 17; B&W. Rendering. **TCI**, vol. 16, n. 5 (May 1982). 16.
    Santoni, G.B. Chicago Lyric Opera: 1913. B&W. Model. **TDT**, vol. XXV, n. 2 (Sum-
        mer 1989). 10.
Giovanni Sebastiano.
    Guglielminetti, Eugenio. Teatro Communale, Bologna: 1970. B&W. Set. **SDW3**, 207.
The Girl Behind the Counter.
    Hicks, Julian. Wyndham's Theatre, London: 1906. B&W. Set. **MCD**, plate 59.
Girl Crazy.
    Oenslager, Donald. Alvin Theatre, NYC: 1930. B&W. Set. **BWM**, 224; Color. Render-
        ing of curtain. **TDO**, facing 40.
The Girl Friend.
    Harker, Phil & F.L. Lyndhurst. Palace Theatre, London: 1927. B&W. Set. **MCD**, plate
        148.
The Girl from Utah.
    Craven, Hawes, T.E. Ryan, Alfred Terraine, & Joseph Hunter. Adelphi Theatre, Lon-
        don: 1913. B&W. Set. **MCD**, plate 96.
The Girl in the Taxi.
    Baruch & Co. Lyric Theatre, Hammersmith, London: 1912. B&W. Set. **MCD**, plate
        94.
The Girl of the Golden West.
    Adams, Ken. Spoleto Festival, Charleston, South Carolina: 1985. B&W. Rendering.
        TCI, vol. 19, n. 9 (Nov 1985). 16.
    Brockman, C. Lance. Centennial Showboat of the University of Minnesota, Minneapo-
        lis: 1985. B&W. Drop. **BSE4**, 16.
    Gros, Ernest. Belasco Theatre, NYC: 1905. B&W. Set. **MCN**, 26, 27.
    Lee, Eugene. Chicago Lyric Opera: 1978. B&W. Model & set. **ASD1**, 75; Color. Set.
        TCI, vol. 18, n. 8 (Oct 1984). 16.
    McCarry, Charles E. (project): 1986. B&W. Rendering. **DDT**, 298. 3 photos.
    Scott, Michael. Metropolitan Opera, NYC: 1991. B&W. Set. **TCI**, vol. 26, n. 1 (Jan
        1992). 8.
    Seger, Richard. American Conservatory Theatre, San Francisco: 1979. B&W. Set.
        TCI, vol. 14, n. 4 (Sep 1980). 20.
Girls of Summer.
    Aronson, Boris. Longacre Theatre, NYC: 1956. B&W. Set. **TAB**, 304.
Giroflé-Girofla.
    Jacoulov, Georges. Kamerny Theater, Moscow: 1922. B&W. Model. **AST**, 134; Color.
        Model. **RSD**, illus. 192; B&W. Set. **RST**, 148, 149. 3 photos; B&W. Set. **SCM**, 92;
        B&W. Set. **TCS2**, plate 166.
Giselle.
    Berman, Eugene. NYC: 1946. B&W. Rendering & curtain. **SDE**, 44, 45.
Giulio Cesare in Eggito.
    Lowery, Nigel. Bavarian State Opera, Munich: 1994. B&W. Set. **TCI**, vol. 29, n. 2
        (Feb 1995). 8.

Giulio Cesare.
> Varona, José. New York City Opera, Lincoln Center: B&W. Set. **TCI**, vol. 14, n. 5 (Oct 1980). 31.

Give Us Europe.
> Shlepyanov, Ilya. Meyerhold Theatre, Moscow: 1924. B&W. Set. **MOT**, between 184 & 185; B&W. Set. **RSD**, illus. 202; B&W. Set. **TCT**, plates 22, 23.

The Glad Death.
> Tovaglieri, Enrico. 1953. B&W. Rendering. **SDE**, 155.

Glamorous Night.
> Messel, Oliver. Theatre Royal, Drury Lane, London: 1935. B&W. Set. **MCD**, plates 177, 178; B&W. Set. **MEM**, 91; B&W. Set. **OMB**, 95.

The Glass Menagerie.
> Arcenas, Loy. Arena Stage, Washington, DC: 1989. B&W and color. Set. **ASD2**, 11, 12, and between 108 & 109; B&W. Model. **DDT**, 61.
> Borges, Jacobo. Teatro La Comedia, Caracas: 1961. B&W. Set. **SDW2**, 243.
> Edlund, Michael. Mankato State University, Minnesota: B&W. Rendering. **BSE2**, 46.
> Lee, Ming Cho. Tyrone Guthrie Theatre, Minneapolis: 1979. B&W. Set. **TCI**, vol. 18, n. 2 (Feb 1984). 19; 1983. B&W. Set. **TCI**, vol. 18, n. 2 (Feb 1984). 15; McCarter Theatre, Princeton, New Jersey: B&W. Set. **TCI**, vol. 25, n. 4 (Apr 1991). 17.
> Mielziner, Jo. Playhouse Theatre, NYC: 1945. B&W. Rendering. **DTT**, 125. Exterior; B&W. Rendering. **DTT**, 127. Interior; B&W. Rendering. **RSD**, illus. 452; B&W. Rendering. **SDA**, 152. 2 photos; B&W. Set. **WTP**, 190, 191. 3 photos.
> Payne, Darwin Reid. B&W. Sketch. **SIP**, 296.

Das Gleichgewicht.
> Herrmann, Karl-Ernst. Salzburg Festival: 1993. B&W. Set. **TCI**, vol. 27, n. 9 (Nov 1993). 18.

Glengarry Glen Ross.
> Griffin, Hayden. National Theatre (Cottesloe), London: 1983. B&W. Set. **BTD**, 89.
> Landwehr, Hugh. Capital Repertory Company, Albany, New York: 1989. B&W. Sketch. **ASD2**, 90, 92; B&W. Rendering. **DDT**, 586.
> Merritt, Michael. Goodman Theatre, Chicago: 1983. B&W. Set. **ASD2**, 138. 2 photos.
> Rigdon, Kevin. Goodman Theatre, Chicago: 1984. B&W. Set. **TCI**, vol. 21, n. 2 (Feb 1987). 31.
> Soule, Robert D. Downstairs Theatre, Trinity Repertory Company, Providence, Rhode Island: 1987. B&W. Set. **TCI**, vol. 22, n. 9 (Nov 1988). 62.

Gli Esami non Finiscono Mai.
> Maccari, Mino. Teatro della Pergola, Italy: 1973. B&W. Set. **SDW4**, illus. 252, 253.

The Glittering Gate.
> Bragdon, Claude. USA: 1933. B&W. Rendering. **TAT**, plate 489.

Gloria.
> Scelzo, Filippo. Maggio Musicale Fiorentino, Florence: 1953. B&W. Rendering. **SDE**, 151.

Gloriana.
> Piper, John. Royal Opera House, Covent Garden, London: 1953. B&W. Set. **CGA**, 144; B&W and color. Rendering. **FCS**, plate 212, color plate 29; B&W and color. Rendering. **SDO**, 245, plate 29.

Glory! Hallelujah!
> Wurtzel, Stuart. American Conservatory Theatre, San Francisco: B&W. Set. **TCI**, vol. 6, n. 5 (Oct 1972). 16; B&W. Set. **TCI**, vol. 14, n. 1 (Jan/Feb 1980). 39.

Die Glückliche Hand.
>   Jones, Robert Edmond. Metropolitan Opera, NYC: 1930. B&W. Rendering. **FCS**,
>   plate 205; B&W. Rendering. **SDO**, 235.
>   Krem, Fritz. State Opera, Berlin: B&W. Set. **SCM**, 66. 2 photos.

Die Gnadiges Fraulein.
>   Lee, Ming Cho. Longacre Theatre, NYC: 1966. B&W. Model. **ASD1**, 98; B&W.
>   Model. **DPT**, 242; B&W. Rendering. **TDT**, n. 24 (Feb 1971). 8; B&W. Model.
>   **SDB**, 38.

The Goat Song.
>   Simonson, Lee. Guild Theatre (Virginia Theatre), NYC: 1926. B&W. Rendering.
>   **BSE4**, 50; B&W. Set. **PLT**, illus. 36, 37, 62; B&W. Set. **SDC**, plate 127. 2 photos;
>   B&W and color. Rendering & set. **TDT**, vol. XXII, n. 3 (Fall 1986). front cover, 7,
>   8. 4 photos.

God is Not Guilty.
>   Dupont, Jacques. Théâtre des Mathurins, Paris: 1941. B&W. Rendering. **SDW1**, 96.

God Loves Us.
>   Thompson, Woodman. Maxine Elliot Theatre, NYC: 1926. B&W. Set. **TCS2**, plate
>   177.

The God of Vengeance.
>   _____. Deutsches Theater, Berlin: 1907. B&W. Set. **MRH**, facing 220.

The Gods of Amsterdam.
>   Hanák, Ján. Statni Divadlo, Kosice, Czechoslovakia: 1959. B&W. Rendering. **SDW2**,
>   41.

The Gods of the Mountain.
>   Zimmerer, Frank J. Punch and Judy Theatre, NYC: 1919. B&W. Set. **MCN**, 45.

Godspell.
>   Wexler, Peter. Mark Taper Forum, Los Angeles: 1971. B&W. Rendering. **TDP**, 121.
>   _____. Cherry Lane Theatre, NYC: 1971. Color. Set. **BWM**, 314.
>   _____. Equity Library Theatre, NYC: B&W. Set. **TCI**, vol. 15, n. 6 (Jun/Jul
>   1981). 24.

Gohiiki Kanjincho.
>   _____. Pomona College: 1987. Color. Set. **TCI**, vol. 22, n. 3 (Mar 1988). 43.

Going Greek.
>   Hubert, René. Gaiety Theatre, London: 1937. B&W. Set. **MCD**, plate 182.

The Gold Diggers.
>   Gros, Ernest. Lyceum Theatre, NYC: 1919. B&W. Set. **MCN**, 48.

Gold Eagle Guy.
>   Oenslager, Donald. Morosco Theatre, NYC: 1934. B&W. Set. **MCN**, 121.

The Golden Apple.
>   Eckart, William & Jean. Phoenix Theatre, NYC: 1954. B&W. Rendering & show
>   curtain. **DDT**, 394, 438, 439. 3 photos; B&W. Rendering. **SDA**, 253; B&W. Ren-
>   dering. **SDB**, 61.

Golden Boy.
>   Gorelik, Mordecai. USA: 1937. B&W. Set. **SDA**, 175.
>   Griffin, Hayden. National Theatre, London: 1984. B&W. Rendering & set. **TCI**, vol.
>   19, n. 9 (Nov 1985). 20, 24.
>   Walton, Tony. Majestic Theatre, NYC: 1964. B&W. Set. **BWM**, 302.

The Golden Coach.
>   Polidori, Gianni. 1952. B&W. Rendering. **SDE**, 133.

The Golden Cockerel.
  Björnson, Maria. Scottish Opera, Edinburgh: B&W. Set. **TCI**, vol. 15, n. 7 (Aug/Sep
    1981). 28.
The Golden Doom.
  Hume, Samuel J. Arts and Crafts Theatre, Detroit: B&W. Set. **TCS2**, plate 62.
  _____. Little Theatre, Citizen House, Bath, England: 1932. B&W. Set. **SCM**,
    36.
The Golden Door.
  Aronson, Boris. (project): 1948. B&W. Rendering. **TAB**, 300.
The Golden Head.
  Masson, André. Odeon Theatre, Paris: 1959. B&W. Rendering. **RSD**, illus. 497; B&W.
    Rendering. **SDW2**, 95.
Golden Rainbow.
  Randolph, Robert. Shubert Theatre, NYC: 1968. B&W. Set. **DPT**, 207.
The Golden Windows.
  Wilson, Robert. Kammerspiele, Munich: 1982. B&W. Rendering & set. **RWT**, 90, 91.
    6 photos; Brooklyn Academy of Music, New York: 1985. B&W and color. Set.
    TDT, vol. XXII, n. 1 (Spring 1986). front cover, 6, 12, 13. 4 photos.
Goldilocks.
  Larkin, Peter. Lunt-Fontanne Theatre, NYC: 1958. B&W. Rendering. **DPT**, 30.
Goldoni E Le Sue 16 Commedie Nuove.
  Paladini, Vinicio. Italy: 1931. B&W. Rendering. **SCM**, 78.
The Golem.
  Aronson, Boris. (project): 1929. B&W. Rendering. **TAB**, 294.
  Luzzati, Emanuele. La Pergola, Florence: 1969. B&W. Rendering & set. **RSD**, illus.
    575, 576; B&W. Rendering & set. **SIO**, 90, 91. 3 photos.
Good.
  Ultz. Warehouse, London: 1981. B&W. Set. **TCI**, vol. 17, n. 7 (Aug/Sep 1983). 37. 2
    photos.
Good Bye Mister Freud.
  Chauveau, Patrick & Michel Lebois. Théâtre de la Porte Saint-Martin, Paris: 1974.
    B&W. Set. **SDW4**, illus. 374, 375.
The Good Earth.
  Simonson, Lee. Guild Theatre (Virginia Theatre), NYC: 1932. B&W. Rendering.
    BSE4, 51; B&W. Rendering. **TDT**, vol. XXII, n. 3 (Fall 1986). 5, 9.
The Good Girl.
  Ratto, Gianni. Campo San Trovaso, Venice: 1950. B&W. Rendering. **SDW1**, 130.
Good Gracious Annabelle.
  Jones, Robert Edmond. Republic Theatre, NYC: 1916. B&W. Set. **SDA**, 198.
The Good Hope.
  _____. Tyrone Guthrie Theatre, Minneapolis: 1995. B&W and color. Set. **TDT**
    vol. XXXI, n. 2 (Spring 1995). Cover, 2.
A Good Little Devil.
  Unitt, Edward G. & Wickes. Republic Theatre, NYC: 1913. B&W. Set. **MCN**, 41.
Good News.
  Oenslager, Donald. 46th Street Theatre, NYC: 1927. B&W. Set. **WMC**, 135.
The Good Person of Szechuan (see *The Good Woman of Setzuan*).
The Good Soldier Schweik.
  Griswold, Mary & John Paoletti. Chicago Opera Theatre: 1981. B&W. Set. **TCI**, vol.
    18, n. 3 (Mar 1984). 24.

Grosz, George & Erwin Piscator. Theater am Nollendorfplatz, Berlin: 1928. B&W.
Set. **NTO**, facing 420. 5 photos; B&W. Set. **RSD**, illus. 241; B&W. Set. **TBB**, 109;
B&W. Set. **TPH**, photo 377.

Heinrich, Rudolf. Komische Oper, Berlin: 1960. B&W. Set. **SDW2**, 53.

Melena, Miroslav. Czechoslovakia: 1987. B&W. Model. **TDT**, vol. XXIII, n. 4 (Winter
1988). 49.

_____. Yiddish Art Theatre (Second Avenue Theatre), NYC: 1937. B&W. Set.
WTP, 108, 109. 5 photos.

The Good Times Are Killing Me.

_____. NYC: Color. Set. **TCI**, vol. 25, n. 9 (Nov 1991). 52.

The Good Woman of Setzuan.

Ali, Sakina Mohamed. Masrah al Geib, Al Kahira, Cairo: 1967. B&W. Set. **SDW3**,
115.

Arcenas, Loy. American Repertory Theatre, Cambridge, Massachusetts: Color. Set.
TCI, vol. 25, n. 3 (Mar 1991). 38.

Aronson, Boris. Stanford Repertory Theatre, California: 1966. B&W. Set. **PST**, 414.

Brill, Robert. La Jolla Playhouse, California: 1994. Color. Set. **TCI**, vol. 28, n. 9 (Nov
1994). 8.

Conklin, John. Williamstown Theatre Festival, Massachusetts: 1973. B&W. Set. **TCI**,
vol. 14, n. 3 (May/Jun 1980). 19.

Feiner, Harry. Missouri Repertory Theatre, Kansas City: 1981. B&W. Rendering.
BSE2, 11.

Freyer, Achim. Volksbühne, Berlin: 1969. B&W. Set. **SDW4**, illus. 241, 242; B&W.
Set. **TCI**, vol. 13, n. 5 (Oct 1979). 21.

Hamel, Niels. Staddsschowburg, Nijmegen, Netherlands: 1968. B&W. Set. **SDW3**,
114.

Long, Yang. China: B&W. Rendering. **TDT**, vol. XXVII, n. 4 (Fall 1991). 24.

Maronek, James E. Goodman Theatre, Chicago: 1960. B&W. Rendering. **SDW2**, 236.

Puigserver, Fabia. Compania Teatre Llure, Spain: 1992. B&W. Set. **TCI**, vol. 26, n. 4
(Apr 1992). 34.

Schmidt, Douglas W. Repertory Theatre of Lincoln Center, NYC: 1970. B&W. Set.
SDW3, 115; B&W. Rendering. **TDT**, vol. XVII, n. 2 (Summer 1981). 17.

Wittstein, Ed. Playhouse in the Park, Cincinnati: B&W. Set. **TCI**, vol. 5, n. 1 (Jan/Feb
1971). 16.

_____. Stanford Repertory Theatre, California: 1966. B&W. Set. **TSY**, 207.

_____. University of North Carolina, Chapel Hill: B&W. Set. **TCI**, vol. 5, n. 1
(Jan/Feb 1971). 13, 14.

The Good-Humoured Ladies.

Pizzi, Pier Luigi. La Fenice, Venice: 1960. Color. Rendering. **SDW2**, 127.

Goodtime Charley.

Ter-Arutunian, Rouben. Palace Theatre, NYC: 1975. B&W. Model. **DPT**, 104.

Götterdämmerung.

Brazda, Jan. Bayerische Staatsoper, Munich: 1976. B&W. Set. **OPE**, 190, 192, 194,
196.

Conklin, John. San Francisco Opera House: 1985. B&W. Sketch & model. **DDT**, 480;
B&W. Set. **TCI**, vol. 20, n. 2 (Feb 1986). 27.

Dudley, William. Beyreuth Festival Theatre: 1983. B&W. Set. **TCI**, vol. 18, n. 3 (Mar
1984). 16.

Heinrich, Rudolf. Opernhaus am Karl-Marx Platz, Leipzig: 1976. B&W. Set. **OPE**,
184, 192, 194, 196, 198.

Israel, Robert. Seattle Opera: 1986/1987. Color. Set. **ASD2**, between 108 & 109; B&W. Set. **TCI**, vol. 22, n. 5 (May 1988). 22. 2 photos.

Koltai, Ralph. English National Opera, London: B&W. Set. **TCI**, vol. 11, n. 1 (Jan/Feb 1977). 13.

Marussig, Guido. La Scala, Milan: 1942. B&W. Rendering. **SDE**, 120.

Peduzzi, Richard. Beyreuth Festival Theatre: 1976. B&W. Set. **OPE**, 191, 192, 194, 196, 198; 1979. B&W. Set. **TCI**, vol. 14, n. 1 (Jan/Feb 1980). 23.

Richter-Forgách, Thomas. Opernhaus, Kassel: 1974. B&W. Rendering. **OPE**, 182, 192, 194, 196, 198, 199.

Schneider-Siemssen, Günther. Grosses Festpielhaus, Salzburg: 1970. B&W and color. Set. **OPE**, 182, 192, 195, 197; Metropolitan Opera, NYC: 1992. B&W. Set. **TCI**, vol. 10, n. 5 (Oct 1976). 18; Color. Set. **TCI**, vol. 27, n. 3 (Mar 1993). 24; B&W. Set. **TCI**, vol. 12, n. 6 (Oct 1978). 31.

Simonson, Lee. Metropolitan Opera, NYC: 1948. B&W. Rendering. **MOM**, 11; B&W. Set. **SDA**, 269; B&W. Set. **TAS**, 160. 2 photos.

Svoboda, Josef. Covent Garden, London: 1976. B&W. Set. **JSS**, 72. Act I, sc. 1; B&W. Set. **JSS**, 74. Act III, sc. 1; B&W. Set. **JSS**, 77; Color. Set. **JSS**, between 54 & 55. Act I; B&W. Set. **OPE**, 186, 192, 195, 196, 198; B&W. Set. **STS**, 85; Grand Theater, Geneva: 1977. B&W. Set. **JSS**, 92. Act III, sc. 1; B&W. Set. **JSS**, 92. Act III, sc. 2; Color. Set. **JSS**, between 54 & 55. Act I, sc. 1; Color. Set. **JSS**, between 54 & 55. Act I, sc. 2.

Wagner, Wieland. Beyreuth Festival Theatre: 1965. B&W and color. Set. **OPE**, 181, 192, 197, 199; B&W. Set. **TCI**, vol. 3, n. 4 (Sep 1969). 29, 33; 1970. Color. Set. **SDW4**, illus. 138, 139.

Wendel, Heinrich. B&W. Set. **OPE**, 48.

Wotruba, Fritz. Deutsches Staatsoper, Berlin: 1967. Color. Rendering. **AST**, 230. 4 photos.

Government Inspector (see *The Inspector General*).

The Governor's Lady.

Gros, Ernest. USA: 1908. B&W. Set. **SDA**, 23. (see caption on pg. 22).

The Grabbing of the Fairy.

Cate, Donald and Regina. Magic Theatre, San Francisco: 1976. B&W. Set. **TCI**, vol. 14, n. 4 (Sep 1980). 23.

La Gran Decision.

_____. INTAR Hispanic American Theatre, NYC: B&W. Set. **TCI**, vol. 13, n. 4 (Sep 1979). 52.

Grand Hotel.

Adar, Arnon. Tel Aviv: B&W. Sketch. **SDL**, 84.

Bernstein, Aline. NYC: 1930. B&W. Set. **SFT**, 293.

Hasait, Max. London: B&W. Set. **SFT**, 295.

Platt, Livingston. 1933. B&W. Set. **SDA**, 232.

Walton, Tony. Martin Beck Theatre, NYC: 1989. B&W. Model. **DDT**, 44; B&W and color. Set. **MBM**, 108, 113, 123; B&W. Show curtain. **MBM**, 13; B&W. Rendering. **SDD**, between 210 & 211; Color. Model & set. **TCI**, vol. 24, n. 1 (Jan 1990). 42, 44; (tour): 1991. Color. Rendering. **TCI**, vol. 25, n. 3 (Mar 1991). 14.

La Grand Macabre.

O'Brien, Timothy. English National Opera, London: 1982. Color. Set. **BTD**, 105.

Grand Street Follies.

Bernstein, Aline. Neighborhood Playhouse, NYC: 1929. B&W. Rendering. **SDD**, between 210 & 211.

The Grapes of Wrath.
>   Rigdon, Kevin. Steppenwolf Theatre, Chicago: 1990. Color. Set. **TCI**, vol. 24, n. 9
>   (Nov 1990). 19; B&W. Set. **TCI**, vol. 23, n. 1 (Jan 1989). 96.

The Grass Harp.
>   Tilton, James. Martin Beck Theatre, NYC: 1971. B&W. Set. **DPT**, 371.
>   Zimmermann, Jörg. Residenz Theater, Munich: B&W. Set. **DSL**, figure 2.8(a).

A Grave Undertaking.
>   Stevens, John Wright. Seattle Repertory Theatre: 1974. B&W. Set. **TCI**, vol. 9, n. 6
>   (Nov/Dec 1975). 14.

Grease.
>   Clark, Bradford. Mankato State University, Minnesota: B&W. Set. **TCI**, vol. 20, n. 5
>   (May 1986). 35.
>   Schmidt, Douglas W. Eden Theatre, NYC: 1972. B&W. Rendering. **ASD1**, 147; B&W.
>   Set. **BMF**, 79; B&W. Set. **BWM**, 313; B&W. Rendering. **DPT**, 64; B&W. Render-
>   ing. **TCI**, vol. 20, n. 5 (May 1986). 34; B&W. Rendering. **TDT**, vol. XVII, n. 2
>   (Summer 1981). 16.

The Great Air Robbery.
>   _____. San Francisco Mime Troupe: 1975. Color. Set. **TCI**, vol. 18, n. 5 (May
>   1984). 11.

Great American Backstage Musical.
>   Klein, Allen Charles. Montgomery Playhouse, San Francisco: 1977. B&W. Set. **TCI**,
>   vol. 11, n. 6 (Nov/Dec 1977). 10.

The Great American Goof.
>   Aronson, Boris. Center Theatre, NYC: 1940. B&W and color. Rendering & model.
>   **TAB**, 16, 70-72, 296. 13 photos.

Great Cyril.
>   Rabinovitch, Isaac. Vakhtangov Theatre, Moscow: 1957. B&W. Rendering. **SDW2**,
>   191.

Great Day in the Morning.
>   Wilson, Robert. Théâtre des Champs-Elysées, Paris: 1982. B&W. Set. **RWT**, 92, 93. 3
>   photos.

The Great Divide.
>   La Ferla, Sandro. Virginia Museum Theatre, Richmond: 1970. Color. Set. **DPT**, be-
>   tween 284 & 285.
>   _____. C.W. Post College, Long Island, New York: 1971. B&W. Set. **TCI**, vol.
>   6, n. 5 (Oct 1972). 24.

Great Expectations.
>   Buderwitz, Tom. Arizona Theatre Company, Tucson: B&W. Set. **SDT**, 297.

The Great Gatsby.
>   Farmer, Peter. Pittsburgh Ballet Theatre: B&W. Set. **SDL**, 4.

The Great God Brown.
>   Aronson, Boris. Lyceum Theatre, NYC: 1972. B&W. Model. **TAB**, 170, 309.
>   Jones, Robert Edmond. Greenwich Village Theatre, NYC: 1926. B&W. Set. **MCN**,
>   73.
>   Heythum, Antonín. National Theatre, Prague: 1928. B&W. Rendering. **TAS**, 98; B&W.
>   Rendering. **TAT**, plates 170, 171.

The Great Hoss Pistol.
>   Rojo, Jerry N. New York University: 1973. B&W. Sketch, model, & set. **TSE**, 170-
>   172. 3 photos.

The Great Magoo.
>   Rosse, Herman. Selwyn Theatre, NYC: 1932. B&W. Rendering. **SDB**, 33, 34.

Straiges, Tony. Hartford Stage, Connecticut: 1982. B&W. Model. **DDT**, 171.

Johnson, Albert R. Center Theatre, NYC: 1934. B&W. Set. **RBS**, 103; B&W. Set. **SDA**, 92, 93. 5 photos.

The Great Waltz.

Johnson, Albert. Center Theatre, NYC: 1934. B&W. Set. **MCN**, 119.

The Great White Hope.

Wagner, Robin. Alvin Theatre, NYC: 1968. B&W. Set. **TCI**, vol. 4, n. 3 (May/Jun 1970). 32.

The Great World Theater.

Roller, Alfred. Kollegienkirche, Salzburg: 1922. B&W. Set. **TPH**, photo 338.

Einsiedeln, Switzerland: 1935. B&W. Set. **TPH**, photo 398.

The Greek Passion.

_____. Indiana University Opera Company: B&W. Set. **TCI**, vol. 15, n. 8 (Oct 1981). 21.

The Greeks.

Hastings. Ohio State University, Columbus: 1988. B&W. Set. **TCI**, vol. 24, n. 10 (Dec 1990). 78.

O'Connor, Charles. University of Southern California, Los Angeles: B&W. Rendering. **SDT**, 291.

Wade, John. Hillberry Repertory Theatre: B&W. Rendering. **SDT**, 64.

The Green Bird.

Dunn, Henry. Theatre de la Jeune Lune, Minneapolis: 1993. B&W. Set. **TCI**, vol. 28, n. 2 (Feb 1994). 6.

Green Fields.

Luftglass, E. Habima, Tel Aviv: 1935. B&W. Set. **SDW2**, 119.

Green Grow the Lilacs.

Sovey, Raymond. Guild Theatre, NYC: 1931. B&W. Set. **MCN**, 101; B&W. Set. **SCM**, 125. 2 photos; B&W. Set. **SDA**, 239. 2 photos.

Jones, Robert Edmond. Mansfield Theatre, NYC: 1930. B&W. Rendering. **REJ**, 73, 75, 77; B&W. Set. **WTP**, 174, 175. 6 photos.

The Green Pastures.

Jones, Robert Edmond. Mansfield Theatre, NYC: 1930. B&W. Set. **MCN**, 96.

The Green Table.

Heckroth, Heinrich. Städtische Bühnen, Essen: 1932. B&W. Rendering & set. **RSD**, illus. 138, 139.

Greenwich Village Follies of 1922.

Greer, Howard. Shubert Theatre, NYC: 1922. B&W. Set. **MCN**, 60.

Greenwillow.

Larkin, Peter. Alvin Theatre, NYC: 1960. Color. Rendering. **TCI**, vol. 23, n. 1 (Jan 1989). 43.

Grind.

Dunham, Clarke. NYC: 1985. B&W. Set. **HPA**, 139; Color. Set. **MBM**, 80, 81, 85; B&W and color. Set. **TCI**, vol. 19, n. 7 (Aug/Sep 1985). 42, 43.

Das Grosse Welttheater.

_____. Deutsches Theater, Berlin: B&W. Set. **SCM**, 62.

_____. Kollegienkirche, Salzburg: B&W. Set. **TCS2**, plates 368, 369.

Grotesques.

Jonson, Raymond. Chicago Little Theatre: B&W. Set. **SDC**, plate 58.

Guan Hanqing.

Jiangang, Mao. China: B&W. Model. **TDT** vol. XXXI, n. 2 (Spring 1995). 9.

La Guardia Vigilante.
> Angelini, Sandro. Teatro delle Novità, Bergamo: 1953. B&W. Rendering. **SDE**, 27.

The Guardsman.
> Burroughs, Robert C. University of Arizona, Tucson: B&W. Set. **SDT**, 117.
> Mielziner, Jo. Garrick Theatre, NYC: 1924. B&W. Set. **MCN**, 68; B&W. Rendering.
> **SDA**, 199.

The Guelder Rose Grove.
> Petritzki, Anatoli. Maly Theatre, Moscow: 1950. B&W. Rendering. **SDW2**, 190.

La Guerre de Troie n' aura pas Lieu.
> Andreu, Mariano. Théâtre de l'Athénée, Paris: 1936. B&W. Set. **SOW**, plate 64;
> B&W. Set. **TPH**, photo 360.
> Kokkos, Yannis. Paris: 1971. B&W. Set. **SDB**, 187.

The Guilded Age.
> Kellogg, Marjorie Bradley. Hartford Stage, Connecticut: B&W. Set. **TCI**, vol. 25, n. 9
> (Nov 1991). 43.

La Guirlande de Campra.
> Harvey, Peter. New York City Ballet, Lincoln Center: 1966. B&W. Rendering. **DPT**,
> 31.

Gustav III.
> Montelius, Olle. State Theatre, Göteborg, Sweden: 1973. B&W. Set. **SDW4**, illus. 181.

Guys and Dolls.
> Edmunds, Kate. Seattle Repertory Theatre: 1985. B&W and color. Set. **TCI**, vol. 20, n.
> 5 (May 1986). 18, 19.
> Fontaine, Joel C. 1979. B&W. Rendering. **BSE1**, 36.
> Gunter, John. National Theatre (Olivier), London: 1982. Color. Set. **BTD**, 166. 3
> photos; B&W. Set. **TDT**, vol. XXV, n. 3 (Fall 1989). 17; B&W. Set. **TDT**, vol.
> XIX, n. 1 (Spring 1983). 9.
> Mielziner, Jo. 46th Street Theatre, NYC: 1950. B&W. Set. **BWM**, 266; B&W. Render-
> ing & elevations. **DPT**, 186. Crap-game; B&W. Rendering. **DPT**, 53. Times Square
> drop; Color. Rendering. **DTT**, 168. Side street off Broadway; Color. Rendering.
> **DTT**, 169. Crap game; B&W. Rendering. **SDW1**, 201; B&W. Set. **TCI**, vol. 20, n.
> 5 (May 1986). 18; B&W. Set. **TMT**, 179; B&W. Set. **WMC**, 265; B&W. Set.
> **WTP**, 246, 247. 4 photos.
> Morton, Mark W. Alliance Theatre, Atlanta: 1985. B&W. Set. **TCI**, vol. 20, n. 5 (May
> 1986). 18.
> Walton, Tony. Martin Beck Theatre, NYC: 1992. Color. Rendering. **DDT**, 24c; Color.
> Model, rendering, & set. **TCI**, vol. 26, n. 7 (Aug/Sep 1992). 5, 40-43. 7 photos.
> Zalon, Paul. Tyrone Guthrie Theatre, Minneapolis: 1983. B&W and color. Set. **TCI**,
> vol. 20, n. 5 (May 1986). 17, 19.

Gyges and his Ring.
> Prätorius, Friedrich. Hebbel-Theater, Berlin: 1948. B&W. Rendering. **SDW1**, 74.
> Hecht, Torsten. State Theatre, Mainz: B&W. Set. **TCS2**, plate 132.
> Linnebach, Adolf. Hoftheater, Dresden: B&W. **TCS2**, plate 188.

The Gyp's Princess.
> Beaton, Cecil. ADC Theatre, Cambridge: 1923. B&W. Rendering. **CBS**, 19.

Gypsy.
> Foy, Kenneth. St. James Theatre, NYC: 1989. B&W and color. Set. **SON**, 31, 56, 57,
> 59.
> Mielziner, Jo. Broadway Theatre, NYC: 1959. Color. Set. **BMF**, 35; B&W. Set. **BMF**,
> 66; Color. Set. **BWM**, 274, 275; B&W. Rendering. **DTT**, 195. Italian restaurant;

B&W. Rendering. **DTT**, 196. Finale; B&W. Rendering. **SDA**, 155; B&W. Set.
SON, 52; B&W. Set. **WMC**, 256.

Randolph, Robert. Winter Garden Theatre, NYC: 1974. B&W. Sketch. **DPT**, 205. 5
scenes; B&W and color. Set. **SON**, 33, 59.

Sandmaier, Robert. Fort Wayne Civic Theatre, Indiana: B&W. Set. **TCI**, vol. 20, n. 5
(May 1986). 32.

_____. Pacific Conservatory of the Performing Arts, Santa Maria, California:
B&W. Set. **TCI**, vol. 20, n. 5 (May 1986). 33.

Gyubal Wahazar.

Coburg, Wally. Towson State College: 1974. B&W. Set. **TCI**, vol. 8, n. 4 (Sep 1974).
4.

-H-

H.M.S. Pinafore.

Scheffler, John. Lehman College Center, Bronx, New York: 1982. B&W. Sketch &
rendering. **DDT**, 185. 2 photos.

Hadibuk.

_____. Habima Studio, Moscow: 1922. B&W. Set. **RST**, 80, 81.

Hadrian of Rome.

Musika, Frantisek. State Theatre, Brno: 1930. B&W. Rendering. **TDT**, n. 42 (Fall
1975). 25.

Hadrian VII.

Fletcher, Robert. American Conservatory Theatre, San Francisco: 1980. B&W. Set.
TCI, vol. 6, n. 5 (Oct 1972). 14.

Williams, Jerry. Alley Theatre, Houston: B&W. Set. **TCI**, vol. 7, n. 3 (May/Jun 1973).
9.

The Haggadah.

Taymor, Julie. Public Theatre, NYC: B&W. Set. **TCI**, vol. 16, n. 8 (Oct 1982). 25.

Hail Scrawdyke! or Little Malcolm and His Struggle Against the Eunuchs.

Merritt, Michael. Goodman Theatre II, Chicago: 1979. B&W. Set. **ASD2**, 131.

Hair.

Hamilton, Rob. Chicago: B&W. Rendering. **TDT**, vol. XXVI, n. 1 (Spring 1990). 10
of insert.

Ming Cho. New York Shakespeare Festival Public Theatre, NYC: 1967. Color. Rendering. **ASD1**, between 70 & 71; Color. Rendering. **SDW3**, 213.

Wagner, Robin. Biltmore Theatre, NYC: 1968. B&W. Sketch. **ASD1**, 161; B&W. Set.
WMC, 349.

The Hairy Ape.

Pitoëff, Georges. Théâtre des Arts, Paris: 1929. B&W. Set. **RSD**, illus. 422; B&W. Set.
SCM, 54; B&W. Set. **TPH**, photo 361.

Stenberg, Vladimir & Georgiy A. Kamerny (Chamber) Theatre, Moscow: 1926. B&W.
Model. **AST**, 135; B&W. Model. **RSD**, illus. 194; B&W and color. Rendering &
set. **RST**, 236. 2 photos; B&W. Set. **SCM**, 88; B&W. Set. **TSS**, 522.

Throckmorton, Cleon & Robert Edmond Jones. Provincetown Playhouse, NYC: 1920.
B&W. Set. **TSS**, 522; 1922. B&W. Set. **TPH**, photo 456.

Vyzga, Bernard. Dartmouth College, Hanover, New Hampshire: 1979. B&W. Render -
ing. **BSE1**, 10. 2 photos.

_____. University of Wisconsin, Madison: B&W. Set. **TDT**, vol. XXVIII, n. 2
(Spring 1992). 5 of insert.

Hajj.
> Archer, Julie. Mabou Mines, NYC: 1983. B&W. Set. **BSE4**, 65.

The Hall.
> Borisch, Frank. Bühnen der Stadt, Magdeburg, Germany: 1969. B&W. Set. **SDW3**,
> 148.

Halloween.
> Bay, Howard. Florida State University, Tallahassee: 1972. Color. Rendering of projec-
> tion design. **CSD**, 65; B&W. Rendering. **SDB**, 193; B&W. Rendering. **TCI**, vol.
> 17, n. 2 (Feb 1983). 17.

The Halloween Tree.
> Dodd, Joseph D. Honolulu Theatre for Youth: 1979. B&W. Rendering. **BSE2**, 9.

Hamlet.
> Akimov, Nikolai. Vakhtangov Theatre, Moscow: 1932. B&W. Rendering. **RSC**, 9;
> B&W. Set. **RST**, 1932; B&W. Set. **SCM**, 90; B&W. Set. **SOS**, 222.
> Altman, Günther. Germany: B&W. Model. **TDT**, vol. XII, n. 3 (Fall 1976). 36.
> Altman, Nathan. Rousski Dramatitcheski Teatr, Kiev: 1954. B&W. **SDW2**, 178.
> Appia, Adolphe. B&W. Rendering. **SDC**, plate 113.
> Barkla, Jack. Tyrone Guthrie Theatre, Minneapolis: 1978. B&W. Set. **TDT**, vol. XXII,
> n. 4 (Winter 1987). 9.
> Bel Geddes, Norman. Broadhurst Theatre, NYC: 1931. B&W. Set. **SDA**, 213; B&W.
> Model. **SOS**, 173; B&W. Model. **SOW**, facing frontispiece, plate 49; B&W. Model
> & set. **TAS**, 166, 167. 4 photos; NYC: 1931. B&W. Model. **TPH**, photo 475.
> Björnson, Maria. Royal Shakespeare Company, GB: 1984. B&W. Set. **BTD**, 53. 4
> photos; B&W. Set. **SDT**, 275.
> Boerner, Edward. University of West Virginia: 1979. B&W. Set. **TCI**, vol. 14, n. 4
> (Sep 1980). 15.
> Borovsky, David. Taganka Theatre, Moscow: 1972. B&W. Set. **SDW4**, illus. 26-30;
> B&W. Set. **TCI**, vol. 12, n. 7 (Nov/Dec 1978). 32.
> Bragdon, Claude. 1918: B&W. Rendering. **SDC**, plate 52.
> Bury, John. Royal Shakespeare Theatre, Stratford-upon-Avon: 1965. B&W. Set. **RSD**,
> illus. 520; Lyttleton, Theatre, London: 1977. B&W. Set. **TCI**, vol. 11, n. 5 (Oct
> 1977). 33.
> Cesarini, Pino. Lake of Garda, Italy: 1953. B&W. Rendering. **SDE**, 57. 2 photos.
> Chaney, Stewart & Jo Mielziner. Empire Theatre, NYC: 1936. B&W. Rendering. **DTT**,
> 93-96. 4 photos; B&W. Set. **SDA**, 214, 215. 4 photos; B&W. Rendering & set.
> **TAS**, 170, 171. 4 photos.
> Conklin, John. Hartford Stage, Connecticut: 1987. B&W. Set. **DDT**, 478; Color. Set.
> **TCI**, vol. 25, n. 9 (Nov 1991). 42.
> Craig, Edward Gordon. 1900. B&W. Rendering. **EGC**, plate 14a; 1901. B&W. Ren-
> dering. **EGC**, plate 14b; 1904. B&W. Rendering. **EGC**, plate 15; B&W. Render-
> ing. **OAT**, 136. Act I, sc. 4; B&W. Rendering. **TDT**, n. 29 (May 1972). 15, 16;
> B&W. Rendering. **TNT**, facing 33; 1907. B&W. Rendering. **COT**, 151; 1907.
> B&W. Rendering. **SOS**, 140; B&W. Rendering. **TNT**, II; 1909. B&W. Model &
> set. **EGC**, plates 17, 18, 20b. 5 photos; Moscow Art Theatre: 1911. B&W. Model.
> **COT**, 144; B&W. Rendering & model. **DMS**, plates 19-21; B&W. Rendering.
> **EGC**, plate 16; B&W. Model. **SDG**, 151; B&W. Model. **SDR**, 18. Act II, sc. 2;
> B&W. Model. **SDR**, 19. Act V, sc. 2; B&W. Rendering. **TNT**, facing 81; 1912.
> B&W. Set. **RSD**, illus. 92; B&W. Rendering. **SDC**, plate 67; B&W. Rendering.
> **TNT**, facing 83.
> Creuz, Serge. Koninklijke Vlaamse Schouwburg, Brussels: 1972. B&W. Set. **SDW4**,
> illus. 25.

Crowley, Bob. Barbican Theatre, London: 1993. Color. Set. **TCI**, vol. 27, n. 4 (Apr 1993). 40, 41. 4 photos.

Dam, Jan Van. B&W. Rendering. **DIT**, plate 114.

Erler, Fritz. Künstlertheater, Munich: 1909. Color. Rendering. **MRH**, facing 48; B&W. Rendering. **TCS2**, plate 59; B&W. Set. **TPH**, photo 333.

Evans, Bill. Kansas Shakespeare Festival: 1972. B&W. Set. **TCI**, vol. 7, n. 2 (Mar/Apr 1973). 8.

Funicello, Ralph. Old Globe Theatre, San Diego: 1990. B&W. Model. **TDT** vol. XXXI, n. 2 (Spring 1995). 16.

Gamrekeli, Irakly. Rustaveli Theatre, Tbilisi: 1925. B&W. Sketch & set. **RST**, 115, 172, 173. 3 photos.

Havemann, Franz. Deutsches Nationaltheater, Weimar. 1960. B&W. Set. **SDW2**, 50.

Hoffman, Vlastislav. National Theatre, Prague: 1926. B&W. Set. **SCM**, 82; B&W. Set. **SDC**, plate 120; B&W. Set. **SOW**, plate 43; B&W. Rendering. **TAS**, 164. 4 photos; B&W. Rendering. **TAT**, plates 184-187; B&W. Set. **TDT**, n. 41 (Summer 1975). 17, back cover.

Hurry, Leslie. New Theatre, London: 1942. B&W. Set. **SDW1**, 177; B&W. Set. **SDG**, 190.

Jones, Robert Edmond. Sam H. Harris Theatre, NYC: 1922. B&W. Rendering. **REJ**, 47, 48; B&W. Sketch. **DFT**, plate 19. Act I, sc. 2: the court; B&W. Sketch. **DFT**, plate 20. Act I, sc. 3: a curtain; B&W. Sketch. **DFT**, plate 21. Act III, sc. 3: a curtain; B&W. Sketch. **DFT**, plate 22. Act III, sc. 4: the Queen's closet; B&W. Sketch. **DFT**, plate 23. Act V, sc. 1: the burial of Ophelia; B&W. Rendering. **DIT**, plate 116.1; B&W. Rendering. **RSD**, illus. 430; B&W. Rendering. **SDA**, 210. 2 photos; B&W. Rendering. **SOS**, 168; B&W. Rendering. **TAS**, 165. 2 photos; B&W. Rendering. **TPH**, photo 472; B&W. Rendering. **TSS**, 526; Haymarket Theatre, London: 1925. B&W. Set. **SOS**, 168.

Juillac, Jean. Grenier de Toulouse, France: 1969. B&W. Model. **SDW3**, 47.

Kochergin, Edward Stepanovich. Krasnoyarsky Theatre, Siberia: 1972. B&W. Model. **TCI**, vol. 11, n. 5 (Oct 1977). 41.

Kokkos, Yannis. Théâtre National de Chaillot, Paris: 1983. B&W. Model. **TDT**, vol. XXIII, n. 4 (Winter 1988). 20.

Lee, Ming Cho. Arena Stage, Washington, DC: 1978. B&W. Set. **ASD1**, 93.

Libakov, Mikhail. Moscow Art Theatre Second Studio: 1924. B&W. Set. **RST**, 172.

Linnebach, Adolf. Mannheim, Germany: 1907. B&W. Rendering. **TPH**, photos 345, 346.

Matcaboji, Mircea. Teatrul National, Cluj, Romania: 1960. B&W. Rendering. **SDW2**, 175.

McDonald, Anthony. Royal Shakespeare Company, GB: 1989. B&W. Set. **TCI**, vol. 25, n. 9 (Nov 1991). 17; B&W. Model. **TDT**, vol. XXVII, n. 4 (Fall 1991). 37.

Merritt, Michael. Wisdom Bridge Theatre, Chicago: 1985. B&W. Set. **ASD2**, 128; Color. Rendering. **BSE5**, 39.

Migid, Adel. (project): B&W. Rendering. **BSE5**, 17.

Minks, Wilfried. Theater am Goetheplatz, Bremen: 1965. B&W. Set. **RSD**, illus. 584; B&W. Set. **TCI**, vol. 12, n. 1 (Jan/Feb 1978). 28.

Mitchell, David. Anspacher Theatre, Public Theatre, NYC: 1967. B&W. Model. **DPT**, 89.

Motley (Margaret Harris, Sophia Harris, & Elizabeth Montgomery). New Theatre, London: 1934. B&W. Sketch & rendering. **TDT**, vol. XXIX, n. 3 (Summer 1993). 26, 28; Shakespeare Memorial Theatre, Stratford-upon-Avon: 1958. B&W. Set.

122   *Hamlet*

SDG, 191; B&W. Sketches & rendering. **TDT**, vol. XXIX, n. 3 (Summer 1993).
    26, 28. 3 photos.
Musika, Frantisek. State Theatre, Brno: 1936. B&W. Rendering. **TDT**, n. 42 (Fall
    1975). 25.
Neher, Caspar. State Theatre, Berlin: 1926. B&W. Rendering. **CBM**, 85; B&W. Set.
    SOS, 211; B&W. Set. **TPH**, photo 425.
Oenslager, Donald. USA: 1933. B&W. Rendering. **TAT**, plate 593; 1936. B&W.
    Rendering. **TAS**, 174. 2 photos; (project): B&W and color. Rendering. **STN**,
    frontispiece, 109-117. 6 photos.
Peduzzi, Richard. Avignon Festival: 1988. B&W. Set. **TCI**, vol. 24, n. 5 (May 1990).
    35.
Pitoëff, Georges. Plainpalais Auditorium, Geneva: 1920. B&W. **RSD**, illus. 423.
Ryndine, Vadim. Teatr Maïakovskovo, Moscow: 1954. B&W. Model. **SDW2**, 192;
    Color. Rendering. **SDW2**, 195.
Schlemmer, Oskar. Volksbühne, Berlin: 1925. B&W. Rendering. **AST**, 154.
Siki, Emil. Madách Szinház, Budapest. 1962. B&W. Set. **SDB**, 44. 2 photos; B&W.
    Set. **SDW2**, 141. 2 photos.
Simonson, Lee. (project): 1933. Color. Rendering. **PLT**, illus. 69-71; B&W and color.
    Rendering. **SDA**, 233, 280, 281. 4 photos; B&W. Rendering. **TAS**, 172, 173. 3
    photos; B&W. Rendering. **TAT**, plate 610; B&W. Rendering. **TPH**, photos 476,
    477.
Smith, Owen W. California State University, Northridge: B&W. Model. **SST**, 121. 3
    photos.
Stern, Ernst. Grosses Schauspielhaus, Berlin: 1920. B&W. Rendering. **MRH**, facing
    69; B&W. Rendering. **MRT**, 69.
Strnad, Oskar. Burgtheater, Vienna: 1923. B&W. Rendering. **RSD**, illus. 94; B&W.
    Rendering. **TCS2**, plates 71, 72.
Svoboda, Josef. Smetana Theatre, Prague: 1959. B&W. Set. **RSD**, illus. 95.Hamlet;
    B&W. Set. **SDW2**, 45; B&W. Model & set. **SJS**, 125. 4 photos; B&W. Set. **STS**,
    56, 57. 3 photos; B&W. Set. **TDT**, vol. XXIII, n. 1 (Spring 1987). 9, 11; National
    Theatre of Belgium, Brussels: 1965. B&W. Set. **RSD**, illus. 546. 3 photos; B&W.
    Set. **SDR**, 22; B&W. Model & set. **SJS**, 125-127. 10 photos; B&W. Set. **TDT**, n. 7
    (Dec 1966). 23.
Takada, Ichiro. Tokyo: 1971. B&W. Set. **SDW3**, 47. 5 photos.
Teodoroff. Rumanian National Theater, Bucharest: 1935. B&W. Set. **TPH**, photo 396.
Van Nerom, Jacques. Chateau de Beersel, Belgium: 1953. B&W. Set. **SDW2**, 32.
Vychodil, Ladislav. Czechoslovakia: B&W. Sketch & set. **TDT**, vol. XXVI, n. 2
    (Summer 1990). 36. 2 photos.
Wahkévitch, Georges. Moscow Art Theatre (Filial Theatre): 1955. B&W. Rendering.
    TOP, 25.
Warre, Michael. Arts Theatre, London: 1945. B&W. Model. **DMS**, plates 46, 47.
Wassberg, Goeran. Royal Dramatic Theatre, Stockholm: 1988. B&W and color. Set.
    TCI, vol. 22, n. 5 (May 1988). 12. 3 photos.
Wijdeveld, H. Th. 1918. B&W. Rendering. **TCS2**, plates 79-81.
Wurtzel, Stuart. American Conservatory Theatre, San Francisco: B&W. Set. **TCI**, vol.
    6, n. 5 (Oct 1972). 14.
_____. 1900. B&W. Set. **TPH**, photo 266.
_____. 1909. B&W. Set. **SDC**, plate 76.
_____. Attic Theatre, Detroit: Color. Set. **TCI**, vol. 25, n. 1 (Jan 1991). 43.
_____. California State University, Northridge: B&W. Set. **SST**, 375.
_____. Deutsches Theater, Berlin: 1909. B&W. Set. **MRH**, facing 68. 2 photos.

_____. Hoftheater, Munich: B&W. Set. **TCS2**, plates 44, 45.

_____. Kingsway Theatre, London: 1925. B&W. Set. **SOS**, 163.

_____. Kronberg Castle, Elsinore, Denmark: 1937. B&W. Rendering. **SOS**, 156;
B&W. Set. **SOW**, plate 45.

_____. Lyric Theatre, Hammersmith, London: 1905. B&W. Set. **SOS**, 130.

_____. Old Vic Theatre, London: 1934. B&W. Set. **TPH**, photo 439.

_____. Old Vic Theatre, London: 1938. B&W. Sketch. **TPH**, photo 444.

_____. Théâtre Antoine, Paris: 1913. B&W. Set. **SOS**, 185.

_____. Théâtre des Arts, Paris: 1926. B&W. Set. **SOS**, 196.

_____. University of Michigan, Ann Arbor: 1980. B&W. Set. **BSE2**, 28.

Hamlet (?).

Tchekhonine, Serge. Leningrad: 1925. B&W. Rendering. **RAG**, 65.

Hamletmachine.

Lemoi, Kyle D. Arizona State University, Tempe: B&W. Set. **TDT**, vol. XXVIII, n. 2
(Spring 1992). 6 of insert.

Mumford, Peter. St. Stephen's Theatre Space, Cardiff: 1985. B&W. Set. **BTD**, 46.

The Hands of Its Enemy,

_____. Mark Taper Forum, Los Angeles: Color. Set. **TCI**, vol. 21, n. 3 (Mar
1987). 26.

The Hanging Judge.

Sheppard, Guy. New Theatre, London: 1952. B&W. Model. **SDW1**, 185. 2 photos.

Hansel and Gretel.

DeFrancesco, Gion. Illinois Opera Theatre, Krannert Center, Urbana: B&W and color.
Model & set. **TDT**, vol. XXX, n. 3 (Summer 1994). 14.

Dunham, Clarke. Connecticut Opera Company, Hartford: 1983. B&W. Set. **DDT**, 84.

Lazaridis, Stefanos. English National Opera, London: 1987. Color. Set. **BTD**, 90. The
angel's sequence.

Thompson, Mark. Australian Opera: 1992. Color. Set. **TCI**, vol. 26, n. 9 (Nov 1992).
10.

Happening by the Sea.

Kantor, Tadeusz. 1967. B&W. Set. **RSD**, illus. 615. Happening.

The Happiness Cage.

Oeschger, Suzanne. Theatre Three, Temple University: B&W. Set. **TDT**, n. 37 (May
1974). 21.

Happy Days.

Bury, John. Lyttleton, Theatre, London: 1976. B&W. Set. **TCI**, vol. 11, n. 5 (Oct
1977). 32.

Herbert, Jocelyn. Royal Court Theatre, London: 1979. B&W. Rendering. **TDT**, vol.
XXX, n. 5 (Fall 1994). 16.

Howard, Pamela. West Yorkshire Playhouse, GB: 1993. Color. Set. **TDT**, vol. XXX, n.
1 (Winter 1994). 18.

Yeargan, Michael. Public Theatre, NYC: 1979. B&W. Set. **TCI**, vol. 17, n. 4 (Apr
1983). 17; B&W. Set. **TCI**, vol. 16, n. 5 (May 1982). 25.

Happy End.

Arnone, John. Arena Stage, Washington, DC: 1984. B&W. Set. **ASD2**, 24, 28.

Neher, Caspar. Theater am Schiffbauerdamm: 1929. B&W. Rendering. **CBM**, 52.

Taylor, Robert U. Martin Beck Theatre, NYC: 1977. B&W. Sketch & set. **TCI**, vol. 11,
n. 5 (Oct 1977). 14. 4 photos.

The Happy Time.

Wexler, Peter. Broadway Theatre, NYC: 1968. B&W and color. Model. **SDT**, 108,
between 152 & 153.

The Hard Nut.
  Lobel, Adrianne. Brooklyn Academy of Music, New York: 1992. Color. Set. **TCI**, vol.
    27, n. 2 (Feb 1993). 53.
Hard Shoulder.
  McCallin, Tanya. Hampstead Theatre, London: 1983. B&W. Set. **BTD**, 52.
Harlequin's Family.
  Faucheur, Yves. Théâtre du Vieux-Columbier, Paris: 1956. B&W. Rendering. **SDW2**,
    90.
The Harmony of the World.
  Schneider-Siemssen, Günther. Theater der Freien Hansestadt, Bremen: 1957. B&W.
    Rendering. **OPE**, 39; B&W. Set. **SDW2**, 70.
Harold and Maude.
  Straiges, Tony. Martin Beck Theatre, NYC: 1980. B&W. Model. **DDT**, 333. 2 photos.
Harrigan and Hart.
  Mitchell, David. Longacre Theatre, NYC: 1985. Color. Set. **TCI**, vol. 19, n. 4 (Apr
    1985). 24.
Harvey Milk.
  Steinberg, Paul. Houston Grand Opera: 1995. Color. Set. **TCI**, vol. 29, n. 4 (Apr
    1995). 31. 2 photos.
Hassan.
  Harris, George W. His Majesty's Theatre, London: 1923. Color. Rendering. **TOP**, 68.
  Pillartz, T.C. Hessiches Landestheater, Darmstadt: B&W. Set. **TCS2**, plate 228.
The Hatter's Castle.
  Komisarjevsky, Theodore. Lyceum Theatre, Edinburgh: 1932. B&W. Set. **SCM**, 28.
Hauptmann.
  Dardenne, James. Cherry Lane Theatre, NYC: 1992. B&W. Set. **TCI**, vol. 26, n. 7
    (Aug/Sep 1992). 12.
Hay Fever.
  Funicello, Ralph. American Conservatory Theatre, San Francisco: B&W. Set. **TCI**,
    vol. 14, n. 4 (Sep 1980). 21.
  Schafer, Lawrence. Avon Theatre, Stratford, Ontario, Canada: 1977. B&W. Set. **TCI**,
    vol. 12, n. 4 (May/Jun 1978). 22.
Haydamaks.
  _____. Malodoi Theatre, Ukraine: 1920. B&W. Set. **RST**, 157.
He Wants to Have Some Fun.
  _____. B&W. Set. **TPH**, photo 330.
He Who Gets Slapped.
  Simonson, Lee. Garrick Theatre, NYC: 1922. B&W. Set. **MCN**, 56; B&W. Set. **PLT**,
    illus. 18; B&W. Set. **TPH**, photo 462.
  Thomas, Christopher. St. Felix Street Playhouse, Brooklyn, NY: 1974. B&W. Set.
    TCI, vol. 8, n. 5 (Oct 1974). 2.
  Wittstein, Ed. Playhouse in the Park, Cincinnati: B&W. Set. **TCI**, vol. 5, n. 1 (Jan/Feb
    1971). 21. 2 photos.
  _____. Paris: Color. Rendering. **CSC**, facing 24.
  _____. Shaw Festival Theatre, Niagara-on-the-Lake, Canada: Color. Set. **TCI**,
    vol. 25, n. 1 (Jan 1991). 37.
He Who Must Die.
  Beyer, Rolf. B&W. Sketch, model, & set. **SDL**, 86. 3 photos.
Heads Up!
  Harker, Joseph & Phil Harker. Palace Theatre, London: 1930. B&W. Set. **MCD**, plate
    162.

Healthy, Wealthy and Wise.
> Pember, Clifford. New Theatre, London: 1930. B&W. Rendering. **SCM**, 36.

Heart's Desire.
> Rigdon, Kevin. Cleveland Playhouse: 1990. Color. Model. **TCI**, vol. 24, n. 10 (Dec 1990). 19.

Heart-throb.
> McGowan, Julian. Bush Theatre, London: 1988. B&W. Set. **BTD**, 84, 85.

Heartbreak House.
> Edwards, Ben. Billy Rose Theatre, NYC: 1959. B&W. Set. **TCI**, vol. 23, n. 7 (Aug/Sep 1989). 51.
> Eisenstein, Sergei M. (project), Moscow: 1922. B&W. Sketch. **RSD**, illus. 184.
> Herbert, Jocelyn. Haymarket Theatre, London: 1983. B&W. Rendering. **TDT**, vol. XXX, n. 5 (Fall 1994). 20.
> Kellogg, Marjorie Bradley. Circle in the Square Theatre, NYC: 1983. B&W. Model. **ASD1**, 65.
> Kimmel, Alan. Playhouse in the Park, Cincinnati: B&W. Set. **BSE4**, 58.
> Levine, Michael. Shaw Festival Theatre, Niagara-on-the-Lake, Canada: B&W. Set. **SDL**, 62; B&W. Set. **TCI**, vol. 22, n. 7 (Aug/Sep 1988). 3.
> Loquasto, Santo. Arena Stage, Washington, DC: 1976. B&W. Sketch. **DDT**, 66.
> Russel, James. B&W. Set. **SDL**, 62.
> Simonson, Lee. Garrick Theatre, NYC: 1920. B&W. Set. **MCN**, 52; B&W. Set. **PLT**, illus. 10, 11.

Heavenly Express.
> Aronson, Boris. Nederlander Theatre, NYC: 1940. B&W. Rendering. **TAB**, 297.

The Heavenly Squadron.
> Marenic, Vladimir. Srpsko Narodno Pozoriste, Novi Sad, Yugoslavia: 1957. B&W. Rendering. **SDW2**, 135.

Hedda Gabler.
> Jenkins, David. Doolittle Theatre, Los Angeles: 1986. B&W. Model. **DDT**, 164, 165. 4 photos.
> Leerhoff, Dick. Actors Theatre of St. Paul: 1981. B&W. Set. **TCI**, vol. 17, n. 7 (Aug/Sep 1983). 20.
> Schultz, Karen. 1981. Color. Set. **DDT**, 152c.

Hedy.
> Hoffman, Vlastislav. National Theatre, Prague: B&W. Set. **TCS2**, plate 270.

The Heidi Chronicles.
> Griswold, Mary. National Jewish Theatre, Skokie, Illinois: 1992. Color. Set. **TCI**, vol. 27, n. 3 (Mar 1993). 43. 2 photos.
> Owen, Paul. Actors Theatre of Louisville: 1992. Color. Set. **TCI**, vol. 27, n. 3 (Mar 1993). 42. 3 photos.
> Ruling, Karl G. Polka Dot Playhouse, Bridgeport, Connecticut: 1992. Color. Set. **TCI**, vol. 27, n. 3 (Mar 1993). 41.

Helen!
> Messel, Oliver. Adelphi Theatre, London: 1932. B&W. Model & set. **MEM**, 35, 86, 87. 3 photos; B&W and color. Rendering & set. **OMB**, 57, 59, 66; B&W. Set. **SCM**, 17, 18.

Helen Retires.
> Kiesler, Frederick. NYC: 1934. B&W. Set. **EIF**, photo 13.

Helena's Husband.
> Hume, Samuel J. 1916. B&W. Set. **TDT**, vol. XX, n. 2 (Summer 1984). 14.

Hélène de Sparte.

Bakst, Léon. Théâtre du Châtelet, Paris: 1912. Color. Rendering. **LBT**, 130.

The Heliotrope Bouquet by Scott Joplin and Louis Chauvin.

Barreca, Christopher. Center Stage, Baltimore: 1991. B&W. Set. **TCI**, vol. 25, n. 5 (May 1991). 10.

Hell-Bent fer Heaven.

Viele, Sheldon K. Klaw Theatre, NYC: 1924. B&W. Set. **MCN**, 65.

Hello Dolly!

Smith, Oliver. St. James Theatre, NYC: 1964. B&W. Rendering & set. **TCI**, vol. 16, n. 4 (Apr 1982). 16, 63; B&W. Set. **WMC**, 325; Theatre Royal, Drury Lane, London: 1965. B&W. Set. **MCD**, plate 222; St. James Theatre, NYC: 1967. B&W and color. Set. **BWM**, 26, 27, 328; B&W. Set. **DPT**, 154; B&W. Set. **DSL**, figure 16.1(a); St. James Theatre, NYC: 1974. B&W. Set. **BWM**, 328, 329.

Thompson, Brian. Australia: 1994. Color. Rendering. **TCI**, vol. 29, n. 3 (Mar 1995). 42, 43. 4 photos.

Kubik, Boris. Germany: B&W. Model. **TDT**, vol. XII, n. 3 (Fall 1976). 33.

Hellzapoppin.

_____. 1977. B&W. Set. **BWM**, 350.

Henry III.

_____. 1910. B&W. Set. **TPH**, photo 243.

Henry IV.

Allio, René. Théâtre de la Cité, Villeurbanne: 1957. Color. Rendering. **RSD**, illus. 571; Color. Rendering. **SOS**, 188.

Beaton, Cecil. Marlowe Dramatic Society, Cambridge: 1924. B&W. Set. **CBS**, 21.

Cesarini, Pino. Roman Theatre, Verona: 1951. B&W. Set. **SDE**, 54. 2 photos.

Chiari, Mario. Piccolo Teatro della Città di Milano: 1961. B&W. Rendering. **SDW2**, 123.

Falleni, Silvano. 1964. B&W. Set. **SIO**, 50.

Fraser, Claude Lovat. Color. Rendering. **TCS2**, color plate 1.

Fredrikson, Kristian & Richard Prins. Victorian Arts Center, Melbourne: 1969. B&W. Set. **SDW3**, 44.

Hess, Ivan E. University of Wisconsin: B&W. Set. **TCI**, vol. 4, n. 5 (Oct 1970). 17.

Kauffer, E. McKnight. Great Britain: B&W. Rendering. **DIT**, plates 24, 25.

Kiesler, Frederick. Philadelphia: 1958. B&W. Set. **EIF**, photo 45.

Sonnabend, Yolande. (project): 1955. B&W. Rendering. **DMS**, plate 58.

Henry IV, part 1.

Lee, Ming Cho. Mark Taper Forum, Los Angeles: 1973. B&W. Set. **DPT**, 137; B&W. Set. **TCI**, vol. 8, n. 1 (Jan/Feb 1974). 12.

Napier, John. Barbican Theatre, London: 1982. B&W. Set. **TDT**, vol. XIX, n. 1 (Spring 1983). 10.

Tsypin, George. New York Shakespeare Festival's Public Theatre: 1991. B&W. Set. **TDT**, vol. XXVII, n. 3 (Summer 1991). 14. 2 photos.

_____. Deutsches Theater, Berlin: 1912. B&W. Model & set. **MRH**, facing 155, between 234 & 235. 3 photos.

Henry IV, part 2.

_____. Deutsches Theater, Berlin: 1912. B&W. Set. **MRH**, facing 236.

_____. Stratford, Ontario: 1965. Color. Set. **SOS**, 243.

Henry IV, parts 1 & 2.

Conklin, John. American Repertory Theatre, Cambridge, Massachusetts: 1994. B&W. Set. **TCI**, vol. 28, n. 3 (Mar 1994). 9.

Henry V.

Craig, Edward Gordon. 1901. B&W. Rendering. **TNT**, facing 21.

Crowley, Bob. Royal Shakespeare Company, GB: 1984. Color. Set. **BTD**, 55.

Elder, Eldon. New York Shakespeare Festival, NYC: 1960. B&W. Model. **EED**, (pages not numbered); B&W. Set. **SDW2**, 234.

Farrah, Abd'Elkader. Royal Shakespeare Theatre, Stratford-upon-Avon: 1975. B&W. Rendering. **TDT**, vol. XIX, n. 3 (Fall 1983). 12. 2 photos.

Heeley, Desmond. Stratford, Ontario: 1965. B&W. Set. **RSD**, illus. 618.

Heslewood, Tom. Great Britain: B&W. Model. **DIT**, plate 28.

Larkin, Grady. 1973. B&W. Set. **TCI**, vol. 9, n. 1 (Jan/Feb 1975). 16.

Mitchell, David. Delacorte Theatre, NYC: 1976. B&W. Model. **ASD1**, 129; B&W. Model. **DDT**, 310. 3 photos.

Moiseiwitsch, Tanya. 1951. B&W. Set. **DOT**, 239.

Motley (Margaret Harris, Sophia Harris, & Elizabeth Montgomery). Old Vic Theatre, London: 1936-37. B&W. Set. **TPH**, photo 442.

Otto, Teo. Burgtheater, Vienna: 1961. Color. Rendering. **SOS**, 261.

Schmidt, Saladin. State Theatre, Bochum: 1927. B&W. Rendering. **SOS**, 210.

Svoboda, Josef. Tyl Theatre, Prague: 1971. B&W. Set. **SJS**, 164. 2 photos; B&W. Set. **STS**, 62.

Henry VI.

McLane, Derek. Theatre for the New City, NYC: 1995. Color. Set. **TCI**, vol. 29, n. 5 (May 1995). 7.

_____. Royal Shakespeare Company, GB: Color. Set. **TCI**, vol. 29, n. 2 (Feb 1995). 33.

Henry VI, part 1.

Napier, John. Barbican Theatre, London: 1982. B&W. Set. **BTD**, 37.

Henry VIII.

Griffin, Hayden. Royal Shakespeare Company, GB: 1984. B&W and color. Sketch & set. **TCI**, vol. 19, n. 9 (Nov 1985). 23, 25.

Harker, Joseph. c. 1900. B&W. Set. **SDG**, 139.

Jones, Robert Edmond. (not produced): 1944. B&W. Rendering. **REJ**, 109 , 111, 113, 115; B&W and color. Rendering. **SDA**, 222, 223, 277, 286, 287. 8 photos; B&W. Rendering. **TDT**, n. 17 (May 1969). 15, 16, 19-21, 24. 6 photos.

Moiseiwitsch, Tanya. Shakespeare Memorial Theatre, Stratford-upon-Avon: 1951. B&W. Set. **SDG**, 182.

_____. American Repertory Theatre, NYC: 1948. B&W. Set. **WTP**, 64, 65. 3 photos.

_____. His Majesty's Theatre, London: 1910. B&W. Set. **SOS**, 128.

Hérakales.

Hoffman, Vlastislav. Municipal Theatre, Prague: 1934. B&W. Rendering. **RSD**, illus. 145.

Ristic, Dusan. Jugoslovensko Dramsko Pozoriste, Beograd: 1959. Color. Rendering. **SDW2**, 137.

Hernani.

Kokkos, Yannis. Théâtre National de Chaillot, Paris: 1985. B&W. Rendering. **TDT**, vol. XXIII, n. 4 (Winter 1988). 22. 6 sketches.

Herod and Miriamne.

_____. Berlin: B&W. Set. **TPH**, photo 244.

Herodiade.

Howland, Gerard. San Francisco Opera: 1994-1995. Color. Model & set. **TCI**, vol. 29, n. 3 (Mar 1995). 33.

Herr von Haucken.
>   Reufersward, Carl Frederik. Royal Opera House, Stockholm. 1965. B&W. Set. **SDR**, 66.
Het Moortje.
>   Wijnberg, Nicolaas. Koninklijken Schouwburg, The Hague: 1957. B&W. Set. **SDW2**, 146.
L'Heure Espagnole.
>   Wijnberg, Nicolaas. Stadsschouwburg, Amsterdam: 1948. B&W. Set. **SDW1**, 140.
Hiawatha.
>   Flood, Marty. National Theatre (Olivier), London: 1980. B&W. Set. **BTD**, 47.
High Button Shoes.
>   Joy, James Leonard. Goodspeed Opera House, East Haddam, Connecticut: Color. Set. **TCI**, vol. 21, n. 9 (Nov 1987). 37.
>   Smith, Oliver. New Century Theatre, NYC: 1947. B&W. Set. **BWM**, 46, 47. 12 photos; B&W. Set. **TCI**, vol. 23, n. 7 (Aug/Sep 1989). 59; B&W. Set. **WTP**, 240.
High Society.
>   Tripp, Tony. Australia: 1993. B&W and color. Set. **TCI**, vol. 27, n. 3 (Mar 1993). 5, 10, 11. 3 photos.
High Tor.
>   Mielziner, Jo. Martin Beck Theatre, NYC: 1937. B&W. Rendering. **DTT**, 103. Phantom Dutchman; B&W. Set. **MCN**, 136; B&W. Rendering. **SOW**, plate 86.
Him.
>   Chepulis, Kyle. New York Shakespeare Festival, NYC: Color. Set. **TCI**, vol. 29, n. 4 (Apr 1995). 43.
Himlens Hemlighet.
>   Berg, Yngye. Intima Teatern, Stockholm: B&W. Set. **TCS2**, plate 139.
Himmlische und Irdische Liebe (Launzi).
>   Jones, Robert Edmond. Plymouth Theatre, NYC: 1923. B&W. Sketch. **DFT**, plate 17. Act V: the tower room.
Hin und Zurück.
>   Moholy-Nagy, Lászlo. Germany: B&W. Set. **SCM**, 57.
Hippolytus.
>   Bakst, Léon. Alexandrinsky Theatre, St. Petersburg: 1902. B&W and color. Rendering & set. **LBT**, 41, 42.
L'Histoire du Soldat.
>   Aronson, Boris. Grand Ballroom, Waldorf-Astoria Hotel, NYC: 1965. B&W. Model. **TAB**, 307.
>   Manzu, Giacomo. Teatro Olimpico, Rome: 1966. B&W. Model. **AST**, 222. 4 photos.
>   Matsoukis, Theophanes. Teatro Nuovo, Milan: 1950. B&W. Rendering. **SDE**, 122. 2 photos.
>   Oenslager, Donald. Jolson's 59th Street Theatre: 1928. B&W. Rendering. **TDO**, 36.
>   _____. State Opera, Berlin: 1925. B&W. Rendering. **TBB**, 126.
The Historic Role of Mr. Pigwa.
>   Zachwatowicz, Krystyna. Teatr Ludowy, Nowa Huta, Poland: 1960. B&W. Set. **SDW2**, 172.
A History of the American Film.
>   Newlin, Forrest A. Southern Methodist University, Dallas: 1981. B&W. Rendering. **BSE2**, 18.
>   Straiges, Tony. Arena Stage, Washington, DC: 1977. B&W. Set. **TCI**, vol. 16, n. 2 (Feb 1982). 17.

Hit the Deck.

> Beatty, John Lee. Goodspeed Opera House, East Haddam, Connecticut: 1977; B&W.
> Set. **TCI**, vol. 12, n. 6 (Oct 1978). 23.

> Harvey & Ward. Belasco Theatre, NYC: 1927. B&W. Set. **WMC**, 105.

> Wenger, John. Belasco Theatre, NYC: 1927. B&W. Set. **TMT**, 103; B&W. Set. **WMC**,
> 105.

Hizzoner!

> Elder, Eldon. Longacre Theatre, NYC: 1989. B&W. Set. **DDT**, 329.

Hogan's Goat.

> Lundell, Kurt. American Place Theatre, NYC: 1966. B&W. Rendering & set. **TCI**, vol.
> 1, n. 1 (Mar/Apr 1967). 26, 27.

Hölderlin.

> Kneidl, Karl. State Theatre, Stuttgart: 1971. B&W. Set. **SDW4**, illus. 281.

> Steiof, Adolf. Deutsches Schauspielhaus, Hamburg: 1971. B&W. Set. **SDW4**, illus.
> 279, 280.

A Hole in the Head.

> Aronson, Boris. Plymouth Theatre, NYC: 1957. B&W and color. Rendering, model, &
> set. **TAB**, 114, 115, 304.

Holeville.

> Landesman, Heidi. Attic Theatre, Brooklyn Academy of Music, New York: 1979.
> B&W. Model. **DDT**, 314.

Holiday Heart.

> Hernandez, Riccardo. Manhattan Theatre Club, NYC: 1995. Color. Set. **TCI**, vol. 29,
> n. 5 (May 1995). 6.

Holle, Weg, Erde.

> Klein, César. Lessing Theater, Berlin: 1919. B&W. Rendering. **RSD**, illus. 142; B&W.
> Rendering. **TPH**, photo 421.

Holy Blood and Crescent Moon.

> Schmidt, Douglas W. Cleveland Opera: 1989. B&W. Model. **TCI**, vol. 23, n. 9 (Nov
> 1989). 18.

The Holy Family.

> Sjöberg, Alf. Royal Dramatic Theatre, Stockholm: B&W. Rendering. **SOW**, plate 59.

Der Holzgeschnitzte Prinz.

> Schlemmer, Oskar. State Theatre, Magdeburg: 1926. B&W. Rendering. **AST**, 155.

Home.

> Cochren, Felix E. Cort Theatre, NYC: 1980. B&W. Model. **DDT**, 250. 3 photos.

> Devine, Michael. LA Public Theatre, Los Angeles: 1982. B&W. Set. **TCI**, vol. 19, n. 7
> (Aug/Sep 1985). 39.

> Payne, Darwin Reid. B&W. Rendering, model, & set. **SIP**, 14, 55, 172; B&W. model
> & rendering. **TCM**, 26, 62, 125, 126. 4 photos.

The Homecoming.

> Bury, John. Royal Shakespeare Company, Aldwych Theatre, London: 1965. B&W.
> Set. **SDR**, 7; 1991. B&W. Set. **TCI**, vol. 26, n. 1 (Jan 1992). 45.

> Gesek, Thaddeus. Yale School of Drama, New Haven, Connecticut: B&W. Set. **SFT**,
> 16, 17.

> Wilke, Ralph A., Jr. Theatre Project Company, St. Louis, Missouri: 1980. B&W. Set.
> **BSE4**, 77.

> _____. Steppenwolf Theatre Company, Chicago: 1989. B&W. Set. **TCR**, 121.

A Homestead Album.

> _____. Cumberland County Playhouse, Crossville, Tennessee: B&W. Set. **TCI**,
> vol. 21, n. 3 (Mar 1987). 24.

L'Homme et ses Fantomes.
> Fuerst, Walter René. Odéon Théâtre, Paris: 1924. B&W. Model. **TCS2**, plate 208.

L'Homme et son Désir.
> Parr, Mme. Sweden: 1927. B&W. Model. **TCS2**, plate 122.

Honor and Offer.
> Wittstein, Ed. Playhouse in the Park, Cincinnati: B&W. Set. **TCI**, vol. 5, n. 1 (Jan/Feb
> 1971). 18.

Hooters.
> McCarry, Charles E. Playwrights Horizons, NYC: 1978. B&W. Rendering. **DDT**, 103;
> B&W. Rendering & set. **TCI**, vol. 13, n. 3 (May/Jun 1979). 30.

Hoppla, Wir Leben!
> Akhvlediana, Elena. Kutaisi, Georgia: 1928. B&W. Set. **RST**, 133.
> _____. Berlin: B&W. Set. **SCM**, 55.

Horatio.
> Eigsti, Karl. Arena Stage, Washington, DC: 1974. B&W. Rendering. **DPT**, 3.
> Larkin, Grady. 1971. B&W. Set. **TCI**, vol. 9, n. 1 (Jan/Feb 1975). 16.

Hospital.
> Helmuth, Suzanne. The Magic Theatre, San Francisco: 1977. B&W. Set. **TCI**, vol. 14,
> n. 4 (Sep 1980). 22.

The Hostage.
> Conklin, John. Arena Stage, Washington, DC: 1972. B&W. Model. **CSD**, 69.

The Hot l Baltimore.
> Radice, Ronald. Circle Theatre, NYC: 1973. B&W. Set. **TCI**, vol. 8, n. 2 (Mar/Apr
> 1974). 9.
> Recht, Raymond C. Center Stage, Baltimore: 1973. B&W. Rendering. **CSD**, 118.

Hot Mikado.
> Karson, Nat. Broadhurst Theatre, NYC: 1939. B&W. Set. **BWM**, 331. 2 photos;
> B&W. Set. **RBS**, 180; B&W. Set. **TMI**, 228.
> _____. Marriot Lincolnshire Theatre, Lincolnshire, Illinois: Color. Set. **TCI**, vol.
> 29, n. 1 (Jan 1995). 45.

Hot Spot.
> Ter-Arutunian, Rouben. 1963. B&W. Set. **BWM**, 347.

Hotel of Follies.
> Price, Rodney. Angels of Light Company, San Francisco: Color. Set. **TCI**, vol. 22, n. 2
> (Feb 1988). 47.

Hotel Paradiso.
> Seger, Richard. American Conservatory Theatre, San Francisco: 1978. B&W. Set.
> **TCI**, vol. 14, n. 4 (Sep 1980). 20. 2 photos.

Hotel Universe.
> Simonson, Lee. Martin Beck Theatre, NYC: 1930. B&W. Set. **MCN**, 97.

Hotspur.
> Tripp, Tony. Melbourne Theatre Company, Australia: 1994. Color. Set. **TCI**, vol. 28, n.
> 10 (Dec 1994). 16.

Hour Glass.
> Craig, Edward Gordon. Abbey Theatre, Dublin: 1910. B&W. Rendering. **SDG**, 151.

House of Agamemnon.
> Maronek, James E. DePaul University, Chicago: 1983. B&W. Set. **BSE4**, 32.

The House of Bernarda Alba.
> Bauer-Ecsy, Leni. State Theatre, Stuttgart: 1953. B&W. Rendering. **SDW1**, 62.
> Beatty, John Lee. Playhouse in the Park, Cincinnati: 1978. B&W. Set. **ASD1**, 9; B&W.
> Set. **TCI**, vol. 12, n. 6 (Oct 1978). 21.

de Paz y Mateo, Alberto. Teatro Municipal, Caracas: 1954. B&W. Model. **SDW2**, 244.

Falleni, Silvano. 1967. B&W. Set. **SIO**, 52.

Kravjansky, Mikulás. Slovak National Theatre, Bratislava: 1957. B&W. Rendering. **SDW2**, 42.

Menconi, Lee. 1979. B&W. Rendering. **BSE1**, 36.

Stewart, Anita C. Theatre Emory: Color. Set. **TCI**, vol. 25, n. 1 (Jan 1991). 44.

Svoboda, Josef. Schlosspark Theatre, Berlin: 1966. B&W. Set. **STS**, 26.

_____. Carnegie-Mellon University, Pittsburgh: 1966. B&W. Set. **TCI**, vol. 7, n. 5 (Oct 1973). 26.

The House of Blue Leaves.

Eigsti, Karl. Truck and Warehouse Theatre, NYC: 1970. B&W. Rendering. **ASD1**, 39; B&W. Rendering. **DPT**, 331.

Saternow, Tim. Seattle Repertory Theatre: B&W and color. Rendering & set. **TDT**, vol. XXX, n. 3 (Summer 1994). 10.

Soule, Robert D. Trinity Square Theatre, Providence, Rhode Island: 1987. Color. Set. **TCI**, vol. 22, n. 9 (Nov 1988). 61.

Walton, Tony. Vivian Beaumont Theatre, Lincoln Center, NYC: 1986. Color. Rendering. **BSE5**, 2; Color. Rendering & set. **TCI**, vol. 21, n. 3 (Mar 1987). 20.

House of Breath.

Lee, Eugene. Trinity Square Theatre, Providence, Rhode Island: 1969. B&W. Set. **TCI**, vol. 5, n. 4 (Sep 1971). 13; B&W. Set. **TDT**, vol. XVIII, n. 2 (Summer 1982). 5.

The House of Connelly.

Throckmorton, Cleon. Martin Beck Theatre, NYC: 1931. B&W. Set. **MCN**, 105.

House of Flowers.

Messel, Oliver. Alvin Theatre, NYC: 1954. B&W. Model & set. **OMB**, 172, 173, 181; B&W. Set. **WMC**, 182.

The House of Women.

Jones, Robert Edmond. Maxine Elliot Theatre, NYC: 1927. B&W. Rendering. **REJ**, 63.

House Party.

Lundell, Kurt. American Place Theatre, NYC: B&W. Set. **TCI**, vol. 8, n. 4 (Sep 1974). 21.

How I Got That Story.

Woodbridge, Patricia. Westside Arts Theatre, NYC: B&W. Set. **TCI**, vol. 16, n. 7 (Aug/Sep 1982). 23.

How the Other Half Loves

Silberstein, Frank. Indiana University Theatre, Bloomington: B&W. Model. **TDT**, vol. XVI, n. 4 (Winter 1980). 5.

How the Steel Was Tempered.

Ounz, Aïmi. Molodejnyj Teatr, Tallinn: 1968. B&W. Rendering. **SDW3**, 119.

How to Get Rid of It.

Jensen, Don F. Astor Place Theatre, NYC: 1974. B&W. Rendering. **DPT**, 87.

How To Succeed in Business Without Really Trying.

Arnone, John. Richard Rodgers Theatre, NYC: 1995. Color. Set. **TCI**, vol. 29, n. 5 (May 1995). cover, 46, 47. 4 photos.

Randolph, Robert. 46th Street Theatre, NYC: 1961. B&W and color. Set. **BWM**, 269, 270; B&W. Set. **DPT**, 208.

Thompson, Brian. Footbridge Theatre, Sidney, Australia: 1993. Color. Set. **TCI**, vol. 27, n. 5 (May 1993). 11.

The Humble and the Offended.
    Dmitriev, Vladimir. Teatr Léninskovo Komsomola, Leningrad: 1956. B&W. Rendering. **SDW2**, 182.
Humpty Dumpty.
    _____. Drury Lane Theatre, London: 1903. B&W. Model. **TPH**, photo 351.
    Pantomime.
Hunger.
    Craig, Edward Gordon. B&W. Rendering. **OAT**, 112, Sc. 1 & 262. Prologue.
Hunger and Thirst.
    Pitoëff, Georges. Berkshire Theatre Festival, Stockbridge, Massachusetts: 1969. B&W. Bas relief. **CSD**, 114.
The Hunger Artist.
    Israel, Robert. Music-Theatre Group/Brooklyn Academy of Music: 1987. B&W. Set. **ASD2**, 54, 55. 3 photos.
Hurlyburly.
    Walton, Tony. Chicago: 1984. B&W. Model. **DDT**, 166.
Hurrah, We Live!
    Traugott, Muller. Piscator Theater, Berlin: 1927. B&W. Rendering & set. **RSD**, illus. 233-237.
The Hussites.
    Hoffman, Vlastislav. Vinohrady Theatre, Prague: 1919. B&W. Rendering. **TDT**, n. 41 (Summer 1975). 16. 2 photos.
Huui-Huui.
    Schmidt, Douglas W. NYSF Public Theatre, St. Clements Church, NYC: 1968. B&W. Set. **TDT**, vol. XVII, n. 2 (Summer 1981). 17.
The Hyacinth Macaw.
    Chepulis, Kyle. Primary Stages, NYC: Color. Set. **TCI**, vol. 29, n. 4 (Apr 1995). 43.
The Hydra.
    Hoffman, Vlastislav. Municipal Theatre, Prague: 1921. B&W. Rendering. **RSD**, illus. 128.
L'Hypothese.
    Chapelle des Penitents Blancs, Avignon: 1987. B&W. Set. **TCI**, vol. 24, n. 5 (May 1990). 33.

-I-

I.
    Strebelle, Olivier. Théâtre Laboratoire Vicinal, Brussels. 1974. B&W. Set. **SDW4**, illus. 391-393. 3 photos.
I Am a Camera.
    Aronson, Boris. Empire Theatre, NYC: 1951. Color. Set. **SDW1**, 195; B&W and color. Rendering & set. **TAB**, 104, 302.
I Am a Man.
    Hernandez, Riccardo. Arena Stage, Washington, DC: 1995. Color. Set. **TCI**, vol. 29, n. 5 (May 1995). 6.
I Am Hong Kong.
    _____. Hong Kong: B&W. Rendering. **TDT** vol. XXXI, n. 2 (Spring 1995). 28.
I and Albert.
    Arrighi, Luciana. B&W. Set. **SST**, 97, 543.
    Orubo, Robert. England: B&W. Set. **DSL**, figure 39.1(c).

I Can Get It for You Wholesale.
_____. 1962. B&W. Set. **BWM**, 272, 273. 4 photos.
I Do! I Do!
Smith, Oliver. 46th Street Theatre, NYC: 1966. Color. Set. **BWM**, 142.
I Married an Angel.
Mielziner, Jo. Shubert Theatre, NYC: 1938. B&W. Set. **WMC**, 123.
I Never Sang for My Father.
Mielziner, Jo. Longacre Theatre, NYC: 1968. B&W. Rendering. **DDT**, 325.
I Remember Mama.
Mitchell, David. Majestic Theatre, NYC: 1979. B&W. Drawing & drop. **DDT**, 219,
403; B&W. Set. **MBM**, 192.
I Want a Child.
Lissitsky, El. (unrealized production) Meyerhold Theatre, Moscow: 1926-1930. B&W.
Model. **MOT**, between 256 & 257; B&W. Model. **AST**, 132. 2 photos; B&W.
Model. **RSD**, illus. 188.
I Was Sitting On My Patio This Guy Appeared I Thought I Was Hallucinating.
Wilson, Robert. Cherry Lane Theatre, NYC: 1977. B&W. Sketches, rendering & set.
RWT, 55-58, 138, 149, 150. 7 photos; B&W. Set. **TCI**, vol. 19, n. 8 (Oct 1985).
22.
I'd Rather Be Right.
Oenslager, Donald. Alvin Theatre, NYC: 1937. B&W. Set. **BWM**, 180; B&W. Set.
RBS, 149. 2 photos; B&W. Rendering. **SDA**, 246; B&W. Rendering. **TDO**, 77;
B&W. Model. **TMI**, 241.
I'm Not Rappaport.
Benson, Gary. Mankato State University, Minnesota: B&W. Set. **TDT**, vol. XXVIII, n.
2 (Spring 1992). 11 of insert.
Walton, Tony. Seattle Repertory Theatre: 1985. B&W. Sketch & set. **DDT**, 148. 2
photos.
I've Got Sixpence.
Aronson, Boris. Ethel Barrymore Theatre, NYC: 1952. B&W. Rendering. **TAB**, 302. 2
photos.
The Ice Wolf.
Hird, Thomas C. California State University, Hayward: 1977. B&W. Set. **BSE1**, 15.
The Iceman Cometh.
Dancy, Virginia & Elmon Webb. Long Wharf Theatre, New Haven, Connecticut: 1972.
B&W. Model. **CSD**, 140; B&W. Set. **DPT**, 100 B&W. Set. **TCI**, vol. 7, n. 5 (Oct
1973). 6. 2 photos.
Edwards, Ben. Lunt-Fontanne Theatre, NYC: 1986. Color. Set. **TCI**, vol. 23, n. 4 (Apr
1989). 50.
Griffin, Hayden. National Theatre, London: 1980. B&W. Set. **TCI**, vol. 19, n. 9 (Nov
1985). 24.
Jones, Robert Edmond. Martin Beck Theatre, NYC: 1946. B&W. Rendering. **REJ**,
123; B&W. Rendering. **SDA**, 205; B&W. Set. **WTP**, 194, 195. 4 photos.
Scott, J. Hutchinson. Arts Theatre Club, London: 1958. B&W. Rendering. **SDW2**, 226.
An Ideal Husband.
Whistler, Rex. London: 1943. B&W. Rendering. **SDB**, 42.
The Idiot.
Benois, Alexander. 1925. B&W. Rendering. **RSC**, 20.
Idiot's Delight.
Simonson, Lee. Shubert Theatre, NYC: 1936. B&W. Set. **MCN**, 130; B&W. Set. **SDA**,
202; B&W. Set. **SOW**, plate 94.

Tsypin, George. Eisenhower Theatre, Washington, DC: 1986. B&W. Set. **ASD2**, 169; B&W. Model. **DDT**, 159.

Idomeneo.

Conklin, John. San Francisco Opera: 1989. B&W and color. Model & set. **TDT**, vol. XXVII, n. 3 (Summer 1991). 12.

Grübler, Ekkehard. Cuvilliés Theatre, Munich: 1976. B&W. Set. **TDT**, vol. XII, n. 1 (Spring 1976). 28; B&W. Set. **TCI**, vol. 11, n. 2 (Mar/Apr 1977). 10.

Jürgens, Helmut. Bavarian State Opera, Munich: 1956. B&W. Set. **SDW2**, 63.

Messel, Oliver. Glyndebourne Festival Opera, England: 1951. B&W. Model. **DMS**, plate 26; B&W. Model. **OMB**, 154; B&W. Set. **SDG**, 188; B&W. Model. **SDW1**, 178.

O'Hearn, Robert. Washington Opera, DC: 1961. B&W. Rendering. **DDT**, 98.

Piot, René. Théâtre des Arts, Paris: 1912. B&W. Rendering. **RSD**, illus. 49.

Ponnelle, Jean-Pierre. Metropolitan Opera, NYC: 1982. B&W and color. Rendering & set. **MOM**, frontispiece & 112-123. 9 photos; B&W. Set. **TCI**, vol. 17, n. 4 (Apr 1983). 8; Salzburg Festival Theatre: 1983. B&W. Set. **DDT**, 29; State Opera, Cologne: B&W. Set. **DSL**, figure 27.1(d); B&W. Set. **SST**, 379, 445.

Sendak, Maurice. Los Angeles Music Center Opera: 1990. B&W. Set. **TDT**, vol. XXVII, n. 3 (Summer 1991). 9.

Steinberg, Paul. Geneva Opera: 1994. Color. Set. **TCI**, vol. 29, n. 4 (Apr 1995). 32, 33; B&W. Set. **TDT** vol. XXXI, n. 2 (Spring 1995). 15.

Svoboda, Josef. State Opera, Vienna: 1971. B&W. Set. **SJS**, 165; B&W. Set. **STS**, 78; National Arts Center, Ottawa: 1981. B&W. Model & set. **STS**, 22, 78, 79. 3 photos.

Zimmermann, Jörg. Salzburg Festival: 1973. B&W. Set. **TCI**, vol. 7, n. 6 (Nov/Dec 1973). 2.

If I Were King.

Unitt, Edward G. Garden Theatre, NYC: 1901. B&W. Set. **MCN**, 17.

The Illusion.

Conklin, John. Hartford Stage, Connecticut: 1990. B&W. Set. **TCI**, vol. 24, n. 4 (Apr 1990). 12; B&W. Set. **TCI**, vol. 25, n. 9 (Nov 1991). 40.

Stewart, Anita C. Tyrone Guthrie Theatre, Minneapolis: 1991. Color. Set. **TCI**, vol. 25, n. 8 (Oct 1991). 20. 2 photos.

TenEyck, Karen. Classic Stage Company, NYC: 1993. Color. Set. **TCI**, vol. 28, n. 3 (Mar 1994). 11.

Wendland, Mark. Trinity Repertory Company, Providence, Rhode Island: 1995. Color. Set. **TCI**, vol. 29, n. 6 (Jun/Jul 1995). 11.

Im Dickicht der Städte.

_____. Germany: 1927. B&W. Set. **TPH**, photo 428.

The Imaginary Invalid.

Benois, Alexander. Moscow Art Theatre: 1911. B&W. Rendering. **FCS**, plate 172. Act I; B&W. Rendering. **SDO**, 194.

Feuerstein, Bedrich. National Theatre, Prague: 1921. B&W. Set. **TCS2**, plates 244, 245; B&W. Set. **TDT**, n. 41 (Summer 1975). 20.

Larkin, Grady. 1973. B&W. Set. **TCI**, vol. 9, n. 1 (Jan/Feb 1975). 17.

Luzzati, Emanuele. Rome: 1952. B&W. Set. **SDE**, 99.

Szekely, Laszlo. Nemzeti Szinhaz, Szeged, Magyarorszag: 1968. B&W. Set. **SDW3**, 72.

Imagination Dead Imagine.

Mabou Mines, NYC: 1984. B&W. **TCI**, vol. 22, n. 9 (Nov 1988). 90.

The Immortal Hour.
Shelving, Paul. Regent Theatre, London: 1922. B&W. Rendering. **TCS2**, plate 226.
The Importance of Being Earnest.
Blackman, Robert. Performing Arts Center, Santa Maria, California: B&W. Set. **TCI**, vol. 14, n. 4 (Sep 1980). 35.
Faulkner, Cliff. South Coast Repertory Theatre, Costa Mesa, California: Color. Set. **TCI**, vol. 20, n. 9 (Nov 1986). 25.
Gjelsteen, Karen. Intiman Theatre/2nd Stage, Seattle: 1977. B&W. Set. **TCI**, vol. 11, n. 6 (Nov/Dec 1977). 96.
McCarry, Charles E. Yale Repertory Theatre, New Haven: B&W. Model. **TDT**, vol. XXVI, n. 1 (Spring 1990). 14 of insert. 2 photos.
Motley (Margaret Harris, Sophia Harris, & Elizabeth Montgomery). Royale Theatre, NYC: 1947. B&W. Set. **WTP**, 134, 135.
Straiges, Tony. Arena Stage, Washington, DC: 1983. B&W. Model. **DDT**, 236; B&W. Set. **TCI**, vol. 18, n. 3 (Mar 1984). 29.
In a Fine Castle.
Montgomery, Richard. Creative Arts Theatre, Kingston, Jamaica. 1970. B&W. Set. **SDW4**, illus. 334.
In Abraham's Bosom.
Throckmorton, Cleon. Provincetown Playhouse, NYC: 1926. B&W. Set. **MCN**, 80.
In Circles.
_____. NYC: B&W. Set. **TCI**, vol. 5, n. 1 (Jan/Feb 1971). 24.
In Closed Time.
Arquitectonica. Brooklyn Academy of Music, New York: 1985. B&W. Set. **TDT**, vol. XXII, n. 1 (Spring 1986). 9.
In Contempt.
Griffeth, Michael J. Miami University Theatre, Ohio: B&W. Set. **TDT**, vol. XIX, n. 3 (Fall 1983). 17.
In Dahomey.
_____. Shaftsbury Theatre, London: 1903. B&W. Set. **MCD**, plates 43, 44.
In His Garden Don Perlimplin Loves Belisa.
Bazaine, Jean. Studio des Champs-Elysées, Paris: 1946. B&W. Rendering. **AST**, 241.
Schlubach, Jan. Deutsches Theater, Göttingen: 1963. B&W. Rendering. **SDW2**, 71.
In Praise of Falling.
_____. Painters Theatre: B&W. Set. **SST**, 203.
In Search of Hakamadare.
Asakura, Setsu. Gekidan-Seigei, Haiyuzo-Gekijo, Tokyo: 1964. B&W. Model. **SDW3**, 152.
In the Boom Boom Room.
Mitchell, David. New York Shakespeare Festival, NYC: 1974. Color. Set. **DSL**, plate VI.
In the Jungle of Cities.
Neher, Caspar. Residenz Theater, Munich: 1923. B&W. Rendering. **CBM**, 78; Color. Rendering. **RSD**, illus. 554; B&W. Set. **TBB**, 24, 75.
In the Matter of J. Robert Oppenheimer.
Wexler, Peter. Repertory Theatre of Lincoln Center, NYC: B&W and color. Model. **SDT**, between 152 & 153, 298.
In the Pasha's Garden.
Kiesler, Frederick. NYC: 1935. B&W. Set. **EIF**, photo 15.

In the Summer House.
> Tsypin, George. Vivian Beaumont Theatre, Lincoln Center, NYC: 1993. Color. Set.
> **TCI**, vol. 27, n. 8 (Oct 1993). 6.

In the Whirlwind.
> Navitskas, Felix. Gosoudarstvennyj Akademitcheskij Teatr Dramy, Vilnius: 1970.
> B&W. Rendering. **SDW3**, 144.

In The Zone.
> _____. Comedy Theatre, NYC: 1917. B&W. Set. **MCN**, 43.

In Time to Come.
> Goffin, Peter. King's Theatre, Hammersmith, London: B&W. Set. **DOT**, 246.

Inadmissible Evidence.
> Herbert, Jocelyn. Royal Court Theatre, London: 1965. B&W. Set. **SDR**, 81.
> Schwab, Per. National Theatre, Oslo: 1965. B&W. Set. **SDR**, 80.

Inching Through the Everglades.
> _____. Provisional Theatre, Los Angeles: B&W. Set. **TCI**, vol. 14, n. 4 (Sep
> 1980). 33.

Incident at Vichy.
> Aronson, Boris. ANTA Washington Square Theatre, NYC: 1964. B&W and color.
> Rendering, model, & set. **TAB**, 161, 162, 307. 4 photos.
> Payne, Darwin Reid. B&W. Model & set. **SDL**, 87. 2 photos; B&W. Model & set.
> **TCM**, xxiv, xxv.
> _____. Playhouse in the Park, Cincinnati: B&W. Set. **TCI**, vol. 14, n. 1 (Jan/Feb
> 1980). 38.

Incidents During a Forced Landing.
> Bill, Max. State Opera, Hamburg: 1966. B&W. Set. **AST**, 236. 4 photos; B&W. Set.
> **SDW3**, 198.

L'Incoronazione de Poppea.
> Evans, Lloyd. New York City Opera: 1973. B&W. Model. **DPT**, 131.
> Jampolis, Neil Peter. Kennedy Center Opera House, Washington, DC: 1973. Color.
> Set. **DPT**, title page.
> Wendel, Heinrich. B&W. Set. **OPE**, 45.

The Incredible Rocky.
> Kallapos, John. California Institute of the Arts: B&W. Set. **DSL**, figure 4.3(b); B&W.
> Set. **SST**, 93.

Les Indes Galantes.
> Fost-Moulene. Opéra de Paris: 1952. B&W. Rendering. **SDW1**, 97.

Indiscretions.
> Lewis, Stephen Brimson. Ethel Barrymore Theatre, NYC: 1995. Color. Model & set.
> **TCI**, vol. 29, n. 4 (Apr 1995). 66. 3 photos.

The Indiad or the India of Their Dreams.
> _____. Cartoucherie Performance Hall, Paris: 1987. Color. Set. **TCI**, vol. 22, n.
> 7 (Aug/Sep 1988). 36.

Indian Love Lyrics.
> Wenger, John. NYC: 1922. B&W. Rendering. **SDB**, 54.

Indians.
> Smith, Oliver. Brooks Atkinson Theatre, NYC: 1969. B&W. Model. **CSD**, 129; B&W.
> Model. **DPT**, 153; B&W. Set. **TCI**, vol. 16, n. 4 (Apr 1982). 17; B&W. Set. **TCI**,
> vol. 7, n. 3 (May/Jun 1973). 18; Color. Set. **TCI**, vol. 23, n. 4 (Apr 1989). 50.
> Vancura, Jan. Czechoslovakia: B&W. Set. **TDT**, vol. XXVII, n. 3 (Summer 1991). 26.

The Indifferent One.
    Bignens, Max. State Theatre, Basel: 1949. B&W. Model. **SDW1**, 113.
Ein Indisches Märchenspiel.
    Hoflehner, Rudolf. Die Tribüne, Vienna: 1954. B&W. Rendering & set. **AST**, 232. 2
       photos.
Inherit the Wind.
    Larkin, Peter. National Theatre, NYC: 1955. B&W. Sketch. **SDB**, 101; B&W. Set.
       TCI, vol. 23, n. 1 (Jan 1989). 40.
    Schmidt, Emile O. Gettysburg College: B&W. Set. **TCI**, vol. 3, n. 2 (Mar/Apr 1969).
       18.
The Inkpot.
    Borges, Jacobo. Teatro ACAT, Valencia, Venezuela: 1965. B&W. Set. **SDW3**, 148.
The Inn.
    Delft, Hep van. Koninklijken Schouwburg, The Hague: 1960. B&W. Set. **SDW2**, 143.
Inner City.
    Wagner, Robin. Ethel Barrymore Theatre, NYC: 1971. B&W. Sketch. **TCI**, vol. 7, n. 6
       (Nov/Dec 1973). 8.
The Innocents.
    Mielziner, Jo. Playhouse Theatre, NYC: 1950. B&W. Rendering. **DTT**, 157.
       Children's pantomime; B&W. Rendering. **DTT**, 158. Ghost scene; B&W. Set.
       SDA, 206.
Inquest.
    Eigsti, Karl. Music Box Theatre, NYC: 1970. B&W. Sketch. **DPT**, 121.
The Insect Comedy.
    Alme, Gunnar. Rogaland Teater, Stavanger, Norway: 1956. B&W. Set. **SDW2**, 151.
    Capek, Josef. National Theatre, Prague: 1922. B&W. Set. **TCS2**, plate 357; B&W. Set.
       TDT, n. 42 (Fall 1975). 23.
    Hampton, Michael. Festival Theater, Cambridge, England: 1927. B&W. Set. **DIT**,
       plate 57; B&W. Set. **TPH**, photo 434.
    Johansen, Svend. Det ny Teater, Copenhagen: 1950. B&W. Rendering. **SDW1**, 56.
    Svoboda, Josef. National Theatre, Prague: 1965. B&W. Set. **SDB**, 143; B&W. Set.
       SJS, 116, 118. 3 photos; B&W. Set. **STS**, 51; B&W. Set. **TDT**, n. 20 (Feb 1970). 4.
    Tomek, Milos. Statni Divadlo, Brno, Czechoslovakia: 1958. B&W. Rendering. **SDW2**,
       46.
Inside U.S.A.
    Ayers, Lemuel. New Century Theatre, NYC: 1948. B&W. Set. **WMC**, 169.
An Inspector Calls.
    Damonte, Marcelo. Histrión-Teatro de Arte, Lima: 1961. B&W. Set. **SDW2**, 163.
    MacNeil, Ian. Lyttleton Theatre, London: 1993. Color. Set. **TCI**, vol. 28, n. 4 (Apr
       1994). 5, 28, 29. 4 photos.
The Inspector General.
    Akimov, Nikolai. Teatr Komedii, Leningrad: 1958. B&W. Set. **SDW2**, 177.
    Bohanetzky, Polly Scranton & Tanya Moiseiwitsch. Stratford Festival Theatre,
       Ontario, Canada: 1985. Color. Set. **TCI**, vol. 20, n. 7 (Aug/Sep 1986). 17.
    Gunter, John. National Theatre (Olivier), London: 1985. B&W. Set. **BTD**, 72; B&W.
       Set. **TDT**, vol. XXV, n. 3 (Fall 1989). 18.
    Hruza, Lubos. Cinoherni Klub, Prague: 1967. B&W. Rendering. **SDW3**, 82.
    Komisarjevsky, Theodore. London: 1926. B&W. Set. **SOW**, plate 68.
    Koniarsky, Helmut. Schlosspark Theatre, Berlin: 1961. B&W. Rendering. **SDW2**, 63.

Lobel, Adrianne. American Repertory Theatre, Cambridge, Massachusetts: 1980.
      B&W. Set. **ASD2**, 102; Yale Repertory Theatre, New Haven, Connecticut: Color.
      Set. **TCI**, vol. 18, n. 1 (Jan 1984). 24.
Merritt, Michael. Goodman Theatre, Chicago: 1986. B&W. Set. **ASD2**, 124, 127;
      Color. Set. **TCI**, vol. 21, n. 2 (Feb 1987). 29.
Meyerhold, Vsevelod, plan; Victor Kisselev, execution. Meyerhold Theatre, Moscow:
      1926. B&W. Set. **MOT**, between 224 & 225 and between 240 & 241; B&W. Set.
      NTO, facing 324; B&W. Sketches & set. **RSD**, illus. 205-207; B&W. Sketch &
      set. **RST**, 191, 224, 225. 3 photos; B&W. Set. **TPH**, photo 412; B&W. Set. **TSS**,
      523.
Paston, Doria. Cambridge Festival Theatre: 1932. B&W. Set. **SDG**, 173.
Patel, Neil. Mandell Weiss Forum, La Jolla Playhouse, California: Color. Set. **TCI**,
      vol. 25, n. 1 (Jan 1991). 40.
(pupils of Pavel Filonov). Leningrad: 1927. Color. Rendering. **RST**, 251.
Rabinovitch, Isaac. Meyerhold Theatre, Moscow: 1920. B&W. Set. **TCS2**, plate 183.
Schultz, Karen. Circle in the Square Theatre, NYC: 1979. B&W. Set. **DDT**, 112.
Svoboda, Josef. National Theatre, Prague: 1948. B&W. Rendering. **SJS**, 134; B&W.
      Rendering. **STS**, 52.
Tröster, Frantisek. National Theatre, Prague: 1936. B&W. Rendering. **TDT**, n. 42 (Fall
      1975). 29.
_____.Katona József Szinház, Kecskemét, Hungary: Color. Set. **TCI**, vol. 24, n.
      5 (May 1990). 39.
_____.Moscow Art Theatre: 1908. B&W. Set. **TSS**, 523.
_____.National Theatre, London: 1985. B&W. Set. **TCI**, vol. 23, n. 2 (Feb
      1989). 39.
An Interest in Strangers.
_____. Theatre X, Milwaukee: B&W. Set. **TCI**, vol. 17, n. 8 (Oct 1983). 29.
Interlock.
Bay, Howard. ANTA Theatre, NYC: 1958. B&W. Set. **SDA**, 206.
The Interlude of Youth.
Shelving, Paul. Malvern: 1934. B&W. Set. **DOT**, 221.
Intermezzo.
Jackness, Andrew. Glimmerglass Opera, Cooperstown, New York: 1990. B&W. Ren-
      dering. **TCI**, vol. 24, n. 7 (Aug/Sep 1990). 34. 2 photos.
Schenk von Trapp, Lothar. Landestheater, Darmstadt: 1929-1930. B&W. Set. **RSD**,
      illus. 250.
Into the Woods.
Straiges, Tony. Martin Beck Theatre, NYC: 1987. B&W. Sketch. **ASD2**, 156; Color.
      Model. **ASD2**, between 108 & 109; B&W. Model & drop. **DDT**, 173, 397. 3
      photos; B&W and color. Set. **MBM**, 40, 41; B&W and color. Set. **SON**, 169, 173,
      176. 4 photos; Color. Set. **TCI**, vol. 22, n. 1 (Jan 1988). 29, 32, 33. 4 photos.
Intolerance.
Svoboda, Josef. Opera Group of Boston: 1965. B&W. Rendering & set. **SDW3**, 208. 3
      photos; B&W. Set. **SJS**, 104. 2 photos.
Intolleranza 1960.
Vedova, Emilio. Teatro La Fenice, Venice: 1961. B&W. Set. **AST**, 243. 4 photos.
Intrigue and Love.
Oechslin, Ary. Ateliertheater, Bern: 1959. B&W. Model. **SDW2**, 112.
The Intruder.
Hume, Samuel J. 1917. B&W. Set. **TDT**, vol. XX, n. 2 (Summer 1984). 14.

The Investigation.
   Palmstierna-Weiss, Gunilla Dramatiska Teatern, Stockholm: 1966. B&W. Model.
      SDW3, 134.
   Puecher, Virginio. Piccolo Teatro, Milan: 1967. B&W. Rendering & set. **RSD**, illus.
      609, 610.
   Schmückle, Hans-Ulrich. Freie Volksbühne, Berlin: 1965. B&W. Model. **SDW3**, 134.
The Invisible People.
   _____. Nashville Children's Theatre: B&W. Set. **TCI**, vol. 5, n. 2 (Mar/Apr
      1971). 10.
Iolanthe.
   Jones, Christine. Glimmerglass Opera, Cooperstown, New York: 1994. Color. Set.
      TCI, vol. 28, n. 9 (Nov 1994). 9.
Ionas and Edme.
   Klicius, Galius. USSR: B&W. Model. **TDT**, vol. XX, n. 1 (Spring 1984). 17.
Iphigenia.
   Dorrer, Valeri. USSR: B&W. **TDT**, vol. XII, n. 3 (Fall 1976). 41.
   Preetorius, Emil. State Theatre, Munich: 1929. B&W. Rendering. **SCM**, 68.
Iphigenia and Other Daughters.
   Sissons, Narelle. Classic Stage Company, NYC: 1995. Color. Set. **TCI**, vol. 29, n. 4
      (Apr 1995). 7.
Iphigenia in Tauris.
   Axer, Otto. Teatr Wspolczesny, Warsaw: 1961. B&W. Set. **SDW2**, 165.
   Barch, Ruddi. Germany: B&W. Set. **SDL**, 33.
   Cambellotti, Duilio. Greek Theatre at Syracuse: 1933. B&W. Model. **TPH**, photo 386.
   Hoflehner, Rudolf. Schauspielhaus, Düsseldorf: 1963. B&W. Set. **AST**, 233.
   Kiesler, Frederick. Barbizon-Plaza Theatre, NYC: 1942. B&W. Sketch. **EIF**, photo 23.
   Masson, André. Festival d'Aix-en-Provence: 1952. B&W. Set. **AST**, 202. 2 photos.
   Napier, John. 1980. B&W. Model. **TDT**, vol. XIX, n. 1 (Spring 1983). 10.
Irene.
   Du Bois, Raoul Pène. Minskoff Theatre, NYC: 1973. B&W. Set. **DPT**, 286; B&W. Set.
      TCI, vol. 7, n. 4 (Sep 1973). 25.
   _____.Adelphi Theatre, London: B&W. Set. **BMF**, 107.
Irma LaDouce.
   Larkin, Grady. 1973. B&W. Set. **TCI**, vol. 9, n. 1 (Jan/Feb 1975). 16.
The Iron Flood.
   _____. Realistic Theatre, Moscow: 1930. B&W. Set. **RST**, 282, 283.
The Iron Man.
   Keegan, Shelagh. Young Vic Theatre, London: 1993. Color. Set. **TCI**, vol. 28, n. 2
      (Feb 1994). 12.
The Island God.
   Berman, Eugene. 1942. B&W. Rendering. **SDE**, 41.
Island of Goats.
   Mielziner, Jo. Fulton Theatre, NYC: 1955. B&W. Rendering. **DTT**, 193. Interior.
It Happened in Irkutsk.
   Perahim, Jules. Teatrul National, Bucharest: 1960. B&W. Model. **SDW2**, 175.
It's a Bird, It's a Plane, It's Superman.
   _____. 1966. B&W. Set. **BWM**, 303. 2 photos.
The Italian Girl in Algiers.
   Feiner, Harry. Pennsylvania Opera Theatre, Pittsburgh: 1985. B&W. Set. **BSE4**, 19.
   Pogany, Willy. Metropolitan Opera, NYC: 1919. B&W. Rendering. **MOM**, 7.

Ponnelle, Jean-Pierre. Metropolitan Opera, NYC: 1979. B&W and color. Set. **MOM**, 124-131. 7 photos.

Siercke, Alfred. State Opera, Hamburg: 1953. B&W. Set. **SDW1**, 78.

Svoboda, Josef. Municipal Theatre, Rio de Janeiro: 1963. B&W. Rendering. **SJS**, 151.

Zeffirelli, Franco. 1952-1953. B&W. Set. **SIO**, 134.

The Italian Straw Hat.

Becker, Victor. National Theatre of the Deaf: 1995. Color. Set. **TCI**, vol. 29, n. 3 (Mar 1995). 62.

Trautvetter, Paul. Carnegie Institute of Technology, Pittsburgh: 1958. B&W. Set. **SDW2**, 238.

Italian-American Reconciliation.

Arcenas, Loy. Cleveland Playhouse: 1989. B&W. Set. **ASD2**, 8.

Ivan Sussanin (or) *The Life of the Tsar.*

Tatlin, Vladimir. Bakhrushin, Museum, Moscow: 1913. B&W. Rendering. **RSD**, illus. 165.

Ivan the Terrible.

Vychodil, Ladislav. Bratislava: 1947. B&W. Model. **TDT**, vol. XV, n. 2 (Summer 1979). 10.

_____.B&W. Set. **TCM**, 114.

Ivanov.

Borovsky, David. 1984. B&W. Model. **TDT**, vol. XVI, n. 1 (Spring 1980). 24; B&W and color. Model. **TDT**, vol. XXIII, n. 4 (Winter 1988). 6, 25.

Csányi, Arpád. Némzeti Színház, Budapest: 1971. B&W. Set. **SDW3**, 91. 2 photos.

Kitaïev, Mark. USSR: 1975. B&W. Model. **TDT**, vol. XXIII, n. 4 (Winter 1988). 27.

Svoboda, Josef. Theatre Behind the Gate, Prague: 1970. B&W. Set. **SDW3**, 90. 2 photos; B&W. Set. **SJS**, 42.

Zborilová, Jana. Czechoslovakia: B&W. Rendering. **TDT**, vol. XXVI, n. 4 (Fall 1990). 27. 4 photos.

Ivona, The Princess of Burgundia.

Roos, Norvid. B&W. Model. **TDT**, vol. XVI, n. 4 (Winter 1980). 13.

-J-

J.B.

Aronson, Boris. ANTA Theatre (Virginia Theatre), NYC: 1958. B&W. Set. **DPT**, 387; B&W. Set. **RSD**, illus. 456; B&W. Set. **SDR**, 56; B&W. Set. **SDW2**, 230; B&W. Rendering. **TCI**, vol. 23, n. 8 (Oct 1989). 10; B&W and color. Rendering, model, & set. **TAB**, 18, 141-144, 305. 9 photos.

Oenslager, Donald. Yale School of Drama, New Haven, Connecticut: 1958. B&W. Rendering. **SDL**, 56; B&W. Rendering. **TDO**, 133; B&W. Rendering. **SDW2**, 237.

Jabez and the Devils.

Lambert, Isabel. Royal Opera House, Covent Garden, London: 1961. B&W. Set. **SDW2**, 219.

Jack and the Beanstalk.

Gardiner, Robert. Seattle Children's Theatre: 1993. Color. Set. **TCI**, vol. 28, n. 3 (Mar 1994). 11.

Jack MacGowran in the Works of Samuel Beckett.

Lee, Ming Cho. New York Shakespeare Festival, NYC: 1970. B&W. Model. **ASD1**, 103.

The Jack the Ripper Revue.
>McCarry, Charles E. Actor's Outlet Theatre: B&W. Set. **TDT**, vol. XXVIII, n. 2 (Spring 1992). 7 of insert.

Jack-in-the-Box.
>Derain, André. Ballets Russes, Paris Opera: 1926. B&W. Rendering. **AST**, 101. 3 photos.

Jackie the Jumper.
>Annals, Michael. Royal Court Theatre, London: 1963. B&W. Rendering. **DMS**, plate 55.

Jacob's Ladder.
>Jampolis, Neil Peter. Opera Theatre, Santa Fe: 1968. B&W. Set. **SDW3**, 187.

A Jade for Don Juan.
>Hegle, Kaare. Det Nye Teater, Oslo: 1948. B&W. Rendering. **SDW1**, 153.

Jake's Women.
>Straiges, Tony. Old Globe Theatre, San Diego: 1990. B&W. Model. **DDT**, 356.

Jamaica.
>Smith, Oliver. Imperial Theatre, NYC: 1957. B&W. Set. **BWM**, 332, 333.

Jan Hus.
>Svoboda, Josef. National Theatre, Prague: 1953. B&W. Set. **SDW1**, 52.

Jane Eyre.
>Edwards, Ben. Belasco Theatre, NYC: 1958. B&W. Set. **DDT**, 285.
>Simonson, Lee. NYC: 1936. B&W. Set. **PLT**, illus. 21; B&W. Set. **SDB**, 41.

January.
>Dobrev, Rumen. Nikola Vapracov Dramatic Theatre, Blagoevgrad, Bulgaria: 1985. B&W. Model. **TDT**, vol. XXIII, n. 4 (Winter 1988). 12.

La Jarre.
>de Chirico, Georgio. Ballets Suédois, Paris: 1924. Color. Rendering. **AST**, 185.

Jarry on the Butte.
>Noël, Jacques. Elysée Montmartre, Paris: 1970. B&W. Rendering & set. **SDW3**, 98, 221.

The Jealous Old Man.
>Muñoz, Gori. Politeama, Buenos Aires: 1947. B&W. Rendering. **SDW1**, 37.

Jeanne au Bucher.
>Benois, Nicola. La Scala, Milan: 1954. B&W. Rendering. **SDE**, 39. 2 photos.

Jeanne d'Arc.
>Bel Geddes, Norman. Paris: 1925. B&W. Model. **TCS2**, plate 70; B&W. Sketches, model, rendering, & set. **TDT**, n. 18 (Oct 1969). 4-11. 11 photos.
>Mork, Lennart. Kungliga Teatern, Stockholm: 1986. Color. Model. **TDT**, vol. XXIII, n. 4 (Winter 1988). 7.

Jeb.
>Mielziner, Jo. Martin Beck Theatre, NYC: 1946. B&W. Rendering. **DTT**, 133. Bar; B&W. Rendering. **DTT**, 134. Parlor interview; B&W. Rendering. **DTT**, 135. Church.

Jedermann.
>Reinhardt, Max. Cathedral Square, Salzburg: 1921. B&W. Set. **TCS2**, plate 373.

Jennie.
>Jenkins, George. Majestic Theatre, NYC: 1963. B&W. Set. **BMF**, 67.

Jenufa.
>Hernon, Paul. Royal Opera House, Covent Garden, London: 1986. B&W. Set. **BTD**, 139.

Skalicky, Jan & Reinhart Zimmerman. Komische Oper, Berlin: 1964. B&W. Model.
   SDW3, 185.
Vychodil, Ladislav. Bratislava: 1986. Color. Set. **TCI**, vol. 21, n. 8 (Oct 1987). 38.
Jeppe on the Hill.
   Aaes, Eric. Det ny Teater, Copenhagen: 1948. B&W. Set. **SDW1**, 55.
Jerome Robbin's Broadway.
   Wagner, Robin. Imperial Theatre, NYC: 1989. B&W and color. Rendering. DDT,
      152d, 347; Color. Set. **MBM**, 32, 33; B&W and color. Set. **TCI**, vol. 23, n. 7 (Aug/
      Sep 1989). 57-59. 4 photos.
Jerry's Girls.
   Tiné, Hal. St. James Theatre, NYC: 1985. B&W. Rendering. **SDT**, 299; National tour,
      USA: c.1986. Color. Rendering. **SDT**, between 152 & 153.
The Jest.
   Jones, Robert Edmond. Plymouth Theatre, NYC: 1919. B&W. Sketch. **DFT**, plate 4.
      Act III: the pillar; B&W. Sketch. **DFT**, plate 5. Act II: Ginevra's chamber; B&W.
      Set. **MCN**, 46; B&W. Rendering. **SDA**, 198; B&W. Set. **SOW**, plate 76.
Jesus Christ Superstar.
   Kanamori, Kaoru. Gékidan-Shiki. Nakano Sun Plaza Hall, Tokyo: 1973. B&W and
      color. Sketch & set. **SDW4**, illus. 409-421; B&W. Set. **TDT**, vol. XII, n. 3 (Fall
      1976). 38.
   Wagner, Robin. B&W. Set. **TCI**, vol. 6, n. 3 (May/Jun 1972). 10, 11. 3 photos; Mark
      Hellinger Theatre, NYC: 1971. Color. Set. **ALW**, 46-49. 6 photos; B&W. Set. **TCI**,
      vol. 5, n. 6 (Nov/Dec 1971). 9; Universal Amphitheatre, Los Angeles: 1972. B&W
      and color. Set. **ALW**, 50, 51; B&W. Set. **DPT**, 388, 389, 394; B&W. Set. **TCI**, vol.
      7, n. 6 (Nov/Dec 1973). 9. 2 photos; Palace Theatre, London: 1972. Color. Set.
      ALW, 55; B&W. Set. **MBM**, 55; B&W. Set. **TCI**, vol. 8, n. 1 (Jan/Feb 1974). 18.
      _____.Jerusalem: 1989. Color. Set. **ALW**, 53.
      _____.Tokyo: 1973. Color. Set. **ALW**, 53.
Jeu de l'Amour et de la Mort.
   Hoffman, Vlastislav. National Theatre, Prague: B&W. Set. **TCS2**, plate 271.
Le Jeune Homme et la Mort.
   Wahkévitch, Georges. Paris: 1948. B&W. Set. **SDE**, 164.
Jeux d'Enfants.
   Miró, Joán. Thêátre de Monte Carlo: 1932. B&W. Rendering. **SDR**, 28.
The Jew of Malta.
   Koltai, Ralph. Royal Shakespeare Company, Aldwych Theatre, London: 1964. Color.
      Model. **SDR**, 40. 3 photos.
Jew Süss.
   Aronson, Boris. Yiddish Art Theatre (Second Avenue Theatre), NYC: 1929. B&W.
      Rendering. **TAB**, 294.
Jewels.
   Harvey, Peter. New York City Ballet, Lincoln Center: 1967. B&W. Model. **DPT**, 365.
The Jewels of the Queen.
   Fisher, Randi & Lennart Mörk. Dramatiska Teatern, Stockholm: 1957. B&W. Set.
      SDW2, 210.
Jim Cooperkop.
   Aronson, Boris. Princess Theatre, NYC: 1930. B&W. Set. **TAB**, 294.
Jimmy Higgins.
   Berezil Theatre, Ukraine: 1923. B&W. Set. **RST**, 159. 2 photos.
Joan at the Stake.
   Bonnat, Yves (Yves-Bonnat). Opéra de Paris: 1951. B&W. Set. **SDW1**, 87.

Joan of Arc.
> Bloumberg, Ilmar. Rousskij Dramatitcheskij Teatr, Riga: 1972. B&W. Set. **SDW4,** illus. 210.

Job.
> Oenslager, Donald. (project): 1941. B&W. Rendering. **TDO,** 103-107. 5 photos.

Jockeys.
> Wexler, Peter. Promenade Theatre, NYC: B&W. Set. **SDT,** 113.

The Jocky Club Stakes.
> Pond, Helen & Herbert Senn. Cape Playhouse, Dennis, Massachusetts: 1973. B&W. Set. **DPT,** 332.

John B. Conquers the World.
> Kourll, Mlroslav. D35 Theatre, Prague. 1934. B&W. Rendering. **RSD,** illus. 284.

John Brown's Body.
> Howard, Pamela. Tramway Theatre, Glasgow: 1990. B&W. Model. **TDT,** vol. XXVII, n. 4 (Fall 1991). 36.
> Landwehr, Hugh. Williamstown Theatre Festival, Massachusetts: 1989. B&W. Show curtain. **DDT,** 511.

John Ferguson.
> Peters, Rollo. Garrick Theatre, NYC: 1919. B&W. Set. **MCN,** 47.

John Gabriel Borkman.
> Lubos, Hruzo. Norway: B&W. Model. **TDT,** vol. XXVII, n. 4 (Fall 1991). 51.
> Stern, Ernst. Deutsches Theater, Berlin: 1917. Color. Rendering. **MRH,** facing 14. 2 photos.

John Murray Anderson's Almanac.
> Du Bois, Raoul Pène. Imperial Theatre, NYC: 1953. B&W. Set. **DPT,** 290; B&W. Set. **SDA,** 253.

Johnny Johnson.
> Oenslager, Donald. 44th Street Theatre, NYC: 1936. B&W. Set. **SOW,** plate 84; B&W. Rendering & set. **TDO,** 70, 71; B&W. Set. **WMC,** 198.

Johnny On a Spot.
> Beatty, John Lee. Brooklyn Academy of Music, New York: 1980. B&W. Rendering. **ASD1,** 5; B&W. Rendering. **TDT,** vol. XVIII, n. 4 (Winter 1982). 6.

Jonny spielt auf (Johnny Strikes Up).
> _____. National Theater, Zagreb: B&W. Projection. **TPH,** photo 373.

Joseph.
> Sharpe, Robert Redington. Liberty Theatre, NYC: 1930. B&W. Rendering. **TDT,** vol. XXVII, n. 1 (Winter 1991). 19.

Joseph and the Amazing Technicolor Dreamcoat.
> Eigsti, Karl. Entermedia Theatre, NYC: 1981/1982. B&W. Set. **ASD1,** 34; B&W and color. Set. **ALW,** 41-44. 5 photos; Color. Rendering. **DDT,** 440a.
> Macie, Tom. University of North Carolina, Wilmington: 1989. B&W. Set. **TCI,** vol. 25, n. 4 (Apr 1991). 74.
> Thompson, Mark. Pantages Theatre, Hollywood, California: 1993. Color. Set. **TCI,** vol. 27, n. 8 (Oct 1993). 5, 38-41. 10 photos.

Josephine, the Mouse Singer.
> Cate, Donald. Magic Theatre, San Francisco: B&W. Set. **TCI,** vol. 14, n. 4 (Sep 1980). 23.
> _____.B&W. Model. **TDT,** vol. XVI, n. 4 (Winter 1980). 15.

The Journey.
> Svoboda, Josef. State Opera, Hamburg: 1969. B&W. Set. **SDL,** 478. 2 photos; B&W. Set. **SJS,** 96. 2 photos; B&W. Set. **TDT,** n. 20 (Feb 1970). 9. 2 photos.

Journey into Hell.
   Douking, Georges. Théâtre Pigalle, Paris: 1947. B&W. Set. **SDW1**, 95.
The Journey of Veniamin III.
   Falk, Robert. State Jewish Theatre, Moscow: 1927. B&W. Set. **RST**, 160.
Journey to Jerusalem.
   Mielziner, Jo. National Theatre, NYC: 1940. B&W. Rendering. **DTT**, 116. Temple
      scene; Color. Rendering. **DTT**, 117. Gate.
Journey's End.
   Conklin, John. Long Wharf Theatre, New Haven, Connecticut: 1979. B&W. Set. **TCI**,
      vol. 14, n. 3 (May/Jun 1980). 23.
Joy Street.
   Levine, Moisei. State Dramatic Theatre, Leningrad: 1932. B&W. Model. **TAT**, plate
      691.
Juarez and Maximilian.
   Simonson, Lee. Theatre Guild, NYC: 1926. B&W. Sketches & set. **TAS**, 132-135. 7
      photos.
Jubilee.
   Mielziner, Jo. Imperial Theatre, NYC: 1935. B&W. Set. **BWM**, 57, 208, 209. 3 pho-
      tos; B&W. Set. **MCN**, 125; B&W. Set. **RBS**, 119. 2 photos; B&W. Set. **WMC**,
      150.
The Judas Applause.
   Taylor, Robert U. Chelsea Theatre Center, Brooklyn, New York: 1969. B&W. Render-
      ing. **DPT**, 90.
The Judge.
   Stegars, Rolf. Suomen Kansallisteatteri, Helsinki: 1963. B&W. Rendering. **SDW3**,
      108.
Die Jüdische Wittwe.
   Crayon. Landestheater, Meiningen: B&W. Rendering. **TCS2**, plate 89.
Judith.
   Aronson, Boris. Her Majesty's Theatre, London: 1962. B&W and color. Rendering &
      set. **TAB**, 137, 306. 4 photos.
   Liberts, Ludolf. National Theatre, Riga: 1925. B&W. Rendering. **TCS2**, plates 248,
      249.
   Ratto, Gianni. La Scala, Milan: 1951. B&W. Rendering. **SDE**, 140.
   Sievert, Ludwig. B&W. Rendering. **DIT**, plate 97.
   _____.Grosses Schauspielhaus, Berlin: B&W. Rendering. **CSC**, facing 164, 168.
Le Juif du Pape.
   Pitoëff, Georges. Théâtre des Arts, Paris: B&W. Set. **SCM**, 54; B&W. Set. **TCS2**, plate
      216.
La Juive.
   Urban, Joseph. Metropolitan Opera, NYC: 1919. Color. Rendering. **MOM**, 9.
Juliet or the Key to Her Dreams.
   Creuz, Serge. Rideau de Bruxelles: 1951. B&W. Set. **SDW1**, 43.
Julieta.
   Musika, Frantisek. National Theatre, Prague: 1938. B&W. Set. **TDT**, n. 42 (Fall 1975).
      25.
   Svoboda, Josef. National Theatre, Prague: 1963. B&W. Rendering. **SJS**, 151.
Julius Caesar.
   Bregni, Paolo. B&W. Model. **SIO**, 17.
   Chitty, Alison. Riverside Studios, London: 1980. B&W. Sketches. **BTD**, 32.
   Coltellacci, Giulio. Roman Theatre, Verona: 1949. B&W. **SDE**, 69.

Craig, Edward Gordon. c.1905. B&W. Rendering. **OAT**, 48. Act II, sc. 2; B&W. Rendering. **TNT**, facing 37; B&W. Sketch. **TPH**, photo 322; B&W. Rendering. **OAT**, 104. Act III, sc. 2; B&W. Rendering. **SDC**, plate 68.

Eigsti, Karl. Playhouse in the Park, Cincinnati: 1984. B&W. Set. **ASD1**, 36.

Faulkner, Cliff. San Diego National Shakespeare Festival: B&W. Set. **TCI**, vol. 14, n. 4 (Sep 1980). 38.

Frycz, Karol. Polski Theater, Warsaw: 1928. B&W. Set. **RSD**, illus. 264; B&W. Set. **SCM**, 85.

Georgiadis, Nicholas. Old Vic Theatre, London: 1961. B&W. Set. **SDW3**, 45.

Klein, Julius V. Hoftheater, Munich: 1909. B&W. Set. **TPH**, photo 344.

Lee, Ming Cho. New York City Opera, Lincoln Center: 1966. Color. Set. **TCI**, vol. 18, n. 2 (Feb 1984). 21.

Leve, Samuel. Mercury Theatre, NYC: 1937. B&W. Set. **SDA**, 120; B&W. Rendering. **SOW**, plate 48.

Padovani, Gianfranco. 1971-1972. B&W. Rendering. **SIO**, 102.

Schmidt, Robert N. Colorado Shakespeare Festival: B&W. Model. **TDT**, vol. XXVIII, n. 2 (Spring 1992). 8 of insert.

Stern, Ernst. Grosses Schauspielhaus, Berlin: 1920. B&W. Rendering. **SOS**, 208.

Straiges, Tony. Yale Repertory Theatre, New Haven: 1976. B&W. Model. **ASD2**, 153; B&W. Model. **DDT**, 237; B&W. Model. **TCI**, vol. 16, n. 2 (Feb 1982). 19.

Tröster, Frantisek. National Theatre, Prague: 1936. B&W. Set. **TDT**, n. 42 (Fall 1975). 28.

Yeargan, Michael. Hartford Stage, Connecticut: B&W. Set. **TCI**, vol. 25, n. 9 (Nov 1991). 43.

Zuffi, Piero. Piccolo Teatro, Milan: 1953. B&W. Rendering. **SDE**, 172, 173. 4 photos; B&W. Set. **SDW1**, 131.

_____.Alliance Theatre, Atlanta: 1984. Color. Set. **TCI**, vol. 21, n. 3 (Mar 1987). 27.

_____.Edison Hotel, NYC: 1950. B&W. Set. **WTP**, 58.

_____.Moscow Art Theatre: 1903. B&W. Set. **SOS**, 118.

_____.New York Shakespeare Festival, NYC: 1988. Color. Set. **TCI**, vol. 22, n. 9 (Nov 1988). 47.

_____.Odéon Theatre, Paris: 1904. B&W. Drawing. **TPH**, photo 279.

Jumbo.

Johnson, Albert R. Hippodrome Theatre, NYC: 1935. B&W. Set. **BWM**, 88; B&W. Set. **WMC**, 121.

Jumpers

Butz, Fritz. Schauspielhaus, Zurich: 1974. B&W. Set. **SDW4**, illus. 378.

_____.Trinity Square Theatre, Providence, Rhode Island: B&W. Set. **TCI**, vol. 9, n. 6 (Nov/Dec 1975). 20, 24.

Jungalbook.

Yanik, Don. Honolulu Theatre for Youth: B&W. Set. **TDT**, vol. XXVIII, n. 2 (Spring 1992). 9 of insert.

Juno and Avas.

Sheintsis, Oleg. Komsomal Theatre, Moscow: Color. Set. **TCI**, vol. 24, n. 2 (Feb 1990). 20; B&W. Model. **TDT**, vol. XX, n. 1 (Spring 1984). 16.

Juno and the Paycock.

Kurtz, Kenneth. Ring Theatre, University of Miami, Florida: B&W. Set. **TCI**, vol. 7, n. 6 (Nov/Dec 1973). 18.

Payne, Darwin Reid. B&W. Sketch. **SIP**, 258.

_____.Long Wharf Theatre, New Haven, Connecticut: B&W. Set. **TCI**, vol. 7,
    n. 5 (Oct 1973). 11.

The Just Vengeance.

_____. Litchfield, England: 1946. B&W. Set. **WTP**, 50, 51.

Justice.

Scandella, Mischa, Teatro Stabile, Torino: 1959. B&W. Rendering. **SDW2**, 131.

-K-

K2.

Belden, Ursula. Pittsburgh Public Theatre: 1984. B&W. Set. **TCI**, vol. 19, n. 5 (May
    1985). 26.

Cosler, Charles. Syracuse Stage, New York: 1982. B&W. Set. **TCI**, vol. 19, n. 5 (May
    1985). 27.

Döepp, John. Theatre by the Sea: 1982. B&W. Set. **TCI**, vol. 19, n. 5 (May 1985). 27.

Dryden, Dan. San Diego Repertory Theatre: 1984. B&W. Set. **TCI**, vol. 19, n. 5 (May
    1985). 27.

Greenleaf, Jamie. Synergy, Anchorage, Alaska: 1984. B&W. Set. **TCI**, vol. 19, n. 5
    (May 1985). 27.

Lee, Ming Cho. Kreeger Theatre, Arena Stage, Washington, DC: 1982. B&W. Set.
    ASD1, 89; B&W. Set. **TCI**, vol. 16, n. 8 (Oct 1982). 16; B&W. Set. **TCI**, vol. 19,
    n. 5 (May 1985). 27; NYC: 1983. B&W. Set. **TCI**, vol. 18, n. 2 (Feb 1984). 15.

Owen, Paul. Actors Theatre of Louisville: Color. Set. **TCI**, vol. 23, n. 3 (Mar 1989).
    34.

Ray, Bill C. Perseverance Theatre, Alaska: B&W. Set. **TCI**, vol. 19, n. 5 (May 1985).
    27.

Weldin, Scott. Empty Space Theatre, Seattle: 1984. B&W. Set. **TCI**, vol. 19, n. 5 (May
    1985). 26.

K: Impressions of Kafka's THE TRIAL.

Arnone, John. Lion Theatre, NYC: 1977. B&W. Set. **ASD2**, 30. 3 photos; B&W. Set.
    TCI, vol. 15, n. 6 (Jun/Jul 1981). 27. 3 photos.

Kabale und Liebe.

Thiersch, Paul. Altes Theater, Leipzig: 1926. B&W. Set. **TCS2**, plates 276, 277.

_____.Vakhtangov Theatre, Moscow: B&W. Set. **SCM**, 87.

Kabuki/Bacchae.

McGillivray, Steven R. University of Oregon: Color. Rendering. **TDT**, vol. XXVIII, n.
    2 (Spring 1992). 14 of insert.

Kaddish.

Scheffler, John. 1971. B&W. Set. **TCI**, vol. 11, n. 5 (Oct 1977). 16.

Kaffehaus.

_____. Kammerspiele, Hamburg: B&W. Set. **TCS2**, plate 269.

Kaiser und Galiläer.

Sturm, Eduard. Schauspielhaus, Düsseldorf: 1924. B&W. Model. **TCS2**, plate 347.

Kanala's Eyes.

Svoboda, Josef. Grand Opera of the Fifth of May, Prague: 1945. B&W. Set. **SJS**, 40. 2
    photos; B&W. Set. **STS**, 39.

The Karl Marx Play.

Eigsti, Karl. American Place Theatre, NYC: 1973. B&W and color. Rendering. **CSD**,
    77, 124; B&W. Rendering. **DPT**, 33.

Karl V.

Haferung, Paul. Städtische Bühnen, Essen: 1950. B&W. Rendering. **SDW1**, 66.

Kaspar.

Roth, Wolfgang. 1972. B&W. Set. **TCI**, vol. 11, n. 5 (Oct 1977). 17. 3 photos.

Kaspariana.

Barba, Eugenio & Bernt Nyberg. Odin Teatret, Holstebro, Denmark: 1967. B&W. Sketch & set. **RSD**, illus. 633, 634; B&W. Sketch & set. **SDW3**, 142. 4 photos.

Kasperlespiele.

Baumeister, Willi. Landestheater, Darmstadt: 1953. B&W. Set. **AST**, 160. 3 photos.

Káta Kabanová.

Björnson, Maria. Scottish Opera, Edinburgh: 1979. B&W. Model. **TDT**, vol. XIX, n. 1 (Spring 1983). 6.

Dreier, Jurgen. Germany: B&W. Model. **TDT**, vol. XX, n. 1 (Spring 1984). 6.

Heinrich, Rudolf. Comic Opera, Berlin: B&W. Set. **TCI**, vol. 15, n. 1 (Jan 1981). 37.

Kinmonth, Patrick. Elgin Theatre, Toronto: 1994. Color. Set. **TCI**, vol. 28, n. 3 (Mar 1994). 14.

Schneider-Siemssen, Günther. San Francisco Opera: 1977. B&W. Set. **TCI**, vol. 12, n. 6 (Oct 1978). 32.

Svoboda, Josef. Grand Opera of the Fifth of May, Prague: 1947. B&W. Set. **SJS**, 40. 4 photos; B&W. Set. **STS**, 46; B&W. Set. **TDT**, vol. XXVIII, n. 5 (Fall 1992). 10; Opera House, Zurich: 1973. B&W. Set. **TDT**, vol. XII, n. 2 (Summer 1976). 12.

Vychodil, Ladislav. Bratislava: 1978. B&W. Set. **TDT**, vol. XV, n. 2 (Summer 1979). 16.

Das Käthchen von Heilbronn.

Freyer, Achim. State Theatre, Stuttgart: 1977. B&W. Set. **TCI**, vol. 13, n. 5 (Oct 1979). 16.

Neher, Caspar. State Theatre, Berlin: 1923. B&W. Rendering. **CBM**, 82.

Katzgraben.

Appen, Karl von. Theater am Schiffbauerdamm, Berlin: 1953. B&W. Set. **SDW2**, 49.

Der Kaufmann von Berlin.

Moholy-Nagy, Lászlo. Piscator Theater, Berlin: 1930. B&W. Set. **SCM**, 56. 2 photos; B&W. Set & technical drawings. **AST**, 147. 4 photos.

Kelly.

Smith, Oliver. Broadhurst Theatre, NYC: 1964. B&W. Rendering. **FCS**, plate 216; B&W. Rendering. **SDO**, 251.

The Kentucky Cycle.

Olich, Michael. Intiman Theatre, Seattle: 1991. Color. Set. **TCI**, vol. 25, n. 8 (Oct 1991). 14; Color. Model & set. **TCI**, vol. 28, n. 1 (Jan 1994). 62. 3 photos.

Key Largo.

Mielziner, Jo. Ethel Barrymore Theatre, NYC: 1939. B&W. Set. **MCN**, 147.

The Key to the Precipice.

Axer, Otto. Scena Kameralna, Teatr Polski, Warsaw: 1956. B&W. Rendering. **SDW2**, 165.

Khovanschina.

Benois, Nicola. La Scala, Milan: 1949. B&W. Rendering. **SDE**, 33.

Lee, Ming Cho. Metropolitan Opera, NYC: 1985. B&W. Model. **DDT**, 192, 193.

Levental, Valery. Bplgarskaja Narodnaja Opera, Sofia: 1966. B&W. Rendering. **SDW3**, 184.

Sonnabend, Yolande. Project for Royal Opera House, London: 1964. Color. Rendering. **DMS**, plate 44.

Kicks.
> Wagner, Robin. 1985. B&W. Model. **ASD1**, 160.

The Kid.
> Lundell, Kurt. American Place Theatre, NYC: 1972. B&W. Set. **DPT**, 349; B&W. Set. **TCI**, vol. 8, n. 4 (Sep 1974). 21.

Kidnapped in London.
> Moiseiwitsch, Tanya. Minneapolis Children's Theatre: 1981. Color. Set. **TCI**, vol. 20, n. 7 (Aug/Sep 1986). 22.

Kiki.
> Gros, Ernest. Belasco Theatre, NYC: 1921. B&W. Set. **MCN**, 55.

The Killer.
> Greter, Johan. Nieuwe de la Mar Theater, Amsterdam: 1960. B&W. Set. **SDW2**, 143.

Killing Game.
> Wisniak, Kazimierz. Teatr im. E. Wiercinskiego, Warsaw: 1973. B&W. Set. **SDW4**, illus. 268-270.
> _____.Shepherd College, Morgantown, West Virginia: Color. Set. **TDT**, vol. XXVIII, n. 2 (Spring 1992). 9 of insert.

The King and I.
> Kimmel, Alan. Casa Mañana, Dallas: B&W. Set. **TCI**, vol. 2, n. 5 (Sep/Oct 1968). 19.
> Mielziner, Jo. St. James Theatre, NYC: 1951. B&W. Set. **BWM**, 17; B&W. Drop. **DDT**, 405; B&W. Rendering. **DTT**, 165. School: night drop; B&W. Rendering. **DTT**, 166. Uncle Tom ballet; B&W. Rendering. **SDA**, 250; B&W. Set. **TMI**, 143, 165, 208; B&W. Set. **TMT**, 180; B&W. Set. **WMC**, 219.
> Wolf, Peter. Minnesota Opera: 1986. Color. Set. **TCI**, vol. 20, n. 8 (Oct 1986). 22.
> _____.University of North Carolina, Greensboro: B&W. Set. **TCI**, vol. 2, n. 3 (May/Jun 1968). 24, 25, 31. 2 photos.

King Bamba.
> Sagert, Horst. Deutsches Theater, Berlin: 1978. B&W. Model. **TDT**, vol. XVI, n. 1 (Spring 1980). 17. 2 photos.

King David.
> Mélat, Maurice. Théâtre du Capitole, Toulouse: 1958. B&W. Set. **SDW2**, 95.
> Schweizer, Richard. Zurich: 1922. B&W. Rendering. **TPH**, photo 400.

The King Goes Forth to France.
> Crowley, Bob. Royal Opera House, Covent Garden, London: 1986. B&W. Set. **BTD**, 144.

King Hunger.
> Gorelik, Mordecai. 1924. B&W. Rendering. **SDB**, 28.

King John.
> Bogaerts, John. Koninklijke Nederlandse Schouwburg, Antwerp: 1969. B&W. Set. **SDW3**, 43.
> Milatz, Ulrich E. State Theatre, Bern: 1972. B&W. Set. **SDW4**, illus. 20, 21.
> Schmidt, Douglas W. Delacorte Theatre, NYC: 1967. B&W. Set. **ASD1**, 151.
> Sporre, Dennis J. University of Illinois, Chicago: B&W. Rendering. **SDT**, 83.

King Lear.
> Altman, Nathan. Bolchoï Dramatitcheski Teatr imeni Gorkovo, Leningrad: 1941. B&W. Model. **SDW2**, 178. 2 photos.
> Appia, Adolphe. 1926. B&W. Rendering. **SDG**, 146; B&W. Rendering. **SOS**, 201; B&W. Rendering. **TCS2**, plates 40, 41; B&W. Sketch. **TPH**, photo 311.
> Bel Geddes, Norman. (project): 1917-1919. B&W. Rendering. **SCM**, 104, 105; B&W. Rendering. **TAT**, plates 505, 506; B&W. Rendering. **SOW**, plate 47; 1926. B&W.

Model. **TCS2**, plate 94; B&W. Rendering. **DOT**, 227; B&W. Model. **SDC**, plate 102.

Brook, Peter. Royal Shakespeare Company, Aldwych Theatre, London: 1964. B&W. Set. **SDW3**, 52.

Carl, Joseph. Habima, Tel Aviv: 1955. B&W. Set. **SDW2**, 118.

Clarke, George Toynbee. Perth Repertory Theatre: 1950. B&W. Rendering. **SDW1**, 174.

Craig, Edward Gordon. 1908. B&W. Rendering. **EGC**, 95; B&W. Woodcut. **TDT**, n. 29 (May 1972). 12.

Crowley, Bob. Royal Shakespeare Company, GB: 1982. B&W. Set. **BTD**, 54.

Czeschka, Carl O. Deutsches Theater, Berlin: 1908. B&W. Set. **DOT**, 210; B&W. Set. **MRH**, facing 138. 2 photos, B&W. Set. **RSD**, illus. 93; B&W. Set. **TCS2**, plates 17, 18.

Dusek, Jan. Czechoslovakia: B&W. Rendering. **TDT**, vol. XXVI, n. 2 (Summer 1990). 38. 3 photos.

Dyer, Chris. Royal Shakespeare Company (The Other Place), London: 1988. Color. Set. **BTD**, 67.

Frigerio, Ezio. Piccolo Teatro di Milano. Teatro Petastasio, Prato: 1973. B&W. Set. **SDW4**, illus. 42-45; B&W. Set. **SIO**, 64, 65.

Griffin, Hayden. National Theatre (Olivier), London: 1986. B&W. Sketch. **BTD**, 88.

Hay, Richard L. Oregon Shakespeare Festival, Ashland: 1985. B&W. Set. **BSE4**, 69.

Kilger, Heinrich. Deutsches Theater, Berlin: 1957. B&W. Set. **SDW2**, 55.

Komisarjevsky, Theodore. Shakespeare Memorial Theatre, Stratford-upon-Avon: 1936. B&W. Set. **SDG**, 181; B&W. Set. **SOS**, 160.

Lee, Eugene. Trinity Square Theatre, Providence, Rhode Island: 1977. B&W. Set. **ASD1**, 82.

Lee, Ming Cho. Vivian Beaumont Theatre, Lincoln Center, NYC: 1962. B&W. Model. **TCI**, vol. 11, n. 1 (Jan/Feb 1977). 6.

Loquasto, Santo. Delacorte Theatre, NYC: 1973. Color. Set. **DPT**, frontispiece.

Lukala, Juha. Turun Kaupunginteatteri, Turku, Finland: 1972. B&W. Set. **SDW4**, illus. 39-41; B&W. Model. **TDT**, vol. XII, n. 3 (Fall 1976). 34.

Nash, Paul. B&W. Rendering. **TCS2**, plate 198.

Oenslager, Donald. (project): 1924. B&W. Rendering. **TDO**, 23.

Ott, Paul. Reussisches Theater, Gera: 1923. B&W. Rendering. **TCS2**, plates 194, 195.

Popov, Assen. National Theater, Sofia, Bulgaria: 1959. B&W. Rendering. **SDW2**, 38.

Richter-Forgach, Thomas. State Theatre, Kassel: 1966. Color. Model. **RSD**, illus. 541.

Ricketts, Charles. Haymarket Theatre, London: 1909. B&W. Rendering. **DIT**, plate 11; B&W. Rendering. **SDG**, 163.

Sonrel, Pierre. Color. Rendering. **SOS**, 187.

Strnad, Oskar. Josefstadter Theater, Vienna: 1920-1927. B&W. Rendering. **TAT**, plate 145; B&W. Rendering. **TCS2**, plate 197.

Svoboda, Josef. Némzeti Színház, Budapest: 1964. B&W. Rendering. **SJS**, 153.

Tischler, Alexander. Jewish State Theatre, Moscow: 1935. B&W. Set. **NTO**, facing 324; B&W. Rendering. **SDW2**, 197; B&W. Set. **TPH**, photo 416.

_____.Gothenburg National Theater, Sweden: B&W. Set. **TPH**, photo 393.

_____.Odéon Theatre, Paris: 1904 B&W. Set. **TCS2**, plates 3, 4; B&W. Set. **TPH**, photo 278.

King Lear (?)

Exter, Alexandra. B&W. Rendering. **RAG**, 25.

The King of Spain.

Wilson, Robert. Anderson Theatre, NYC: 1969. B&W. Set. **RWT**, 11.

The King of the Candle.
> Carrozzino, Jorge. El Galpon, Montevideo: 1969. Color. Rendering. **SDW3**, 104.
> Eichbauer, Helio. Teatro Oficina, São Paulo: 1967. Color. Rendering & set. **SDW3**, 104. 3 photos.
> Prieto, Carmen. El Galpon, Montevideo: 1969. Color. Rendering. **SDW3**, 104.

The King of the Castle.
> Adshead, Mary. Liverpool Playhouse, England: 1924. B&W. Rendering. **SCM**, 26.

The King of Yvetot.
> Carelman, Jacques. Opéra de Strasbourg: 1961. B&W. Set. **SDW3**, 192.

King Priam.
> Kenny, Sean. Royal Opera House, Covent Garden, London: 1962. B&W. Set. **SDW3**, 199.

The King Stag.
> Gugel, Fabius von. Landestheater, Darmstadt: 1959. B&W. Rendering. **SDW2**, 59.
> Yeargan, Michael. American Repertory Theatre, Cambridge, Massachusetts: 1984. Color. Set. **TCI**, vol. 24, n. 8 (Oct 1990). 42; Color. Set. **TCI**, vol. 22, n. 3 (Mar 1988). 51.
> _____. American Repertory Theatre at Teatro Espanol, Madrid: 1988. B&W. Set. **TCI**, vol. 23, n. 5 (May 1989). 35.

King's Rhapsody.
> Delany, Edward. Palace Theatre, London: 1949. B&W. Set. **MCD**, plate 197.

Kinkaku-ji.
> Hasegawa, Kanbei. Kabuki-za, Tokyo: B&W. Set. **SDW1**, 142.

Kismet.
> Ayers, Lemuel. Stoll Theatre, London: 1955. Color. Set. **BMF**, 35; B&W. Set. **MCD**, plate 208.

A Kiss Is Just a Kiss.
> McCarry, Charles E. Manhattan Punch Line Theatre, NYC: 1983. B&W. Rendering. **DDT**, 102.

Kiss Me Kate.
> Ayers, Lemuel. New Century Theatre, NYC: 1948. B&W. Set. **BWM**, 213-215. 3 photos; B&W. Set. **TMT**, 173; B&W. Set. **WMC**, 155. 2 photos; B&W. Set. **WTP**, 244, 245. 4 photos; Coliseum, London: 1951. Color. Set. **BMF**, 70; B&W. Set. **MCD**, plate 201.
> Da Costa, Liz. Royal Shakespeare Company, GB: 1987. B&W. Set. **BTD**, 161.
> Dudley, William. Royal Shakespeare Company, GB: 1986. B&W. Act curtain. **TDT**, vol. XXV, n. 3 (Fall 1989). 23.

Kiss of the Spider Woman.
> Sirlin, Jerome. Toronto: 1992. Color. Set. **TCI**, vol. 27, n. 5 (May 1993). 5, 36, 37. 4 photos.
> _____. South Coast Repertory Theatre, Costa Mesa, California: Color. Set. **TCI**, vol. 27, n. 2 (Feb 1993). 44.

The Kitchen.
> Herbert, Jocelyn. Royal Court Theatre, London: 1959. B&W. Set. **TDT**, vol. XXX, n. 5 (Fall 1994). 15. 2 photos; Color. Set. **TCI**, vol. 28, n. 7 (Aug/Sep 1994). 16.
> Lanphier, Dawn. University of Wisconsin, Madison: B&W. Set. **TDT**, vol. XXVIII, n. 2 (Spring 1992). 13 of insert.
> _____. The Acting Company tour: 1979. B&W. Set. **TCI**, vol. 15, n. 5 (May 1981). 23.

Das Klagelied.
> Baumeister, Willi. Landestheater, Stuttgart: 1927. B&W. Rendering. **AST**, 158.

Die Klofrau (The Toilet Attendant).
>   Von Emde, Boris. Templehof Airport, Berlin: 1994. B&W. Set. **TCI**, vol. 29, n. 3 (Mar 1995). 9.

Die Kluge (The Wise Woman).
>   Schafer, Lawrence. Macmillan Theatre, Toronto: 1966. B&W. Set. **TDT**, n. 7 (Dec 1966). 17-19. 5 photos; B&W. Model. **SDW3**, 196.

Kyldex 1.
>   Schöffer, Nicolas. State Opera, Hamburg: 1973. B&W. Set. **RSD**, illus. 472. 4 photos; Color. Set. **SDW4**, illus. 308-312.

The Knack.
>   La Ferla, Sandro. Virginia Museum Theatre, Richmond: 1970. B&W. Rendering. **DPT**, 119.

Knee Play 1.
>   _____. Walker Arts Center, Minneapolis: 1984. B&W. Set. **TCI**, vol. 19, n. 8 (Oct 1985). 24.

Knickerbocker Holiday.
>   Mielziner, Jo. Ethel Barrymore Theatre, NYC: 1938. B&W. Set. **MCN**, 142; B&W. Set. **RBS**, 169. 2 photos; B&W. Set. **WMC**, 199.

The Knight of the Rose.
>   Kautskj, Robert. La Scala, Milan: 1952. B&W. Set. **SDE**, 111.

The Knitting Shop.
>   Bjarnason, Gunnar. Pjodleikhusid Reykjavik: 1966. B&W. Set. **SDW3**, 119.

Knock.
>   Jouvet, Louis. Comédie des Champs-Élysées, Paris: 1924. B&W. Rendering. **RSD**, illus. 404; B&W. Rendering. **SDC**, plate 122. 2 photos.
>   Neher, Caspar. Deutsches Theater, Berlin: B&W. Rendering. **CBM**, 83.

Knock Knock.
>   Beatty, John Lee. Circle Repertory Theatre, NYC: 1976. B&W. Rendering & set. **TCI**, vol. 12, n. 6 (Oct 1978). 18, 19; B&W. Set. **TCI**, vol. 10, n. 3 (May/Jun 1976). 24; B&W. Set. **TCI**, vol. 16, n. 5 (May 1982). 28. 2 photos.

Knockout.
>   Eigsti, Karl. Helen Hayes Theatre, NYC: 1979. Color. Rendering. **ASD1**, between 70 & 71.

The Knot Garden.
>   O'Brien, Timothy. Royal Opera House, Covent Garden, London: 1970. B&W. Set. **SDW3**, 199; B&W. Set. **TDT**, vol. XIX, n. 3 (Fall 1983). 8.

Kongi's Harvest.
>   Soyinka, Wole. School of Drama Arts Theatre, Ibadan, Nigeria: 1965. B&W. Set. **SDW3**, 162.

Kordian.
>   Kolodziej, Marian. Teatr Nowy, Lodz: 1969. B&W. Set. **SDW3**, 82.
>   _____. Laboratory Theater, Opole, Poland: 1962. B&W. Sketch. **RSD**, illus. 631.

Krakatit.
>   Kolar, Zbynek. Czechoslovakia: B&W. Model. **TDT**, vol. XX, n. 1 (Spring 1984). 9.

Der Kreidekreis.
>   Hrska, Alexander Vladimir. National Theatre, Prague: 1926. B&W. Set. **TCS2**, plate 246.

Kristina.
>   Öberg, Barbara W. State Theatre, Norrköping, Sweden: 1961. B&W. Set. **SDW2**, 211. 2 photos.

Krutnava.
    Svoboda, Josef. National Theatre, Prague: 1973. B&W. Set. **TDT**, vol. XII, n. 2 (Summer 1976). 10.
Kukirol.
    Stenberg, Vladimir & Georgiy A. Russia: 1925. B&W. Rendering. **TCI**, vol. 24, n. 7 (Aug/Sep 1990). 8.
Kumagaya's Battle Headquarters.
    Hasegawa, Kanbei. Kabuki-za, Tokyo: 1952. B&W. Rendering. **SDW1**, 143.

-L-

L-Train to Eldorado.
    Buchmuller, Eva. Squat Theatre, NYC: 1988. Color. Set. **TCI**, vol. 22, n. 9 (Nov 1988). 12.
La Cage aux Folles.
    Mitchell, David. Palace Theatre, NYC: 1983. B&W and color. Model & set. **ASD1**, between 70, 71, 121; B&W. Set. **MBM**, 23, 154; B&W and color. Set. **TCI**, vol. 17, n. 9 (Nov/Dec 1983). 17-19. 6 photos.
Labyrinth.
    Kooning, Willem de. NYC: 1946. B&W. Rendering. **ASC**, 26.
    Van Eyck, Aldo. Amsterdam: 1966. B&W. Set. **SDW3**, 216. 2 photos.
The Labyrinth of the World and the Paradise of the Heart.
    Svoboda, Josef. (not produced): 1967. B&W. Model. **SJS**, 20.
Le Lache.
    Pitoëff, Georges. Théâtre des Arts, Paris: B&W. Set. **TCS2**, plate 200.
Lâcheté.
    Bakst, Léon. Théâtre Kousnetzoff, Paris: B&W. Rendering. **DIT**, plate 72; B&W. Rendering. **TCS2**, plate 230.
Ladies and Gentlemen.
    Aronson, Boris. Martin Beck Theatre, NYC: 1939. B&W. Set. **TAB**, 296.
The Ladies' Battle.
    Weigersma, Friso. Stadsschouwburg, Amsterdam: 1953. B&W. Set. **SDW1**, 139.
Lady Be Good!
    Harker, Joseph & Phil Harker. Empire Theatre, London: 1926. B&W. Set. **MCD**, plate 142.
    Sicangco, Eduardo. Goodspeed Opera House, East Haddam, Connecticut: Color. Show curtain. **TCI**, vol. 21, n. 9 (Nov 1987). 37.
The Lady from the Sea.
    Fjell, Kai. National Theater, Oslo: 1951. B&W. Set. **SDW2**, 151.
    Oenslager, Donald. Little Theatre, NYC: 1934. B&W. Rendering. **TDO**, 51.
    Svoboda, Josef. Milan: 1991. Color. Set. **TDT**, vol. XXX, n. 5 (Fall 1994). 38.
Lady Godiva.
    Ivo, Lode. Nationaal Toneel, Antwerp: 1948. B&W. Set. **SDW1**, 45.
Lady in the Dark.
    Baldwin, Phillip. Skylight Opera Theatre, Milwaukee: 1991. Color. Set. **TCI**, vol. 26, n. 1 (Jan 1992). 14.
    Horner, Harry. Alvin Theatre, NYC: 1941. B&W. Set. **BWM**, 263. 3 photos; B&W. Set. **SDA**, 236, 237. 3 photos; B&W. Set. **SOW**, plates 103, 104.
Lady Macbeth from Minsk.
    Barsacq, Alberte. Frankfurt Opera: 1993. Color. Set. **TCI**, vol. 27, n. 5 (May 1993). 11.

Borovsky, David. Teatr Opery i Baleta, Chevtchenko, SSSR: 1965. B&W. Model. **SDW3**, 200.

Brown, Paul. Metropolitan Opera, NYC: 1994. Color. Set. **TCI**, vol. 29, n. 2 (Feb 1995). 6.

Guttuso, Renato. La Fenice, Venice: 1947. B&W. Rendering. **SDW1**, 126.

Lazaridis, Stefanos. English National Opera, London: 1987. B&W. Set. **BTD**, 128, 129.

_____.Chicago Lyric Opera: 1983. Color. Set. **TCI**, vol. 18, n. 7 (Aug/Sep 1984). 42.

Lady Precious Stream.

Gillette, A.S. University of Iowa, Iowa City: 1945. B&W. Set. **TDP**, 81.

Lady Thief.

Vychodil, Ladislav. Prague: 1962. B&W. Set. **TDT**, vol. XV, n. 2 (Summer 1979). 15.

Lady Windermere's Fan.

Beaton, Cecil. Theatre Royal, Haymarket, London: 1945. B&W. Set. **BTD**, 18; B&W. Rendering. **CBS**, 34; B&W. Set. **SOW**, plate 73; B&W. Set. **WTP**, 132, 133; Curran Theatre, San Francisco: 1946. Color. Set. **CBS**, 18; NYC: 1946/1947. B&W. Sketch. **CBS**, 37; B&W. Set. **WTP**, 132; Phoenix Theatre, London: 1966. Color. Set. **CBS**, 36; B&W. Rendering. **CBS**, 59. Acts II & III.

_____. National Opera, Sofia, Bulgaria: B&W. Set. **SCM**, 83.

The Lady's Not for Burning.

Boyce, Raymond. New Zealand Players Co., Wellington: 1953. B&W. Set. **SDW1**, 141.

Messel, Oliver. Globe Theatre, London: 1949. B&W. Set. **OMB**, 136, 137; B&W. Set. **WTP**, 166, 167. 5 photos.

Lake Lyul.

Shestakov, Victor. Theatre of the Revolution, Moscow: 1923. B&W. Model. **RSD**, illus. 182; B&W. Sketch, model & set. **RST**, 102, 136.

Lakeboat.

Merritt, Michael. Goodman Theatre, Chicago: 1982. B&W. Set. **ASD2**, 129.

Lamp at Midnight.

Fielding, Eric. Brigham Young University, Provo, Utah: 1979. B&W. Model. **BSE2**, 14.

La Lampara.

Carra, Carlo. La Scala, Milan: 1957. Color. Rendering. **AST**, 188.

Land of Men.

Santa Rosa, Thomas. Teatro Ginastico, Rio de Janeiro: 1947. B&W. Set. **SDW1**, 50.

The Land of Smiles.

Johnstone, Alick. Theatre Royal, Drury Lane, London: 1931. B&W. Set. **MCD**, plate 169.

Land of the Dragon.

Payne, Tap R. University of Minnesota, Morris: 1980. B&W. Set. **BSE2**, 19.

Land's End.

Oenslager, Donald. Playhouse Theatre, NYC: 1946. B&W. Rendering. **TDO**, 117.

Landscape.

Bury, John. Royal Shakespeare Company, Aldwych Theatre, London: 1969. B&W. Model. **TDT**, vol. XII, n. 3 (Fall 1976). 36.

Landscape of the Body.

Tsypin, George. Goodman Theatre, Chicago: 1988. B&W. Model. **DDT**, 405.

Wulp, John. Academy Festival Theatre, Lake Forest: B&W. Set. **TCI**, vol. 13, n. 1 (Jan/Feb 1979). 24.

Landscape-Silence.
> Bury, John. Royal Shakespeare Company, Aldwych Theatre, London: 1969. B&W. Set. **SDW3**, 153.

A Large Dead Animal.
> Appel, Karel. Grand Théâtre Gooiland, Hilversum, Netherlands: 1963. B&W. Set. **SDW3**, 138.

Largo Desolato.
> Zídek, Ivo. Prague: 1990. B&W. Rendering & set. **TDT**, vol. XXVIII, n. 2 (Spring 1992). 37, 41.

The Lark.
> Malclés, Jean Dénis. Théâtre Montparnasse, Paris: 1953. Color. Rendering. **RSD**, illus. 494.
> Mielziner, Jo. Longacre Theatre, NYC: 1955. B&W. Rendering. **DMS**, plate 29; Color. Rendering. **DTT**, 198. Study for burning at the stake; Color. Rendering. **DTT**, 199. Throne room; Color. Rendering. **SDA**, 292; B&W. Rendering. **SDW2**, 237.
> Ratto, Gianni. Maria della Costa, São Paulo: 1954. B&W. Rendering. **SDW1**, 129.

Lark Rise.
> Dudley, William. National Theatre (Cottesloe), England: 1978. B&W. Set. **TCI**, vol. 18, n. 1 (Jan 1984). 36; B&W. Set. **TDT**, vol. XIX, n. 1 (Spring 1983). 12.

Lass wehen die Zeit.
> Hoflehner, Rudolf. Kleines Theater der Josefstadt, Vienna: 1957. B&W. Set. **AST**, 232.

The Last Love.
> Dorsey, Kent. Studio Arena Theatre, Buffalo: Color. Set. **TCI**, vol. 25, n. 8 (Oct 1991). 49.

The Last Meeting of the Knights of the White Magnolia.
> Eigsti, Karl. Arena Stage, Washington, DC: 1975. B&W. Sketch & Set. **ASD1**, 31; B&W. Sketch. **DPT**, 97.
> Faulkner, Cliff. Third Step Theatre (South Coast Repertory), Costa Mesa, California: 1977. B&W. Set. **TCI**, vol. 14, n. 4 (Sep 1980). 36.

The Last Mile.
> Throckmorton, Cleon. USA: B&W. Set. **SCM**, 111.

The Last Night of Don Juan.
> Reynolds, James. Greenwich Village Theatre, NYC: 1926. B&W. Set. **SDC**, plate 59.

The Last Ones.
> Acquart, André. Théatre National Daniel Sorano, Dakar: 1965. B&W. Sketches, model & set. **SDW3**, 55. 3 photos.
> Svoboda, Josef. Tyl Theatre, Prague: 1966. B&W. Set. **DSL**, figure 1.1(b); B&W. Set. **SJS**, 100-102. 5 photos; B&W. Set. **STS**, 67, 70. 3 photos; B&W. Set. **TDT**, vol. XIX, n. 3 (Fall 1983). 15; B&W. Set. **TDT**, n. 7 (Dec 1966). 24; B&W. Set. **TDT**, n. 20 (Feb 1970). 5. 2 photos.

The Last Paradise.
> Toffolutti, Ezio. Volksbühne, Berlin: 1973. B&W. Set. **SDW4**, illus. 297.

The Last Pierrot.
> Drabik, Vincent. B&W. Set. **SCM**, 84.

The Last Savage.
> Montresor, Beni. Metropolitan Opera, NYC: 1963. B&W. Rendering. **MOM**, 15; Spoleto Festival, Charleston, South Carolina: 1981. B&W. Set. **TCI**, vol. 16, n. 5 (May 1982). 17. 2 photos.

The Last Supper.
> Hayes, Dermot. Royal Court Theatre, London: 1988. B&W. Set. **BTD**, 77.

The Last Temptations.
 Taivassalo, Reino. Oulun Teatteri, Oulun, Finland: 1961. B&W. Set. **SDW2**, 207.
The Late Christopher Bean.
 Bernstein, Aline. Henry Miller's Theatre, NYC: 1932. B&W. Set. **SDA**, 201.
The Late Shakespeares.
 Chitty, Alison. National Theatre (Cottesloe), England: 1988. Color. Set. **BTD**, 34.
Laughing in the Sea Wind.
 Sheffield, Ann. Occidental College, Los Angeles: 1982. B&W. Rendering. **TCI**, vol.
  17, n. 7 (Aug/Sep 1983). 8.
Laughter on the 23rd Floor.
 Walton, Tony. Richard Rodgers Theatre, NYC: 1994. Color. Set. **TCI**, vol. 28, n. 2
  (Feb 1994). 7.
Lazarus Laughed.
 Bel Geddes, Norman. USA: 1926. B&W. Model. **TCS2**, plate 69; B&W. Model. **SDC**,
  plate 101.
Lea.
 Stegars, Rolf. Suomen Kansallisteatteri, Helsinki: 1951. B&W. Set. **SDW1**, 159.
The Leading Lady.
 Oenslager, Donald. Nederlander Theatre, NYC: 1948. B&W. Rendering. **DPT**, 361;
  B&W. Rendering. **SDB**, 43; B&W. Rendering. **TDO**, 119.
Leah Kleschna.
 Gates, Frank E. & E.A. Morange. Manhattan Theatre, NYC: 1904. B&W. Set. **MCN**,
  24.
Lear.
 Freyer, Achim. Schiller Theater, Berlin: 1973. B&W. Set. **SDW4**, illus. 355, 356;
  B&W. Set. **TCI**, vol. 13, n. 5 (Oct 1979). 18.
 Ponnelle, Jean-Pierre. San Francisco Opera: 1981. B&W. Model & set. **TDT**, vol.
  XVII, n. 3 (Fall 1981). 4, 5. 3 photos.
The Learned Ladies.
 Funicello, Ralph. Denver Center, Colorado: 1980. B&W. Set. **ASD1**, 51.
 Prévost, Robert. Théâtre du Nouveau Monde, Montréal: 1960. Color. Rendering.
  SDW2, 51.
 Ross, Carolyn L. Missouri Repertory Theatre, Kansas City: 1981. B&W. Set. **BSE4**,
  38.
 _____. Dallas, Texas: 1949. B&W. Set. **SOW**, plate 110.
 _____. South Coast Repertory Theatre, Costa Mesa, California: B&W. Set. **TCI**,
  vol. 13, n. 5 (Oct 1979). 32.
Leave It to Me!
 Johnson, Albert R. Imperial Theatre, NYC: 1938. B&W. Set. **RBS**, 171. 2 photos;
  B&W. Set. **WMC**, 152.
Leben des Orest.
 de Chirico, Georgio. Krolloper, Berlin: 1930. B&W. Model & set. **AST**, 182. 4 photos.
Left-Handed.
 Popov, Dimitri. Teatr Mouzkomedii, Leningrad: 1959. Color. Rendering. **SDW2**, 185.
The Legend.
 Wyspianski, Stanislaw. Municipal Theatre, Lvov: 1905. B&W. Rendering. **RSD**, illus.
  96.
The Legend of Joseph.
 de Chirico, Georgio. La Scala, Milan: 1951. B&W. Rendering & set. **AST**, 184. 4
  photos; B&W. Rendering. **SDE**, 62, 63. 3 photos.

The Legend of Kaupo.
    Freibergs, A. USSR: Color. Model. **TDT**, vol. XII, n. 3 (Fall 1976). 35.
    Kroder, Olghert. Dramatitcheskij Teatr imeni Leona Pegla, Valmiera: 1973. B&W. Set.
        SDW4, illus. 367.
Legend of Lovers.
    Elder, Eldon. Plymouth Theatre, NYC: 1951-1952. B&W. Rendering. **EED**, (pages not
        numbered).
    _____. Yale School of Drama, New Haven, Connecticut: B&W. Set. **SDL**, 59.
The Legend of Ochrid.
    Sokolic, Dorian. Narodno Kazaliste, Rijeka: 1957. B&W. Rendering. **SDW2**, 136.
Legend of the Invisible City of Kitezh and the Maiden of Sevronia.
    Dunkel, Eugene. 1924. B&W. Rendering. **RSC**, 29.
    Kitaïev, Mark. Opera House, Brooklyn Academy of Music: 1995. Color. Set. **TCI**, vol.
        29, n. 5 (May 1995). 10.
The Legend of the Rood.
    St. John's Cathedral, NYC: 1971. B&W. Set. **TCI**, vol. 6, n. 3 (May/Jun 1972). 17.
The Legend of Tzar Saltan.
    Lissim, Simon. Grand Théâtre du Lycée, Barcelona: 1924. B&W. Rendering. **RSC**, 47;
        B&W. Rendering. **TCS2**, plate 233.
Legs Diamond.
    Mitchell, David. Mark Hellinger Theatre, NYC: 1988. B&W. Model. **DDT**, 311.
Lend Me a Tenor.
    Walton, Tony. Royale Theatre, NYC: 1989. B&W. Set. **SDL**, 61.
Lenny.
    Wagner, Robin. Brooks Atkinson Theatre, NYC: 1970/1971. B&W. Set. **ASD1**, 163;
        B&W. Set. **DPT**, 390, 391; B&W. Set. **DSL**, figures 1.1(a), 2.7(e); B&W. Set.
        SDB, 195; B&W. Set. **TCI**, vol. 5, n. 6 (Nov/Dec 1971). 7.
Leon and Lena and Lenz.
    Tsypin, George. Tyrone Guthrie Theatre, Minneapolis: 1987. B&W. Set. **ASD2**, 172;
        Color. Model. **DDT**, 440d; Color. Set. **TCI**, vol. 25, n. 2 (Feb 1991). 37.
Leonce and Lena.
    Ciulei, Liviu. Teatrul Lucia Sturdza Bulandra, Bucharest: 1970. Color. Set. **SDW4**,
        illus. 130.
    Troike, Gero. Volksbühne, Berlin: 1978. B&W. Model. **TDT**, vol. XVI, n. 1 (Spring
        1980). 16.
    Walser, Karl. Lessing Theatre, Berlin: 1913. B&W. Rendering. **AST**, 30. 3 photos.
A Lesson from Aloes.
    Straiges, Tony. Center Stage, Baltimore: 1981. B&W. Set. **ASD2**, 144; B&W. Model.
        DDT, 586; B&W. Set. **TCI**, vol. 16, n. 2 (Feb 1982). 14; B&W. Set. **TCI**, vol. 20,
        n. 2 (Feb 1986). 20.
    Yeargan, Michael. Yale Repertory Theatre, New Haven: 1980. B&W. Set. **TCI**, vol.
        14, n. 5 (Oct 1980). 79.
Let 'Em Eat Cake.
    Johnson, Albert R. Imperial Theatre, NYC: 1933. B&W. Set. **BWM**, 228.
Let's Get a Divorce.
    Averyt, Bennett. Asolo State Theatre, Sarasota, Florida: B&W. Set. **TCI**, vol. 13, n. 5
        (Oct 1979). 36.
A Letter for Queen Victoria.
    Harvey, Peter & Robert Wilson. ANTA Theatre, NYC: 1974. Color. Set. **MBM**, 190;
        B&W. Set. **TCI**, vol. 19, n. 8 (Oct 1985). 23; B&W. Set. **RWT**, 33-36, 38-41. 7
        photos.

Kolouch, Fred. Théâtre des Variétés, Paris: 1974. B&W. Set. **SDW4**, illus. 405.

Les Liaisons Dangereuses.

Crowley, Bob. Music Box Theatre, NYC: 1987. Color. Set. **TCI**, vol. 21, n. 7 (Aug/ Sep 1987). 26, 27, 31. 3 photos.

Howland, Gerard. San Francisco Opera: 1994-1995. Color. Model & set. **TCI**, vol. 29, n. 3 (Mar 1995). 33, 36.

Jennings, Gary: Academy Theatre, Atlanta: 1988. Color. Set. **TCI**, vol. 23, n. 2 (Feb 1989). 50.

Ladwehr, Hugh. Williamstown Theatre Festival, Massachusetts: 1988. Color. Set & painter's elevations. **TCI**, vol. 23, n. 2 (Feb 1989). 48. 3 photos.

Lee, Eugene. Dallas Theatre Center: 1988. Color. Set. **TCI**, vol. 23, n. 2 (Feb 1989). 51; Color. Set. **TCI**, vol. 23, n. 9 (Nov 1989). 59.

Tilton, James. Mirror Repertory Company, Belfast, Maine: 1988. B&W. Set. **TCI**, vol. 23, n. 2 (Feb 1989). 49.

Vychodil, Ladislav. Czechoslovakia: B&W. Rendering & set. **TDT**, vol. XXVII, n. 3 (Summer 1991). 26. 2 photos.

The Liar.

Barth, Ruodi. Komödie, Basel: 1950. B&W. Rendering. **SDW1**, 113.

Macie, Tom. Hillberry Repertory Theatre: B&W. Sketch, rendering, & set. **SDT**, 127-129.

The Libation Bearers.

Riddell, Richard. Stanford University, California: 1976. B&W. Set. **TCI**, vol. 11, n. 3 (May/Jun 1977). 24.

Libel!

Sovey, Raymond. Henry Miller's Theatre, NYC: 1936. B&W. Set. **SOW**, plate 88.

Liberty.

Baumeister, Willi. Deutsches Theater, Stuttgart: 1920. B&W. Set. **RSD**, illus. 243.

Libuse.

Vychodil, Ladislav. Prague: 1968. B&W. Set. **TDT**, vol. XV, n. 2 (Summer 1979). 15.

Lieber Georg.

Langhoff, Matthias. Theatertreffen, Berlin: 1980. B&W. Set. **TCI**, vol. 14, n. 6 (Nov/ Dec 1980). 39. 2 photos.

Liebestrank.

Ponnelle, Jean-Pierre. Hamburg Opera: 1977. B&W. Set. **TCI**, vol. 12, n. 3 (Mar/Apr 1978). 16.

The Life and Adventures of Nicholas Nickleby.

Benson, Tom. University of Arizona, Tucson: B&W. Sketches & set. **TDP**, 24, 26. 5 photos.

Dermot, Neil Peter Jampolis, & John Napier. Plymouth Theatre, NYC: 1981. B&W. Set. **TCI**, vol. 15, n. 9 (Nov/Dec 1981). 12-15. 5 photos.

Napier, John. Royal Shakespeare Company, GB: 1980. Color. Model. **BTD**, 38.

Life and Death of an American.

Bay, Howard. Maxine Elliot Theatre: 1939. B&W. Rendering. **NTO**, facing 300; B&W. Rendering. **SDB**, 190; B&W. Set. **SOW**, plate 87; B&W. Drop. **TCI**, vol. 17, n. 2 (Feb 1983). 11.

The Life and Times of Joseph Stalin.

Polakov, Lester. Brooklyn Academy of Music, New York: 1973. B&W. Rendering. **CSD**, 115; B&W. Set. **TCI**, vol. 9, n. 3 (May/Jun 1975). 16-19. 6 photos.

Wilson, Robert. Copenhagen: 1973. B&W. Set. **RWT**, 28-31. 4 photos.

The Life and Times of Sigmund Freud.
 Wilson, Robert. Brooklyn Academy of Music, New York: 1969. B&W. Set. **RWT**, 12-
   14. 3 photos.
A Life in the Theatre.
 Beatty, John Lee. Theatre de Lys, NYC: 1977. B&W. Rendering. **DDT**, 548; B&W.
   Rendering. **TCI**, vol. 12, n. 6 (Oct 1978). 18.
Life is a Dream.
 Arcenas, Loy. American Repertory Theatre, Cambridge, Massachusetts: 1989. B&W.
   Set. **ASD2**, 14; Color. Set. **TCI**, vol. 25, n. 3 (Mar 1991). 39.
 Artaud, Antonin. Théâtre du Vieux-Columbier, Paris: 1922. B&W. Rendering. **RSD**,
   illus. 394.
 Mancera, Antonio. Teatro Fabregas, Mexico: 1964. B&W. Rendering. **DMS**, plate 37.
   2 photos.
 Wang, Ru Jun. (project): B&W. Rendering. **TDT**, vol. XXVIII, n. 2 (Spring 1992). 15
   of insert.
The Life of Galileo (see also *Galileo*).
 Assman, Jost. State Theatre, Norrköping-Linköping, Sweden: 1970. B&W. Set.
   SDW3, 112. 3 photos.
 Damiani, Luciano. Piccolo Teatro, Milan: 1963. B&W. Rendering & set. **RSD**, illus.
   578-581; B&W. Set. **SIO**, 38-40. 3 photos.
 Herbert, Jocelyn. National Theatre (Olivier), London: 1980. B&W. Sketches & set.
   BTD, 69. 5 photos; B&W. Set. **TCI**, vol. 15, n. 5 (May 1981). 13.
 Neher, Caspar. Theater am Schiffbauerdamm, Berlin: 1957. B&W. Rendering & set.
   RSD, illus. 562-565.
The Life of Man.
 Egorov, V.E. Moscow Art Theatre: 1907. B&W. Rendering. **MOT**, between 48 & 49;
   B&W. Set. **RSD**, illus. 32, 33.
 Navarro, Oscar. Teatro Experimental de la Universidad de Chile, Santiago: 1949.
   B&W. Rendering. **SDW1**, 54.
Life of Orestes.
 Wong, Carey. Portland Opera, Oregon: 1975. B&W. Set. **TCI**, vol. 10, n. 4 (Sep 1976).
   23. 2 photos; B&W. Set. **TCI**, vol. 12, n. 5 (Sep 1978). 39.
Life With Father.
 Boros, Frank. Pittsburgh Public Theatre: 1985. Color. Set. **TCI**, vol. 21, n. 7 (Aug/Sep
   1987). 32.
 Stevens, John Wright. Seattle Repertory Theatre: 1974. B&W. Set. **TCI**, vol. 9, n. 6
   (Nov/Dec 1975). 14.
Life With Mother.
 Oenslager, Donald. Empire Theatre, NYC: 1948. B&W. Rendering. **DPT**, 21; B&W.
   Rendering & set. **TDO**, 121-123. 3 photos.
Light o' Love.
 Mai, Wolfgang. Komödie, Basel: 1973. B&W. Set. **SDW4**, illus. 187, 188.
 Ter-Arutunian, Rouben. Akademietheater, Vienna: 1972. B&W. Set. **SDW4**, illus. 189,
   190.
Light Up the Sky.
 Phillips, Van. Purdue University: B&W. Set. **SST**, 18.
The Lighted Factory.
 Madau Diaz, Antonello. Teatro Comunale, Bologna: 1971. B&W. Set. **SDW3**, 207.
The Lights of London.
 Craig, Edward Gordon. 1901. B&W. Rendering. **TNT**, facing 17.

Lilac Time.

   Prévost, Robert. Théâtre du Nouveau Monde, Montréal: 1958. B&W. Set. **SDW2**, 40.

   Ryan, E.H. Lyric Theatre, Hammersmith, London: 1922. B&W. Set. **MCD**, plate 122.

Lilian.

   Edwards, Ben. Ethel Barrymore Theatre, NYC: 1986. Color. Set. **TCI**, vol. 23, n. 4
      (Apr 1989). 51.

Liliom.

   Pitoëff, Georges. Comédie des Champs-Élysées, Paris: 1923. B&W and color. Render-
      ing & set. **RSD**, illus. 384, 418, 419; B&W. Set. **TSS**, 524. 2 photos.

   Simonson, Lee. Garrick Theatre, NYC: 1921. B&W. Set. **MCN**, 54; B&W. Set. **PLT**,
      illus. 12-17; B&W. Set. **SDC**, plate 44; B&W. Set. **SOW**, plate 78; B&W. Set.
      TAS, 120-122. 6 photos; B&W. Set. **TSS**, 525. 2 photos.

   _____. NYC: 1947. B&W. Set. **WTP**, 124. 4 photos.

Liluli.

   Masereel, Franz. Art and Action, Paris: 1922. B&W. Projection designs. **RSD**, illus.
      389.

Lincoln.

   King, Lawrence. Chelsea Theatre Center, Brooklyn, New York: 1976. B&W. Set. **TCI**,
      vol. 11, n. 5 (Oct 1977). 12, 13.

The Lion and the Jewel.

   _____. University of Michigan, Ann Arbor: 1993. B&W. Set. **TDT**, vol. XXX,
      n. 5 (Fall 1994). 61.

The Lion and the Mouse.

   Physioc, Joseph. Lyceum Theatre, NYC: 1905. B&W. Set. **MCN**, 28.

Lips Together, Teeth Apart.

   Beatty, John Lee. Manhattan Theatre Club, NYC: 1991. B&W. Rendering. **DDT**, 30.

The Litigants.

   Rinfret, Jean-Claude. Comédie Canadienne, Théatre Club, Montréal: 1959. B&W.
      Rendering. **SDW2**, 40.

The Little Clay Cart.

   Bernstein, Aline. Neighborhood Playhouse, NYC: 1924. B&W. Set. **SDC**, plate 62.

The Little Donkey Porfirion.

   Zahorski, Lech. Teatr Kameralny, Warsaw: 1958. B&W. Set. **SDW2**, 172.

Little Eyolf.

   Appia, Adolphe. 1923. B&W. Sketch. **TPH**, photo 310; B&W. Rendering. **TSS**, 505.

   Katsioula, Elina. Yale Repertory Theatre, New Haven: B&W. Set. **TCI**, vol. 20, n. 3
      (Mar 1986). 8.

   Stenersen, Christian. National Theatre, Oslo: 1949. B&W. Rendering. **SDW1**, 155.

The Little Foxes.

   Bay, Howard. National Theatre, NYC: 1939. B&W. Set. **MCN**, 144; B&W. Set. **SDA**,
      203; B&W. Set. **TCI**, vol. 17, n. 2 (Feb 1983). 19. 2 photos; B&W. Set. **TDT**, n. 19
      (Dec 1969). 20; B&W. Set. **WTP**, 177; B&W. Set. **TDT**, n. 19 (Dec 1969). 21;
      London: 1982. B&W. Set. **TCI**, vol. 17, n. 2 (Feb 1983). 19.

   Jackness, Andrew. Martin Beck Theatre, NYC: 1981. B&W. Set. **DDT**, 354; B&W.
      Set. **DSL**, figure 16.2(a).

   Svoboda, Josef. National Theatre, Prague: 1948. B&W. Set. **STS**, 64.

   _____. North Carolina School of the Arts, Winston-Salem: 1972. B&W. Set.
      TCI, vol. 6, n. 5 (Oct 1972). 20.

The Little Hut.

   Wahkévitch, Georges. Nouveautés, Paris: 1947. B&W. Set. **SDW1**, 107.

   _____. B&W. Set. **WTP**, 120, 121. 4 photos.

Little Johnny Jones.
> Beatty, John Lee. Goodspeed Opera House, East Haddam, Connecticut: 1980. B&W.
> Set. **TCI**, vol. 15, n. 8 (Oct 1981). 29; B&W. Set. **TCI**, vol. 21, n. 9 (Nov 1987).
> 37.
> _____. Liberty Theatre, NYC: 1904. B&W. Set. **MBM**, 220.

Little Lili.
> de Nobili, Lila. A.B.C., Paris: 1951. B&W. Set. **SDW1**, 102.

Little Malcolm and His Struggle Against the Eunuchs.
> Loquasto, Santo. Experimental Theatre, Yale University, New Haven, Connecticut:
> 1967. B&W. Set. **TCI**, vol. 7, n. 5 (Oct 1973). 18.

Little Mary Sunshine.
> _____. University of Illinois, Urbana: B&W. Set. **TCI**, vol. 24, n. 5 (May 1990).
> 68.

Little Me.
> Randolph, Robert. Lunt-Fontanne Theatre, NYC: 1962. Color. Set. **BWM**, 118, 119;
> Color. Set. **MBM**, 208.

Little Moon of Alban.
> Mielziner, Jo. Longacre Theatre, NYC: 1960. B&W. Rendering. **DTT**, 207. Street;
> B&W. Rendering. **DTT**, 208. Finale.

Little Murders.
> Jackness, Andrew. Second Stage, Chicago: 1987. B&W. Rendering. **BSE5**, 37.

A Little Night Music.
> Aronson, Boris. Shubert Theatre, NYC: 1973. Color. Set. **BWM**, 324. 2 photos; B&W.
> Model. **CSD**, 37; B&W. Set. **HPA**, 108; B&W. Set. **HPR**, 205; Color. Set. **SON**,
> 41, 106, 107, 110. 6 photos; B&W and color. Set. **TAB**, 253-258, 309. 8 photos;
> Color. Show curtain. **TAB**, 259; Color. Set. **TMT**, plate 14; London: 1973. B&W.
> Set. **TAB**, 259.
> Weldin, Scott. Wichita State University, Kansas: B&W. Set. **TCI**, vol. 11, n. 3 (May/
> Jun 1977). 27.

The Little Shop of Horrors.
> _____. Orpheum Theatre, NYC: 1982. Color. Set. **MBM**, 173.
> _____. Theatrical Outfit, Atlanta: Color. Set. **TCI**, vol. 22, n. 3 (Mar 1988). 57.

The Little Show.
> Mielziner, Jo. Music Box Theatre, NYC: 1929. B&W. Rendering. **DTT**, 71. "Moanin'
> Low."

Liubov Yarovaya.
> Karakachev, Gueorgui. National Theater, Sofia, Bulgaria: 1959. B&W. Rendering.
> **SDW2**, 37.
> Menshutin, Nikolai. Maly Theatre, Moscow: 1926. B&W. Model & set. **RST**, 212,
> 213. 3 photos.

Livin' Dolls.
> Beatty, John Lee. Manhattan Theatre Club, NYC: 1982. B&W. **ASD1**, 11.

The Living Corpse.
> Korovin, Konstantin. Moscow Art Theatre: 1911. B&W. Set. **TPH**, photo 300.

La Locandiera.
> Benois, Alexander. Moscow Art Theatre: B&W. Rendering. **TCS2**, plates 9, 10.
> Visconti-Tosi. Eliseo, Rome: 1953. Color. Set. **SDW1**, 123.

Lock Up Your Daughters.
> Kenny, Sean. Mermaid Theatre, London: 1959. B&W. Set. **MCD**, plate 212.

Lohengrin.
> Elson, Charles. Metropolitan Opera, NYC: 1953. B&W. Rendering. **SDL**, 34; B&W.
> Rendering. **SDW1**, 197.
> Fedorovsky, Feodor. Bolshoi Theatre, Moscow: 1923. B&W. Model. **AST**, 134.
> Komisarjevsky, Theodore. Moscow Soviet Opera: 1918. B&W. Rendering. **SCM**, 29.
> Lynch, Thomas. Seattle Opera: 1994. Color. Set. **TCI**, vol. 28, n. 8 (Oct 1994). 9.
> Preetorius, Emil. State Opera, Berlin: 1930. B&W. Rendering. **SCM**, 68; La Scala,
> Milan: 1953. B&W. Rendering. **SDE**, 135.
> Steinberg, Paul. Grand Theater, Geneva: 1994. Color. Set. **TCI**, vol. 29, n. 4 (Apr
> 1995). 5; B&W. Set. **TDT** vol. XXXI, n. 2 (Spring 1995). 16.
> Uecker, Günther. Beyreuth Festival Theatre: 1979. B&W. Set. **TCI**, vol. 14, n. 1 (Jan/
> Feb 1980). 23.
> Wagner, Wieland. Beyreuth Festival Theatre: 1960. B&W. Set. **SDW2**, 73.

I Lombardi alla prima Crociata.
> Sironi, Mario. Teatro Comunale, Florence: 1948. B&W. Rendering. **AST**, 192; B&W.
> Rendering. **SDE**, 153.

Loneliness.
> Svoboda, Josef. B&W. Set. **DSL**, figure 1.1(c).

Long Day's Journey into Night.
> Dancy, Virginia & Elmon Webb. Promenade Theatre, NYC: 1971. B&W. Model & set.
> **DPT**, 85.
> Dusek, Jan. Czechoslovakia: 1983. B&W. Rendering. **TDT**, vol. XXVI, n. 4 (Fall
> 1990). 25, 26; B&W. Model. **TDT**, vol. XXIII, n. 4 (Winter 1988). 49.
> Edwards, Ben. Yale Repertory Theatre, New Haven: 1988. B&W. Set. **TCI**, vol. 23, n.
> 7 (Aug/Sep 1989). 49.
> Hays, David. Helen Hayes Theatre, NYC: 1956. B&W. Set. **TCI**, vol. 23, n. 8 (Oct
> 1989). 43.
> Hein, Keith. Morgan Theatre, California: B&W. Set. **TCI**, vol. 14, n. 4 (Sep 1980). 47.
> Payne, Darwin Reid. B&W. Sketch. **SIP**, 238.
> Phillips, Jason. Center Stage, Baltimore: 1969. B&W. Set. **TCI**, vol. 7, n. 3 (May/Jun
> 1973). 12.
> Phillips, Van. Purdue University: B&W. Set. **SST**, 262.
> _____. Playhouse in the Park, Cincinnati: B&W. Set. **TCI**, vol. 14, n. 1 (Jan/Feb
> 1980). 38.

Long Time Since Yesterday.
> McClennahan, Charles. New Federal Theatre, NYC: 1985. B&W. Set. **ASD2**, 120.

The Long Voyage Home.
> Remson, Ira. Playwright's Theatre, NYC: 1917. B&W. Set. **MCN**, 44.

A Long Way from Home.
> Kerz, Leo. Maxine Elliot Theatre, NYC: 1948. B&W. Set. **SDW1**, 198.

Look After Lulu.
> Beaton, Cecil. Henry Miller's Theatre, New York: 1959. Color. Rendering & set. **CBS**,
> 35.

Look Back in Anger.
> Gillette, A.S. University of Iowa, Iowa City: 1969. B&W. Rendering. **TDP**, 13.
> _____. Asolo State Theatre, Sarasota, Florida: 1968. B&W. Set. **TCR**, 107.

Look Homeward Angel.
> Beatty, John Lee. Yale School of Drama, New Haven, Connecticut: 1972. Color.
> Rendering. **ASD1**, between 70 & 71.

Mielziner, Jo. Ethel Barrymore Theatre, NYC: 1957. B&W. Rendering. **DPT**, 52; Color. Rendering. **DTT**, 210. Porch scene; B&W. Rendering. **DTT**, 211. Bedroom scene; Color. Rendering. **SDA**, 293; B&W. Set. **SDB**, 37.

Look Ma, I'm Dancin'!

Smith, Oliver. Adelphi Theatre, NYC: 1948. B&W. Set. **BWM**, 103. 2 photos.

Look to the Lilies.

Mielziner, Jo. Lunt-Fontanne Theatre, NYC: 1970. B&W. Sketch. **TCI**, vol. 4, n. 3 (May/Jun 1970). 18.

Looking for the Wind in the Field.

Gansonskaya, Liona. USSR: B&W. Rendering. **TDT**, vol. XX, n. 1 (Spring 1984). 17.

The Lords of the West.

Jones, Robert Edmond. (project): 1942. B&W. Rendering. **REJ**, 107.

Lorenzaccio.

Gunter, John. National Theatre (Olivier), London: 1983. B&W. Set. **BTD**, 72, 73.

_____. Chicago Lyric Opera: c. 1930. B&W. Model & backdrop. **TDT**, vol. XXV, n. 2 (Summer 1989). 12. 2 photos.

A Loss of Roses.

Aronson, Boris. Eugene O'Neill Theatre, NYC: 1959. B&W. Set. **TAB**, 306.

The Lost Boys.

Bradley, Scott. American Repertory Theatre, Cambridge, Massachusetts: Color. Set. **TCI**, vol. 25, n. 1 (Jan 1991). 34.

The Lost Fairy Tale.

Svoboda, Josef. Laterna Magika, Prague: 1975. B&W. Set. **STS**, 118.

Lost in the Stars.

Jenkins, George. Music Box Theatre, NYC: 1949. B&W. Set. **WMC**, 204.

Walentin, Arne. Folketertret, Oslo: 1952. B&W. Set. **SDW2**, 154.

Lost Melody.

Johansen, Svend. Odense Teater, Odense, Denmark: 1936. Color. Rendering. **SDW1**, 57.

Louis Ferdinand.

Pillartz, T.C. B&W. Set. **SDC**, plate 123.

Louis Riel.

Laufer, Murray. O'Keefe Centre, Toronto: 1967. B&W. Set. **SDW3**, 209. 3 photos.

Louise.

Utrillo, Maurice. Opéra-Comique, Paris: 1950. B&W. Rendering. **AST**, 109.

_____. New York City Opera, Lincoln Center: B&W. Set. **TCI**, vol. 7, n. 1 (Jan/Feb 1973). 18.

Love! Valour! Compassion!

Arcenas, Loy. 1994. Color. Rendering. **TCI**, vol. 29, n. 1 (Jan 1995). 6.

Love Among the Ruins.

Aronson, Boris. (project): 1951. B&W. Rendering. **TAB**, 302.

Love and Death.

Feuerstein, Bedrich. Vinohrady Theatre, Prague: 1923. B&W. Set. **TDT**, n. 41 (Summer 1975). 20.

Love and Intrigue.

Finke, Jochen. Kammerspiele, Berlin: 1972. B&W. Set. **SDW4**, illus. 115-117.

Reinking, Wilhelm. Schiller Theatre, Berlin: 1955. B&W. Set. **SDW1**, 80.

Love and Peace.

Mumcu, Hüseyin. Devlet Tiyatrosu, Ankara, Turkey: 1960. B&W. Rendering. **SDW2**, 214.

Love for Love.
>   de Nobili, Lila. National Theatre Company, Old Vic, London: 1966. B&W. Set. **SDR,**
>   6.
>   Higgins, Douglas. Phoenix Theatre, NYC: 1974. B&W. Rendering. **TCI,** vol. 8, n. 6
>   (Nov/Dec 1974). 14. 2 photos.
>   Jones, Robert Edmond. Provincetown Playhouse, NYC: 1925. B&W. Sketch. **DFT,**
>   plate 28.
>   Sporre, Dennis J. B&W. Drawing & set. **TCI,** vol. 5, n. 6 (Nov/Dec 1971). 18, 19, 21.
>   4 photos.
>   Whistler, Rex. Phoenix Theatre, London: 1943. B&W. Rendering. **TPH,** photo 432.
>   _____. Great Britain: 1947. B&W. Set. **WTP,** 128, 129. 8 photos.

The Love for Three Oranges.
>   Anisfeld, Boris. Chicago Opera House: 1921. B&W. Set. **SDC,** plate 53. 2 photos;
>   B&W. Set. **TCS2,** plate 236.
>   Bay, Howard. 1939. B&W. Rendering. **SDB,** 192; B&W. Rendering. **TCI,** vol. 17, n. 2
>   (Feb 1983). 11.
>   Oenslager, Donald. (project); B&W. Rendering. **STN,** 167-177. 6 photos.
>   Scandella, Mischa. Spoleto Festival, Charleston, South Carolina: 1962. Color. Render-
>   ing. **RSD,** illus. 463.
>   Svoboda, Josef. Smetana Theater, Prague: 1963. B&W. Rendering & set. **SJS,** 136. 2
>   photos; B&W. Rendering. **STS,** 66; B&W. Rendering & set. **TDT,** n. 20 (Feb
>   1970). 12, 13.

Love from Judy.
>   Sutcliffe, Berkeley. Saville Theatre, London: 1952. B&W. Set. **MCD,** plate 202.

Love in Buffalo.
>   Casler, Richard. Yale School of Drama, New Haven, Connecticut: B&W. Set. **SFT,**
>   116, 117. 8 photos.

Love Letters on Blue Paper.
>   Elder, Eldon. Syracuse Stage, New York: 1977-1978. B&W. Model. **EED,** (pages not
>   numbered).

Love Life.
>   Aronson, Boris. 46th Street Theatre, NYC: 1948. B&W and color. Rendering & set.
>   **TAB,** 86-88, 90-94, 301. 25 photos.

The Love of Don Perlimplin and Belisa in the Garden.
>   Clavé, Antoni. Théâtre des Champs-Elysées, Paris: 1952. B&W. Model. **SDW1,** 90.
>   _____. National Technical Institute for the Deaf: B&W. Set. **TCI,** vol. 3, n. 1
>   (Jan/Feb 1969). cover.

The Love of Four Colonels.
>   _____. London: 1950. B&W. Set. **WTP,** 168. 2 photos.

The Love of the Three Kings.
>   Urban, Joseph. Boston Opera: 1913. B&W. Set. **SDC,** plate 57.

Love the Sorcerer.
>   Brayer, Yves. Opéra de Paris: 1943. B&W. Rendering. **SDW1,** 88.

Love's Labor's Lost.
>   Beaton, Cecil. Old Vic Company, New Theatre, London: 1954. B&W. Sketch. **CBS,**
>   49.
>   Donnelly, Mark. University of Arizona, Tucson: B&W. Set. **SDT,** 293.
>   Erven, Charles E. Colorado Shakespeare Festival: 1980. B&W. Rendering. **BSE2,** 10.
>   Gliese, Rochus. Staatliches Schauspielhaus, Berlin: 1930. Color. Rendering. **SOS,** 213.
>   Klingeelhoefer. Folger Library Theatre, Washington, DC: 1987. B&W. Model. **BSE5,**
>   15.

Lee, Ming Cho. New York Shakespeare Festival, NYC: 1965. B&W. Set. **DMS**, plate
    54.
MacArthur, Molly. Old Vic Theatre, London: 1949. B&W. Set. **TPH**, photo 441.
Malina, Jaroslav: National Theatre, Prague: B&W. Set. **TDT**, vol. XXVII, n. 3 (Sum-
    mer 1991). 23. 4 photos.
O'Brien, Timothy. Great Britain: B&W. Model. **TDT**, vol. XXVII, n. 4 (Fall 1991). 37.
Stewart, Anita C. Playmakers Repertory Company, Paul Green Theatre, Chapel Hill,
    North Carolina: Color. Set. **TCI**, vol. 25, n. 3 (Mar 1991). 47.
Toms, Carl. National Theatre, London: 1968. B&W. Set. **TCI**, vol. 6, n. 1 (Jan/Feb
    1972). 17.
_____. Brattle Theatre, Cambridge, Massachusetts: B&W. Set. **WTP**, 70, 71. 6
    photos.
_____. Yale Repertory Theatre, New Haven: B&W. Set. **SDL**, 72.
Love's Triumph.
Gischia, Léon. Théâtre National Populaire, Lyon: 1956. B&W. Set. **SDW2**, 92.
The Lovelies and the Dowdies.
Kantor, Tadeusz. Cricot Theater, Cracow: 1973. B&W. Set. **RSD**, illus. 637. Photo
    taken at Edinburgh Festival.
The Lover's Tears on the Tomb of the Beloved.
Feres, Sarah. Teatro da Paz, Belém do Para, Brasil: 1966. B&W. Set. **SDW3**, 175.
The Lovers.
Remisoff, Nicolai. B&W. Rendering. **RSC**, 49.
Lovers from the Kiosk.
Feuerstein, Bedrich. Estates Theatre, Prague. 1932. B&W. Set. **TDT**, n. 41 (Summer
    1975). 21.
The Lower Depths.
Buckingham, William. University of Minnesota, Minneapolis: 1978. B&W. Model.
    BSE1, 32; B&W. Set. **TCI**, vol. 13, n. 3 (May/Jun 1979). 38.
Ciulei, Liviu. Teatrul Municipal, Bucharest: 1960. B&W. Set. **SDW2**, 173.
Davis, Janice. (project): B&W. Model. **TCI**, vol. 16, n. 2 (Feb 1982). 27.
Elder, Eldon. (project): 1949. B&W. Rendering. **EED**, (pages not numbered). 2 pho-
    tos.
Fara, Libor. Cinoherni Klub, Prague: 1971. B&W. Model & set. **SDW3**, 95. 2 photos.
Galup, Mario. Teatro Universitario, Montevideo: 1957. B&W. Set. **SDW2**, 241.
Loquasto, Santo. Arena Stage, Washington, DC: 1977. B&W. Set. **ASD1**, 111.
Simov, Victor Andréiévich. Moscow Art Theatre: 1902. B&W. Set. **RSD**, illus. 13.
Suhr, Edward. Volksbühne, Berlin: B&W. Set. **TCS2**, plate 104.
_____. Kleines Theater, Berlin: 1903. B&W. Set. **MRH**, facing 71.
_____. B&W. Set. **TPH**, photo 329.
Loyalty.
Hasegawa, Kanbei. Kabuki-za, Tokyo: 1951. B&W. Set. **SDW1**, 143.
LSD-Just the High Points.
Clayburg, Jim. Performing Arts Garage, NYC: 1986. B&W. Set. **TCI**, vol. 23, n. 5
    (May 1989). 47.
Lucia di Lammermoor.
Corrodi, Annelies. B&W. Set. **DSL**, figure 39.11, pg. 428; B&W. Set. **SST**, 558.
Howland, Gerard. San Francisco Opera: 1994-1995. Color. Model. **TCI**, vol. 29, n. 3
    (Mar 1995). 33.
Pecktal, Lynn. Teatro Municipal, Santiago, Chile: 1970. B&W. Rendering. **DPT**, 317.
    Act III, sc. 2.
Svoboda, Josef. Macerata: 1993. B&W. Set. **TDT**, vol. XXX, n. 5 (Fall 1994). 41.

_____. Basel: 1967. B&W. Set. **TCI**, vol. 4, n. 4 (Sep 1970). 23.

Lucifer and the Lord.

Acquart, Claude. Théâtre National Populaire, Lyon: 1968. B&W. Model. **SDW3**, 119.

Bondt, Werner de. Belgium: B&W. Model. **TCI**, vol. 13, n. 6 (Nov/Dec 1979). 24.

Kosinski, Jan. Teatr Dramatyczny, Warsaw: 1960. B&W. Rendering. **SDW2**, 167.

Labisse, Félix. Théâtre Antoine, Paris: 1951. Color. Rendering. **SDW1**, 103.

Lenneweit, H.W. Municipal Theatre, Frankfurt am Main: 1964. B&W. Rendering. **SDR**, 67.

Maximowna, Ita. Schiller Theatre, Berlin: 1952. B&W. Set. **SDW1**, 71.

Polidori, Gianni. 1962. B&W. Set. **SIO**, 112.

Luck, Pluck, & Virtue.

Lobel, Adrianne. La Jolla Playhouse, California: 1993. Color. Set. **TCI**, vol. 27, n. 8 (Oct 1993). 7.

The Lucky Shipwreck.

Schwab, Per. Den Nationale Scene, Bergen, Norway: 1949. B&W. Rendering. **SDW1**, 155.

Lucrece.

Jones, Robert Edmond. Belasco Theatre, NYC: 1930. B&W. Set. **SDA**, 211; B&W. Set. **SCM**, 99.

Lucrezia Borgia.

Varona, José. Vancouver Opera: 1972. Color. Rendering. **DPT**, between 124 & 125. Act II, sc. 2; Color. Rendering. **DPT**, between 124 & 125. Prologue; B&W. Rendering. **TCI**, vol. 14, n. 5 (Oct 1980). 33.

Luisa Miller.

Tovaglieri, Enrico. Maggio Musicale Fiorentino, Florence: 1937. B&W. Rendering. **SDE**, 157.

Lulu.

Arnone, John. La Jolla Playhouse, California: 1988. Color. Set. **ASD2**, between 108 & 109.

Herbert, Jocelyn. Metropolitan Opera, NYC: 1977. B&W and color. Rendering & set. **MOM**, 132-143. 10 photos; B&W. Set. **TCI**, vol. 11, n. 4 (Sep 1977). 14; B&W. Set. **TCI**, vol. 18, n. 3 (Mar 1984). 19.

Klein, Allen Charles. Vienna State Opera: 1983. B&W. Rendering. **DDT**, 8. 2 photos.

Lobel, Adrianne. 1981. Color. Set. **DDT**, 440a. 2 photos.

Vernet, Thierry. Grand Theater, Geneva: 1971. B&W. Rendering. **SDW3**, 192. 3 photos.

_____. Santa Fe Opera: B&W. Set. **TCI**, vol. 15, n. 7 (Aug/Sep 1981). 66. 2 photos.

Lulu Belle.

Joseph Wickes' Studio. Belasco Theatre, NYC: 1926. B&W. Set. **MCN**, 74.

Luminous Moss.

Kanamori, Kaoru. Nissei Gekijo, Tokyo: 1973. B&W. Set. **SDW4**, illus. 277.

Lute Song.

Jones, Robert Edmond. Plymouth Theatre, NYC: 1944. B&W. Rendering. **SDA**, 249; B&W. Sketch. **DFT**, plate 35. The blue pavilion in the palace of Prince Nieou; B&W. Rendering & set. **REJ**, 117, 119, 121, 138. 5 photos; B&W. Set. **WTP**, 84, 85.

Luther.

Falleni, Silvano. 1967. B&W. Set. **SIO**, 52.

Herbert, Jocelyn. Royal Court Theatre, London: 1961. B&W. Set. **SDW2**, 216. 2 photos.

Lydie Breeze.
　　Rigdon, Kevin. Steppenwolf Theatre, Chicago: 1986. Color. Set. **TCI**, vol. 21, n. 2
　　　　(Feb 1987). 29.
Lysistrata.
　　Anderson, Nels. Louisiana State University Theatre, Baton Rouge: Color. Set. **TCI**,
　　　　vol. 21, n. 3 (Mar 1987). 22.
　　Bel Geddes, Norman. USA: 1928. B&W. Set. **SCM**, 103; B&W. Set. **SDA**, 213.
　　Beyer, Rolf. Hopkins Center, Dartmouth College, Hanover, New Hampshire: 1971.
　　　　B&W. Set. **DPT**, 102.
　　Hegle, Kaare. Carl Johan Scenen, Oslo: 1951. B&W. Set. **SDW1**, 153.
　　Itô, Kisaku. Haiyuza, Tokyo: 1954. B&W. Set. **SDW1**, 149.
　　Öberg, Barbara W. State Theatre, Norrköping, Sweden: 1957. B&W. Set. **SDW2**, 211.
　　Olivastro, John J. Southern Illinois University, Edwardsville: 1981. B&W. Set. **BSE2**,
　　　　24, 39.
　　Rabinovitch, Isaac. Musical Studio, Moscow Art Theater: 1923. B&W. Set. **RSD**, illus.
　　　　197; B&W. Set. **TCS2**, plate 169; B&W. Set. **SDC**, plate 119.
　　Saint-Phalle, Niki de. State Theatre, Kassel: 1966. B&W. Set. **RSD**, illus. 487.
　　Stern, Ernst. Berlin: 1908. B&W. Set. **SDB**, 29.
　　Upor, Tibor. Vigszinház, Budapest. 1959. B&W. Set. **SDW2**, 142.
　　＿＿＿＿＿. Grosses Schauspielhaus, Berlin: B&W. Set. **MRH**, facing 17; B&W. Set.
　　　　TCS2, plate 370.
　　＿＿＿＿＿. Moscow Art Theatre: 1919. B&W. Set. **TPH**, photos 304, 305.

-M-

M. Butterfly.
　　Ishioka, Eiko. Eugene O'Neill Theatre, NYC: 1988. Color. Set. **TCI**, vol. 22, n. 8 (Oct
　　　　1988). 54; Color. Set. **TCI**, vol. 22, n. 5 (May 1988). 9.
M. Monsieur's Theatre (The Box Office).
　　Tanaka, Béatrice. Théâtre de l'Alliance Française, Paris: 1962. B&W. Model. **SDW2**,
　　　　36.
Ma Rainey's Black Bottom.
　　McClennahan, Charles. Yale Repertory Theatre, New Haven: 1984. B&W. Sketch &
　　　　set. **ASD2**, 110, 116.
　　Soule, Robert D. Downstairs Theatre, Trinity Repertory Company, Providence, Rhode
　　　　Island: 1987. Color. Set. **TCI**, vol. 22, n. 9 (Nov 1988). 63.
Macbeth.
　　Aaes, Eric. Det Kongelige Teater, Copenhagen: 1938. B&W. Model. **SDW1**, 55.
　　Abril, Jean Philippe. Théâtre National de Strasbourg: 1970. B&W. Model. **SDW3**, 96.
　　Acquart, André. Théâtre de l'Est Parisien: 1965. B&W. Sketches, model & set. **SDW3**,
　　　　55. 3 photos.
　　Alkazi, Ebrahim. Theatre Unit, Jai Hind College Theatre, Bombay: 1956. Color.
　　　　Model. **SDW2**, 115.
　　Axer, Otto. Teatr Polski, Warsaw: 1964. B&W. **SDW3**, 53. 4 photos.
　　Baumeister, Willi. Deutsches Theater, Stuttgart: 1921. B&W. Rendering. **AST**, 158.
　　Boehlke, Bain. Southern Theatre, Minneapolis: 1983. B&W. Set. **TCI**, vol. 17, n. 7
　　　　(Aug/Sep 1983). 21.
　　Boehm, Herta. Teatro Comunale, Florence: 1951. B&W. Set. **SDW1**, 62; B&W. Set.
　　　　SDE, 48.
　　Bradshaw, Laurence. (project): Color. Rendering. **DIT**, plate 61.

Brulin, Tone. Reizend Volkstheater, Antwerp: 1948. B&W. Rendering. **SDW1**, 43.
Cagli, Corrado. La Scala, Milan: 1959. B&W. Rendering. **SDW2**, 122; B&W. Rendering. **SIO**, 140. 2 photos.
Carrick, Edward A. Shakespeare Memorial Theatre, Stratford-upon-Avon: 1949. Color. Rendering. **DMS**, plate 45; B&W. Rendering. **SDW1**, 173.
Ciulei, Liviu. Teatrul Lucia Sturdza Bulandra, Bucharest: 1968. B&W. Set. **SDW3**, 59. 3 photos.
Corrodi, Annelies. B&W and color. Rendering & model. **DSL**, figure 39.1(b), plate III; B&W. Model. **SST**, 543.
Craig, Edward Gordon. B&W. Rendering. **OAT**, 118. Act V, sc. 5; B&W. Rendering. **OAT**, 280; B&W. Rendering. **SDC**, plates 69, 70; B&W. Sketch. **TPH**, photo 320; 1906. B&W. Rendering. **COT**, 149; B&W. Rendering. **TNT**, facing 64; Theatersammlung, Vienna (unproduced): 1908. B&W. Rendering. **COT**, 150; B&W. Rendering. **FCS**, plate 169. Act II; B&W. Rendering. **RSD**, illus. 80; B&W. Rendering. **SDO**, 191; B&W. Rendering. **TNT**, facing 69; 1909. B&W. Rendering. **TNT**, facing 71, 73, 75, 77; 1910. B&W. Rendering. **TNT**, facing 79; 1913. B&W. Rendering. **RSD**, illus. 81, 82; 1928. B&W. Rendering. **TDT**, n. 29 (May 1972). 11. Act II, sc. 2.
Dare, Daphne. Mark Hellinger Theatre, NYC: 1988. Color. Set. **TCI**, vol. 22, n. 7 (Aug/Sep 1988). 112.
Diouf, Ibou. Théatre National Daniel Sorano, Dakar: 1969. B&W and color. Sketch & set. **SDW3**, 56, 57. 9 photos.
Doboujinsky, Mstislav. Theatre of Tragedy, Petrograd: 1918. B&W. Sketch. **RST**, 111.
Dyer, Chris. Royal Shakespeare Company, GB: 1982. B&W. Set. **SDT**, 272.
Eisenstein, Sergei & Sergei Yutkevich. Central Educational Theatre, Moscow: 1922. B&W. Sketch. **RST**, 112.
Gliese, Rochus & Knut Ström. Munich: B&W. Rendering. **DIT**, plate 106; B&W. Rendering. **SDC**, plate 56.
Hay, Richard L. Oregon Shakespeare Festival, Ashland: 1979. B&W. Set. **TCI**, vol. 13, n. 4 (Sep 1979). 31.
Heinrich, Rudolf. Bavarian State Opera, Munich: 1967. B&W. Set. **SDW3**, 181. 2 photos.
Hembrow, Victor. Great Britain: B&W. Rendering. **DIT**, plate 19; B&W. Sketch. **TPH**, photo 431.
Howland, Gerard. San Francisco Opera: 1994-1995. Color. Model & set. **TCI**, vol. 29, n. 3 (Mar 1995). 33, 34, 36. 4 photos.
Jones, Robert Edmond. Apollo Theatre, NYC: 1921. B&W. Set. **CSD**, 11; B&W. Sketch. **DFT**, plate 12. Act I, sc. 1: the three witches; B&W. Sketch. **DFT**, plate 13. Act I, sc. 5: the letter scene; B&W. Sketch. **DFT**, plate 14. Act III, sc. 4: the banquet scene; B&W. Rendering. **DOT**, 226; B&W. Rendering. **PST**, 386. Act III, sc. 4; B&W. Rendering. **REJ**, 39, 41; B&W. Rendering. **RSD**, illus. 431, 432; B&W. Drawings, model, rendering, & set. **SDA**, 65-67, 339-351. 29 photos; B&W. Rendering. **SDC**, plate 116; B&W. Rendering. **SDT**, 35; B&W. Rendering. **SOS**, 172; B&W. Rendering. **SOW**, plate 81; B&W. Rendering. **TAT**, plate 553; B&W. Model. **TCS2**, plate 201; B&W. Rendering. **TPH**, photos 473, 474; B&W. Rendering. **TSY**, 177; (not produced): 1938. B&W. Rendering. **FCS**, plate 206. Act V, sc. 1; B&W. Rendering. **SDO**, 236; (not produced): 1946. B&W. Rendering. **FCS**, plate 207. Act V, sc. 1; B&W. Rendering. **REJ**, 127; B&W. Rendering. **SDO**, 237; (not produced): B&W. Rendering. **REJ**, 129.
Jorgulesco, Jonel. Boston Repertory Theatre: B&W. Rendering. **TCS2**, plate 361.

Karson, Nat. Lafayette Theatre, NYC: 1936. B&W. Set. **SOS**, 179; B&W. Rendering. **SOW**, plate 42.

Komisarjevsky, Theodore. Shakespeare Memorial Theatre, Stratford-upon-Avon: 1933. B&W. Rendering. **SCM**, 29; B&W. Set. **SOS**, 161; B&W. Rendering. **TPH**, photo 437.

Lee, Eugene. Trinity Square Theatre, Providence, Rhode Island: 1969. B&W. Set. **SDW3**, 58. 2 photos.

Luzzati, Emanuele. 1971. B&W. Set. **SIO**, 94.

Macke, August. Schauspielhaus, Düsseldorf: 1906. B&W. Sketches. **AST**, 36.

Majewski, Andrej. Color. Rendering. **DSL**, plate II; B&W & color. Rendering. **SST**, 5, plate III.

Minks, Wilfried. Bremen: 1966. B&W. Set. **TCI**, vol. 12, n. 1 (Jan/Feb 1978). 28.

Neher, Caspar. Hamburg: 1944. B&W. Set. **SDB**, 20; Charlottenburg Opera, Berlin: B&W. Set. **SCM**, 61.

O'Hearn, Robert. American Shakespeare Festival, Stratford, Connecticut: 1961. B&W. Rendering. **DDT**, 299.

Pitoëff, Georges. Plainpalais Auditorium, Geneva: 1921. B&W. Rendering & set. **RSD**, illus. 424, 425; B&W. Set. **TCS2**, plate 117.

Refn, Helge. Det kongelige Teater, Copenhagen: 1944. B&W. Rendering. **SDW1**, 61.

Reiman, Walter. State Theatre, Berlin: B&W. Rendering. **TCS2**, plates 130, 131.

Scandella, Mischa. 1966-1967. B&W. Rendering. **SIO**, 128.

Scheffler, John. 1979. Color. Set. **DDT**, 312d.

Schmidt, Douglas W. American Shakespeare Festival, Stratford, Connecticut: 1973. B&W. Rendering. **ASD1**, 142; B&W. Rendering. **CSD**, 127. Heath; B&W. Rendering. **CSD**, 127. Sleepwalking scene.

Schumacher, Fritz. B&W. Rendering. **DIT**, plate 91.

Senghor, Line. Théatre National Daniel Sorano, Dakar: 1969. B&W and color. Sketch & set. **SDW3**, 56, 57. 9 photos.

Serban, Milenko. Jugoslovensko Dramsko Pozoriste, Beograd: 1956. B&W. Set. **SDW2**, 136.

Soehnlein, Kurt. Germany: B&W. Rendering. **TAT**, plate 403.

Stegars, Rolf. Suomen Kansallisteatteri, Helsinki: 1964. B&W. Set. **SDW3**, 54. 2 photos.

Stern, Ernst. Deutsches Theater, Berlin: 1916. Color. Rendering. **MRH**, facing 232.

Svoboda, Josef. Tyl Theatre, Prague: 1969. B&W. Set. **SJS**, 41; Zurich: 1985. B&W. Set. **TCI**, vol. 21, n. 8 (Oct 1987). 35.

Turina, Drago. Teatar I TD, Zagreb, Yugoslavia: 1974. B&W. Set. **SDW4**, illus. 47-52.

Tvadze, D.M. Rustaveli Georgian Drama Theatre, Tbilisi: 1963. B&W. Rendering. **TDT**, n. 33 (May 1973). 15.

Unruh, Del & Ione. Southwest Repertory Theatre, Norman, Oklahoma: 1976. B&W. Model. **BSE1**, 34. 2 photos; B&W. Set. **TDT**, vol. XVII, n. 1 (Spring 1981). 11. 5 photos.

Upor, Tibor. National Theatre, Budapest: B&W. Rendering. **SCM**, 75.

Varga, Joseph A. Virginia Museum Theatre, Richmond: 1983. B&W. Rendering. **BSE3**, 39.

Wagner, Robin. Arena Stage, Washington, DC: B&W. Set. **TCI**, vol. 5, n. 6 (Nov/Dec 1971). 13.

Walton, Tony. Color. Set. **TCI**, vol. 22, n. 7 (Aug/Sep 1988). 112.

Welcke, Stefan. Svenska Teatern, Helsinki: 1945. B&W. Model. **SDW1**, 159.

Wenig, Josef. National Theatre, Prague: 1916. B&W. Rendering. **TDT**, n. 41 (Summer 1975). 15.

Yeargan, Michael. Folger Library Theatre, Washington, DC: Color. Set. **TCI**, vol. 22, n. 5 (May 1988). 50. 2 photos.

Yodice, Robert. Juilliard School of Music, NYC: 1973. B&W. Rendering. **CSD**, 145.

Zuffi, Piero. Piccolo Teatro, Milan: 1952. B&W. Rendering. **SDE**, 170, 171. 3 photos.

_____. Arena Stage, Washington, DC: 1966. B&W. Set. **TCI**, vol. 19, n. 7 (Aug/Sep 1985). 44.

_____. Berezil Theatre, Ukraine: 1924. B&W. Set. **RST**, 164.

_____. produced by the Federal Theater: B&W. Set. **TPH**, photo 478.

_____. His Majesty's Theatre, London: 1911. B&W. Set. **SOS**, 127.

_____. Krannert Center, Champaign-Urbana, Illinois: B&W. Set. **TCI**, vol. 6, n. 1 (Jan/Feb 1972). 30, 31.

_____. Royal Opera House, Stockholm. B&W. Rendering. **CSC**, facing 54.

_____. Salzburg: B&W. Set. **TCI**, vol. 11, n. 2 (Mar/Apr 1977). 21. 2 photos.

_____. State Opera, Berlin: B&W. Set. **SCM**, 61.

_____. Yale Repertory Theatre, New Haven: B&W. Set. **TCI**, vol. 6, n. 3 (May/Jun 1972). 26.

_____. 1942. B&W. Set. **WTP**, 68. 2 photos.

_____. 1946. B&W. Set. **WTP**, 68, 69. 3 photos.

Macbett.

Ciulei, Liviu. Kammerspiele, Munich: 1973. B&W. Set. **SDW4**, illus. 267.

Machandel.

Schultz, Johannes. Tanztheater, Germany: 1989. B&W. Set. **TCI**, vol. 23, n. 9 (Nov 1989). 11.

Machinal.

MacNeil, Ian. Lyttleton Theatre, London: 1993. Color. Set. **TCI**, vol. 28, n. 4 (Apr 1994). 30, 31. 3 photos.

May, Henry. University of California, Berkeley: 1981. B&W. Set. **TCI**, vol. 15, n. 8 (Oct 1981). 10.

The Machine Wreckers.

Miller, Kenny. Glasgow Citizens Theatre: 1985. B&W. Set. **BTD**, 64.

Mack and Mabel.

Wagner, Robin. Majestic Theatre, NYC: 1974. B&W. Set. **TCI**, vol. 8, n. 6 (Nov/Dec 1974). 6.

Mad Forest.

Draghici, Marina. Pittsburgh Public Theatre: 1993. Color. Set. **TCI**, vol. 27, n. 3 (Mar 1993). 7.

Mad Joan.

Wahkévitch, Georges. Comédie Française, Paris: 1949. B&W. Rendering. **SDW1**, 108.

Mad Tristan.

Dali, Salvador. International Ballet, NYC: 1944. B&W. Rendering. **RSD**, illus. 483, 484.

A Mad World.

Kellogg, Marjorie Bradley. La Jolla Playhouse, California: 1983. Color. Set. **TCI**, vol. 21, n. 8 (Oct 1987). 26.

Madame Butterfly.

Bregni, Paolo. B&W. Model. **SIO**, 17.

Chiment, Marie Anne. Opera Theatre of St. Louis: Color. Set. **TCI**, vol. 27, n. 9 (Nov 1993). 40.

Dunham, Clarke. Chicago Lyric Opera: 1982. B&W. Set & show curtain. **DDT**, 395, 587; Color. Set. **TCI**, vol. 18, n. 8 (Oct 1984). 16.

Fedorovitch, Sophie. Royal Opera House, Covent Garden, London: 1950. B&W.
    Rendering. **SDW1**, 175.
Foujita, Tajakawa. La Scala, Milan: 1951. B&W. Rendering. **SDE**, 87.
Lazaridis, Stefanos. English National Opera, London: 1984. B&W. Set. **BTD**, 129.
Moholy-Nagy, László. Krolloper, Berlin: 1933. B&W. **RSD**, illus. 260; B&W. Set.
    SCM, 58.
Nagasaka, Motohiro. Metropolitan Opera, NYC: 1957. B&W. Rendering. **MOM**, 14.
Payne, Darwin Reid. B&W. Sketch. **SIP**, 263.
Preetorius, Emil. State Opera, Berlin: 1928. B&W. Rendering. **SCM**, 68.
Salzer, Beeb. Baltimore Opera Company: B&W. Rendering. **TDT**, n. 39 (Dec 1974). 8.
    2 photos.
Scott, Michael. Metropolitan Opera, NYC: 1995. Color. Set. **TCI**, vol. 29, n. 4 (Apr
    1995). 10.
Steinberg, Paul. Flanders Opera: 1994. Color. Set. **TCI**, vol. 29, n. 4 (Apr 1995). 30.
Zimmerman, Reinhart. Comic Opera, Berlin: B&W. Set. **TCI**, vol. 15, n. 1 (Jan 1981).
    37; B&W. Model. **TDT**, vol. XVI, n. 1 (Spring 1980). 17.
_____. Brooklyn Academy of Music, New York: B&W. Set. **TCI**, vol. 1, n. 2
    (May/Jun 1967). 14.
Madame Bovary.
Baty, Gaston. Théâtre Montparnasse, Paris: 1936. B&W. Set. **SOW**, plate 65; B&W.
    Set. **TPH**, photo 359.
Madame Pompadour.
Harker, Joseph, Phil Harker, & Alfred Terraine. Daly's Theatre, London: 1923. B&W.
    Set. **MCD**, plate 125.
Mme. Sand.
Peters, Rollo. B&W. Set. **SDC**, plate 45.
Made in Bangkok.
Arnone, John. Mark Taper Forum, Los Angeles: 1988. B&W. Set. **ASD2**, 16.
Mademoiselle Colombe.
Aronson, Boris. Longacre Theatre, NYC: 1954. B&W and color. Rendering & set.
    TAB, 108, 109, 303. 5 photos.
Mlle. Modiste.
Emens, Homer. Knickerbocker Theatre, NYC: 1905. B&W. Set. **TMI**, 98; B&W. Set.
    WMC, 15.
The Madman and the Nun.
Kantor, Tadeusz. Teatr Cricot 2, Crakow: 1963. B&W. Set. **SDW3**, 101. 3 photos.
The Madras House.
Howard, Pamela. Lyric Theatre, Hammersmith, London: 1992. Color. Set. **TDT**, vol.
    XXX, n. 1 (Winter 1994). 20.
The Madwoman of Chaillot.
Bérard, Christian. Théâtre de l'Athénée, Paris: 1945. B&W. Set. **SDB**, 66; B&W. Set.
    SDW1, 83; B&W. Set. **WTP**, 118, 119. 4 photos.
Krohg, Guy. Det Norske Teatret, Oslo: 1951. B&W. Set. **SDW1**, 154.
Porteous, Cameron. Shaw Festival Theatre, Niagara-on-the-Lake, Canada: B&W and
    color. Set. **SDL**, 4, plates 8-17.
Il Maestro di Cappella.
Vagnetti, Gianni. Maggio Musicale Fiorentino, Florence: 1949. B&W. Rendering.
    SDE, 157.
Magdalena.
Bay, Howard. Los Angeles: 1948. B&W. Rendering. **SDB**, 72; B&W. Rendering.
    TDT, n. 19 (Dec 1969). 23.

The Magic Flute.

Brown, Zack. Washington Opera, DC: 1990. B&W. Set. **TDT**, vol. XXVII, n. 3 (Summer 1991). 11. 2 photos; B&W. Set. **TDT**, vol. XXVII, n. 2 (Spring 1991). 36.

Chagall, Marc. Metropolitan Opera, NYC: 1967. B&W. Set. **ASC**, 36; Color. Rendering. **AST**, 62, 63; Color. Set. **DPT**, Facing 29; B&W and color. Rendering & set. **MOM**, 236-247. 8 photos; B&W and color. Set. **OPE**, 93, 102, 105, 109, 110.

Chiment, Marie Anne. Santa Fe Opera: Color. Rendering & set. **TCI**, vol. 27, n. 9 (Nov 1993). 38, 39. 5 photos.

Colavecchia, Franco. Blossom Theatre, Cleveland, Ohio. 1985. B&W. Rendering. **DDT**, 211.

Conklin, John. Opera Theatre of St. Louis: 1984. B&W. Set. **TDT**, vol. XXVII, n. 2 (Spring 1991). 36.

Craig, Russell. Opera North, Leeds, England: 1984. B&W. Set. **BTD**, 124. 2 photos.

Crowley, Bob. English National Opera, London: 1988. Color. Set. **BTD**, 144.

Damiani, Luciano. Grosses Festspielhaus, Salzburg: 1974. B&W. Sketches & set. **SDW4**, illus. 106-112.

Heinrich, Rudolf. Comic Opera, Berlin: 1954/1960. B&W. Set. **SDB**, 74; B&W. Set. **TCI**, vol. 15, n. 1 (Jan 1981). 36; Staatsoper, Vienna: 1974. B&W. Set. **OPE**, 98, 100, 104; Opernhaus am Karl-Marx Platz, Leipzig: 1975. B&W. Set. **OPE**, 108, 110.

Hockney, David. Glyndebourne Festival Opera, England: 1978. Color. Model & set. **HPS**, 62, 66, 67, 106-111, 116, 118, 120. 25 photos; B&W. Set. **TCI**, vol. 13, n. 3 (May/Jun 1979). 21; San Francisco Opera: 1987. B&W. Set. **TDT**, vol. XXVII, n. 2 (Spring 1991). 36; San Francisco Opera: 1990. Color. Set. **TDT**, vol. XXVII, n. 3 (Summer 1991). 8.

Horner, Harry. Metropolitan Opera, NYC: 1955. B&W. Rendering. **MOM**, 14.

Keienberg, Eberhard. B&W. Model. **TDT**, vol. XVI, n. 1 (Spring 1980). 17.

Kiesler, Frederick. NYC: 1940. B&W. Drawing. **EIF**, photo 22; 1949. B&W. Set. **EIF**, photo 38.

Lobel, Adrianne. Glyndebourne Festival Opera, England: 1990. Color. Set. **ASD2**, between 108 & 109. 2 photos; B&W. Set. **DDT**, 6. 4 photos.

Luzzati, Emanuele. Glyndebourne Festival Opera, England: 1963. B&W. Set. **SDR**, 77.

Majewski, Andrej. Color. Rendering. **SST**, plate II.

Messel, Oliver. Royal Opera House, Covent Garden, London: 1947. B&W. Set. **CGA**, 132; Color. Rendering. **MEM**, 115. Gauze; B&W. Set. **OMB**, 133.

Montresor, Beni. New York City Opera, Lincoln Center: 1966. B&W. Set. **TCI**, vol. 16, n. 5 (May 1982). 16; B&W. Set. **TCI**, vol. 7, n. 1 (Jan/Feb 1973). 16; B&W. Set. **TCI**, vol. 4, n. 1 (Jan/Feb 1970). 17.

Neuman-Spallart, Gottfried. Staatsakademie für Musik, Vienna: 1952. B&W. Set. **SDW2**, 158.

Otto, Teo. Grosses Festspielhaus, Salzburg: 1967. B&W and color. Rendering & set. **OPE**, 94, 100, 103, 104, 107, 108, 110.

Ponnelle, Jean-Pierre. Opernhaus, Cologne: 1972. B&W. Set. **OPE**, 96, 101, 103, 104, 106, 109, 110.

Prabhavalkar, Nigel. Cambridge Arts Theatre: 1987. B&W. Set. **BTD**, 116.

Rychtarik, Richard. Metropolitan Opera, NYC: 1941. B&W. Rendering. **MOM**, 11.

Sendak, Maurice. Houston Grand Opera: 1979/1981. B&W. Set. **TCI**, vol. 18, n. 4 (Apr 1984). 45; B&W. Model. **TDT**, vol. XXVII, n. 3 (Summer 1991). 8; B&W. Set. **TDT**, vol. XXVII, n. 2 (Spring 1991). 36.

Siercke, Alfred. State Opera, Hamburg: 1951. B&W. Rendering. **SDW1**, 78.

Skalicki, Wolfram. Opernhaus, Graz, Austria: 1956. B&W. Set. **SDW2**, 162.
Slevogt, Max. Project, Staatsoper, Berlin: 1928. B&W. Rendering. **AST**, 35.
Svoboda, Josef. B&W. Set. **TDT**, n. 7 (Dec 1966). 24, 25; National Theatre, Prague:
    1957. B&W. Set. **STS**, 44; Tyl Theatre, Prague: 1961. B&W. Set. **SDW2**, 45;
    B&W. Set. **SJS**, 43. 2 photos; Bayerische Staatsoper, Munich: 1970. B&W. Set.
    OPE, 95, 100, 102, 104, 106, 108, 110; Prague: 1993. B&W. Set. **TDT**, vol. XXX,
    n. 5 (Fall 1994). 41.
Tannenberg, Winkler. B&W. Rendering. **DIT**, plate 89.
Vancura, Jan. Czechoslovakia: 1986. B&W. Rendering. **TDT**, vol. XXIX, n. 1 (Winter
    1993). 18, 22; B&W. Model. **TDT**, vol. XXVII, n. 4 (Fall 1991). 46.
Vychodil, Ladislav. Prague: 1986. B&W. Rendering. **TCI**, vol. 21, n. 8 (Oct 1987). 36.
Yeargan, Michael. Nancy, France: 1980. B&W. Set. **TCI**, vol. 16, n. 5 (May 1982). 26.
    2 photos.
_____. Cincinnati Conservatory of Music: Color. Set. **TDT**, vol. XXVI, n. 1
    (Spring 1990). 13 of insert.
_____. Mannheim National Theatre: B&W. Set. **TCI**, vol. 4, n. 4 (Sep 1970). 22.
The Magistrate.
Toms, Carl. Chichester Festival Theatre, England: B&W. Set. **TCI**, vol. 6, n. 1 (Jan/
    Feb 1972). 16.
The Magnanimous Cuckold.
Popova, Lyubov. Meyerhold Theatre, Moscow: 1922. B&W. Model. **AST**, 135; B&W.
    Rendering. **DIT**, plate 110; B&W. Set. **MOT**, between 160 & 161. 2 photos; B&W.
    Rendering. **PST**, 411; B&W. Sketch & set. **RSD**, illus. 173-175; B&W. Rendering.
    SDC, plate 118; B&W. Set. **TAB**, 7; B&W. Sketch. **TCR**, 85; B&W. Set. **TCS2**,
    plate 174; B&W. Set. **TCT**, plates 17-19; B&W. Set. **TPH**, photo 409; B&W.
    Rendering. **TSY**, 198.
The Mahabharata.
Brook, Peter. Brooklyn Academy of Music, New York: 1987. B&W and color. Set.
    TCI, vol. 21, n. 9 (Nov 1987). 7, 27-30. 6 photos.
Maid of Orleans.
Minks, Wilfried. Hamburg: 1960. B&W. Set. **TCI**, vol. 12, n. 1 (Jan/Feb 1978). 31.
The Maids.
Alarcon, Enrique & Victor Garcia. Teatro Poliorama, Barcelona: 1968. B&W. Set.
    SDW3, 124.
Castillo, Carlos. Club de Teatro de Lima: 1959. B&W. Set. **SDW2**, 163.
Engelbach, Claude. Comédie de Saint-Etienne, France: 1971. B&W. Model. **SDW3**,
    124.
Esbjornson, David. Classic Stage Company, NYC: 1993. Color. Set. **TCI**, vol. 27, n.
    10 (Dec 1993). 8.
Mail.
Baral, Vicki & Gerry Hariton. Pasadena Playhouse, California: 1987. Color. Set. **TCI**,
    vol. 22, n. 2 (Feb 1988). 51.
Major Barbara.
Arcenas, Loy. American Repertory Theatre, Cambridge, Massachusetts: Color. Set.
    TCI, vol. 25, n. 3 (Mar 1991). 38.
Arent, Benno von. Theater am Kurfürstendamm, Berlin: 1926. B&W. Set. **TPH**, photo
    427.
Landwehr, Hugh. Center Stage, Baltimore: 1987. B&W. Set. **ASD2**, 83.
Oenslager, Donald. Morosco Theatre, NYC: 1956. B&W. Rendering. **DPT**, 360;
    B&W. Rendering. **TDO**, 130, 131.

Porteous, Cameron. Shaw Festival Theatre, Niagara-on-the-Lake, Canada: Color. Set. **TCI**, vol. 22, n. 7 (Aug/Sep 1988). 61.

Sharpe, Robert Redington. Guild Theatre (Virginia Theatre), NYC: 1928. B&W. Set. **TCR**, 62.

Straiges, Tony. Arena Stage, Washington, DC: 1981. B&W. Set. **TCI**, vol. 16, n. 2 (Feb 1982). 15.

A Majority of One.

Oenslager, Donald. Shubert & Barrymore Theatres, NYC: 1959. B&W. Drawings, model, & set. **SDA**, 192-195. 9 photos.

Majority of Two.

Joy, Michael. Centaur Theatre, Montreal: 1984. Color. Set. **TCI**, vol. 18, n. 9 (Nov/ Dec 1984). 39.

Makbeth.

Rojo, Jerry N. Performance Garage, NYC: 1969. B&W. Rendering, model, & set. **CSD**, 20, 21, 120; B&W. Rendering. **SDW3**, 53; B&W. Set. **TCI**, vol. 5, n. 4 (Sep 1971). 14. 2 photos; B&W. Rendering & set. **TSE**, 105, 106, 110, 113.

The Makropoulos Secret.

Björnson, Maria. Welsh National Opera: 1978. B&W. Set. **TDT**, vol. XIX, n. 1 (Spring 1983). 6.

Campbell, Patton. New York City Opera, Lincoln Center: B&W. Set. **TCI**, vol. 7, n. 1 (Jan/Feb 1973). 16. 2 photos.

Paston, Doria. Festival Theater, Cambridge, England: 1932. B&W. Set. **SCM**, 30.

Sharpe, Robert Redington. Pasadena Playhouse, California: B&W. Set. **SDC**, plate 91.

Svoboda, Josef. National Theatre, Prague: 1965. B&W. Set. **SDR**, 65; B&W. Set. **SJS**, 137. 2 photos; B&W. Set. **TDT**, n. 20 (Feb 1970). 14. 2 photos.

Maksim Crnojevic.

Denic, Miomir. Narodno Pozoriste, Beograd: 1967. B&W. Set. **SDW3**, 85. 3 photos.

Malbrouck s'en va-t-en guerre.

Jouvet, Louis. Comédie des Champs-Élysées, Paris: 1925. B&W. Rendering. **RSD**, illus. 403; B&W. Rendering. **SCM**, 48.

The Male Animal.

Bourne, Mel. City Center, NYC: 1952. B&W. Set. **WTP**, 208. 2 photos.

La Malédiction.

Sliwinski, Stanislas. Teatr Maly, Warsaw: B&W. Set. **TCS2**, plate 209.

Malvaloca.

Thompson, Woodman. 48th Street Theatre, NYC: 1922. B&W. Set. **SDC**, plate 51. 2 photos; B&W. Set. **TCS2**, plates 73, 74.

Mame.

Eckart, William & Jean. Winter Garden Theatre, NYC: 1966. B&W. Rendering. **CSD**, 76; B&W. Rendering. **SDB**, 61; **TMT**, 212.

Les Mamelles de Tirésias.

Hockney, David. Metropolitan Opera, NYC: 1981. B&W and color. Rendering & set. **HPS**, 126, 146-159, 164-166. 14 photos; B&W. Set. **TCI**, vol. 18, n. 4 (Apr 1984). 42.

Man and Superman.

Dahlstrom, Robert A. American Conservatory Theatre, San Francisco: 1976. B&W. Set. **TCI**, vol. 14, n. 4 (Sep 1980). 18, 19.

Kochergin, Edward Stepanovich. Shaw Festival Theatre, Niagara-on-the-Lake, Canada: 1989. B&W. Set. **TCI**, vol. 23, n. 8 (Oct 1989). 15.

Koltai, Ralph. National Theatre, London: 1981. B&W. Set. **TDT**, vol. XIX, n. 3 (Fall 1983). 10.

Stover, Frederick. Alvin Theatre, NYC: 1947. B&W. Set. **WTP**, 148, 149.
Man and the Masses.
    Shestakov, Victor. Theatre of the Revolution, Moscow: 1923. B&W. Rendering. **RSD**, illus. 183.
    Simonson, Lee. Theatre Guild, NYC: 1924. B&W. Set. **PLT**, illus. 32-35; B&W. Set. **TAS**, 130, 131. 5 photos; B&W. Set. **TSS**, 512, 513. 4 photos.
Man and the Shadow.
    Zaki, Samir. Masrah al Geib, Al Kahira, Cairo: 1970. B&W. Set. **SDW3**, 140.
Man Better Man.
    Minshall, Peter. Dartmouth College, Hanover, New Hampshire: 1975. B&W. Set. **TCI**, vol. 9, n. 5 (Oct 1975). 12, 13. 3 photos.
A Man for All Seasons.
    Gischia, Léon. T.N.P., Paris: 1963. Color. Rendering. **RSD**, illus. 535.
    Lee, Eugene. Trinity Square Theatre, Providence, Rhode Island: 1974. B&W. Set. **DPT**, 35; B&W. Set. **TDT**, vol. XVIII, n. 2 (Summer 1982). 9.
    Motley (Margaret Harris, Sophia Harris, & Elizabeth Montgomery). Globe Theatre, London: 1960. Color. Rendering. **SDW2**, 221.
    Oman, Julia Trevelyan. Chichester Festival Theatre, England: 1987. B&W. Set. **BTD**, 80.
    _____. Mummers Theatre, Oklahoma City: B&W. Set. **TCI**, vol. 5, n. 3 (May/Jun 1971). 9.
The Man from Cordova.
    Luzzati, Emanuele. Piccola Scala, Milan: 1959. B&W. Rendering. **SDW2**, 129.
The Man in the Moon.
    Kruschenick, Nicholas. Tyrone Guthrie Theatre, Minneapolis: 1968. Color. Set. **ASC**, 13.
The Man in the Raincoat.
    Wilson, Robert. Theater der Welt, Cologne: 1981. B&W. Set. **RWT**, 86. 2 photos.
The Man of Honor.
    Fini, Léonor. Théâtre Marigny, Paris: 1960. B&W. Rendering. **SDW2**, 91.
Man of La Mancha.
    Brockman, C. Lance. University of Minnesota, Minneapolis: B&W. Set. **TDT**, n. 36 (Feb 1974). 29.
    Payne, Darwin Reid. B&W. Model. **SIP**, 7.
    Bay, Howard. ANTA Washington Square Theatre, NYC: 1965. B&W. Rendering. **CSD**, 61; B&W. Rendering. **DPT**, 325; B&W. Rendering. **SFT**, 6; B&W. Rendering & set. **TCI**, vol. 17, n. 2 (Feb 1983). 17; B&W. Set. **TDT**, n. 5 (May 1966). 25.
    Stenberg, Enar. G. USSR: B&W. Rendering. **TDT**, vol. XII, n. 3 (Fall 1976). 42.
The Man of Mode.
    Ettinger, Daniel H. University of Hawaii, Honolulu: 1979. B&W. Set & painter's elevation. **BSE1**, 6.
    Firth, Tazeena & Timothy O'Brien. Royal Shakespeare Company, Aldwych Theatre, London: 1971. B&W. Set. **TDT**, vol. XIX, n. 3 (Fall 1983). 9.
The Man Outside.
    Bruland, Arne. Studioteatret, Oslo: 1948. B&W. Model. **SDW1**, 152.
Man to Man.
    Christie, Bunny. Traverse Theatre, Edinburgh: 1987. B&W. Set. **BTD**, 60.
The Man Who Came to Dinner.
    Oenslager, Donald. Music Box Theatre, NYC: 1939. B&W. Set. **MCN**, 146; B&W. Set. **WTP**, 182, 183. 4 photos.

The Man Who Did Not Come Back.
   Ichijô, Tatsuo. Hitotsubashi Hall, Tokyo: 1957. B&W. Rendering. **SDW2**, 147.
The Man Who Married a Dumb Wife.
   Jones, Robert Edmond. Wallack's Theatre, NYC: 1915. B&W. Sketch. **DFT**, plate 1;
      B&W. Rendering. **NTO**, facing 180; B&W. Rendering. **REJ**, 31; B&W. Rendering
      & set. **SDA**, 50, 51. 3 photos; B&W. Rendering. **SDC**, plate 54; B&W. Rendering.
      SDD, between 210 & 211; B&W. Rendering. **SOW**, plate 74; B&W. Sketch. **TPH**,
      photo 458.
The Man Who Was Thursday.
   Hoffman, Vlastislav. National Theatre, Prague: 1927. B&W. Rendering. **RSD**, illus.
      276; B&W. Rendering. **TDT**, n. 41 (Summer 1975). 17.
   Vesnin, Alexandr A. Kamerny Theater, Moscow: 1923. B&W. Model. **RSD**, illus. 193,
      B&W. Set. **RST**, 154, 155; B&W. Set. **TCS2**, plate 175.
The Man with the Briefcase.
   _____. Theatre of the Revolution, Moscow: 1928. B&W. Set. **RST**, 230.
The Man With the Flower in His Mouth.
   Gelpi, Germén. Teatro Argentino de la Plata: 1953. B&W. Rendering. **SDW1**, 34.
A Man's a Man.
   Neher, Caspar. Hessiches Landestheater, Darmstadt: 1926. B&W. Rendering & set.
      CBM, 19; B&W. Drawing & set. **TBB**, 27, 90; B&W. Set. **TCS2**, plate 105;
      Volksbühne, Berlin: 1928. B&W. Rendering. **CBM**, 50.
   Okajima, Sigeo. Japan: B&W. Model. **TDT**, vol. XX, n. 1 (Spring 1984). 7.
   Sprott, Eoin. Tyrone Guthrie Theatre, Minneapolis: 1970. B&W. Set. **TCI**, vol. 9, n. 1
      (Jan/Feb 1975). 10.
   Stein, Douglas O. La Jolla Playhouse, California: 1986. B&W and color. Set. **TCI**,
      vol. 21, n. 8 (Oct 1987). 27, 28.
   _____. Berlin: 1931. B&W. Set. **TBB**, 171. 3 photos.
Mandragola.
   Ristic, Dusan. Narodno Pozoriste, Beograd: 1972. B&W. Set. **SDW4**, illus. 15-17.
   Rosse, Herman. NYC: 1925. B&W. Rendering. **SDC**, plate 96.
Manfred.
   Sturm, Eduard. Schauspielhaus, Düsseldorf: B&W. Model. **TCS2**, plate 348.
Mannequin's Ball.
   Heythum, Antonín. D34 Theatre, Prague: 1933. B&W. Rendering. **TDT**, n. 41 (Sum-
      mer 1975). 23.
Manoeuvres in Ingolstadt.
   Neher, Caspar. Theater am Schiffbauerdamm: 1929. B&W. Rendering & set. **CBM**,
      53.
Manon.
   Brown, Zack. Washington Opera, DC: 1991. B&W and color. Rendering. **DDT**, 152a,
      267.
   Eck, Marsha Louis. New York City Opera: 1968. B&W. Rendering. **DPT**, 36. Act I.
   Hordijk, Gérard. Stadsschouwburg, Amsterdam: 1949. B&W. Set. **SDW1**, 137.
   Hudson, Richard. Royal Northern College of Music, GB: 1987. B&W. Model. **BTD**,
      147.
   Klein, Allen Charles. Kennedy Center Opera House, Washington, DC: 1974. B&W.
      Sketch. **DPT**, 120. Act III, sc. 1; B&W. Rendering. **DPT**, 187. Act IV, sc. 2.
   _____. Covent Garden, London: 1977. B&W. Set. **CGA**, 192.
Manon Lescaut.
   Crayon. 1949. Metropolitan Opera, NYC: B&W. Rendering. **CSD**, 38; B&W. Render-
      ing. **MOM**, 11.

Heeley, Desmond. Metropolitan Opera, NYC: 1980. B&W. Rendering. **DDT**, 155;
  B&W and color. Rendering & set. **MOM**, 147-150. 5 photos; B&W. Set. **TCI**, vol.
  14, n. 6 (Nov/Dec 1980). 15.
Malina, Jaroslav. Czechoslovakia: B&W. Rendering & set. **TDT**, vol. XXVI, n. 2
  (Summer 1990). 36, 37. 3 photos.
Naccarato, John. Seattle Opera: 1981. Color. Set. **TCI**, vol. 20, n. 8 (Oct 1986). 21.
The Manure Cart.
  Vanerelli, Mario. Teatro El Nacional, Buenos Aires: 1953. B&W. Rendering. **SDW1**,
  38.
A Map of the World.
  Griffin, Hayden. National Theatre, London: 1982. B&W and color. Rendering & set.
  TCI, vol. 19, n. 9 (Nov 1985). 19, 25.
Mar I Cel.
  Amenós, Montse & Isidre Prunés. Dagoll Dagom Company, Barcelona: 1988. Color.
  Set. **TCI**, vol. 27, n. 1 (Jan 1993). 3, 43.
Marat/Sade.
  Aronson, Boris. Stanford Players, Stanford University: 1976. B&W. Set. **PST**, 441.
  Conklin, John. Williamstown Theatre Festival, Massachusetts: 1966. B&W. Set. **TCI**,
  vol. 14, n. 3 (May/Jun 1980). 19.
  Darling, Robert Edward. Williamstown Theatre Festival, Massachusetts: 1990. B&W.
  Set. **TCI**, vol. 24, n. 8 (Oct 1990). 17; B&W. Set. **TCR**, 112.
  Egemar, Christian. Den Nationale Scene, Bergen, Norway: 1970. B&W. Set. **SDW3**,
  135.
  Jacobs, Sally. Martin Beck Theatre, NYC: 1965. B&W. Set. **TDT**, n. 5 (May 1966).
  23, back cover; Aldwych Theatre, London: B&W. Set. **SIP**, 221, 231.
  La Ferla, Sandro. Virginia Museum Theatre, Richmond: 1969. B&W. Set. **DPT**, 349. 2
  photos.
  Muraoka, Alan E. New York University Tisch School of the Arts, NYC: 1983. B&W.
  Rendering. **BSE3**, 33.
  Nieva, Francisco. Teatro Español, Madrid: 1968. B&W. Set. **SDW3**, 221.
  Palmstierna-Weiss, Gunilla. Schiller Theater, Berlin: 1964. B&W. Set. **SDW3**, 135;
  B&W. Set. **TCI**, vol. 12, n. 7 (Nov/Dec 1978). 41; Royal Dramatic Theatre,
  Stockholm: 1965/1966. B&W. Set. **RSD**, illus. 592; B&W. Set. **TCI**, vol. 12, n. 7
  (Nov/Dec 1978). 40.
  Sherman, Loren. Whole Theatre Company, Montclair, New Jersey: 1982. B&W.
  Model. **DDT**, 258.
Marathon '33.
  Curreri, Alan. Eureka Theatre, San Francisco: B&W. Set. **TCI**, vol. 14, n. 4 (Sep
  1980). 24.
  Levine, Michael. Shaw Festival Theatre, Niagara-on-the-Lake, Canada: Color. Set.
  TCI, vol. 22, n. 7 (Aug/Sep 1988). 60.
Marathon Dancing.
  Chepulis, Kyle. En Garde Arts, West 23rd Street Masonic Hall, NYC: 1994. B&W.
  Set. **TCI**, vol. 28, n. 5 (May 1994). 9.
Marching Song.
  Bay, Howard. Bayes Theatre, NYC: 1937. B&W. Set. **DPT**, 329; B&W. Set. **SOW**,
  plate 85; B&W. **TCI**, vol. 17, n. 2 (Feb 1983). 11.
Marco Millions.
  Funicello, Ralph. American Conservatory Theatre, San Francisco: 1988. Color. Set.
  TCI, vol. 23, n. 1 (Jan 1989). 15.

Simonson, Lee. Guild Theatre, NYC: 1928. B&W. Set. **DOT**, 223; B&W. Set. **MCN**, 88; B&W. Set. **PLT**, illus. 39-46, 61; B&W. Set. **SDA**, 220, 221. 4 photos; B&W. Set. **TAS**, 138, 139, 143, 144. 7 photos; B&W. Set. **TSS**, 528, 529. 3 photos.
Margarete in Aix.
Brade, Helmut & Ezio Toffolutti. Volksbühne, Berlin: 1973. B&W. Set. **SDW4**, illus. 319-323.
Maria Golovin.
Ter-Arutunian, Rouben. New York City Opera: 1958. B&W. Sketch. **CSD**, 39; Color. Rendering. **SDW2**, 231.
Maria Malibran.
Kiesler, Frederick. NYC: 1936. B&W. Sketches, rendering & set. **EIF**, photo 16-19.
Maria Pineda.
Stenersen, Christian. National Theater, Oslo: 1956. B&W. Set. **SDW2**, 154.
Maria Stuart (see also *Mary Stuart*).
Shipulin, M.N. Mayakovsky Drama Theatre, Dyushambe: 1959. B&W. Rendering. **TDT**, n. 33 (May 1973). 17.
Sievert, Ludwig. Frankfurt, Germany; B&W. Rendering. **CSC**, facing 112, 114.
Sturm, Eduard. Schauspielhaus, Düsseldorf: 1926. B&W. Model. **TCS2**, plate 190.
Le Mariage Forcé.
Rutherston, Albert. St. James Theatre, London: 1913. B&W. Model. **DIT**, plate 55; B&W. Model. **SDG**, 161; B&W. Model. **TPH**, photo 429.
Marie Tudor.
Gischia, Léon. Festival of Avignon: 1955. B&W. Set. **RSD**, illus. 532.
Les Mariés de la Tour Eiffel.
Lagut, Irene. 1921. B&W. Set. **TCS2**, plate 259.
Marija.
Falleni, Silvano. 1965. B&W. Set. **SIO**, 51.
Marinka.
Bay, Howard. Winter Garden Theatre, NYC: 1945. B&W. Rendering. **SDW1**, 192.
Mario and the Magician.
Levine, Michael: Elgin Theatre, Toronto: 1992. B&W. Set. **TCI**, vol. 26, n. 7 (Aug/ Sep 1992). 16.
Marketa Lazarová.
Zídek, Ivo. Prague: 1987. B&W. Rendering. **TDT**, vol. XXVIII, n. 2 (Spring 1992). 37.
Marlborough's Campaign.
Capek, Josef. Vinohrady Theatre, Prague: 1929. B&W. Rendering. **TDT**, n. 42 (Fall 1975). 24.
La Marquesa Rosalinda.
Nieva, Francisco. Teatro Español, Madrid: 1970. Color. Set. **SDW3**, 93; B&W. Set. **SDW4**, illus. 194.
Marquis von Keith.
Pirchan, Emil. State Theatre, Berlin: 1920. B&W. Rendering & set. **RSD**, illus. 134, 137; B&W. Set. **SDC**, plate 125. 2 photos; B&W. Set. **TCS2**, plate 106; B&W. Set. **TPH**, photo 423.
Rose, Jürgen. Kammerspiele, Munich: 1970. Color. Set. **SDW4**, illus. 191.
Marriage.
Vychodil, Ladislav. Prague: 1963. B&W. Set. **TDT**, vol. XV, n. 2 (Summer 1979). 15.
_____. Theatre for Young Spectators, Moscow: B&W. Set. **SCM**, 91.
The Marriage.
Dart, Paul. Shared Experience, England: 1984. B&W. Sketch. **BTD**, 28.

The Marriage Market.
>   Ryan, E.H. & Alfred Terraine. Daly's Theatre, London: 1913. B&W. Set. **MCD**, plates
>   100, 101.

The Marriage of Bette and Boo.
>   Sherman, Loren. Newman Theatre, NYC: 1985. B&W. Model. **DDT**, 201. 6 photos;
>   Color. Set. **TCI**, vol. 21, n. 4 (Apr 1987). 35.
>   Smith, Vicki. Arizona Theatre Company, Tucson: B&W. Set. **SDT**, 116.

The Marriage of Figaro.
>   Blane, Sue. Welsh National Opera. 1987. B&W. Set. **BTD**, 108, 109.
>   Brown, Zack. San Francisco Opera: 1982. B&W. Rendering & set. **TDT**, vol. XXVII,
>   n. 3 (Summer 1991). 10. 2 photos; B&W. Rendering. **TDT**, vol. XXVII, n. 2
>   (Spring 1991). 37.
>   Carcano, Emilio & Olimpio Hruska. Spoleto Festival, Charleston, South Carolina:
>   1989. Color. Set. **TCI**, vol. 24, n. 5 (May 1990). 29.
>   Colasanti, Veniero. Teatro Quirino, Rome: 1946. B&W. Rendering. **SDE**, 66.
>   Conklin, John. Juilliard School of Music, NYC: 1988. B&W. Model. **TDT**, vol.
>   XXVII, n. 3 (Summer 1991). 13.
>   Dorsey, Kent. American Conservatory Theatre, San Francisco: Color. Set. **TCI**, vol.
>   25, n. 8 (Oct 1991). 46.
>   Edwards, Norman. Eastman Theatre, Rochester, NY: B&W. Set. **SDC**, plate 124.
>   Feiner, Harry. Bronx Opera: 1990. B&W. Set. **TDT**, vol. XXVII, n. 3 (Summer 1991).
>   6.
>   Fielding, Eric. Brigham Young University, Provo, Utah: 1978. B&W. Set. **TDT**, vol.
>   XXVII, n. 3 (Summer 1991). 6.
>   Fuerst, Walter René. Odéon Théâtre, Paris: B&W. Set. **TCS2**, plate 110; Krolloper,
>   Berlin: B&W. Set. **TCS2**, plate 111.
>   Golovin, Alexander. Moscow Art Theatre: 1927. B&W. Set. **RST**, 221, 222.
>   Heinrich, Rudolf. Bavarian State Opera, Munich: B&W. Set. **TCI**, vol. 10, n. 6 (Nov/
>   Dec 1976). 15, 16
>   Hudson, Richard. English National Opera, London: 1991. B&W. Model. **TDT**, vol.
>   XXVIII, n. 2 (Spring 1992). 21.
>   Lazaridis, Stefan & Michael Stennett. Covent Garden, London: 1971. B&W. Set.
>   **CGA**, 180.
>   Liotta, Vincent. Pennsylvania Opera Theatre: B&W. Set. **TCI**, vol. 18, n. 3 (Mar
>   1984). 27.
>   Lobel, Adrianne. Pepsico Summerfare, Purchase, New York: 1988. B&W. Sketch &
>   set. **ASD2**, 104, 105. Act III; B&W. Set. **DDT**, 369; B&W. Set. **TDT**, vol. XXVII,
>   n. 3 (Summer 1991). 14.
>   Messel, Oliver. Glyndebourne Festival Opera, England: 1955. B&W. Rendering.
>   **MEM**, 156; B&W. Model & set. **OMB**, 182, 183; Metropolitan Opera, NYC:
>   1959. B&W. Set. **OMB**, 190, 191.
>   Montresor, Beni. Tyrone Guthrie Theatre, Minneapolis: 1982. B&W. Set. **TCI**, vol. 17,
>   n. 7 (Aug/Sep 1983). 21; Color. Set. **TCI**, vol. 18, n. 7 (Aug/Sep 1984). 40.
>   Olich, Michael. Seattle Opera: 1989. B&W. Set. **TDT**, vol. XXVII, n. 3 (Summer
>   1991). 6.
>   Ponnelle, Jean-Pierre. Salzburg Festival: 1976. B&W. Set. **TCI**, vol. 12, n. 3 (Mar/Apr
>   1978). 19.
>   Stern, Ernst. Color. Rendering. **MRH**, facing 226.
>   Vancura, Jan. Stavoske Theatre, Prague: 1988. B&W. Rendering. **TDT**, vol. XXIX, n.
>   1 (Winter 1993). 18; Color. Rendering. **TDT**, vol. XXVII, n. 4 (Fall 1991). 6.

_____. Redoutensaal, Hofburg Palace, Vienna: Color. Rendering. **CSC**, frontis
 piece & facing 186; B&W. Sketch. **TPH**, photo 340.
The Marriage of Mr. Mississippi.
 Znamenacek, Wolfgang. Kammerspiele, Munich: 1952. Color. Rendering. **RSD**, illus.
 461; B&W. Set. **SDW1**, 80.
Marriages of Convenience.
 Viudes, Vicente. Teatro María Guerrero, Madrid: 1961. B&W. Set. **SDW2**, 82.
Martha.
 Smith, Oliver. Metropolitan Opera, NYC: 1961. B&W. Set. **TCI**, vol. 16, n. 4 (Apr
 1982). 62.
Martin Guerre.
 Yeargan, Michael. Hartford Stage, Connecticut. 1993. B&W. Set. **TCI**, vol. 27, n. 4
 (Apr 1993). 8.
Martine.
 Chitty, Alison. National Theatre (Lyttleton), England: 1985. B&W. Set. **BTD**, 33.
Le Martyre de Saint Sébastien.
 Bakst, Léon. Théâtre du Châtelet, Paris. 1911. B&W. Rendering. **DIT**, plate 71; B&W
 and color. Rendering & set. **LBT**, 122, 123; B&W. Rendering. **TCS2**, plate 231.
Mary.
 _____. Equity Library Theatre, NYC: B&W. Set. **TCI**, vol. 15, n. 6 (Jun/Jul
 1981). 25.
Mary C. Brown and the Hollywood Sign.
 Wagner, Robin. Shubert Theatre, Century City, Los Angeles: 1972. B&W. Set. **DPT**,
 393; B&W. Set. **TCI**, vol. 7, n. 6 (Nov/Dec 1973). 8. 2 photos.
Mary of Scotland.
 Jones, Robert Edmond. Alvin Theatre, NYC: 1933. B&W. Set. **MCN**, 114.
Mary Stuart. (see also *Maria Stuart*).
 Colasanti, Veniero. Valle, Rome: 1952. B&W. Set. **SDW1**, 122.
 Gunzinger, Eduard. State Theatre, Basel: 1952. B&W. Rendering. **SDW1**, 115.
 Karavan, Dani. Cameri, Tel Aviv: 1961. B&W. Set. **SDW2**, 119. 3 photos.
 McDonald, Anthony. Greenwich Theatre, London: 1988. B&W. Set. **BTD**, 40.
 Oenslager, Donald. Phoenix Theatre, NYC: 1957. B&W. Rendering. **DMS**, plate 28;
 B&W. Rendering. **TDO**, 132.
 Svoboda, Josef. Zurich: 1984. Color. Set. **TCI**, vol. 21, n. 8 (Oct 1987). 34.
 Westerman, Wyda. Nationaal Toneel, Antwerp: 1951. B&W. Rendering. **SDW1**, 48.
The Mask of Orpheus.
 Herbert, Jocelyn. English National Opera, The Coliseum, London: 1986. Color.
 Sketches & set. **BTD**, 134, 135. 4 photos; B&W. Rendering. **TDT**, vol. XXX, n. 5
 (Fall 1994). 22.
The Masked Ball.
 Maximowna, Ita. State Opera, Vienna: 1958. B&W. Set. **SDW2**, 65. 2 photos.
 Oenslager, Donald. Central City Opera House, Colorado: 1967. B&W. Rendering.
 TDO, 138.
 Skawonius, Sven Erik. Royal Opera House, Stockholm. 1958. B&W. Set. **SDR**, 54.
 Wijnberg, Nicolaas. Stadsschouwburg, Amsterdam: 1951. B&W. **SDW1**, 140.
The Masque of London.
 Craig, Edward Gordon. (project): 1901. B&W. Rendering. **TNT**, facing 19; 1904.
 B&W. Rendering. **OAT**, frontispiece; B&W. Rendering. **TNT**, facing 27.
Masquerade.
 Golovin, Alexander. Alexandrinsky Theatre, Moscow: 1917. B&W. Set. **MOT**, be-

180   *Mass Appeal*

tween 96 & 97; B&W. Rendering. **RSD**, illus. 27; B&W and color. Rendering &
    set. **RST**, 34, 36, 37.
Prowse, Philip. Citizen's Theatre of Glasgow: 1976. B&W. Set. **TCI**, vol. 15, n. 7
    (Aug/Sep 1981). 22.
Mass Appeal.
Placido, Stephen, Jr. Burt Reynolds Dinner Theatre, Stuart, Florida: 1983. Color. Set.
    TCI, vol. 21, n. 3 (Mar 1987). 23.
The Massacre at Paris.
Peduzzi, Richard. Théâtre National Populaire, Villeurbanne, France: 1972. B&W. Set.
    SDW4, illus. 64-69.
Masse Mensch.
Strohbach, Hans. Volksbühne, Berlin: 1921. B&W and color. Rendering. **CSC**, facing
    148, 150, 152, 154, 156; B&W. Rendering. **NTO**, facing 276.
The Master Builder.
Aronson, Boris. Phoenix Theatre, NYC: 1955. B&W. Set. **TAB**, 110, 111. 3 photos.
Hudson, Richard. Royal Shakespeare Company, GB: 1989. B&W. Model & set. **TDT**,
    vol. XXVIII, n. 2 (Spring 1992). 23. 3 photos.
Wulp, John. Kennedy Center, Washington, DC: B&W. Set. **TCI**, vol. 13, n. 1 (Jan/Feb
    1979). 25.
Master Builder Manole.
Musatescu, Sanda. Teatrul Giulesti, Bucharest: 1968. B&W. Set. **SDW3**, 105.
Master Harold...and the boys.
Funicello, Ralph. Seattle Repertory Theatre: 1984. B&W. Set. **ASD1**, 44.
Sinkkonen, Eric. San Diego Repertory Theatre: 1986. B&W. Rendering. **BSE5**, 23.
Master of Thornfield.
Edwards, Ben. B&W. Model. **SFT**, 111.
Master Olof.
Molander, Olav & Sven-Eric Skawonius. Royal Dramatic Theatre, Stockholm: B&W.
    Rendering. **TAT**, plate 469.
Master Pathelin.
Landi, Angelo Maria. Siena: 1948. B&W. Rendering. **SDE**, 95.
Martin, Tyr. State Theatre, Malmö, Sweden: 1951. B&W. Set. **SDW2**, 210.
Feuerstein, Bedrich. Theatre at International Exhibit of Decorative Arts, Paris: 1925.
    B&W. Rendering. **TDT**, n. 41 (Summer 1975). 20.
Mata Hari.
_____. Washington, DC: B&W. Set. **BWM**, 349.
The Matchmaker.
Yeargan, Michael. La Jolla Playhouse, California: 1987. Color. Set. **TCI**, vol. 21, n. 8
    (Oct 1987). 25.
Mathis der Maler.
Schneider-Siemssen, Günther. Opera House, Nürnberg: B&W. Rendering. **OPE**, 53.
Il Matrimonio Segreto.
Ganeau, François. Festival d'Aix-en-Provence: 1951. Color. Rendering. **SDW1**, 103.
Matrimonium.
Owens, Paul. Actors Theatre of Louisville: 1979. B&W. Set. **TCI**, vol. 14, n. 6 (Nov/
    Dec 1980). 43.
A Matter of Gravity.
Edwards, Ben. Broadhurst Theatre, NYC: 1976. B&W. Rendering. **DDT**, 125; B&W.
    Rendering. **TCI**, vol. 23, n. 7 (Aug/Sep 1989). 53.

Matthew the Honest.
> Melena, Miroslav. Studio Y, Prague: B&W. Set. **TDT**, vol. XXVII, n. 2 (Spring 1991). 30. 2 photos.

Mattress.
> Boley, James. St. Nicholas Theatre, Chicago: 1977. B&W. Rendering. **TCI**, vol. 12, n. 1 (Jan/Feb 1978). 8.

Maude Gonne Says No to the Poet.
> Kavelin, John. Mark Taper Forum, Los Angeles: B&W. Set. **TCI**, vol. 14, n. 4 (Sep 1980). 46.

Maulwerke.
> Freyer, Achim. Hochschule der Künste, Berlin: 1977. B&W. Set. **TCI**, vol. 13, n. 5 (Oct 1979). 18.

Mavra.
> Guglielminetti, Eugenio. Teatro Communale, Bologna: 1970. B&W. Set. **SDW3**, 189.

Maya.
> Baty, Gaston. Studio des Champs-Elysees, Paris: 1924. B&W. Set. **RSD**, illus. 413; B&W. Set. **SCM**, 48.

Maydays.
> Gunter, John. Royal Shakespeare Company, GB: 1983. Color. Set. **BTD**, 71.

The Mayor of Zalamea.
> Boehm, Herta. Deutsches Schauspielhaus, Hamburg: 1961. B&W. Set. **SDW2**, 57.
> Griffin, Hayden. Teatro Stabile di Genova: B&W. Sketches. **TCI**, vol. 19, n. 9 (Nov 1985). 22, 23. 6 photos.

Mazel Tov.
> Chagall, Marc. State Jewish Theatre, Moscow: 1921. B&W. Rendering & set. **RSD**, illus. 210.

Mazeppa.
> _____. Amsterdam: Color. Set. **TCI**, vol. 27, n. 1 (Jan 1993). 3.

McTeague: A Tale of San Francisco.
> Tsypin, George. Berkeley Repertory Theatre, California: 1992. Color. Set. **TCI**, vol. 26, n. 4 (Apr 1992). 11.

Me and Molly.
> Horner, Harry. 1948. B&W. Set. **TPH**, photo 485.

Me and My Girl.
> Johns, Martin. Haymarket Theatre, Leicester, England: 1984. B&W. Set. **BTD**, 158. 3 photos; B&W. Set. **MBM**, 27. 2 photos.
> _____. North Shore Music Theatre, Beverly, Massachusetts: Color. Set. **TCI**, vol. 24, n. 9 (Nov 1990). 43.

Measure for Measure.
> Beisker, Heinz. State Theatre, Braunschweig: 1950. B&W. Rendering. **SDW1**, 63.
> Bloodgood, William. Berkeley Repertory Theatre, California: 1981. B&W. Set. **TCI**, vol. 15, n. 8 (Oct 1981). 8.
> Cernescu, Dinu & Sorin Haber. Theatrul Giulesti, Bucharest: 1971. B&W. Set. **SDW4**, illus. 36-38.
> Funicello, Ralph. Mark Taper Forum, Los Angeles: 1985. B&W. Set. **DDT**, 83.
> Landwehr, Hugh. Seattle Repertory Theatre: 1989. B&W. Sketch & set. **ASD2**, 80, 81; B&W. Rendering. **DDT**, 488.
> Lemaire, Claude. Théâtre du Parvis, Brussels: 1972. B&W. Set. **SDW4**, illus. 31-35.
> Loquasto, Santo. Delacorte Theatre, NYC: 1975. B&W. Sketch. **ASD1**, 117; B&W. Sketch. **TDT**, vol. XVII, n. 3 (Fall 1981). 19.

Martin-Davies, Ashley. Royal Shakespeare Theatre, Stratford-upon-Avon: 1994. Color.
Set. **TCI**, vol. 29, n. 6 (Jun/Jul 1995). 12.
McGarity, Michael. Trinity Square Theatre, Providence, Rhode Island: 1994. Color.
Set. **TCI**, vol. 28, n. 5 (May 1994). 6.
Minks, Wilfried. Theater der Freien Hansestadt, Bremen: 1967. B&W. Set. **SDW3**, 50;
B&W. Set. **TCI**, vol. 12, n. 1 (Jan/Feb 1978). 28.
Thompson, Mark. Royal Shakespeare Company, GB: 1987. B&W. Set. **BTD**, 57. 2
photos.
Underdown, William. Comédie de l'Est, Strasbourg: 1966. B&W. Model. **SDW3**, 50.
The Measures Taken.
Youens, Frederic. B&W. Set. **SDL**, 80, 366.
Mechinal.
Jones, Robert Edmond. Plymouth Theatre, NYC: 1928. B&W. Rendering. **REJ**, 69.
Medea.
Barendse, Ferry. Koninklijke Vlaamse Schouwburg, Brussels: 1960. B&W. Set.
SDW3, 29.
Coutaud, Lucien. Maggio Musicale Fiorentino, Florence: 1953. B&W. Rendering.
SDE, 74.
Davison, Peter J. Longacre Theatre, NYC: 1994. Color. Set. **TCI**, vol. 28, n. 7 (Aug/
Sep 1994). 10.
Edwards, Ben. 1947. B&W. Set. **TCI**, vol. 23, n. 7 (Aug/Sep 1989). 54; Cort Theatre,
NYC: 1982. B&W. Model. **DDT**, 178.
Fiume, Salvatore. La Scala, Milan: 1953. B&W. Rendering. **SDE**, 84, 85. 4 photos.
Guglielminetti, Eugenio. 1971. B&W. Set. **SIO**, 82. 2 photos.
Gunzinger, Eduard. State Theatre, Basel: 1959. B&W. Rendering. **SDW2**, 110.
Jonson, Raymond. Chicago Little Theatre: B&W. Set. **SDC**, plate 83.
Masson, André. Opéra de Paris: 1940. B&W. Set. **AST**, 201. 4 photos.
Mitchell, Robert D. Circle in the Square Theatre, NYC: 1972. B&W. Model. **DDT**, 81;
Mt. Lycabettos Theatre, Athens: 1976. B&W. Rendering. **DDT**, 81; Salonika,
Greece: 1976. B&W. Set. **DDT**, 81; Herod Atticus Theatre, Athens: 1985. B&W.
Model & set. **DDT**, 81. 3 photos.
Raffaëlli, Michel. Royan Festival: 1967. B&W. Sketches. **RSD**, illus. 545.
Sagert, Horst. Germany: 1979. B&W. Model. **TDT**, vol. XVI, n. 1 (Spring 1980). 15. 2
photos.
Sköld, Otte. Sweden: B&W. Set. **SOW**, plate 33.
Ward, Anthony. Royal Exchange Theatre, Manchester, England: 1991. B&W. Set.
TCI, vol. 27, n. 4 (Apr 1993). 44.
Wilson, Robert. Kennedy Center, Washington, DC: 1981. B&W. Rendering & set.
RWT, 89. 3 photos.
_____. Chicago Little Theater: 1913. B&W. Set. **TPH**, photo 452.
_____. University of Wisconsin, Madison: 1987. B&W. Set. **TDT**, vol. XXIV, n.
2 (Summer 1988). 46.
_____. B&W. Set. **WTP**, 30-32.
The Medium.
Armistead, Horace. Ethel Barrymore Theatre, NYC: 1947. B&W. Rendering. **SDW1**,
189; B&W. Rendering. **TPH**, photo 486; B&W. Set. **WTP**, 212, 213. 4 photos.
Aston, Tom A. Opera Overtures Company, Michigan: 1968. B&W. Set. **TCI**, vol. 3, n.
2 (Mar/Apr 1969). 17.
La Ferla, Sandro. Yubinchokin Hall, Tokyo: 1974. B&W. Rendering. **DPT**, 331.

Meet Me in St. Louis.
>   Anderson, Keith. Gershwin Theatre, NYC: 1989. Color. Model. **TCI**, vol. 23, n. 9 (Nov 1989). 47. 2 photos.

Mefistofele.
>   Anisfeld, Boris. Metropolitan Opera, NYC: 1923. Color. Rendering. **TDT**, vol. XXIX, n. 3 (Summer 1993). 17.
>   Mitchell, David. New York City Opera, Lincoln Center: 1969. B&W. Set. **TCI**, vol. 7, n. 1 (Jan/Feb 1973). 16; B&W. Set. **TCI**, vol. 4, n. 1 (Jan/Feb 1970). 18; 1974. B&W. Set. **DPT**, 22.

Die Meistersinger von Nürnberg.
>   Haferung, Paul. Städtische Bühnen, Essen: 1950. B&W. Model. **SDW1**, 66.
>   Heinrich, Rudolf. Opernhaus Leipzig: 1960. B&W. Set. **SDW2**, 53.
>   Jürgens, Helmut. Bayerische Staatsoper, Munich: 1963. B&W and color. Rendering & set. **OPE**, 165, 172, 175, 176, 179.
>   Marussig, Guido. La Scala, Milan: 1942. B&W. Rendering. **SDE**, 120.
>   O'Hearn, Robert. Metropolitan Opera, NYC: 1962. B&W. Set. **DDT**, 92; Color. Rendering. **DPT**, between 124 & 125. Act I.
>   Rose, Jürgen. Staatsoper, Vienna: 1975. B&W and color. Set. **OPE**, 169, 172, 175, 176, 178.
>   Schneider-Siemssen, Gunther. Grosses Festspielhaus, Salzburg: 1974. B&W and color. Rendering & set. **OPE**, 168, 173, 174, 177, 179.
>   Villa, Gianni. 1952. B&W. Rendering. **SDE**, 162.
>   Wagner, Wieland. Beyreuth Festival Theatre: 1956. B&W. Set. **SDW2**, 73; 1963. B&W and color. Set. **OPE**, 166, 173, 174, 177, 178; 1968. B&W and color. Set. **OPE**, 167, 172, 174, 176, 178.
>   Hudson, Richard. Royal Opera House, Covent Garden, London: 1993. Color. Set. **TCI**, vol. 28, n. 1 (Jan 1994). 12.
>   Roller, Alfred. State Opera, Vienna: Color. Rendering. **CSC**, facing 56.
>   Schneider-Siemssen, Günther. Metropolitan Opera, NYC: 1993. Color. Set. **TCI**, vol. 27, n. 3 (Mar 1993). 27.
>   Svoboda, Josef. National Theatre, Prague: 1978. B&W. Set. **JSS**, 95. Act I; B&W. Set. **JSS**, 95. Act III, sc. 1.

Melo.
>   Wayne, Rollo. Ethel Barrymore Theatre, NYC: 1931. B&W. Set. **SCM**, 116. 2 photos.

The Member of the Wedding.
>   Christopher, Roy. B&W. Set. **SCT**, 276. Television scenery.
>   Gillette, J. Michael. B&W. Rendering & model. **TDP**, 78, 125.
>   Polakov, Lester. Empire Theatre, NYC: 1950. B&W. Rendering. **DDT**, 37; B&W. Rendering. **TPH**, photo 489; B&W. Set. **WTP**, 203. 2 photos.

A Memory of Two Mondays.
>   Aronson, Boris. Coronet Theatre (Eugene O'Neill Theatre), NYC: 1955. B&W and color. Rendering & set. **TAB**, 106, 304; B&W. Rendering. **TDT**, vol. XXV, n. 3 (Fall 1989). 14.

Men In White.
>   Gorelik, Mordecai. Broadhurst Theatre, NYC: 1934. B&W. Set. **MCN**, 112; B&W. Sketches. **SDA**, 240, 241. 6 photos.

The Menaechmi.
>   Aronson, Boris. Yale School of Drama, New Haven, Connecticut: 1964. B&W. Set. **PST**, 59.

Menschen.
>   Moholy-Nagy, Lászlo. 1923. B&W. Rendering. **AST**, 146. 2 photos.

Le Menteur.
> Floriet, Bernard, Herat Sellner, & Brigitte Tribouilloy. Maison de la Culture, Grenoble: 1970. B&W. Set. **SDW3**, 67.

Mephisto.
> Mnouchkine, Ariane. Theatertreffen, Berlin: 1980. B&W. Set. **TCI**, vol. 14, n. 6 (Nov/ Dec 1980). 36, 38.

Méphistophélès.
> Cesarini, Pino. Arena, Verona: 1949. B&W. Rendering. **SDE**, 52, 53. 4 photos.
> Luzzati, Emanuele. Teatro Comunale, Florence: 1954. B&W. Rendering. **SDE**, 105. 2 photos.

Mercadet l'Affarista.
> Scandella, Mischa. 1969-1970. B&W. Rendering. **SIO**, 131.

The Merchant.
> Oenslager, Donald. Yale School of Drama, New Haven, Connecticut: 1939. B&W. Set. **WTP**, 44.

The Merchant of Hearts.
> Prampolini, Enrico. Théâtre de la Madeleine, Paris: 1927. B&W and color. Rendering & set. **RSD**, illus. 336, 337, 341.

The Merchant of Venice.
> Alkazi, Ebrahim. Theatre Unit, Meghdoot Terrace Theatre, Bombay: 1958. Color. Model. **SDW2**, 115. 2 photos.
> Allio, René. Schauspielhaus, Bochum: 1973. B&W. Set. **SDW4**, illus. 22.
> Blanch, Lesley. Shakespeare Memorial Theatre, Stratford-upon-Avon: 1932. B&W. Rendering. **TAT**, plate 208.
> Craig, Edward Gordon. 1902. B&W. Rendering. **COT**, 147.
> Egemar, Christian. Den Nationale Scene, Bergen, Norway: 1969. B&W. Set. **SDW3**, 43.
> Exter, Alexandra. B&W. Rendering. **RAG**, 30; (project): B&W. Rendering. **RSC**, 39.
> Geddes, Tony. New Zealand: B&W. Rendering. **TDT**, vol. XXVII, n. 4 (Fall 1991). 21.
> Heeley, Desmond. Stratford Festival Theatre, Ontario, Canada: 1970. B&W. Set. **TCI**, vol. 7, n. 2 (Mar/Apr 1973). 10.
> Heythum, Antonín. National Theatre, Prague: 1930. B&W. Rendering. **TAT**, plate 172; B&W. Rendering & set. **TDT**, n. 41 (Summer 1975). 23. 2 photos.
> Howard, Pamela. Chichester Festival Theatre, England: 1985. B&W. Rendering & set. **TDT**, vol. XXIV, n. 2 (Summer 1988). 50. 2 photos.
> Orlik, Emil. Deutsches Theater, Berlin: 1905. B&W. Set. **MRH**, facing 212, 213. 3 photos; B&W. Set. **TCS2**, plates 11, 12.
> Paston, Doria. Festival Theater, Cambridge, England: 1932. B&W. Set. **SCM**, 31.
> Stern, Ernst. Deutsches Theater, Berlin: 1913. B&W. Rendering. **MRH**, facing 212; B&W. **MRT**, 59; B&W. Rendering. **SOS**, 205. 2 photos.
> Strnad, Oskar. Josefstadter Theater, Vienna: B&W. Set. **TCS2**, plates 32, 33.
> Tilton, James. American Conservatory Theatre, San Francisco: 1970. B&W. Set. **DPT**, 377.
> Wijdewelt, H. Th. B&W. Set. **DIT**, plate 113.
> _____. Campo San Trovaso, Venice: 1934. B&W. Sketch & set. **SOS**, 207.
> _____. Center Stage, Baltimore: B&W. Set. **TCI**, vol. 7, n. 3 (May/Jun 1973). 14.
> _____. NYC: B&W. Set. **TPH**, photo 263.
> _____. Old Vic Theatre, London: 1960. B&W. Set. **SOS**, 274.
> _____. Théâtre Antoine, Paris: 1917. B&W. Rendering. **SOS**, 184.
> _____. Vienna: 1934. B&W. Set. **TPH**, photo 341.

_____. 1922. B&W. Set. **TPH**, photo 268.

_____. (unproduced), Cirque Mendrano, Paris: B&W. Rendering. **CSC**, facing 208.

The Merchant of Yonkers.

Aronson, Boris. Guild Theatre (Virginia Theatre), NYC: 1938. B&W. Set. **TAB**, 62, 296. 3 photos.

Mercy Street.

Higgins, Douglas. St. Clement's Church, NYC: B&W. Set. **TCI**, vol. 6, n. 3 (May/Jun 1972). 21.

Merlin.

Malina, Jaroslav. Czechoslovakia: B&W. Rendering & set. **TDT**, vol. XXVI, n. 2 (Summer 1990). 37. 3 photos.

Wagner, Robin. Mark Hellinger Theatre, NYC: 1983. B&W. Set. **TDT**, vol. XIX, n. 4 (Winter 1983). 8, 9.

Wareing, John. University of Arizona, Tucson: B&W. Model. **SDT**, 283.

Merrily We Roll Along.

Lee, Eugene. Alvin Theatre, NYC: 1981. B&W and color. Set. **MBM**, 42, 45, 86, B&W and color. Set. **SON**, 40, 147-151. 6 photos; B&W. Set. **TCI**, vol. 18, n. 8 (Oct 1984). 19; B&W. Set. **TCI**, vol. 19, n. 8 (Oct 1985). 18.

McCarry, Charles E. (project): 1986. B&W. Rendering. **DDT**, 477. 2 photos.

Sherman, Loren. Mandell Weiss Forum, La Jolla Playhouse, California: Color. Set. **TCI**, vol. 19, n. 8 (Oct 1985). 18; Color. Set. **TCI**, vol. 21, n. 8 (Oct 1987). 30.

The Merry Widow.

Brown, Zack. 1984. Color. Rendering. **DDT**, 312a.

Keller, Ronald E. Virginia Opera: B&W. **TDT**, vol. XXVI, n. 1 (Spring 1990). 12 of insert.

Varona, José. Deutsche Oper, Berlin: 1979. B&W. Rendering. **DDT**, 281; B&W. Set. **TCI**, vol. 14, n. 5 (Oct 1980). 30. 2 photos.

Yeargan, Michael. Welsh National Opera: 1984. B&W. Set. **ASD2**, 189.

_____. Daly's Theatre, London: 1907. B&W. Set. **BMF**, 20.

The Merry Wives of Windsor.

Beyer, Rolf. Hopkins Center, Dartmouth College, Hanover, New Hampshire: 1977. Color. Rendering of backdrop. **DDT**, 152a.

Chifrine, Nisson. Teatr Mossovieta, Moscow: 1957. B&W. Rendering. **SDW2**, 180.

Ensor, A.C. Everyman Theatre, Hampstead, London: B&W. Model. **DIT**, plate 56.

Marenic, Vladimir. Srpsko Narodno Pozoriste, Novi Sad, Yugoslavia: 1966. Color. Rendering. **SDW3**, 48.

Motley (Margaret Harris, Sophia Harris, & Elizabeth Montgomery). Shakespeare Memorial Theatre, Stratford-upon-Avon: 1955. B&W. Set. **DMS**, plates 30-32.

Slevogt, Max. Neues Theater, Berlin: 1904. B&W. Rendering. **TPH**, photo 325.

The Merry Wives of Windsor, Texas.

Rupnik, Kevin. Duke University, Durham, North Carolina: 1989. B&W. Set. **TCI**, vol. 24, n. 3 (Mar 1990). 22.

Merry-go-round.

Kalinauskas, Vytautas. Dramos Teatras, Panevezys: 1971. B&W. Set. **SDW4**, illus. 278.

Merton of the Movies.

_____. Equity Library Theatre, NYC: B&W. Set. **TCI**, vol. 15, n. 6 (Jun/Jul 1981). 24.

Metamorphosis.
> Durfee, Duke (scenic supervisor). Mark Taper Forum, Los Angeles: 1989. B&W. Set.
> **TCI**, vol. 23, n. 5 (May 1989). 24.

Metaphysics of the Two-headed Calf.
> Monod, Jean. Nouveau Théatre de Poche, Geneva: 1971. B&W. Set. **SDW4**, illus. 215.

Metropolis.
> Koltai, Ralph. Piccadilly Theatre, London: 1989. B&W. Set. **BTD**, 168. 2 photos;
> B&W. Model. **TDT**, vol. XXVII, n. 4 (Fall 1991). 37.

Metti, Una Sera a Cena.
> Pizzi, Pier Luigi. 1967. B&W. Set. **SIO**, 107.

The Mexican.
> Eisenstein, Sergei. Proletkult Theatre, Moscow: 1920. B&W. Sketch. **RST**, 129.

Midsummer.
> Bay, Howard. 1953. B&W. Sketch. **SDB**, 98.

Midsummer Dream in the Workhouse.
> Walentin, Arne. Det Norske Teatret, Oslo: 1951. B&W. Set. **DOT**, 241; B&W. Set.
> **SDW1**, 155.

The Midsummer Marriage.
> Cairns, Tom & Antony McDonald. Opera North, Leeds, England: 1985. Color. Set.
> **BTD**, 145.
> Don, Robin. San Francisco Opera: 1983. B&W. Set. **BTD**, 123.
> Hepworth, Barbara. Covent Garden, London: 1955. B&W. Set. **AST**, 220; B&W. Set.
> **CGA**, 145.
> Lazaridis, Stefanos. English National Opera, London: 1985. Color. Model. **BTD**, 130.
> 2 photos.

A Midsummer Night's Dream.
> Bailey, James. Shakespeare Memorial Theatre, Stratford-upon-Avon: 1949. B&W.
> Rendering. **DMS**, plate 27.
> Bury, John. Glyndebourne Festival Opera, England: 1981. B&W. Set. **BTD**, 114, 115;
> Color. Set. **TCI**, vol. 26, n. 1 (Jan 1992). 47.
> Craven, Hawes. 1901. B&W. Rendering. **SDT**, 260.
> Czelényi, Jósef. Katona József Szinház, Kecskemét, Hungary: 1959. B&W. Set.
> **SDW2**, 139. 2 photos.
> Dahlstrom, Robert A. University of Washington, Seattle: Color. Set. **TCI**, vol. 22, n. 1
> (Jan 1988). 36; University of British Columbia, Vancouver: Color. Set. **SCT**,
> between 152 & 153. 4 settings.
> Dudley, William. Royal Shakespeare Company, Stratford-upon-Avon: 1986. B&W.
> Set. **TDT**, vol. XXV, n. 3 (Fall 1989). 19.
> Duer, Fred. Studio Arena Theatre, Buffalo: 1984. B&W. Set. **TCI**, vol. 19, n. 4 (Apr
> 1985). 10.
> Falleni, Silvano. 1963. B&W. Set. **SIO**, 48.
> Firth, Tazeena & Timothy O'Brien. Sydney Opera House, Australia: 1978. Color.
> Model. **BTD**, 102.
> Gough, Philip. Liverpool Repertory Theatre, England: 1928. B&W. Set. **SCM**, 35.
> Harvey, Peter. 1979. Color. Rendering. **DDT**, 24b.
> Heinrich, Rudolf. Comic Opera, Berlin: B&W. Set. **TCI**, vol. 15, n. 1 (Jan 1981). 36.
> Israel, Robert. Minneapolis Center Opera: B&W. Set. **TCI**, vol. 4, n. 5 (Oct 1970). 23.
> Jacobs, Sally. Royal Shakespeare Theatre, Stratford-upon-Avon: 1971. B&W. Set.
> **SDT**, 273. 2 photos; B&W. Set. **SIP**, 248; Color. Set. **SOS**, 280; B&W. Set. **TCI**,
> vol. 5, n. 4 (Sep 1971). 23. 2 photos; B&W. Set. **TCI**, vol. 5, n. 3 (May/Jun 1971).

23; B&W. Set. **TCR**, 117; American Conservatory Theatre, San Francisco: B&W. Set. **TSY**, 217.

Jampolis, Neil Peter. Eric Harvie Theatre, Banff, Alberta, Canada 1984. B&W. Set. **DDT**, 477.

Kokoschka, Oskar. (not produced): Color. Rendering. **AST**, 211. Act I, sc. 3.

Labenz, Craig. Intiman Theatre, Seattle: 1991. Color. Set. **TCI**, vol. 26, n. 3 (Mar 1992). 36.

Landesman, Heidi. The Acting Company tour: 1980. B&W. Set. **TCI**, vol. 15, n. 5 (May 1981). 24; Arena Stage, Washington, DC: 1981. B&W. Model. **DDT**, 166; Newman Theatre, NYC: 1981. B&W. Model. **DDT**, 167; Delacorte Theatre, NYC: 1982. B&W. Set. **ASD2**, 68.

Luzzati, Emanuele. 1972. B&W. Set. **SIO**, 94.

Makkonen, Tina. Finland: B&W. Model. **TDT**, vol. XXVII, n. 4 (Fall 1991). 53.

Malina, Jaroslav. ABC Theatre, Prague: B&W. Set. **TDT**, vol. XXIII, n. 1 (Spring 1987). 6, 7, 12, 13. 3 photos.

Marron, Bill & Catherine Martin. Australian Opera, Edinburgh Festival: 1994. Color. Set. **TCI**, vol. 29, n. 1 (Jan 1995). 9.

Messel, Oliver. Old Vic Theatre, London: 1937. B&W. Set. **MEM**, 98, 99; B&W. Set. **OMB**, 108, 109; B&W. Set. **TPH**, photo 443.

Montresor, Beni. Tyrone Guthrie Theatre, Minneapolis: 1985. Color. Set. **TCI**, vol. 20, n. 1 (Jan 1986). 16.

Mörner, Stellan. Kungliga Teatern, Stockholm: 1956. B&W. Set. **SDW2**, 210.

Motley (Margaret Harris, Sophia Harris, & Elizabeth Montgomery). c. 1950. Color. Rendering. **DDT**, 312a.

Napier, John. B&W. Model. **TDT**, vol. XVI, n. 1 (Spring 1980). 22. 2 photos.

Nash, Paul. B&W. Rendering. **SDC**, plate 89.

Payne, Darwin Reid. B&W. Rendering. **SIP**, 56.

Piper, John. Royal Opera House, Covent Garden, London: 1961. B&W. Set. **SDW2**, 224.

Roller, Alfred. Austria: B&W. Rendering. **SCM**, 70.

Serroni, J.C. SESC Anchieta, São Paulo, Brazil: 1979. Color. Set. **TCI**, vol. 28, n. 4 (Apr 1994). 38.

Stern, Ernst. Deutsches Theater, Berlin: 1913. B&W. Model. **RSD**, illus. 109; Color. Rendering. **SOS**, 213; B&W. Set. **TPH**, photos 326, 327.

Straiges, Tony. Yale Repertory Theatre, New Haven: 1975. B&W. Set. **DDT**, 238; B&W. Set. **TCI**, vol. 10, n. 1 (Jan/Feb 1976). 72. 2 photos.

Svoboda, Josef. National Theatre, Prague: 1963. B&W. Model. **SJS**, 68. 4 photos.

Walser, Karl. Künstlertheater, Munich: 1909. Color. Rendering. **AST**, 29. Act IV, sc. 9.

Ward, Anthony. Royal Shakespeare Company, GB: Color. Set. **TCI**, vol. 29, n. 2 (Feb 1995). 32. 3 photos.

Wijnberg, Nicolaas. Stadsschouwburg, Amsterdam: 1961. B&W. Set. **SDW3**, 42.

Wilkinson, Norman. Shakespeare Memorial Theatre, Stratford-upon-Avon: 1933. B&W. Set. **SCM**, 21; B&W. Set. **SDC**, plate 80; B&W. Set. **SDG**, 160; Savoy Theatre, London: B&W. Set. **TCS2**, plates 140, 141.

Weger, Dwight. Oak Theatre, Olivet College, Michigan: 1969. B&W. Rendering & set. **TCI**, vol. 3, n. 5 (Oct 1969). 20-23. 4 photos.

Yeargan, Michael. Hartford Stage, Connecticut: 1988/1989. B&W. Set. **ASD2**, 174; B&W. Set. **SDL**, 367; B&W. Set. **TCI**, vol. 23, n. 7 (Aug/Sep 1989). 14; B&W and color. Set. **TCI**, vol. 25, n. 9 (Nov 1991). 40, 41.

_____. American Repertory Theatre, Cambridge, Massachusetts: B&W. Set. **TCI**, vol. 15, n. 8 (Oct 1981). 26, 27. 3 photos.

_____. Indiana University Theatre, Bloomington: B&W. Set. **BSE2**, 35.
_____. International Theatre Festival, Chicago: 1990. B&W. Set. **TCI**, vol. 24, n. 5 (May 1990). 39.
_____. Magnus Theatre, Thunder Bay, Ontario: B&W. Set. **TCI**, vol. 18, n. 2 (Feb 1984). 30.
_____. Neues Theater, Berlin: 1905. B&W. Set. **MRH**, between 10 & 11. 3 photos.
_____. NYC: B&W. Set. **TPH**, photo 263.
_____. Stratford Festival Theatre, Ontario, Canada: 1977. B&W. Set. **TCI**, vol. 12, n. 4 (May/Jun 1978). 16.
_____. Tomlinson Theatre, Temple University, Philadelphia: 1970. B&W. Set. **TCI**, vol. 5, n. 5 (Oct 1971). 26, 27. 3 photos.
_____. Vienna: 1925. B&W. Set. **TPH**, photo 328.
_____. 1988. Color. Set. **TCI**, vol. 27, n. 4 (Apr 1993). 30.
Midsummer's Morning Madness.
_____. Playhouse in the Park, Cincinnati: B&W. Set. **TCI**, vol. 5, n. 2 (Mar/Apr 1971). 12, 13. 3 photos.
Miguel Mañara.
Lucke, Christiane. Comédie de la Loire, Tours: 1963. B&W. Model. **SDW2**, 93.
Mihal, Daughter of Saul.
Berger, Genia. Habima, Tel Aviv: 1941. B&W. Rendering. **SDW2**, 117.
Mikado 2050.
_____. Candlewood Playhouse, New Fairfield, Connecticut: Color. Set. **TCI**, vol. 22, n. 7 (Aug/Sep 1988). 19.
The Mikado.
Arnold, Richard. Northern Illinois University, DeKalb, Illinois: Color. Set. **SST**, plate XII.
Blackman, Robert. Performing Arts Center, Santa Maria, California: 1974. B&W. Set. **TCI**, vol. 14, n. 4 (Sep 1980). 35.
Gorey, David. Carnegie-Mellon University, Pittsburgh: Color. Set. **TCI**, vol. 18, n. 4 (Apr 1984). 43.
Lobel, Adrianne. Chicago Lyric Opera: 1983. B&W. Set. **ASD2**, 94; B&W. Set. **ASD2**, 98; Color. Set. **TCI**, vol. 18, n. 1 (Jan 1984). 26; Color. Set. **TDT**, vol. XXI, n. 2 (Summer 1985). front cover.
Whitney, Michael J. Stratford Festival Theatre, Ontario, Canada: Color. Set. **TCI**, vol. 18, n. 9 (Nov/Dec 1984). 38.
The Military Lover.
Billa, Bernard. Théâtre Populaire Romand. La Chaux-de-Fonds, Switzerland: 1973. B&W. Set. **SDW4**, illus. 97.
Milk and Honey.
Bay, Howard. Martin Beck Theatre, NYC: 1961. B&W. Set. **BWM**, 305. 2 photos.
The Mill.
Svoboda, Josef. Slovak National Theatre, Bratislava: 1965. B&W. Rendering. **SJS**, 46.
The Millionairess.
Bailey, James. President Theatre, NYC: 1950. B&W. Set. **WTP**, 140.
Heythum, Antonín. National Theatre, Prague: 1936. B&W. Rendering. **SOW**, plates 60, 61.
_____. Shaw Festival Theatre, Niagara-on-the-Lake, Canada: B&W. Set. **TCI**, vol. 12, n. 4 (May/Jun 1978). 23.
The Mines of Sulfer.
Schmidt, Douglas W. Juilliard School of Music, NYC: 1967. B&W. Sketch. **DPT**, 114.

Minick.
Thompson, Woodman. Booth Theatre, NYC: 1925. B&W. Set. **SDA**, 199.
Minna von Barnhelm.
Kilger, Heinrich. Deutsches Theater, Berlin: 1960. B&W. Rendering. **SDW2**, 55.
Minnie Mouse and the Tapdancing Buddha.
Cate, Donald. The Magic Theatre, San Francisco: 1978. B&W. Set. **TCI**, vol. 14, n. 4 (Sep 1980). 23.
Minnikin and Mannikin.
Rotha, Paul. Great Britain: B&W. Rendering. **DIT**, plate 32.
Il Mio Carso.
Luzzati, Emanuele. 1969. B&W. Set. **SIO**, 89.
The Miracle.
Bel Geddes, Norman. Century Theatre, NYC: 1924. B&W. Set. **MCN**, 66; B&W and color. Rendering. **MRH**, between 6 & 7, between 248 & 249, facing 314. 3 photos; B&W. Rendering. **SDD**, between 210 & 211.
Stern, Ernst. Olympia Theatre, London: 1911. B&W. Rendering. **DOT**, 211; B&W and color. Rendering. **MRH**. facing 264, 304; B&W. Rendering. **RSD**, illus. 114, 115; B&W. Set. **SCM**, 18; B&W. Rendering. **SDG**, 167; B&W. Rendering. **TSY**, 176; Schumann Circus, Berlin: 1914. B&W. Rendering. **MRH**, facing 288; Westfalenhalle, Dortmund: B&W. Set. **TCI**, vol. 7, n. 6 (Nov/Dec 1973). 24. 2 photos.
Strnad, Oskar. Zirkus Renz, Vienna: 1927. B&W. Rendering. **TCS2**, plates 371, 371; Lyceum Theatre, London. 1932. B&W. Set. **MEM**, 81; B&W. Set. **OMB**, 74, 75.
Miracle at Verdun.
Simonson, Lee. Martin Beck Theatre, NYC: 1931. B&W. Rendering. **BSE4**, 51; B&W. Set. **SCM**, 113; B&W. Set. **TAS**, 150, 151. 4 photos; B&W. Rendering & set. **TDT**, vol. XXII, n. 3 (Fall 1986). 9, 10.
Miracle in the Gorbals.
Burra, Edward. Princes Theatre, London: 1944. B&W. Model. **SDW1**, 170.
The Miracle of St. Anthony.
_____. Moscow Art Theatre Third Studio: 1921. B&W. Set. **RST**, 79. 2 photos.
The Miracle Worker.
Jenkins, George. Playhouse Theatre, NYC: 1959. B&W. Rendering. **TCI**, vol. 14, n. 2 (Mar/Apr 1980). 24; B&W. model & rendering. **TDT**, n. 25 (May 1971). 12, 13; (tour): B&W. Rendering & set. **TDT**, n. 25 (May 1971). 10, 14, 15. 4 photos.
Kenny, Sean. B&W. Set. **TCI**, vol. 2, n. 1 (Jan/Feb 1968). 33.
Miracolo d'Amore.
Isreal, Robert. Spoleto Festival, Charleston, South Carolina: 1988. B&W. Set. **ASD2**, 48; B&W. Set. **TCI**, vol. 22, n. 7 (Aug/Sep 1988). 24; B&W. Set. **TCI**, vol. 24, n. 5 (May 1990). 30; New York Shakespeare Festival, NYC: 1988. Color. Set. **TCI**, vol. 24, n. 9 (Nov 1990). 39.
The Miraculous Mandarin.
Daydé, Bernard. O.R.T.F., Paris: 1967. B&W. Model. **SDW3**, 188.
The Mirror.
Janosa, Lajos. Vigszinhaz, Budapest: 1969. B&W. Set. **SDW3**, 219.
Misalliance.
Armstrong, Will Steven. Yale School of Drama, New Haven, Connecticut: 1957. B&W. Set. **SDW2**, 229.
Arnold, Richard. Northern Illinois University, DeKalb, Illinois: Color. Set. **SCT**, between 152 & 153.
Burroughs, Robert C. Fords Theatre, Washington, DC: B&W. Set. **SDT**, 292.

Döepp, John. Asolo State Theatre, Sarasota, Florida: B&W. Set. **TDP**, 116.

Frankish, Leslie. Shaw Festival Theatre, Niagara-on-the-Lake, Canada: 1990. Color. Set. **TCI**, vol. 24, n. 7 (Aug/Sep 1990). 10.

Ficello, Ralph. South Coast Repertory Theatre, Costa Mesa, California: 1988. B&W. Model. **DDT**, 170; Color. Set. **TCI**, vol. 22, n. 7 (Aug/Sep 1988). 13.

McLane, Derek. American Repertory Theatre, Cambridge, Massachusetts: 1992. Color. Set. **TCI**, vol. 26, n. 4 (Apr 1992). 14.

Smith, Raynette Halvorson. Loyola University, New Orleans: B&W. Set. **TCI**, vol. 16, n. 7 (Aug/Sep 1982). 35.

Strike, Maurice. Shaw Festival Theatre, Niagara-on-the-Lake, Canada: 1972. B&W. Set. **TCI**, vol. 22, n. 7 (Aug/Sep 1988). 64.

_____. Shaw Festival Theatre, Niagara-on-the-Lake, Canada: B&W. Set. **TCI**, vol. 12, n. 4 (May/Jun 1978). 23.

The Misanthrope.

Armistead, Horace. Loeb Drama Center, Harvard University: 1962. B&W. Set. **SFT**, 13.

Atkinson, Patrick. Missouri Summer Repertory Theatre, Columbia: 1981. B&W. Rendering. **BSE2**, 6.

Capek, Josef. National Theatre, Prague: B&W. Set. **TCS2**, plate 146.

Engelbach, Claude. Maison de la Culture, Amiens: 1969. B&W. Model. **SDW3**, 71.

Jenkins, David. Williamstown Theatre Festival, Massachusetts: 1973. B&W. Set. **DPT**, 93.

Moiseiwitsch, Tanya. National Theatre, Old Vic, London: 1973. B&W. Set. **SDW4**, illus. 79.

Tsypin, George. La Jolla Playhouse, California: 1989. B&W. Set. **ASD2**, 170, 171.

_____. Mummers Theatre, Oklahoma City: B&W. Set. **TCI**, vol. 5, n. 3 (May/Jun 1971). 7, 9.

_____. State Theatre, Salzburg: B&W. Set. **TCI**, vol. 11, n. 2 (Mar/Apr 1977). 20.

The Mischief of Being Clever.

Tröster, Frantisek. Vinohrady Theatre, Prague: 1947. B&W. Rendering. **SDW1**, 53.

The Miser.

Arnone, John. Hartford Stage, Connecticut: 1990. B&W. Set. **ASD2**, 26.

Beyer, Rolf. Hopkins Center, Dartmouth College, Hanover, New Hampshire: 1968. B&W. Set. **DDT**, 284.

Funicello, Ralph. South Coast Repertory Theatre, Costa Mesa, California: 1993. B&W. Set. **TDT** vol. XXXI, n. 2 (Spring 1995). 16.

Gilseth, Thom. Phoenix Little Theatre, Arizona: B&W. Set. **SDT**, 118.

Landwehr, Hugh. Center Stage, Baltimore: 1982. Color. Set. **ASD2**, between 108 & 109.

Luzzati, Emanuele. 1954. B&W. Rendering. **SDE**, 106.

Minks, Wilfried. Theater der Freien Hansestadt, Bremen: 1964. B&W. Rendering. **SDW3**, 72.

Pelletier, Jacques. Théâtre du Nouveau Monde, Montréal: 1951. B&W. Set. **SDW2**, 40.

Wittstein, Ed. Playhouse in the Park, Cincinnati: B&W. Set. **TCI**, vol. 5, n. 1 (Jan/Feb 1971). 18.

Wong, Carey. Oregon Shakespeare Festival, Portland: Color. Set. **TCI**, vol. 27, n. 9 (Nov 1993). 10.

_____. Centenary College, Louisiana: 1961. Color. Set. **MOR**, 45.

Les Misérables.
>   Napier, John. Royal Shakespeare Company, London: 1985. B&W. Set. **BTD**, 150;
>   B&W and color. Set. **TCI**, vol. 20, n. 9 (Nov 1986). 32, 33, 35. 4 photos; Broad-
>   way Theatre, NYC: 1987. B&W. Set. **DDT**, 596; Color. Set. **MBM**, 129, 132, 133.

Le Miserie di Monsù Travet.
>   Guglielminetti, Eugenio. B&W. Set. **SIO**, 80.

Misery and Nobless.
>   Cristini, Cesare M. Teatro San Carlo, Naples: 1953. B&W. Rendering. **SDE**, 73.

The Miss Firecracker Contest.
>   Beatty, John Lee. Manhattan Theatre Club, NYC: 1984. B&W. Rendering. **DDT**, 543.

Miss Havisham's Fire.
>   Conklin, John. New York City Opera, Lincoln Center: 1979. B&W. Model. **ASD1**, 19;
>   B&W. Model. **DDT**, 483; B&W. Model. **TCI**, vol. 14, n. 3 (May/Jun 1980). 23.

Miss Julie.
>   Schleef, Einar. Germany: B&W. Set. **TDT**, vol. XII, n. 3 (Fall 1976). 34.

Miss Liberty.
>   Smith, Oliver. Imperial Theatre, NYC: 1949. B&W. Set. **BWM**, 245.

Miss Lulu Bett. Viele,
>   Sheldon K. Belmont Theatre, NYC: 1920. B&W. Set. **MCN**, 53.

Miss Saigon.
>   Napier, John. London: 1989. Color. Set. **TCI**, vol. 24, n. 1 (Jan 1990). 22; Broadway
>   Theatre, NYC: 1991. B&W. Set. **DDT**, 7, 595; Color. Set. **MBM**, 136, 137; B&W.
>   Set. **TCI**, vol. 25, n. 8 (Oct 1991). 24; Color. Set. **TCI**, vol. 25, n. 4 (Apr 1991).
>   35, 38. 5 photos.

Miss Underground.
>   Aronson, Boris. (not produced): 1943. B&W and color. Rendering. **TAB**, 17, 299.

*Mr. BURT his MEMORY of Mr. WHITE his FANTASY of Mr. DUNSTABLE his
   MUSICK/PAGODE.*
>   MacDonald, Kim. La Jolla Museum of Contemporary Art, California: 1974. Color.
>   Set. **ASC**, 32.

Mr. Cinders.
>   Harker, Joseph & Phil Harker. Adelphi Theatre, London: 1929. B&W. Set. **MCD**, plate
>   161.

Mr. Gilhooley.
>   Mielziner, Jo. Broadhurst Theatre, NYC: 1930. B&W. Rendering. **DTT**, 76. Bedroom.

Mr. Gogol and Mr. Preen.
>   Beatty, John Lee. Mitzi Newhouse Theatre, Lincoln Center, NYC: 1991. B&W. Ren-
>   dering. **DDT**, 545.

Mister Johnson.
>   Eckart, William & Jean. Martin Beck Theatre, NYC: 1956. B&W. Rendering. **DDT**,
>   264 & 324; B&W. Rendering. **SDW2**, 233.

Mister Magridge Junior.
>   Akimov, Nikolai. Volnaia Comedia, Leningrad: 1924. B&W. Model. **RSD**, illus. 190.

Mr. Perrichon's Journey.
>   Dignimont. Comédie Française, Paris: 1946. B&W. Rendering. **SDW1**, 94.

Mr. Pickwick's Christmas.
>   Barkla, Jack. Children's Theatre Company, Minneapolis: B&W. Set. **TCI**, vol. 17, n. 7
>   (Aug/Sep 1983). 29.

Mister Puntila and His Chauffer Matti.
>   Gropman, David. Yale Repertory Theatre, New Haven: 1977. B&W. Set. **ASD2**, 40,
>   41; B&W. Rendering. **DDT**, 170.

Haferung, Paul. Theater der Stadt, Bonn: 1956. Color. Rendering. **SDW2**, 61.
Mister Roberts.
  Mielziner, Jo. Alvin Theatre, NYC: 1948. B&W. Set. **WTP**, 198, 199. 7 photos.
Mistero Buffo.
  Corso, Arturo. Koninklijke Muntschouwburg, Brussels: 1972. B&W. Set. **SDW4**, illus. 306.
Mithridate, King of Pontus.
  _____. Salzburg Festival: 1971. B&W. Set. **TDT**, n. 28 (Feb 1972). front cover.
Moby Dick.
  Guglielminetti, Eugenio. 1972. B&W. Set. **SIO**, 86. 2 photos.
Modell Beatrice.
  Arle, Asmund & Yngve Larson. Dramatiska Teatern, Stockholm: 1954. B&W. Set. **SDW2**, 208.
A Modern Dream.
  Palitzsch, Hans Heinrich. Landestheater, Linz: 1968. B&W. Set. **RSD**, illus. 595.
Moisasur's Magic Curse.
  Kokoschka, Oskar. Burgtheater, Vienna: 1960. B&W. Set. **SDW2**, 157.
The Moliére Comedies.
  Stein, Douglas O. Roundabout Theatre, NYC: 1995. Color. Set. **TCI**, vol. 29, n. 3 (Mar 1995). 6.
Der Mond.
  Bauer-Ecsy, Leni. B&W. Set. **SIP**, 298.
The Monkey and the Quiver.
  Hasegawa, Kanbei. Kabuki-za, Tokyo: Color. Rendering. **SDW1**, 146.
Monna Vanna.
  Urban, Joseph. Boston: 1912. B&W. Set. **TPH**, photo 450.
Monologue about Marriage.
  Kochergin, Edward Stepanovich. Gorky Theatre, Leningrad: B&W. Model. **TCI**, vol. 11, n. 5 (Oct 1977). 38. 2 photos; Leningradskij Akademitcheskij Teatr Komedii, Leningrad: 1973. B&W. Set. **SDW4**, illus. 368.
Monsieur Beaucaire.
  Bonnat, Yves (Yves-Bonnat). Opéra-Comique, Paris: 1955. Color. Rendering. **SDW1**, 85.
Monsieur de Pourceaugnac.
  Cassandre, A.M. Comédie Française, Paris: 1948. B&W. Rendering. **SDW1**, 89.
Montag aus Licht.
  Dyer, Chris. La Scala, Milan: 1988. B&W. Set. **BTD**, 125.
Monte Cassino.
  Baumeister, Willi. Städtische Bühnen, Essen: 1949. B&W. Sketch & rendering. **AST**, 159. 3 photos.
Montezuma.
  Lee, Ming Cho. Juilliard School, Lincoln Center, NYC: 1982. B&W. Set. **TCI**, vol. 20, n. 3 (Mar 1986). 25.
A Month in the Country.
  Conklin, John. Williamstown Theatre Festival, Massachusetts: 1978. B&W. Set. **TCI**, vol. 14, n. 3 (May/Jun 1980). 17.
  Doboujinsky, Mstislav. Moscow Art Theatre: 1909. B&W. Rendering. **DOT**, 206; B&W. Model. **TCS2**, plates 7, 8; 1919. B&W and color. Rendering. **FCS**, plate 176, color plate 19. Act I; B&W. Rendering. **RSC**, 28; B&W and color. Rendering. **SDO**, 199, plate 19.
  Shervashidze, Alexander. Théâtre du Marais, Brussels: B&W. Set. **TCS2**, plate 51.

Taylor, Robert U. Colonnades Theatre Lab, NYC: B&W. Set. **TCI**, vol. 11, n. 1 (Jan/Feb 1977). 24.

Monument to Kleist.

Freyer, Achim. State Theatre, Stuttgart: 1977. B&W. Set. **TCI**, vol. 13, n. 5 (Oct 1979). 16.

The Moon.

Siercke, Alfred. State Opera, Hamburg: 1951. B&W. Rendering. **SDW1**, 79.

A Moon for the Misbegotten.

Edwards, Ben. Morosco Theatre, NYC: 1973. B&W. Set. **DPT**, 177; B&W. Set. **DSL**, frontispiece; B&W. Sketches. **TCI**, vol. 23, n. 7 (Aug/Sep 1989). 53.

Hay, Richard L. Oregon Shakespeare Festival, Ashland: B&W. Set. **SDL**, 75.

Jones, Robert Edmond. Hanna Theatre, Cleveland: 1947. B&W. Rendering. **SDW1**, 198.

_____. Cohoes Music Hall, Albany, New York: 1977. B&W. Set. **TCI**, vol. 12, n. 6 (Oct 1978). 26.

_____ Theatre Calgary: B&W. Set. **TCI**, vol. 18, n. 2 (Feb 1984). 31.

The Moon is Blue.

Chaney, Stewart. Henry Miller's Theatre, New York: 1951. B&W. Set. **SDW1**, 194.

The Moon of the Caribbees.

Throckmorton, Cleon. Provincetown Playhouse, NYC: B&W. Set. **SDC**, plate 49.

Moon on a Rainbow Shawl.

Galup, Mario. Teatro Universitario, Montevideo: 1959. B&W. Set. **SDW2**, 242.

Moonchildren.

McClennahan, Charles. Second Stage, NYC: 1987. Color. Set. **ASD2**, between 108 & 109.

Moose Murders.

Kellogg, Marjorie Bradley. Eugene O'Neill Theater, NYC: 1983. B&W. Set. **ASD1**, 66.

Mörder, Hoffnung der Frauen.

Schlemmer, Oskar. Landestheater, Stuttgart: 1921. Color. Rendering. **AST**, 153.

More Fun Than Bowling.

Dunham, Clarke. Pennsylvania Stage Company, Allentown: 1987. B&W. Set. **DDT**, 476.

_____. Addison Centre Theatre, Addison, Texas: Color. Set. **TCI**, vol. 26, n. 5 (May 1992). 46.

More Light.

Don, Robin. Bush Theatre, London: 1987. B&W. Set. **BTD**, 40.

More Stately Mansions.

Edwards, Ben. Broadhurst Theatre, NYC: 1967. B&W. Rendering & drop. **DDT**, 27, 404; B&W. Rendering. **DPT**, 24.

The Morning Bride.

Van Nerom, Jacques. Théâtre Royal des Galeries, Brussels: 1959. B&W. Set. **SDW2**, 32.

Morning's at Seven.

Hein, Keith. Theatre Forty, California: B&W. Set. **TCI**, vol. 14, n. 4 (Sep 1980). 47.

Morocco.

Yeargan, Michael. Hartford Stage, Connecticut: 1987. B&W. Set. **ASD2**, 184; B&W. Set. **SDL**, 72.

Morowitz Hamlet.

Phillips, Van. Purdue University: B&W. Set. **SST**, 446.

La Mort de Sparta.
 Jouvet, Louis. Théâtre du Vieux-Columbier, Paris: 1921. B&W. Set. **RSD**, illus. 107.
Morts sans Sépulture.
 Masson, André. Théâtre Antoine, Paris: 1946. B&W. Set. **AST**, 202.
La Moscheta.
 Luzzati, Emanuele. 1970. B&W. Set. **SIO**, 93. 2 photos.
Moscow!
 Dmitriev, Vladimir(?). (not produced): 1926. B&W. Sketch. **RST**, 200.
Moses and Aaron.
 Bury, John. Royal Opera House, Covent Garden, London: 1965. B&W. Set. **CGA**,
  163; B&W. Set. **RSD**, illus. 594; B&W. Set. **SDB**, 77; Color. Set. **SDR**, 49; B&W.
  Set. **TCI**, vol. 26, n. 1 (Jan 1992). 49.
 Freyer, Achim. New York City Opera, Lincoln Center: 1990. Color. Set. **TCI**, vol. 24,
  n. 9 (Nov 1990). 13.
 Haferung, Paul. State Theatre, Zurich: 1957. B&W. Rendering. **RSD**, illus. 455; B&W.
  Set. **SDW2**, 60.
 Heinrich, Rudolf. State Opera, Vienna: 1973. B&W. Set. **SDW4**, illus. 205-208.
 Raffaëlli. Michel. State Opera, Berlin: 1961. B&W. Set. **SDW2**, 100.
 Wendel, Heinrich. Deutsches Oper am Rhein, Düsseldorf-Duisburg: 1968. B&W. Set.
  SDW3, 187.
The Most Happy Fella.
 Beatty, John Lee. Goodspeed Opera House, East Haddam, Connecticut: 1991. Color.
  Rendering. **TCI**, vol. 25, n. 6 (Aug/Sep 1991). 14.
 Mielziner, Jo. Imperial Theatre, NYC: 1956. B&W. Set. **BWM**, 268.
 Sicangco, Eduardo. Music Theatre of Wichita, Kansas: 1985. B&W. Drop. **BSE4**, 40.
The Mother.
 Angelini, Sandro. Teatro delle Novità, Bergamo: 1951. B&W. Rendering. **SDE**, 26.
 Borovsky, David. Taganka Theatre, Moscow: 1969. B&W. Rendering. **SDW3**, 96;
  B&W. Rendering. **TCI**, vol. 12, n. 7 (Nov/Dec 1978). 35.
 Kiesler, Frederick. NYC: 1942. B&W. Set. **EIF**, photo 24.
 Kolodziej, Marian. Teatr Wybrzeze, Gdansk: 1969. B&W. Set. **SDW3**, 102.
 Neher, Caspar. Komödienhaus, Berlin: 1932. B&W. Rendering. **CBM**, 57; B&W.
  Rendering & set. **TBB**, 40, 118; Theater am Schiffbauerdamm, Berlin: 1951.
  B&W. Set. **CBM**, 57; B&W. Set & projection. **TBB**, 162, 175, 180. 5 photos.
 Ryndine, Vadim. Teatr Maïakovskovo, Moscow: 1948. B&W. Rendering. **SDW2**, 192.
 Shtoffer, Jacob. Krasnaya Presnya (Realistic) Theatre, Moscow: 1932. B&W. Set.
  NTO, facing 364; B&W. Sketch & set. **RSD**, illus. 223, 224; B&W. Set. **RST**, 285.
  2 photos; B&W. Set. **TPH**, photo 408; B&W. Set. **SCM**, 93; B&W. Set. **TSE**, 7.
  _____. Berlin: B&W. Set. **TPH**, photo 245.
  _____. San Francisco Mime Troupe: B&W. Set. **TCI**, vol. 14, n. 4 (Sep 1980).
  32.
Mother Courage and Her Children.
 Lee, Ming Cho. The Acting Company tour: B&W. Set. **TCI**, vol. 15, n. 5 (May 1981).
  23.
 Merritt, Michael. Wisdom Bridge Theatre, Chicago: 1981. B&W. Set. **ASD2**, 130.
 Neher, Caspar. Schauspielehaus, Zürich: 1946. B&W. Rendering. **CBM**, 60.
 Otto, Teo. Schauspielehaus, Zürich: 1941. B&W. Model. **RSD**, illus. 558, 559; B&W.
  Rendering. **TBB**, 122.
 Padovani, Gianfranco. 1969-1970. B&W. Model. **SIO**, 100. 4 photos.
 Rojo, Jerry N. Performance Garage, NYC: 1975. B&W. Rendering & set. **TSE**, 140-
  152. 8 photos.

Rozier, Daniele. Théâtre des Quartiers d'Ivry-Théatre des Amandiers, Nanterre, France: 1973. B&W. Sketch. **SDW4**, illus. 240.

Svoboda, Josef. Tyl Theatre, Prague: 1970. B&W. Set. **SJS**, 160, 162. 6 photos; B&W. Set. **STS**, 63.

Williams, F. Elaine. Bucknell University Theatre, Lewisburg, Pennsylvania: 1983. B&W. Rendering. **BSE3**, 42.

_____. Deutsches Theater, Berlin: 1949. B&W. Set. **TBB**, 152.

_____. Germany: B&W. Set. **TCR**, 97.

_____. Pennsylvania State University, University Park: Color. Set. **TDT**, vol. XXVIII, n. 2 (Spring 1992). 12 of insert.

_____. Theater am Schiffbauerdamm, Berlin: 1951. B&W. Set. **TBB**, 48; B&W. Set. **DSL**, 178.

_____. Zurich: 1941. B&W. Set. **TBB**, 152.

_____. B&W. Set. **TCR**, 99.

Mother Hicks.

Cochran, Randel R. Stage One: The Louisville Children's Theatre, Kentucky: 1985. B&W. Set. **BSE4**, 76.

Crome, Sara. University of Illinois, Urbana: 1989. B&W. Set. **TDT**, vol. XXVI, n. 2 (Summer 1990). 63.

The Mother of Christ.

Bel Geddes, Norman. B&W. Model. **SDC**, plate 101.

The Mother of Gregory.

Theater of the Golden Bough, Carmel: 1924. B&W. Set. **TPH**, photo 453.

Mother of Pearl.

Messel, Oliver. Gaiety Theatre, London: 1933. B&W. Set. **MEM**, 90.

The Mother of Us All.

Eckart, William & Jean. 1986. Color. Rendering. **DDT**, 152d.

Indiana, Robert. Tyrone Guthrie Theatre, Minneapolis: 1967. B&W. Set. **ASC**, 14.

Kiesler, Frederick. 1947. B&W. Sketches. **EIF**, photo 48, 49.

The Mound Builders.

Beatty, John Lee. Circle Repertory Theatre, NYC: 1975. B&W. Rendering. **DPT**, 23; B&W. Set. **TCI**, vol. 9, n. 3 (May/Jun 1975). 2; B&W. Set. **TCI**, vol. 12, n. 6 (Oct 1978). 20.

The Mountain Bride.

Ciller, Josef. Martin, Czechoslovakia: 1986. B&W. Model. **TDT**, vol. XXVIII, n. 2 (Spring 1992). 35; B&W. Model. **TDT**, vol. XXIII, n. 4 (Winter 1988). 49.

Mountain Language.

Taylor, Michael. National Theatre (Lyttleton), London: 1988. B&W. Set. **BTD**, 80.

Mourning Becomes Electra.

Aronson, Boris. Metropolitan Opera, NYC: 1967. B&W. Rendering. **DPT**, 77; B&W. Set. **SDL**, 70; B&W. Sketch, model, & set. **TAB**, 208-211, 213, 214, 307. 9 photos.

Hoffman, Vlastislav. National Theatre, Prague: 1934. B&W. Rendering. **TDT**, n. 41 (Summer 1975). 18.

Jones, Robert Edmond. Guild Theatre, NYC: 1931. B&W. Set. **MCN**, 107; B&W. Rendering. **REJ**, 83; B&W. Set. **SDA**, 200. 3 photos.

Prampolini, Enrico. Rome: 1942. B&W. Rendering. **SDE**, 136.

The Mousetrap.

Holland, Anthony. London: 1952. B&W. Set. **TCI**, vol. 22, n. 5 (May 1988). 41.

Pecktal, Lynn. Barter Theatre, Abingdon, Virginia: 1958. B&W. Set. **DDT**, 368.

Mrs. Bumpstead-Leigh.

Dodge, D. Frank. Lyceum Theatre, NYC: 1911. B&W. Set. **MCN**, 38.

Mrs. McThing.
> Polakov, Lester. Martin Beck Theatre, NYC: 1952. B&W. Rendering. **DDT**, 183, 284. 3 photos.

Mrs. Murray's Farm.
> Beatty, John Lee. Circle Repertory Theatre, NYC: 1976. B&W. Set. **TCI**, vol. 12, n. 6 (Oct 1978). 21.

Mrs. Warren's Profession.
> Mitchell, David. Vivian Beaumont Theatre, Lincoln Center, NYC: 1976. B&W. Set. **TCI**, vol. 10, n. 3 (May/Jun 1976). 24.

Mrs. Wiggs of the Cabbage Patch.
> _____. Savoy Theatre, NYC: 1904. B&W. Set. **MCN**, 23.

Much Ado About Nothing.
> Blackman, Robert. Solvang Festival Theatre, California: 1977. B&W. Set. **TCI**, vol. 14, n. 4 (Sep 1980). 35.
> Cesarini, Pino. Roman Theatre, Verona: 1951. B&W. Rendering & set. **SDE**, 55.
> Drury, Walter. Shakespeare Memorial Theatre, Stratford-upon-Avon: 1923. B&W. Set. **SDG**, 178, 179.
> Jones, Robert Edmond. (project): 1920. B&W. Rendering. **SDA**, 208. 2 photos.
> Koltai, Ralph. Royal Shakespeare Company, GB: 1982. B&W. Set. **SDT**, 275; Color. Set. **TDT**, vol. XIX, n. 3 (Fall 1983). front cover.
> Lee, Ming Cho. Delacorte Theatre, NYC: 1968. B&W. **SDB**, 60; Delacorte Theatre, NYC: 1972. B&W. Model. **CSD**, 92; Color. Set. **TCI**, vol. 29, n. 3 (Mar 1995). 7; B&W. Set. **TCI**, vol. 7, n. 2 (Mar/Apr 1973). 9.
> Moiseiwitsch, Tanya. Shakespeare Festival Theatre, Stratford, Ontario: 1958. B&W. Set. **SDW2**, 39, 220.
> Peters, Philip. University of Montana, Missoula: 1980. B&W. Set. **BSE2**, 21.
> Refn, Helge. National Theatre, Oslo: 1946. B&W. Model. **SDW1**, 61.
> Ryndine, Vadim. Vakhtangov Theatre, Moscow: 1936. B&W. Rendering. **SDW2**, 191.
> Seger, Richard. American Conservatory Theatre, Geary Theatre, San Francisco: 1981. B&W. Set. **TCI**, vol. 15, n. 4 (Apr 1981). 42.
> Stern, Ernst. Deutsches Theater, Berlin: 1912. Color. Rendering. **MRH**, facing 12. 2 photos; B&W. Set. **TCS2**, plate 27.
> _____. Phoenix Theatre, London: 1952. B&W. Set. **SOS**, 247.
> _____. New York Shakespeare Festival, NYC: Color. Set. **TCI**, vol. 23, n. 4 (Apr 1989). 50.

Mud.
> Duthie, Diane. Theatre for the New City, NYC: 1984. B&W. Set. **BSE4**, 90.

The Murder at Cherry Hill.
> _____. Empire State Institute for the Performing Arts: Color. Set. **TCI**, vol. 22, n. 5 (May 1988). 49.

Murder at the Howard Johnson's.
> Eigsti, Karl. John Golden Theatre, NYC: 1979. B&W. Rendering. **ASD1**, 35.

Murder in the Cathedral.
> Falleni, Silvano. 1970. B&W. Set. **SIO**, 53.
> Koltai, Ralph. Sadler's Wells Opera House, London: 1962. Color. Model. **DMS**, plate 41.
> Vesseur, Wim. Stadsschouwburg, Amsterdam: 1949. B&W. **SDW1**, 139.
> Zuffi, Piero. La Scala, Milan: 1957. B&W. Set. **SDW2**, 134. 2 photos.
> _____. Hobart College, Geneva, New York: 1939. B&W. Set. **WTP**, 52, 53.

Murder on the Nile.

Detweiler, Lowell. Actors Theatre of Louisville: 1987. Color. Set. **TCI**, vol. 22, n. 5 (May 1988). 40.

Murderer, Hope of Women.

Sievert, Ludwig. State Opera, Frankfurt: 1922. B&W. Rendering. **CSC**, facing 32; B&W. Rendering. **FCS**, plate 194; B&W. Rendering. **SDO**, 222; B&W. Rendering. **TCS2**, plate 207.

Museum.

Ward, Randy. Virginia Technological University Theatre: Color. Set. **TCI**, vol. 21, n. 3 (Mar 1987). 25.

Music Cure.

Kerr, Mary. Shaw Festival Theatre, Niagara-on-the-Lake, Canada: 1982. Color. Set. **TCI**, vol. 18, n. 9 (Nov/Dec 1984). 39.

Music Hall Sidelights.

Arnone, John. Lion Theatre, NYC: B&W. Set. **TCI**, vol. 13, n. 4 (Sep 1979). 53; B&W. Set. **TCI**, vol. 15, n. 6 (Jun/Jul 1981). 28.

Music in the Air.

Urban, Joseph. Alvin Theatre, NYC: 1932. B&W. Set. **BWM**, 171; B&W. Set. **RBS**, 71; B&W. Set. **WMC**, 63.

The Music Man.

Bay, Howard. Majestic Theatre, NYC: 1957. Color. Set. **BWM**, 298, 299; B&W. Rendering. **SDA**, 252; B&W. Rendering. **SDB**, 57, 109; B&W. Rendering. **TCI**, vol. 17, n. 2 (Feb 1983). 16; B&W. Drop. **TCI**, vol. 20, n. 5 (May 1986). 20.

Pecktal, Lynn. 1979. Color. Set. **DDT**, 312d.

Sibbald, George. Corning Summer Theatre, NY: 1985. B&W. Set. **TCI**, vol. 20, n. 5 (May 1986). 21.

The Musical Comedy Murders of 1940.

Potts, David. Circle Repertory Theatre, NYC: 1987. B&W. Set. **TCI**, vol. 22, n. 5 (May 1988). 33, 37.

A Musical Nightmare.

Gould, Peter David. Stage West: 1987. Color. Set. **TCI**, vol. 22, n. 5 (May 1988). 39.

Mutiny!

Dudley, William. Piccadilly Theatre, London: B&W. Set. **TCI**, vol. 20, n. 2 (Feb 1986). 33.

Mutiny of the Machines.

Bolshoi Theatre, Moscow: 1924. B&W. Set. **RST**, 135.

Muzeeka.

Harvey, Peter. Provincetown Playhouse, NYC: 1968. B&W. Backdrop. **DPT**, 293.

My Fair Lady.

Donnelly, Mark. Pacific Conservatory of the Performing Arts, Santa Maria, California: B&W. Set. **SDT**, 282. Act I, sc. 1.

Kimmel, Alan. Casa Mañana, Dallas: B&W. Set. **TCI**, vol. 2, n. 5 (Sep/Oct 1968). 20.

Smith, Oliver. Mark Hellinger Theatre, NYC: 1956. B&W and color. Set. **BWM**, 282, 283; B&W. Set. **CBS**, 100; B&W. Set. **DPT**, 159; B&W. Rendering. **SDA**, 254, 255. 3 photos; B&W. Rendering. **SDW2**, 239; B&W. Rendering. **TCI**, vol. 16, n. 4 (Apr 1982). 14; B&W. Rendering of show curtain. **TDT**, vol. XXIV, n. 3 (Fall 1988). 17; B&W. Set. **TMT**, 184, 185. 3 photos; B&W. Set. **WMC**, 244. 4 photos; Theatre Royal, Drury Lane, London: 1958. B&W. Set. **MCD**, plate 209; NYC: 1976. B&W. Drop. **DDT**, 406; (tour): 1981. B&W. Rendering & set. **TCI**, vol. 16, n. 4 (Apr 1982). 14; B&W. Set. **TCI**, vol. 15, n. 2 (Feb 1981). 19. 2 photos; NYC: 1993. Color. Set. **TCI**, vol. 28, n. 3 (Mar 1994). 31, 32. 4 photos.

My Father's House.
   Odin Teatret, Holstebro, Denmark: 1972. B&W. Sketch & set. **SDW4**, illus. 155-162.
My Favorite Year.
   Lynch, Thomas. Vivian Beaumont Theatre, Lincoln Center, NYC: 1992. Color. Set.
      TCI, vol. 27, n. 3 (Mar 1993). 5, 30, 31. 5 photos.
My Foot My Tutor.
   Luft, Jochen. Forumtheater, Berlin: 1970. B&W. Set. **SDW4**, illus. 394.
My Four Angels.
   Echave, José. Teatro Solis, Montevideo: 1956. B&W. Rendering. **SDW2**, 241.
My Friend.
   Shlepyanov, Ilya. Theatre of the Revolution, Moscow: 1932. B&W. Set. **RST**, 278,
      279. 3 photos.
My Friend Kolka.
   Knoblock, Boris. Tsentralnyi Detski Teatr, Moscow: 1959. B&W. Model. **SDW2**, 187.
My Heart's in the Highlands.
   Andrews, Herbert. Group Theatre, USA: 1939. B&W. Set. **SOW**, plate 99.
My Kinsman, Major Molyneaux.
   Wulp, John. American Place Theatre, NYC: B&W. Set. **TCI**, vol. 13, n. 1 (Jan/Feb
      1979). 25.
My Masters.
   Kellogg, Marjorie Bradley. La Jolla Playhouse, California: 1983. Color. Set. **TCI**, vol.
      21, n. 8 (Oct 1987). 26.
My Miracle.
   Ohasi, Jasuhiro. Japan: B&W. Model. **TDT**, vol. XX, n. 1 (Spring 1984). 42.
My Mocking Happiness.
   Kochergin, Edward Stepanovich. Teatr imeni Komissarjevskoy, Leningrad: 1968.
      B&W. Set. **SDW3**, 122.
My Mother, My Father and Me.
   Bay, Howard. Plymouth Theatre, NYC: 1963. B&W. Backdrop. **SDB**, 196.
My One and Only.
   Lobel, Adrianne. St. James Theatre, NYC: 1983. Color. Set. **MBM**, 105; Color. Col-
      lage. **TCI**, vol. 18, n. 1 (Jan 1984). 25. 2 photos.
My Poor Marat.
   Russia: B&W. Set. **TCM**, 115.
My Three Angels.
   Aronson, Boris. Morosco Theatre, NYC: 1953. B&W. Rendering. **TAB**, 303.
The Mysteries.
   Dudley, William. National Theatre (Cottesloe), England: 1985. B&W. Set. **BTD**, 44,
      45.
Mysteries and Smaller Pieces.
   _____. American Center, Paris: 1964. B&W. Set. **RSD**, illus. 625.
The Mysteries of the Canary Islands.
   Yutkevich, Sergei. Mastfor, Moscow: 1923. B&W. Sketch. **RST**, 100.
Mystery Bouffe.
   Kiselev, Viktor. Teatr RSFSR 1, Moscow: 1921. B&W. Model. **MOT**, between 144 &
      145.
   Malevich, Kasimir. Theatre of Musical Drama, Petrograd: 1921. B&W. Model. **TCT**,
      plate 14.
   Mayakovsky, Vladimir. Petrograd: 1918. B&W. Rendering. **RST**, 65.
   Tischler, Alexander. Teatr Satiry, Moscow: 1957. B&W. **SDW2**, 198.

The Mystery of Edwin Drood.
Belli, Keith. Arkansas Repertory Theatre, Little Rock: Color. Set. **TCI**, vol. 23, n. 4 (Apr 1989). 55.
Bottari, Michael & Ronald Case. An Evening Dinner Theatre, Elmsford, New York: Color. Set. **TCI**, vol. 23, n. 4 (Apr 1989). 53.
Gilseth, Thom. Phoenix Little Theatre, Arizona: Color. Set. **TCI**, vol. 23, n. 4 (Apr 1989). 53.
Rager, John. Landers Theatre, Springfield, Missouri: Color. Set. **TCI**, vol. 23, n. 4 (Apr 1989). 53.
Shaw, Bob. Delacorte Theatre, NYC: 1985. Color. Set. **MBM**, 172; Color. Set. **TCI**, vol. 20, n. 1 (Jan 1986). 23.

-N-

N (Nijinsky).
Kaplevich, Pasha. Theatre Agency BOGIS, Russia: 1992. B&W. Set. **TDT**, vol. XXX, n. 5 (Fall 1994). 35, 36. 3 photos.
Nabucco.
Benois, Nicola. New York City Opera, Lincoln Center: B&W. Set. **TCI**, vol. 16, n. 8 (Oct 1982). 22.
Fiume, Salvatore. La Scala, Milan: 1958. B&W. Rendering. **SDW2**, 126.
Lazaridis, Stefanos. Bregenz Festival, Austria: 1994. B&W and color. Set. **TCI**, vol. 28, n. 3 (Mar 1994). 40, 41. 4 photos.
Marussig, Guido. La Scala, Milan: 1947. B&W. Rendering. **SDE**, 121. 2 photos.
Svoboda, Josef. Zurich: 1968. B&W. Set. **STS**, 101; Covent Garden, London: 1972. B&W. Set. **TDT**, vol. XII, n. 2 (Summer 1976). 22; Czechoslovakia: 1985. B&W. Model. **TDT**, vol. XXIII, n. 4 (Winter 1988). 50; Zurich: 1986. Color. Set. **TCI**, vol. 21, n. 8 (Oct 1987). 36.
Nachfolge Christi-spiel.
Reigbert, Otto. Kammerspiele, Munich: B&W. Rendering. **TAT**, plate 384.
Naked Hamlet.
Mitchell, David. Anspacher Theatre, NYC: 1967. B&W. Set. **ASD1**, 131.
Nala and Damayanti.
King, Edith. King Coit School, USA: B&W. Set. **SOW**, plate 35.
The Names of Powers.
Szajna, Josef. Teatr Ludowy, Nowa Huta, Poland: 1957. B&W. Set. **SDW2**, 170.
Napoleon.
Klein, César. State Theatre, Berlin: 1922. B&W. Rendering. **CSC**, facing 126; B&W. Rendering. **RSD**, illus. 132, 133; B&W. Rendering. **TCS2**, plate 93.
Napoli Milionaria.
Ward, Anthony. Royal National Theatre, London: 1991. Color. Set. **TCI**, vol. 27, n. 4 (Apr 1993). 44.
Narcisa Garay, a Woman for Crying.
Pedreira, Luis Diego. Teatro Carpa Belgrano, Buenos Aires: 1959. B&W. Rendering. **SDW2**, 26.
The Narrow Road to the Deep North.
Acquart, André. Théâtre de Nice-Cote d'Azur, Nice: 1969. B&W. Model. **SDW3**, 163.
_____. Addison Centre Theatre, Addison, Texas: Color. Set. **TCI**, vol. 26, n. 5 (May 1992). 47.
Natalia Tarpova.
_____. Kamerny Theatre, Moscow: 1929. B&W. Set. **RST**, 231. 3 photos.

Nathan the Wise.
    Kilger, Heinrich. Deutsches Theater, Berlin: 1966. B&W. Rendering & set. **SDW3**, 77.
        5 photos.
National Health.
    _____. Long Wharf Theatre, New Haven, Connecticut: B&W. Set. **TCI**, vol. 9,
        n. 6 (Nov/Dec 1975). 24.
Native Son.
    Morcom, James Stewart. St. James Theatre, NYC: 1941. B&W. Rendering. **DDT**, 170;
        B&W. Set. **WTP**, 184, 185. 4 photos.
Naughty-Naught.
    Dunkel, Eugene. American Music Hall, NYC: 1937. B&W. Set. **RBS**, 141.
The Naval Battle.
    Strenger, Friedhelm. Germany: B&W. Set. **DSL**, figure 27.1(a). Die Seeschlacht.
The Neapolitan Desease.
    Zídek, Ivo. Prague: 1988. B&W. Rendering. **TDT**, vol. XXVIII, n. 2 (Spring 1992).
        36.
Neapolitan Fete.
    Ratto, Gianni. La Pergola, Florence: 1950. B&W. Set. **SDW1**, 130.
Ned Kelly.
    Boyce, Raymond. New Zealand Players Co., Wellington: 1953. B&W. Model. **SDW1**,
        141.
Ned McCobb's Daughter.
    Bernstein, Aline. John Golden Theatre, NYC: 1926. B&W. Set. **MCN**, 78.
Nefertiti.
    Kirkpatrick, Sam. Blackstone Theatre, Chicago: 1977. B&W. Set. **TCI**, vol. 11, n. 6
        (Nov/Dec 1977). 16-19. 6 photos.
Nelligan.
    Goyette, Claude. Canada: B&W. Model. **TDT**, vol. XXVII, n. 4 (Fall 1991). 21.
Nerone.
    _____. Milan: 1924. B&W. Model. **TDT**, vol. XXV, n. 2 (Summer 1989). 11.
The Nest of the Woodgrouse.
    Sherman, Loren. Newman Theatre, NYC: 1984. B&W. Set. **DDT**, 61.
New Cranks.
    Toms, Carl. Lyric Opera House, Hammersmith, London: 1960. B&W. Rendering.
        SDW2, 228.
New Jerusalem.
    Arnone, John. Public Theatre, NYC: 1979. B&W. Set. **TCI**, vol. 15, n. 6 (Jun/Jul
        1981). 28.
New Year's Eve.
    Pimenov, Youri. Vakhtangov Theatre, Moscow: 1945. B&W. Rendering. **SDW2**, 190.
News of the Day.
    Reinking Wilhelm. Landestheater, Darmstadt: 1929-1930. B&W. Set. **RSD**, illus. 251.
Nick and Nora.
    Schmidt, Douglas W. Marquis Theatre, NYC: 1991. B&W. Rendering. **TCI**, vol. 24, n.
        8 (Oct 1990). 37.
Night and Day.
    Toms, Carl. ANTA Theatre, NYC: 1980. B&W. Set. **TCI**, vol. 14, n. 2 (Mar/Apr
        1980). 6.
A Night at the Chinese Opera.
    Hudson, Richard. Kent Opera, GB: 1987. B&W. Set. **BTD**, 146, 147. 2 photos.

The Night Before Christmas.
    Aronson, Boris. Morosco Theatre, NYC: 1941. B&W. Rendering. **TAB**, 297.
The Night Bell.
    Sciltian, Gregorio. Piccola Scala, Milan: 1957. B&W. Rendering. **SDW2**, 132.
Night Flight.
    Douking, Georges. Opéra-Comique, Paris: 1961. B&W. Sketch. **SDW2**, 89.
Night Flowers.
    Amenós, Montse & Isidre Prunés. Dagoll Dagom Company, Barcelona: 1991. Color.
        Set. **TCI**, vol. 27, n. 1 (Jan 1993). 42. 2 photos.
A Night in Old Peking.
    Ultz. Lyric Theatre, Hammersmith, London: B&W. Set. **TCI**, vol. 17, n. 7 (Aug/Sep
        1983). 38. 2 photos.
A Night in the Old Market.
    Falk, Robert. State Jewish Theatre, Moscow: 1924. B&W. Set. **RSD**, illus. 214, 215;
        B&W. Set. **TCS2**, plate 103.
'night Mother.
    Edwards, Jack. Tyrone Guthrie Theatre, Minneapolis: 1984. B&W. Set. **TCI**, vol. 19,
        n. 5 (May 1985). 22.
    Landesman, Heidi. John Golden Theatre, NYC: 1983. B&W. Set. **TCI**, vol. 19, n. 5
        (May 1985). 22.
Night of the Auk.
    Bay, Howard. Playhouse Theatre, NYC: 1956. B&W. Sketch & model. **SDB**, 112;
        B&W. Set. **TCI**, vol. 17, n. 2 (Feb 1983). 16; B&W. Set. **TDT**, n. 19 (Dec 1969).
        23.
Night of the Iguana.
    Belden, Ursula. Cleveland Playhouse B&W and color. Model & set. **TDT**, vol. XXX,
        n. 3 (Summer 1994). 4.
    Rasmussen, Thomas F. University of Southern California, Los Angeles: 1973. B&W.
        Model. **CSD**, 116.
    Smith, Oliver. Royale Theatre, NYC: 1961. B&W. Set. **DPT**, 156.
Night on the Old Market Place.
    _____. Moscow State Jewish Theater: 1928. B&W. Set. **TPH**, photo 415.
Night Over Taos.
    Jones, Robert Edmond. 48th Street Theatre, NYC: 1932. B&W. Rendering. **REJ**, 85.
The Nightingale.
    Schlemmer, Oskar. State Theatre, Breslau: 1929. Color. Rendering. **AST**, 156; Color.
        Rendering. **RSD**, illus. 355.
Nights of Wrath.
    Labisse, Félix. Théâtre Marigny, Paris: 1946. B&W. Set. **RSD**, illus. 496.
Nine.
    Miller, Lawrence. 46th Street Theatre, NYC: 1982. Color. Set. **MBM**, 96, 97, 104;
        B&W. Set. **TCI**, vol. 16, n. 7 (Aug/Sep 1982). 16-19. 9 photos; B&W. Set. **TCI**,
        vol. 19, n. 5 (May 1985). 17; Color. Set. **TCI**, vol. 21, n. 7 (Aug/Sep 1987).
        22; (tour): 1982. Color. Set. **TCI**, vol. 21, n. 7 (Aug/Sep 1987). 22.
The 1940's Radio Hour.
    Gropman, David. St. James Theatre, NYC: 1979. B&W. Set. **TCI**, vol. 23, n. 8 (Oct
        1989). 47.
Nixon in China.
    Lobel, Adrianne. Houston Grand Opera: 1987. B&W. Set. **TCI**, vol. 22, n. 1 (Jan
        1988). 10; produced by the Houston Grand Opera at the Edinburgh Festival: 1988.
        B&W and color. Set. **TCI**, vol. 23, n. 5 (May 1989). 43, 44. 3 photos.

No Exit.
>   Kiesler, Frederick. Biltmore Theatre, NYC: 1946. B&W. Sketches & set. **EIF**, photo
>   29-34.

No Man's Land.
>   _____. Roundabout Theatre, NYC: 1994. B&W. Set. **TCI**, vol. 28, n. 4 (Apr
>   1994). 7.

No More Heroes in Thebes.
>   Svoboda, Josef. Balustrade Theatre, Prague: 1962. B&W. Set. **SJS**, 54.

No Place to Be Somebody.
>   Kerz, Leo. Arena Stage, Washington, DC: B&W. Set. **TDT**, n. 39 (Dec 1974). front
>   cover.

No Strings.
>   Hays, David. 54th Street Theatre, NYC: 1962. Color. Set. **BWM**, 198; B&W. Set.
>   **WMC**, 226.

No Time for Sergeants.
>   Larkin, Peter. Alvin Theatre, NYC: 1955. B&W. Set. **TCI**, vol. 23, n. 1 (Jan 1989). 41;
>   B&W. Set. **SDW2**, 236.

No, No Nanette.
>   Du Bois, Raoul Pène. 46th Street Theatre, NYC: 1971. B&W. Set. **TCI**, vol. 14, n. 1
>   (Jan/Feb 1980). 20; B&W. Set. **TCI**, vol. 7, n. 4 (Sep 1973). 25; B&W. Set. **BWM**,
>   250; B&W. Set. **DPT**, 289; B&W. Set. **TCI**, vol. 5, n. 6 (Nov/Dec 1971). 10.

Nobody Loves an Albatross.
>   Kellner, Peggy J. Old Globe Theatre, San Diego: B&W. Rendering. **SDT**, 291.

Les Noces.
>   Benois, Nicola. La Scala, Milan: 1954. B&W. Rendering. **SDE**, 38. 2 photos.
>   Goncharova, Natalia. Théâtre de la Gaité-Lyrique, Paris: 1923. B&W. Rendering.
>   **AST**, 55. Sc. 4.

Noises Off.
>   Drake, Jim. Dickinson College, Carlisle, Pennsylvania: B&W. Set. **TDT**, vol. XXIX,
>   n. 5 (Fall 1993). 36.
>   Evancho, Mark. New Jersey Shakespeare Festival: B&W. Sketch. **TCI**, vol. 22, n. 1
>   (Jan 1988). 41.
>   Funicello, Ralph. Seattle Repertory Theatre: B&W. Set. **TCI**, vol. 22, n. 1 (Jan 1988).
>   40. 2 photos.
>   Layman, David. Midland Theatre, Texas: Color. Set. **TCI**, vol. 22, n. 1 (Jan 1988). 39.
>   Rothman, Gerald. Kingsboro Community College, New York: Color. Set. **TCI**, vol.
>   22, n. 1 (Jan 1988). 38.
>   _____. Theatre Tesseract, Milwaukee: B&W. Set. **TCI**, vol. 24, n. 4 (Apr 1990).
>   43.

Non si sa Come.
>   Falleni, Silvano. 1972. B&W. Set. **SIO**, 53.

Nora.
>   Falabella, John. (project): 1986. B&W. Rendering. **DDT**, 320. 6 photos.

Norma.
>   Barlow, Alan. Covent Garden, London: 1952. B&W. Set. **CGA**, 142.
>   Ceroli, Mario. La Scala, Milan: 1972-1973. B&W. Set. **SIO**, 141-143. 4 photos.
>   Elson, Charles. Metropolitan Opera, NYC: 1954. B&W. Rendering. **SDW1**, 197.
>   Prampolini, Enrico. Teatro San Carlo, Naples: 1953. B&W. Rendering. **SDE**, 137.
>   Stevens, John Wright. Houston, Cincinnati, and Philadelphia Opera Companies: B&W.
>   Rendering. **SDT**, 279.

Toms, Carl. San Diego Opera: 1976. B&W. Set. **TCI**, vol. 13, n. 3 (May/Jun 1979). 28.

The Normal Heart.

Malolepsy, John F. University of New Mexico Theatre: B&W. Set. **TDT**, vol. XXVI, n. 1 (Spring 1990). 13 of insert. 2 photos.

The Nose.

Perdziola, Robert. Santa Fe Opera: 1987. B&W. Rendering. **DDT**, 170; B&W. Set. **TCI**, vol. 21, n. 8 (Oct 1987). 19.

Not for Children.

MacLiammoir, Michael. Dublin Gate Theatre: B&W. Set. **SOW**, plate 58.

The Notebooks of Leonardo Da Vinci.

Bradley, Scott. Goodman Theatre, Chicago: 1993. Color. Set. **TCI**, vol. 28, n. 1 (Jan 1994). 6.

Notes of a Madman.

Kochergin, Edward Stepanovich. Taganka Theatre, Moscow: 1978. B&W. Model. **TCI**, vol. 11, n. 5 (Oct 1977). 41.

Nothing Sacred.

Kerr, Mary. Centre Stage, Toronto: 1988. Color. Set. **TCI**, vol. 22, n. 8 (Oct 1988). 16.
_____. Arena Stage, Washington, DC: Color. Set. **TCI**, vol. 25, n. 2 (Feb 1991). 50.

November Dictum.

Szajna, Josef. Warsaw: 1969. B&W. Set. **SDB**, 184

November Night.

Wajda, Andrej. Teatr Stary Im., Crakow: B&W. Set. **TCI**, vol. 15, n. 4 (Apr 1981). 12.

Now for Hamlet.

Akimov, Nikolai. Crooked Mirror Theatre, Leningrad: 1930. B&W. Rendering. **FCS**, plate 183; B&W. Rendering. **SDO**, 209.

Noye's Flude.

_____. St. George's Church, NYC: 1964. B&W. Set. **TCI**, vol. 6, n. 3 (May/Jun 1972). 14. 3 photos.

Nucléa.

Calder, Alexander. Théâtre National Populaire, Lyon: 1952. B&W. Set. **AST**, 217; B&W. Set. **RSD**, illus. 469.

Nuit des Quatre-Temps.

Marty, André. Théâtre du Jorat, Mézieres, Switzerland: 1912. B&W. Rendering. **TPH**, photo 399.

Numance.

Masson, André. Opéra de Paris: 1940. B&W. Set. **AST**, 200. 3 photos.

The Nutcracker.

Aronson, Boris. Kennedy Center, Washington, DC: 1976. Color. Show curtain. **TAB**, 282; Color. Sketch, model, & set. **TAB**, 283-289, 309. 15 photos.

Bailey, James. La Scala, Milan: 1957. B&W. Rendering. **SDW2**, 215.

Baird, Campbell. Oregon Ballet Theatre: 1993. Color. Rendering. **TCI**, vol. 27, n. 9 (Nov 1993). 70. 2 photos.

Lobel, Adrianne. Théâtre Royal de la Monnaie, Brussels: 1991. B&W. Model. **TCI**, vol. 25, n. 1 (Jan 1991). 6. 3 photos.

O'Hearn, Robert. San Francisco Ballet: 1968. Color. Rendering. **DPT**, between 124 & 125. Act II, sc. 2.

Sicangco, Eduardo. Kravis Center, West Palm Beach: 1992. B&W. Rendering. **DDT**, 366; Color. Set. **TCI**, vol. 27, n. 2 (Feb 1993). 6.

Ter-Arutunian, Rouben. New York State Theatre, Lincoln Center, NYC: 1964. B&W.
Set. **DPT**, 294.

-O-

O Mistress Mine.
_____. London: 1944. B&W. Set. **WTP**, 163. 3 photos.
O, Evening Star!
Chaney, Stewart. Empire Theatre, NYC: 1936. B&W. Rendering. **SOW**, plate 89.
The Obedient Daughter.
Colasanti, Veniero. Teatro La Fenice, Venice: 1949. B&W. Set. **SDE**, 66, 67; B&W.
Set. **SDW1**, 122.
Oberon.
Svoboda, Josef. Bavarian State Opera, Munich: 1968. B&W. Set. **DSL**, figure 27.1(c);
B&W. Model & set. **SJS**, 68, 69. 3 photos; B&W. Set. **SST**, 378; B&W. Set. **TCI**,
vol. 5, n. 1 (Jan/Feb 1971). 30. 2 photos.
The Octette Bridge Club.
Beatty, John Lee. Music Box Theatre, NYC: 1985. B&W. Set. **TDT**, vol. XXII, n. 4
(Winter 1987). 18.
October.
Stenberg, Georgiy A. 1919. B&W. Rendering. **RAG**, 58.
The Octoroon.
_____. C.W. Post College, Long Island, New York: 1968. B&W. Set. **TCI**, vol.
6, n. 5 (Oct 1972). 22.
The Odd Couple.
Smith, Oliver. Plymouth Theatre, NYC: 1965. B&W. Set. **TCI**, vol. 16, n. 4 (Apr
1982). 17.
Ode.
Tchelitchew, Pavel. Sarah Bernhardt Theatre, Paris: 1928. B&W. Rendering. **RSD**,
illus. 329. Ballet-Russes.
Odysseus.
Svoboda, Josef. Prague: 1982. B&W. Model. **TDT**, vol. XXIII, n. 4 (Winter 1988). 49;
B&W and color. Set. **TDT**, vol. XXIV, n. 4 (Winter 1988). front cover, 17-27. 6
photos; Laterna Magika, Prague: 1987. B&W. Set. **STS**, 18, 101, 120. 4 photos
The Odyssey.
Anemoyannis, Georges. Ellinikon Laikon Théâtron. Théâtron Calouta, Athens: 1960.
B&W. Rendering. **SDW2**, 103.
Oedipus.
Beck, Julian. Living Theatre, NYC: 1967. B&W. Set. **SDW3**, 24.
Boll, André. Opéra de Paris: 1937. B&W. Set. **SDW1**, 87.
Bonnat, Yves (Yves-Bonnat). Théâtre Romain, Lyon: 1962. B&W. Model. **SDW3**, 200.
Bragaglia, Anton Giulia. Italy: B&W. Rendering. **SCM**, 76.
Clonis, Cl. Archaion Théatron, Delphi: 1952. B&W. Set. **SDW1**, 109.
Cocteau, Jean. Théâtre des Champs-Elysées, Paris: 1952. B&W. Sketch. **SDW1**, 93.
Dulberg, Ewald. Krolloper, Berlin: 1928. B&W. Drawing. **RSD**, illus. 70.
Edwards, Norman. Greek Theatre, University of California, Berkeley: 1922. B&W.
Set. **TCS2**, plates 376, 377.
Eren, Refik. Devlet Tiyatrosu, Ankara, Turkey: 1959. B&W. Set. **SDW2**, 214.
Ezell, John. Wisconsin Union Theatre, Madison: 1968. B&W. Model. **SDW3**, 190.
Farrah, Abd'El Kader. Sadler's Wells Opera House, London: 1960. B&W. Set. **SDW2**,
90.

Fletcher, Robert. American Conservatory Theatre, San Francisco: 1970. B&W. Set. **TSY**, 41.

Gonçalves, Martin. Teatro do Estudante, Pernambuco, Brasil: 1948. B&W. Set. **SDW1**, 49.

Grey, Terence. Cambridge Festival Theatre: B&W. Set. **SDG**, 184.

Grübler, Ekkehard. State Opera, Munich: 1970. B&W. Set. **OPE**, 68.

Heeley, Desmond. Tyrone Guthrie Theatre, Minneapolis: 1972. Color. Set. **TCI**, vol. 22, n. 8 (Oct 1988). 61; B&W. Set. **TSY**, 35.

Hoffman, Vlastislav. National Theatre, Prague: 1932. B&W. Rendering. **TDT**, n. 41 (Summer 1975). 18.

Jones, Robert Edmond. Metropolitan Opera, NYC: 1930. B&W. Rendering. **REJ**, 81; B&W. Rendering & set. **SDA**, 95.

Kiesler, Frederick. NYC: 1948. B&W. Rendering. **EIF**, photo 36.

Kosinski, Jan. Warsaw Opera: 1962. B&W. Set. **RSD**, illus. 509.

Lazaridis, Stefanos. Opera North, Leeds, England: 1981. B&W. Set. **BTD**, 128.

Lowery, Nigel. Great Britain: B&W. **TDT**, vol. XXVII, n. 4 (Fall 1991). 36.

Mataré, Ewald. Deutsches Oper am Rhein, Düsseldorf-Duisburg: 1964. B&W. Model. **AST**, 234.

Mertz, Franz. Landestheater, Darmstadt: 1952. B&W. Set. **DSL**, 282; B&W. Set. **RSD**, illus. 516; B&W. **SDW1**, 73; B&W. Set. **TSY**, 42.

Mitchell, Robert D. Epidaurus Theatre, Athens: 1982. B&W. Rendering & set. **DDT**, 75. 4 photos.

Neher, Caspar. Vienna State Opera: 1958. B&W. Rendering. **RSD**, illus. 517.

Orlik, Emil. Circus Schumann, Berlin: 1910. B&W. Sketches. **MRH**, facing 32, 119. 3 photos; B&W. Rendering. **TPH**, photo 336.

Payne, Darwin Reid. B&W. Model. **SIP**, 15.

Picasso, Pablo. Picasso, Pablo. Théâtre des Champs-Elysées, Paris: 1947. B&W. Set. **AST**, 79; 1951. B&W. Set. **SDW1**, 105.

Pillartz, T.C. Hessiches Landestheater, Darmstadt: 1922. B&W. Rendering. **DIT**, plate 99; B&W. **RSD**, illus. 72; B&W. Set. **SDC**, plate 106; B&W. Set. **TPH**, photo 426.

Pizzi, Pier Luigi. 1968-1969. B&W. Rendering. **SIO**, 107.

Poppe, Catherine. California State University, Hayward: 1981. B&W. Set. **TCI**, vol. 16, n. 7 (Aug/Sep 1982). 10.

Ristic, Dusan. Opera Narodnog Pozorista, Beograd: 1967. B&W. Set. **SDW3**, 190.

Roller, Alfred. Schumann Circus, Berlin: 1910. B&W. Rendering. **RSD**, illus. 110.

Rossi, Enzo. Teatro San Carlo, Naples: 1953. B&W. Rendering. **SDE**, 146.

Sagert, Horst. Deutsches Theater, Berlin: 1966. B&W. Set. **SDW3**, 26, 27. 8 photos.

Savinio, Alberto. La Scala, Milan: 1948. B&W. Rendering. **AST**, 186; B&W. Rendering. **SDE**, 147.

Stern, Ernst. Schumann Circus, Berlin: 1910. B&W. Set. **TCS2**, plate 366.

Svoboda, Josef. Smetana Theatre, Prague: 1963. B&W. Set. **RSD**, illus. 73; B&W. Set. **SJS**, 56, 57; B&W. Set. **STS**, 61; Czechoslovakia: 1987. B&W. Model. **TDT**, vol. XXIII, n. 4 (Winter 1988). 50.

Sylbert, Paul. New York City Opera, Lincoln Center: 1959. B&W. Set. **TCI**, vol. 15, n. 7 (Aug/Sep 1981). 31.

Tsypin, George. B&W. Set. **TDT** vol. XXXI, n. 2 (Spring 1995). 16.

Wotruba, Fritz. 1964. B&W. Sketch. **AST**, 239; Burgtheater, Vienna: 1967. B&W. Sketch. **AST**, 237; B&W. Sketch, model, & set. **RSD**, illus. 464, 465-467; B&W. Set. **SDW2**, 162.

_____. Old Vic Theatre, London: 1945. B&W. Set. **TPH**, photo 447.

_____. Southern Methodist University, Dallas: 1972. B&W. Set. **TCI**, vol. 6, n. 5 (Oct 1972). 21.

Oedipus (Seneca).

Clayburg, Jim. Performing Arts Garage, NYC: 1977. B&W. Set. **TDT**, vol. XIV, n. 2 (Summer 1978). 29.

Oedipus at Colonus.

Bakst, Léon. Alexandrinsky Theatre, St. Petersburg: 1904. B&W. Set. **LBT**, 45.

Falleni, Silvano. 1961. B&W. Set. **SIO**, 48.

Oedipus Rex (see *Oedipus*).

Oedipus Tyrannos-Antigone.

Svoboda, Josef. Smetana Theatre, Prague: 1963. B&W. Set. **SDW3**, 25.

Oedipus Tyrannos (see *Oedipus*).

Oedipus, King of Thebes.

Bertin, Emile. Paris: 1919. B&W. Set. **RSD**, illus. 113.

Oedipus, Oedipus at Colonus, Antigone.

Svoboda, Josef. Theatre Behind the Gate, Prague: 1971. B&W. Set. **SDW3**, 20, 21. 5 photos; B&W. Set. **SJS**, 164. 4 photos; B&W. Set. **STS**, 20.

Oesterreichische Komödie.

Strnad, Oskar. Josefstadter Theater, Vienna: 1927. B&W. Set. **TCS2**, plate 30.

Of Mice and Men.

Flournoy, Sue. East Texas State University Playhouse, Commerce: 1985. B&W. Rendering. **BSE4**, 81.

Lee, Eugene. Trinity Square Theatre, Providence, Rhode Island: 1981. B&W. Sketches. **ASD1**, 83.

Oenslager, Donald. Music Box Theater, NYC: 1937. B&W. Set. **SOW**, plates 92, 93; B&W. Rendering. **TDO**, 79.

_____. Hartford Stage, Connecticut: Color. Set. **TCI**, vol. 21, n. 4 (Apr 1987). 34.

_____. Oklahoma State College: 1972. B&W. Set. **TCI**, vol. 6, n. 5 (Oct 1972). 20.

Of Thee I Sing.

Mielziner, Jo. Music Box Theater, NYC: 1931. B&W. Set. **BMF**, 34; B&W. Set. **BWM**, 60, 226, 227. 3 photos; B&W. Set. **HPA**, 12; B&W. Set. **MCN**, 108; B&W. Set. **RBS**, 57; B&W. Set. **SCM**, 123.

Ofeo.

Chicago Lyric Opera: 1910. B&W. Model. **TDT**, vol. XXV, n. 2 (Summer 1989). 14.

The Officer's Revolt.

Schmückle, Hans-Ulrich. Freie Volksbühne, Berlin: 1966. B&W. Model. **SDW3**, 130; B&W. Model. **RSD**, illus. 510.

Oh! Calcutta!

Tilton, James. Eden Theatre, NYC: 1972. B&W. Set. **TCI**, vol. 3, n. 6 (Nov/Dec 1969). 12-15. 5 photos; B&W. Set. **TCI**, vol. 4, n. 1 (Jan/Feb 1970). 15.

Oh! Oh!! Delphine!!!

Hann, Walter, R.C. McCleery, & Conrad Tritschler. Shaftsbury Theatre, London: 1913. B&W. Set. **MCD**, plate 95.

Oh, Hell.

Beatty, John Lee. Mitzi Newhouse Theatre, Lincoln Center, NYC: 1989. B&W. Rendering. **DDT**, 11.

Oh, Kay!

Foy, Kenneth. Richard Rodgers Theatre, NYC: 1990. Color. Rendering. **DDT**, 152c; Color. Set. **MBM**, 28, 29.

_____. C.W. Post College, Long Island, New York: 1969. B&W. Set. **TCI**, vol. 6, n. 5 (Oct 1972). 23.

Oh, Lady! Lady!

_____. Princess Theater, NYC: 1918. B&W. Set. **BWM**, 162, 163.

Oil City Symphony.

Schissler, Jeffrey. Circle in the Square Downtown, NYC: 1988. B&W. Set. **TCI**, vol. 22, n. 3 (Mar 1988). 29.

Oklahoma!

Ayers, Lemuel. St. James Theatre, NYC: 1943. B&W. Set. **BWM**, 14, 15, 186, 187. 4 photos; B&W. Set. **CSD**, 14; B&W. Set. **HOB**, 77; B&W. Set. **TCI**, vol. 20, n. 5 (May 1986). 36; B&W. Set. **TMI**, 135, 175, 236; B&W. Set. **TMT**, 152. 2 photos; Color. Set. **TMT**, plate 8; B&W. Set. **WMC**, 210, 211. 3 photos; B&W. Set. **WTP**, 228, 229. 5 photos; Theatre Royal, Drury Lane, London: 1947. B&W. Set. **BMF**, 44; B&W. Set. **MCD**, plate 194.

Bakkom, James. Chimera Theatre Company, St. Paul, Minnesota: B&W. Set. **TCI**, vol. 20, n. 5 (May 1986). 36.

Sullivan, Gary. Wagner Community College, Staten Island, NY: B&W. Set. **TCI**, vol. 20, n. 5 (May 1986). 37.

The Old Foolishness.

Jones, Robert Edmond. (project): 1942. B&W. Rendering. **REJ**, 105.

Oenslager, Donald. Windsor Theatre, NYC: 1940. Color. Rendering. **TDO**, facing 96.

Old Heads and Young Hearts.

Diss, Eileen. Chichester Festival Theatre, England: 1980. B&W. Set. **TCI**, vol. 15, n. 5 (May 1981). 13.

The Old Ladies.

Pemberton, Reece. Lyric Theatre, Hammersmith, London: 1950. B&W. Rendering. **TOP**, 75.

The Old Maid.

Chaney, Stewart. Empire Theatre, NYC: 1935. B&W. Set. **MCN**, 122; B&W. Set. **SDA**, 201.

Old Music.

Whistler, Rex. London: 1938. B&W. Set. **SOW**, plate 72.

The Old Ones.

Heinrich, Rudolf. Kammerspiele, Munich: 1973. B&W. Set. **SDW4**, illus. 348.

Old Times.

Kellogg, Marjorie Bradley. Roundabout Theatre, NYC: 1983. B&W. Set. **ASD1**, 61.

Loquasto, Santo. Mark Taper Forum, Los Angeles: 1972. B&W. Set. **ASD1**, 112; B&W. Set. **TCI**, vol. 7, n. 5 (Oct 1973). 19. 2 photos; B&W. Set. **TDT**, vol. XVII, n. 3 (Fall 1981). 21. 2 photos.

O'Brien, Timothy. Theatre Royal, Haymarket, London: 1985. Color. Set. **BTD**, 35.

The Old Woman Broods.

Krakowski, Wojciech. Teatr Wspolczesny, Warsaw: 1969. B&W. Set. **SDB**, 202; B&W. Set. **SDW3**, 141.

_____. La Mama ETC, NYC: B&W. Set. **TCI**, vol. 8, n. 2 (Mar/Apr 1974). 20.

_____. Teatr Narodowy, Poland: B&W. Set. **TCI**, vol. 15, n. 4 (Apr 1981). 14.

Oleanna.

Merritt, Michael. Orpheum Theatre, NYC: 1993. B&W. Set. **TCI**, vol. 27, n. 3 (Mar 1993). 8.

Olive chez les Negres.

Hugo, Jean. Théâtre des Champs-Elysées, Paris: 1926. B&W. Set. **TCS2**, plate 113.

Oliver!
    Kenny, Sean. Imperial Theatre, NYC: 1963. Color. Set. **BMF**, 191.
    Payne, Darwin Reid. B&W. Model. **TCM**, 84; B&W. Model. **SIP**, 54.
    Ward, Anthony. Palladium, London: 1994. Color. Set. **TCI**, vol. 29, n. 4 (Apr 1995).
        38, 39.
Olivia.
    Craven, Hawes. Lyceum Theatre, London: 1900. B&W. Rendering. **SDT**, 270.
Olympia.
    Conti, Primo. Maggio Musicale Fiorentino, Florence: 1950. B&W. Rendering. **SDE**,
        70.
Olympus on My Mind.
    Stapleton, Christopher. Mainstage Productions: 1986. B&W. Rendering. **BSE5**, 23.
Omphale.
    Reinhardt, Andreas. Theater am Schiffbauerdamm, Berlin: 1972. B&W and color. Set.
        SDW4, illus. 313-315.
On All Fours.
    Wisniak, Kazimierz. Teatr Dramatyczny, Warsaw: 1972. B&W. Set. **SDW4**, illus. 286.
On Board.
    Jon-And, John. Royal Dramatic Theatre, Stockholm: 1927. B&W. Set. **NTO**, facing
        292.
On the Air.
    Zentis, Robert. CAST Theatre, Los Angeles: 1979. B&W. Set. **TCI**, vol. 14, n. 4 (Sep
        1980). 43.
On the Bum.
    Moyer, Allen. Playwrights Horizons, NYC: 1992. Color. Set. **TCI**, vol. 27, n. 2 (Feb
        1993). 10.
On the High Seas.
    Vanek, Marian. Divadlo na Korze, Bratislava: 1969. B&W. Set. **SDW3**, 151.
On the Open Road.
    Eastman, Donald. Martinson Hall, Public Theatre, NYC: 1993. B&W. Set. **TCI**, vol.
        27, n. 5 (May 1993). 7.
On the Razzle.
    Straiges, Tony. Arena Stage, Washington, DC: 1982. B&W. Set. **ASD2**, 149.
    Toms, Carl. National Theatre (Lyttleton), London: 1981. B&W. Set. **BTD**, 78. 2
        photos.
On the Town.
    Olsen, Stephan. Goodspeed Opera House, East Haddam, Connecticut: 1993. Color.
        Rendering. **TCI**, vol. 27, n. 8 (Oct 1993). 70. 3 photos.
    Smith, Oliver. Adelphi Theatre, NYC: 1944. B&W. Set. **BWM**, 65, 90, 91; B&W. Set.
        HPA, 150; B&W. Rendering. **SDB**, 62; B&W. Set. **TCI**, vol. 16, n. 4 (Apr 1982).
        12. 2 photos; B&W. Set. **WMC**, 231. 2 photos; B&W. Set. **WTP**, 236, 237. 6
        photos.
On the Twentieth Century.
    Wagner, Robin. St. James Theatre, NYC: 1978. B&W. Sketch of backdrop & set.
        ASD1, 164, 165; B&W and color. Sketches, model, & set. **BWM**, 72-81. 25
        photos; B&W. Set. **DSL**, figure 2.7(b); B&W. Set. **HPR**, 255; B&W. Model & set.
        TCI, vol. 12, n. 4 (May/Jun 1978). 12, 13. 6 photos; Color. Set. **TCI**, vol. 18, n. 8
        (Oct 1984). 15; B&W. Set. **TCI**, vol. 14, n. 1 (Jan/Feb 1980). 18.
On the Verge or The Geography of Yearning.
    Arnone, John. John Houseman Theatre, NYC: 1987. B&W. Set. **ASD2**, 21; B&W. Set.
        DDT, 174. 4 photos.

Straiges, Tony. Center Stage, Baltimore: 1984. B&W. Set. **ASD2**, 155; Color. Set.
    TCI, vol. 20, n. 9 (Nov 1986). 18.
On the Waterfront.
    Mitchell, David. 1985. B&W. Model. **ASD1**, 125; (project): 1990. B&W. Model.
        DDT, 308. 2 photos.
    Potts, David. Cleveland Playhouse: B&W. Set. **TCI**, vol. 23, n. 1 (Jan 1989). 96.
On Your Toes.
    Brown, Zack. Virginia Theatre, NYC: 1983. B&W. Rendering. **DDT**, 154.
    Harker, Joseph & Phil Harker. Palace Theatre, London: 1937. B&W. Set. **MCD**, plate
        180.
    Mielziner, Jo. Imperial Theatre, NYC: 1936; B&W. Set. **RBS**, 127; B&W. Set. **WMC**,
        121.
Once in a Lifetime.
    Arcenas, Loy. American Repertory Theatre, Cambridge, Massachusetts: 1991. Color.
        Set. **TCI**, vol. 25, n. 3 (Mar 1991). 36, 37.
    Cirker & Robbins. Music Box Theatre, NYC: 1930. B&W. Set. **MCN**, 98.
    Napier, John. Royal Shakespeare Company, GB: 1979. B&W. Set. **BTD**, 37. 2 photos.
Once On This Island.
    Arcenas, Loy. Playwrights Horizons, NYC: 1990. B&W. Painter's elevations. **ASD2**,
        2; B&W. Model. **DDT**, 178; Color. Set. **TCI**, vol. 24, n. 8 (Oct 1990). 35.
    _____. Birmingham Repertory Theatre, England: 1994. Color. Set. **TCI**, vol. 28,
        n. 9 (Nov 1994). 5.
Once Upon a Mattress.
    Eckart, William & Jean. Phoenix and Alvin Theatres, NYC: 1959. B&W. Rendering.
        DDT, 363; B&W. Set. **TCI**, vol. 20, n. 5 (May 1986). 30. 2 photos.
    Sineath, Pat. Lexington Musical Theatre: B&W. Set. **TCI**, vol. 20, n. 5 (May 1986).
        31. 2 photos.
    Stell, W. Joseph. Richmond Professional Institute, Virginia: 1965. B&W. Set. **TCI**,
        vol. 1, n. 5 (Nov/Dec 1967). 13, 15-17. 9 photos.
Once Upon a Tailor.
    Aronson, Boris. Cort Theatre, NYC: 1955. B&W. Rendering. **TAB**, 303.
Ondine.
    Acquart, André. France: B&W. Model. **TDT**, vol. XX, n. 1 (Spring 1984). 6.
    Gröning, Karl. Deutsches Schauspielhaus, Hamburg: 1946. B&W. Rendering. **SDW1**,
        65.
    Larkin, Peter. NYC: 1954. B&W. Set. **TCI**, vol. 23, n. 1 (Jan 1989). 40.
    Tchelitchew, Pavel. Théâtre de l'Athénée, Paris: 1939. B&W and color. Rendering.
        FCS, plate 209, color plate 30; B&W. Set. **RSD**, illus. 405; B&W and color.
        Rendering of backdrop. **SDO**, 240, plate 30; B&W. Rendering. **TPH**, photo 365.
One Flew Over the Cuckoo's Nest.
    Idoine, Chris. Pacific Conservatory of the Performing Arts, Santa Maria, California:
        1978. B&W. Set. **TCI**, vol. 13, n. 3 (May/Jun 1979). 36.
    Jenkins, David. Kreeger Theatre, Arena Stage, Washington, DC: 1973. B&W. Set.
        CSD, 27.
    Larkin, Grady. 1972. B&W. Set. **TCI**, vol. 9, n. 1 (Jan/Feb 1975). 16.
    Owen, Paul. Actors Theatre of Louisville: 1974. Color. Set. **TCI**, vol. 23, n. 3 (Mar
        1989). 34.
110 in the Shade.
    Smith, Oliver. Broadhurst Theatre, NYC: 1963. B&W. Set. **BWM**, 307.

One Third of a Nation.
> Bay, Howard. Vassar College, Poughkeepsie, New York: 1937. B&W. Sketch. **SDB**, 188; B&W. Rendering. **TCI**, vol. 17, n. 2 (Feb 1983). 9; Adelphi Theatre, NYC: 1938. B&W. Set. **DPT**, 324; B&W. Set. **SDA**, 125; B&W. Set. **SDB**, 89; B&W. Set. **SIP**, 310; B&W. Set. **TCI**, vol. 17, n. 2 (Feb 1983). 9; B&W. Set. **TPH**, photo 479.

1,000 Airplanes on the Roof.
> Sirlin, Jerome. (tour): 1988. Color. Set. **TCI**, vol. 22, n. 10 (Dec 1988). 10.

1000 Franks Reward.
> Farrah, Abd'El Kader. Comédie de l'Est, Strasbourg: 1961. B&W. Set. **SDW2**, 89.

One Touch of Venus.
> Bay, Howard. Imperial Theatre, NYC: 1943. B&W. Set. **WMC**, 203.

One-Way Pendulum.
> Hugoké. Koninklijke Nederlandse Schouwburg, Antwerp: 1963. B&W. Set. **SDW3**, 139.

The Only Jealousy of Emer.
> _____. La Mama ETC, NYC: 1970. B&W. Set. **TCI**, vol. 8, n. 2 (Mar/Apr 1974). 21; B&W. Set. **TCI**, vol. 20, n. 1 (Jan 1986). 25.

An Opera for Three Butts.
> Vancura, Jan. Czechoslovakia: B&W. Model. **TDT**, vol. XX, n. 1 (Spring 1984). 8.

Die Operetta.
> Svoboda, Josef. Schiller Theatre, Berlin: 1972. B&W. Set. **STS**, 92; B&W. Set. **TDT**, vol. XII, n. 2 (Summer 1976). 31.

Ophelia and the Words.
> Bohrer, Robert. Theater am Neumarkt, Zürich: 1971. B&W. Set. **SDW4**, illus. 332, 333.

The Optimistic Tragedy.
> Bossoulaev, Anatoli. Dramatitcheski Teatr imeni Puochkina, Leningrad: 1955. B&W. Rendering. **SDW2**, 179.
> Herrmann, Karl-Ernst. Schaubühne am Halleschen Ufer, Kreuzberg, Germany: 1972. B&W. Set. **TCI**, vol. 13, n. 1 (Jan/Feb 1979). 18.
> Ryndine, Vadim. Kamerny Theater, Moscow: 1933. B&W. Rendering. **RSD**, illus. 218; B&W. Rendering & set. **RST**, 286, 287. 4 photos; B&W. Rendering. **SDW2**, 191.
> Svoboda, Josef. National Theatre, Prague: 1957. B&W. Rendering. **SJS**, 59; B&W. Set. **STS**, 24; B&W. Set. **TDT**, vol. XII, n. 2 (Summer 1976). 32.
> Vychodil, Ladislav. Bratislava: 1957. B&W. Rendering. **TDT**, vol. XV, n. 2 (Summer 1979). 11.

The Orchid.
> Craven, Hawes. Gaiety Theatre, London: 1903. B&W. Set. **MCD**, plate 49.

Orchids in the Moonlight.
> Spatz-Rabinowitz, Elaine. Loeb Drama Center, Boston: 1981. B&W. Set. **TCI**, vol. 16, n. 8 (Oct 1982). 14.

An Ordinary Woman.
> Mozuras, Vitalijus. Dramos Teatras, Panevzys: 1972. B&W. Set. **SDW4**, illus. 318.

Oreste.
> Polidori, Gianni. South America: 1951. B&W. Rendering. **SDW1**, 128.

The Oresteia.
> Nonnis, Franco. Teatro Stabile dell'Aquila, Italy: 1970. B&W. Set. **SDW3**, 17.
> Elder, Eldon. Ypsilanti Greek Festival Theatre, Michigan: 1966-1967. B&W. Rendering. **EED**, (pages not numbered).

Herbert, Jocelyn. National Theatre (Olivier), London: 1981. B&W. Rendering. **TDT**, vol. XXX, n. 5 (Fall 1994). 18; B&W. Model. **TDT**, vol. XIX, n. 1 (Spring 1983). 8.

Job, Enrico. Cooperativa Tuscolano, Spoleto, Italy: 1973. B&W. Set. **SDW4**, illus. 1-7.

Labisse, Félix. Théâtre Marigny, Paris: 1955. B&W. Set. **SDW2**, 93.

Roller, Alfred. Schumann Circus, Berlin: 1911. B&W. Set. **MRH**, facing 33; B&W. Set. **RSD**, illus. 112.

Orestes.

Chepulis, Kyle. NYC: Color. Set. **TCI**, vol. 29, n. 4 (Apr 1995). 41.

Orfeo (see also *Orpheus and Eurydice*).

Oenslager, Donald. New York City Opera: 1960. B&W. Rendering. **SDW2**, 237; Color. Rendering. **TDO**, facing 8; B&W. Rendering. **TDO**, 134; .

Ponnelle, Jean-Pierre. Opernhaus, Zurich: 1978. B&W. Set. **TCI**, vol. 12, n. 7 (Nov/Dec 1978). 4. 2 photos.

Orghast.

Lee, Eugene, Franne Lee, & Jean Monod, Festival de Shiraz, Persepolis, Iran: 1971. B&W. Set. **SDW4**, illus. 295, 296.

L'Orione.

Bury, John. Santa Fe Opera: Color. Set. **TCI**, vol. 26, n. 1 (Jan 1992). 48.

Orlando Furioso.

Bertacca, Uberto. Teatro Libero, Rome: 1970. B&W. Set. **RSD**, illus. 639-641; B&W. Set. **SDW3**, 33. 3 photos.

Imero Fiorentino Associates. Bryant Park, NYC: B&W. Set. **TCI**, vol. 5, n. 4 (Sep 1971). 7, 9, 10, 24, 25. 6 photos.

Nannini, Elena. Teatro Libero di Roma: 1970. B&W. Set. **SDW3**, 33. 3 photos.

Orlando.

McDonald, Anthony. Scottish Opera, Edinburgh: 1984. B&W and color. Set. **BTD**, 131.

Spatz-Rabinowitz, Elaine. Loeb Drama Center, Boston: 1981. B&W. Set. **TCI**, vol. 16, n. 8 (Oct 1982). 15.

L'Ormindo.

McCarry, Charles E. Pennsylvania Opera Theatre, Philadelphia: 1981. B&W. Rendering. **DDT**, 476. 2 photos.

Montresor, Beni. Chamber Opera Theatre of New York: 1982. B&W. Set. **TCI**, vol. 18, n. 3 (Mar 1984). 27.

The Orphan.

Loquasto, Santo. Public Theatre, NYC: 1973. B&W. Set. **TCI**, vol. 7, n. 5 (Oct 1973). 18.

Orphans.

Eigsti, Karl. Pittsburgh Public Theatre: 1987. B&W. Set. **DDT**, 188; Color. Set. **TCI**, vol. 21, n. 7 (Aug/Sep 1987). 35.

Orphée (see also *Orpheus and Eurydice*).

Isreal, Robert. American Repertory Theatre, Cambridge, Massachusetts: 1993. B&W. Set. **TCI**, vol. 27, n. 8 (Oct 1993). 10.

Majewski, Andrej. B&W. Model. **DSL**, figure 16.3(b); B&W. Model. **SST**, 263.

Orpheus (see *Orpheus and Eurydice*).

Orpheus and Eurydice.

Appia, Adolphe. Jacques Delcroze Institute, Hellerau: 1912-13. B&W. Set. **RSD**, illus. 67; Théâtre des Champs-Elysées, Paris: 1926. B&W. Rendering. **DOT**, 209; B&W. Rendering. **RSD**, illus. 61; B&W. Sketch. **TPH**, photo 312; B&W. Rendering.

WLA, 111; Maddermarket Theatre, Norwich, England: 1926. B&W. Rendering.
   BSE4, 47. Descent into Hell."; B&W. Rendering. **BSE4**, 47. "Elysian Fields.";
   B&W. Rendering. **TCS2**, plate 38.
Fedorovitch, Sophie. Covent Garden, London: 1953. B&W. Set. **CGA**, 141.
Golovin, Aleksandr. Marinsky Theatre, St. Petersburg: 1911. B&W. Set. **MOT**, be-
   tween 64 & 65.
Jones, Robert Edmond. Central City Opera House, Colorado: 1941. B&W. Rendering.
   BSE2, 48. "The Elysian Fields."
Kiesler, Frederick. NYC: c. 1943. B&W. Set. **EIF**, photo 26.
Lynch, Thomas. Seattle Opera: 1988. B&W. Rendering. **DDT**, 587.
Montonati, Bruno. 1951. B&W. Rendering. **SDE**, 124.
Reinking, Wilhelm. Deutsches Staatsoper, Berlin: 1961. B&W. Set. **SDW2**, 69.
Schavernoch, Hans. Komische Oper, Berlin: 1991. Color. Set. **TCI**, vol. 25, n. 2 (Feb
   1991). 12.
Tchelitchew, Pavel. Metropolitan Opera, NYC: 1935. B&W. Rendering. **MOM**, 10.
Ter-Arutunian, Rouben. Hamburg Staatsoper: 1963. B&W. Renderings. **DPT**, 106. "Le
   Tombeau D'Eurydice" and "L'Enfer"; B&W. Rendering. **DPT**, 107. "L'Elysée".
_____. Viennese State Opera, Reitschule, Salzburg: 1948. B&W. Set. **TPH**,
   photo 342.
Orpheus Descending.
Aronson, Boris. Martin Beck Theatre, NYC: 1957. B&W and color. Rendering & set.
   TAB, 116, 117. 4 photos.
Smith, Raynette Halvorsen. Stephens College, Columbia, Missouri: 1977. B&W.
   Rendering. **BSE2**, 20.
Orpheus in the Underworld.
Daydé, Bernard. Städtische Bühnen, Cologne: 1958. B&W. Model. **SDW2**, 88.
Fischer, Hans. Corsotheater, Zürich: 1938. B&W. Rendering. **SDW1**, 115.
Rée, Max. Copenhagen: 1921. Color. Rendering. **MRH**, facing 8, 130, 131. 3 photos.
Scarfe, Gerald. English National Opera, London: 1985. B&W and color. Set. **BTD**,
   140.
Svoboda, Josef. Operetta Theatre, Moscow: 1965. B&W. Rendering. **STS**, 89.
Osamene.
Svoboda, Josef. National Theatre, Prague: 1961. B&W. Set. **SDR**, 65.
Ostend Masks.
Schultz, Rudolf. Opernhaus, Hanover: 1960. B&W. Rendering. **SDW2**, 71.
L'Osteria della Pergola.
Zimelli, Umberto. Italy: 1932. B&W. Rendering. **SCM**, 77.
Otello.
Brown, Zack. Washington Opera, DC: 1992. Color. Rendering. **TCI**, vol. 27, n. 3 (Mar
   1993). 6.
Haferung, Paul. Städtische Bühnen, Essen: 1949. B&W. Rendering. **SDW1**, 66.
Howland, Gerard. San Francisco Opera: 1994-1995. Color. Model & set. **TCI**, vol. 29,
   n. 3 (Mar 1995). cover, 33, 35, 36. 4 photos.
Marussig, Guido. 1948. B&W. Rendering. **SDE**, 119.
Schneider-Siemssen, Günther. Salzburg Festival: 1968. B&W. Set. **TCI**, vol. 27, n. 3
   (Mar 1993). 28.
Skalicki, William. San Diego Opera: 1986. Color. Set. **TCI**, vol. 20, n. 8 (Oct 1986).
   22.
Svoboda, Josef. Opéra de Paris: 1976. B&W. Set. **STS**, 93; Grand Theater, Geneva:
   1980. B&W. Set. **STS**, 101; Color. Set. **TDT**, vol. XXVIII, n. 5 (Fall 1992). 9.

Zeffirelli, Franco. Metropolitan Opera, NYC: 1972. B&W and color. Set. **MOM**, 154-163. 10 photos.

_____. English National Opera, London: 1982. B&W. Set. **TCI**, vol. 19, n. 4 (Apr 1985). 21.

Othello.

Barker, Rochelle. Pennsylvania State University, University Park: 1988. B&W. Set. **TDT**, vol. XXV, n. 3 (Fall 1989). 37.

Bragdon, Claude. Shubert Theatre, NYC: 1925. B&W. Drawing. **FCS**, plate 197; B&W. Sketch. **SDO**, 225.

Exter, Alexandra. B&W. Rendering. **RAG**, 28. 2 photos.

Jones, Robert Edmond. USA: 1933. B&W. Rendering. **TAS**, 81. 2 photos; B&W. Rendering. **TAT**, plate 565; Central City Opera House, Colorado: 1934. B&W. Rendering. **BSE2**, 51; New Amsterdam Theatre, NYC: 1937. B&W. Rendering. **REJ**, 91, 93.

Klein, César. B&W. Rendering. **TCS2**, plate 252.

Mihara, Yasuhiro. Tokyo: 1969. B&W. Set. **SDW3**, 51.

Otskheli, Petr. (project), Tbilisi: 1932. B&W. Rendering. **RST**, 293.

Pirchan, Emil. State Theatre, Berlin: 1921. B&W. Rendering. **CSC**, facing 128, 130, 132,134; B&W. Rendering. **DIT**, plate 90; B&W and color. Rendering & set. **RSD**, illus. 129, 131; B&W. Rendering. **SDC**, plate 109. (Drawing by Robert Edmond Jones); Color. Rendering. **SOS**, 214, 215; B&W. Rendering. **SOW**, plate 41; B&W. Set. **TCS2**, plates 126-129. 4 photos.

Sanchez, Alberto. Teatro Universitario, Caracas: 1968. B&W. Set. **SDW3**, 51.

Schneider-Siemssen, Günther. Grosses Festspielhaus, Salzburg: 1970. B&W. Set. **TDT**, n. 27 (Dec 1971). 15.

Svoboda, Josef. National Theatre, Prague: 1959. B&W. Rendering. **SJS**, 149.

_____. Gothenburg National Theater, Sweden: B&W. Set. **TPH**, photo 392.

The Other Animals.

Bury, John. Theatre Royal, Stratford East, London: 1954. B&W. Set. **DMS**, plate 51.

The Other History of Hamlet.

Orsini, Humberto. Teatro Estudio 67, Caracas: 1967. B&W. Set. **SDW3**, 47.

Other People's Money.

Jenkins, David. Minetta Lane Theatre, NYC: 1989. B&W. Model. **DDT**, 439.

Other Worlds.

Byrne, John. Royal Court Theatre, London: 1982. B&W. Set. **BTD**, 58. 2 photos.

Otto Dix.

Svoboda, Josef. Berlin. 1993. Color. Set. **TDT**, vol. XXX, n. 5 (Fall 1994). 38.

Our Country's Good.

Barreca, Christopher. Hartford Stage, Connecticut: B&W. Set. **TCI**, vol. 25, n. 3 (Mar 1991). 5, 41.

Hartwell, Peter. Mark Taper Forum, Los Angeles: B&W. Set. **TCI**, vol. 25, n. 3 (Mar 1991). 42.

Jackness, Andrew. Repertory Theatre of St. Louis: Color. Set. **TCI**, vol. 25, n. 3 (Mar 1991). 43.

Olich, Michael. Empty Space Theatre, Seattle: 1991. Color. Set. **TCI**, vol. 26, n. 3 (Mar 1992). 37.

Our Friends of the North.

Ultz. Other Place, Stratford: B&W. Set. **TCI**, vol. 17, n. 7 (Aug/Sep 1983). 39.

Our Honor and Our Power.

Refn, Helge. Det kongelige Teater, Copenhagen: 1936. B&W. Set. **SDW1**, 60.

Our Hotheads.
    Svoboda, Josef. National Theatre, Prague: 1979. B&W. Model. **STS**, 66.
Our House.
    _____. Mobius Theatre, University of Connecticut: 1974. B&W. Set. **TSE**, 55.
Our Milan.
    Damiana, Luciano. Piccolo Teatro della Città di Milano: 1955. B&W. Rendering.
        SDW2, 125.
Our Miss Gibbs.
    Harker, Joseph. B&W. Set. **MCD**, plate 78.
Our Town.
    Orphanidis, Stelios. Kentrikon-Katerinas, Athens: 1945. B&W. Rendering. **SDW1**,
        110.
    Sovey, Raymond. Henry Miller's Theatre, NYC: 1938. B&W. Set. **MCN**, 140; B&W.
        Set. **NTO**, facing 436; B&W. Set. **SDA**, 120; B&W. Set. **SOW**, plate 100; B&W.
        Set. **WTP**, 178, 179. 4 photos.
    Straiges, Tony. Center Stage, Baltimore: 1983. B&W. Set. **ASD2**, 152.
    Mielziner, Jo. Lyceum Theatre, NYC: 1973. Color. Rendering. **CSD**, 144. Opening:
        backstage; B&W. Rendering. **DDT**, 36; B&W. Rendering. **DPT**, 51.
Out of Gas on Lover's Leap.
    Gianfrancesco, Edward. WPA Theatre, NYC: 1984. B&W. Set. **TCI**, vol. 20, n. 4 (Apr
        1986). 36.
Out of This World.
    Ayers, Lemuel. New Century Theatre, NYC: 1950. B&W. Set. **BWM**, 217; B&W. Set.
        SDA, 156; B&W. Set. **SDW1**, 191; B&W. Set. **WTP**, 48.
The Outburst at Chiozza.
    Svoboda, Josef. National Theatre, Prague: 1961. B&W. Set. **STS**, 53.
Over Here!
    Schmidt, Douglas W. Shubert Theatre, NYC: 1974. B&W. Model. **ASD1**, 137; B&W.
        Rendering. **DPT**, 62; B&W. Rendering. **DPT**, 63. "Fan" paint sketch; B&W and
        color. Rendering. **SDT**, 281, and between 152 & 153; B&W. Rendering & set.
        TCI, vol. 8, n. 3 (May/Jun 1974). 6-8. 5 photos; B&W. Rendering. **TDT**, vol.
        XVII, n. 2 (Summer 1981). 19.
Overlord.
    Bevan, Frank. 1929. B&W. Set. **SFT**, 89.
Overture.
    Wilson, Robert. Musée Galliera, Paris: 1972. B&W. Set. **RWT**, 24-27. 4 photos.
Ovidiu.
    Marosin, Mircea. Teatrul de Stat, Constanta, Romania: 1957. B&W. Set. **SDW2**, 174.
The Owners of the Keys.
    Svoboda, Josef. Tyl Theatre, Prague: 1962. B&W. Set. **RSD**, illus. 598; B&W. Set.
        SJS, 114, 115; B&W. Set. **STS**, 17.

-P-

Pacific Overtures.
    Aronson, Boris. Winter Garden Theatre, NYC: 1976. Color. Set. **BWM**, 4, 5, 326. 3
        photos; B&W. Model. **DDT**, 10; B&W. Set. **DSL**, figure 27.1(e); B&W. Set. **HPA**,
        114, 116, 117, 119. 4 photos; B&W. Set. **HPR**, 234; B&W and color. Set. **SON**,
        36, 116, 117, 119-121. 6 photos; B&W and color. Model & set. **TAB**, 20, 263, 265-
        269, 272, 275-279, 309. 26 photos; Color. Show curtain. **TAB**, 262; B&W. Set.
        TCI, vol. 18, n. 8 (Oct 1984). 14; B&W. Set. **TCI**, vol. 14, n. 1 (Jan/Feb 1980). 18;

B&W. Set. **TCI**, vol. 19, n. 5 (May 1985). 24, 25; B&W. Model & set. **TCI**, vol. 10, n. 1 (Jan/Feb 1976). 8-11. 8 photos; Color. Model. **TDT**, vol. XXV, n. 3 (Fall 1989). 8, 9; B&W. Set. **WMC**, 292; **TCI**, vol. 19, n. 5 (May 1985). 25.

Provenza, Rasario. Yale School of Drama, New Haven, Connecticut: B&W. Set. **TCI**, vol. 19, n. 5 (May 1985). 24.

I Pagliacci.

Armistead, Horace. Metropolitan Opera, NYC: 1950. B&W. Rendering. **MOM**, 14.

Bay, Howard. Carnegie Hall, NYC: 1940. B&W. Rendering. **TCI**, vol. 17, n. 2 (Feb 1983). 13.

Bregni, Paolo. 1968. B&W. Rendering. **SIO**, 18, 19. 4 photos.

Zeffirelli, Franco. Metropolitan Opera, NYC: 1970. B&W and color. Set. **MOM**, 40-55. 15 photos.

Pain.

Capek, Josef. Municipal Theatre, Prague: B&W. Set. **TCS2**, plate 274.

Paint Your Wagon.

Smith, Oliver. Shubert Theatre, NYC: 1951. B&W. Set. **SDW1**, 205; B&W. Set. **WMC**, 241.

_____. His Majesty's Theatre, London: 1953. B&W. Set. **BMF**, 103.

Painting Churches.

Landesman, Heidi. Second Stage & Lamb's Theatre, NYC: 1983. B&W. Set. **TCI**, vol. 19, n. 5 (May 1985). 18; B&W. Model & set. **ASD2**, 70, 71; B&W. Set. **DDT**, 259.

Landwehr, Hugh. Center Stage, Baltimore: 1984-1985. Color. Set. **TCI**, vol. 20, n. 2 (Feb 1986). 16.

McCarry, Charles E. Portland Stage Company, Maine: 1987. B&W. Model. **DDT**, 259; Color. Set. **TDT**, vol. XXVIII, n. 2 (Spring 1992). 7 of insert.

The Pajama Game.

Anania, Michael. New York City Opera, Lincoln Center: 1989. B&W and color. Rendering & set. **TCI**, vol. 23, n. 5 (May 1989). 26, 27. 4 photos; Paper Mill Playhouse, Milburn, New Jersey: 1989. Color. Set. **TCI**, vol. 24, n. 2 (Feb 1990). 63.

Ayers, Lemuel. St. James Theatre, NYC: 1954. B&W. Set. **BWM**, 94; B&W. Set. **HPA**, 28; B&W. Set. **HPR**, 19; B&W. Set. **SDW1**, 191.

Pal Joey.

Lynch, Thomas. Goodman Theatre, Chicago: 1988. B&W. Rendering. **DDT**, 9.

Mielziner, Jo. Ethel Barrymore Theatre, NYC: 1940. B&W. Set. **BWM**, 185; B&W. Set. **CSD**, 16; B&W. Rendering. **DTT**, 114. Pet shop; B&W. Set. **WMC**, 127, 128.

Smith, Oliver. Princes Theatre, London: 1954. B&W. Set. **MCD**, plate 207.

Pallas Athene Weeps.

Siercke, Alfred. Hamburg Staatsoper: 1955. B&W. Set. **SDW2**, 72.

Pamela's Bag.

Lanc, Émile. Rideau de Bruxelles: 1955. B&W. Set. **SDW2**, 29.

Panama Hattie.

Du Bois, Raoul Pène. 46th Street Theatre, NYC: 1940. B&W. Set. **BWM**, 211.

Panic.

Mielziner, Jo. Imperial Theatre, NYC: 1934. B&W. Rendering. **RSD**, illus. 449; B&W. Rendering. **DTT**, 83.

Pantagleize.

Elder, Eldon. Walt Whitman Hall, Brooklyn College Opera Theatre, New York: 1973. B&W. Rendering. **CSD**, 78; B&W. Rendering. **EED**, (pages not numbered). 2 photos.

Loquasto, Santo. Kreeger Theatre, Arena Stage, Washington, DC: 1971. B&W. Set.
TCI, vol. 7, n. 5 (Oct 1973). 19.
Pantomime Espagnole.
Exter, Alexandra. (project): 1926. B&W. Rendering. RSC, 37.
Papp.
Lundell, Kurt. American Place Theatre, NYC: 1968. B&W. Set. DPT, 86.
The Parachutists.
Pace. Studio des Champs-Élysées, Paris: 1963. Color. Model. SDW2, 97.
Parade.
Hockney, David. Metropolitan Opera, NYC: 1981. B&W. Set. TCI, vol. 15, n. 6 (Jun/
Jul 1981). 10. 4 photos; B&W. Set. TCI, vol. 16, n. 9 (Nov/Dec 1982). 31; B&W
and color. Model & set. MOM, 167-175. 9 photos.
Paradise Lost.
Aronson, Boris. Longacre Theatre, NYC: 1935. B&W. Set. TAB, 295.
Paradise North Side.
Serroni, J.C. SESC Anchieta, São Paulo, Brazil: 1988. B&W. Set. TCI, vol. 28, n. 4
(Apr 1994). 39.
Parallelepiped.
Prampolini, Enrico. Svandovo Theatre, Prague: 1921. B&W. Rendering. RSD, illus.
338.
Parisian Comedy.
Egg, Lois. Akademietheater, Vienna: 1960. B&W. Rendering. SDW2, 155.
La Parisienne.
_____. B&W. Set. SIP, 58.
Parisol 4 Marisol.
_____. Gramercy Arts Theatre, NYC: 1963. B&W. Set. RSD, illus. 613. Hap-
pening.
The Park.
Cairns, Tom. Crucible Theatre, Sheffield, England: 1988. B&W. Set. BTD, 48.
Park.
Phillips, Jason. Center Stage, Baltimore: B&W. Set. TCI, vol. 7, n. 3 (May/Jun 1973).
14.
Il Parlamento di Ruzzante.
Scandella, Mischa. Teatro La Fenice, Venice: 1951. B&W. Rendering. SDE, 151.
Parnell.
Chaney, Stewart. Ethel Barrymore Theatre, NYC: 1935. B&W. Set. CSD, 16.
Parsifal.
Appia, Adolphe. 1922. B&W. Sketch. RSD, illus. 62; B&W. Rendering. SOW, plate
55; B&W. Rendering. TCR, 74. Act I; WLA, 93. Act II.
Benois, Alexander. B&W. Rendering. RSC, 20.
Brazda, Jan. Royal Opera House, Stockholm: 1963. B&W. Set. SDR, 20.
Griffin, Hayden. Royal Opera House, Covent Garden, London: 1988. B&W. Sketch.
BTD, 107.
Heinrich, Rudolf. Hamburg: 1967. B&W. Set. SDB, 76.
Neher, Caspar. La Scala, Milan: 1950. B&W. Rendering. SDE, 125, 126
O'Hearn, Robert. Metropolitan Opera, NYC: 1970. B&W. Rendering. DDT, 95.
Schneider-Siemssen, Günther. Bavarian State Opera, Munich: B&W. Set. SCT, 30;
B&W. Set. TCI, vol. 11, n. 2 (Mar/Apr 1977). 18.
Sievert, Ludwig. Opera House, Frerburg, Germany: 1913. B&W. Rendering. FCS,
plate 193. Act I, sc. 1; B&W. Rendering. SDO, 221.
Urban, Joseph. Metropolitan Opera, NYC: 1919. B&W. Rendering. FCS, plate 200.

Act II, sc. 2; B&W. Rendering. **SDO**, 229; B&W. Rendering. **SOW**, plate 57;
B&W. Set. **TPH**, photo 319; Paris: B&W. Set. **SDC**, plate 47.

Wagner, Wieland. Beyreuth Festival Theatre: 1951. B&W. Set. **SDW1**, 81; 1955.
B&W. Set. **SDB**, 39; 1959. B&W. Set. **RSD**, illus. 550.

Wagner, Wolfgang. Beyreuth Festival Theatre: 1961. B&W. Set. **TDT**, n. 29 (May
1972). 7.

Wendel, Heinrich. B&W. Set. **OPE**, 46. Scene 1; B&W. Set. **OPE**, 46. Scene 6.

Wildermann, Hans. State Theatre, Breslau: B&W. **TCS2**, plate 187.

_____. Beyreuth Festival Theatre: 1977. B&W. Set. **TCI**, vol. 11, n. 2 (Mar/Apr
1977). 17.

_____. Germany: B&W. Set. **TCI**, vol. 19, n. 2 (Feb 1985). 22, 23. 3 photos.

Pas d'Acier.

Jacoulov, Georges. Sarah Bernhardt Theatre, Paris: 1927. B&W. Model. **RSD**, illus.
201. Ballet-Russes; B&W. Model. **TCS2**, plate 164.

Pas de Deux.

Francois, André. Opéra de Paris: 1960. B&W. Rendering. **SDW2**, 91.

Passion.

Lobel, Adrianne. Plymouth Theatre, NYC: 1994. Color. Model & set. **TCI**, vol. 28, n.
8 (Oct 1994). 38-41. 11 photos.

The Passion.

National Theatre (Cottesloe), England: 1980. B&W. Set. **TCI**, vol. 18, n. 1 (Jan 1984).
36.

The Passion of Dracula.

Hotopp, Michael J. Ed Sullivan Theatre, NYC: 1981. B&W. Set. **TCI**, vol. 15, n. 8
(Oct 1981). 19. Televised version.

Passion of General Franco.

Raffaëlli, Michel. State Theatre, Kassel: 1967. B&W. Set. **SDW3**, 145.

The Passion of Jonathan Wade.

Schneider-Siemssen, Günther. Seattle: 1990. Color. Set. **TCI**, vol. 27, n. 3 (Mar 1993).
27.

The Passionate Heart.

Krymov, Nikolai. Moscow Art Theatre: 1926. B&W. Sketch. **RST**, 180.

Past Tense.

Landwehr, Hugh. Hartford Stage, Connecticut: 1977. B&W. Set. **ASD2**, 88.

La Pastourelle.

Schoukhaeff, Vassily. Chauve-Souris, Moscow: B&W. Rendering. **TCS2**, plate 234.

The Path of Thunder.

Dorrer, Valeri. Teatr Opery i Baleta imeni Kirova, Leningrad: 1958. B&W. Rendering.
SDW2, 183.

The Patience of the Poor.

Fenneker, Josef. Theater am Kurfürstendamm, Berlin: 1951. B&W. Rendering. **SDW1**,
63.

Les Patineurs.

Chappell, William. Sadler's Wells Theatre, London: 1937. B&W. Rendering. **SDW1**,
174.

Patio/Porch.

Arnone, John. B&W. Set. **TCI**, vol. 15, n. 6 (Jun/Jul 1981). 29.

La Patisserie Enchantée.

Zak, Leon. B&W. Rendering. **RSC**, 59.

Patrie.

Jambon and Bailly. Comédie Française, Paris: 1901. B&W. Set. **TPH**, photo 252.

The Patriot.
> Bel Geddes, Norman. Majestic Theatre, NYC: 1928. B&W. Rendering. **SDB**, 40;
>> B&W. Rendering. **SDT**, 37.

Le Pauvre Matelot.
> Oenslager, Donald. Academy of Music, Philadelphia: 1937. B&W.
>> Rendering. **SDA**, 266; B&W. Rendering. **SOW**, plate 83; B&W. Rendering. **TDO**,
>> 75.

Payer of Promises.
> Del Neri, Cino. Teatro Brasileiro de Comédia, São Paulo: 1961. B&W. Set. **SDW2**, 35.

Peace.
> Puigserver, Fabia. Teatre Español, Madrid: 1969. B&W. Set. **SDW3**, 32; B&W. Set.
>> **TDT**, vol. XII, n. 3 (Fall 1976). 39.

The Pearl Fishers.
> O'Hearn, Robert. New York City Opera, Lincoln Center: 1980. B&W. Set. **TCI**, vol.
>> 15, n. 4 (Apr 1981). 38.

Pedro Malazarte.
> Santa Rosa, Thomas. Teatro Municipal, Rio de Janeiro: 1952. Color. Rendering.
>> **SDW1**, 41.

Peer Gynt.
> Bay, Howard. 1939. B&W. Rendering. **SDB**, 50.
> Burroughs, Robert C. University of Arizona, Tucson: 1965. Color. Rendering. **SDT**,
>> 278, and between 152 & 153.
> Conklin, John. Yale School of Drama, New Haven, Connecticut: 1966. B&W. Set.
>> **TCI**, vol. 25, n. 9 (Nov 1991). 42; B&W. Set. **TDT**, n. 9 (May 1967). front cover.
> Funicello, Ralph. Pacific Conservatory of the Performing Arts, Santa Maria, Califor-
>> nia: 1974. B&W. Set. **ASD1**, 47.
> Geyling, Remigius. Burgtheater, Vienna: 1924. B&W. Set. **TCS2**, plate 359; B&W.
>> Set. **TPH**, photo 370.
> Herrmann, Karl-Ernst. Schaubühne am Halleschen Ufer, Berlin: 1971. B&W. Sketch
>> & set. **SDW4**, illus. 163-168; B&W. Set. **TCI**, vol. 13, n. 1 (Jan/Feb 1979). 18.
> Jürgens, Helmut. State Opera, Munich: 1952. B&W. Rendering. **SDW1**, 69.
> Lee, Eugene. Trinity Square Theatre, Providence, Rhode Island: 1975. B&W. Set.
>> **TDT**, vol. XVIII, n. 2 (Summer 1982). 5.
> Lee, Ming Cho. New York Shakespeare Festival, NYC: 1969. B&W. Model. **RSD**,
>> illus. 543; B&W. **SDB**, 49; B&W. Model. **TDT**, n. 24 (Feb 1971). 7; B&W. Model.
>> **TDT**, n. 24 (Feb 1971). front cover.
> Loquasto, Santo. Tyrone Guthrie Theatre, Minneapolis: 1983. B&W. Model. **ASD1**,
>> 111; B&W. Model. **DDT**, 387; B&W. Set. **TCI**, vol. 17, n. 7 (Aug/Sep 1983). 24.
> Maximowna, Ita. Deutsches Schauspielhaus, Hamburg: 1952. B&W. Set. **SDW1**, 71.
> May, Henry. Zellerbach Playhouse, University of California, Berkeley: 1972. B&W.
>> Rendering. **CSD**, 104.
> Minks, Wilfried. Bremen: 1968. B&W. Set. **TCI**, vol. 12, n. 1 (Jan/Feb 1978). 29.
> Pemberton, Reece. Old Vic Theatre, London: 1943. B&W. Model. **SDW1**, 180.
> Raheng, Rahé. National Theatre, Bergen, Norway: 1903. B&W. Rendering. **TPH**,
>> photo 287; B&W. Set. **TPH**, photo 288.
> Sharir, David. Ha' Teatron Haleumi Habimah, Tel-Aviv: 1971. B&W. Set. **SDW3**, 84.
> Shelley, John. Festival Theater, Cambridge, England: 1932. B&W. Set. **SCM**, 31.
> Simonson, Lee. Garrick Theatre, NYC: 1923. B&W. Set. **PLT**, illus. 30, 31; B&W.
>> Sketches & set. **TAS**, 126, 127. 5 photos.
> Vanek, Joe. Gate Theatre, London: Color. Set. **TCI**, vol. 28, n. 1 (Jan 1994). 39.

Zitelli, Fabrizio. Maggio Musicale Fiorentino, Florence: 1951. B&W. Rendering. **SDE**, 169.

Peg O' My Heart.

Faulkner, Cliff. Fourth Step Theatre (South Coast Repertory), Costa Mesa, California: 1978. B&W. Set. **TCI**, vol. 14, n. 4 (Sep 1980). 36.

Law, H. Robert (studio). Cort Theatre, NYC: 1912. B&W. Set. **MCN**, 40; B&W. Set. **SDA**, 27.

Peggy.

Harker, Joseph. Gaiety Theatre, London: 1911. B&W. Set. **MCD**, plate 87.

Peggy Ann.

Laverdet, London & Marc-Henri. Daly's Theatre, London: B&W. Rendering. **DIT**, plate 66.

The Pelican.

Svoboda, Josef. Louvain: 1989. B&W. Set. **TDT**, vol. XXX, n. 5 (Fall 1994). 42.

Pelléas and Mélisande.

Bouchène, Dimitri. La Scala, Milan: 1953. B&W. Rendering. **SDE**, 50. 2 photos.

Bragaglia, Anton Giulia. Italy: B&W. Sketch. **TPH**, photo 381.

Chihuly, Dale. Seattle Opera: 1993. Color. Model. **TCI**, vol. 27, n. 5 (May 1993). 62. 2 photos.

Evans, Lloyd. New York City Opera, Lincoln Center: 1970. B&W. Rendering & set. **TCI**, vol. 7, n. 1 (Jan/Feb 1973). 12, 13. 4 photos; 1974. B&W. Set. **DPT**, 292.

Freyer, Achim. Opernhaus, Cologne: 1974. B&W. Rendering. **OPE**, 218, 220, 224, 226; State Theatre, Cologne: 1979. B&W. Set. **DSL**, figure 2.7(c&d); B&W. Set. **SST**, 46, 47.

Heeley, Desmond. Metropolitan Opera House, NYC: 1972. B&W. Set. **OPE**, 216, 223, 224.

Hugo, Valentine. Opéra-Comique, Paris: 1947. B&W. Rendering. **SDW1**, 98.

Janoir, Jean. Opéra de Lyon: 1962. B&W. Set. **SDW2**, 92.

Jones, Robert Edmond. (project): 1921. B&W. Sketch. **DFT**, plate 15. Act IV, sc. 3: the fountain; B&W. Rendering. **PST**, 388. Act IV, sc. 3; B&W. Rendering. **REJ**, 45; Color. Rendering. **RSD**, illus. 433; B&W. Rendering. **SDL**, 33; B&W. Rendering. **TCS2**, plate 204; B&W. Rendering. **TSY**, 181; (project): c. 1940. B&W. Rendering. **REJ**, 97.

Jouvet, Louis. Garrick Theatre, NYC: 1919. B&W. Set. **RSD**, illus. 103.

Klein, César. Wallner Theater, Berlin: B&W. Rendering. **TCS2**, plate 253.

Ponnelle, Jean-Pierre. Bavarian State Opera, Munich: 1973. B&W. Rendering. **OPE**, 217, 221, 222, 225, 227, 228; B&W. Set. **TCI**, vol. 12, n. 3 (Mar/Apr 1978). 16.

Robertson, Patrick. Glyndebourne Festival Opera, England: 1976. B&W. Set. **TDT**, vol. XIX, n. 3 (Fall 1983). 4.

Santa Rosa, Thomas. Teatro Municipal, Rio de Janeiro: 1944. B&W. Set. **SDW1**, 50.

Schneider-Siemssen, Günther. Staatsoper, Vienna: 1962. B&W and color. Rendering. **OPE**, 215, 221, 222, 225, 227, 229.

Sharpe, Robert Redington. (project): 1927. B&W. Rendering. **TDT**, vol. XXVII, n. 1 (Winter 1991). 19.

Strosser, Pierre. Opéra de Lyon: 1983. B&W. Set. **TCI**, vol. 20, n. 3 (Mar 1986). 12.

Svoboda, Josef. Covent Garden, London: 1969. B&W. Set. **RSD**, illus. 601; B&W. Model & set. **SJS**, 73, 74. 7 photos; B&W. Set. **TDT**, n. 20 (Feb 1970). 10. 2 photos.

Ter-Arutunian, Rouben. Spoleto Festival, Charleston, South Carolina: 1966. B&W. Set. **SDB**, 69; B&W. Set. **SDR**, 76; B&W. Set. **TCI**, vol. 5, n. 5 (Oct 1971). 11;

Teatro alla Scala, Milan: 1973. B&W. Rendering & set. **OPE**, 215, 220, 223, 226, 228.

Urban, Joseph. Metropolitan Opera, NYC: 1925. B&W. Rendering. **TCS2**, plates 224, 225.

_____. Belgian National Theatre: 1963. B&W. Set. **TSY**, 182.

_____. San Francisco Opera: 1965. B&W. Set. **TSY**, 179.

Pendulum.

Sharir, David. Lahakat Machol Bat-Sheva, Tel-Aviv: 1974. B&W. Set. **SDW4**, illus. 351, 352.

Penguin Touquet.

Foreman, Richard & Heidi Landesman. Public Theatre, NYC: 1981. B&W. Set. **TCI**, vol. 15, n. 5 (May 1981). 6.

Penny for a Song.

_____. Seattle Repertory Theatre: 1978. B&W. Set. **TCI**, vol. 16, n. 3 (Mar 1982). 52.

Penny Pantomime.

Acquart, André. Odeon Theatre, Paris: 1961. B&W. Rendering. **SDW2**, 83.

Penthesilea.

Marillier, Jacques. Théâtre Hébertot, Paris: 1955. B&W. Set. **SDW2**, 95.

Mertz, Franz. Stadtische Buhnen, Frankfurt: 1961. B&W. Model. **SDW2**, 66.

Oechslin, Ary. State Theatre, Bern: 1968. B&W. Model. **SDW3**, 81.

Sievert, Ludwig. Schauspielhaus, Frankfurt: B&W. Set. **TCS2**, plate 118.

People of Budapest.

Weyl, Roman. Volksbühne, Berlin: 1960. B&W. Set. **SDW2**, 56.

The People of Stalingrad.

Chifrine, Nisson. Tsentralnyi Teatr Sovietskoï Armii, Moscow: 1944. B&W. Rendering. **SDW2**, 180.

The People's Malakhy.

Meller, Vadim. Berezil Theatre, Ukraine: 1928. B&W. Set. **RST**, 235. 2 photos.

Perchance to Dream.

Carl, Joseph. Hippodrome, London: 1945. B&W. Set. **MCD**, plate 192.

Perelà, Uomo di Fumo.

Ghiglia, Lorenzo. 1971. B&W. Set. **SIO**, 74.

Perfect Lives (Private Parts).

_____. Almeida Theatre, London: Color. Set. **TCI**, vol. 17, n. 8 (Oct 1983). 16.

La Peri.

Mitchell, Robert D. Paris Opéra Ballet: 1967. B&W. Rendering. **DPT**, 29.

Pericles.

Conklin, John. Hartford Stage, Connecticut: 1987. B&W. Set. **DDT**, 485; B&W. Set. **SDL**, 35; B&W. Set. **SDL**, 74; Color. Set. **TCI**, vol. 25, n. 9 (Nov 1991). 38, 39.

Fievez, Jean-Marie. Théâtre National de Belgique, Brussels: 1973. B&W. Set. **SDW4**, illus. 53.

Firth, Tazeena & Timothy O'Brien. Royal Shakespeare Theatre, Stratford-upon-Avon: 1969. B&W. Set. **SDW3**, 62. 3 photos.

Griffin, Hayden. Teatro Stabile di Genova: Color. Rendering. **TCI**, vol. 19, n. 9 (Nov 1985). 20.

Hay, Richard L. Oregon Shakespeare Festival, Ashland: B&W and color. Set. **TDT**, vol. XXVI, n. 1 (Spring 1990). 10 of insert. 2 photos.

Ormerod, Nick. Cheek by Jowl, England: 1984. B&W. Set. **BTD**, 41.

Sainthill, Loudon. Shakespeare Memorial Theatre, Stratford-upon-Avon: 1958. B&W. Rendering. **SDW2**, 226.

Pericole.

Bartz, Axel & Bill Passmore. Sydney Opera House, Australia: 1993. Color. Model. **TCI**, vol. 27, n. 5 (May 1993). 12.

Periférie.

Capek, Josef. Czechoslovakia: B&W. Set. **SCM**, 81. 2 photos.

Period Dances.

Zídek, Ivo. Ustí nad Lábem, Czechoslovakia: 1980. B&W. Rendering. **TDT**, vol. XXVIII, n. 2 (Spring 1992). 36.

The Persecution and Assassination of Jean-Paul Marat as Performed by the Inmates of the Asylum of Charenton under the Direction of the Marquis de Sade. (see *Marat/ Sade.*)

The Persians.

Aronson, Boris. De Niewe Komedie of the Hague: 1962. B&W. Set. **PST**, 16.

Noya, Italo. Asociación de Artistas Aficionados, Lima: 1953. B&W. Set. **SDW2**, 164.

Vesseur, Wim. Amsterdam: 1963. B&W. Set. **SDW3**, 18.

Peter and the Wolf.

Asplin, Wilfred. Tivoli Theatre, Sydney: 1952. B&W. Set. **SDW1**, 39.

Peter Grimes.

Firth, Tazeena & Timothy O'Brien. Storan Theater, Götesborg: 1979. Color. Set. **BTD**, 101.

Moiseiwitsch, Tanya. Royal Opera House, Covent Garden, London: 1947. B&W. Set. **CGA**, 134; B&W. Model. **SDW1**, 179; Color. Rendering. **TOP**, 139; Metropolitan Opera, NYC: 1967. B&W and color. Set. **MOM**, 176-186. 6 photos.

Peter Pan.

Barnes, Robert. Florida State University, Tallahassee: B&W. Set. **TDP**, 119.

Conklin, John. Actors Theatre of Louisville: Color. Set. **TCI**, vol. 23, n. 3 (Mar 1989). 39.

Dancy, Virginia & Elmon Webb. Alliance Theatre, Atlanta: 1978. B&W. Rendering. **BSE3**, 17; B&W. Rendering. **DDT**, 42, 337.

Gros, Ernest. Empire Theatre, NYC: 1905. B&W. Set. **MCN**, 25.

Hotopp, Michael J. & James Leonard Joy. Lunt-Fontanne Theatre, NYC: 1990. B&W. Set. **TCI**, vol. 25, n. 3 (Mar 1991). 26.

Porteous, Cameron. Shaw Festival Theatre, Niagara-on-the-Lake, Canada: B&W and color. Sketch & set. **TCI**, vol. 22, n. 7 (Aug/Sep 1988). 62, 63.

Ross, Carolyn L. Denver Center, Colorado: B&W and color. Rendering & set. **TDT**, vol. XXVI, n. 1 (Spring 1990). 16 of insert.

———, LaGrange College, Georgia: 1981. B&W. Set. **TCI**, vol. 18, n. 5 (May 1984). 24.

La Petite Catherine.

Larionov, Michel. Paris: B&W. Rendering. **SCM**, 45.

The Petrified Forest.

Fritzsche, Max. Schauspielhaus, Bochum: 1954. B&W. Rendering. **SDW1**, 64.

Kellner, Peggy J. University of Arizona, Tucson: B&W. Model. **SDT**, 286; B&W. Model. **TDP**, 13.

Petrouchka.

Benois, Alexander. Théâtre du Chatelet, Paris: 1911. B&W. Rendering. **RSD**, illus. 41; B&W. Rendering. **SDE**, 32; B&W. Rendering. **SDR**, 26; 1925. B&W. Rendering. **RSD**, illus. 43. Ballet-Russes; Vienna State Opera: 1956. B&W. Rendering. **RSC**, 22. 2 photos.

Doboujinsky, Mstislav. Loukomoriye Theater, Moscow: 1908. B&W. Rendering. **RSD**, illus. 26.

Soudeikine, Serge. Metropolitan Opera, NYC: 1925. B&W. Rendering. **TCS2**, plate 237.

Tichy. Prague: 1948. B&W. Rendering. **SDB**, 71.

Pfarr Pedr.

Neher, Caspar. Darmstadt, Germany: 1941. B&W. Set. **CBM**, 90.

Phaedra.

Aronson, Boris. University of Kansas City: 1958. B&W. Set. **PST**, 234.

Bakst, Léon. Théâtre National de l'Opera, Paris: 1923. B&W and color. Rendering. **LBT**, 226, 227. 4 photos.

Bauer-Ecsy, Leni. State Theatre, Stuttgart: 1951. B&W. Rendering. **SDW1**, 62.

Bertin, Emile. Théâtre Montparnasse, Paris: 1940. B&W. Set. **RSD**, illus. 417.

Cocteau, Jean. Opéra de Paris: 1950. B&W. Sketch & set. **AST**, 121. 4 photos.

Joukovski, Arik & Elisabeth de Wée. Forest National, Brussels. 1974. Color. Set. **SDW4**, illus. 80-85.

Nemes, Erik. Hungary: c.1929. B&W. Rendering. **SCM**, 75.

Vesnin, Alexandr A. Kamerny Theater, Moscow: 1921/1923. Color. Model. **RSD**, illus. 156; B&W. Sketch & set. **TCT**, plates 27, 29. 3 photos; B&W. Rendering. **RAG**, 73; B&W. Model & set. **RST**, 150. 2 photos; B&W. Set. **TCS2**, plate 151.

_____. Kamerny Theatre, Moscow: B&W. Set. **SDC**, plate 114.

_____. Théâtre Montparnasse, Paris: 1948. B&W. Set. **TPH**, photo 364.

_____. University of Kansas City: 1958. B&W. Set. **TSY**, 101.

A Phantasmagoria Historia of D. Johan Fausten Magister, PhD, MD, DD, DL, etc.

Dunham, Clarke. Truck and Warehouse Theatre, NYC: 1973. B&W. Set. **DDT**, 85.

Phantom.

Anania, Michael. Paper Mill Playhouse, Milburn, New Jersey: 1993. Color. Model. **TCI**, vol. 27, n. 8 (Oct 1993). 8.

Foser, Bill. Candlelight Dinner Playhouse, Chicago: 1992. B&W. Set. **TCI**, vol. 26, n. 7 (Aug/Sep 1992). 12.

The Phantom of the Opera.

Björnson, Maria. Her Majesty's Theatre, London: 1986. B&W and color. Set. **ALW**, 186-188, 190, 191. 8 photos; B&W and color. Sketches & set. **BTD**, 156, 157. 3 photos; Color. **DDT**, 24c; B&W. Set. **HPR**, 351, 357; Color. Set. **TCI**, vol. 21, n. 1 (Jan 1987). 10; Color. Set. **TCI**, vol. 22, n. 2 (Feb 1988). 32-35. 5 photos; Majestic Theatre, NYC: 1988. B&W and color. Set. **MBM**, 6, 68, 70; Color. Set. **TCI**, vol. 23, n. 2 (Feb 1989). 16; B&W. Model. **TCI**, vol. 22, n. 2 (Feb 1988). 36; Tokyo: Color. Set. **ALW**, 187.

The Philadelphia Story.

Hird, Thomas C. 1977. B&W. Set. **BSE1**, 32.

Jones, Robert Edmond. Shubert Theatre, NYC: 1939. B&W. Set. **MCN**, 145; B&W. Rendering. **REJ**, 95; B&W. Set. **SDA**, 203.

Philadelphia, Here I Come!

Beatty, John Lee. Professional Theatre in Residence, Queens, NY: 1975. B&W. Rendering. **DPT**, 333.

Kurtz, Kenneth. Ring Theatre, University of Miami, Florida: B&W. Set. **TCI**, vol. 7, n. 6 (Nov/Dec 1973). 21. 3 photos.

The Philanthropist.

Landwehr, Hugh. Long Wharf Theatre, New Haven, Connecticut: 1992. Color. Set. **TCI**, vol. 26, n. 3 (Mar 1992). 19.

Philoctetes.

Rose, Jürgen. Residenz Theater, Munich: 1968. B&W. Set. **SDW3**, 19.

Turina, Drago. Teatar I TD, Zagreb, Yugoslavia: 1972. B&W. Set. **SDW4**, illus. 12.

Phoebe's Got 3 Sisters.
　　＿＿＿＿＿. Color. Set. **TCI**, vol. 25, n. 1 (Jan 1991). 47.
A Phoenix Too Frequent.
　　＿＿＿＿＿. Mummers Theatre, Oklahoma City: B&W. Set. **TCI**, vol. 5, n. 3 (May/
　　Jun 1971). 9.
A Photograph. ．
　　Davis, Collis & David Mitchell. 1978. B&W. Model. **TCI**, vol. 13, n. 1 (Jan/Feb
　　1979). 33.
The Photographer.
　　＿＿＿＿＿. Color. Set. **TCI**, vol. 24, n. 8 (Oct 1990). 41.
The Physicists.
　　Bury, John. Royal Shakespeare Company, Aldwych Theatre, London: 1963. B&W.
　　Set. **SIP**, 65.
　　Straiges, Tony. McCarter Theatre Company: B&W. Model. **TCI**, vol. 16, n. 2 (Feb
　　1982). 18.
Pickwick.
　　Kenny, Sean. 46th Street Theatre, NYC. 1965. B&W. Set. **TCI**, vol. 2, n. 1 (Jan/Feb
　　1968). 32.
The Pickwick Club.
　　Viliams, Piotr. Moscow Art Theatre: 1934. B&W. Set. **SDW2**, 199.
Picnic.
　　Conklin, John. Actors Theatre of Louisville: 1993. Color. Set. **TCI**, vol. 27, n. 4 (Apr
　　1993). 11.
　　Donnelly, Mark. Cerritos College, California: B&W. Set. **SDT**, 287.
　　Mielziner, Jo. Music Box Theatre, NYC: 1953. B&W. Set. **WTP**, 209.
Picnic in the Field.
　　Grübler, Ekkehard. Stadtische Buhnen, Frankfurt: 1959. B&W. Rendering. **SDW2**, 60.
The Picture of Dorian Gray.
　　MacNeil. Ian. Lyric Theatre, Hammersmith, London: 1994. Color. Set. **TCI**, vol. 29, n.
　　2 (Feb 1995). 7.
Pictures at an Exhibition.
　　Aronson, Boris. International Theatre, Columbus Circle, NYC: 1944. B&W and color.
　　Rendering & set. **TAB**, 82, 299.
　　Kandinsky, Vassily. Friedrich-Theatre, Dessau: 1928. Color. Rendering. **AST**, 141;
　　Color. Rendering. **RSD**, illus. 330-332.
Pierre Pathelin.
　　Simonson, Lee. NYC: 1916. B&W. Set. **TPH**, photo 457.
Pierrot Funeste.
　　Bragaglia, Anton Giulia. Italy: B&W. Rendering. **SCM**, 76.
La Pietra del Paragone.
　　Chiari, Mario. 1958-1959. B&W. Set. **SIO**, 28, 29. 3 photos.
The Pilgrim of Love.
　　Hammond, Aubrey. Great Britain: 1925. B&W. Rendering. **DIT**, plate 7.
Pillar of Fire.
　　Mielziner, Jo. USA: 1942. Color. Rendering. **DTT**, 118; B&W. Rendering. **DTT**, 119;
　　Color. Rendering. **SDA**, 284.
Pillars of the Community.
　　Funicello, Ralph. American Conservatory Theatre, San Francisco: 1974. B&W. Set.
　　ASD1, 51.

Pinkville.
>   Roth, Wolfgang. American Place Theatre, NYC: 1971. B&W. Rendering. **CSD**, 121;
>   B&W. Set. **TCI**, vol. 6, n. 3 (May/Jun 1972). 21.

Pinocchio.
>   Delu, Dahl. Minneapolis Children's Theatre: 1979. B&W. Rendering. **BSE1**, 22.

Pins and Needles.
>   Syrjala, Sointu. Labor Stage, NYC: 1937. B&W. Set. **RBS**, 152, 153. 4 photos.

Pinwheel.
>   Oenslager, Donald. Neighborhood Playhouse, NYC: 1927. B&W. Rendering. **SDA**,
>   274; B&W. Rendering. **SDB**, 23; B&W. Set. **TCS2**, plate 181; B&W. Rendering.
>   **TDO**, 31.

Pipe Dream.
>   Mielziner, Jo. Shubert Theatre, NYC: 1955. B&W. Rendering. **DPT**, 54; B&W. Ren-
>   dering. **DTT**, 191. Lab scene; B&W. Rendering. **SDA**, 154; B&W. Set. **WMC**,
>   221.

Pippa Dances.
>   _____. Lessing Theatre, Berlin: 1906. B&W. Set. **TPH**, photo 292.

Pippin.
>   Walton, Tony. Imperial Theatre, NYC: 1972. Color. Set. **BWM**, 315; B&W. Render-
>   ing. **CSD**, 139; B&W. Rendering & set. **DDT**, 55. 5 photos; B&W. Set. **DPT**, 65;
>   B&W. Set. **TCI**, vol. 14, n. 1 (Jan/Feb 1980). 18; B&W. Set. **TCI**, vol. 7, n. 4 (Sep
>   1973). 25; Color. Set. **TCI**, vol. 28, n. 3 (Mar 1994). 33; B&W. Set. **TCI**, vol. 11,
>   n. 3 (May/Jun 1977). 9.

The Pirate.
>   Ayers, Lemuel. Theatre Guild, NYC: 1942. B&W. Set. **SDA**, 260, 261. 5 photos;
>   B&W. Rendering. **SOW**, plate 105; B&W. Set. **SDB**, 37.

The Pirates of Penzance.
>   Leach, Wilford & Bob Shaw. Delacorte Theatre, NYC: 1980. B&W. Set. **MBM**, 26;
>   B&W. Set. **TCI**, vol. 15, n. 6 (Jun/Jul 1981). 12, 13; B&W. Set. **TCI**, vol. 20, n. 1
>   (Jan 1986). 23.

La Pisanella.
>   Bakst, Léon. Théâtre du Châtelet, Paris: 1913. B&W and color. Rendering & set. **LBT**,
>   163-165. 5 photos; Color. Rendering. **TCS2**, color plate 5.

Plain and Fancy.
>   _____. Equity Library Theatre, NYC: B&W. Set. **TCI**, vol. 15, n. 6 (Jun/Jul
>   1981). 25.

The Plantagenets.
>   Crowley, Bob. Royal Shakespeare Company, Barbican Centre, London: 1988. Color.
>   Sketches. **BTD**, 55. 16 drawings; B&W. Sketches. **TCI**, vol. 23, n. 4 (Apr 1989).
>   112. 6 photos.

Platée.
>   Montresor, Beni. Opéra de Paris: B&W. Set. **TCI**, vol. 16, n. 5 (May 1982). 16.

Platonov.
>   Guglielminetti, Eugenio. Teatro Stabile, Torino: 1958. B&W. Set. **SDW2**, 126.
>   Pignon, Edouard. Théâtre National Populaire, Lyon: 1956. B&W. **SDW2**, 99.
>   Vychodil, Ladislav. B&W. Model. **TDT**, vol. XXIII, n. 4 (Winter 1988). 28.

Play Mas.
>   Lobel, Adrianne. Goodman Theatre, Chicago: 1981. B&W. Set. **ASD2**, 109.

Play Memory.
>   Dunham, Clarke. Longacre Theatre, NYC: 1984. Color. Set. **DDT**, 312c.

The Play of Daniel.

_____. Cloisters Museum, NYC: B&W. Set. **TCI**, vol. 6, n. 3 (May/Jun 1972). 16.

The Play of Love and Death.

Vychodil, Ladislav. Prague: 1964. B&W. Set. **TDT**, vol. XV, n. 2 (Summer 1979). 15; Bratislava: 1973. B&W. Rendering. **TDT**, vol. XV, n. 2 (Summer 1979). 16.

The Play of Robin and Marion.

Kiesler, Frederick. NYC: 1952. B&W. Sketch. **EIF**, photo 42.

Play Strindberg.

Navon, Arieh. Teatron Ha Cameri, Tel Aviv: 1971. B&W. Rendering. **SDW4**, illus. 180.

The Play's the Thing.

Anderson, Cletus. Pittsburgh Public Theatre: Color. Set. **TCI**, vol. 21, n. 7 (Aug/Sep 1987). 32.

Easley, Holmes. Roundabout Theatre, NYC: 1973. B&W. Set. **TCI**, vol. 8, n. 2 (Mar/Apr 1974). 13.

Messel, Oliver. Booth Theatre, NYC: 1948. B&W. Set. **WTP**, 125.

_____. Henry Miller's Theatre, NYC: 1926. B&W. Set. **MCN**, 77.

The Playboy of the Western World.

Chagall, Marc. (not produced): 1920-1921. B&W. Rendering. **RSD**, illus. 208.

Donnelly, Mark. South Coast Repertory Theatre, Costa Mesa, California: 1983. B&W. Model. **BSE5**, 35.

Mostafa, Ramzi. Loeb Drama Center, Harvard University: 1962. B&W. Set. **SFT**, 14.

Palkovic, Tim. State University of New York, Plattsburgh: B&W. Rendering. **TDT**, vol. XXX, n. 3 (Summer 1994). 41; B&W. Sketch. **TDT**, vol. XX, n. 3 (Fall 1984). 7.

Slayton, Kati. Loretto-Hilton Center, Webster Groves, Missouri: 1974. B&W. Model & set. **TCI**, vol. 9, n. 1 (Jan/Feb 1975). 15.

Van Lint, Louis. Spectacles du Palais, Brussels: 1944. B&W. Set. **SDW1**, 48.

_____. Dennis, Massachusetts: 1946. B&W. Set. **WTP**, 154, 155. 6 photos.

Plenty.

Griffin, Hayden. National Theatre, London: 1978. B&W. Set. **TCI**, vol. 19, n. 9 (Nov 1985). 25.

Gunter, John. Plymouth Theatre, NYC: 1983. Color. Set. **TCI**, vol. 22, n. 9 (Nov 1988). 49.

The Plough and the Stars.

Dancy, Virginia & Elmon Webb. Syracuse Stage, New York: 1977. B&W. Model & set. **DDT**, 210, 211. 5 photos.

Feiner, Harry. Brandeis University, Waltham, Massachusetts: 1977. B&W. Rendering. **BSE2**, 12.

_____. Hudson Theatre, NYC: 1927. B&W. Set. **MCN**, 86.

Pluck a Star.

Deckwitz, Franz. Amsterdamsche Vrouwelijke Studenten Vereeniging. Stadsschouwburg, Amsterdam: 1957. Color. Rendering. **SDW2**, 137.

Plutus.

Moralis, Yannis. Théâtron Technis, Athens: 1957. B&W. Rendering. **SDW2**, 104.

The Poem of the Axe.

Shlepyanov, Ilya. Theatre of the Revolution, Moscow: 1931. B&W. Set. **RST**, 276, 277. 3 photos.

The Poem of the Storm.

Vilks, Girts. Dailes Teatri, Riga: 1960. B&W. Rendering. **SDW2**, 200. 2 photos.

Poison.
> Levin, Mark. Leningrad Academic Theatre of Drama: 1925. B&W. Set. **RST**, 184. 2
> photos.

The Police.
> Kosinski, Jan. Teatr Dramatyczny, Warsaw: 1958. B&W. Set. **SDW2**, 167.

Polly.
> Taylor, Robert U. Chelsea Theatre Center, Brooklyn, New York: B&W. Drop. **TCI**,
> vol. 11, n. 1 (Jan/Feb 1977). 24, 25. 8 photos.

Polytope de Cluny.
> Xenakis, Iannis. Musee de Cluny, Paris: 1972. B&W. Set. **RSD**, illus. 600.

The Poor Bride.
> Dmitriev, Vladimir. Moscow Art Theatre: 1929. B&W. Rendering. **SDW2**, 182.

The Poor Sailor.
> Kiesler, Frederick. NYC: 1948. B&W. Set. **EIF**, photo 35.

Poppea's Coronation.
> Clerici, Fabrizio. La Fenice, Venice: 1949. B&W. Rendering. **SDW1**, 121.

Poppie Nongena.
> Ringbom, Jon. St. Clement's Church, NYC: 1983. B&W. Set. **TCI**, vol. 17, n. 4 (Apr
> 1983). 10.

Poppy God.
> Wenger, John. Hudson Theatre, NYC: 1921. B&W. Set. **DIT**, plate 115.

Porgy.
> Throckmorton, Cleon. Guild Theatre, NYC: 1927. B&W. Set. **DSL**, figure 27.1(b;
> B&W. Set. **MCN**, 85; B&W. Set. **SCM**, 132; B&W. Set. **SOW**, plate 96.

Porgy and Bess.
> Gunter, John. Glyndebourne Festival Opera, England: 1986. B&W. Set. **BTD**, 120.
> Jankus, Yozak. Russia: 1967. B&W and color. Rendering. **FCS**, plate 184, color plate
> 24; B&W and color. Rendering. **SDO**, 210, plate 24.
> O'Hearn, Robert. Bregenz Festival, Austria: 1971. B&W. Set. **TCI**, vol. 11, n. 2 (Mar/
> Apr 1977). 22; B&W and color. Set. **MOM**, 188-199. 9 photos.
> Randolph, Robert. Uris Theatre, NYC: 1976. Color. Set. **BWM**, 232, 233; Houston
> Grand Opera: 1976. B&W. Set. **TCI**, vol. 11, n. 1 (Jan/Feb 1977). 8.
> Roth, Wolfgang. Ziegfeld Theatre, NYC: c.1953. B&W. Set. **WTP**, 210, 211. 3 photos.
> Schmidt, Douglas W. Arie Crown Theatre, Chicago: 1983. B&W. Rendering. **ASD1**,
> frontis; B&W. Rendering & model. **DDT**, 145, 160. 4 photo; B&W. Set. **TCI**, vol.
> 17, n. 7 (Aug/Sep 1983). 12.
> Soudeikine, Serge. Alvin Theater, NYC: 1935. B&W. Set. **BMF**, 40; B&W. Set.
> **BWM**, 231; B&W. Set. **RBS**, 116, 117. 3 photos; B&W. Set. **TMT**, 132, 134;
> B&W. Set. **WMC**, 97, 98.

La Porta Fedele.
> Recchi, Ugo. Teatro delle Novità, Bergamo: 1953. B&W. Rendering. **SDE**, 143.

The Possessed.
> Wajda, Andrej. Stary Teatr, Cracow: 1971. B&W. Set. **SDW4**, illus. 145.

Postcard from Morocco.
> Isackes, Richard M. Illinois Opera Theatre, Krannert Center, Urbana: 1985. Color.
> Rendering. **BSE5**, 14; Color. Rendering. **SCT**, between 152 & 153.

The Pot.
> Herrmann, Karl-Ernst. Schaubühne am Halleschen Ufer, Berlin: 1973. B&W. Set.
> **SDW4**, illus. 143, 144.

A Pound of Flesh.
Serebrovskij, Vladimir. Teatr imeni Ermolovoj, Moscow: 1965. B&W. Model. **SDW3,** 139.
Poverty and Nobility.
Navon, Arieh. Cameri, Tel Aviv: 1960. B&W. Set. **SDW2,** 120.
Power and Truth.
Ciulei, Liviu. Teatrul Lucia Sturdza Bulandra, Bucharest: 1973. B&W. Set. **SDW4,** illus. 331.
The Power of Darkness.
Simonson, Lee. 1919. B&W. Set. **PLT,** illus. 4, 5.
_____. B&W. Set. **MRH,** facing 59.
Pravda.
Brill, Robert. Oregon Shakespeare Festival, Ashland: 1995. Color. Set. **TCI,** vol. 29, n. 5 (May 1995). 8.
Griffin, Hayden. National Theatre (Olivier), London: 1985. B&W. Set. **BTD,** 89.
Pre-Paradise Sorry Now.
Brill, Robert. Sledgehammer Theatre, San Diego: Color. Set. **TCI,** vol. 26, n. 1 (Jan 1992). 36.
Prelude to a Kiss.
Arcenas, Loy. South Coast Repertory Theatre, Costa Mesa, California: 1988. B&W. Set. **ASD2,** 10; Helen Hayes Theatre, NYC: 1990. B&W. Set. **ASD2,** 9.
Les Présages.
Masson, André. Théátre de Monte Carlo: 1933. B&W. Rendering. **SDR,** 28.
Present Laughter.
Oenslager, Donald. Plymouth Theatre, NYC: 1946. B&W. Set. **SDA,** 205.
The Pretenders.
Cloffe. Royal Opera House, Stockholm. 1966. B&W. Set. **SDR,** 66.
Craig, Edward Gordon. 1926. B&W. Rendering. **COT,** 145, 146; B&W. Rendering. **DOT,** 208; B&W. Sketch. **TPH,** photo 323.
Prettybelle.
_____. c.1970. B&W. Set. **BWM,** 348.
Le Preziose Ridicole.
Jones, Robert Edmond. Metropolitan Opera, NYC: 1930. B&W. Rendering. **REJ,** 79.
The Price.
Aronson, Boris. Morosco Theatre, NYC: 1968. B&W. Model & set. **TAB,** 164, 165, 308. 4 photos.
Mitchell, David. Harold Clurman Theatre, NYC: 1979. B&W. Set. **TCI,** vol. 13, n. 4 (Sep 1979). 50.
Scandella, Mischa. 1969-1970. B&W. Rendering. **SIO,** 130.
Pride and Prejudice.
Mielziner, Jo. Music Box Theatre, NYC: 1935. B&W. Set. **SFT,** 258, 259. 3 photos.
Whistler, Rex. St. James Theatre, London: 1936. B&W. Rendering. **SDW1,** 187.
Il Prigioniero.
Polidori, Gianni. 1964. B&W. Rendering. **SIO,** 116.
Prince Igor.
Fedorovsky, Feodor. Bolshoi Theatre, Moscow: 1934. B&W. Rendering. **SDW2,** 184.
Lee, Ming Cho. New York City Opera, Lincoln Center: B&W. Set. **TCI,** vol. 7, n. 1 (Jan/Feb 1973). 18.
Suominen, Paul. Suomen Kansallisoppera, Helsinki. 1959. B&W. Rendering. **SDW2,** 205.

Prince of Homburg.
    Thomas, Christopher. 1977. B&W. Set. **TCI**, vol. 11, n. 5 (Oct 1977). 16. 2 photos.
    Sturm, Eduard. Schauspielhaus, Düsseldorf: 1925. B&W. Set. **TCS2**, plate 133.
The Prince of Pilsen.
    Burridge, Walter. Shaftsbury Theatre, London: 1904. B&W. Set. **MCD**, plate 50.
Princess Brambilla.
    Jacoulov, Georges. Kamerny Theater, Moscow: 1920. Color. Model. **RSD**, illus. 176;
        Color. Rendering & set. **RST**, 144, 145, 147.
Princess Charming.
    Tritschler, Conrad. Palace Theatre, London: 1926. B&W. Set. **MCD**, plate 143.
Princess Ivona.
    Brotherston, Lez. Actors Touring Company, England: 1988. B&W. Set. **BTD**, 88.
The Prisoner.
    Boland, Bridgette. Centenary College, Louisiana: 1963. B&W. Rendering. **MOR**, 4.
    Kiesler, Frederick. Opera Theatre, NYC: 1951. B&W. Sketch. **EIF**, photo 41; B&W.
        Rendering. **SDE**, 111.
Private Lives.
    Calthrop, Gladys. Phoenix Theatre, London: 1930. B&W. Sketch. **TOP**, 71.
    Elson, Charles. Harris Theatre, Chicago:: 1947. B&W. Set. **WTP**, 161.
A Private View.
    Kellogg, Marjorie Bradley. New York Shakespeare Festival, NYC: 1983. B&W.
        Model. **ASD1**, 64.
Privates on Parade.
    Sherman, Loren. Roundabout Theatre, NYC: 1989. B&W. Set. **TCI**, vol. 23, n. 8 (Oct
        1989). 11.
Processional.
    Gorelik, Mordecai. Garrick Theatre, NYC: 1925. B&W. Rendering. **TPH**, photo 468.
Processo a Gesù.
    Guglielminetti, Eugenio. 1968. B&W. Set. **SIO**, 77.
Processo per Magia.
    Falleni, Silvano. 1967. B&W. Set. **SIO**, 51.
The Prodigal Son.
    Rouault, Georges. Sarah Bernhardt Theatre, Paris: 1929. B&W. Rendering. **AST**, 112.
        2 photos; B&W. Rendering. **RSD**, illus. 298, 299. Ballet-Russes.
        _____. B&W. Set. **MRH**, facing 220.
A Profitable Post.
    Shestakov, Victor. Theatre of the Revolution, Moscow: 1923. B&W. Set. **RST**, 176,
        177.
Proibito da Chi?
    Scandella, Mischa. 1970-1971. B&W. Rendering. **SIO**, 131. 2 photos.
Promenade.
        _____. NYC: B&W. Set. **TCI**, vol. 4, n. 3 (May/Jun 1970). 32.
Prometheus.
    Appia, Adolphe. 1910. B&W. Rendering. **WLA**, 105, 107. Acts I & III.
    Rajkai, György. Körszinház. Hungary: 1961. B&W. Model. **SDW2**, 142.
    Svoboda, Josef. Bavarian State Opera, Munich: 1968. B&W. Set. **RSD**, illus. 608;
        B&W. Set. **SDW3**, 196; B&W. Model & set. **SJS**, 107. 4 photos; B&W. Set. **STS**,
        2, 75; B&W. Set. **TCI**, vol. 5, n. 1 (Jan/Feb 1971). 28, 29. 3 photos; B&W. Set.
        TCI, vol. 4, n. 1 (Jan/Feb 1970). 35; B&W. Set. **TDT**, vol. XXIV, n. 4 (Winter
        1988). 12; B&W. Set. **TDT**, n. 20 (Feb 1970). 8. 2 photos; La Scala, Milan: 1972.
        B&W. Set. **TDT**, vol. XII, n. 2 (Summer 1976). 16.

Prometheus Bound.
    Camurati, Jacques. Théâtre du Tertre, Paris: 1959. B&W. Set. **SDW2**, 87.
    Decamp, Olivier. Comédie Française, Festival de Lyon-Charbonniere: 1954. B&W.
        Set. **SDW2**, 88.
    Oenslager, Donald. Yale School of Drama, New Haven, Connecticut: 1939. B&W.
        Rendering. **SDL**, 38. 4 photos; B&W. Rendering. **TDO**, 94, 95; (project): B&W.
        Rendering. **STN**, 31-41. 6 photos.
    _____. Stanford Repertory Theatre, California: 1966. B&W. Set. **TSY**, 26;
        B&W. Set. **TDT**, n. 12 (Feb 1968). 14.
The Promise.
    Moukosseeva, Margarita. Tsentralnyj Teatr Sovietskoj Armii, Moscow: 1965. B&W.
        Rendering. **SDW3**, 122.
Promises, Promises.
    Wagner, Robin. Shubert Theatre, NYC: 1968. B&W. Set. **BWM**, 312; B&W. Set. **TCI**,
        vol. 3, n. 3 (May/Jun 1969). cover, 7-9. 3 photos; B&W. Set. **WMC**, 352.
Propaganda plays.
    Otto, Teo. Kassel: 1926. B&W. Set. **RSD**, illus. 228, 229.
Le Prophète.
    Urban, Joseph. Metropolitan Opera, NYC: B&W. Rendering. **TCS2**, plate 189.
    Wexler, Peter. Metropolitan Opera, NYC: 1977. B&W. Set. **TCI**, vol. 11, n. 4 (Sep
        1977). 14.
Proserpine and the Stranger.
    Vanarelli, Mario. Teatro de Verano, Buenos Aires: 1957. B&W. Rendering. **SDW2**, 26.
Proteus.
    Coutaud, Lucien. Comédie de Paris: 1955. B&W. Rendering. **SDW2**, 87.
    Creuz, Serge. Maison de la Culture, Rennes: 1970. Color. Set. **SDW3**, 94. 2 photos.
The Provocation.
    Calder, Alexander. Comédie de Bourges: 1963. B&W. Model. **AST**, 217; B&W. **RSD**,
        illus. 470.
Prúy Tiresiovy.
    Mrkvicka, Teige & Zelenka. Prague: 1926. B&W. Set. **SDB**, 186.
Psyche.
    Craig, Edward Gordon. Theatersammlung, Vienna: 1907. B&W. Rendering. **OAT**,
        176; B&W. Rendering. **RSD**, illus. 83.
Public Chant Before Two Electric Chairs.
    Monloup, Hubert. T.N.P., Paris: 1961. B&W and color. Rendering & set. **RSD**, illus.
        511-513.
Public Enemy.
    Tröster, Frantisek. Estates Theatre, Prague: 1935. B&W. Set. **TDT**, n. 42 (Fall 1975).
        28.
Pueblo.
    _____. Arena Stage, Washington, DC: B&W. Set. **TCI**, vol. 5, n. 5 (Oct 1971).
        23.
Pump Boys and Dinettes.
    Johnson, Doug & Christopher Nowak. Princess Theatre, NYC: 1982. B&W. Set. **TCI**,
        vol. 16, n. 9 (Nov/Dec 1982). 26.
Punch and the Child.
    Armistead, Horace. City Center, New York: 1947. B&W. Rendering. **SDW1**, 189.
Purgatory in Ingolstadt.
    Herrmann, Karl-Ernst. Schaubühne am Halleschen Ufer, Berlin: 1972. B&W. Set.
        SDW4, illus. 254, 255.

Purge.
> _____. American Contemporary Theatre, Buffalo: 1974. B&W. Set. **TDT**, vol.
> XIV, n. 2 (Summer 1978). 35.

I Puritani.
> de Chirico, Georgio. Teatro Comunale, Florence: 1933. B&W. Rendering. **AST**, 183.
> Lee, Ming Cho. Metropolitan Opera, NYC: 1976. B&W and color. Rendering & set.
> **MOM**. 203-210. 6 photos.

Purlie.
> Davis, Peter. Performing Arts Center, Santa Maria, Califronia: 1978. B&W. Set. **TCI**,
> vol. 14, n. 4 (Sep 1980). 34.
> Edwards, Ben. Broadway Theatre, NYC: 1970. B&W. Set. **BWM**, 334; B&W. Set.
> **DPT**, 181; B&W. Rendering. **DPT**, 182; B&W. Set. **TCI**, vol. 7, n. 3 (May/Jun
> 1973). 20; B&W. Set. **TCI**, vol. 23, n. 7 (Aug/Sep 1989). 50.
> Tilton, James. (TV version): B&W. Set. **TCI**, vol. 18, n. 7 (Aug/Sep 1984). 32.

Purlie Victorious.
> Edwards, Ben. 1959. B&W. Rendering. **SDD**, between 210 & 211. Act I, sc. 1; 1961.
> Color. Rendering. **DDT**, 152b.

The Purple Dust.
> Polakov, Lester. Cherry Lane Theatre, NYC: 1956. B&W. Rendering. **DPT**, 187.

Put Them All Together.
> Gianfrancesco, Edward. 1980. Color. Set. **TCI**, vol. 20, n. 4 (Apr 1986). 35. 2 photos.

La Putta Onorata.
> Ratto, Gianni. Venice: 1950. B&W. Set. **SDE**, 140.

Pygmalion.
> Blane, Sue. Citizen's Theatre of Glasgow: B&W. Set. **TCI**, vol. 15, n. 7 (Aug/Sep
> 1981). 26.
> Conklin, John. Roundabout Theatre, NYC: 1991. Color. Set. **TCI**, vol. 25, n. 5 (May
> 1991). 12.
> Elder, Eldon. Queens Playhouse, Flushing, NY: 1972-1973. B&W. Rendering. **EED**,
> (pages not numbered).
> Oenslager, Donald. Ethel Barrymore Theatre, NYC: 1945. B&W. Rendering. **TDO**,
> 111; 1948. B&W. Set. **WTP**, 150, 151. 3 photos.

-Q-

Quadrille.
> Beaton, Cecil. Phoenix Theatre, London: 1952. B&W. Set. **SDW1**, 170; B&W. Set.
> **WTP**, 162. 3 photos.

The Quarrels in Chioggia.
> Guillaumot, Bernard. Studio Théatre de Vitry, France: 1968. B&W. Model. **SDW3**, 75.
> Ristic, Dusan. Narodno Pozoriste, Beograd: 1973. B&W. Set. **SDW4**, illus. 98.

Queen after Death.
> Oudot, Roland. Comédie Française, Paris: 1942. B&W. Rendering. **SDW1**, 105.

The Queen and the Rebels.
> Aronson, Boris. (project): 1960. B&W. Rendering. **TAB**, 306.
> Francini, Mauro. Teatro Brasileiro de Comédia, São Paulo: 1957. B&W. Set. **SDW2**,
> 35.

The Queen of Spades.
> Chupiatov, Leonid. Malyi Opera, Leningrad: 1935. B&W. Set. **MOT**, between 304 &
> 305.
> Dmitriev, Vladimir. Bolshoi Theatre, Moscow: 1944. B&W. Rendering. **SDW2**, 181.

Hartman, Dominik. B&W. Rendering. **SDR**, 51.

Messel, Oliver. Royal Opera House, Covent Garden, London: 1950. B&W. Set. **OMB**, 152; B&W. Rendering. **SDW1**, 178.

Polidori, Gianni. Teatro Comunale, Florence: 1952. B&W. Rendering. **SDW1**, 128.

Svoboda, Josef. National Arts Center, Ottawa: 1976. B&W. Set. **STS**, 48.

The Quest.

Piper, John. Sadler's Wells Ballet, London: 1943. B&W. Set. **BTD**, 20.

Quiet Flows the Don.

Volkov, Boris. Mouzikalnyi Teatr imeni Stanislavskovo i Nemirovitcha-Dantchenko, Moscow: 1936. B&W. Set. **SDW2**, 201.

A Quiet Place.

Gropman, David. La Scala, Milan & The Kennedy Center, Washington, DC: 1984. B&W. Models & set. **ASD2**, 44-46. 4 photos.

Lynch, Thomas. Vienna State Opera: 1986. B&W. Rendering. **DDT**, 158. 2 photos.

Quilters.

_____. Omaha Community Playhouse, Nebraska: 1989. B&W. Set. **TCI**, vol. 24, n. 3 (Mar 1990). 35.

Quo Vadis.

Craven, Hawes. Lyceum Theatre, London: 1900. B&W. Rendering. **SDT**, 261.

-R-

R.U.R.

Aronson, Boris. Ethel Barrymore Theatre, NYC: 1942. B&W. Rendering. **TAB**, 298.

Feuerstein, Bedrich. National Theatre, Prague: 1921. B&W. Rendering. **TDT**, n. 41 (Summer 1975). 19.

Gorelik, Mordecai. B&W. Rendering. **SDC**, plate 90.

Hoffman, Vlastislav. National Theatre, Prague: 1929. B&W. Rendering. **RSD**, illus. 277; B&W. Rendering. **TAT**, plate 193.

Kiesler, Frederick. Theater am Kufürstendamm, Berlin: 1922. B&W. Set. **EIF**, photo plate 1; B&W. Set. **TCS2**, plates 158, 159; B&W. **RSD**, illus. 382.

Simonson, Lee. Garrick Theatre, NYC: 1922. B&W. Set. **MCN**, 61; B&W. Set. **TCR**, 79.

Ra.

Smith, Jerrard & Diane. Comus Music Theatre, Ontario Science Center, Canada: B&W. Set. **TCI**, vol. 18, n. 3 (Mar 1984). 26.

Rabelais.

_____. France: B&W. Set. **SIP**, 173; B&W. Set. **TCM**, 28.

Radamisto.

Heckroth, Heinrich. Handel Festival, Gottingen: 1927. B&W. Set. **RSD**, illus. 249.

Raduz znd Mahulena.

Svoboda, Josef. National Theatre, Prague: 1970. B&W. Set. **SJS**, 72. 2 photos.

Rags.

Foy, Kenneth. (project): 1988. B&W. Rendering. **DDT**, 103.

Montresor, Beni. Mark Hellinger Theatre, NYC: 1986. B&W. Set. **MBM**, 223.

The Raid of the Ranquels.

Gelpi, Germén. Teatro Casino, Buenos Aires: 1954. B&W. Rendering. **SDW1**, 34.

Rain.

Conklin, John. Hartford Stage, Connecticut: 1978. B&W. Model. **ASD1**, 27; B&W. Model. **DDT**, 484.

The Rainbow Pass.
　　_____. China: B&W. Set. **SOW**, plate 51.
Rainforest.
　　Warhol, Andy. Odeon Theatre, Paris: 1970. B&W. Set. **RSD**, illus. 485.
Raisin.
　　Taylor, Robert U. 46th Street Theatre, NYC: 1973. Color. Model. **CSD**, 105; B&W.
　　　　Model. **DPT**, 129. Front and top views.
The Rake's Progress.
　　Bellman, Willard F. California State University, Northridge: Color. Set. **DSL**, plate
　　　　VIII; Color. Set. **SST**, plate XVI.
　　Bergling, Birger. Royal Opera House, Stockholm. 1961. B&W. Set. **SDR**, 52.
　　Firth, Tazeena & Timothy O'Brien. Royal Opera House, Covent Garden, London:
　　　　1979. B&W. Set. **BTD**, 101; B&W. Set. **TDT**, vol. XIX, n. 3 (Fall 1983). 8.
　　Hockney, David. Glyndebourne Festival Opera, England: 1975. Color. Rendering,
　　　　model, & set. **HPS**, 60, 70, 71, 74, 79, 80, 82-84, 90-97, 103. 38 photos.
　　Hudson, Richard. Chicago Lyric Opera: Color. Model. **TCI**, vol. 29, n. 3 (Mar 1995).
　　　　55.
　　Lancaster, Osbert. Festival Opera House, Glyndebourne: 1953. B&W. Rendering.
　　　　SDW2, 220.
　　Ratto, Gianni. La Scala, Milan: 1951. B&W. Rendering. **SDW2**, 130.
　　Scharsich, Lothar. Comic Opera, Berlin: 1978. B&W. Set. **TCI**, vol. 15, n. 1 (Jan
　　　　1981). 34, 36.
　　Svoboda, Josef. National Theatre, Prague: 1972. B&W. Set. **TDT**, vol. XII, n. 2 (Sum-
　　　　mer 1976). 22.
　　Whistler, Rex. Royal Opera House, Covent Garden, London: 1974. B&W. Set. **CGA**,
　　　　184.
Ramayana.
　　Knoblock, Boris. Tsentralnyi Detski Teatr, Moscow: 1960. B&W. Model. **SDW2**, 187.
The Rape in Harem.
　　Ratto, Gianni. La Scala, Milan: 1952. B&W. Rendering. **SDE**, 141.
The Rape of Lucrece.
　　Piper, John. Ziegfeld Theatre, NYC: 1948. B&W. Set. **SDG**, 189.
　　_____. Cincinnati Conservatory of Music: Color. Set. **SDL**, plate 23-4. 2 photos.
Rare Area.
　　Sirlin, Jerome. University of California, Berkeley: 1986. Color. Model. **TCI**, vol. 22,
　　　　n. 1 (Jan 1988). 34.
Rashomon.
　　Itô, Juichi. Shinjuku Koma, Tokyo: 1961. B&W. Rendering. **SDW2**, 147.
Rasputin.
　　Colavecchia, Franco. New York City Opera: 1988. B&W. Rendering. **DDT**, 171.
　　Traugott, Muller. Piscator Theater, Berlin: 1928. B&W. Set. **RSD**, illus. 239, 240.
Die Räuber.
　　Gamrekeli, Irakly. Rustaveli Theatre, Tbilisi: 1933/1934. B&W. Rendering & set.
　　　　RST, 269, 290, 291. 4 photos; B&W. Rendering. **SDW2**, 184
　　Hein, Peter. Volksbühne, Berlin: 1971. B&W. Set. **SDW4**, illus. 118-123.
　　Minks, Wilfried. Theater der Freien Hansestadt, Bremen: 1966. B&W. Set. **RSD**, illus.
　　　　583; B&W. Set. **SDW3**, 81; B&W. Set. **TCI**, vol. 12, n. 1 (Jan/Feb 1978). 30.
　　Orlik, Emil. Deutsches Theater, Berlin: 1908. B&W. Rendering. **FCS**, plate 189. Act
　　　　II, sc. 3; B&W. Rendering. **SDO**, 215; B&W. Set. **TCS2**, plate 13.
　　Richter, Kurt. Grosses Schauspielhaus, Berlin: 1921. B&W. Rendering. **MRH**, be-
　　　　tween 156, 157. 2 photos.

Walter, Paul. National Theater, Mannheim: 1957. B&W. Set. **RSD**, illus. 621.
Le Rayon des Jouets.
Wahkévitch, Georges. Teatro de la Madeleine, Paris: B&W. Rendering. **SDE**, 167.
Razzia.
Martin, Karlheinz. Lessing Theatre, Berlin: B&W. Set. **TCS2**, plate 281.
Real Reel.
Ferbus, Jean-Pol & Frédéric Flamand. Théâtre Laboratoire Vicinal, Brussels: 1971.
B&W. Set. **SDW3**, 168.
The Real Thing.
Recht, Raymond C. Pittsburgh Public Theatre: 1985. B&W. Set. **TCI**, vol. 20, n. 2
(Feb 1986). 10.
Walton, Tony. Plymouth Theatre, NYC: 1984. B&W. Set. **DDT**, 373; Color. Rendering
& set. **TCI**, vol. 18, n. 5 (May 1984). 20. 3 photos.
Rebecca.
Bartau. Théâtre de Paris: 1946. B&W. Rendering. **SDW1**, 84.
Rebel Women.
Beatty, John Lee. New York Shakespeare Festival, NYC: 1976. B&W. Rendering.
ASD1, 2; B&W. Rendering. **TCI**, vol. 12, n. 6 (Oct 1978). 21.
Recriminal Minds.
Chepulis, Kyle. NYC: Color. Set. **TCI**, vol. 29, n. 4 (Apr 1995). 41.
The Recruiting Officer.
Appen, Karl von. Theater am Schiffbauerdamm, Berlin: 1955. B&W. Rendering.
SDW2, 49. 2 photos.
Corrigan, Robert. B&W. Set. **TDT**, n. 19 (Dec 1969). 32. 2 photos.
Red and Blue.
Arnone, John. Public Theatre's Other Stage, NYC: 1982. B&W. **ASD2**, 19. 9 views;
B&W. Sketch. **DDT**, 157.
The Red General.
Mielziner, Jo. 1929. B&W. Rendering. **DTT**, 73. Railroad station; B&W. Rendering.
DTT, 74. War scene.
Red Gloves.
_____. B&W. Set. **WTP**, 113. 3 photos.
Red Hot and Blue!
Oenslager, Donald. Alvin Theatre, NYC: 1936. B&W. Set. **BWM**, 203; B&W. Render-
ing. **SDA**, 246; B&W. Rendering. **TDO**, 67; B&W. Set. **WMC**, 150.
Red House.
Jesurun, John. La Mama ETC, NYC: 1984. Color. Set. **TCI**, vol. 19, n. 7 (Aug/Sep
1985). 46.
The Red Mill.
_____. Knickerbocker Theatre, NYC: 1906. B&W. Set. **BWM**, 11.
The Red Navy Man.
_____. B&W. Set. **TBB**, 207.
Red Noses.
Brown, Bado. Florida State University, Tallahassee: Color. Set. **TCI**, vol. 26, n. 3 (Mar
1992). 39.
Weldin, Scott. Goodman Theatre, Chicago: 1987. B&W. Set. **TCI**, vol. 21, n. 10 (Dec
1987). 20.
The Red Orient.
You Beijing Wen Hua Gong Zuozhe, Gong Ren, Nong Min, Xue Sheng Jiti Bian.
Beijing: 1965. B&W. Set. **SDW3**, 174.

The Red Poppy.
> Aronson, Boris. Music Hall Theatre, Cleveland: 1943. B&W. Rendering. **TAB**, 298.
> Kourilko, Mikhäil. Bolshoi Theatre, Moscow: 1949. B&W. Set. **SDW2**, 188.

Red River.
> Schultz, Karen. Goodman Theatre, Chicago: 1983. B&W. Rendering. **DDT**, 170.

The Red Robins.
> _____. St. Clement's Church, NYC: 1978. Color. Set. **TCI**, vol. 18, n. 4 (Apr 1984). 28, 29.

Red Roses for Me.
> Bay, Howard. Booth Theatre, NYC: 1955. B&W. Rendering. **TCI**, vol. 17, n. 2 (Feb 1983). 55.

The Red Shoes.
> Buck, Gene Davis. Children's Theatre Company, Minneapolis: B&W. Set. **TCI**, vol. 17, n. 7 (Aug/Sep 1983). 31.
> Landesman, Heidi. Gershwin Theatre, NYC: 1994. Color. Set. **TCI**, vol. 28, n. 3 (Mar 1994). 13.

The Red Women's Detachment.
> Zhongguo Wujutuan Jiti Gaibian. Beijing: 1970. B&W. Set. **SDW3**, 174.

Redemption.
> Jones, Robert Edmond. Plymouth Theatre, NYC: 1918. B&W. Rendering. **REJ**, 33.

Redwood Curtain.
> Beatty, John Lee. Old Globe Theatre, San Diego: 1993. B&W. Set. **TCI**, vol. 27, n. 4 (Apr 1993). 8; Brooks Atkinson Theatre, NYC: 1993. B&W. Rendering. **DDT**, 469.

Regarding November.
> Szajna, Josef. Wyspianski Theater, Katowice: 1969. B&W. Set. **RSD**, illus. 556.

Le Régiment qui passe.
> Doboujinsky, Mstislav. Chauve-Souris, Moscow: B&W. Rendering. **SDC**, plate 94; Color. Rendering. **TCS2**, color plate 3.

Regina Uliva.
> Marchi, Mario Vellani. La Scala, Milan: 1949. B&W. Rendering. **SDE**, 117. 2 photos.

Regina.
> Yeargan, Michael. Long Wharf Theatre, New Haven, Connecticut: 1988. B&W. Set. **ASD2**, 181; B&W. Set. **TCI**, vol. 22, n. 7 (Aug/Sep 1988). 29.

The Rehearsal.
> Ward, Anthony. Almeida Theatre, London: 1990. Color. Set. **TCI**, vol. 27, n. 4 (Apr 1993). 43.

Rehearsal for Love.
> Malclés, Jean Dénis. Théâtre Marigny, Paris: 1950. B&W. Rendering. **SDW1**, 101.

La Reja.
> Toms, Carl. Sadler's Wells Opera House, London: 1959. B&W. Rendering. **SDW2**, 228.

Relache.
> Picabia, Francis. Ballets Suédois, Paris (not performed): 1924. B&W. Set. **RSD**, illus. 328; B&W. Set. **TCS2**, plate 155.

The Relapse.
> Aronson, Boris. American Conservatory Theatre, San Francisco: 1970. B&W. Set. **PST**, 254; B&W. Set. **TSY**, 113.

The Reluctant Dragon.
> _____. Seattle Children's Theatre: Color. Set. **TCI**, vol. 26, n. 1 (Jan 1992). 39.

The Remarkable Mr. Pennypacker.
> Edwards, Ben. Coronet Theatre (Eugene O'Neill Theatre), NYC: 1953. B&W. Rendering. **DDT**, 163.

Remembrance.
> Falabella, John. Huntington Theatre, Boston: 1987. B&W. Rendering. **DDT**, 244.

Remembrances in a Louisville Harem.
> Phillips, Van. Purdue University, Lafayette, Indiana: 1976. B&W. Rendering. **BSE1**, 18.

Renard.
> Larionov, Michel. Opéra de Paris: 1922. Color. Rendering. **RSD**, illus. 295. Ballet-Russes.
> Prampolini, Enrico. Teatro delle Arte, Rome: 1940. B&W. Rendering. **SDE**, 135.

The Representative.
> Kerz, Leo. Freie Volksbühne, Berlin: 1963. B&W. Set. **SDW3**, 157.

Requiem for a Heavyweight.
> Kellogg, Marjorie Bradley. Long Wharf Theatre, New Haven, Connecticut: 1984. B&W. Set. **ASD1**, 63; Martin Beck Theatre, NYC: 1985. B&W. Model. **DDT**, 88.

Requiem for a Nun.
> Barkla, Jack. Tyrone Guthrie Theatre, Minneapolis: B&W. Set. **TCI**, vol. 17, n. 7 (Aug/Sep 1983). 23; Color. Set. **TCI**, vol. 18, n. 7 (Aug/Sep 1984). 41.
> Otto, Teo. Schauspielehaus, Zürich: 1955. B&W. Set. **SDW2**, 111.

The Resistible Rise of Arturo Ui.
> Acquart, André. T.N.P., Paris: 1969. Color. Set. **RSD**, illus. 540.
> Conklin, John. Williamstown Theatre Festival, Massachusetts: 1972. B&W. Model. **DDT**, 482. 2 photos; B&W. Set. **TCI**, vol. 14, n. 3 (May/Jun 1980). 18; 1979. B&W. Model. **ASD1**, 15; B&W. Set. **BSE4**, 79.
> Eigsti, Karl. Arena Stage, Washington, DC: 1974. B&W. Set. **TCI**, vol. 8, n. 3 (May/Jun 1974). 2.
> Scandella, Mischa. 1961. B&W. Rendering. **SIO**, 122.
> _____. Lunt-Fontanne Theatre, NYC: 1959. B&W. Set. **TBB**, 53.

The Respectful Prostitute.
> Gundlach, Robert. New Stages Theatre, NYC: 1948. B&W. Set. **WTP**, 114, 115. 4 photos.

Ressurection.
> Kolar, Zbynek. Czechoslovakia: B&W. Model. **TDT**, vol. XX, n. 1 (Spring 1984). 11.
> Koltai, Ralph. Prague: 1962. B&W. Set. **SDB**, 88.
> _____. Moscow Art Theatre: 1930. B&W. Set. **RST**, 298; B&W. Set. **SCM**, 87.

Return.
> Xinglin, Liu. China: B&W. Model. **TDT** vol. XXXI, n. 2 (Spring 1995). 11.

The Return of Peter Grimm.
> _____. 1911. B&W. Set. **SDC**, plate 43.

The Return of the Prodigal.
> Beaton, Cecil. Globe Theatre, London: 1948. B&W. Set. **CBS**, 39.

Return of Ulysses.
> Zimmerman, Reinhart. Copenhagen: 1969. B&W. Set. **SDB**, 140.

Return to the Forbidden Planet.
> Ford, Rodney. London: 1990. Color. Model. **TCI**, vol. 25, n. 8 (Oct 1991). 11.

Reuben, Reuben.
> Eckart, William & Jean. Shubert Theatre, Boston: 1955. B&W and color. Rendering. **DDT**, 153, 312d; B&W. Rendering. **SDT**, 43.

Reunion in Vienna.
    Toms, Carl. B&W. Set. **TCI**, vol. 6, n. 1 (Jan/Feb 1972). 17.
Revenge.
    Kosinski, Jan. Panstwowy Teatr Polski, Poznan: 1951. B&W. Set. **SDW1**, 157.
Revenge of the Space Pandas.
    Zoller, Buz. University of Texas, Austin: B&W. Set. **TDT**, vol. XXIV, n. 2 (Summer
        1988). 47. 2 photos.
The Revenger's Tragedy.
    Brill, Robert. Sledgehammer Theatre, San Diego: B&W. Set. **TDT** vol. XXXI, n. 2
        (Spring 1995). 16.
    Howard, Pamela. West Yorkshire Playhouse, GB: 1992. Color. Model. **TDT**, vol.
        XXX, n. 1 (Winter 1994). 19.
    Minks, Wilfried. Hamburg: 1972. B&W. Set. **TCI**, vol. 12, n. 1 (Jan/Feb 1978). 28.
    Winsor, William J. The Ohio State University, Columbus: B&W. Set. **TDT**, vol. XXVI,
        n. 1 (Spring 1990). 16 of insert.
Revolution in Krähwinkel.
    Stern, Ernst. Deutsches Theater, Berlin: 1908. B&W. Rendering. **MRH**, facing 20.
The Revolution Must End With the Perfection of Happiness.
    Moscoso, Roberto. Théâtre du Soleil, Vincennes, France: 1970. B&W. Set & ground
        plan. **SDW4**, illus. 379-384. 6 photos.
Revolution of the Heavenly Orbs.
    Roberts, Thom. Cricket Theatre, Minneapolis: 1980. B&W. Set. **TCI**, vol. 17, n. 7
        (Aug/Sep 1983). 20.
Der Revolutionär.
    Crayon. Kleines Theater, Berlin: 1919. B&W. Rendering. **TPH**, photo 422.
The Revolutionary City Belongs to this World.
    Bauchau, B., R. Moscoso, J. N. Cordier, A. Ferreira, Cl. Forget, G. Cl. Francois, L. de
        Grandmaison, & A. Salomon. Théâtre du Soleil, Vincennes, France: 1972. B&W.
        Set & ground plan. **SDW4**, illus. 385-390. 6 photos.
Rex.
    Conklin, John. Lunt-Fontanne Theatre, NYC: 1976. Color. Model. **DDT**, 152b; B&W.
        Set. **TCI**, vol. 11, n. 3 (May/Jun 1977). 11.
Reynard.
    Montresor, Beni. Spoleto Festival, Charleston, South Carolina: 1986. B&W. Set. **TCI**,
        vol. 20, n. 9 (Nov 1986). 12.
Reynard the Fox.
    _____. B&W. Set. **TCI**, vol. 4, n. 1 (Jan/Feb 1970). 19.
Das Rheingold.
    Appia, Adolphe. Basel: 1923. B&W. Sketch. **SDB**, 17; B&W. Rendering. **WLA**, 99.
    Conklin, John. San Francisco Opera: 1985. B&W. Model & rendering. **DDT**, 125, 481;
        Color. Set. **TCI**, vol. 20, n. 2 (Feb 1986). 26.
    Dudley, William. Beyreuth Festival Theatre: 1983. Color. Set. **BTD**, 119. Act I; B&W.
        Set. **TCI**, vol. 18, n. 3 (Mar 1984). 17. Isreal, Robert. Seattle Opera: 1986. B&W.
        Set. **ASD2**, 56.
    Isreal, Robert. Seattle Opera: 1990. Color. Set. **TCI**, vol. 24, n. 9 (Nov 1990). 38.
    Koltai, Ralph. English National Opera, London: B&W. Set. **TCI**, vol. 11, n. 1 (Jan/Feb
        1977). 13. 2 photos.
    Linnebach, Adolphe & Pasetti. National Theater, Munich: B&W. Rendering. **CSC**,
        facing 64, 76.
    Peduzzi, Richard. Beyreuth Festival Theatre: 1976. B&W. Set. **TCI**, vol. 11, n. 2 (Mar/
        Apr 1977). 16, 17; B&W. Set. **TCI**, vol. 14, n. 1 (Jan/Feb 1980). 22; 1979. B&W.

Set. **TCI**, vol. 14, n. 1 (Jan/Feb 1980). 22.

Roller, Alfred. Court Opera of Vienna: 1905. B&W. Sketch. **TPH**, photo 318.

Schneider-Siemssen, Günther. Metropolitan Opera, NYC: 1992. B&W. Set. **TCI**, vol. 10, n. 5 (Oct 1976). 18; Color. Set. **TCI**, vol. 27, n. 3 (Mar 1993). 24.

Sievert, Ludwig. Frieburg-in-Breisgau: 1912. B&W. Rendering. **RSD**, illus. 69.

Simonson, Lee. Metropolitan Opera, NYC: 1948. B&W and color. Rendering & set. **SDA**, 268, 290; B&W. Set. **TAS**, 154. 2 photos; Color. Rendering. **TAS**, facing frontispiece.

Svoboda, Josef. Royal Opera House, Covent Garden, London: 1974. B&W. Set. **CGA**, 190; B&W. Set. **JSS**, 60. Sc. 2; B&W. Set. **JSS**, 62. Sc. 3; B&W. Set. **JSS**, 63; Color. Set. **JSS**, between 54 & 55. Sc. 1; B&W. Set. **STS**, 84; B&W. Set. **TDT**, vol. XII, n. 2 (Summer 1976). 28. 3 photos; Grand Theater, Geneva: 1975. B&W. Set. **JSS**, 82. Sc. 1; B&W. Set. **JSS**, 84; Color. Set. **JSS**, between 54 & 55. Sc. 4; B&W. Model. **STS**, 86; B&W. Set. **TDT**, vol. XII, n. 2 (Summer 1976). 27; Roman Amphitheatre, Orange, France: 1988. B&W. Set. **TDT**, vol. XXVIII, n. 5 (Fall 1992). 18.

Wagner, Weiland. Beyreuth Festival Theatre: 1952. B&W. Set. **JSS**, 18; 1969/1970. B&W. Set. **TCI**, vol. 3, n. 4 (Sep 1969). 33; B&W. Set. **TCI**, vol. 14, n. 1 (Jan/Feb 1980). 22.

Wagner, Wolfgang. Beyreuth Festival Theatre: 1970. B&W. Set. **SDW4**, illus. 131, 135, 136; B&W. Set. **TDT**, n. 29 (May 1972). 14. Sc. 2.

Wendel, Heinrich. B&W. Set. **OPE**, 47. Final scene.

_____. (based on Appia's ideas). Theater Municipal, Basel: 1924. B&W. Set. **RSD**, illus. 63, 64.

_____. Mannheim National Theatre: B&W. Set. **TCI**, vol. 4, n. 4 (Sep 1970). 22.

Rhinocéros.

Kantor, Tadeusz. Stary Teatr, Cracow: 1961. B&W. Set. **RSD**, illus. 477.

Wich, Harry. Stadsschouwburg, Amsterdam: 1960. B&W. Rendering. **SDW2**, 146.

Rhythm Ranch.

Anania, Michael. Paper Mill Playhouse, Milburn, New Jersey: Color. Rendering. **TCI**, vol. 24, n. 2 (Feb 1990). 64. 3 photos.

Ricercare.

Ter-Arutunian, Rouben. American Ballet Theater, NYC: 1966. B&W. Set. **CSD**, 47.

Rich and Famous.

Yodice, Robert. LA Public Theatre, Los Angeles: 1982. B&W. Set. **TCI**, vol. 19, n. 7 (Aug/Sep 1985). 40.

Richard II.

Bury, John. Shakespeare Memorial Theatre, Stratford-upon-Avon: B&W. Model. **SDG**, 194.

Firth, Tazeena & Timothy O'Brien. Brooklyn Academy of Music, New York: 1974. B&W. Set. **TCI**, vol. 8, n. 2 (Mar/Apr 1974). 2.

Ffolkes, David. St. James Theatre, NYC: 1937. B&W. Set. **MCN**, 137.

Öberg, Barbara W. State Theatre, Norrköping, Sweden: 1958. B&W. Set. **SDW2**, 211.

Warre, Michael. New Theatre, London: 1947. Color. Rendering. **DMS**, plate 34; B&W. Model. **DOT**, 241; B&W. Model. **SDW1**, 186.

Richard III.

Aronson, Boris. Old Globe Theatre, San Diego: 1972. B&W. Set. **PST**, 128.

Babic, Ljubo. National Theatre, Zagreb: B&W. Rendering. **TCS2**, plate 119.

Benson, Tom. Utah Shakespeare Festival: B&W. Rendering. **SDT**, 280.

Blackman, Robert. American Conservatory Theatre, San Francisco: 1974. B&W. Set. **SST**, 446; B&W. Set. **TCI**, vol. 14, n. 4 (Sep 1980). 18, 19.

Ceroli, Mario. Teatro Stabile, Torino: 1968. B&W. Set. **AST**, 224. 3 photos.

Dare, Daphne. Stratford Festival Theatre, Ontario, Canada: 1977. B&W. Set. **TCI**, vol. 12, n. 4 (May/Jun 1978). 22.

Dudley, William. Royal Shakespeare Company, Stratford-upon-Avon: 1984. B&W. Set. **TDT**, vol. XXV, n. 3 (Fall 1989). 24.

Ericson, Sven. Dramatiska Teatern, Stockholm: 1947. B&W. Rendering. **SDW1**, 163.

Herbert, Jocelyn. Shakespeare Memorial Theatre, Stratford-upon-Avon: 1961. B&W. Set. **TDT**, vol. XXX, n. 5 (Fall 1994). 18.

Jones, Robert Edmond. Plymouth Theatre, NYC: 1920. B&W. Sketch. **DFT**, plate 6. Act I, sc. 2: the wooing of Lady Anne; B&W. Sketch. **DFT**, plate 7. Gloster's soliloquy; B&W. Sketch. **DFT**, plate 8. Act I, sc. 4: Clarence in prison; B&W. Sketch. **DFT**, plate 9. Act V, sc. IV: a gibbet; B&W. Rendering. **DIT**, plate 117.2; B&W. Rendering. **REJ**, 37; B&W. Rendering. **RSD**, illus. 429; B&W. Rendering. **SDA**, 209. 2 photos; B&W. Rendering. **TPH**, photo 471; B&W. Rendering & set. **TSS**, 518, 519. 3 photos; (project): 1941. B&W. Rendering. **REJ**, 101, 103; B&W. Rendering. **TDT**, vol. XXIV, n. 4 (Winter 1988). 11.

Jozwick, Tim. Repertory Theatre of St. Louis. B&W. Set. **TCI**, vol. 15, n. 9 (Nov/Dec 1981). 20.

Kerz, Leo. (not produced): 1948. B&W. Model. **SDA**, 234, 235. 4 photos.

Kieling, Johanna & Andreas Reinhardt. Deutsches Theater, Berlin: 1972. B&W. Set. **SDW4**, illus. 19.

Koltai, Ralph. National Theatre, London: B&W. Rendering. **SDL**, 42. 2 photos.

Lee, Ming Cho. Delacorte Theatre, NYC: 1966. B&W. Set. **SDB**, 45; B&W. Set. **TCI**, vol. 18, n. 2 (Feb 1984). 16.

Loquasto, Santo. Delacorte Theatre, NYC: 1983. B&W. Set. **ASD1**, 106; Color. Set. **TCI**, vol. 18, n. 5 (May 1984). 10; 1989. B&W. Set. **SDL**, 11.

Malclés, Jean Dénis. Théâtre Montparnasse-Gaston Baty, Paris: 1964. B&W. Rendering. **SDW3**, 35.

Nordgreen, Eric. Det kongelige Teater, Copenhagen: 1951. B&W. Rendering. **SDW1**, 59.

Payne, Darwin Reid. B&W. Model. **TCM**, 112, 113.

Pirchan, Emil. State Theatre, Berlin: 1920. B&W and color. Rendering. **CSC**, facing 136, 138, 140, 142, 144, 146; B&W. Rendering & set. **RSD**, illus. 135, 136; B&W. Rendering. **SOS**, 209; B&W. Set. **TCS2**, plate 123.

Sinkkonen, Eric. California Shakespeare Festival, Berkeley: 1994. Color. Model. **TCI**, vol. 28, n. 8 (Oct 1994). 7.

Tahara, Eiji. Tokyo: 1965. Color. Model. **SDW3**, 36.

Tischler, Alexander. Great Dramatic Theater, Moscow: 1935. B&W. Rendering. **RSD**, illus. 219; B&W. Rendering. **SDW2**, 197. 3 photos; B&W. Rendering. **SOS**, 220; B&W. Rendering. **TPH**, photo 407.

Vakalo, Georges. Paris: B&W. Rendering. **SDE**, 161.

Wierchowicz, Zofia. Teatry Dramatyczne, Szczecin, Poland: 1967. B&W. Sketches & set. **TDT**, n. 11 (Dec 1967). 24-29. 10 photos.

_____. Germany: B&W. Set. **TPH**, photo 424.

Richard of Bordeaux.

Motley (Margaret Harris, Sophia Harris, & Elizabeth Montgomery). New Theatre, London: 1933. B&W. Set. **SCM**, 21.

Ride a Cock Horse.

Bardon, Henry. Piccadilly Theatre, London: 1965. B&W. Rendering. **DMS**, plates 59, 60.

The Ride Across Lake Constance.

Humm, Ambrosius. Theater am Neumarkt, Zürich: 1972. B&W. Set. **SDW4**, illus. 396.

Roos, Norvid. B&W. Model. **TDT**, vol. XVI, n. 4 (Winter 1980). 14.

Right Mind.

_____. American Conservatory Theater, Geary Theatre, San Francisco: 1989. B&W. Set. **TCI**, vol. 23, n. 10 (Dec 1989). 17.

Right You Are.

Tilton, James. Lyceum Theatre, NYC: 1966. B&W. Set. **TCI**, vol. 1, n. 1 (Mar/Apr 1967). 23.

Right You Are If You Think You Are.

Matthews, William. B&W. Set. **SDL**, 69.

Pizzi, Pier Luigi. Teatro Valle, Rome: 1972. B&W. Set. **SDW4**, illus. 195-198.

Rigoletto.

Angelopoulos, Marius. Ethnike Lyrike Skene, Athens: 1948. B&W. Rendering. **SDW1**, 109.

Benois, Nicola. State Opera, Vienna: 1962. B&W. Set. **SDW2**, 121.

Berman, Eugene. Metropolitan Opera, NYC: 1951. B&W. Rendering. **SDB**, 66; B&W. Rendering. **SDE**, 46, 47. 4 photos; B&W. Rendering. **SDW1**, 193; B&W. Rendering & set. **TCM**, xxi. 2 photos.

Brown, Zack. Opera House, Kennedy Center, Washington, DC: 1983. B&W. Rendering. **DDT**, 161.

Calva, Aldo. Teatro Comunale, Florence. 1949. B&W. Rendering. **SDE**, 52.

Guangjian, Gao. China: B&W. Model. **TDT** vol. XXXI, n. 2 (Spring 1995). 9.

Iliprandi, Gian Carlo. 1952. B&W. Rendering. **SDE**, 91.

Moiseiwitsch, Tanya. Metropolitan Opera, NYC: 1978. B&W. Set. **TCI**, vol. 20, n. 7 (Aug/Sep 1986). 19.

Robertson, Patrick & Rosemary Vercoe. English National Opera, London: 1982. Color. Set. **BTD**, 100; B&W. Set. **TCI**, vol. 19, n. 4 (Apr 1985). 20, 21.

Svoboda, Josef. Grand Opera of the Fifth of May, Prague: 1947. B&W. Set. **SJS**, 138, 139. 4 photos; B&W. Set. **TDT**, n. 20 (Feb 1970). 15-17. 4 photos; Smetana Theatre, Prague: 1954. B&W. Set. **STS**, 23; B&W. Set. **TDT**, vol. XXVIII, n. 5 (Fall 1992). 12; Macerata: 1993. Color. Set. **TDT**, vol. XXX, n. 5 (Fall 1994). 38.

Zeffirelli, Franco. Théâtre de la Monnaie, Brussels: 1960. B&W. Set. **SDW2**, 133.

Rigonda.

Vardaunis, Edgars. Teatr Opery i Baleta Latviiskoï, Riga: 1959. B&W. Rendering. **SDW2**, 199.

The Rimers of Eldritch.

Malolepsy, John F. University of New Mexico, Albuquerque: 1979. B&W. Model. **BSE1**, 16.

Warburton, Jeffrey L. University of Arizona, Tucson: B&W. Set. **SDT**, 290.

Rinaldo.

Negin, Mark. Metropolitan Opera, NYC: 1984. B&W. Model & set. **TCI**, vol. 18, n. 9 (Nov/Dec 1984). 44, 46. 4 photos.

The Ring Around the Ankle.

Lehto, Leo. Suomen Kansallisteatteri, Helsinki. 1959. B&W. Set. **SDW2**, 204.

Ring Around the Moon.

Barsacq, André. Théâtre de l'Atelier, Paris: 1947. B&W. Set. **SDW1**, 84.

Messel, Oliver. Globe Theatre, London: 1950. B&W. Set. **MEM**, 26, 120, 121; B&W. Set. **OMB**, 141; B&W. Rendering. **SDW1**, 178; B&W. Model. **TDT**, vol. XXIII, n. 3 (Fall 1987). 28.

Der Ring des Nibelungen.

    Conklin, John. San Francisco Opera: 1985. Color. Rendering & model. **TCI**, vol. 21, n. 5 (May 1987). 28.

    Dudley, William. Beyreuth Festival Theatre: 1983. B&W. Rendering. **BTD**, 118. Hall of the Gibichungs.

    Heinrich, Rudolf. Leipzig: 1973-1976. B&W. Set. **TCI**, vol. 10, n. 6 (Nov/Dec 1976). 17.

    Manthey, Axel. Frankfurt Opera: 1987. B&W. Set. **TCI**, vol. 21, n. 10 (Dec 1987). 18.

    Oenslager, Donald. (project): 1927. B&W. Rendering. **SDC**, plate 104; B&W. Rendering. **TCS2**, plate 381; B&W. Model & rendering. **TDO**, 25, 26.

    Shock, Amy. Arizona Opera: 1994. Color. Rendering of projection designs. **TCI**, vol. 28, n. 3 (Mar 1994). 62.

    Simond, Anne-Marie & Pierre. Lausanne: 1969. B&W. Model. **SDW3**, 180.

    Svoboda, Josef. Orange: 1988. B&W. Sketch & set. **TDT**, vol. XXX, n. 5 (Fall 1994). 41.

    Wagner, Wolfgang. Beyreuth Festival Theatre: 1970. B&W. Sketches. **SDW4**, illus. 132-134.

    _____. Deutsche Oper, Berlin: 1989. B&W and color. Set. **TCI**, vol. 23, n. 5 (May 1989). 45. 3 photos.

    _____. Seattle Opera: 1987. Color. Set. **TCI**, vol. 22, n. 5 (May 1988). 47. 3 photos.

The Rink.

    Larkin, Peter. Martin Beck Theatre, NYC: 1983. Color. Rendering. **DDT**, 24a; B&W. Set. **MBM**, 159; Color. Rendering. **TCI**, vol. 23, n. 1 (Jan 1989). 43.

Rio Rita.

    _____. Prince Edward Theatre, London: 1930. B&W. Set. **MCD**, plate 163.

Ripa Albastra.

    Mohirta, T. Rumania: B&W. Rendering. **TDT**, vol. XII, n. 3 (Fall 1976). 43.

The Rise and Fall of the City of Mahagonny.

    Feitscher, Vicki. Australia: B&W. Model. **TDT**, vol. XX, n. 1 (Spring 1984). 10.

    Herbert, Jocelyn. Metropolitan Opera, NYC: 1979. B&W. Sketches. **BTD**, 133. 4 photos.

    Isreal, Robert. Los Angeles Music Center Opera: 1990. Color. Set. **TCI**, vol. 24, n. 9 (Nov 1990). 36.

    Koltai, Ralph. Sadler's Wells Opera House, London: 1963. B&W. Set. **DMS**, plate 53; B&W. Set. **SDW3**, 197.

    Neher, Caspar. Neues Theatre, Leipzig: 1930. B&W. Rendering. **CBM**, 49. 2 photos; Theater am Kurfürstendamm, Berlin: 1931. B&W. Rendering. **RSD**, illus. 561.

    Rapp, Jacques. Opéra de Lyon: 1970. B&W. Set. **SDW3**, 197.

    Straiges, Tony. Yale Repertory Theatre, New Haven: 1974. B&W. Rendering. **CSD**, 130. Act II, sc. 13; B&W. Set. **TCI**, vol. 16, n. 2 (Feb 1982). 19.

    Wexler, Peter. Metropolitan Opera, NYC: 1979. B&W. Set. **TCI**, vol. 14, n. 6 (Nov/Dec 1980). 14. 2 photos.

    Yeargan, Michael. Yale Repertory Theatre, New Haven: 1978. B&W. Set. **TCI**, vol. 13, n. 3 (May/Jun 1979). 46.

    Zimmerman, Reinhart. Comic Opera, Berlin: B&W. Set. **TCI**, vol. 15, n. 1 (Jan 1981). 36.

    _____. Deutsches Kammermusik, Baden-Baden: 1927. B&W. Set. **TBB**, 29.

The Rise of a Frog.

    Kohno, Kunio. Mitsukoshi, Tokyo: 1952. B&W. Rendering. **SDW1**, 150.

The Rise of Silas Lapham.
> Simonson, Lee. 1919. B&W. Set. **PLT**, illus. 1.

The Risen People.
> Crabb, Sally. Gaiety Theatre, Dublin: 1994. Color. Set. **TCI**, vol. 29, n. 2 (Feb 1995). 7.

Rites of Spring.
> Svoboda, Josef. National Theatre, Prague: 1972. B&W. Set. **TDT**, vol. XII, n. 2 (Summer 1976). 15.

The Rivals.
> Barratt, Watson. Shubert Theatre, NYC: 1942. B&W. Set. **WTP**, 130, 131. 3 photos.
> Chaney, Stewart. Old Vic Theatre, London: 1938. B&W. Rendering. **SOW**, plate 40.
> Coble, McKay. Playmakers Repertory Company, Paul Green Theatre, Chapel Hill, North Carolina: Color. Set. **TCI**, vol. 25, n. 3 (Mar 1991). 46.
> Gunter, John. National Theatre (Olivier), London: 1983. Color. Set. **BTD**, 70.
> Maronek, James E. DePaul/Goodman School of Drama, Chicago: 1982. B&W. Rendering. **BSE3**, 31.
> Messel, Oliver. Criterion Theatre, London: 1945. B&W. Set. **MEM**, 107; B&W and color. Rendering & set. **OMB**, 70, 120, 121.
> Sheffield, Ann. Indiana Repertory Theatre: Color. Set. **TCI**, vol. 25, n. 1 (Jan 1991). 42.
> Toms, Carl. Chichester Festival Theatre, England: 1971. B&W. Set. **TCI**, vol. 6, n. 1 (Jan/Feb 1972). 15.
> Zdravkovic, Margo. Brandeis University, Waltham, Massachusetts: B&W. Set. **TCI**, vol. 23, n. 9 (Nov 1989). 54.

The River Mouth.
> Yoshida, Kenkishi. Tsukiji Shogekijo, Tokyo: 1939. B&W. Set. **SDW1**, 151.

The Road to Mecca.
> McCarry, Charles E. City Theatre, Pittsburgh, PA: B&W. Set. **TDT**, vol. XXVIII, n. 2 (Spring 1992). 7 of insert.

Roar China.
> Efimenko, Sergei. Meyerhold Theatre, Moscow: 1926. B&W. Set. RST, 234; B&W. Set. **SCM**, 86.
> Simonson, Lee. Theatre Guild, NYC: 1930. B&W. Set. **PLT**, illus. 48-51; B&W. Set. **RSD**, illus. 435; B&W. Set. **SCM**, 112. 2 photos; B&W. Set. **SDA**, 99-101. 4 photos; B&W. Set. **TAS**, 148, 149. 5 photos.

Roar Like a Dove.
> Jensen, Don F. Ogunquit Playhouse, Ogunquit, Maine: 1960. B&W. Set. **DPT**, 92.

The Roar of the Greasepaint, The Smell of the Crowd.
> English, Gary. University of Arizona Repertory Theatre, Tucson: B&W. Rendering. **SDT**, 66.
> _____. United States International University: 1972. B&W. Set. **TCI**, vol. 6, n. 5 (Oct 1972). 21.

The Roaring Girl.
> Dyer, Chris. Royal Shakespeare Company, GB: 1983. B&W. Set. **BTD**, 67; B&W. Model. **TDT**, vol. XX, n. 1 (Spring 1984). 19.

The Robber Bridegroom.
> Butsch, Tom. Chanhassen Dinner Theatre, Minnesota: B&W. Set. **TCI**, vol. 14, n. 5 (Oct 1980). 25.
> Schmidt, Douglas W. Biltmore Theatre, NYC: 1976. B&W. Set. **TCI**, vol. 10, n. 6 (Nov/Dec 1976). 10.

Roberta.
> Robinson, Clark. New Amsterdam Theatre, NYC: 1933. B&W. Set. **RBS**, 91; B&W. Set. **WMC**, 64; B&W. Set. **BWM**, 172.

Roberto Devereaux.
> Lee, Ming Cho. New York City Opera, Lincoln Center: 1970. B&W and color. Rendering. **SDT**, 278, and between 152 & 153; Color. Set. **TCI**, vol. 18, n. 2 (Feb 1984). 21; B&W. Rendering. **ASD1**, 95; B&W. Set. **DPT**, 243; B&W. Set. **TCI**, vol. 7, n. 1(Jan/Feb 1973). 14. 2 photos.

Robespierre.
> Schmuckle, Hans-Ulrich. Freie Volksbuhne, Berlin: 1963. B&W. Set. **RSD**, illus. 500; B&W. Rendering. **SDB**, 89.

Robinson and Crusoe.
> _____. Teatro dell'angolo, Italy: B&W. Set. **TCR**, 131.

Rock 'n Roll! The First Five Thousand Years.
> Ravitz, Mark. St. James Theatre, NYC: 1982. Color. Set. **MBM**, 184

The Rocky Horror Show.
> Thompson, Brian. Belasco Theatre, NYC: 1975. B&W. Set. **BMF**, 80.
> _____. Omaha Community Playhouse, Nebraska: 1988. Color. Set. **TCI**, vol. 24, n. 3 (Mar 1990). 34.

Rodelinda.
> Vancura, Jan. Czechoslovakia: B&W. Set. **TDT**, vol. XXVII, n. 3 (Summer 1991). 27.
> Varona, José. Holland Festival: 1973. Color. Model. **CSD**, 66; B&W. Set. **TCI**, vol. 14, n. 5 (Oct 1980). 31.
> Yeargan, Michael. Welsh National Opera: 1981. B&W. Set. **TCI**, vol. 16, n. 5 (May 1982). 26.

Rodeo.
> Smith, Oliver. USA: 1940. Color. Rendering. **SDA**, 285; B&W. Rendering. **TDT**, vol. XVI, n. 1 (Spring 1980). 13.

Rodogune.
> Pace. Sarah Bernhardt Theatre, Paris: 1960. B&W. Set. **SDW2**, 96.

Le Roman de Fauvel.
> Wareing, John. Waverly Consort, NYC: B&W. Model. **SDT**, 284.

The Romance of the Rose.
> Hume, Samuel J. 1917. B&W. Set. **TDT**, vol. XX, n. 2 (Summer 1984). 15.

Romance.
> Wenger, John. Playhouse Theatre, NYC: 1921. B&W. Rendering. **SDB**, 53.

Romeo and Juliet.
> Acquart, André. Théâtre Gérard Philipe, Saint-Denis, France: 1969. Color. Set. **SDW3**, 36.
> Anania, Michael. Lake George Opera Festival: 1985. Color. Set. **TCI**, vol. 20, n. 8 (Oct 1986). 25.
> Andrews, Paul. Birmingham Royal Ballet: 1992. B&W. Set. **TCI**, vol. 27, n. 3 (Mar 1993). 19.
> Barkhin, Sergei. USSR: B&W and color. Rendering & set. **TDT**, vol. XIX, n. 1 (Spring 1983). front cover, 20. 3 photos.
> Bernstein, Aline. Civic Repertory Theatre, NYC: 1930. B&W. Set. **SCM**, 118; B&W. Set. **SOW**, plate 50.
> Cesarini, Pino. Roman Theatre, Verona: 1954. B&W. Rendering & set. **SDE**, 57, 58. 3 photos.
> Conklin, John. Hartford Ballet: 1980. Color. Model. **ASD1**, between 70 & 71, back cover.

Craig, Edward Gordon. (unproduced): 1904. B&W. Rendering. **FCS**, plate 168. Act I, sc. 5; B&W. Rendering. **OAT**, 224. Act I, sc. 5; B&W. Rendering. **SDO**, 190.

Dimou, Fotini. Victory Theatre, NYC: 1991. Color. Set. **TCI**, vol. 25, n. 4 (Apr 1991). 19.

Ericson, Sven. Dramatiska Teatern, Stockholm: 1953. B&W. Set. **SDW1**, 163.

Ernst, Max. Opéra, Monte Carlo: 1926. Color. Rendering. **AST**, 117; B&W. Rendering. **RSD**, illus. 302, 303. Ballet-Russes.

Exter, Alexandra. Kamerny Theatre, Moscow: 1921. B&W and color. Rendering & set. **RST**, 168-170. 4 photos; B&W. Model. **TCS2**, plate 153; B&W. Set. **TPH**, photo 403.

Franz, Ernest. Narodno Gledalisce, Ljubljana: 1940. B&W. Set. **SDW1**, 134.

Georgiadis, Nicholas. Covent Garden, London: 1971. B&W. Set. **CGA**, 176.

Hall, Peter J. & Franco Zeffirelli. Old Vic Theatre, London: 1960. B&W. Set. **SDW2**, 133; Color. Set. **SOS**, 262.

Hanson, Debra. Stratford Festival Theatre, Ontario, Canada: 1992. Color. Set. **TCI**, vol. 26, n. 9 (Nov 1992). 29.

Jacobs, Sally. Royal Shakespeare Company, Stratford-upon-Avon: 1970. B&W. Model. **SDW3**, 39-41. 3 photos.

Jakab, William. Carnegie-Mellon University, Pittsburgh: B&W and color. Set. **TDT**, vol. XXX, n. 3 (Summer 1994). 15. 2 photos.

Kanamori, Kaoru. Tokyo: 1970. B&W. Set. **SDW3**, 37. 4 photos.

Koltai, Ralph. Royal Shakespeare Company, Stratford-upon-Avon: 1980. B&W. Set. **TCI**, vol. 15, n. 5 (May 1981). 12.

Lee, Ming Cho. Circle in the Square Theatre, NYC: 1977. B&W. Model. **DDT**, 198.

Levental, Valery. Teatr Opery i Baleta, Novossibirsk: 1964. B&W. Rendering. **SDW3**, 193.

Macdermott, Norman. Everyman Theatre, Hampstead, London: 1921. B&W. Set. **TCS2**, plate 77.

Merritt, Michael. Goodman Theatre, Chicago: 1988. B&W. Set. **ASD2**, 134.

Messel, Oliver. Broadhurst Theatre, NYC: 1951. B&W and color. Model & set. **MEM**, 127-129. 2 photos; B&W. Set. **OMB**, 152.

Mielziner, Jo. 1931. B&W. Rendering. **SDD**, between 210 & 211; B&W. Rendering. **DTT**, 85. Verona; 1934. B&W. Rendering. **DTT**, 86. Mantua; Color. Rendering. **DTT**, 87. Juliet's garden.

Motley (Margaret Harris, Sophia Harris, & Elizabeth Montgomery). Shakespeare Memorial Theatre, Stratford-upon-Avon: 1954. B&W. Set. **PST**, 155.

Payne, Darwin Reid. B&W. Rendering. **TDT** vol. XXXI, n. 2 (Spring 1995). 50; B&W. Rendering. **TDT**, vol. XXX, n. 3 (Summer 1994). 31; B&W. Sketch. **SIP**, 280, 282.

Pecktal, Lynn. (project): 1960. B&W. Rendering. **DDT**, 364. 2 photos.

Pitoëff, Georges. Théâtre des Mathurins, Paris: 1922. Color. Rendering. **RSD**, illus. 426, 427; 1937. B&W. Set. **TPH**, photo 362.

Rossman, Zdenek. National Theatre, Prague: 1954. B&W. Rendering. **SDW1**, 51.

Roszkopfova, Marta. Czechoslovakia: B&W. Rendering & set. **TDT**, vol. XXVI, n. 2 (Summer 1990). 33-35. Multiple images.

Shimizu, Kesatoshi. Tokyo: 1968. B&W. Model. **SDW3**, 37.

Sinkkonen, Eric. California Shakespeare Festival, Berkeley: 1994. Color. Model. **TCI**, vol. 28, n. 8 (Oct 1994). 7.

Stephenson, Andrew. Maddermarket Theatre, Norwich, England: B&W. Rendering. **SDC**, plate 100.

Straiges, Tony. Tyrone Guthrie Theatre, Minneapolis: 1979. B&W. Set. **TCI**, vol. 16, n. 2 (Feb 1982). 18.

Svoboda, Josef. National Theatre, Prague: 1963. B&W. Model. **SDW3**, 38; B&W. Model & set. **SJS**, 109-111. 7 photos; B&W. Set. **STS**, 63; B&W. Set. **TDT**, n. 7 (Dec 1966). 24; Municipal Theatre, Cologne: 1969. B&W. Model. **SJS**, 112.

Takada, Ichiro. Tokyo: 1971. B&W. Model. **SDW3**, 38.

Vychodil, Ladislav. Oslo: 1985. Color. Set. **TCI**, vol. 21, n. 8 (Oct 1987). 38.

Walser, Karl. Deutsches Theater, Berlin: 1907. B&W and color. Rendering. **FCS**, plate 188, color plate 20. Act I, sc. 1; B&W. Rendering & set. **MRH**, facing 81-83. 3 photos; B&W and color. Rendering. **SDO**, 214, plate 20.

Wareing, John. University of Arizona, Tucson: B&W. Set. **SDT**, 285.

Yoshida, Kenkishi. Asahi-Kaikan, Osaka: 1948. B&W. Model. **SDW1**, 150.

_____. Folger Library Theatre, Washington, DC: 1972. B&W. Set. **TCI**, vol. 7, n. 2 (Mar/Apr 1973). 9.

_____. Gothenburg National Theater, Sweden: B&W. Set. **TPH**, photo 391.

_____. Long Wharf Theatre, New Haven, Connecticut: B&W. Set. **TCI**, vol. 15, n. 9 (Nov/Dec 1981). 16. 2 photos.

_____. Louisburg College, North Carolina: B&W. Set. **TDT**, vol. XIX, n. 3 (Fall 1983). 15.

_____. Moscow Chamber Theatre: 1921. B&W. Set. **SOS**, 218.

_____. Royal Shakespeare Company, Stratford-upon-Avon: 1976. B&W. Set. **TDT**, vol. XIV, n. 2 (Summer 1978). 20.

_____. Théâtre des Mathurins, Paris: 1937. B&W. Rendering & set. **SOS**, 199.

_____. Wayne State University, Detroit: B&W. Set. **TDT**, vol. XXVI, n. 1 (Spring 1990). 24 of insert.

_____. 1930. B&W. Set. **SOS**, 177.

_____. Color. Set. **SDL**, plates 23-2b.

Roméo et Juliette (Shakespeare-Cocteau).

Hugo, Jean. Théâtre de la Cigale, Paris: 1924. B&W. Set. **TCS2**, plates 256, 257.

Romeo, Juliet, and the Darkness.

Svoboda, Josef. National Theatre, Prague: 1962. B&W. Set. **SJS**, 96. 2 photos.

Romulus the Great.

Grübler, Ekkehard. Frankfurt State Theatre: 1965. B&W. Set. **TDT**, n. 14 (Oct 1968). 23.

Sulzbachner, Max. Friedrich Dürrenmatt, Basel: 1950. B&W. Rendering. **SDW1**, 116.

Room Service.

Barkla, Jack. Tyrone Guthrie Theatre, Minneapolis: 1982. B&W. Set. **TCI**, vol. 17, n. 7 (Aug/Sep 1983). 29.

Belden, Ursula. Pittsburgh Public Theatre: B&W. Set. **TCI**, vol. 21, n. 7 (Aug/Sep 1987). 35.

Roots.

Herbert, Jocelyn. Belgrade Theatre, Coventry, GB: 1959. B&W. Rendering. **TDT**, vol. XXX, n. 5 (Fall 1994). 15.

The Rope Dancers.

Aronson, Boris. Cort Theatre, NYC: 1957. B&W and color. Rendering & set. **TAB**, 118, 119, 305. 3 photos.

The Rose and the Ring.

Hammond, Aubrey. Wyndham's Theatre, London: 1925. B&W. Rendering. **DIT**, plate 7; B&W. Rendering. **TCS2**, plate 227.

The Rose of the Rancho.

Gros, Ernest. Belasco Theatre, NYC: 1906. B&W. Set. **MCN**, 30.

Rose Marie.
> Gates & Morange studio. Imperial Theatre, NYC: 1924. B&W. Set. **TMT**, 62.
> Harker, Joseph & Phil Harker. Theatre Royal, Drury Lane, London: 1925. B&W. Set.
> MCD, plate 136.

The Rose Tattoo.
> Aronson, Boris. Martin Beck Theatre, NYC: 1951. Color. Rendering. **DDT**, 24c;
> B&W. Set. **SDW1**, 190; B&W and color. Rendering & set. **TAB**, 101, 102, 302. 3
> photos; B&W. Rendering. **TPH**, photo 488.
> Landwehr, Hugh. Williamstown Theatre Festival, Massachusetts: 1989. B&W. Set.
> **ASD2**, 76.

Rosencrantz and Guildenstern are Dead.
> Oechslin, Ary. State Theatre, Bern: 1968. B&W. Model. **SDW3**, 167.
> Rose, Jürgen. Schiller Theater, Berlin: 1967. B&W. Set. **SDW3**, 166. 2 photos.
> Tosa, Yoshi. Parade Theatre, Sydney: 1969. B&W. Set. **SDW3**, 167.

Der Rosenkavalier.
> Bosquet, Thierry. Théâtre Royal de la Monnaie, Brussels: 1962. B&W. Rendering.
> **SDW2**, 27.
> Fischer-Dieskau, Mathias. Chatelet Theatre Musical de Paris: 1993. Color. Set. **TCI**,
> vol. 27, n. 10 (Dec 1993). 14.
> Ironside, Robin. Covent Garden, London: 1947. B&W. Set. **CGA**, 133.
> Jürgens, Helmut. Munich: B&W. Set. **TCI**, vol. 11, n. 2 (Mar/Apr 1977). 11.
> O'Hearn, Robert. Metropolitan Opera, NYC: 1969. B&W. Set. **DPT**, 9.
> Roller, Alfred. Dresden: 1911. B&W. Set. **MRH**, between 12 & 13. 3 photos.
> Rose, Jürgen. Munich: B&W. Set. **TCI**, vol. 11, n. 2 (Mar/Apr 1977). 11.
> Wonder, Erich. Frankfurt Opera: 1992. Color. Set. **TCI**, vol. 27, n. 3 (Mar 1993). 12.
> _____. Salzburg: B&W. Set. **TCI**, vol. 11, n. 2 (Mar/Apr 1977). 11.

Rosmersholm.
> Craig, Edward Gordon. 1906. B&W. Rendering. **TNT**, facing 64.
> Fiala, Jeffrey A. University of Massachusetts, Amherst: 1974. B&W. Rendering. **CSD**,
> 79.
> Griffin, Hayden. Teatro Stabile di Genova: B&W. Rendering. **TCI**, vol. 19, n. 9 (Nov
> 1985). 21.
> Lee, Eugene. Trinity Square Theatre, Providence, Rhode Island: 1977. B&W. Set.
> **ASD1**, 73; B&W. Set. **TDT**, vol. XVIII, n. 2 (Summer 1982). 9.
> _____. Lessing Theatre, Berlin: 1906. B&W. Set. **TPH**, photo 291.
> _____. Norwegian National Theatre, Christiania: 1906. B&W. Set. **TPH**, photo
> 286.

Le Rossignol.
> Hockney, David. Metropolitan Opera, NYC: 1981. Color. Set. **BTD**, 112; B&W. Set.
> **TCI**, vol. 16, n. 9 (Nov/Dec 1982). 31.
> Soudeikine, Serge. Metropolitan Opera, NYC: 1925. B&W. Rendering. **MOM**, 8.
> _____. Lessing Theatre, Berlin: 1906. B&W. Set. **TPH**, photo 291.Santa Fe
> Opera: B&W. Set. **SST**, 303.

Rothchild's Violin.
> _____. 1990. Color. Set. **TCI**, vol. 27, n. 4 (Apr 1993). 30.

The Rothschilds.
> Bury, John. Lunt-Fontanne Theatre, NYC: 1970. B&W. Model & set. **TCI**, vol. 4, n. 6
> (Nov/Dec 1970). 22-26. 5 photos; B&W. Set. **TCI**, vol. 26, n. 1 (Jan 1992). 49.

Rough Crossing.
> Toms, Carl. National Theatre (Lyttleton), London: 1984. B&W. Set. **BTD**, 78. 2
> photos.

_____. Indiana Repertory Theatre: Color. Set. **TCI**, vol. 25, n. 9 (Nov 1991). 55.
Round Heads and Pointed Heads.
_____. Riddersalen Theatre, Copenhagen: 1936. B&W. Set. **TBB**, 42.
The Rout.
_____. Maly Theatre, Moscow: 1932. B&W. Set. **RST**, 280.
The Rover.
  Beatty, John Lee. Goodman Theatre, Chicago: 1989. Color. Set. **TCI**, vol. 23, n. 7
     (Aug/Sep 1989). 20.
Rowena's Room.
  Reaney, Mark. University of Kansas, Lawrence: B&W. Sketches. **TDT**, vol. XXV, n. 2
     (Summer 1989). 25.
The Royal Family.
  Burroughs, Robert C. University of Arizona, Tucson: B&W. Set. **SDT**, 281.
  Reynolds, James. Selwyn Theatre, NYC: 1927. B&W. Set. **MCN**, 87.
Royal Hunt of the Sun.
  Annals, Michael. ANTA Theatre, NYC: 1965. B&W. Sketches. **SDB**, 97.
Royal Palace.
  Heckroth, Heinrich. Opernhaus, Essen: 1929. B&W. Rendering. **RSD**, illus. 252.
Roza.
  Okun, Alexander. Mark Taper Forum, Los Angeles: 1987. B&W. Set. **HPA**, 52; Color.
     Set. **MBM**, 89 B&W and color. Rendering & set. **TCI**, vol. 21, n. 9 (Nov 1987).
     46.
The Rules of the Game.
  Pizzi, Pier Luigi. 1966. B&W. Set. **SIO**, 105. 2 photos.
The Ruling Class.
  La Ferla, Sandro. Goodman Theatre, Chicago: 1972. Color. Rendering. **CSD**, 84;
     B&W. Rendering. **DPT**, 355.
Rumors.
  Straiges, Tony. Broadhurst Theatre, NYC: 1988. B&W. Set. **ASD2**, 148.
The Run.
  _____. Realistic Theatre, Moscow: 1932. B&W. Set. **RST**, 284. 2 photos.
Rusalka.
  Kunishima, Yoshiko. Japan: 1986. Color. Model. **TDT**, vol. XXIII, n. 4 (Winter 1988).
     7.
  Lazaridis, Stefanos. English National Opera, London: 1983. Color. Set. **BTD**, 130;
     B&W. Set. **SDL**, 4; B&W. Model. **TDT**, vol. XXIII, n. 4 (Winter 1988). 33; Color.
     Model. **TDT**, vol. XXIII, n. 4 (Winter 1988). 6.
  Rätz, Christian. Spoleto Festival, Charleston, South Carolina: 1988. B&W. Set. **TCI**,
     vol. 22, n. 7 (Aug/Sep 1988). 24; B&W. Set. **TCI**, vol. 24, n. 5 (May 1990). 30.
  Schneider-Siemssen, Günther. Seattle Opera: 1991. Color. Set. **TCI**, vol. 27, n. 3 (Mar
     1993). 26.
  Svoboda, Josef. National Theatre, Prague: 1960. B&W. Rendering. **SJS**, 150; 1991.
     B&W. Set. **STS**, 41; B&W and color. Set. **TDT**, vol. XXX, n. 5 (Fall 1994). 37, 41.
The Rush Hour.
  Borovsky, David. Taganka Theatre, Moscow: 1969. B&W. Model. **SDW3**, 140.
Russia.
  _____. Brooklyn Academy of Music, New York: 1985. Color. Set. **TCI**, vol. 20,
     n. 1 (Jan 1986). 26.
The Russian People.
  Aronson, Boris. Guild Theatre (Virginia Theatre), NYC: 1942. B&W. Rendering.
     TAB, 298.

Rutherford and Son.
> Brown, Penny. New End Theatre, London: 1988. Color. Set. **BTD**, 66.

Ruy Blas.
> Hugo, Jean. Comédie Française, Paris: 1950. B&W. Rendering. **SDW1**, 98.
> Jones, Robert Edmond. Central City Opera House, Colorado: 1938. B&W. Rendering. **SOW**, plate 91.

-S-

Sacrifice to the Wind.
> Toronczyk, Jerzy. Teatr Osterwy, Lublin, Poland: 1957. B&W. Set. **SDW2**, 171.

Sadie Thompson.
> Aronson, Boris. Alvin Theater, NYC: 1944. B&W and color. Rendering & set. **TAB**, 83.

Sadko.
> Younovitch, Sophia. Teatr Opery i Baleta imeni Kirova, Leningrad: 1953. B&W. Rendering. **SDW2**, 202.

Safe Sex.
> Falabella, John. Lyceum Theatre, NYC: 1987. B&W. Rendering. **DDT**, 156. Act I: "Manny and Jake."; B&W. Rendering. **DDT**, 156. Act I: "On Tidy Endings."; B&W. Rendering. **DDT**, 156. Act II: "Safe Sex."

The Saga of Soimaresti.
> Vaselesco, Valer. Opera de Stat, Cluj, Romania: 1959. B&W. Rendering. **SDW2**, 176.

The Saga of the Folkungs.
> Skawonius, Sven Erik. Sweden: B&W. Set. **DSL**, 84.

La Sagra della Primavera.
> Marini, Marino. La Scala, Milan: 1972-1973. B&W. Set. **SIO**, 149-151. 4 photos.

The Sailor Who Fell from Grace with the Sea.
> Steinberg, Paul. San Francisco Opera: 1991. Color. Set. **TCI**, vol. 29, n. 4 (Apr 1995). 34.

The Saint.
> Jones, Robert Edmond. Provincetown Playhouse, NYC: 1924. B&W. Sketch. **DFT**, plate 24. The portico of a seminary at Las Flores, New Mexico.

Saint François d'Assise.
> Tsypin, George. Grosses Festspielhaus, Salzburg: 1992. Color. Model. **TCI**, vol. 26, n. 8 (Oct 1992). 9.

St. Jacobs Fahrt.
> Frey, Maxim. B&W. Rendering. **DIT**, plate 101.

St. Joan.
> Bel Geddes, Norman. Théâtre de la Porte Saint-Martin, Paris: 1925. B&W. Rendering. **RSD**, illus. 438.
> Galliard-Risler, Francine. Centre dramatique de l'Est, Colmar, France: 1949. B&W. Set. **SDW1**, 97.
> Ghika. Basilikon Théatron, Athens: 1951. B&W. Rendering. **SDW1**, 109.
> Hays, David. Vivian Beaumont Theatre, Lincoln Center, NYC: 1967-1968. B&W. Set. **TCI**, vol. 2, n. 6 (Nov/Dec 1968). 33.
> Kantor, Tadeusz. Teatr Stary, Crakow: 1956. B&W. Set. **SDW2**, 166.
> Lee, Ming Cho. Seattle Repertory Theatre: 1979. B&W. Set. **TCI**, vol. 18, n. 2 (Feb 1984). 18.
> Moiseiwitsch, Tanya. Tyrone Guthrie Theatre, Minneapolis: 1963. B&W. Set. **TCI**, vol. 20, n. 7 (Aug/Sep 1986). 23.

Pecktal, Lynn. Trinity Square Theatre, Providence, Rhode Island: 1966. B&W. Set.
    DPT, 16.
Ricketts, Charles. New Theatre, London: 1924. B&W. Set, act drop, & tapestry cur-
    tain. **TDC**, 120-129. 5 photos.
Sovey, Raymond. Garrick Theatre, NYC: 1923. B&W. Set. **MCN**, 64.
Stenberg, Vladimir & Georgiy A. Kamerny (Chamber) Theatre, Moscow: 1924. B&W.
    Model. **AST**, 134; Color. Rendering. **RST**, 171; B&W. Set. **SCM**, 89;
    Theatersammlung, Vienna: 1924. Color. Rendering. **RSD**, illus. 196.
Svoboda, Josef. Tyl Theatre, Pilsen: 1961. B&W. Rendering. **SJS**, 150; Czechoslova-
    kia: 1983. B&W. Model. **TDT**, vol. XXIII, n. 4 (Winter 1988). 50.
_____. Pioneer Theatre Company, Salt Lake City: 1989. B&W. Set. **TCR**, 63.
St. Joan at the Stake.
Svoboda, Josef. Zurich: 1983. Color. Set. **TCI**, vol. 21, n. 8 (Oct 1987). 34.
Saint Joan of America.
Fernandez, Salvador & Raúl Oliva. Teatro Nacional de Cuba, Havana: 1960. B&W.
    Set. **SDW2**, 48.
St. Joan of the Stockyards.
Appen, Karl von. Theater am Schiffbauerdamm, Berlin: 1968. B&W. Rendering & set.
    SDW3, 110. 6 photos.
Frigerio, Ezio. 1970. B&W. Set. **SIO**, 58-61. 3 photos.
Neher, Caspar. Deutsches Schauspielhaus, Hamburg: 1959. B&W. Set. **TBB**, 36.
Nemteanu, Dan. Helsingen Kaupunginteatteri, Helsinki: 1972. B&W. Set. **SDW4**,
    illus. 233-237.
Otto, Teo. Municipal Theatre, Frankfurt am Main: 1963. B&W. Rendering. **SDR**, 46.
Palmstierna-Weiss, Gunilla. Municipal Theatre, Stockholm: 1969. B&W. Set. **RSD**,
    illus. 593; B&W. Set. **TCI**, vol. 12, n. 7 (Nov/Dec 1978). 42, 43.
Schade, Gerhard. State Theatre, Dresden: 1961. B&W. Set. **SDW2**, 56.
Tovaglieri, Enrico. 1953. B&W. Rendering. **SDE**, 156.
St. Louis Woman.
Ayers, Lemuel. Martin Beck Theatre, NYC: 1946. B&W. Set. **BWM**, 253, 254.
St. Luke's Passion.
Wendel, Heinrich. B&W. Set. **OPE**, 48.
St. Matthew Passion.
Lee, Ming Cho. San Francisco Opera: 1973. B&W. Set. **DPT**, 7.
The Saint of Bleeker Street.
Salzer, Beeb. Baltimore Opera Company: 1973. B&W. Rendering. **CSD**, 122. Act I,
    sc. 2; B&W. Rendering. **TDT**, n. 39 (Dec 1974). 11.
St. Petersburg Dreams (Crime and Punishment).
Vassiliev, Alexandre. Teatr Mossovieta, Moscow: 1969. B&W. Rendering. **SDW3**, 83.
    2 photos.
Sakuntala.
Grünewald, Isaac. National Dramatic Theatre, Stockholm: B&W. Rendering. **TPH**,
    photo 389.
Salad Days.
Robertson, Patrick. Theatre Royal, Bristol: 1954. B&W. Set. **MCD**, plate 206.
Salammbo.
Franceschi, Edgar. Ridiculous Theatre, NYC: Color. Set. **TCI**, vol. 20, n. 3 (Mar
    1986). 34, 35.
Salomé.
Bakst, Léon. Théâtre du Châtelet, Paris: 1912. Color. Rendering. **LBT**, 158.
Buchholz, Gerhard T. Wiesbaden: B&W. Set. **TCS2**, plate 214.

Bury, John. Royal Opera House, Covent Garden, London: 1988. Color. Set. **BTD**, 115.

Dali, Salvador. Covent Garden, London: 1949. B&W. Set. **AST**, 199. 4 photos; B&W. Set. **CGA**, 136.

Exter, Alexandra. Kamerny Theater, Moscow: 1917. Color. Model. **RSD**, illus. 155; B&W and color. Rendering, model & set. **RST**, 31, 32; B&W. Set. **TCS2**, plate 152; B&W. Set. **TPH**, photo 402.

Fülöp, Zoltán. Allami Operház, Budapest: 1958. B&W. Rendering. **SDW2**, 140.

Heckroth, Heinrich. State Theatre, Münster: B&W. Set. **TCS2**, plate 148.

Heinrich, Rudolf. Metropolitan Opera, NYC: 1964. B&W. Rendering. **MOM**, 15; B&W. Set. **TCI**, vol. 10, n. 5 (Oct 1976). 15; English National Opera, London: B&W. Sketches & set. **TCI**, vol. 10, n. 6 (Nov/Dec 1976). 14. 4 photos.

Herwig, Curt. Stadtbühnen, Magdeburg: 1925. B&W. Set. **TCS2**, plate 279.

Jampolis, Neil Peter. Netherlands Opera, Amsterdam: 1974. Color. Model. **DPT**, between 124 & 125.

Kruse, Max. Kleines Theater, Berlin: 1902. B&W. Rendering. **MRT**, 16; B&W. Set. **TPH**, photo 324.

Mörner, Stellan. Kungliga Teatern, Stockholm: 1954. B&W. Rendering. **SDW1**, 167.

Oenslager, Donald. Metropolitan Opera, NYC: 1933. B&W. Rendering. **MOM**, 10.

Ricketts, Charles. King's Hall, Covent Garden, London: 1906. B&W. Rendering. **SDT**, 271; B&W. Rendering. **TDC**, 24; B&W. Sketch. **TPH**, photo 353.

Sievert, Ludwig. Germany: 1925. B&W. Rendering. **TAT**, plate 397.

Svoboda, Josef. Montreal: 1985. B&W. Set. **TDT**, vol. XXVIII, n. 5 (Fall 1992). 16; B&W. Model. **TDT**, vol. XXIII, n. 4 (Winter 1988). 50; Berlin: 1990. Color. Set. **TDT**, vol. XXX, n. 5 (Fall 1994). 38.

Wecus, Walter von. State Theatre, Düsseldorf: B&W. Set. **TCS2**, plate 149.

_____. Gran Teatre del Liceu, Barcelona: 1992. Color. Set. **TCI**, vol. 26, n. 4 (Apr 1992). 34.

Salonika.

_____. New York Shakespeare Festival, NYC: 1985. Color. Set. **TCI**, vol. 21, n. 4 (Apr 1987). 34.

Salvation Nell.

Dodge, D. Frank & Ernest Gros. Hackett Theatre, NYC: 1908. B&W. Set. **MCN**, 32; B&W. Set. **SDA**, 24. 2 photos.

Same Old Moon.

Vanek, Joe. London: Color. Set. **TCI**, vol. 28, n. 1 (Jan 1994). 39.

Same Time Next Year.

Butsch, Tom. Chanhassen Dinner Theatre, Minnesota: B&W. Set. **TCI**, vol. 14, n. 5 (Oct 1980). 25.

Sampiero Corso.

Bezombes, Roger. Festival de Bordeaux, France: 1956. B&W. Rendering. **SDW2**, 85.

Samson.

Bragaglia, Anton Giulia. Italy: B&W. Rendering. **SCM**, 76.

Forray, Gabor. National Opera, Budapest: B&W. Set. **TDT**, n. 38 (Oct 1974). 14.

Messel, Oliver. Royal Opera House, Covent Garden, London: 1958. B&W. Set. **OMB**, 185.

O'Brien, Timothy. Royal Opera House, Covent Garden, London: 1985. B&W. Set. **BTD**, 105.

Samson et Dalila.

Cairns, Tom. Bregenz Festival, Austria: 1988. Color. Set. **BTD**, 141.

250 *Sant'Alessio*

Grünewald, Isaac. Royal Opera House, Stockholm. 1921. B&W. Rendering. **CSC**, facing 120, 122; B&W. Rendering. **RSD**, illus. 141; B&W. Rendering. **TCS2**, plate 222; B&W. Rendering. **TPH**, photo 390.
Marussig, Guido. La Scala, Milan: 1950. B&W. Rendering. **SDE**, 121.
Schmidt, Douglas W. San Francisco Opera: 1980. Color. Rendering. **ASD1**, between 70 & 71; B&W. Rendering. **DDT**, 140, 141; B&W. Set. **TCI**, vol. 17, n. 9 (Nov/Dec 1983). 21; B&W. Set. **TDT**, vol. XXII, n. 4 (Winter 1987). 13.
Sant'Alessio.
Ponnelle, Jean-Pierre. Salzburg Festival: 1977. B&W. Set. **TCI**, vol. 12, n. 3 (Mar/Apr 1978). 17. 4 photos.
Santa Claus.
Kiesler, Frederick. B&W. Sketch. **EIF**, photo 46.
Santos Vega.
Benavente, Saulo. Teatro Solis, Montevideo: 1952. B&W. Rendering. **SDW1**, 33.
Saratoga.
Beaton, Cecil. Winter Garden Theatre, NYC: 1959. Color. Set. **CBS**, 36; B&W. Set. **WMC**, 183.
The Satin Slipper.
Coutaud, Lucien. Comédie Française, Paris: 1943. B&W. Rendering. **SDW1**, 94.
Haferung, Paul. Schauspielhaus, Bochum: 1953. B&W. Rendering. **SDW1**, 66.
Saturday, Sunday, Monday.
La Ferla, Sandro. Asolo State Theatre, Sarasota, Florida: B&W. Set. **TCI**, vol. 13, n. 5 (Oct 1979). 36.
Saturday's Children.
_____. Booth Theatre, NYC: 1927. B&W. Set. **MCN**, 82.
Satyagraha.
Isreal, Robert. Rotterdam, Amsterdam, Utrecht, The Hague, The Netherlands: 1980. Color. Set. **TCI**, vol. 24, n. 9 (Nov 1990). 37; B&W. Set. **TDT**, vol. XVII, n. 2 (Summer 1981). 10, 11. 6 photos; Brooklyn Academy of Music, New York: 1981. Color. Set. **ASD2**, between 108 & 109.
Savages.
Funicello, Ralph. Seattle Repertory Theatre: 1982. B&W. Set. **ASD1**, 46.
Straiges, Tony. Center Stage, Baltimore: 1981. B&W. Set. **ASD2**, 143; B&W. Set. **TCI**, vol. 16, n. 8 (Oct 1982). 25.
Savannah Bay.
McLeish, Iona. Foco Novo: 1988. B&W. Set. **BTD**, 68.
Savonarola.
Barsacq, André. Piazza de la Signoria: 1935. B&W. Set. **RSD**, illus. 108.
Sayonara.
Anania, Michael. Paper Mill Playhouse, Milburn, New Jersey: 1987. B&W. Set. **TCI**, vol. 21, n. 10 (Dec 1987). 24.
Says I, Says He.
Jenkins, David. Mark Taper Forum, Los Angeles: 1979. B&W. Set. **TCI**, vol. 14, n. 4 (Sep 1980). 40.
Scandal in the Valley of St. Florian.
Molka, Viktor. Narodno Gledalisce, Ljubljana: 1951. B&W. Model. **SDW1**, 134.
Scapin the Trickster.
Bérard, Christian. Théâtre Marigny, Paris: 1949. B&W. Rendering. **SDW1**, 82.
Scapino.
Pate, Catherine. University of New Hampshire: 1978. B&W. Set. **TCI**, vol. 13, n. 3 (May/Jun 1979). 38.

Prévost, Robert. Canada: B&W. Model. **TDT**, vol. XVI, n. 1 (Spring 1980). 25.
Schmidt, Douglas. Old Globe Theatre, San Diego: 1984. B&W. Set. **TDT** vol. XXXI,
  n. 2 (Spring 1995). 16.
Sousa, Larry. (project): B&W. Rendering. **TDT**, vol. XXVI, n. 1 (Spring 1990). 24 of
  insert.
Scarlet Letter.
Patel, Neil. Classic Stage Company, NYC: 1994. Color. Set. **TCI**, vol. 29, n. 1 (Jan
  1995). 7.
Scenes from a Marriage.
Howland, Gerald. Royal Shakespeare Company, GB: 1986. B&W. Sketch. **BTD**, 46.
Der Schatzgräber.
Pirchan, Emil. B&W. Rendering. **CSC**, facing 60.
Schéhérazade.
Bakst, Léon. Théâtre National de l'Opera, Paris: 1910. B&W. Rendering. **CSD**, 44;
  Color. Rendering. **LBT**, 94, 95; Color. Rendering. **RSD**, illus. 37; B&W. Render-
  ing. **SDC**, plate 63; B&W. Rendering. **SDG**, 169.
Marchi, Mario Vellani. La Scala, Milan: 1950. B&W. Rendering. **SDE**, 118.
Scherz, Satire, Ironie und tiefere Bedeutung.
Gade, Svend. Kleines Theater, Berlin: 1915. B&W. Set. **TPH**, photo 418.
Schluck and Jau.
Ulyanov, Nikolai. Studio Theater, Moscow: 1905. B&W. Set. **MOT**, between 48 & 49;
  B&W. Rendering. **RSD**, illus. 24.
The School for Husbands.
Burroughs, Robert C. University of Arizona, Tucson: B&W. Rendering. **SDT**, 284.
Simonson, Lee. Theatre Guild, NYC: 1933. B&W. Rendering. **FCS**, plate 201; B&W.
  Rendering. **SDO**, 230.
The School for Scandal.
Aronson, Boris. Queen's Theatre, London: 1937. B&W. Set. **PST**, 308; B&W. Set.
  TSY, 125.
Beaton, Cecil. Old Vic Company, New Theatre, London: 1947. B&W. Rendering.
  CBS, 40, 41.
Hurwitz, Albert. Arena Stage, Washington, DC: 1950. B&W. Set. **TCI**, vol. 18, n. 3
  (Mar 1984). 30.
Schmidt, Douglas W. The Acting Company, NYC: 1972. B&W. Set. **BSE4**, 55.
Svoboda, Josef. National Theatre, Prague: 1972. B&W. Set. **TDT**, vol. XII, n. 2 (Sum-
  mer 1976). 14.
———. Gate Theatre, London: Color. Set. **TCI**, vol. 28, n. 1 (Jan 1994). 41.
The School for Wives.
Arnone, John. Hartford Stage, Connecticut: B&W. Set. **TCI**, vol. 25, n. 9 (Nov 1991).
  43.
Bérard, Christian. Théâtre de l'Athénée, Paris: 1937. B&W and color. Rendering &
  set. **RSD**, illus. 406-409; B&W. Set. **SDW1**, 82, 83; B&W. Set. **SOW**, plate 38.
Ciller, Josef. Martin, Czechoslovakia: 1969. B&W. Rendering. **TDT**, vol. XXVIII, n. 2
  (Spring 1992). 34.
Davison, Peter J. Almeida Theatre, London: 1993. B&W. Set. **TCI**, vol. 28, n. 4 (Apr
  1994). 13.
Daydé, Bernard. Det Kongelige Teater, Köbenhavn: 1970. B&W. Set. **SDW3**, 67.
Howard, Pamela. National Theatre (Lyttleton), London: 1986. B&W. Set. **TDT**, vol.
  XXIV, n. 2 (Summer 1988). 48.
Schwab, Per. National Theatre, Oslo: 1965. B&W. Set. **SDR**, 70.
Siercke, Alfred. Hamburg Staatsoper: 1958. B&W. Rendering. **SDW2**, 72.

Stegars, Rolf. Suomen Kansallisteatteri, Helsinki. 1959. B&W. Set. **SDW2**, 206.

Survage, Leopold. Paris: 1935. B&W. Rendering. **SDE**, 153.

The Schooling of Don Quixote.

Kysela, Frantisek. Vinohrady Theatre, Prague: 1914. B&W. Rendering. **TDT**, n. 41 (Summer 1975). 15. 2 photos.

Schwanda the Piper.

Schenk von Trapp, Lothar. Hessiches Landestheater, Darmstadt: 1930. B&W. **RSD**, illus. 246.

Die schweigsame Frau.

Jürgens, Helmut. State Opera, Munich: 1962. B&W. Set. **OPE**, 67.

Schweik in the Second World War.

Damiani, Luciano. 1961-1962. B&W. Set. **SIO**, 35-37. 4 photos.

Dudley, William. National Theatre (Olivier), London: 1982. B&W. Set. **BTD**, 56.

_____. Ruhrfestspiele, Recklinghausen: 1967. B&W. Rendering. **RSD**, illus. 582.

_____. Municipal Theatre, Frankfurt am Main: 1959. B&W. Set. **TBB**, 55.

Screenplay.

Eigsti, Karl. Arena Stage, Washington, DC: 1983. B&W. Set. **DDT**, 157; B&W. Set. **TCI**, vol. 18, n. 3 (Mar 1984). 28.

The Screens.

Acquart, André. Odeon Theatre, Paris: 1966. B&W. Set. **RSD**, illus. 538; Color. Set. **SDW3**, 127. 2 photos.

Mitchell, Robert D. Chelsea Theatre Center, Brooklyn, New York: B&W. Set. **TCI**, vol. 8, n. 2 (Mar/Apr 1974). 16.

Rose, Jürgen. Residenz Theater, Munich: 1968. Color. Set. **SDW3**, 126. 5 photos.

Tsypin, George. Tyrone Guthrie Theatre, Minneapolis: 1989/1990. B&W. Set. **ASD2**, 159, 168; B&W. Set. **DDT**, 24; B&W. Set. **TCI**, vol. 24, n. 1 (Jan 1990). 15; B&W. Set. **TCI**, vol. 24, n. 8 (Oct 1990). 42; Color.Set. **TCI**, vol. 25, n. 2 (Feb 1991). 39; B&W. Model. **TDT**, vol. XXVII, n. 3 (Summer 1991). 11.

Se Questo è un Uomo.

Polidori, Gianni. 1966. B&W. Rendering. **SIO**, 117.

Sea Marks.

Jordan, Dale and Leslie Taylor. Players Theatre, NYC: B&W. Set. **TCI**, vol. 16, n. 7 (Aug/Sep 1982). 27.

The Seagull.

Annals, Michael. Tel Aviv: 1971. B&W. Rendering. **SDB**, 101, 102. Acts I-IV. 4.

Arnone, John. La Jolla Playhouse, California: 1985/1986. B&W. Set. **ASD2**, 21; B&W. Set. **TCI**, vol. 21, n. 8 (Oct 1987). 29.

Darling, Robert Edward. Williamstown Theatre Festival, Massachusetts: 1974. B&W. Set. **TCI**, vol. 14, n. 3 (May/Jun 1980). 18.

Faulkner, Cliff. South Coast Repertory Theatre, Costa Mesa, California: Color. Rendering & set. **TCI**, vol. 20, n. 9 (Nov 1986). 29.

Isackes, Richard M. Illinois Repertory Theatre: B&W. Rendering & set. **TDT**, vol. XXVI, n. 1 (Spring 1990). 2, 12 of insert. Act I.

Jackness, Andrew. Yale Repertory Theatre, New Haven: 1979. B&W. Set. **TCI**, vol. 13, n. 4 (Sep 1979). 8.

Jordanov, Ljubomir. Ivan Vazov National Academic Theatre, Sofia: B&W. Set. **TDT**, vol. XXIII, n. 4 (Winter 1988). 37.

Kerz, Leo. Center Stage, Baltimore: 1968. B&W. Set. **TCI**, vol. 7, n. 3 (May/Jun 1973). 14.

Kokkos, Yannis. Théâtre National de Chaillot, Paris: 1984. Color. Rendering. **TDT**, vol. XXIII, n. 4 (Winter 1988). 6. 2 photos.

Kolodziej, Marian. Teatr Ateneum Im. Stefana Jaracza, Poland: B&W. Set. **TCI**, vol. 15, n. 4 (Apr 1981). 15.

Leahy, Gerry. Florida State University, Tallahassee: Color. Set. **TCI**, vol. 26, n. 3 (Mar 1992). 41.

McDonald, Anthony. American Repertory Theatre, Cambridge, Massachusetts: 1991. Color. Set. **TCI**, vol. 26, n. 5 (May 1992). 12.

Strzelecki, Zenobiusz. Teatr Polski, Warsaw: 1959. B&W. Rendering. **SDW2**, 169.

Svoboda, Josef. Tyl Theatre, Prague: 1960. B&W. Rendering. **SDW2**, 44; B&W. Rendering & set. **SJS**, 62. 3 photos; B&W. Set. **STS**, 58; B&W. Rendering. **TDT**, vol. XXVIII, n. 5 (Fall 1992). 12; Theatre Beyond the Gate, Prague: 1972. B&W. Set. **STS**, 25; B&W. Set. **TDT**, vol. XII, n. 2 (Summer 1976). 31; Louvain: 1988. Color. Set. **TDT**, vol. XXX, n. 5 (Fall 1994). 38.

Taylor, Robert U. Colonnades Theatre Lab, NYC: B&W. Sketch. **TCI**, vol. 11, n. 1 (Jan/Feb 1977). 24.

Tsypin, George. Eisenhower Theatre, Washington, DC: 1985. B&W. Set. **ASD2**, 163; B&W. Model. **DDT**, 410.

Yeargan, Michael. Public Theatre, NYC: 1980. B&W. Set. **TCI**, vol. 17, n. 4 (Apr 1983). 16; B&W. Set. **TCI**, vol. 16, n. 5 (May 1982). 24. 3 photos.

Zboril, M. Czechoslovakia: B&W. Rendering. **TDT**, vol. XII, n. 3 (Fall 1976). 43.
_____. American National Theatre, Washington, DC: 1985. Color. Set. **TCI**, vol. 20, n. 9 (Nov 1986). 19.

The Searcher.

Oenslager, Donald. Yale School of Drama, New Haven, Connecticut: 1930. B&W. Rendering. **TDO**, 39, 40.

Seascape.

Hird, Thomas C. California State University, Hayward: 1979. B&W. Set. **BSE2**, 16.

Tilton, James. Shubert Theatre, NYC: 1975. Color. Set. **DPT**, Facing 28.

Season in the Sun.

Aronson, Boris. Cort Theatre, NYC: 1950. B&W and color. Rendering & set. **TAB**, 98, 301.

Seat of Justice.

Mostafa, Ramzi. Al Gaama al Amrikia, Al Kahiro, Cairo: 1971. B&W. Set. **SDW3**, 108.

Sebastian.

La Ferla, Sandro. Harkness Ballet, Harkness Theatre, New York: 1974. B&W. Rendering. **CSD**, 91; B&W. Scrim. **DPT**, 311.

The Second Man.

Mielziner, Jo. Guild Theatre, NYC: 1927. B&W. Set. **MCN**, 83.

Second Sons: A Story of Rugby, Tennessee.

Harman, Leonard. Cumberland County Playhouse, Crossville, Tennessee: 1985. B&W. Set. **BSE4**, 25; Color. Set. **SCT**, between 152 & 153; B&W. Set. **TCI**, vol. 22, n. 3 (Mar 1988). 100.

The Second-hand Dealer.

Ivo, Lode. Koninklijke Vlaamse Opera, Antwerp: 1963. B&W. Set. **SDW2**, 28.

The Secret.

Svoboda, Josef. Prague: 1973. B&W. Set. **TDT**, vol. XII, n. 2 (Summer 1976). 14.

The Secret Garden.

Landesman, Heidi. Virginia Stage Company, Norfolk: 1989. Color. Set. **ASD2**, between 108 & 109; St. James Theatre, NYC: 1991. Color. Model. **TCI**, vol. 25, n. 4

(Apr 1991). 12; B&W and color. Model & set. **TCI**, vol. 25, n. 8 (Oct 1991). 7, 42-44. 6 photos.

El Secreto a voces.

_____. Svando Teatr, Prague: 1922. B&W. Set. **TCS2**, plate 247.

See Hear.

Sirlin, Jerome. American Music Theatre Festival, Philadelphia: 1985. Color. Model. **TCI**, vol. 22, n. 1 (Jan 1988). 34.

Seesaw.

Wagner, Robin. Uris Theatre, NYC: 1973. Color. Set. **BWM**, 137; B&W. Photomontages. **DPT**, 124; B&W. Set. **TCI**, vol. 7, n. 4 (Sep 1973). 25.

Segel am Horizont.

Müller, Traugott. Volksbühne, Berlin: 1924. B&W. Set. **TCS2**, plate 125.

Der Seidene Schuh (The Silk Shoe).

Toffolutti, Ezio. Landestheater, Salzburg: 1986. B&W. Set. **TCI**, vol. 20, n. 4 (Apr 1986). 8.

Semi Mode.

Prowse, Philip. Citizen's Theatre of Glasgow: B&W. Set. **TCI**, vol. 15, n. 7 (Aug/Sep 1981). 25.

Semion Kotko.

Levental, Valery. Akademitcheskij Bolsoj Teatr Soyouza SSR, Moscow: 1970. B&W. Set. **SDW4**, illus. 224.

Semiramis.

Iacovleff, Alexandre. Opéra de Paris: 1934. B&W. Rendering. **RSC**, 43.

Sempronio, the Hairdresser and the Little Men.

Vigón, Ruben. Teatro Nacional de Cuba, Havana: 1962. B&W. Rendering. **SDW2**, 48.

Senora Carrar's Rifles.

_____. Salle Adyar, Paris: 1937. B&W. Set. **TBB**, 45.

Sept Chansons.

Barbey, Valdo. B&W. Rendering. **DIT**, plate 103.

September 8.

Padovani, Gianfranco. 1970-1971. B&W. Rendering. **SIO**, 101.

Il Seraglio.

Firth, Tazeena. Storan Theater, Götesborg: 1986. B&W. Set. **BTD**, 104.

Seraphic Dialogue.

Noguchi, Isamu. 1955. B&W. Set. **CSD**, 46. Dance.

Serenading Louie.

Belden, Ursula. Pittsburgh Public Theatre: B&W. Set. **TCI**, vol. 21, n. 7 (Aug/Sep 1987). 36.

Serious Money.

Dorsey, Kent. Berkeley Repertory Theatre, California: Color. Set. **TCI**, vol. 25, n. 8 (Oct 1991). 47.

Hartwell, Peter. New York Shakespeare Festival, NYC: 1987. Color. Set. **TCI**, vol. 22, n. 2 (Feb 1988). 10.

Sergeant Musgrave's Dance.

Damiani, Luciano. 1967. B&W. Rendering. **SIO**, 46. 3 photos.

Freudenberger, Daniel. Loeb Drama Center, Harvard University: 1967. B&W. Set. **SFT**, 15.

Herbert, Jocelyn. Royal Court Theatre, London: 1959. Color. Rendering. **DMS**, plate 33.

The Servant of Two Masters.

Creuz, Serge. Comédie de l'Est, Strasbourg: 1962. B&W. Set. **SDW2**, 28. 2 photos.

Frigerio, Ezio. Piccolo Teatro della Città di Milano: 1973. B&W. Set. **SDW2**, 125; B&W. Set. **SIO**, 66, 67. 3 photos.

Renard, Raymond. Théâtre de la Poche, Brussels: 1958. B&W. Set. **SDW2**, 31.

Smith, Russell. Furman University, Greenville, South Carolina: 1980. B&W. Rendering. **TCI**, vol. 15, n. 7 (Aug/Sep 1981). 7.

Stern, Ernst. Kammerspiele, Munich: 1907. B&W. Rendering. **MRH**, facing 20.

Takata, Ichiro. Haiyuza, Tokyo: 1962. B&W. Set. **SDW2**, 150.

Ultz. Cambridge Theatre Company: 1982. B&W. Set. **TCI**, vol. 17, n. 7 (Aug/Sep 1983). 38.

I Sette Peccati.

Chiari, Mario. 1955-1956. B&W. Set. **SIO**, 25-27. 3 photos.

The Seven Brothers.

Puumalainen, Kaj. Turun Kaupunginteatteri, Turku (Suomi): 1972. B&W. Set. **SDW4**, illus. 177, 178.

The Seven Deadly Sins.

Heckroth, Heinrich. Stadtische Buhnen, Frankfurt: 1960. B&W. Rendering. **SDW2**, 63.

Karavan, Dani. Ha-Cameri Haysraeli, Isreal: 1972. B&W. Set. **SDW4**, illus. 238.

Loquasto, Santo. Yale Repertory Theatre, New Haven: 1971. B&W. Set. **TCI**, vol. 7, n. 5 (Oct 1973). 18.

Svoboda, Josef. Schauspielhaus, Düsseldorf: 1990. B&W. Sketch & set. **TDT**, vol. XXX, n. 5 (Fall 1994). 42.

Ter-Arutunian, Rouben. NYC: 1958. B&W. Set. **SDB**, 24.

_____. Juilliard School, Lincoln Center, NYC: 1990. Color. Set. **TCI**, vol. 27, n. 4 (Apr 1993). 29.

The Seven Deadly Sins of the Lower Middle Class.

Prowse, Philip. Citizen's Theatre of Glasgow: B&W. Set. **TCI**, vol. 15, n. 7 (Aug/Sep 1981). 23.

Seven Keys to Baldpate.

Lee, Eugene. Dallas Theatre Center: 1984. B&W. Sketch & set. **ASD1**, 78, 79.

The Seven Princesses.

Jones, Robert Edmond. (project): 1919. B&W. **SDC**, plate 117; B&W. Rendering. **TCS2**, plate 196.

Seven Ways to Cross a River.

Fievez, Jean-Marie. Théâtre de l'Espirit Frappeur, Brussels: 1973. B&W. Set. **SDW4**, illus. 370-373.

1789.

Moscoso, Roberto. Sports Stadium, Milan: 1970. B&W. Set. **RSD**, illus. 642-644.

1793.

_____. Vincennes: 1972. B&W. Sketch & set. **RSD**, illus. 645-647.

1776.

Mielziner, Jo. 46th Street Theatre, NYC: 1969. B&W. Set. **BWM**, 313; B&W. Rendering. **CSD**, 108; B&W. Rendering. **DDT**, 246. 2 photos; B&W. Rendering. **DPT**, 55; B&W. Rendering. **SDB**, 63. 2 photos; B&W. Rendering & set. **TCI**, vol. 4, n. 3 (May/Jun 1970). 18, 24, 25. 5 photos.

_____. North Shore Music Theatre, Beverly, Massachusetts: Color. Set. **TCI**, vol. 24, n. 9 (Nov 1990). 41.

Sganarelle.

Yeargan, Michael. Yale Repertory Theatre, New Haven: 1978. B&W. Set. **TCI**, vol. 16, n. 5 (May 1982). 25. 2 photos; Loeb Drama Center, Boston: 1978. B&W. Set. **TCI**, vol. 12, n. 5 (Sep 1978). 26-29. 18 photos.

Shackles.
> Eich, Harry. De Haagse Comedie, Koninklijke Schouwburg, Den Haag: 1971. B&W.
>   Set. **SDW4**, illus. 193.

The Shadow.
> Akimov, Nikolai. Teatr Komedii, Leningrad: 1940. B&W. Rendering. **SDW2**, 177.

The Shadow Box.
> Scheffler, John. Asolo State Theatre, Sarasota, Florida: B&W. Set. **TCI**, vol. 13, n. 5
>   (Oct 1979). 37.

Shadow of a Gunman.
> Bainbridge, Martyn. Theatre Royal, Plymouth, England: 1986. B&W. Set. **BTD**, 77.

The Shaughraun.
> Dudley, William. National Theatre, London: 1988. Color. Set. **TCI**, vol. 23, n. 1 (Jan
>   1989). 10; B&W. Set. **TDT**, vol. XXV, n. 3 (Fall 1989). 22.

She Always Said, Pablo.
> Paoletti, John. Goodman Theatre, Chicago: 1987. B&W. Set. **BSE5**, 35; Color. Set.
>   **BSE5**, back cover.

She Loves Me.
> Baldasso, Carl A. Equity Library Theatre, NYC: B&W. Set. **TCI**, vol. 20, n. 5 (May
>   1986). 27.
> Eckart, William & Jean. Eugene O'Neill Theatre, NYC: 1963. Color. Set. **BWM**, 295;
>   B&W. Set. **HPA**, 34; B&W. Set. **HPR**, 87; B&W. Set. **TCI**, vol. 20, n. 5 (May
>   1986). 26.
> Landwehr, Hugh. Center Stage, Baltimore: Color. Set. **TCI**, vol. 20, n. 5 (May 1986).
>   26.
> Morton, Mark W. Alliance Theatre, Atlanta: Color. Set. **TCI**, vol. 20, n. 5 (May 1986).
>   26.
> Pass, Paul de. Carnegie-Mellon University, Pittsburgh: 1971. B&W. Set. **TCI**, vol. 7,
>   n. 5 (Oct 1973). 27.
> Walton, Tony. Roundabout Theatre, NYC: 1993. Color. Model & set. **TCI**, vol. 27, n.
>   7 (Aug/Sep 1993). 70. 5 photos.

She Stoops to Conquer.
> _____. Milwaukee Repertory Theatre: Color. Set. **TCI**, vol. 24, n. 4 (Apr 1990).
>   40.

The She-devil.
> Castillo, Carlos. Nuevo Teatro, Lima: 1959. B&W. Set. **SDW2**, 163.

The Sheep Well.
> Navarro, Oscar. Teatro Experimental de la Universidad de Chile, Santiago: 1952.
>   B&W. Set. **SDW1**, 54.
> Cortezo, Victor. Teatro Español, Madrid: 1962. B&W. Set. **SDW2**, 77.

Shelter.
> Walton, Tony. Golden Theatre, NYC: 1973. B&W. Set. **DDT**, 58.

Shenandoah.
> Anania, Michael. Paper Mill Playhouse, Milburn, New Jersey: Color. Set. **TCI**, vol.
>   24, n. 2 (Feb 1990). 66.
> Jensen, Bob. Plays-in-the-Park, Edison, New Jersey: B&W. Set. **TCI**, vol. 14, n. 3
>   (May/Jun 1980). 41.

The Shepherd King.
> Conklin, John. Glimmerglass Opera, Cooperstown, New York: 1991. B&W. Model.
>   **TDT**, vol. XXVII, n. 3 (Summer 1991). 13.

Sherlock Holmes.
> Toms, Carl. Aldwych Theatre, London: 1974. B&W. Set. **TCI**, vol. 14, n. 1 (Jan/Feb

1980). 18; B&W. Set. **TCI**, vol. 9, n. 1 (Jan/Feb 1975). 21. 2 photos.

_____. Alaska Repertory Theatre, Anchorage: B&W. Set. **TCI**, vol. 13, n. 2 (Mar/Apr 1979). 25. 2 photos.

Sherlock's Last Case.
Soule, Robert D. Trinity Square Theatre, Providence, Rhode Island: 1988. B&W. Set. **TCI**, vol. 22, n. 9 (Nov 1988). 60.

Sherry!
Randolph, Robert. Alvin Theatre, NYC: 1967. B&W. Rendering & set. **TCI**, vol. 1, n. 1 (Mar/Apr 1967). 12-15. 5 photos.

The Ship.
Marussig, Guido. Italy: 1932. B&W. Rendering. **TPH**, photo 379.

The Shoemaker's Holiday.
Lagrange, Jacques. Théâtre National Populaire, Lyon: 1959. B&W. Model. **SDW2**, 93.
Leve, Samuel & Orson Welles. Mercury Theatre, NYC: 1938. B&W. Set. **MCN**, 139; B&W. Set. **SOW**, plate 37.

The Shoemaker's Wife.
Ganeau, François. Grenier de Toulouse, France: 1960. B&W. Rendering. **SDW2**, 92.
Luzzati, Emanuele. La Fenice, Venice: 1959. Color. Rendering. **SDW2**, 127.
Moralis, Yannis. Vassilikon Théâtron, Athens: 1958. B&W. Rendering. **SDW2**, 104. 2 photos.
Vos, Marik. Dramatiska Teatern, Stockholm: 1956. B&W. Set. **SDW2**, 212.

Shogun: The Musical.
Sherman, Loren. Marquis Theatre, NYC: 1990. B&W and color. Set. **DDT**, 24a, 31, 587; Color. Set. **TCI**, vol. 24, n. 10 (Dec 1990). 11; Color. Set. **TCI**, vol. 28, n. 3 (Mar 1994). 33; B&W. Model. **TCI**, vol. 24, n. 8 (Oct 1990). 36. 5 photos.

Short Eyes.
Mitchell, David. Vivian Beaumont Theatre, Lincoln Center, NYC: 1974. B&W. Set. **ASD1**, 126; B&W. Model. **CSD**, 110.

_____. Karamu Theatre, Cleveland: B&W. Set. **TDT**, vol. XV, n. 4 (Winter 1979). 15.

A Short Happy Life.
Mielziner, Jo. 1961. B&W. Rendering. **DTT**, 213. Prologue; B&W. Rendering. **DTT**, 214. Jungle scene; B&W. Rendering. **DTT**, 215. Transformation: Venice.

The Shot.
_____. Theatre of Working Youth (TRAM), Leningrad: 1929. B&W. Set. **RST**, 244. 2 photos.

Shout Up a Morning.
Arnone, John. La Jolla Playhouse, California: Color. Set. **TCI**, vol. 21, n. 8 (Oct 1987). 27.

Show Boat.
Anania, Michael. Paper Mill Playhouse, Milburn, New Jersey: 1989. Color. Set. **TCI**, vol. 23, n. 9 (Nov 1989). 26. Staged for television
Bay, Howard. Ziegfeld Theatre, NYC: 1946. B&W. Rendering. **SDB**, 111; B&W. Rendering & set. **TCI**, vol. 17, n. 2 (Feb 1983). 18; B&W. Set. **TMI**, 127; B&W. Set. **WTP**, 220, 221. 4 photos; Los Angeles Civic Light Opera Company: 1953. B&W. Rendering. **DPT**, 327; NYC: 1954. B&W. Rendering. **SDB**, 58; B&W. Rendering. **TCI**, vol. 17, n. 2 (Feb 1983). 18.
Butsch, Tom. Chanhassen Dinner Theatre, Minnesota: B&W. Set. **TCI**, vol. 14, n. 5 (Oct 1980). 24.
Harker, Joseph & Phil Harker. Theatre Royal, Drury Lane, London: 1928. B&W. Set. **MCD**, plate 153.

Kimmel, Alan. Casa Mañana, Dallas: B&W. Set. **TCI**, vol. 2, n. 5 (Sep/Oct 1968). 19.

Lee, Eugene. Main Stage Theatre, Toronto: 1994. B&W and color. Model & set. **TCI**, vol. 28, n. 2 (Feb 1994). 5, 26-28. 7 photos.

Smith, Oliver. Lincoln Center, NYC: 1966. Color. Set. **BWM**, 168, 169.

Urban, Joseph. Ziegfeld Theater, NYC: 1927. B&W. Set. **BMF**, 32; B&W. Set. **BWM**, 166, 167; B&W. Set. **HPA**, 11; B&W. Set. **SDA**, 244; B&W. Set. **TMI**, 116; B&W. Set. **WMC**, 61.

_____. NYC: 1971. Color. Set. **TMT**, plate 7.

_____. Palace Theatre, London: c.1970. Color. Set. **BMF**, 140.

The Show is On.

Minelli, Vincent. Winter Garden Theatre, NYC: 1936. B&W. Set. **RBS**, 137.

The Show-Off.

Cornell, Allen. Pittsburgh Public Theatre: Color. Set. **TCI**, vol. 21, n. 7 (Aug/Sep 1987). 37.

Mikulewicz, Bill. Arizona Theatre Company, Tucson: 1979. B&W. Set. **TCI**, vol. 14, n. 3 (May/Jun 1980). 40.

The Sicilian Vespers.

Grübler, Ekkehard. Munich: B&W. Set. **TCI**, vol. 11, n. 2 (Mar/Apr 1977). 18.

Röthlisberger, Max. State Theatre, Zurich: 1951. B&W. Set. **SDW1**, 119.

Svoboda, Josef. State Opera, Hamburg: 1969. B&W. Set. **SJS**, 66. 3 photos; B&W. Set. **TDT**, n. 20 (Feb 1970). 10; Metropolitan Opera, NYC: 1974. B&W. Set. **STS**, 97.

Side By Side By Sondheim.

Docherty, Peter. Music Box Theatre, NYC: 1977. Color. Set. **SON**, 2, 3.

Kissel, David. Paper Mill Playhouse, Milburn, New Jersey: Color. Set. **TCI**, vol. 20, n. 5 (May 1986). 24.

Siebenstein.

Rochus-Gliese. State Theatre, Berlin: B&W. Rendering. **SCM**, 59. Act III.

The Siege of Corinth.

Benois, Nicola. Metropolitan Opera, NYC: B&W. Set. **TCI**, vol. 10, n. 5 (Oct 1976). 17.

Crespi, Maria Grazia. 1953. B&W. Sketch. **SDE**, 71.

Ratto, Gianni. Florence: 1949. B&W. Rendering. **SDE**, 138.

Siegfried.

Benois, Nicola. La Scala, Milan: 1950. B&W. Rendering. **SDE**, 34.

Bonnat, Yves (Yves-Bonnat). Centre dramatique de l'Est, Colmar, France: 1951. B&W. Rendering. **SDW1**, 87.

Brazda, Jan. Kungliga Teatern, Stockholm: 1970. B&W. Rendering. **SDW3**, 180.

Isreal, Robert. Seattle Opera: 1986. B&W. Set. **ASD2**, 52; 1990. Color. Set. **TCI**, vol. 24, n. 9 (Nov 1990). 38.

Peduzzi, Richard. Beyreuth Festival Theatre: 1976. B&W. Set. **TCI**, vol. 11, n. 2 (Mar/ Apr 1977). 17.

Preetorius, Emil. Beyreuth Festival Theatre: 1937. B&W. Set. **JSS**, 17. Act III, sc. 2.

Schneider-Siemssen, Günther. Metropolitan Opera, NYC: 1967-1972. B&W. Set. **TCI**, vol. 10, n. 5 (Oct 1976). 18; B&W. Set. **TCI**, vol. 12, n. 6 (Oct 1978). 31.

Simonson, Lee. Metropolitan Opera, NYC: 1948. B&W. Set. **SDA**, 269; B&W. Set. **TAS**, 157. 2 photos.

Svoboda, Josef. Royal Opera House, Covent Garden, London: 1975. B&W. Set. **JSS**, 68. Act III, sc. 1; B&W. Set. **JSS**, 68; B&W. Set. **JSS**, 70. Act II; Color. Set. **JSS**, between 54 & 55. Act I; B&W. Set. **STS**, 83; B&W. Model. **TDT**, vol. XII, n. 2 (Summer 1976). 30; B&W. Set. **TDT**, vol. XV, n. 1 (Spring 1979). 8; Grand The-

ater, Geneva: 1976. B&W. Set. **JSS**, 88. Act II; B&W. Set. **JSS**, 90. Act III, sc. 1;
Color. Set. **JSS**, between 54 & 55. Act I; Color. Set. **TDT**, vol. XXVIII, n. 5 (Fall
1992). 9; Czechoslovakia: B&W. Model. **TDT**, vol. XVI, n. 1 (Spring 1980). 29.
Wagner, Wieland. Beyreuth Festival Theatre: 1951. B&W. Set. **RSD**, illus. 548.
Wagner, Wolfgang. Beyreuth Festival Theatre: 1964. B&W. Set. **JSS**, 20. Act III, sc. 2;
1970. B&W. Set. **TDT**, n. 29 (May 1972). 10. Act II.
Wendel, Heinrich. B&W. Set. **OPE**, 47. Final scene.
Wotruba, Fritz. Deutsches Staatsoper, Berlin: 1967. B&W. Set. **AST**, 231. 4 photos.
Il Signor Bruschino.
Pizzi, Pier Luigi. 1956-1957. B&W. Rendering. **SIO**, 104.
The Signs of the Zodiac.
Prieto, Julio. Palacio de Bellas Artes, Mexico: 1951. B&W. Set. **SDW1**, 135.
Silence.
Bury, John. National Theatre, London: 1969. B&W. Set. **TDT**, vol. XIX, n. 3 (Fall
1983). 7.
The Silence of the Dead.
Feher, Miklos. Vigszinhaz, Budapest: 1973. B&W. Set. **SDW4**, illus. 276.
The Silent Canary.
Heythum, Antonín. Osvobozene Theatre, Prague: 1937. B&W. Set. **RSD**, illus. 280.
The Silent Woman.
Hugo, Jean. L'Atelier, Paris: 1925. Color. Rendering. **TCS2**, color plate 4. 2 photos.
Silk Stockings.
Mielziner, Jo. Imperial Theatre, NYC: 1955. B&W. Rendering. **DTT**, 180.
"Commissar's office."
The Silver Cord.
Throckmorton, Cleon. John Golden Theatre, NYC: 1926. B&W. Set. **MCN**, 79.
The Silver Dream of Salome.
Czerniawski, Jerzy. Teatr Narodowy, Poland: B&W. Set. **TCI**, vol. 15, n. 4 (Apr 1981).
13.
Silverlake.
Brotherston, Lez. Camden Festival, GB: 1987. B&W. Model. **BTD**, 138.
Simon Boccanagra.
Svoboda, Josef. National Theatre, Prague: 1971. B&W. Set. **TDT**, vol. XII, n. 2 (Sum-
mer 1976). 21.
Fielding, David. English National Opera, London: 1986. B&W. Set. **BTD**, 106. 2
photos.
Frigerio, Ezio. 1972. B&W. Rendering. **SIO**, 63. 2 photos.
Simoun.
Fuerst, Walter René. Odéon Théâtre, Paris: B&W. Model. **TCS2**, plate 218.
Simpatico.
_____. Downtown Art Co., NYC: 1993. Color. Set. **TCI**, vol. 27, n. 4 (Apr
1993). 6.
Simple Takes a Wife.
Synek, Vladimir. Divadlo S.K. Neumanna, Prague: 1959. B&W. Rendering. **SDW2**,
46.
The Simpleton.
Itô, Kisaku. Geijutsuza, Tokyo: 1960. B&W. Set. **SDW2**, 150.
The Simpleton of the Unexpected Isles.
Simonson, Lee. Guild Theatre, NYC: 1935. B&W. Set. **TAS**, 152. 2 photos.
Sinfonia Argentina.
Muñoz, Gori. Teatro Avenida, Buenos Aires: 1952. B&W. Rendering. **SDW1**, 37.

Sing for Your Supper.
    Andrews, Herbert. Adelphi Theatre, NYC: 1939. B&W. Set. **RBS**, 181.
Singin' in the Rain.
    Loquasto, Santo. Gershwin Theatre, NYC: 1985. B&W. Set. **TCI**, vol. 19, n. 8 (Oct
        1985). 42.
        _____. (tour): B&W. Set. **TCI**, vol. 21, n. 7 (Aug/Sep 1987). 22.
The Singing Globe.
    Bel Geddes, Norman. USA: B&W. Model. **TCS2**, plate 386.
The Sinking of the Titanic.
    Rupprecht, Martin. Deutsche Oper, Berlin: 1979. B&W. Set. **TCI**, vol. 14, n. 1 (Jan/
        Feb 1980). 17.
Sinner and Saint.
    Pedersen, Ove C. Det kongelige Teater, Copenhagen: 1940. B&W. Rendering. **SDW1**,
        60.
Sire Halewijn.
    Geenens, Robert. Nederlands Kamertoneel, Antwerp: 1957. B&W. Set. **SDW2**, 29.
Sirocco.
    Pillartz, T.C. B&W. Set. **SDC**, plate 123.
Sister Josephine.
    Muñoz, Gori. Teatro La Comedia, Argentina: 1958. Color. Rendering. **SDW2**, 33.
The Sisters Rosensweig.
    Beatty, John Lee. Ethel Barrymore Theatre, NYC: 1993. B&W. Rendering. **DDT**, 350.
The Sistuhs.
        _____. Karamu Theatre, Cleveland: B&W. Set. **TDT**, vol. XV, n. 4 (Winter
        1979). 13.
Situation Comedy.
    Blake, Warner. Carnegie-Mellon University, Pittsburgh: 1971. B&W. Set. **CSD**, 51;
        B&W. Set. **TCI**, vol. 7, n. 5 (Oct 1973). 22.
Six Characters in Search of an Author.
    Aronson, Boris. American Conservatory Theatre, Stanford Summer Festival: 1966.
        B&W. Set. **PST**, 412.
    Baldessari, Luciano. Italy: 1932. B&W. Rendering. **SCM**, 79; B&W. Rendering. **SDE**,
        29; B&W. Rendering. **TPH**, photo 380.
    Owen, Paul. Actors Theatre of Louisville: Color. Set. **TCI**, vol. 23, n. 3 (Mar 1989).
        38.
    Schmidt, Willi. Burgtheater, Vienna: 1959. B&W. Rendering. **SDW2**, 70.
    Smith, Gary. New York City Opera: 1959. B&W. Set. **SDW2**, 238.
    Svoboda, Josef. Theatre Studio, Louvain: 1984. B&W. Set. **STS**, 96, 101.
    Villa, Gianni. 1953. B&W. Rendering. **SDE**, 162.
    Yeargan, Michael. American Repertory Theatre, Cambridge, Massachusetts: 1984.
        B&W. Sketches. **ASD2**, 188; B&W. Set. **BSE4**, 102.
        _____. American Conservatory Theatre, San Francisco: 1966. B&W. Set. **TSY**,
        201.
        _____. American Repertory Theatre at Teatro Espanol, Madrid: 1988. B&W.
        Set. **TCI**, vol. 23, n. 5 (May 1989). 35.
        _____. Stanford University, California: 1951. B&W. Set. **TSY**, 202.
        _____. 1936. B&W. Set. **TCR**, 87.
Six Degrees of Separation.
    Walton, Tony. Mitzi Newhouse Theatre, Lincoln Center, NYC: 1990. Color. Model.
        TCI, vol. 24, n. 8 (Oct 1990). 22.

Six Wings for Everybody.
>   Bergner, Yossl. Habima, Tel Aviv: 1958. B&W. Set. **SDW2**, 118.

Skating Rink.
>   Léger, Fernand. Théâtre des Champs-Elysées, Paris: 1922. B&W. Rendering. **AST**, 96;
>   B&W. Set. **RSD**, illus. 321; B&W. Set. **TCS2**, plate 260.

The Skin of Our Teeth.
>   Conklin, John. Long Wharf Theatre, New Haven, Connecticut: 1970. B&W. Set. **TCI**,
>   vol. 14, n. 3 (May/Jun 1980). 22; B&W. Set. **TCI**, vol. 7, n. 5 (Oct 1973). 8.
>   Cory, Lauren. Berkeley Repertory Theatre, California: B&W. Set. **TCI**, vol. 14, n. 4
>   (Sep 1980). 30.
>   Furse, Roger. Phoenix Theatre, London: 1945. Color. Rendering. **TOP**, 77.
>   Johnson, Albert R. Plymouth Theatre, NYC: 1942. B&W. Set. **WTP**, 186, 187. 5
>   photos.
>   Martin, Denis. Théâtre National, Brussels: 1949. B&W. Set. **SDW1**, 46.
>   Otto, Theo. Schauspielhaus, Zürich: 1943-44. B&W. Rendering. **TPH**, photo 401.
>   Payne, Darwin Reid. B&W. Model. **TCM**, 146.
>   Schmidt, Douglas W. Playhouse in the Park, Cincinnati: 1966. B&W. Set. **ASD1**, 149
>   Stein, Douglas O. Tyrone Guthrie Theatre, Minneapolis: 1990. Color. Set. **TCI**, vol.
>   24, n. 10 (Dec 1990). 22.

Skinflint Out West.
>   Conklin, John. Hartford Stage, Connecticut: 1967. B&W. Set. **ASD1**, 21.

Skipper Next to God.
>   Aronson, Boris. Maxine Elliot Theatre, NYC: 1948. B&W. Rendering. **TAB**, 301.

Skutarewshy.
>   Damiani, Luciano. Teatro della Soffitta, Bologna: 1951. B&W. Set. **SDE**, 77.

Skyscraper.
>   Randolph, Robert. Lunt-Fontanne Theatre, NYC: 1965. B&W. Set. **DPT**, 206.

Skyscrapers.
>   Jones, Robert Edmond. Metropolitan Opera, NYC: 1926. B&W. Rendering. **REJ**, 59;
>   B&W. Rendering. **SDA**, 273.

The Slab Boys.
>   Hicks, Grant. Traverse Theatre, Edinburgh: 1978. B&W. Set. **BTD**, 83.

Slaughter on Tenth Avenue.
>   Mielziner, Jo. New York City Ballet: 1985-1986. B&W. Rendering. **TCI**, vol. 20, n. 10
>   (Dec 1986). 12. Original 1936 design for On Your Toes.

Slave Ship.
>   Lee, Eugene. Chelsea Theatre Center, Brooklyn, New York: 1969. B&W. Sketch.
>   **ASD1**, 76. Top view; B&W. Sketch & elevation. **DPT**, 91; B&W. Set. **SDB**, 198;
>   B&W. Set. **SDW3**, 162; B&W. Sketch & set. **TCI**, vol. 5, n. 4 (Sep 1971). 12. 4
>   photos.

Slavs! (Thinking About the Longstanding Problems of Virtue and Happiness).
>   Patel, Neil. New York Theatre Workshop, NYC: 1995. Color. Set. **TCI**, vol. 29, n. 3
>   (Mar 1995). 7.

The Sleep.
>   Vincenzi, Simon. British tour: 1987. B&W. Set. **BTD**, 68.

A Sleep of Prisoners.
>   _____. St. James Church, NYC: 1951. B&W. Set. **WTP**, 54, 55.

The Sleeping Beauty.
>   Gamlin, Yngve. Kungliga Teatern, Stockholm: 1955. B&W. Set. **SDW1**, 164.
>   Larrain, Raymond de. Théâtre des Champs-Elysées, Paris: 1961. B&W. Set. **SDW2**,
>   94.

Varona, José. Théâtre National de L'Opéra, Paris: 1974. B&W. Model. **DPT**, 4; 1977. Color. Rendering. **DDT**, 152a.

The Sleeping Princess.

Messel, Oliver. 1946. B&W. Model. **DOT**, 242.

Sleepy Hollow.

Mielziner, Jo. St. James Theatre, NYC: 1948. B&W. Rendering. **DTT**, 152. Church yard.

Sleight of Hand.

Sherman, Loren. Cort Theatre, NYC: 1987. B&W. Model. **DDT**, 550, 551.

Sleuth.

Brumley, Keith. Alaska Repertory Theatre, Anchorage: 1986. Color. Set. **TCI**, vol. 22, n. 5 (May 1988). 31.

Thurn, Nancy. American Stage Festival, Milford, New Hampshire: 1987. B&W. Set. **TCI**, vol. 21, n. 9 (Nov 1987). 12.

Toms, Carl. Music Box Theatre, NYC: 1970. B&W. Set. **TCI**, vol. 6, n. 1 (Jan/Feb 1972). 14.

Trimble, David. Coconut Grove Theatre, Miami: 1985. B&W. Set. **TCI**, vol. 22, n. 5 (May 1988). 37.

_____. Merrimack Regional Theatre, Lowell, Massachusetts: B&W. Set. **TCI**, vol. 15, n. 2 (Feb 1981). 67.

Sly Fox.

Jenkins, George. Broadhurst Theatre, NYC: 1976. B&W. Set. **TCI**, vol. 11, n. 4 (Sep 1977). 10.

Small Miracle.

Aronson, Boris. John Golden Theatre, NYC: 1934. B&W. **TAB**, 295.

Small War on Murray Hill.

Aronson, Boris. Ethel Barrymore Theatre, NYC: 1957. B&W. Set. **TAB**, 304.

Smierc na Gruszy.

Szajna, Josef. Warsaw: 1968. B&W. Set. **SDB**, 184.

Smile.

Schmidt, Douglas W. Lunt-Fontanne Theatre, NYC: 1986. B&W and color. Set. **TCI**, vol. 21, n. 1 (Jan 1987). 19, 21-23. 5 photos.

Smoky Joe's Cafe.

Landesman, Heidi. NYC: 1995. Color. Set. **TCI**, vol. 29, n. 5 (May 1995). 48, 49. 4 photos.

The Snow Ball.

Schmidt, Douglas W. Huntington Theatre, Boston: 1991. B&W. Set. **TCI**, vol. 25, n. 9 (Nov 1991). 25.

The Snow Knight.

Bonnat, Yves (Yves-Bonnat). Grande Théâtre de l'Opéra, Nancy, France: 1957. B&W. Rendering. **SDW2**, 86. 2 photos.

The Snow Maiden.

Aronson, Boris. Metropolitan Opera, NYC: 1942. Color. Rendering. **TAB**, 80.

The Snow Queen.

Svoboda, Josef. Laterna Magika, Prague: 1979. B&W. Set. **STS**, 119; B&W. Set. **STS**, 120.

_____. University of Texas, Austin: B&W. Set. **TCI**, vol. 19, n. 9 (Nov 1985). 34.

Snow White.

Bouchène, Dimitri. Opéra de Paris: 1950. B&W. Rendering. **SDW1**, 88.

So ist das Leben.
   Walser, Karl. Neues Theater, Berlin: 1903. B&W. Rendering. **AST**, 31.
So This is Love.
   Harker, Joseph & Phil Harker. Winter Garden Theatre, London. 1928. B&W. Set.
      MCD, plate 152.
Soda Jerk at HOME.
   Youmans, James. Contemporary Theatre and Art: Color. Set. **TCI**, vol. 25, n. 1 (Jan
      1991). 46.
Sodom and Gomorrah.
   Kiesler, Frederick. NYC: 1950. B&W. Sketch. **EIF**, photo 40.
The Soga Brothers' Meeting.
   Hasegawa, Kanbei. Kabuki-za, Tokyo: B&W. Set. **SDW1**, 143.
Der Sohn.
   Reigbert, Otto. Kammerspiele, Munich: B&W. Rendering. **TPH**, photo 420.
The Soldier and the Witch.
   Chapelain-Midy. Sarah Bernhardt Theatre, Paris: 1946. B&W. Rendering. **SDW1**, 90.
The Soldiers.
   Koltai, Ralph. Opéra de Lyon: 1983. B&W and color. Model & set. **BTD**, 126, 127.
   Minks, Wilfried. Freie Volksbühne, Berlin: 1967. B&W. Set. **SDW3**, 157.
   Svoboda, Josef. Bavarian State Opera, Munich: 1969. B&W. Set. **RSD**, illus. 603, 604;
      B&W. Set. **SDW3**, 205. 3 photos; B&W. Set. **SJS**, 98, 99. 5 photos; B&W. Set.
      STS, 80; B&W. Set. **TCI**, vol. 5, n. 1 (Jan/Feb 1971). 26, 27. 5 photos; 1977.
      B&W. Set. **STS**, 81. 2 photos; B&W. Set. **TCI**, vol. 11, n. 2 (Mar/Apr 1977). 19.
   Wendel, Heinrich. Deutsches Oper am Rhein, Düsseldorf-Duisburg: 1971. B&W. Set.
      SDW3, 204. 2 photos.
Solitaire.
   Heeley, Desmond. Sadler's Wells Theatre Ballet, London: 1956. B&W. Rendering.
      SDW2, 216.
Solitaire, Double Solitaire.
   Lundell, Kurt. Long Wharf Theatre at the Edinburgh Festival: 1972. B&W. Set. **TCI**,
      vol. 13, n. 3 (May/Jun 1979). 15; Long Wharf Theatre, New Haven, Connecticut:
      1972. B&W. Set. **TCI**, vol. 7, n. 5 (Oct 1973). 7. 2 photos.
Solomon and Balkis.
   Kiesler, Frederick. NYC: 1942. B&W. Set. **EIF**, photo 25.
Someone Who'll Watch Over Me.
   Don, Robin. Booth Theatre, NYC: 1993. B&W. Set. **TCI**, vol. 27, n. 2 (Feb 1993). 11.
Something for the Boys
   Bay, Howard. Alvin Theatre, NYC: 1943. B&W. Rendering. **DPT**, 41; B&W. Render-
      ing. **SDA**, 252; B&W. Set. **TCI**, vol. 17, n. 2 (Feb 1983). 12.
Something's Afoot.
   Hardie, Peter. Spokane Civic Theatre: 1986. Color. Set. **TCI**, vol. 22, n. 5 (May 1988).
      35.
   Holamon, Ken. Pennsylvania State University, University Park: B&W. Set. **TCI**, vol.
      12, n. 5 (Sep 1978). 40, 41. 6 photos.
The Son.
   Sievert, Ludwig. National Theater, Mannheim: 1918. B&W. Rendering. **RSD**, illus.
      118.
Son of Man and the Family.
   Lee, Eugene. Trinity Square Theatre, Providence, Rhode Island: 1970. B&W. Set.
      ASD1, 71; B&W. Set. **TDT**, vol. XVIII, n. 2 (Summer 1982). 6.

Song and Dance.

Wagner, Robin. Royale Theatre, NYC: 1985. Color. Set. **MBM**, 73.

_____. Palace Theatre, London: 1979. Color. Set. **ALW**, 96. 2 photos.

The Song of Jacob Zulu.

_____. Plymouth Theatre, NYC: 1993. B&W. Set. **TCI**, vol. 27, n. 5 (May 1993). 48.

Song of Singapore.

Beatty, John Lee. 17 Irving Place, NYC: 1991. B&W. Set. **TCI**, vol. 25, n. 6 (Aug/Sep 1991). 32.

The Song of the Lusitanian Bogey.

Ahmed, Samir. Masrah al Geib, Al Kahira, Cairo: 1971. B&W. Set. **SDW3**, 136.

Burbridge, Edward. Circle Theatre, NYC: B&W. Set. **TCI**, vol. 8, n. 2 (Mar/Apr 1974). 11.

Depero, Fortunato. (not produced): 1917. B&W. Model. **RSD**, illus. 345.

Keserü, Ilona. Katona Jozsef Szinhaz, Budapest: 1970. B&W. Set. **SDW3**, 222.

Mau, Waltraut, Ilse Träbing, & Klaus Weiffenbach. Schaubühne am Halleschen Ufer, Berlin: 1967. B&W. Set. **SDW3**, 136.

McCarthy, Dessis. B&W. Set. **SDL**, 211.

Palmstierna-Weiss, Gunilla. Scala Theatre, Stockholm: 1967. Color. Rendering. **RSD**, illus. 589; B&W. Set. **TCI**, vol. 12, n. 7 (Nov/Dec 1978). 40.

_____. Carnegie-Mellon University, Pittsburgh: B&W. Set. **TCI**, vol. 7, n. 5 (Oct 1973). 26.

Le Songe Argenté de Salonica.

Drabik, Vincent. Teatr Polski, Warsaw: B&W. Set. **TCS2**, plate 239.

La Sonnambula.

Brown, Zack. Terrace Theatre, Washington, DC: 1984. B&W. Rendering. **DDT**, 301.

Sophisticated Ladies.

Kuper, Yuri. Russia: 1988. Color. Set. **TCI**, vol. 23, n. 5 (May 1989). 37. 2 photos.

Walton, Tony. Lunt-Fontanne Theatre, NYC: 1981. B&W. Set. **DDT**, 316; Color. Set. **MBM**, 188, 189; National tour, USA: B&W. Drop. **DDT**, 397.

The Sorceress.

Rabinovitch, Isaac. State Jewish Theatre, Moscow: 1922. B&W. Set. **RSD**, illus. 212, 213; B&W. Model & set. **RST**, 161. 2 photos; B&W. Set. **TCS2**, plate 178.

Sorochinsky Fair.

Goncharova, Natalia. Théâtre des Champs-Elysées, Paris: 1926. Color. Rendering. **SDR**, 15. Act drop.

The Sorrows of Frederick.

Touhy, Susan. Fourth Step Theatre (South Coast Repertory), Costa Mesa, California: 1978. B&W. Set. **TCI**, vol. 14, n. 4 (Sep 1980). 37.

A Sound of Hunting.

Leve, Samuel. Lyceum Theatre, NYC: 1945. B&W. Set. **SDW1**, 199.

The Sound of Music.

Black, F. Scott. Essex Community College, Baltimore: 1982. Color. Set. **TCI**, vol. 20, n. 5 (May 1986). 23.

Joseph, Larry. University of Hawaii, Hilo: Color. Set. **TCI**, vol. 20, n. 5 (May 1986). 22.

Smith, Oliver. Lunt-Fontanne Theater, NYC: 1959. Color. Set. **BMF**, 88; Color. Set. **BWM**, 196, 197; B&W. Set. **TCI**, vol. 16, n. 4 (Apr 1982). 15; B&W. Set. **TCI**, vol. 20, n. 5 (May 1986). 22; Color. Set. **TMT**, plate 8; B&W. Set. **WMC**, 223; Palace Theatre, London: 1961. B&W. Set. **MCD**, plate 214.

Sour Angelica.
>Bliese, Thomas H. University of Iowa, Iowa City: B&W. Set. **BSE1**, 14.

South.
>Wahkévitch, Georges. Paris: 1953. B&W. Set. **SDB**, 48; B&W. Set. **SDW1**, 108.

South Africa Amen.
>Bosserdet, Jean. Centre Dramatique de Lausanne-Vidy, Lausanne: 1971. B&W. Set. **SDW3**, 161.

South of the 38th Parallel.
>Tischler, Alexander. Novyi Teatr, Leningrad: 1951. B&W. Rendering. **SDW2**, 198.

South Pacific.
>Aronson, Boris. Cort Theatre, NYC: 1943. B&W. Set. **TAB**, 298.
>Baral, Vicki & Gerry Hariton. (tour): 1987. Color. Set. **TCI**, vol. 22, n. 2 (Feb 1988). 51; Color. Set. **TCI**, vol. 22, n. 2 (Feb 1988). 51.
>Jackness, Andrew. Dorothy Chandler Pavilion, Los Angeles: 1985. B&W. Model. **DDT**, 164, 165. 4 photos.
>Mielziner, Jo. Majestic Theatre, NYC: 1949. B&W. Set. **BWM**, 193, 194; B&W Rendering of drop. **DTT**, 139. Bali Ha'i; B&W. Rendering of transformation drop. **DTT**, 140. Bali Ha'i; B&W. Set. **SDA**, 251; B&W. Set. **TMT**, 174; B&W. Set. **WMC**, 218; B&W. Set. **WTP**, 243. 2 photos.
>Thompson, Brian. Australian tour: 1993. Color. Set. **TCI**, vol. 27, n. 8 (Oct 1993). 11.

South Sea Island Fantasy.
>Rosse, Herman. 1926. B&W. Set. **TCS2**, plate 143.

Southern Cross.
>Becker, Victor. Alliance Theatre, Atlanta: 1989. B&W. Set. **TCI**, vol. 23, n. 10 (Dec 1989). 10.

The Spaniard of Brabant.
>Van Nerom, Jacques. Rotterdam: 1961. B&W. Set. **DMS**, plate 39.

The Spanish Citizen of Brabant.
>Norden, Hans van. De Rotterdamse Schouwburg, Rotterdam. 1961. B&W. Set. **SDW2**, 144.

The Spanish Triangle.
>Neuman-Spallart, Gottfried. Akademietheater, Vienna: 1955. B&W. Set. **SDW2**, 161.

Speed-the-Plow.
>Eigsti, Karl. Pittsburgh Public Theatre: 1991. Color. Set. **TCI**, vol. 25, n. 4 (Apr 1991). 14.

Spiel des Lebens.
>Reighert, Otto. Kammerspiele, Munich: B&W. Rendering. **TCS2**, plates 254, 255.

Splendid's.
>Arroyo, Eduardo. Berliner Schaubühne: 1995. Color. Set. **TCI**, vol. 29, n. 3 (Mar 1995). 12.

Spoils of War.
>Jackness, Andrew. Music Box Theatre, NYC: 1988. Color. Model. **TCI**, vol. 22, n. 10 (Dec 1988). 14.

Spokesong.
>Devine, Michael. Fourth Step Theatre (South Coast Repertory), Costa Mesa, California: 1978. B&W. Set. **TCI**, vol. 14, n. 4 (Sep 1980). 37.

Spookhouse.
>Stabile, Bill. Playhouse 91, NYC: 1984. B&W. Rendering. **BSE4**, 99.

The Spotted Tiger.
>Dar, Ruth. Teatron Ironi Haifa, Isreal: 1974. B&W. Set. **SDW4**, illus. 350.

The Spring Torrent.
  Pimenov, Youri. Tsentralnyi Teatr Sovietskoï Armii, Moscow: 1953. B&W. Model.
    SDW2, 190.
Spring Violins.
  Kovalenko, Evgheni & Valentina Krivocheina. Teatr Maïakovskovo, Moscow: 1959.
    B&W. Set. **SDW2**, 188. 2 photos.
Spring's Awakening.
  Arcenas, Loy. Vassar College, Poughkeepsie, New York: 1986. B&W. Set. **DDT**, 586.
  Brown, Zack. (project): 1975. B&W. Rendering. **DDT**, 9.
  Kouril, Miroslav. D36 Theatre, Prague: 1936. B&W. Set. **RSD**, illus. 285; B&W. Set.
    TDT, n. 42 (Fall 1975). 31. 2 photos.
  Minks, Wilfried. B&W. Set. **TCI**, vol. 12, n. 1 (Jan/Feb 1978). 30. 5 photos. The
Squabbles of Chioggia.
  _____. Venice: 1936. B&W. Set. **TPH**, photo 385.
Squire Puntila and His Servant Matti.
  Laufer, Murray. St. Lawrence Center, Toronto: 1971. B&W. Set. **SDW3**, 116.
  Neher, Caspar. Deutsches Theater, Berlin: 1949. B&W. Rendering & set. **CBM**, 62;
    B&W. Set. **TBB**, 51, 157, 163.
  Reinhardt, Andreas. Deutsches Staatsoper, Berlin: 1966. B&W. Set. **SDR**, 71; B&W.
    Rendering. **SDW3**, 194.
  Soumbatashvili, Iossif. Tsentralnyj Teatr Sovietskoj Armii, Moscow: 1966. B&W.
    Rendering. **SDW3**, 116. 3 photos.
  _____. B&W. Set. **SDL**, 69.
Stage Door.
  Oenslager, Donald. Music Box Theatre, NYC: 1936. B&W. Set. **MCN**, 133.
Staircase.
  Kerz, Leo. Center Stage, Baltimore: B&W. Set. **TCI**, vol. 7, n. 3 (May/Jun 1973). 14.
Stallerhof.
  Heising, Ulrich & Karl Kneidl. Berliner Theatertreffen, Berlin: 1973. B&W. Set.
    SDW4, illus. 408.
The Stamp of the Devil.
  Denic, Miomir. Narodno Pozoriste, Beograd: 1971. B&W. Set. **SDW4**, illus. 345.
Stanoje Glavas.
  Denic, Miomir. Narodno Pozoriste, Beograd: B&W. Model. **SDW1**, 133.
The Star.
  Jones, Robert Edmond. (project): 1925. B&W. Sketch. **DFT**, plate 25. Sc. 2: "The
    astrologer on the bridge."
Star and Garter.
  Horner, Harry. Music Box Theatre, NYC: 1942. B&W. Set. **SDB**, 59.
Star Turns Red.
  Bonnat, Yves (Yves-Bonnat). Maison des Jeunes et de la Culture, Colombes, France:
    1967. B&W. Model. **SDW3**, 98.
Starlight Express.
  Napier, John. Apollo Victoria, London: 1984. Color. Set. **ALW**, 143; B&W. Model &
    set. **BTD**, 154. 2 photos; Gershwin Theatre, NYC: 1987. B&W and color. Set.
    ALW, 146-150. 5 photos; B&W. Set. **DDT**, 588; B&W and color. Set. **MBM**, 65,
    66; B&W. Set. **TCI**, vol. 21, n. 5 (May 1987). 8; (tour): 1990. B&W and color. Set.
    TCI, vol. 24, n. 8 (Oct 1990). 44, 47; Bochum, Germany: Color. Set. **ALW**, 151.
The Start.
  Shtoffer, Jacob. Krasnaya Presnya (Realistic) Theatre, Moscow: 1931. B&W. Set.
    NTO, facing 364; B&W. Sketch & set. **RSD**, illus. 221, 222.

State of Siege.

Baltus. Théâtre Marigny, Paris: 1948. B&W. Set. **SDW1**, 84.

Statements After an Arrest.

_____. Stanford University, California: Color. Set. **TDT**, vol. XXVI, n. 1 (Spring 1990). 15 of insert.

States of Shock.

Stabile, Bill. American Place Theatre, NYC: 1991. Color. Set. **TCI**, vol. 25, n. 6 (Aug/Sep 1991). 19.

Status Quo Vadis.

Burbridge, Edward. Brooks Atkinson Theatre, NYC: 1973. B&W. Set. **TCI**, vol. 7, n. 3 (May/Jun 1973). 23.

The Steadfast Tin Soldier.

Mitchell, David. New York City Ballet, Lincoln Center: 1976. B&W. Set. **ASD1**, 135.

Steambath.

Mitchell, David. Truck and Warehouse Theatre, NYC: 1970. B&W. Sketch. **ASD1**, 123; B&W. Set. **DPT**, 84.

Steaming

Kellogg, Marjorie Bradley. Brooks Atkinson Theatre, NYC: 1982. Color. Model. **ASD1**, between 70 & 71.

Tiramani, Jenny. Theatre Royal, Stratford East, London: 1981. B&W. Set. **BTD**, 77.

Steel Magnolias.

Dorsey, Kent. Arizona Theatre Company, Tucson: Color. Set. **TCI**, vol. 24, n. 2 (Feb 1990). 58.

_____. Alley Theatre, Houston: Color. Set. **TCI**, vol. 24, n. 2 (Feb 1990). 58.

_____. Oregon Shakespeare Festival, Ashland: B&W. Set. **TCI**, vol. 24, n. 2 (Feb 1990). 60.

_____. Salt Lake Acting Company: Utah: B&W. Set. **TCI**, vol. 24, n. 2 (Feb 1990). 60.

_____. Topeka Civic Theatre, Kansas: B&W. Set. **TCI**, vol. 24, n. 2 (Feb 1990). 60.

The Steel Workers.

Soumbatashvili, Iossif. Moskovskij Khoudojestvennyj Akademitcheskij Teatr imeni Gorkogo, Moscow: 1972. B&W. Set. **SDW4**, illus. 353, 354.

Stella.

_____. Redoutensaal, Hofburg Palace, Vienna: 1922. B&W. Set. **MRH**, facing 163.

Stempenyu, The Fiddler

Aronson, Boris. Yiddish Art Theatre (Second Avenue Theatre), NYC: 1929. B&W. Set. **TAB**, 46, 294.

Stevedore.

Syrjala, Sointu. Civic Repertory Theatre, NYC: 1934. B&W. Set. **MCN**, 118.

The Stick Wife.

Yeargan, Michael. Hartford Stage, Connecticut: 1987. B&W. Set. **ASD2**, 180.

_____. Manhattan Theatre Club, NYC: Color. Set. **TCI**, vol. 25, n. 9 (Nov 1991). 53.

The Stickiness of Gelatine.

McDonald, P.J. Weber & Fields Music Hall, NYC: 1902. B&W. Set. **MCN**, 19.

Sticks and Bones.

Loquasto, Santo. Anspacher Theatre, Public Theatre, NYC: 1972. B&W. Set. **TCI**, vol. 7, n. 5 (Oct 1973). 17.

Stiffelio.
>   Scott, Michael. Metropolitan Opera, NYC: 1994. Color. Set. **TCI**, vol. 28, n. 1 (Jan
>   1994). 7.

Still Life.
>   Glenn, David. Scene Shop, Arena Stage, Washington, DC: B&W. Set. **TCI**, vol. 18, n.
>   3 (Mar 1984). 28.

Stomp.
>   _____. University of Texas, Austin: B&W. Set. **TCI**, vol. 5, n. 4 (Sep 1971). 10.

The Stone Flower.
>   Virsaladze, Soliko. Teatr Opery i Baleta imeni Kirova, Leningrad: 1957. B&W. Set.
>   **SDW2**, 201.

The Stone Guest.
>   Benois, Alexander. Moscow Art Theatre: 1915. B&W. Rendering. **RSC**, 23.

Stop the World - I Want to Get Off.
>   Kenny, Sean. Queen's Theatre, London: 1961. B&W. Sketch. **SDW2**, 218.

The Storm.
>   Stenberg, Vladimir & Georgiy A. Kamerny (Chamber) Theatre, Moscow: 1924. B&W.
>   Model. **AST**, 135; B&W and color. Rendering & set. **RST**, 174, 175.
>   Volkov, Boris. Moscow Trades Union Theatre: 1925. B&W. Set. **RST**, 209. 3 photos.

Storm Over Gothland.
>   Traugott, Muller. Volksbühne, Berlin: 1927. B&W. Set. **RSD**, illus. 231.

The Storming of the Winter Palace.
>   Annekov, George. Winter Palace Square, Petrograd: 1920. B&W. Rendering. **RAG**,
>   18; Color. Rendering. **RSC**, 14; B&W. Rendering & set. **RSD**, illus. 148-150.

The Story of a Real Man.
>   Svoboda, Josef. National Theatre, Prague: 1961. B&W. Rendering. **SDW2**, 44; B&W.
>   Rendering. **SJS**, 50.
>   Zolotariev, Nicolaï. Bolshoi Theatre, Moscow: 1960. B&W. Rendering. **SDW2**, 202. 2
>   photos.

The Story of Bertoldo.
>   Scandella, Mischa. B&W. Rendering. **SIO**, 124. 3 photos.

The Story of the Glorius Ressurection of Our Lord.
>   Stopka, Andrzej. National Theatre, Warsaw: 1962. B&W. Set. **RSD**, illus. 504.

The Story of Tobias and Sara.
>   Acquart, André. Bühnen der Stadt, Cologne, Germany: 1961. B&W. Rendering.
>   **SDW2**, 83.

The Story of Uriah.
>   Schakhine, Gila. Bamat Hasachkanim, Tel-Aviv: 1967. B&W. Model. **SDW3**, 140.

The Story of Vasco.
>   Greter, Johan. Stadsschouwburg, Arnhem: 1959. B&W. Rendering. **SDW2**, 144.
>   Strenger, Friedhelm. Landestheater, Hanover: 1958. B&W. Rendering. **SDW2**, 71.

The Strange Case of Dr. Jekyll and Mr. Hyde.
>   Vychodil, Ladislav. Lyceum Theatre, San Diego: 1986. B&W. Rendering. **TCI**, vol.
>   21, n. 2 (Feb 1987). 12; B&W. Rendering. **TCI**, vol. 21, n. 8 (Oct 1987). 38.

A Strange Escapade at the Basile Circus.
>   Tanaka, Béatrice. Maison des Jeunes et de la Culture, Meudon, France: 1969. B&W.
>   Set. **SDW3**, 160.

Strange Fruit.
>   Jenkins, George. Royale Theatre, NYC: 1945. B&W. Set. **WTP**, 188, 189. 5 photos.

Strange Interlude.
>   Hughes, Allen Lee. NYC: Color. Set. **TCI**, vol. 20, n. 2 (Feb 1986). 13.

Levine, Michael. Nederlander Theatre, NYC: 1985. B&W. Set. **TCI**, vol. 23, n. 2 (Feb 1989). 38.

Mielziner, Jo. John Golden Theatre, NYC: 1928. B&W. Set. **MCN**, 89.

Rossi, Vittorio. Teatro Verdi, Padova: 1972. B&W. Set. **SDW4**, illus. 220, 221.

The Stranger.

Aronson, Boris. Playhouse Theatre, NYC: 1945. B&W. Rendering. **TAB**, 299.

La Straniera.

Halmen, Pet. Spoleto Festival, Charleston, South Carolina: 1989. B&W and color. Set. **TCI**, vol. 24, n. 5 (May 1990). 29, 30; B&W. Set. **TCI**, vol. 23, n. 7 (Aug/Sep 1989). 9.

Straying.

Svoboda, Josef. (not produced): 1942-43. B&W. Rendering. **SJS**, 52. 2 photos.

The Stream.

Kôno, Kunio. Geijutsuza, Tokyo: 1957. Color. Rendering. **SDW2**, 149.

Streamline.

Beaton, Cecil. Palace Theatre, London: 1934. Color. Rendering. **CBS**, 17.

Street Scene

Janco, Marcel. Ohel, Tel Aviv: 1948. Color. Rendering. **SDW2**, 107.

Mielziner, Jo. Adelphi Theatre, NYC: 1929. B&W. Set. **BWM**, 264; Color. Rendering. **DTT**, 149. Night; B&W. Rendering. **DTT**, 150. Day; B&W. Set. **MCN**, 93; B&W. Rendering. **SCM**, 121; B&W. Rendering & set. **SDA**, 86. 2 photos.

Pecktal, Lynn. Yale School of Drama, New Haven, Connecticut: 1959. Color. Collage. **DPT**, between 284 & 285.

Sylbert, Paul. New York City Opera, Lincoln Center: 1959. B&W. Set. **TCI**, vol. 15, n. 7 (Aug/Sep 1981). 31.

_____. Houston Grand Opera: Color. Set. **TCI**, vol. 28, n. 4 (Apr 1994). 46.

The Street Singer.

Harker, Joseph & Phil Harker. Lyric Theatre, Hammersmith, London: 1924. B&W. Set. **MCD**, plate 129.

A Streetcar Named Desire.

Bloodgood, William. Oregon Shakespeare Festival, Ashland: 1977. B&W. Set. **TCI**, vol. 11, n. 6 (Nov/Dec 1977). 8.

Dancy, Virginia & Elmon Webb. Long Wharf Theatre, New Haven, Connecticut: B&W. Set. **TCI**, vol. 7, n. 5 (Oct 1973). 8.

Funicello, Ralph. 1984. Color. Set. **DDT**, 152c.

Mielziner, Jo. Ethel Barrymore Theatre, NYC: 1947. B&W. Rendering. **DTT**, 143. Scene at entrance; B&W. Rendering. **DTT**, 144. Houses backdrop; B&W Rendering. **SDA**, 153. 3 photos; B&W. Rendering. **SDW1**, 202. 3 photos; B&W. Set. **WTP**, 197.

Owen, Paul. Actors Theatre of Louisville: 1986. Color. Set. **TCI**, vol. 23, n. 3 (Mar 1989). 35.

Packard, Stephen. New American Theatre, Rockford, IL: Color. Set. **TDT**, vol. XXVI, n. 1 (Spring 1990). 14 of insert.

Payne, Darwin Reid. B&W. Set. **SIP**, 151; B&W. Rendering. **SIP**, 250; B&W. Rendering. **SIP**, 251.

Pisoni, Edward. B&W. Set. **SDL**, 376, 377.

Sabo, Jonathan. Hillberry Repertory Theatre: B&W. Set. **SDT**, 277.

Schmidt, Douglas W. St. James Theatre, NYC: 1973. B&W. Rendering. **DPT**, 19; Repertory Theatre of Lincoln Center, NYC: 1973. Color. Set. **TCI**, vol. 27, n. 4 (Apr 1993). 33; B&W. Rendering. **TDT**, vol. XVII, n. 2 (Summer 1981). 18.

The Streets of New York.
  Peters, Rollo. 48th Street Theatre, NYC: 1931. B&W. Set. **SCM**, 102.
Strider.
  Belcher, Richard. Seattle Repertory Theatre: B&W. Set. **TCI**, vol. 16, n. 7 (Aug/Sep
    1982). 34.
Strife.
  Bury, John. National Theatre, London: 1978. B&W. **TCI**, vol. 13, n. 6 (Nov/Dec
    1979). 25; B&W. Model. **TDT**, vol. XVI, n. 1 (Spring 1980). 24.
A Stroll in the Air.
  Noël, Jacques. Odéon-Théatre de France, Paris: 1963. B&W. Rendering. **SDW2**, 96;
    B&W. Rendering. **SDW3**, 129. 3 photos.
Strontium.
  Schönberg, Lars-Henrik. Collegium Artium, Helsinki: 1968. B&W. Set. **SDW3**, 220.
The Stubbornness of Geraldine.
  Physioc, Joseph. Garrick Theatre, NYC: 1902. B&W. Set. **MCN**, 18.
The Student Prince.
  Meyer, Eloise. Eastside Playhouse, NYC: 1976. B&W. Set. **TCI**, vol. 10, n. 5 (Oct
    1976). 4. 2 photos.
The Stuff We are Made Of.
  Colin, Paul. Théâtre de la Renaissance, Paris: 1947. B&W. Rendering. **SDW1**, 93.
Sturmflut (Storm Flood or *Tidal Wave).*
  Suhr, Edward. Volksbühne, Berlin: 1926. B&W. Set. **RSD**, illus. 232; B&W. Set. **TBB**,
    108; B&W. Set. **TCS2**, plate 280; B&W. Set. **TPH**, photo 376.
Suddenly Last Summer.
  Payne, Darwin Reid. B&W. Model & set. **TCM**, xxvi, xxvii, 68; B&W. Model. **TDP**,
    125.
The Suffering of Young Werther.
  Kouril, Miroslav. D38 Theatre, Prague: 1938. B&W. Set. **TDT**, n. 42 (Fall 1975). 31.
Sugar Babies.
  Du Bois, Raoul Pène. Mark Hellinger Theatre, NYC: 1979. B&W. Set. **TCI**, vol. 14, n.
    1 (Jan/Feb 1980). 8.
  _____. Omaha Community Playhouse, Nebraska: 1987. Color. Set. **TCI**, vol.
    24, n. 3 (Mar 1990). 32.
The Suicide.
  Leistikov, Ivan. Meyerhold Theatre, Moscow: B&W and color. Rendering. **RST**, 262-
    264. 5 photos.
  Loquasto, Santo. ANTA Washington Square Theatre, NYC: 1980. B&W. Sketch.
    ASD1, 109; B&W. Rendering. **DDT**, 66; B&W. Sketch. **TDT**, vol. XVII, n. 3 (Fall
    1981). 19.
  Melena, Miroslav. Czechoslovakia: B&W. Set. **TDT**, vol. XXVI, n. 2 (Summer 1990).
    38.
  Rees, Rick. University of Minnesota, Minneapolis: B&W. Model. **TDT**, vol. XXVI, n.
    1 (Spring 1990). 22 of insert.
Sullivan and Gilbert.
  Falabella, John. Huntington Theatre, Boston: 1985. B&W. Rendering. **DDT**, 335. 5
    photos.
Sultana Hürrem.
  Eren, Refik. Devlet Tiyatrosu, Ankara, Turkey: 1959. B&W. Set. **SDW2**, 213.
Summer.
  Capek, Josef. National Theatre, Prague: 1926. B&W. Set. **TDT**, n. 42 (Fall 1975). 24.

Straiges, Tony. Manhattan Theatre Club, NYC: 1983. B&W. Model. **ASD2**, 150; B&W. Model. **DDT**, 291.

Summer and Smoke.

Mielziner, Jo. Music Box Theatre, NYC: 1948. B&W. Rendering. **DTT**, 154. Full set; B&W. Rendering. **DTT**, 155. Restaurant set; B&W. Rendering. **SDA**, 154.

Pemberton, Reece. Duchess Theatre, London: 1952. B&W. Rendering. **SDW1**, 183.

Pond, Helen & Herbert Senn. Cape Playhouse, Dennis, Massachusetts: 1973. B&W. Set. **DPT**, 93.

Summer Folk.

Kralj, Matthias. Theatertreffen, Berlin: 1980. B&W. Set. **TCI**, vol. 14, n. 6 (Nov/Dec 1980). 38.

_____. Trinity Square Theatre, Providence, Rhode Island: 1989. B&W. Set. **TCI**, vol. 23, n. 10 (Dec 1989). 23.

Summer Play, White Comedy.

Takada, Ichiro. Kizashi. Haiyuza-Gekijo, Tokyo: 1970. B&W. Model. **SDW3**, 80.

Summertree.

_____. Tomlinson Theatre, Temple University, Philadelphia: B&W. Set. **TCI**, vol. 5, n. 5 (Oct 1971). 28.

Summit Conference.

Prowse, Philip. Citizen's Theatre of Glasgow: B&W. Set. **TCI**, vol. 15, n. 7 (Aug/Sep 1981). 24.

Sumurûn.

Stern, Ernst. Kammerspiele, Berlin: 1910. B&W and color. Sketches & rendering. **MRH**, between 208 & 209, facing 226. 3 photos; B&W. Rendering. **MRT**, 43; B&W. Rendering. **SDC**, plate 46; Color. Rendering. **TOP**, 127.

Sun Up.

Liebetrau, Oscar. Provincetown Playhouse, NYC: 1923. B&W. Set. **MCN**, 62.

A Sunday in August.

Svoboda, Josef. Tyl Theatre, Prague: 1958. B&W. Set. **SJS**, 61, 62. 3 photos; B&W. Set. **STS**, 54; B&W. **TDT**, vol. XXVIII, n. 5 (Fall 1992). 12.

Sunday in the Park With George.

English, Gary. Pittsburgh Public Theater: B&W. Set. **TCI**, vol. 21, n. 9 (Nov 1987). 51. 2 photos.

Seger, Richard. American Conservatory Theatre, San Francisco: 1986. Color. Set. **TCI**, vol. 21, n. 9 (Nov 1987). 49.

Straiges, Tony. Playwrights Horizons, NYC: 1983. Color. Model. **DDT**, 24a; Booth Theatre, NYC: 1984. B&W. Set. **ASD2**, 157; B&W. Set. **BSE4**, 92; B&W Model **DDT**, 232; B&W and color. Set. **MBM**, 48-50. 3 photos; B&W and color. Set. **SON**, 154, 157, 159, 163, 165; B&W and color. Set. **TCI**, vol. 18, n. 7 (Aug/Sep 1984). 24-27. 5 photos; Color. Set. **TCI**, vol. 28, n. 3 (Mar 1994). 33; Color. Set. **TCI**, vol. 27, n. 8 (Oct 1993). 35; Color. Set. **TMT**, plate 14.

Wallace, Bill. Hamline University, St. Paul, Minnesota: 1987. Color. Set. **TCI**, vol. 21, n. 9 (Nov 1987). 48. 2 photos.

Sundown Beach.

Aronson, Boris. Actors Studio, NYC: 1948. B&W. Rendering. **TAB**, 301.

The Sunken Town.

Humm, Ambrosius. State Theatre, St. Gallen, Switzerland: 1950. B&W. Rendering. **SDW1**, 115.

Sunrise at Campobello.

Alswang, Ralph. Cort Theatre, NYC: 1958. B&W. Rendering. **SDT**, 42. Act III, sc. 3.

Sunset Boulevard.
   Napier, John. Adelphi Theatre, London: 1993. Color. Set. **TCI**, vol. 28, n. 1 (Jan
      1994). 42-44. 8 photos; Color. Set. **TCI**, vol. 29, n. 2 (Feb 1995). 41.
Sunset/Sunrise.
   _____. Actors Theatre of Louisville: 1980. B&W. Set. **TCI**, vol. 15, n. 4 (Apr
      1981). 16. 2 photos.
The Sunshine Boys.
   Lundell, Kurt. Lunt-Fontanne Theatre, NYC: 1974. B&W. Set. **DPT**, 331.
Suor Angelica.
   Heeley, Desmond. San Francisco Opera: 1988. B&W. Rendering. **DDT**, 477.
La Surprise de l'Amour.
   Jouvet, Louis. Théâtre du Vieux-Columbier, Paris: 1920. B&W. Sketch. **RSD**, illus.
      105; B&W. Set. **TCS2**, plate 48.
The Survival of St. Joan.
   Harvey, Peter. Anderson Theatre, NYC: 1971. B&W. Sketch. **DPT**, 20.
The Survivors.
   Aronson, Boris. Playhouse Theatre, NYC: 1948. B&W. Set. **TAB**, 301.
Susannah.
   Scheffler, John. Houston Grand Opera: 1972. B&W. Rendering. **DDT**, 476.
   Sylbert, Paul. New York City Opera, Lincoln Center: 1958. B&W. Set. **TCI**, vol. 15, n.
      7 (Aug/Sep 1981). 31.
Suspense.
   Bleynie, Claude. Aix-les-Bains, France: 1957. B&W. Rendering. **SDW2**, 85.
The Suzanna Play.
   Svoboda, Josef. Municipal Theatre, Frankfurt am Main: 1968. B&W. Set. **SJS**, 96. 2
      photos.
Svanda the Bagpiper.
   Svoboda, Josef. Volksoper, Vienna (not performed): 1963. B&W. Rendering. **SJS**, 152.
Svätopluk.
   Svoboda, Josef. National Theatre, Prague: 1960. B&W. Set. **SJS**, 62. 2 photos; B&W.
      Set. **TDT**, n. 7 (Dec 1966). 24.
   Tröster, Frantisek. National Theatre, Bratislava: 1934/1935. B&W. Set. **TDT**, n. 42
      .(Fall 1975). 28; B&W. Model. **RSD**, illus. 274.
   Vychodil, Ladislav. Bratislava: 1970. B&W. Model. **TDT**, vol. XV, n. 2 (Summer
      1979). 16.
The Swan.
   Rosse, Herman (Acts 1 & 3). Cort Theatre, NYC: 1923. B&W. Set. **MCN**, 63.
   Tortora, Michael. Contemporary American Theatre Festival, Shepherdstown, West
      Virginia: B&W and color. Set. **TDT**, vol. XXX, n. 3 (Summer 1994). 12. 2 photos.
   Youmans, James. New York Shakespeare Festival, NYC: 1993. B&W. Set. **TCI**, vol.
      28, n. 2 (Feb 1994). 8.
Swan Lake.
   Hurry, Leslie. Sadler's Wells Ballet, London: 1942. B&W. Set. **BTD**, 20.
   Simonson, Lee. USA: 1937. B&W. Rendering. **SDA**, 275.
   Ter-Arutunian, Rouben. NYC: 1962. B&W. **SDB**, 68.
Sweeney Todd.
   Harman, Leonard. Bijou Theatre, Knoxville, Tennessee: 1983. B&W. Rendering.
      BSE3, 25.
   Jones, Russell. University of Kentucky, Lexington: B&W and color. Model & set.
      TDT, vol. XXX, n. 3 (Summer 1994). 7.
   Lee, Eugene. Uris Theatre, NYC: 1979. B&W. Sketch. **ASD1**, 81; B&W. Set. **ASD1**,

84; B&W. Set. **BWM**, 327; B&W. Set. **HPA**, 121, 122; B&W. Set. **HPR**, 290; Color. Set. **MBM**, 36; B&W and color. Set. **SON**, 124, 126, 129, 133, 144. 7 photos; B&W. Set. **TCI**, vol. 14, n. 1 (Jan/Feb 1980). 18; B&W. Set. **TCI**, vol. 15, n. 2 (Feb 1981). 13; Color. Set. **TCI**, vol. 18, n. 8 (Oct 1984). 17; B&W. Set. **TCI**, vol. 22, n. 5 (May 1988). 35; B&W. Set. **TDT**, vol. XVIII, n. 2 (Summer 1982). 7. Set under construction; B&W. Set. **WMC**, 293; London: 1980. B&W. Set. **TCI**, vol. 15, n. 2 (Feb 1981). 12.

Tilford, Joe. Wright State University, Dayton, Ohio : 1983. B&W. Set. **TCI**, vol. 18, n. 3 (Mar 1984). 8.

Sweet and Low.

Mielziner, Jo. 46th Street Theatre, NYC: 1930. Color. Rendering. **DTT**, 69. "Three Cabbies."; Color. Rendering. **SDA**, frontispiece.

Sweet Bird of Youth.

Mielziner, Jo. Martin Beck Theatre, NYC: 1959. B&W. Rendering. **DTT**, 203. Finale.

_____. (tour): 1987. B&W. Set. **TDT**, vol. XXII, n. 4 (Winter 1987). 10.

Sweet Bye and Bye.

Aronson, Boris. Shubert Theatre, New Haven: 1946. B&W and color. Sketches & rendering. **TAB**, 84, 300. 3 photos.

Sweet Charity.

Lacy, Robin. Ohio State University, Columbus: 1973. B&W. Set. **TDT**, n. 35 (Dec 1973). 14.

Randolph, Robert. Palace Theatre, NYC: 1966. B&W. Set. **TCI**, vol. 2, n. 6 (Nov/Dec 1968). 22, 24-29. Multiple images; 1986. Color. Set. **TCI**, vol. 28, n. 3 (Mar 1994). 32.

Sweet Kitty Bellairs.

_____. 1903. B&W. Set. **TPH**, photo 267.

Sweet Medicine.

Webster, Dan. University of Illinois, Urbana: 1978. B&W. Set. **TCI**, vol. 13, n. 3 (May/Jun 1979). 38.

Sweet of You To Say So.

Tilton, James. Lyceum Theatre, NYC: 1966. B&W. Set. **TCI**, vol. 1, n. 1 (Mar/Apr 1967). 22.

Sweet Orthodoxy.

Ristic, Dusan. Atelje 212 Beograd: 1970. B&W. Set. **SDW4**, illus. 261.

Sweet River.

Oenslager, Donald. 51st Street Theatre, NYC: 1936. Color. Rendering. **TDO**, facing 64.

Swing.

Wagner, Robin. Playhouse, Wilmington, Delaware: 1980. Color. Set. **TCI**, vol. 18, n. 4 (Apr 1984). 54.

The Swing Mikado.

Rickabaugh, Clive. New Yorker Theatre, NYC: 1939. B&W. Set. **RBS**, 180.

The Sword of Damocles.

Nyvlt, Vladimir. Divadlo cs. Armady, Prague: 1959. B&W. Rendering. **SDW2**, 43.

Swords.

Jones, Robert Edmond. National Theatre, NYC: 1921. B&W. Sketch. **DFT**, plate 16. A Castle in Calabria; B&W. Rendering. **REJ**, 43; B&W. Rendering. **SDC**, plate 77.

Les Sylphides.

Benois, Alexander. Ballets Russes, Paris Opera: 1909. B&W. Rendering. **RSD**, illus. 44.

Sylvia's Real Good Advice.
  Ryan, Thomas M. Organic Theatre, Chicago: 1991. Color. Set. **TCI**, vol. 25, n. 9 (Nov 1991). 22.
Symphonie Fantastique.
  Svoboda, Josef. National Opera, Paris: 1975. B&W. Set. **TDT**, vol. XII, n. 2 (Summer 1976). 15.
Symphonie Italienne.
  Berman, Eugene. (not produced): 1939. B&W. Rendering. **FCS**, plate 208.
Il Systema della Dolcezza.
  Angelini, Sandro. Teatro delle Novità, Bergamo: 1951. B&W. Rendering. **SDE**, 26.

-T-

T Bone N Weasel.
  Patel, Neil. Center Stage, Baltimore: 1992. Color. Set. **TCI**, vol. 27, n. 2 (Feb 1993). 7.
Tadpole.
  _____. Mark Taper Forum, Los Angeles: 1973. B&W. Set. **TCI**, vol. 8, n. 1 (Jan/Feb 1974). 14.
Taira no Masakado.
  Itô, Juichi. Tsukiji Shogekijo, Tokyo: 1944. B&W. Rendering & ground plan. **SDW1**, 144, 145. 3 photos.
Take a Chance.
  Throckmorton, Cleon. Apollo Theatre, NYC: 1932. B&W. Set. **WMC**, 108.
Take the Fool Away.
  Kautskj, Robert. Burgtheater, Vienna: 1956. B&W. Set. **SDW2**, 157.
Takhir i Zoukhra.
  Tchemodourov, Evgheni. Teatr Opery i Baleta, Stalinabad: 1945. B&W. Rendering. **SDW2**, 194.
Taking Steps.
  Smith, Vicki. Arizona Theatre Company, Tucson: B&W. Model. **SDT**, 287.
Tale of a Horse.
  Kochergin, Edward Stepanovich. Gorky Theatre, Leningrad: 1976. B&W. Model. **TCI**, vol. 11, n. 5 (Oct 1977). 40.
The Tale of Genji.
  Yasuda, Yukihiko. Kabuki-za, Tokyo: 1954. B&W. Rendering. **SDW1**, 151.
A Tale Told.
  Beatty, John Lee. Circle Repertory Theatre, NYC: 1981. B&W. Rendering. **ASD1**, 5; B&W. Rendering. **TDT**, vol. XVIII, n. 4 (Winter 1982). 7.
Tales from the Vienna Woods.
  Herrmann, Karl-Ernst. Schaubühne am Halleschen Ufer, Berlin: 1972. B&W and color. Set. **SDW4**, illus. 256, 257; B&W. Set. **TCI**, vol. 13, n. 1 (Jan/Feb 1979). 18.
The Tales of Hoffmann.
  Bignens, Max. Theater am Gartnerplatz, Munich: 1966. B&W. Rendering. **RSD**, illus. 454.
  Dreier, Jürgen. Städtische Bühnen, Wuppertal: 1973. B&W. Set. **OPE**, 203, 206, 209, 211, 213.
  Dudley, William. Covent Garden, London: 1980. B&W. Model. **TDT**, vol. XIX, n. 1 (Spring 1983). 11.
  Dunham, Clarke. Walnut Street Theatre, Philadelphia: 1975. B&W. Set. **DDT**, 23.
  Kiesler, Frederick. NYC: 1939. B&W. Set. **EIF**, photo 20.

Moholy-Nagy, Lászlo. State Opera, Berlin: 1929. B&W and color. Rendering. **AST**, 144, 145. 5 photos; B&W. Set. **NTO**, facing 396; B&W and color. Model, rendering, & set. **RSD**, illus. 253-259; B&W. Set. **SCM**, 57. Act III.

Neher, Caspar. Bühnen der Stadt, Cologne, Germany: 1961. B&W. Set. **SDW2**, 67.

Pasetti, Leo. Munich: B&W. Rendering. **SCM**, 59.

Peduzzi, Richard. Théâtre de l'Opera, Paris: 1974. B&W. Set. **OPE**, 205, 206, 208, 210, 212.

Savinio, Alberto. La Scala, Milan: 1949. B&W. Rendering. **AST**, 187. 2 photos; B&W. Rendering. **SDE**, 148. 2 photos.

Schneider-Siemssen, Günther. Metropolitan Opera, NYC: 1982. B&W and color. Model & set. **MOM**, 56-67. 13 photos; B&W. Set. **TCI**, vol. 17, n. 5 (May 1983). 8.

Soherr, Hermann. Deutsche Oper am Rhein, Düsseldorf: 1969. B&W. Set. **OPE**, 202, 206, 208, 210.

Stros, Ladislav. National Theatre, Prague: 1971. B&W. Set. **OPE**, 202, 207, 208, 213.

Svoboda, Josef. Grand Opera of the Fifth of May, Prague: 1946. B&W. Rendering & set. **SJS**, 131, 132. 4 photos; B&W. Rendering & set. **STS**, 14, 15, 40. 3 photos; State Theatre, Ostrava, Czechoslovakia: 1947. B&W. Rendering. **SJS**, 132; B&W. Rendering. **STS**, 21, 41; Laterna Magika, Prague: 1959. B&W. Rendering. **SJS**, 132; 1962. B&W. Rendering. **STS**, 117; Deutsches Staatsoper, Berlin: 1969. B&W. Rendering. **SJS**, 132; Municipal Theatre, Frankfurt am Main: 1970. B&W. Set. **SJS**, 132.

Varona, José. Sydney Opera House: 1974. B&W and color. Set. **OPE**, 204, 207, 209, 211, 212.

_____. Chicago Lyric Opera: c. 1910. Color. Model. **TDT**, vol. XXV, n. 2 (Summer 1989). 8, 9.

Tales of the Lost Formicans.

Odorisio, Rob. Philadelphia Drama Guild: Color. Set. **TCI**, vol. 26, n. 1 (Jan 1992). 40.

The Talisman.

Zídek, Ivo. Pilsen: 1985. B&W. Rendering. **TDT**, vol. XXVIII, n. 2 (Spring 1992). 36.

Talley's Folly.

Beatty, John Lee. Circle Repertory Theatre, NYC: 1979. B&W. Rendering. **ASD1**, 13; Color. Rendering. **DDT**, 152a; B&W. Rendering. **TDT**, vol. XVIII, n. 4 (Winter 1982). 5; Mark Taper Forum, Los Angeles: 1979. Color. Rendering. **DDT**, 152a; Brooks Atkinson Theatre, NYC: 1980. Color. Rendering. **DDT**, 152a; B&W. Set. **TCI**, vol. 16, n. 5 (May 1982). 29.

Tamara.

Checchi, Robert. Seventh Regiment Armoury, NYC: 1987. B&W. Rendering & set. **TCI**, vol. 22, n. 2 (Feb 1988). 12.

Tamburlaine the Great.

Bury, John. National Theatre (Olivier), London: 1976. B&W. Set. **TCI**, vol. 11, n. 5 (Oct 1977). 32.

Hurry, Leslie. Old Vic Theatre, London: 1951. Color. Rendering. **SDW1**, 171.

Tamerlano.

Don, Robin. Opéra de Lyon: 1984. Color. Set. **BTD**, 123.

The Taming of the Shrew.

Armstrong, Will Steven. American Shakespeare Festival, Stratford, Connecticut: B&W. Model & set. **TCI**, vol. 1, n. 1 (Mar/Apr 1967). 17, 18. 3 photos.

Colonello, Attilio. Piccolo Teatro, Trieste: 1959. B&W. Rendering. **SDW2**, 124.

Conklin, John. California Shakespearean Festival, Visalia: 1979. B&W. Set. **TCI**, vol. 14, n. 4 (Sep 1980). 38. 4 photos.

Craig, Edward Gordon. 1908. B&W. Rendering. **COT**, 148.

DePuy, Peggy J. Webster Conservatory, St. Louis: 1981. B&W. Rendering & set. **BSE2**, 23, 31, 38.

Dyer, Chris. Royal Shakespeare Theatre, Stratford-upon-Avon: 1978. B&W. Model. **TDT**, vol. XIX, n. 1 (Spring 1983). 5.

Frazer, Anne. Old Tote Theatre Company, Parade Theatre, Sydney: 1972. B&W. Set. **SDW4**, illus. 24.

Fuerst, Walter René. Odéon Theatre, Paris: 1924. B&W. Set. **TCS2**, plate 267; B&W. Set. **TPH**, photo 356.

Funicello, Ralph. American Conservatory Theatre, San Francisco: 1976. B&W. TV set. **ASD1**, 48. Television production.

Gilliam, Steve. Colorado Shakespeare Festival: 1989. B&W. Set. **TCI**, vol. 23, n. 9 (Nov 1989). 25.

Hancock, Carolyn. Theatre Guild, NYC: 1935. B&W. Set. **WTP**, 77.

Howard, Pamela. Royal Shakespeare Company, GB: 1985. B&W. Set. **TDT**, vol. XXIV, n. 2 (Summer 1988). 5.

Lazaridis, Stefanos. Royal Shakespeare Company, GB: 1987. B&W. Set. **BTD**, 81.

Pátek, J. Czechoslovakia: B&W. Model. **TDT**, vol. XVI, n. 1 (Spring 1980). 27.

Stone, Alex. Shakespeare Memorial Theatre, Stratford-upon-Avon: 1960. B&W. Model. **SDW2**, 227.

Ter-Arutunian, Rouben. 1956. B&W. Sketch. **SDB**, 165. For TV production

_____. Alabama Shakespeare Festival, Anniston: 1978. B&W. Set. **TCI**, vol. 13, n. 2 (Mar/Apr 1979). 23.

_____. Centenary College, Louisiana: Color. Set. **MOR**, 101.

_____. Equity Library Theatre, NYC: B&W. Set. **TCI**, vol. 15, n. 6 (Jun/Jul 1981). 22.

_____. Globe Theatre, Hofstra University: B&W. Set. **TCI**, vol. 7, n. 2 (Mar/Apr 1973). 11.

_____. Globe Theatre, Odessa, Texas: 1972. B&W. Set. **TCI**, vol. 7, n. 2 (Mar/Apr 1973). 9.

_____. Maddermarket Theatre, Norwich, England: B&W. Set. **SDG**, 158.

_____. Seattle Repertory Theatre: 1980. B&W. Set. **TCI**, vol. 16, n. 3 (Mar 1982). 54.

Tamu Tamu.

_____. Juilliard School, Lincoln Center, NYC: 1987. Color. Set. **TCI**, vol. 27, n. 4 (Apr 1993). 29.

Tancredi.

Cagli, Corrado. Maggio Musicale Fiorentino, Florence: 1952. B&W. Rendering. **SDE**, 51.

Tango.

Fielding, Eric. Goodman Theatre, Chicago: 1985. B&W. Rendering. **BSE4**, 21; B&W. Set. **TCI**, vol. 21, n. 5 (May 1987). 41.

Mercer, Thomas Travix. Carnegie-Mellon University, Pittsburgh: 1971. B&W. Set. **CSD**, 49.

Tango Argentina.

Orezzoli, Hector & Claudio Segovia. M Hellinger Theatre, NYC: 1985. Color. Set. **MBM**, 184.

Tannhäuser.

> Darling, Robert Edward. Seattle Opera: 1984. B&W. Set. **TCI**, vol. 20, n. 8 (Oct 1986). 25.
>
> Howland, Gerard. San Francisco Opera: 1994-1995. Color. Model. **TCI**, vol. 29, n. 3 (Mar 1995). 32, 33.
>
> Schenk von Trapp, Lothar. Hessiches Landestheater, Darmstadt: 1929-1930. B&W. Set. **RSD**, illus. 247.
>
> Schneider-Siemssen, Günther. Metropolitan Opera, NYC: 1977. B&W and color. Rendering & set. **MOM**, 212-221. 7 photos; B&W. Sketch & set. **TCI**, vol. 12, n. 6 (Oct 1978). 28, 30. 4 photos.
>
> Svoboda, Josef. State Opera, Hamburg: 1969. B&W. Set. **JSS**, 33. Act I, sc. 1; B&W. Set. **JSS**, 34. Act III; B&W. Set. **SJS**, 75, 76. 3 photos; Covent Garden, London: 1973. B&W. Set. **JSS**, 34. Act I, sc. 2; B&W. Set. **JSS**, 38. Act II, Wartburg scene; Color. Set. **JSS**, between 54 & 55. Act I, sc. 1; Color. Set. **JSS**, between 54 & 55. Act I, sc. 1; B&W. Set. **RSD**, illus. 602; B&W. Set. **TDT**, vol. XII, n. 2 (Summer 1976). 19.
>
> Toren, Roni. Bavarian State Opera, Munich: 1994. B&W. Set. **TCI**, vol. 29, n. 2 (Feb 1995). 8.
>
> Tsypin, George. Chicago Lyric Opera: 1988. B&W. Sketch. **ASD2**, 161; B&W. Model. **DDT**, 171; B&W. Set. **TCI**, vol. 23, n. 2 (Feb 1989). 10; B&W. Rendering. **TDT**, vol. XXVII, n. 3 (Summer 1991). 18.
>
> Wagner, Wieland. Beyreuth Festival Theatre: 1954. B&W. Set. **SDW1**, 81; 1964. B&W. Set. **SDW3**, 179; 1965. Color. Set. **RSD**, illus. 547; 1966. B&W. Set. **TDT**, n. 29 (May 1972). 12. Act I.

The Tap Dance Kid.

> DePass, Paul & Michael J. Hotopp. Broadhurst Theatre, NYC: 1983. Color. Set. **MBM**, 1, 168, 169.

Tapestry in Gray.

> Oenslager, Donald. Shubert Theatre, NYC: 1935. B&W. Set. **SDA**, 216; B&W. Set. **TDO**, 61.

The Tartar's Fair.

> Zídek, Ivo. Prague: 1988. B&W. Rendering. **TDT**, vol. XXVIII, n. 2 (Spring 1992). 36.

Tartuffe.

> Akimov, Nikolai. Gosdrama Theater, Leningrad: 1929. B&W. Model. **RSD**, illus. 191; B&W. Set. **RST**, 294, 295. 3 photos.
>
> Allio, René. Théâtre de la Cité, Villeurbanne: 1962. B&W. Set. **RSD**, illus. 574; B&W. Set. **SDW2**, 84.
>
> Aronson, Boris. Stanford Repertory Theatre, California: 1965. B&W. Set. **PST**, 235; B&W. Set. **TSY**, 5.
>
> Barkhin, Sergei. Moskovskij Teatr Dramy i Komedii na Taganke, Moscow: 1968. B&W. Set. **SDW3**, 68. 3 photos.
>
> Braque, Georges. Théâtre de l'Athénée, Paris: 1950. B&W. Rendering. **AST**, 86; B&W. Rendering. **RSD**, illus. 412.
>
> Funicello, Ralph. Seattle Repertory Theatre: 1988. B&W. Set. **DDT**, 374.
>
> Loquasto, Santo. Williamstown Theatre Festival, Massachusetts: 1969. B&W. Set. **TCI**, vol. 14, n. 3 (May/Jun 1980). 18; B&W. Set. **TCI**, vol. 7, n. 5 (Oct 1973). 18.
>
> Monloup, Hubert. Théâtre National Populaire, Villeurbanne, France: 1974. B&W and color. Set. **SDW4**, illus. 71-78.
>
> Nieva, Francisco. Spain: Color. Rendering. **TDT**, vol. XII, n. 3 (Fall 1976). 26.

Perdziola, Robert. McCarter Theatre, Princeton, New Jersey: 1988. Color. Set. **TCI**,
vol. 23, n. 2 (Feb 1989). 14.

Ragey, Joe. Virginia Stage Company, Norfolk: 1983. B&W. Set. **BSE4**, 78.

Schillingowsky, P. State Theatre, Leningrad: 1930. B&W. Sketch. **TPH**, photo 406.

Stern, Ernst. Deutsches Theater, Berlin: 1906. B&W. Set. **MRT**, 37.

Vychodil, Ladislav. Bratislava: 1946. B&W. Set. **TDT**, vol. XV, n. 2 (Summer 1979).
10.

Williams, Jerry. Alley Theatre, Houston: B&W. Set. **TCI**, vol. 7, n. 3 (May/Jun 1973).
7. 2 photos.

Wurtzel, Stuart. American Conservatory Theatre, San Francisco: 1967. B&W. Set.
TSY, 5.

_____. California Institute of the Arts Modular Theatre: B&W. Set. **TCI**, vol. 7,
n. 6 (Nov/Dec 1973). 15.

_____. Malodoi Theatre, Ukraine: 1919. B&W. Set. **RST**, 157.

_____. Tyrone Guthrie Theatre, Minneapolis: 1984. B&W. Set. **TCI**, vol. 20, n.
3 (Mar 1986). 26.

*Tartuffe, or rather the Life, Loves, Self-censorship and Death on Stage of Seigneur
Molière, our Contemporary.*

Padovani, Gianfranco. Teatro Stabile di Genova: 1971. B&W. Set. **SDW4**, illus. 222,
223.

A Taste of Honey.

Smith, Oliver. Lyceum Theatre, NYC: 1960. B&W. Sketch. **DDT**, 77.

_____. Black Swan Theatre, Ashland, Oregon: 1977. B&W. Set. **TCI**, vol. 13, n.
4 (Sep 1979). 39.

Taverner.

Koltai, Ralph. Royal Opera House, Covent Garden, London: 1972. B&W. Set. **CGA**,
181; B&W. Set. **TCI**, vol. 11, n. 1 (Jan/Feb 1977). 10, 11. 4 photos; Color. Model.
TDT, vol. XII, n. 3 (Fall 1976). 26.

Tea and Sympathy.

Mielziner, Jo. Ethel Barrymore Theatre, NYC: 1953. B&W. Set. **SDA**, 229.

The Teacher Bulbus.

_____. Meyerhold Theatre, Moscow: B&W. Set. **SCM**, 93.

Teahouse of the August Moon.

Larkin, Peter. Martin Beck Theatre, NYC: 1953. B&W. Set. **TCI**, vol. 23, n. 1 (Jan
1989). 41.

Teddy.

Travis, Warren. Berkeley, California: 1976. B&W. Sketches. **TCI**, vol. 14, n. 4 (Sep
1980). 27. 2 photos.

Teddy and Alice.

Wagner, Robin. Minskoff Theatre, NYC: 1987. B&W. Models & backdrop. **DDT**, 345.
3 photos.

The Telephone.

Ganeau, François. Festival di Aix en Provence: 1951. B&W. Set. **SDE**, 89.

Vossen, Frans. Kleine Komedie, Amsterdam: 1969. B&W. Set. **SDW3**, 201.

The Tempest.

Adducci, Alexander F. Northern Illinois University, DeKalb, Illinois: B&W. Set. **SCT**,
83.

Arnone, John. Arena Stage, Washington, DC: 1984. B&W. Set. **ASD2**, 21.

Arzadun, Nestor de & J. Monod. Round House, London: 1968. B&W. Set. **RSD**, illus.
638.

Benson, Susan. Stratford Festival Theatre, Ontario, Canada: 1992. Color. Set. **TCI**, vol. 26, n. 9 (Nov 1992). 29. 2 photos.

Ciulei, Liviu. Tyrone Guthrie Theatre, Minneapolis: 1981. B&W. Set. **TCI**, vol. 17, n. 7 (Aug/Sep 1983). 23.

Conklin, John. Tyrone Guthrie Theatre, Minneapolis: 1991. Color. Set. **TCI**, vol. 26, n. 2 (Feb 1992). 11.

Daszewski, Wladislaw. Teatr Wojska Polskiego, Lodz: 1947. B&W. Set. **SDW1**, 156.

Dorsey, Kent. Folger Library Theatre, Washington, DC: Color. Set. **TCI**, vol. 25, n. 8 (Oct 1991). 48.

Edwards, Ben. Stratford, Connecticut: B&W. Set. **TCI**, vol. 7, n. 2 (Mar/Apr 1973). 11.

Ferguson, John: Stratford Festival Theatre, Ontario, Canada: 1976. B&W. Set. **TCI**, vol. 12, n. 4 (May/Jun 1978). 22.

Fielding, David. Royal Shakespeare Company, GB: 1988. Color. Set. **BTD**, 87.

Fletcher, Robert. American Conservatory Theatre, San Francisco: B&W. Set. **TCI**, vol. 6, n. 5 (Oct 1972). 14.

Fontanels, Manuel. Odéon Théâtre, Paris: B&W. Rendering. **TCS2**, plate 199.

Funicello, Ralph. Old Globe Theatre, San Diego: 1991. Color. Set. **TCI**, vol. 25, n. 9 (Nov 1991). 14.

Hajek, Otto Herbert. Burgtheater, Vienna: 1968. B&W. Rendering. **AST**, 235.

Hudson, Richard. Old Vic Theatre, London: 1988. B&W. Set. **BTD**, 59.

Jeter, Richard. Williams College Theatre, Williamstown, Massachusetts: 1973. B&W. Set. **TCI**, vol. 8, n. 3 (May/Jun 1974). 4.

Kiesler, Frederick. Martha's Vineyard: 1954. B&W. Set. **EIF**, photo 44.

Knight, Michael. Pitlochry Festival Theatre, Scotland: 1978. B&W. Set. **TCI**, vol. 12, n. 6 (Oct 1978). 57.

Lee, Ming Cho. Mark Taper Forum, Los Angeles: 1979. Color. Set. **ASD1**, between 70 & 71; B&W. Set. **TCI**, vol. 18, n. 2 (Feb 1984). 19; B&W. Set. **TCI**, vol. 14, n. 4 (Sep 1980). 41.

Messel, Oliver. Old Vic Theatre, London: 1940. B&W. Set. **MEM**, 101; B&W. Set. **OMB**, 111.

Minks, Wilfried. Theater der Freien Hansestadt, Bremen: 1970. B&W. Set. **SDW3**, 64. 3 photos; Hamburg: 1976. B&W. Set. **TCI**, vol. 12, n. 1 (Jan/Feb 1978). 31.

Motley (Margaret Harris, Sophia Harris, & Elizabeth Montgomery). Alvin Theatre, NYC: 1944/1945.B&W. Set. **SOW**, plate 106; B&W. Set. **WTP**, 66, 67.

Neighbor, David. Thiel College, Pennsylvania: Color. Set. **SST**, plate V.

Phillips, Jason. Center Stage, Baltimore: 1969. B&W. Set. **TCI**, vol. 7, n. 3 (May/Jun 1973). 12.

Plate, Roberto. Avignon Festival: B&W. Set. **TCI**, vol. 24, n. 5 (May 1990). 33.

Ratto, Gianni. Boboli Gardens, Florence: 1949. B&W. Set. **SDE**, 139.

Ross, Carolyn L. Hopkins Center, Dartmouth College, Hanover, New Hampshire: 1976. B&W. Set. **BSE1**, 28.

Sainthill, Loudon. Shakespeare Memorial Theatre, Stratford-upon-Avon: 1951. Color. Rendering. **LST**, 19, 23.

Schmidt, Douglas W. Old Globe Theatre, San Diego: 1982. B&W. Set. **DDT**, 146.

Sheringham, George. c.1932. B&W. Rendering. **SCM**, 37.

Stern, Ernst. Volksbühne, Berlin: 1915. B&W. Rendering. **SOS**, 206; B&W. Model. **TCS2**, plate 345.

Taylor, Robert U. (project): 1968. Color. Rendering. **DPT**, between 124 & 125.

Tomlinson, Charles D. McCarter Theatre, Princeton, New Jersey: B&W. Set. **TCI**, vol. 1, n. 4 (Sep/Oct 1967). 37.

Walentin, Arne. Det Norske Teatret, Oslo: 1959. B&W. Set. **SDW2**, 154.

Ward, Anthony. Swan Theatre, Worcester, England: 1987. Color. Set. **BTD**, 50.

Yeargan, Michael. Hartford Stage, Connecticut: 1985. Color. Set. **TCI**, vol. 20, n. 4 (Apr 1986). 23; B&W. Set. **TCI**, vol. 19, n. 10 (Dec 1985). 8.

_____. Denver Center, Colorado: 1982. B&W. Set. **TCI**, vol. 17, n. 8 (Oct 1983). 29.

_____. King Coit School, USA: B&W. Set. **WTP**, 66, 67.

Tempo.

_____. Vakhtangov Theatre, Moscow: 1930. B&W. Set. **RST**, 275. 2 photos.

The Temporary Mrs. Smith.

Oenslager, Donald. 1946. B&W. Rendering. **TDO**, 124.

The Temptation of Saint Anthony.

Autant, Edouard. Laboratory Art and Action, Paris: 1931. B&W. Set. **RSD**, illus. 386.

Ten Days That Shook the World.

Tarassov, Alexandr. Moskovskij Teatr Dramy i Komedii na Taganke, Moscow: 1965. B&W. Set. **SDW3**, 102. 3 photos.

Ten Little Indians.

Durfee, Duke. Empire State Institute for the Performing Arts: B&W. Set. **TCI**, vol. 22, n. 5 (May 1988). 7, 41.

Ten Million Ghosts.

Oenslager, Donald. St. James Theatre, London: 1936. B&W. Rendering. **TDO**, 63.

Ten Nights in a Bar Room.

Campbell, Jean. Birmingham Repertory Theatre, England: 1932. B&W. Set. **SCM**, 35.

Tenderloin.

Beaton, Cecil. 46th Street Theatre, NYC: 1960. B&W and color. Set. **BWM**, 294. 2 photos; B&W. Set. **WMC**, 299.

Les Tentations de la Bergere ou l' amour vainqueur.

Gris, Juan. Ballets Russes, Monte Carlo: 1924. Color. Rendering. **AST**, 85.

The Tenth Commandment.

Aronson, Boris. Yiddish Art Theatre (Second Avenue Theatre), NYC: 1926. B&W. Rendering, model, & set. **BAT**, 8, 23, 24, 26, 27, 29; B&W. Model. **SDB**, 21; B&W. Set. **SDC**, plate 121; B&W. Rendering, model, & set. **TAB**, 39, 42-46. 11 photos; B&W. Model. **TDT**, vol. XXV, n. 3 (Fall 1989). 13.

The Tents of the Arabs.

Hume, Samuel J. Arts and Crafts Theatre, Detroit: 1916. B&W. Set. **SDC**, plate 88; B&W. Set. **TDT**, vol. XX, n. 2 (Summer 1984). 13; B&W. Set. **TPH**, photo 454.

Terra Nova.

Colavecchia, Franco. Asolo State Theatre, Sarasota, Florida: 1981. B&W. Rendering. **DDT**, 468. 2 photos.

Feiner, Harry. Missouri Repertory Theatre, Kansas City: 1982. B&W. Rendering. **BSE3**, 21.

Gillette, J. Michael. Color. Set. **TDP**, 103, 106, 107. 5 photos.

Koltai, Ralph. Denmark: 1981. B&W. Set. **TDT**, vol. XIX, n. 3 (Fall 1983). 9.

Mikulewicz, Bill. (project) Eugene O'Neill Memorial Theater Center, Waterford, Connecticut: B&W. Rendering. **TCI**, vol. 13, n. 3 (May/Jun 1979). 32.

Wexler, Peter. Mark Taper Forum, Los Angeles: 1978. B&W. Set. **TCI**, vol. 14, n. 4 (Sep 1980). 40.

_____. Mark Taper Forum, Los Angeles: Color. Set. **TCI**, vol. 27, n. 2 (Feb 1993). 45.

Tete d'or.
> Masson, André. Théâtre de France, Odéon, Paris: 1959. B&W. Rendering. **AST**, 204. Act III.

Tetes de rechange.
> Baty, Gaston. Studio des Champs-Elysees, Paris: 1926. B&W. Set. **RSD**, illus. 414.

Tetnould.
> Gamrekeli, Irakly. Rustaveli Theatre, Tbilisi: 1932. B&W. Rendering. **TAT**, plate 711.

Thamar.
> Goncharova, Natalia. 1925. B&W and color. Rendering. **FCS**, plate 178, color plate 21.

Thark.
> Strike, Maurice. Shaw Festival Theatre, Niagara-on-the-Lake, Canada: B&W. Set. **TCI**, vol. 12, n. 4 (May/Jun 1978). 23. 2 photos.

That Boy Pete.
> Chailloux, Roger & Peter Oosthoek. Stadsschouwburg, Haarlem, Netherlands: 1970. B&W. Set. **SDW4**, illus. 376, 377.

That Championship Season
> Loquasto, Santo. Booth Theatre, NYC: 1972. B&W. Set. **TCI**, vol. 7, n. 5 (Oct 1973). 17; B&W. Set. **TDT**, vol. XVII, n. 3 (Fall 1981). 21.

That Serious He-Man Ball.
> McClennahan, Charles. American Place Theatre, NYC: 1987. B&W. Set. **ASD2**, 120.

That's It, Folks.
> Sherman, Loren. Playwrights Horizons, NYC: 1983. B&W. Set. **TCI**, vol. 17, n. 8 (Oct 1983). 10. 3 photos.

Their Day.
> Svoboda, Josef. National Theatre, Prague: 1959. B&W. Set. **RSD**, illus. 607; B&W. Set. **SJS**, 94. 4 photos; B&W. Set. **STS**, 55; B&W. Set. **TDT**, n. 7 (Dec 1966). 25.

Theodora.
> Heckroth, Heinrich. State Theatre, Münster: 1927. B&W. Set. **RSD**, illus. 143; B&W. Model. **TCS2**, plates 120, 121.

There and Back.
> _____. Stanford Opera Theatre, California: 1962. B&W. Set. **TSY**, 23.

There Was a Little Girl.
> Mielziner, Jo. Cort Theatre, NYC: 1960. B&W. Rendering. **DTT**, 205. Parking lot attack.

Theresa's Birthday.
> Soumbatashvili, Iossif. Teatr Poushkina, Moscow: 1961. B&W. Set. **SDW3**, 120.

Thésée.
> Dethomas, Maxime. Théâtre des Arts, Paris: 1913. B&W. Rendering. **RSD**, illus. 48.

Thesmophoriazusae.
> Heythum, Antonín. Osvobozene Theatre, Prague: 1926. B&W. Set. **RSD**, illus. 278; B&W. Set. **TDT**, n. 41 (Summer 1975). 22.

They (Oni).
> Szajna, Josef. Teatr Kameralny, Cracow: 1968. B&W. Rendering. **RSD**, illus. 553.

They Handcuffed the Flowers.
> Kramer, Simon. De Brakke Gronde, Amsterdam: 1970. B&W. Set. **SDW4**, illus. 343.

They Shall Not Die.
> Gorelik, Mordecai. (project): 1934. B&W. Rendering. **NTO**, facing 428; B&W. Rendering. **RSD**, illus. 446.
> Simonson, Lee. Royale Theatre, NYC: 1934. B&W. Set. **MCN**, 116.

They're Playing Our Song.
> Schmidt, Douglas W. Imperial Theatre, NYC: 1979. B&W. Projection. **ASD1**, 139;
>> B&W. Rendering. **TDT**, vol. XVII, n. 2 (Summer 1981). 21. 3 photos.

The Thief.
> _____. Art and Action, Paris: 1922. B&W. Set. **RSD**, illus. 385.

Thief-woman from London.
> Vychodil, Ladislav. Prague: 1962. B&W. Rendering. **SDB**, 77.

Thieves' Carnival.
> Vakalo, Georges. Basilikon Théatron, Athens: 1950. Color. Rendering. **SDW1**, 111.

Thing Number 2.
> _____. Playhouse in the Park, Cincinnati: B&W. Set. **TCI**, vol. 5, n. 2 (Mar/Apr
> 1971). 13, 27.

Third & Oak.
> Owen, Paul. Actors Theatre of Louisville: 1978. Color. Set. **TCI**, vol. 23, n. 3 (Mar
> 1989). 35.

The Third Sound of the Bells.
> Zelenka, Frantisek. Czechoslovakia: B&W. Rendering. **TDT** vol. XXXI, n. 2 (Spring
> 1995). 42.

Third Symphony.
> Wendel, Heinrich. Wuppertaler Bühnen, Wuppertal: 1960. B&W. Set. **SDW2**, 74.

Thirteen Suns of the Rue Saint Blaise.
> Monloup, Hubert. Théâtre de l'Est Parisien: 1968. B&W. Set. **SDW3**, 145.

This Evening at Samarcande.
> Douking, Georges. Thêátre de la Renaissance, Paris: 1951. B&W. Set. **SDW1**, 95.

This is Goggle.
> Aronson, Boris. McCarter Theatre, Princeton, New Jersey: 1958. B&W. Rendering.
> **TAB**, 305.

This Is the Army.
> Koenig, John. Broadway Theatre, NYC: 1942. B&W. Set. **BWM**, 240, 241.

Thomas More, A Man for All Seasons (see *A Man for All Seasons*).

The Thousand Cranes.
> Itô, Kisaku. Kabuki-za, Tokyo: 1952. B&W. Rendering. **SDW1**, 144, 145.

Three Birds Alighting on a Field.
> Jacobs, Sally. Manhattan Theatre Club, NYC: 1994. Color. Set. **TCI**, vol. 28, n. 4 (Apr
> 1994). 8.

Three Blind Men.
> Payne, Darwin Reid. B&W. Sketch. **SIP**, 238.

The Three Cuckolds.
> Moon, Jill. La Jolla Playhouse, California: Color. Set. **TCI**, vol. 21, n. 8 (Oct 1987).
> 26.

The Three Estates.
> Macewen, Molly. Assembly Hall, Edinburgh: 1948. B&W. Set. **DMS**, plate 38.

Three Men on a Horse.
> Aronson, Boris. Playhouse Theatre, NYC: 1935. B&W. Set. **TAB**, 58, 59. 3 photos.
> Beatty, John Lee. Royal Alexandra Theatre, Toronto: 1987. B&W. Rendering. **DDT**,
> 547.

The Three Musketeers.
> Urban, Joseph. Lyric Theatre, NYC: 1928. B&W. Set. **MCN**, 90; B&W. Set. **WMC**,
> 39.
> Zelenka, Frantisek. Vinohrady Theatre, Prague: 1934. B&W. Rendering. **TDT**, n. 42
> (Fall 1975). 26.

Three Postcards.
  Arcenas, Loy. South Coast Repertory Theatre, Costa Mesa, California: 1987. B&W.
    Model. **ASD2**, 5; B&W. Model. **DDT**, 35.
The Three Sisters.
  Dmitriev, Vladimir. Moscow Art Theatre: 1940. B&W. Set. **DMS**, plate 24; B&W. Set.
    SDW2, 181.
  Holland, Anthony. Aldwych Theatre, London: 1950. B&W. Rendering. **SDW1**, 176.
  Moiseiwitsch, Tanya. Tyrone Guthrie Theatre, Minneapolis: B&W. Set. **TCI**, vol. 20,
    n. 7 (Aug/Sep 1986). 23.
  Motley (Margaret Harris, Sophia Harris, & Elizabeth Montgomery). Ethel Barrymore
    Theatre, NYC: 1942. B&W. Set. **TCR**, 67; B&W. Set. **WTP**, 100-103. 8 photos.
  O'Brien, Timothy. Royal Shakespeare Company, GB: 1988. B&W. Set. **BTD**, 36.
  Perina, Peter. Canada: 1986. B&W. Model. **TDT**, vol. XXIII, n. 4 (Winter 1988). 29.
  Pizzi, Pier Luigi. 1964. B&W. Rendering & set. **SIO**, 104.
  Staheli, Paul. American Conservatory Theatre, San Francisco: 1969. B&W. Set. **TCI**,
    vol. 6, n. 5 (Oct 1972). 14.
  Straiges, Tony. Williamstown Theatre Festival, Massachusetts: 1976. B&W. Sketch.
    ASD2, 155; B&W. Set. **TCI**, vol. 14, n. 3 (May/Jun 1980). 18.
  Svoboda, Josef. National Theatre, London: 1967. B&W. Set. **SJS**, 48, 49. 3 photos;
    B&W. Set. **STS**, 99.
  Zeffirelli, Franco. Elisco, Rome: 1953. B&W. Set. **SDE**, 168, 169; B&W. Rendering.
    SDW1, 132.
  _____. Moscow Art Theatre: B&W. Set. **SDC**, plate 42. early 20th century.
Three Waltzes.
  Barratt, Watson. Majestic Theatre, NYC: 1937. B&W. Set. **RBS**, 157.
Three's a Crowd.
  Johnson, Albert R. Selwyn Theatre, NYC: 1930. B&W. Set. **MCN**, 99; B&W. Set.
    RBS, 34.
The Threepenny Opera.
  Conklin, John. Williamstown Theatre Festival, Massachusetts: 1974. B&W. Set. **TCI**,
    vol. 14, n. 3 (May/Jun 1980). 18; 1992. Color. Set. **TCI**, vol. 26, n. 8 (Oct 1992). 8.
  Frigerio, Ezio. Teatro Metastasio, Prato, Italy: 1973. B&W. Set. **SDW4**, illus. 231,
    232; B&W. Set. **SIO**, 66.
  Fritzsche, Max. Théâtre des Nations, Paris: 1957. B&W. Set. **SDW2**, 58.
  Herbert, Jocelyn. Lunt-Fontanne Theatre, NYC: 1989. Color. Model. **TCI**, vol. 23, n. 9
    (Nov 1989). 44. 2 photos.
  Jampolis, Neil Peter. Eric Harvie Theatre, Banff, Alberta, Canada: 1980. B&W. Set.
    DDT, 370.
  Maronek, James E. Goodman Theatre, Chicago: 1970. B&W. Rendering. **CSD**, 103.
  Neher, Caspar & Cleon Throckmorton. Empire Theatre, NYC: 1933. B&W. Set.
    BWM; 260; 1944. B&W. Set. **HPA**, 16. 2 photos; B&W. Set. **RBS**, 81.
  Neher, Caspar. Theater am Schiffbauerdamm, Berlin: 1928. B&W. Rendering & set.
    CBM, 50, 103, 104. 4 photos; B&W. Rendering. **RSD**, illus. 560; B&W. Set. **TBB**,
    30, 161.
  Otto, Teo. Municipal Theatre, Frankfurt am Main: 1965. B&W. Set. **SDR**, 67.
  Reinhardt, Andreas. Theater des Westerns, Berlin: 1987. B&W. Set. **TCI**, vol. 22, n. 1
    (Jan 1988). 14.
  Roth, Wolfgang. State Theatre, Munich: 1974. B&W. Set. **TDT**, n. 42 (Fall 1975). 18.
  Stenberg, Vladimir & Georgiy A. Kamerny Theatre, Moscow: 1930. B&W and color.
    Rendering & set. **RST**, 240, 241. 3 photos; B&W. Set. **TBB**, 208.
  Sujan. Bratislava: 1966. B&W. Rendering. **SDB**, 76.

Svoboda, Josef. Municipal Theatre, Zurich: 1972. B&W. Set. **TDT**, vol. XII, n. 2 (Summer 1976). 20. 2 photos.

_____. Stanford University, California: 1982. B&W. Set. **BSE4**, 37.

Throstlebeard.

Schwenk, Eberhard. Städtische Bühnen, Magdeburg: 1959. Color. Rendering. **SDW2**, 51.

Through the Leaves.

Stein, Douglas O. New York Shakespeare Festival's Public Theatre: 1984. B&W. Set. **BSE4**, 100; 1990. B&W. Set. **TCI**, vol. 24, n. 9 (Nov 1990). 27.

The Thrust.

Burgos, Emilio. Teatro Lara, Madrid: 1960. B&W. Rendering. **SDW2**, 76.

Thunder Rock.

Gorelik, Mordecai. Mansfield Theatre, NYC: 1939. B&W. Rendering. **RSD**, illus. 447; B&W and color. Rendering & set. **SDA**, 175, 289; Color. Rendering. **SDW1**, 195.

The Thunderstorm.

Medunetsky, K. & Vladimir A. Stenberg. Kamerny Theater, Moscow: 1924. B&W. Model. **RSD**, illus. 195.

Thyestes.

Luzzatti, Lele. Valle, Rome: 1953. B&W. Rendering. **SDW1**, 127.

The Thyme and Dragon's Death.

Koniarsky, Helmut. State Theatre, Stuttgart: 1955. B&W. Set. **SDW1**, 70.

Ti-jean and His Brothers.

Beyer, Rolf. Hopkins Center, Dartmouth College, Hanover, New Hampshire: 1971. B&W. Set. **DPT**, 103.

The Tidings Brought to Mary.

Appia, Adolphe. 1914. B&W. Set. **SDC**, plate 111.

Franko, Rodolfo. Teatro Odeon, Buenos Aires: 1940. B&W. Rendering. **SDW1**, 34.

Salzman, Alexander von. Jacques Delcroze Institute, Hellerau: 1913. B&W. **RSD**, illus. 68.

Simonson, Lee. Theatre Guild, NYC: 1922/1924. B&W. Set. **PLT**, illus. 26-29; B&W. Set. **SDA**, 212. 2 photos; B&W. Set. **TAS**, 123. 2 photos; B&W. Set. **TCS2**, plate 61; B&W. Set. **TSS**, 510, 511.

Vesnin, Alexandr A. Kamerny Theatre, Moscow: 1920. B&W. Sketch & set. **RST**, 152, 153; B&W. Set. **TCS2**, plate 150; B&W. Set. **TCT**, plate 26.

Tieste.

Luzzati, Emanuele. Rome: 1952. B&W. Rendering & set. **SDE**, 103, 104.

Tiger at the Gates.

Hays, David. Vivian Beaumont Theatre, Lincoln Center, NYC: 1967-1968. B&W. Set. **TCI**, vol. 2, n. 6 (Nov/Dec 1968). 33.

Kanamori, Kaoru. Gekidan-Shiki. Nissei Gekijo, Tokyo: 1969. B&W. Set. **SDW3**, 99.

Otto, Teo. Schauspielehaus, Zürich: 1949. B&W. Rendering. **SDW1**, 117.

Sainthill, Loudon. Apollo Theatre, London: 1955. Color. Rendering. **LST**, 41.

Til Eulenspiegel.

Bay, Howard. (project): B&W. Sketches. **SDB**, 96; B&W. Rendering. **SDW1**, 192.

Jones, Robert Edmond. Metropolitan Opera, NYC: 1916. B&W. Sketch. **DFT**, plate 3. Before the cathedral; B&W. Rendering. **SDA**, 273; B&W. Rendering. **TCS2**, plate 242.

Timbuktu.

Straiges, Tony. Martin Beck Theatre, NYC: 1978. B&W. Sketch. **ASD2**, 150; B&W. Set. **TCI**, vol. 12, n. 4 (May/Jun 1978). 14, 15. 3 photos; B&W. Set. **TCI**, vol. 16, n. 2 (Feb 1982). 18.

Time.
Napier, John. Dominion Theatre, London: 1986. B&W and color. Set. **BTD**, 162, 163.
The Time of the Cuckoo.
Edwards, Ben. Empire theatre, NYC: 1952. B&W. Drop. **DDT**, 404; Color. Drop.
TCI, vol. 23, n. 7 (Aug/Sep 1989). 55.
The Time of Your Life.
Aronson, Boris. Shubert Theatre, New Haven: 1939. B&W. Rendering. **SOW**, plate
102; B&W. Rendering. **TAB**, 61.
Barratt, Watson. Booth Theatre, NYC: 1939. B&W. Set. **TAB**, 61; B&W. Set. **WTP**,
181. 4 photos.
Lynch, Thomas. Goodman Theatre, Chicago: 1985. B&W. Rendering. **BSE4**, 89.
_____. C.W. Post College, Long Island, New York: 1972. B&W. Set. **TCI**, vol.
6, n. 5 (Oct 1972). 25.
Time Remembered.
Doeve, J.F. De Nederlandse Comedie, Amsterdam: 1951. B&W. Rendering. **SDW1**,
137.
Timon of Athens.
Dyer, Chris. Royal Shakespeare Company, GB: 1981. B&W. Set. **TDT**, vol. XIX, n. 1
(Spring 1983). 5.
Launay, Michel. Théâtre des Bouffes du Nord, Paris: 1974. B&W. Set. **SDW4**, illus.
57-63
Turina, Drago. Hrvatsko narodno kazaliste, Zagreb, Yugoslavia: 1973. B&W. Set.
SDW4, illus. 54-56.
Yeargan, Michael. Yale Repertory Theatre, New Haven: B&W. Set. **TCI**, vol. 14, n. 5
(Oct 1980). 80.
Tin Hau, Goddess of Heaven.
_____. B&W. Set. **TDT** vol. XXXI, n. 2 (Spring 1995). 27.
The Tinker's Wedding.
Humm, Ambrosius. Theater am Neumarkt, Zürich: 1974. B&W. Set. **SDW4**, illus.
202.
Tintypes.
Blake, Kathleen. Skylight Comic Opera, Milwaukee: B&W. Set. **TCI**, vol. 20, n. 5
(May 1986). 25.
Tiny Alice.
Farrah, Abd'El Kader. Royal Shakespeare Company, Aldwych Theatre, London: 1970.
B&W. Set. **SDW3**, 150.
Wurtzel, Stuart. American Conservatory Theatre, San Francisco: 1967. B&W. Set.
TCI, vol. 6, n. 5 (Oct 1972). 12; NYC: 1969. B&W. Set. **TCI**, vol. 14, n. 1 (Jan/
Feb 1980). 38.
Tip-Toes.
Beatty, John Lee. Goodspeed Opera House, East Haddam, Connecticut: 1978. B&W.
Sketch & set. **TCI**, vol. 12, n. 6 (Oct 1978). 22, 23. 3 photos.
Tirésias.
Lancaster, Osbert. Jubilee Hall, Aldeburgh, England: 1958. B&W. Rendering. **SDW2**,
219; Color. Rendering. **TOP**, 31.
'Tis Pity She's a Whore.
Ciller, Josef. Zagreb: 1984. B&W. Model. **TDT**, vol. XXVIII, n. 2 (Spring 1992). 34.
Glossop, Roger. National Theatre (Olivier), London: 1988. B&W. Set. **BTD**, 52.
_____. B&W. Set. **SDL**, 172.
Titus.
Erni, Hans. Salzburg Festival Theatre: 1949. B&W. Rendering. **SDW1**, 114.

Wendel, Heinrich. B&W. Set. **OPE**, 45.

Titus Andronicus.

　　Aronson, Boris. Oregon Shakespeare Festival, Ashland: 1974. B&W. Set. **PST**, 80.

　　Brook, Peter. Shakespeare Memorial Theatre, Stratford-upon-Avon: 1955. B&W. Set.
　　　　DMS, plates 48, 49; B&W. Set. **SDW2**, 216.

　　Luzzati, Emanuele. 1968. B&W. Set. **SIO**, 88.

　　McLane, Derek. Theatre for New Audience, NYC: 1994. Color. Set. **TCI**, vol. 28, n. 5
　　　　(May 1994). 6.

　　Stockemer, Richard. B&W. Rendering. **BSE2**, 41.

To Die for Grenada.

　　Berliner, Charles. Cleveland Playhouse: 1986. Color. Rendering. **BSE5**, 14; B&W.
　　　　Rendering. **TCI**, vol. 21, n. 8 (Oct 1987). 45.

To Die, Perchance to Dream.

　　Rodriguez, Aida & Beatriz Tosar. Teatro Solis, Montevideo: 1953. B&W. Set. **SDW2**,
　　　　242.

To Kill a Mockingbird.

　　Moran, Jim. Clarence Brown Theatre Company, Knoxville, Tennessee: B&W. Set.
　　　　TDT, vol. XXVIII, n. 2 (Spring 1992). 8 of insert.

Tobacco Road.

　　Proett, Daniel. George Street Playhouse, New Brunswick, New Jersey: B&W. Set.
　　　　TCI, vol. 14, n. 3 (May/Jun 1980). 44.

　　Sharpe, Robert Redington. Masque Theatre, NYC: 1933. B&W. Sketch & set. **TDT**,
　　　　vol. XXVII, n. 1 (Winter 1991). 16. 2 photos.

　　Yeargan, Michael. Long Wharf Theatre, New Haven, Connecticut: 1985. B&W. Set.
　　　　ASD2, 183.

　　_____. Playhouse in the Park, Cincinnati: B&W. Set. **TCI**, vol. 14, n. 1 (Jan/Feb
　　　　1980). 39. 2 photos.

Tod eines Jägers.

　　Schneider-Siemssen, Günther. Salzburg Festival: 1977. B&W. Set. **TCI**, vol. 12, n. 6
　　　　(Oct 1978). 33.

Today a Little Extra.

　　_____. Actors Theatre of Louisville: 1980. B&W. Set. **TCI**, vol. 15, n. 4 (Apr
　　　　1981). 17.

Today is a Holiday.

　　Burgos, Emilio. Teatro María Guerrero, Madrid: 1955. Color. Rendering. **SDW2**, 79.

Today the Sun Still Sets on Atlantida.

　　Svoboda, Josef. National Theatre, Prague: 1956. B&W. Set. **STS**, 19.

Toller.

　　Minks, Wilfried. 1968. B&W. Set. **TCI**, vol. 12, n. 1 (Jan/Feb 1978). 30.

　　Peduzzi, Richard. Théâtre National Populaire, Villeurbanne, France: 1973. B&W. Set.
　　　　SDW4, illus. 298-305.

Tom Jones.

　　Belden, Ursula. Pittsburgh Public Theatre: 1982. B&W. Set. **BSE4**, 73.

　　Lee, Eugene. Dallas Theatre Center: 1984. B&W. Set. **ASD1**, 68.

　　_____. Trinity Square Theatre, Providence, Rhode Island: B&W. Set. **TCI**, vol.
　　　　9, n. 6 (Nov/Dec 1975). 25.

Tommy.

　　Arnone, John. La Jolla Playhouse, California: 1992. Color. Set. **TCI**, vol. 26, n. 9 (Nov
　　　　1992). 7; St. James Theatre, NYC: 1993. Color. Set. **TCI**, vol. 27, n. 7 (Aug/Sep
　　　　1993). cover, 7, 26-30. 12 photos.

Tomorrow's Monday.
> Beatty, John Lee. Circle Repertory Company, NYC: 1985. B&W. Rendering. **DDT**, 542.

Tonight We Improvise (Pirandello).
> Padovani, Gianfranco. 1971-1972. B&W. Rendering. **SIO**, 102.

Too Clever By Half.
> Hudson, Richard. Old Vic Theatre, London: 1988. Color. Set. **BTD**, 59; B&W. Set. **TDT**, vol. XXVIII, n. 2 (Spring 1992). 21.

Too Funny for Words.
> Johnson, Carlos. Grupo de Arte Dramatico del Instituto Chileno-Francés de Cultura, Santiago: 1952. B&W. Rendering. **SDW1**, 54.

Too True to Be Good.
> Jorgulesco, Jonel. Guild Theatre, NYC: 1932. B&W. Set. **SCM**, 132.
> Köpeczi-Bócz, István. Budapest: 1968. B&W. Rendering. **SDW3**, 87. 2 photos.
> Kruger, Halina. Poland: B&W. Model. **SCM**, 84; B&W. Rendering. **TPH**, photo 395.

The Tooth of Crime.
> Conklin, John. Hartford Stage, Connecticut: 1986. B&W. Set. **TCI**, vol. 20, n. 5 (May 1986). 8.
> Dorsey, Kent. Berkeley Repertory Theatre, California: Color. Set. **TCI**, vol. 25, n. 8 (Oct 1991). 49.
> Rojo, Jerry N. Frederick Wood Theatre, Vancouver,: 1973. B&W. Set. **CSD**, 22; B&W. Set. **TSE**, 15, 132-136. 4 photos.

Torquato Tasso.
> Egg, Lois. Akademietheater, Vienna: 1960. B&W. Set. **SDW2**, 155.
> Finke, Jochen. Deutsches Theater, Berlin: 1975. B&W. Model. **TDT**, vol. XVI, n. 1 (Spring 1980). 16.
> Minks, Wilfried. Theater der Freien Hansestadt, Bremen: 1969. B&W. Set. **SDW3**, 78; B&W. Set. **TCI**, vol. 12, n. 1 (Jan/Feb 1978). 28.
> _____. Deutsches Theater, Berlin: B&W. Set. **MRH**, facing 231. 2 photos.
> _____. Edinburgh Festival: 1994. Color. Set. **TCI**, vol. 29, n. 1 (Jan 1995). 9.

La Torre Rossa.
> Bragaglia, Anton Giulio. Teatro degli Indipendenti, Rome: 1925. B&W. **TCS2**, plate 156.

Tosca.
> Beck, Peter Dean. Hawaii Opera Theatre, Honolulu: 1986. Color. Set. **TCI**, vol. 20, n. 8 (Oct 1986). 21.
> Klein, Allen Charles. San Diego Opera: 1974. B&W. Set. **DPT**, 348; Tulsa Opera: 1985. B&W. Set. **TCI**, vol. 20, n. 8 (Oct 1986). 21.
> Lazaridis, Stefanos. Maggio Musicale Fiorentino, Florence: 1986. B&W. Set. **BTD**, 128.
> Oenslager, Donald. New York City Opera: 1966. B&W. Set. **DPT**, 358. Act I; B&W. Painter's elevations. **SDB**, 120; B&W. Model. **TDO**, 137.
> Ponnelle, Jean-Pierre. San Francisco Opera: 1976. B&W. Set. **TCI**, vol. 12, n. 3 (Mar/Apr 1978). 14, 16.
> Svoboda, Josef. Grand Opera of the Fifth of May, Prague: 1947. B&W. Set. **SJS**, 52; B&W. Set. **STS**, 47.
> _____. Basel: 1963. B&W. Set. **TCI**, vol. 4, n. 4 (Sep 1970). 23.

Total Eclipse.
> Fievez, Jean-Marie. Théâtre du Rideau de Bruxelles: 1973. B&W. Set. **SDW4**, illus. 407.

Griffin, Hayden. Lyric Theatre, Hammersmith, London: B&W. Rendering. **TCI**, vol. 19, n. 9 (Nov 1985). 20.

A Touch of the Poet.

Axtell, Barry. Northern Arizona State University, Phoenix: 1978. B&W. Rendering. **BSE1**, 13.

Edwards, Ben. Helen Hayes Theatre, NYC: 1958. B&W. Rendering. **DPT**, 179; B&W. Rendering & set. **TCI**, vol. 1, n. 3 (Jul/Aug 1967). 24-27. 3 photos; B&W. Rendering. **TCI**, vol. 23, n. 7 (Aug/Sep 1989). 3, 53.

Jones, Robert Edmond. (project): 1946. B&W. Rendering. **REJ**, 125.

The Tourist Guide.

Bechtler, Hildegard. Almeida Theatre, London: 1987. B&W. Set. **BTD**, 74.

Toussaint.

Björnson, Maria. English National Opera, London Coliseum: 1977. B&W. Set. **TCI**, vol. 15, n. 5 (May 1981). 15; B&W. Set. **TDT**, vol. XIX, n. 1 (Spring 1983). 6.

Tovarich.

Sovey, Raymond. Plymouth Theatre, NYC: 1936. B&W. Set. **MCN**, 132.

The Tower.

Essman, Manuel. USA: 1933. B&W. Rendering. **TAT**, plate 501.

The Tower of Babel.

Gronovsky, Tadeusz. Polski Theater, Warsaw: 1927. B&W. Set. **RSD**, illus. 270, 271.

The Town at Dawn.

Kitaïev, Mark. Theatr Younogo Zritelia, Riga: 1970. B&W. Set. **SDW4**, illus. 259, 260.

Toys in the Attic.

Bay, Howard. Hudson Theatre, NYC: 1960. B&W. Set. **SDB**, 43; B&W. Set. **TCI**, vol. 17, n. 2 (Feb 1983). 14.

Tragedia Cloveka.

Vychodil, Ladislav. Bratislava: B&W. Model. **TDT**, n. 38 (Oct 1974). back cover.

The Tragedy of Man.

Varga, Matyas. Némzeti Színház, Budapest: 1961. B&W. Model. **SDW2**, 142.

The Tragedy of Nothing.

Aronson, Boris. Irving Place Theatre, NYC: 1927. B&W. Model. **BAT**, 21; B&W. Rendering. **TAB**, 293.

The Tragedy of Thomas Andros.

Scott, Henry III. Circle Theatre, NYC: B&W. Set. **TCI**, vol. 8, n. 2 (Mar/Apr 1974). 8. 2 photos.

Transfiguration.

Baumeister, Willi. Deutsches Theater, Stuttgart: 1920. B&W. Sketches. **RSD**, illus. 244, 245.

Neppach, Robert. Tribune, Berlin: 1919. B&W. Rendering. **RSD**, illus. 123.

Translations.

Davis, Ashley Martin. Plymouth Theatre, NYC: 1995. Color. Model & set. **TCI**, vol. 29, n. 5 (May 1995). 62. 3 photos.

Diss, Eileen. Hampstead Theatre, London: 1981. B&W. Set. **BTD**, 61.

Reaney, Mark. Chapman Theatre, Tulsa, Oklahoma: 1986. Color. Set. **BSE5**, 21.

The Transparent City.

Bergallo, Armando & Hector Vilche. Holland: 1979. Color. Set. **TDT**, vol. XX, n. 1 (Spring 1984). front cover.

Transposed Heads.

Okun, Alexander. B&W. Set. **TCI**, vol. 21, n. 9 (Nov 1987). 46.

Der Traum, ein Leben.
>Strohbach, Hans. B&W. Rendering. **CSC**, facing 44.

Traumspiel.
>Gade, Svend. Barnowsky Bühnen, Berlin: B&W. Rendering. **TCS2**, plates 210, 211.

Traveler in the Dark.
>Lee, Ming Cho. Mark Taper Forum, Los Angeles: 1985. B&W. Sketch & model. **DDT**, 194, 195; B&W. Set. **TCI**, vol. 19, n. 7 (Aug/Sep 1985). 38.

Traveller Without Luggage.
>Messel, Oliver. ANTA Theatre, NYC: 1964. B&W. Model. **OMB**, 223.

Travelling Companions.
>Nordgreen, Eric. Det kongelige Teater, Copenhagen: 1949. B&W. Rendering. **SDW1**, 59.

La Traviata.
>Bosquet, Thierry. Opéra National. Théatre Royal de la Monnaie, Brussels: 1974. B&W and color. Set. **SDW4**, illus. 140-142.
>
>Colasanti, Veniero & John Moore. Teatro Bellini: Catania, Italy: 1959. B&W. Rendering. **SDW2**, 123.
>
>Gunter, John. Glyndebourne Festival Opera, England: 1987. B&W. Set. **BTD**, 120.
>
>Heeley, Desmond. Chicago Lyric Opera: 1993. Color. Set. **TCI**, vol. 27, n. 10 (Dec 1993). 12.
>
>Heinrich, Reinhard. Semper Opera, Dresden: 1987. B&W. Set. **TCI**, vol. 21, n. 10 (Dec 1987). 16.
>
>Lorenzen, William A. Purdue University: B&W. Set. **SST**, 446.
>
>Schoukhaeff, Vassily. Chauve-Souris, Moscow: B&W. Rendering. **TCS2**, plate 235.
>
>Smith, Oliver. Metropolitan Opera, NYC: 1957. B&W. Renderings. **DPT**, 157. Acts II & III.
>
>Svoboda, Josef. Macerata: 1992. B&W and color. Set. **TDT**, vol. XXX, n. 5 (Fall 1994). 38, 42.
>
>Varona, José. Netherlands Opera, Amsterdam: 1974. B&W. Model. **DPT**, 117.
>
>Yodice, Robert. Juilliard School, Lincoln Center, NYC: B&W. Set. **TCI**, vol. 10, n. 3 (May/Jun 1976). 11.
>
>_____. Covent Garden, London: 1930. B&W. Set. **CGA**, 113.
>
>_____. Madison Opera, Wisconsin: 1985. B&W. Set. **BSE4**, 24.

Treasure.
>_____. Leningrad Theatre for Young Spectators: 1934. B&W. Set. **SOW**, plate 67.

The Treatment.
>Schuette, James. New York Shakespeare Festival, NYC: 1993. B&W. Set. **TCI**, vol. 28, n. 1 (Jan 1994). 9.

A Tree Grows in Brooklyn.
>Mielziner, Jo. Alvin Theatre, NYC: 1951. B&W. Set. **BWM**, 252; B&W. Rendering. **DTT**, 173. Laundry scene; B&W. Rendering. **DTT**, 174. Rooftops; B&W. Rendering. **DTT**, 175.

The Triadic Ballet.
>Schlemmer, Oskar. Landestheater, Stuttgart: 1920. B&W and color. Rendering & set. **RSD**, illus. 356, 357.

The Trial.
>Labisse, Félix. Théâtre Marigny, Paris: 1947. B&W. Set. **RSD**, illus. 495; B&W. Set. **SDW1**, 99.
>
>Prampolini, Enrico. Rome: 1949. B&W. Rendering. **SDE**, 136.
>
>Schmidt, Willi. Schlosspark Theatre, Berlin: 1950. B&W. Set. **SDW1**, 74.

Schultz, Rudolf. Landestheater, Hanover: 1951. B&W. Rendering. **SDW1**, 77.
Vychodil, Ladislav. Stockholm: 1977. B&W. Rendering. **TDT**, vol. XV, n. 2 (Summer 1979). 16.
_____. NYC: 1952. B&W. Set. **WTP**, 116, 117. 4 photos.
The Trial of Lucullus.
Neher, Caspar. State Opera, Berlin: 1951. B&W. Set. **SDW1**, 72.
The Trial of the Catonsville Nine.
_____. Mark Taper Forum, Los Angeles: 1971. B&W. Set. **TCI**, vol. 8, n. 1 (Jan/Feb 1974). 17.
The Trial: A Funhouse.
Kollenborn, Greg. California Institute of the Arts: 1975. B&W. Set. **TCI**, vol. 13, n. 5 (Oct 1979). 32.
A Tribute to Lili Lamont.
Beatty, John Lee. Circle Repertory Company, NYC: 1976. B&W. Set. **TCI**, vol. 12, n. 6 (Oct 1978). 21.
The Tricks of Scapin.
Köpeczi-Bócz, István. Madách Szinház, Budapest. 1959. B&W. Rendering. **SDW2**, 139.
Le Triomphe de l' Amour.
Gischia, Léon. T.N.P., Paris: 1955. B&W. Set. **RSD**, illus. 536.
I Trionfi del Petrarca.
Bernard, Roger & Joelle Roustan. Forest National, Brussels: 1974. B&W. Set. **SDW4**, illus. 289-294.
Trip to the Coast.
Breyer, Gaston. Teatro de los Independientes, Buenos Aires: 1956. B&W. Set. **SDW2**, 25.
The Trip to the Country.
Chiari, Mario. Piccolo Teatro, Milan: 1954-55. B&W. Set. **SDW1**, 121.
Trip to the Moon.
Zimmerman, Reinhart. Comic Opera, Berlin: B&W. Set. **TCI**, vol. 15, n. 1 (Jan 1981). 36.
Triple-A Plowed Under.
Hermanson, Hjalmar. Biltmore Theatre, NYC: 1936. B&W. Set. **NTO**, facing 396; B&W. Set. **RSD**, illus. 448.
Tristan and Isolde.
Allinson, Adrian. Great Britain: B&W. Rendering. **DIT**, plate 40.
Appia, Adolphe. Milan: 1923. B&W. Sketch. **JSS**, 15. Act III; B&W. Rendering. **TAS**, 96, 97. 4 photos; B&W. Rendering. **TCS2**, plate 34; B&W. Rendering. **TDT**, n. 38 (Oct 1974). 20, 21. Act II; B&W. Rendering. **TSS**, 506, 507. 3 photos; B&W. Rendering. **WLA**, 97. 2 photos, Act III.
Bury, John. Covent Garden, London: 1971. B&W. Set. **TDT**, vol. XIX, n. 3 (Fall 1983). 7.
Fortuny, Mariano. Metropolitan Opera, NYC: 1909. B&W. Rendering. **MOM**, 7.
Fuerst, Walter René. Odéon Theatre, Paris: 1923. B&W. Sketches. **TCS1**, plates 43, 44. 9 drawings.
Hockney, David. Los Angeles Music Center Opera: 1987. Color. Model. **BTD**, 112. Act I; Color. Set. **TCI**, vol. 22, n. 3 (Mar 1988). 22.
Hoffman, Vlastislav. National Theatre, Prague: 1924. B&W. Rendering. **TDT**, n. 41 (Summer 1975). 17.
Oenslager, Donald. Academy of Music, Philadelphia: 1934. B&W. Rendering. **CSD**, 13; B&W. Rendering. **SDA**, 266; B&W. Rendering. **STN**, 221-225. 3 photos;

B&W and color. Rendering. **TDO**, xv, 56, 57. 3 photos; B&W. Rendering. **TPH**, photo 467.

Roller, Alfred. Court Opera of Vienna: 1903. B&W. Rendering. **TCS2**, plate 186; B&W. Sketches. **TPH**, photo 317.

Schneider-Siemssen, Gunther. Metropolitan Opera, NYC: 1971. B&W and color. Set. **MOM**, 228-235. 5 photos; B&W. Rendering. **OPE**, 40. Act 1; B&W. Rendering. **OPE**, 40. Act 1.

Shervashidze, Alexander. Marinsky Theatre, St. Petersburg: 1909. B&W. Set. **MOT**, between 64 & 65.

Stroem, Carl Johan. Royal Opera House, Stockholm. 1966. B&W. Set. **SDR**, 53.

Svoboda, Josef. B&W. Set. **SDL**, 470; Hesse State Theatre, Wiesbaden: 1967. B&W. Set. **JSS**, 41; B&W. Set. **SJS**, 66; B&W. Set. **STS**, 59; Cologne, Germany: 1967. B&W. Set. **JSS**, 42; Beyreuth Festival Theatre: 1974/1975. B&W. Set. **JSS**, 44; B&W. Model. **JSS**, 47 and between 54 & 55. Act III; Color. Set. **JSS**, between 54 & 55. Act II; B&W. Set. **STS**, 82, 95. 3 photos; B&W. Set. **TDT**, vol. XII, n. 2 (Summer 1976). 17, 18. Acts II & III; B&W. Set. **TCI**, vol. 14, n. 1 (Jan/Feb 1980). 22; Grand Theater, Geneva: 1978. B&W. Set. **JSS**, 50, 51. Act II; B&W and color Set. **JSS**, 51 and between 54 & 55. Act I; Color. Set. **JSS**, between 54 & 55. Act III; B&W. Set. **STS**, 23; B&W. Set. **TDT**, vol. XXVIII, n. 5 (Fall 1992). 16. Act I; Color. Set. **TDT**, vol. XXVIII, n. 5 (Fall 1992). 9.

Wagner, Wieland. Beyreuth Festival Theatre: B&W. Set. **TCI**, vol. 3, n. 4 (Sep 1969). 30; 1952. B&W. Set. **JSS**, 19. Act III; 1962. B&W. Set. **RSD**, illus. 552.

Wonder, Erich. Beyreuth Festival Theatre: 1993. B&W. Set. **TCI**, vol. 28, n. 1 (Jan 1994). 13.

The Triumph of Love.

Culbert, John. Court Theatre, Chicago: 1993. Color. Set. **TCI**, vol. 28, n. 2 (Feb 1994). 9.

Gallo, David. Classic Stage Company, NYC: 1994. Color. Set. **TCI**, vol. 28, n. 6 (Jun/Jul 1994). 10.

The Triumph of St. Joan.

Kiesler, Frederick. NYC: 1951. B&W. Sketch. **EIF**, photo 43.

Le Troiane (Euripides/Sartre).

Polidori, Gianni. 1965. B&W. Rendering. **SIO**, 116.

Troilus and Cressida.

Acquart, André. Odeon Theatre, Paris: 1964. B&W. 6 sketches & set. **RSD**, illus. 537, 539; B&W. Sketches & set. **SDW3**, 49. 9 photos.

Döepp, John. Shakespeare Summer Festival, Washington, DC: 1972. B&W. Rendering. **CSD**, 74.

Falleni, Silvano. Maggio Musicale Fiorentino, Florence: 1949. B&W. Rendering. **SDE**, 78.

Haferung, Paul. Städtische Bühnen, Essen: 1952. Color. Rendering. **SDW1**, 75.

Koltai, Ralph. Royal Shakespeare Company, GB: 1985. B&W. Model. **BTD**, 31.

Koniarsky, Helmut. State Theatre, Stuttgart: 1952. B&W. Set. **SDW1**, 70.

Polidori, Gianni. 1964. B&W. Set. **SIO**, 114, 115.

Straiges, Tony. Yale Repertory Theatre, New Haven: 1976. B&W. Set. **TCI**, vol. 16, n. 2 (Feb 1982). 15.

Vesseur, Wim. Koninklijken Schouwburg, The Hague: 1959. B&W. Rendering. **SDW2**, 145.

Ward, Anthony. Royal Shakespeare Company, GB: 1991. Color. Set. **TCI**, vol. 27, n. 4 (Apr 1993). 45.

Zeffirelli, Franco. Giardino di Boboli, Florence: 1949. B&W. Set. **DOT**, 245; B&W. **SDW1**, 132.
_____. Angus Bowmer Theatre, Ashland, Oregon: B&W. Set. **TCI**, vol. 7, n. 2 (Mar/Apr 1973). 10.
_____. Germany: B&W. Set. **TCM**, 95.
_____. Old Vic Theatre, London: 1955. B&W. Set. **SOS**, 271.
Trojan Incident.
Bay, Howard. St. James Theatre: 1938. B&W. Set. **TCI**, vol. 17, n. 2 (Feb 1983). 10.
The Trojan War Will Not Take Place.
Seger, Richard. American Conservatory Theatre, Geary Theatre, San Francisco: 1981. B&W. Set. **TCI**, vol. 15, n. 4 (Apr 1981). 42.
The Trojan Women.
Eichbauer, Helio. Teatro Glaucio Gil, Rio de Janeiro: 1967. B&W. Set. **SDW3**, 29.
Mataré, Ewald. Wuppertaler Bühnen, Wuppertal: 1962. B&W. Model. **AST**, 234.
_____. Old Vic Theatre, London: 1955. B&W. Set. **SOS**, 271.University of Texas, Austin: B&W. Set. **TDT**, vol. XXVI, n. 1 (Spring 1990). 23 of insert.
The Trojans.
Cairns, Tom. Welsh National Opera: 1987. Color. Set. **BTD**, frontispiece.
Pond, Helen & Herbert Senn. Opera Company of Boston: 1971. B&W. Model. **DPT**, 365.
Preetorius, Emil. State Opera, Berlin: 1931. B&W. Rendering. **SCM**, 68.
Svoboda, Josef. Grand Theater, Geneva: 1974/1975. B&W. **STS**, 88; B&W. Set. **TDT**, vol. XII, n. 2 (Summer 1976). 25. 4 photos.
Wagner, Robin. Vienna State Opera: 1976. B&W. Set. **ASD1**, 156.
Wexler, Peter. Metropolitan Opera, NYC: 1973. B&W. Model. **CSD**, 141; B&W. Model. **DPT**, 133; B&W. Set. **DPT**, 69; B&W. Set. **SDL**, 55; B&W. Model. **SDT**, 45; B&W. Set. **TDT**, n. 39 (Dec 1974). back cover.
Trommeln in der Nacht (Drums in the Night).
Sievert, Ludwig. Schauspielhaus, Frankfurt: 1923. B&W. Rendering. **TCS2**, plate 206.
Tropical Proxy.
_____. Eureka Theatre, San Francisco: B&W. Set. **TCI**, vol. 14, n. 4 (Sep 1980). 24.
The Troubador's Mirror.
Sebregts, Lode. Nationaal Toneel, Antwerp: 1960. B&W. Set. **SDW2**, 32.
The Trousers-The Snob-1913.
Bignardi, Giancarlo. Teatro delle Arte, Rome: 1973. B&W. Set. **SDW4**, illus. 211-213.
Il Trovatore.
Barburini, Gilberto. Italy: 1952. B&W. Rendering. **SDE**, 29.
Cristini, Cesare M. Teatro San Carlo, Naples: 1953. B&W. Rendering. **SDE**, 72. 2 photos.
Fortunato, Franz. 1952. B&W. Rendering. **SDE**, 88.
Howland, Gerard. San Francisco Opera: 1994-1995. Color. Model. **TCI**, vol. 29, n. 3 (Mar 1995). 33.
Kravjansky, Mikulás. Statne Divadlo Ostrava, Czechoslovakia: 1966. B&W. Rendering. **SDW3**, 182. 2 photos.
Labò, Savino. La Scala, Milan: 1943. B&W. Rendering. **SDE**, 93.
Mitchell, David. Opéra de Paris: 1973. B&W. Model. **DPT**, 118. Prison set.
Ostroff, Boyd. Indianapolis Opera Company: 1982. Color. Set. **TCI**, vol. 20, n. 8 (Oct 1986). 24.
Svoboda, Josef. Grand Opera of the Fifth of May, Prague: 1947. B&W. Rendering. **SJS**, 148; Komische Oper, Berlin: 1966. B&W. Model. **SJS**, 58. 2 photos.

Wendel, Heinrich. Deutsches Oper am Rhein, Düsseldorf-Duisburg: B&W. Set. **SDR**, 50.

Yeargan, Michael. Opera North, Leeds, England: 1983. B&W. Set. **ASD2**, 189.

Tru.

_____. Color. Set. **TCI**, vol. 24, n. 8 (Oct 1990). 52.

Truckline Café.

Aronson, Boris. Belasco Theatre, NYC: 1946. B&W. Set. **TAB**, 300.

True Blue and Trembling.

Parkman, Russell. Yale School of Drama, New Haven, Connecticut: Color. Set. **TCI**, vol. 25, n. 1 (Jan 1991). 39.

True West.

Billings, James. American Southwest Theatre Company: B&W. Drawing. **TDP**, 84.

Edmunds, Kate. Hasty Pudding Club, Boston: 1981. B&W. Set. **TCI**, vol. 16, n. 8 (Oct 1982). 14.

Truffles in the Soup.

Schmidt, Douglas W. Seattle Repertory Theatre: 1989. B&W. Set. **DDT**, 138.

Tsar Feodor Ivanovitch.

Kumankov, J. USSR: Color. Rendering. **TDT**, vol. XII, n. 3 (Fall 1976). 26.

Sapoundoff, Klaudius. Moscow Art Theatre: 1898-1912. B&W. Set. **TCS2**, plate 6.

_____. Moscow Art Theatre: 1922. B&W. Set. **DOT**, 207; B&W. Set. **TPH**, photo 297.

Stelletsky, Dimitri. Alexandrinsky Theatre, St. Petersburg: 1915. B&W. Rendering. **RSC**, 55.

Turandot.

Anisfeld, Boris. (not produced): 1926. Color. Rendering. **TDT**, vol. XXIX, n. 3 (Summer 1993). 21.

Beaton, Cecil. Metropolitan Opera, NYC: 1960. B&W. Rendering. **MOM**, 12; Royal Opera House, Covent Garden, London: 1963. B&W. Set. **CBS**, 76.

Clerici, Fabrizio. La Scala, Milan: 1961-1962. B&W. Rendering & set. **SIO**, 144, 145.

Colasanti, Veniero. Teatro Olympico, Vicenza: 1952. B&W. Rendering. **SDW1**, 122.

Exter, Alexandra. Moscow: 1922. B&W. Set. **TPH**, photo 404.

Fanto, E. State Opera, Dresden: B&W. Set. **TCS2**, plate 356.

Firth, Tazeena & Timothy O'Brien. Vienna State Opera: 1983. Color. Set. **BTD**, 102, 103.

Guglielminetti, Eugenio. 1969. B&W. Set. **SIO**, 78.

Jacobs, Sally. Royal Opera House, Covent Garden, London: 1984. B&W. Set. **BTD**, 121.

Montresor, Beni. New York City Opera, Lincoln Center: B&W. Rendering. **TCI**, vol. 16, n. 5 (May 1982). 16.

Nivinsky, Ignati. Vakhtangov Theatre, Moscow: 1922. B&W. Set. **DIT**, plate 80; B&W. Rendering. **RSD**, illus. 160-162; B&W. Set. **RST**, 82, 83. 4 photos; B&W. **TAB**, 6; B&W. Rendering. **TAT**, plate 718; B&W. Set. **TCS2**, plate 167.

Roller, Alfred. Salzburg Festival Theatre: 1926. B&W. Sketch. **TPH**, photo 334.

Steinberg, Paul. Welsh National Opera: 1994. Color. Set. **TCI**, vol. 29, n. 4 (Apr 1995). cover, 33.

Stern, Ernst. Deutsches Theater, Berlin: 1911. B&W. Rendering. **FCS**, plate 192; Color. Renderings of drops. **MRH**, facing 40. 2 photos; B&W. Rendering. **SDO**, 218, 219.

Svoboda, Josef. Grand Theater, Geneva: 1976. B&W. Set. **STS**, 73.

_____. Covent Garden, London: 1947. B&W. Set. **CGA**, 134.

_____. Dallas Opera: B&W. Set. **TCI**, vol. 16, n. 9 (Nov/Dec 1982). 24.

_____. Third Studio, Moscow Art Theatre: B&W. Set. **DOT**, 214.
Turandot or the Congress of the Whitewashers.
    Appen, Karl von. Theater am Schiffbauerdamm, Berlin: 1973. B&W. Set. **SDW4**,
        illus. 243-247.
    Sagert, Horst. Schauspielehaus, Zürich: 1969. Color. Rendering. **RSD**, illus. 588.
Turangalila.
    Ernst, Max. Opéra de Paris: 1968. B&W. Rendering. **AST**, 119. 4 photos.
Turcaret.
    Acquart, André. Théâtre de l'Est Parisien: 1965. B&W. Set. **SDW3**, 74.
The Turk in Italy.
    Conklin, John. New York City Opera, Lincoln Center: 1978. B&W. Set. **TCI**, vol. 14,
        n. 3 (May/Jun 1980). 23.
    Zeffirelli, Franco. 1955. B&W. Set. **SIO**, 136; La Scala, Milan: 1957. B&W. Set. **TCI**,
        vol. 13, n. 3 (May/Jun 1979). 16.
The Turn of the Screw.
    Isreal, Robert. Santa Fe Opera: 1983. B&W. Set. **ASD2**, 51.
    Piper, John. Sadler's Wells Theatre, London: 1954. B&W. Rendering. **SDB**, 67; B&W.
        Rendering. **SDR**, 44;. B&W. Rendering. **SDW1**, 184.
    Robertson, Patrick & Rosemary Vercoe. English National Opera, London: 1979.
        B&W. Set. **BTD**, 92; B&W. Sketches & set. **SDL**, 80, 472, 473. 6 photos; B&W.
        Set. **TDT**, vol. XIX, n. 3 (Fall 1983). 5.
    Venza, Jàc. New York City Opera, Lincoln Center: B&W. Set. **TCI**, vol. 7, n. 1 (Jan/
        Feb 1973). 19.
        _____. Eastman Theatre, Rochester, NY: B&W. Set. **TCI**, vol. 17, n. 7 (Aug/Sep
        1983). 33.
        _____. English National Opera, London: 1984. B&W. Set. **TCI**, vol. 19, n. 4
        (Apr 1985). 20.
The Tutor.
    Neher, Caspar. Theater am Schiffbauerdamm, Berlin: 1950. B&W. Rendering. **CBM**,
        110. 2 photos; B&W. Set. **TBB**, 59.
Twang!!
    Messel, Oliver. Shaftsbury Theatre, London: 1965. B&W. Model. **OMB**, 225.
Twelfth Night.
    Babic, Ljubo. National Theatre, Zagreb: 1924. B&W. Model. **TCS2**, plate 112; Na-
        tional Theatre, Prague: B&W. Set. **SDC**, plate 87.
    Berman, Eugene. (not produced): 1938. B&W. Rendering. **TPH**, photo 483.
    Beyer, Rolf. Dartmouth College, Hanover, New Hampshire: 1968. B&W. Paint eleva-
        tions. **DDT**, 65.
    Cairns, Tom. Crucible Theatre, Sheffield, England: 1987. B&W. Set. **BTD**, 49.
    Chaney, Stewart. St. James Theatre, NYC: 1940. B&W. Rendering & set. **SDA**, 258,
        259. 5 photos.
    Craven, Hawes. 1901. B&W. Rendering. **SDG**, 138.
    Curiel, Nicolas. Teatro Universitario de la Universidad Central de Venezuela, Caracas:
        1962. B&W. Set. **SDW2**, 243.
    de Nobili, Lila. Shakespeare Memorial Theatre, Stratford-upon-Avon: 1958. Color.
        Set. **SOS**, 261.
    Eigsti, Karl. Playhouse in the Park, Cincinnati: 1979. B&W. Set. **ASD1**, 38.
    Favorski, Vladimir. Moscow Art Theatre Studio II: 1934. B&W. Model. **SDW2**, 183;
        B&W. Model. **RSD**, illus. 220.
    Feiner, Harry. North Carolina Shakespeare Festival, High Point: 1980. B&W. Set.
        BSE2, 13.

Funicello, Ralph. Old Globe Theatre, San Diego: Color. Set. **TCI**, vol. 29, n. 2 (Feb 1995). 32.

Furse, Roger. Old Vic Theatre, London: 1950. B&W. Rendering. **SDW1**, 175.

Hudson, Richard. Goodman Theatre, Chicago: 1992. B&W and color. Model & set. **TDT**, vol. XXVIII, n. 2 (Spring 1992). front cover, 19, 22.

Inglessi, Marion. Brandeis University, Waltham, Massachusetts: B&W. Set. **TCI**, vol. 23, n. 9 (Nov 1989). 54.

Jouvet, Louis. Théâtre du Vieux Colombier, Paris: B&W. Set. **TCS2**, plate 49.

Marosin, Mircea. Teatrul Municipal, Bucharest: 1956. B&W. Rendering. **SDW2**, 174.

Mörner, Stellan. Dramatiska Teatern, Stockholm: 1946. B&W. Rendering. **SDW1**, 167.

Navon, Arieh. Cameri, Tel Aviv: 1959. B&W. Set. **SDW2**, 120.

O'Brien, Timothy. Great Britain: B&W. Model. **TDT**, vol. XXVII, n. 4 (Fall 1991). 37.

Palmstierna-Weiss, Gunilla. Royal Dramatic Theatre, Stockholm: 1975. B&W. Model & set. **TCI**, vol. 12, n. 7 (Nov/Dec 1978). 40.

Pizzi, Pier Luigi. Teatre Eliseo, Rome: 1961. B&W. Rendering. **SDW2**, 130.

Pride, Malcolm. Shakespeare Memorial Theatre, Stratford-upon-Avon: 1955. B&W. Set. **SOS**, 251.

Robinson, T.O. Northampton Repertory Theatre, England: 1933. B&W. Rendering. **SCM**, 27.

Schmidt, Douglas W. Center Theatre Group/Mark Taper Forum, Los Angeles: 1981. B&W. Set. **BSE4**, 57.

Sheringham, George. Shakespeare Memorial Theatre, Stratford-upon-Avon: 1932. B&W. Rendering. **SCM**, 37; B&W. Set. **SDG**, 177; B&W. Rendering. **TPH**, photo 438.

Sovey, Raymond. Maxine Elliott's Theatre, NYC: 1930. B&W. Set. **SCM**, 124. 2 photos; B&W. Set. **SDA**, 238. 2 photos.

Stern, Ernst. Deutsches Theater, Berlin: 1907. B&W. Rendering. **MRH**, facing 237.

Surrey, Kit. Royal Shakespeare Company, GB: 1987. B&W. Set. **BTD**, 46.

Svoboda, Josef. 1991. B&W. Set. **TDT**, vol. XXX, n. 5 (Fall 1994). 41.

Ter-Arutunian, Rouben. American Shakespeare Festival, Stratford, Connecticut: 1960. B&W. Set. **SDW2**, 240.

Urban, Joseph. 1915. B&W. Rendering. **TPH**, photo 470.

Van Dalsum, Albert. Stadsschouwburg, Amsterdam: 1947. B&W. Set. **SDW1**, 136.

Vychodil, Ladislav. Bratislava: 1962. B&W. Set. **TDT**, vol. XV, n. 2 (Summer 1979). 14.

Wilkinson, Norman. London: B&W. Set. **SDC**, plate 60; B&W. Set. **TPH**, photo 352.

_____. Carnegie-Mellon University, Pittsburgh: 1973. B&W. Set. **TCI**, vol. 7, n. 5 (Oct 1973). 24.

_____. Folger Library Theatre, Washington, DC: 1971. B&W. Set. **TCI**, vol. 7, n. 2 (Mar/Apr 1973). 10.

_____. Hopkins Center, Dartmouth College, Hanover, New Hampshire: B&W. Set. **SFT**, 16.

_____. Künstlertheater, Munich: 1908. B&W. Set. **TPH**, photo 343.

_____. Naples: 1950. B&W. Set. **SOS**, 264.

_____. Sanders Theatre, Cambridge, GB: 1909. B&W. Set. **SOS**, 84.

_____. Savoy Theatre, London: 1912. B&W. Set. **SOS**, 143.

_____. Théâtre du Vieux-Columbier, Paris: 1914. B&W. Set. **SOS**, 190.

_____. University of California, Santa Cruz: B&W. Set. **TCI**, vol. 12, n. 4 (May/Jun 1978). 34.

20,000.
>   Aronson, Boris. Kamerny Theatre, Moscow: 1920's. B&W. Set. **TAB**, 6; B&W. Set.
>   **TPH,** photo 414.

The Twin Rivals.
>   Ultz. Pit/Barbican Center, London: B&W. Set. **TCI**, vol. 17, n. 7 (Aug/Sep 1983). 38.

Two by Two.
>   Hays, David. Imperial Theatre, NYC: 1970. B&W. Set. **BWM**, 199; B&W. Set. **TCI**,
>   vol. 5, n. 1 (Jan/Feb 1971). 7.

Two Gentlemen of Verona.
>   Haymann, Henry. Three River Shakespeare Festival, Pittsburgh: B&W. Set. **SDL**, 71.
>   Lee, Ming Cho. New York Shakespeare Festival & St. James Theatre, NYC: 1971.
>   B&W. Rendering. **ASD1**, 86; B&W. Set. **BMF**, 77; B&W. Set. **TCI**, vol. 18, n. 2
>   (Feb 1984). 17; B&W. Set. **WMC**, 350.
>   Reimer, Tom. Aalborg Teater, Denmark: 1972. B&W. Set. **SDW4**, illus. 329.

The Two Ogres.
>   Vidrovitch, Nina. Théâtre de Bourgogne: 1958. B&W. Set. **SDW2**, 102.

Two on an Island.
>   Mielziner, Jo. Broadhurst Theatre, NYC: 1940. Color. Rendering. **DTT**, 105. Taxicab
>   set; B&W. Rendering. **DTT**, 106. Rooftops.

Two Saints.
>   Recht, Raymond C. Center Stage, Baltimore: 1973. B&W. Set. **TCI**, vol. 7, n. 3 (May/
>   Jun 1973). 14. 2 photos.

Two Shakespearean Actors.
>   Jenkins, David. Cort Theatre, NYC: 1991. B&W. Model. DDT, 436; Lincoln Center,
>   NYC: 1992. B&W and color. Set. **TCI**, vol. 26, n. 4 (Apr 1992). 40, 41.

2x2=5.
>   Aronson, Boris. Civic Repertory Theatre, NYC: 1927. B&W. Set. **BAT**, 6; B&W.
>   Rendering & set. **TAB**, 11, 293.

Tyl.
>   Moulaert, René. Het Vlaamsche Volkstoneel, Brussels: B&W. Set. **TCS2**, plate 179.

Typografica.
>   Balla, Giacomo. (project): 1914. B&W. Rendering. **RSD**, illus. 350.

The Tzaddik.
>   Aronson, Boris. Newman Theatre, NYC: 1974. B&W. Set. **TAB**, 309.

-U-

Ubu Enchainé.
>   Ernst, Max. Comédie des Champs-Élysées, Paris: 1937. B&W. Set. **AST**, 118.

Ubu Roi.
>   Conklin, John. Hartford Stage, Connecticut: 1973. B&W. Set. **TCI**, vol. 14, n. 3 (May/
>   Jun 1980). 23.
>   Hockney, David. Royal Court Theatre, London: 1966. B&W. Set. **SDR**, 42.
>   Themerson, Francizka. Marionetteatern-Dramaten, Stockholm: 1968. B&W. Set. **RSD**,
>   illus. 459, 60; B&W. Set. **SDW3**, 220.
>   Wiley, William. San Francisco Mime Troupe: 1963. B&W. Set. **ASC**, 24.

Ulysses in Nighttown.
>   Wittstein, Ed. Winter Garden Theatre, NYC: 1973. Color. Rendering. **DPT**, Facing 28;
>   B&W. Set. **TCI**, vol. 14, n. 1 (Jan/Feb 1980). 18.
>   Wendel, Heinrich. Deutsches Oper am Rhein, Düsseldorf-Duisburg: 1970. B&W. Set.
>   **SDW3**, 198. 2 photos.

The Umbrellas of Cherbourg.
>   Yeargan, Michael. Public Theatre, NYC: 1978. B&W. Set. **TCI**, vol. 16, n. 5 (May 1982); B&W. Set. **TDT**, vol. XV, n. 4 (Winter 1979). 25, 26. 5 photos.

Un Ballo in Maschera.
>   Neher, Gaspar. State Opera, Berlin: 1932. B&W. Set. **SCM**, 60. Act III.

Una delle Utime Domeniche di Carnovale.
>   Padovani, Gianfranco. 1968-1969. B&W. Set & curtain. **SIO**, 98. 2 photos.

Uncle Harry.
>   Bay, Howard. Broadhurst Theatre, NYC: 1942. B&W. Set. **TCI**, vol. 17, n. 2 (Feb 1983). 54.

Uncle Maroje.
>   Serban, Milenko. Jugoslovensko Dramsko Pozoriste, Beograd: 1949. B&W. Set. **SDW2**, 135.

Uncle Tom's Cabin.
>   Oenslager, Donald. Alvin Theatre, NYC: 1933. B&W. Rendering. **SDT**, 39; B&W. Rendering. **STN**, 207, 209

Uncle Vanya.
>   Cairns, Tom. Crucible Theatre, Sheffield, England: 1987. B&W. Set. **BTD**, 49.
>   Dmitriev, Vladimir. Moscow Art Theatre: 1947. B&W. Set. **DMS**, plate 25; B&W. Set. **SDW2**, 182.
>   Egemar, Christian. Den Nationale Scene, Bergen, Norway: 1971. B&W. Set. **SDW4**, illus. 185.
>   Freyer, Ilona. Schlosspark Theater, Berlin: 1976. B&W. Set. **TCI**, vol. 11, n. 2 (Mar/ Apr 1977). 26.
>   Jensen, John. Pittsburgh Public Theatre: 1977. B&W. Set. **TCI**, vol. 14, n. 6 (Nov/Dec 1980). 33.
>   Kochergin, Edward Stepanovich. 1982. B&W. Model. **TDT**, vol. XXIII, n. 4 (Winter 1988). 25.
>   Landwehr, Hugh. Old Globe Theatre, San Diego: 1989. B&W. Set. **ASD2**, 87.
>   Levental, Valery. 1984. B&W. Model. **TDT**, vol. XXIII, n. 4 (Winter 1988). 25.
>   Loquasto, Santo. Williamstown Theatre Festival, Massachusetts: 1972 B&W. Set. **TCI**, vol. 7, n. 5 (Oct 1973). 18; La Mama Annex, NYC: 1983. B&W. Set. **ASD1**, 108.
>   Pán, Jozef. Katona József Szinház, Budapest: 1952. B&W. Set. **SDW2**, 141.
>   Pitoëff, Georges. B&W. Rendering. **CSC**, facing 124.
>   Starowieyska, Eva. Kammerspiele, Munich: 1972. B&W. Set. **SDW4**, illus. 184.
>   Tosi, Piero. Teatre Eliseo, Rome: 1955. B&W. Rendering. **SDW2**, 132. 3 photos.
>   Tsarouchis, John. Vassilikon Théâtron, Athens: 1953. B&W. Set. **SDW2**, 106.
>   Wonder, Erich. Cologne, Germany: 1980. Color. Set. **TCI**, vol. 20, n. 8 (Oct 1986). 33.
>   Yeargan, Michael. Center Stage, Baltimore: Color. Set. **TCI**, vol. 24, n. 1 (Jan 1990). 48.
>   Zídek, Ivo. Prague: 1990. B&W. Rendering. **TDT**, vol. XXVIII, n. 2 (Spring 1992). 36. Act IV.

Uncle's Dream.
>   _____. Moscow Art Theatre: 1929. B&W. Set. **RST**, 297. 2 photos.

Uncommon Women.
>   Mikulewicz, Bill. (project) Eugene O'Neill Memorial Theater Center, Waterford, Connecticut: B&W. Rendering. **TCI**, vol. 13, n. 3 (May/Jun 1979). 32.

Uncommon Women and Others.
>   _____. Lucille Lortel Theatre, NYC: 1994. Color. Set. **TCI**, vol. 29, n. 1 (Jan 1995). 7.

_____. Invisible Theatre, Tuscon, Arizona: B&W. Set. **TCI**, vol. 15, n. 7 (Aug/
Sep 1981). 66.

The Unconquered.

Aronson, Boris. Biltmore Theatre, NYC: 1940. B&W. Model. **TAB**, 296.

Under Gaslight.

_____. Carnegie-Mellon University, Pittsburgh: 1972. B&W. Set. **TCI**, vol. 7, n.
5 (Oct 1973). 26, 27.

Under Milkwood.

Bauer-Ecsy, Leni. Schiller Theatre, Berlin: 1957. B&W. Set. **SDW2**, 57.

Gesek, Thaddeus. Powerhouse Theatre, Vassar College: Color. Rendering. **TCI**, vol.
24, n. 10 (Dec 1990). 53.

_____. Centenary College, Louisiana: 1967. Color. Set. **MOR**, 104.

Under the Gas Lights.

Gauer, Glenn. B&W. Set. **SDL**, 242.

Under Two Flags.

Burroughs, Robert C. University of Arizona, Tucson: B&W. Rendering. **SDT**, 288.

Gros, Ernest. Garden Theatre, NYC: 1901. B&W. Set. **MCN**, 16.

Undiscovered Country.

Jenkins, David. Hartford Stage, Connecticut: 1980. B&W. Set. **TCI**, vol. 16, n. 1 (Jan
1982). 14.

Lobel, Adrianne. Arena Stage, Washington, DC: 1982. B&W. Sketch. **ASD2**, 97.

The Undivine Comedy.

Drabik, Vincent. Boguslawski Theater, Warsaw: 1926. B&W. Set. **RSD**, illus. 263.

Pronaszko, Andrzej. Wielki Theater, Lvov: 1935. B&W. Set. **RSD**, illus. 267.

The Unexpected Guest.

_____. Cohoes Music Hall, Albany, New York: 1977. B&W. Set. **TCI**, vol. 12,
n. 6 (Oct 1978). 27.

The Unknown Soldiers.

Rindin, V. Kamerny Theatre, Moscow: 1932. B&W. Model. **TAT**, plate 729.

The Unnamable.

_____. American Contemporary Theatre, Buffalo: 1972. B&W. Set. **TDT**, vol.
XIV, n. 2 (Summer 1978). 35.

The Unsinkable Molly Brown.

Smith, Oliver. Winter Garden Theatre, NYC: 1960. B&W. Set. **BWM**, 300. 2 photos.

The Untamed.

Lindblad, Gunnar. State Theatre, Norrköping-Linköping, Sweden: 1949. B&W. Set.
SDW1, 166.

Der Untergang Karthagos.

Neher, Caspar. Darmstadt, Germany: 1938. B&W. Set. **CBM**, 90.

Untilovsk.

_____. Moscow Art Theatre: 1928. B&W. Set. **RST**, 247. 2 photos.

Unwounded.

Avellana, Lamberto V. Cultural Center of the Philippines Theatre, Manila: 1971.
B&W. Set. **SDW4**, illus. 186.

Up in Central Park.

Bay, Howard. Century Theatre, NYC: 1945. B&W. Set. **CSD**, 18; B&W. Rendering.
DPT, 328; B&W. Rendering. **SDA**, 252; B&W. Rendering. **SDB**, 56; B&W.
Rendering. **SDL**, 54; B&W. Rendering. **SDW1**, 192; B&W. Rendering. **TCI**, vol.
17, n. 2 (Feb 1983). 13; B&W. Rendering. **TDT**, n. 19 (Dec 1969). 22; B&W. Set.
WMC, 48.

Uptown Its Hot.
   McPhillips, Tom. Lunt-Fontanne Theatre, NYC: 1986. Color. Set. **MBM**, 185.
Urfaust.
   Raffaëlli, Michel. Schauspielehaus, Zürich: 1970. B&W. Set. **SDW3**, 78.
   Stern, Ernst. Deutsches Theater, Berlin: 1920. Color. Rendering. **MRH**, facing 140 &
      between 238 & 239, between 240 & 241, between 242 & 243. 5 photos.
Uriel Acosta.
   Altman, Nathan. Jewish State Theatre, Moscow: 1922. B&W and color. model &
      rendering. **RST**, 72, 73; B&W. Model. **TCS2**, plates 170-173. 4 photos.
L'Urlo.
   Scandella, Mischa. 1967. B&W. Rendering. **SIO**, 126, 127. 4 photos.
The Utter Glory of Morrissey Hale.
   Bay, Howard. Mark Hellinger Theatre, NYC: 1979. B&W. Rendering. **TCI**, vol. 17, n.
      2 (Feb 1983). 55.

-V-

V for Vietnam.
   Grund, Manfred. Volksbühne, Berlin: 1969. B&W. Set. **SDW3**, 220.
The Vagabond King.
   Reynolds, James. Winter Garden Theatre, London. 1927. B&W. Set. **MCD**, plate 147.
Valentine and Valentina.
   Blackman, Robert. American Conservatory Theatre, San Francisco: B&W. Set. **TCI**,
      vol. 14, n. 4 (Sep 1980). 35.
   Borovsky, David. Taganka Theatre, Moscow: 1978. B&W. Rendering. **TCI**, vol. 12, n.
      7 (Nov/Dec 1978). 35.
Valmouth.
   Walton, Tony. Lyric Theatre, Hammersmith, London: 1958. B&W. Set. **BMF**, 102;
      B&W. Rendering & show curtain. **DDT**, 106, 107, 394. 5 photos; B&W. Set.
      MCD, plate 211.
The Value of Names.
   Kellogg, Marjorie Bradley. Hartford Stage, Connecticut: 1984. B&W. Model. **DDT**,
      89.
   Ragey, Joe. People's Light & Theatre Company, Malvern, Pennsylvania: 1983. B&W.
      Set. **BSE4**, 72.
The Vampires.
   Lobel, Adrianne. Astor Place Theatre, NYC: 1984. B&W. Sketches & set. **ASD2**, 100,
      101; B&W. Set. **TDT**, vol. XXI, n. 2 (Summer 1985). 32; B&W. Set. **TDT** vol.
      XXXI, n. 2 (Spring 1995). 16.
Vanessa.
   Beaton, Cecil. Metropolitan Opera, NYC: 1958. B&W. Rendering. **CBS**, 74.
   _____. 1991. Color. Set. **TCI**, vol. 27, n. 4 (Apr 1993). 31.
Vanities.
   Arnone, John. Mark Taper Forum, Los Angeles: B&W. Set. **TCI**, vol. 15, n. 6 (Jun/Jul
      1981). 29.
   Cornwell, Bruce. Hippodrome, Gainesville, Florida: B&W. Set. **TCI**, vol. 15, n. 2 (Feb
      1981). 67.
   Jensen, John. Pittsburgh Public Theatre: B&W. Set. **TCI**, vol. 14, n. 6 (Nov/Dec
      1980). 32. 3 photos.
   _____. Cohoes Music Hall, Albany, New York: 1977. B&W. Set. **TCI**, vol. 12,
      n. 6 (Oct 1978). 27.

Vanna Lupa.
>   Annigoni, Pietro. Maggio Musicale Fiorentino, Florence: 1949. B&W. Rendering.
>   **SDE**, 28. 2 photos.

Vanquished by Voodoo.
>   Chepulis, Kyle. NYC: Color. Set. **TCI**, vol. 29, n. 4 (Apr 1995). 40.

Vasantasena (The Little Clay Cart).
>   Geyling, Remigius. Burgtheater, Vienna: 1926. B&W. Projection. **TPH**, photo 371.

The Venetian Twins.
>   Micunis, Gordon Jules. Tyrone Guthrie Theatre, Minneapolis: 1970. B&W. Rendering.
>   **CSD**, 107; B&W. Model & set. **DPT**, 99.
>   Padovani, Gianfranco. 1963-1964. B&W. Set. **SIO**, 97.

Venice Preserved.
>   Costa, Valeria. Piccolo Teatro, Rome: 1949. B&W. Set. **SDW2**, 124.
>   Craig, Edward Gordon. 1904. B&W. Rendering. **EGC**, plate 7; B&W. Rendering.
>   **OAT**, 148; B&W. Rendering. **TNT**, facing 29, 30.
>   Oenslager, Donald. Yale School of Drama, New Haven, Connecticut: 1933. B&W.
>   Rendering. **STN**, 149-151. 5 photos.

Venus Observed.
>   Haferung, Paul. Städtische Bühnen, Essen: 1951. B&W. Rendering. **SDW1**, 66.

Vereda da Salvação.
>   Serroni, J.C. Brazil: Color. Set. **TCI**, vol. 28, n. 4 (Apr 1994). 37.

Die Verlobung in San Domingo.
>   Otto, Teo. Bavarian State Theatre, Munich: 1963. B&W. Set. **TDT**, n. 2 (Oct 1965). 8.

Veronica's Room.
>   Schmidt, Douglas W. Music Box Theatre, NYC: 1973. Color. Rendering. **DPT**, be-
>   tween 124 & 125; B&W. Rendering. **TDT**, vol. XVII, n. 2 (Summer 1981). 18.

Very Good Eddie.
>   DeWolf, Elsie. Princess Theatre, NYC: 1915. B&W. Set. **MCN**, 42; B&W. Set. **TMI**,
>   114.

I Vespri Siciliani.
>   Benois, Nicola. La Scala, Milan: 1952. B&W. Rendering. **SDE**, 35.
>   Pizzi, Pier Luigi. 1970-1971. B&W. Rendering. **SIO**, 108, 109. 4 photos.
>   Svoboda, Josef. Metropolitan Opera, NYC: 1974. B&W. Set. **TCI**, vol. 16, n. 9 (Nov/
>   Dec 1982). 30.

The Vestal.
>   Zuffi, Piero. La Scala, Milan: 1954. B&W. Rendering. **SDW2**, 134.

Vetsera does not Bloom for Everybody.
>   Refn, Helge. Frederiksberg Teater, Copenhagen: 1950. Color. Rendering. **SDW1**, 57.

Victims of Duty.
>   Rojo, Jerry N. Le Petit Théâtre du Vieux Carré, New Orleans: 1967. B&W. Set. **TSE**,
>   2, 158-163. 5 photos.

Victoria Regina.
>   Whistler, Rex. Broadhurst Theatre, NYC: 1935. B&W. Set. **DSL**, figure 16.3(a);
>   B&W. Rendering. **FCS**, plate 211. Act III, sc. 2; B&W. Set. **MCN**, 128; B&W.
>   Rendering. **SDO**, 242, 243.

Victory Over the Sun.
>   Malevich, Kasimir. Luna Park Theatre, St. Petersburg: 1913. B&W. Rendering. **AST**,
>   129; B&W. Sketches. **RSD**, illus. 152-54; Color. Sketches. **RST**, 28. 2 photos;
>   B&W. Rendering & set. **TDT**, vol. XXVI, n. 4 (Fall 1990). 10. 1980 recreation of
>   setting.

La Vida Breve.

> Fiume, Salvatore. La Scala, Milan: 1951. B&W. Rendering. **SDE**, 81. 2 photos.

> Prampolini, Enrico. Teatro San Carlo, Naples: 1952. B&W. Rendering. **SDE**, 137.

La Vida es sueño.

> Wenig, Josef. National Theatre, Prague: B&W. Set. **TCS2**, plate 273.

La Vie Parisienne.

> Martin, Denis. Théâtre National, Brussels: 1950. B&W. Set. **SDW1**, 46.

Vienna: Lusthaus.

> Isreal, Robert. Lenox Arts Center: 1986. Color. Set. **TCI**, vol. 21, n. 4 (Apr 1987). 37.

Vietnam Discourse.

> Asakura, Setsu. Haiyuza-Gekijo, Tokyo: 1968. B&W. Set. **SDW3**, 137.

> Palmstierna-Weiss, Gunilla Städtische Bühnen, Frankfurt: 1968. B&W. Set. **SDW3**, 137; B&W. Set. **RSD**, illus. 590; B&W. Set. **TCI**, vol. 12, n. 7 (Nov/Dec 1978). 38, 39.

A View from the Bridge.

> Adar, Arnon. Habima, Tel Aviv: 1956. B&W. Rendering. **SDW2**, 117.

> Aronson, Boris. Coronet Theatre (Eugene O'Neill Theatre), NYC: 1955. B&W. Set **SDW2**, 230; B&W and color. Rendering & set. **TAB**, 18, 107.

> Garbuglia, Mario. Teatre Eliseo, Rome: 1958. B&W. Set. **SDW2**, 126.

> Landwehr, Hugh. Studio Arena Theatre, Buffalo: 1986. B&W. Set. **TCI**, vol. 21, n. 5 (May 1987). 16.

> Vychodil, Ladislav. Slovak National Theatre, Bratislava: 1959. B&W. Rendering. **TDT**, vol. XV, n. 2 (Summer 1979). 12; B&W. Rendering. **TDT**, n. 38 (Oct 1974). 26.

The Vikings at Helgeland.

> Craig, Edward Gordon. Imperial Theatre, London: 1903. B&W. Rendering. **EGC**, plates 6a, 6b; B&W and color. Rendering. **RSD**, illus. 55, 74, 75; B&W. Rendering. **TDT**, n. 29 (May 1972). 11. Act IV; B&W. Rendering. **TDT**, n. 29 (May 1972). 4.

> Lauterer, Arch. USA: 1933. B&W. Model. **TAT**, plate 582.

Violostries.

> Soto, Jésus-Raphaël. Maison de la Culture, Amiens: 1969. B&W. Set. **RSD**, illus. 492.

Virgin Soil Upturned.

> Chifrine, Nisson. Tsentralnyi Teatr Sovietskoï Armii, Moscow: 1957. B&W. Model. **SDW2**, 180.

Virineya.

> Zolotariev, Nicolaï. Mouzikalnyi Teatr imeni Stanislavskovo i Nemirovitcha Dantchenko, Moscow: 1967. B&W. Rendering. **SDW3**, 214.

> _____. 1925. B&W. Set. **RST**, 210, 211. 3 photos.

The Visions of Simone Machard.

> Falleni, Silvano. 1963-1964. B&W. Set. **SIO**, 49. 2 photos.

> Lobel, Adrianne. La Jolla Playhouse, California: Color. Set. **TCI**, vol. 18, n. 1 (Jan 1984). 26.

> Otto, Teo. Städtische Bühnen, Frankfurt: 1957. B&W. Set. **TBB**, 54.

The Visit.

> Burbridge, Edward. Phoenix Theatre, NYC: 1973. B&W. Set. **TCI**, vol. 8, n. 6 (Nov/ Dec 1974). 17.

> Hill, Hainer. Germany: B&W. Model. **TDT**, vol. XII, n. 3 (Fall 1976). 33.

> Huszti, Douglas A. (project): B&W. Rendering. **TDT**, vol. XXVIII, n. 2 (Spring 1992). 12 of insert.

Lee, Eugene. Trinity Square Theatre, Providence, Rhode Island: 1986. B&W and
    color. Set. **TCI**, vol. 22, n. 9 (Nov 1988). 59, 62.
Lopez, Frank. (project): 1974. B&W. Rendering. **CSD**, 99; B&W. Sketch. **DPT**, 120.
    Act II.
Parker, W. Oren. Yale School of Drama, New Haven, Connecticut: 1963. B&W. Set.
    SFT, 119.
Steinberg, Paul. Goodman Theatre, Chicago: 1991. B&W. Set. **TCI**, vol. 25, n. 6
    (Aug/Sep 1991). 31.
Stowe, Laura. University of California, Irvine: 1981. B&W. Rendering. **BSE2**, 22.
    _____. B&W. Rendering. **SDL**, 84.
The Visit of the Old Lady.
    Darling, Robert Edward. San Francisco Opera: 1972. B&W. Rendering. **CSD**, 73.
Viteazul.
    Ciulei, Liviu. Teatrul de Nord: 1970. B&W. Set. **RSD**, illus. 514, 515.
Vivat! Vivat Regina!
    Toms, Carl. Chichester Festival Theatre, England: 1970. B&W. Set. **TCI**, vol. 6, n. 1
    (Jan/Feb 1972). 12, 13.
Vivisection.
    Svoboda, Josef. Laterna Magika, Prague: 1987. B&W. Set. **STS**, 119; B&W. Set. **TDT**,
    vol. XXIV, n. 4 (Winter 1988). 19, 20.
Vladimir Mayakovsky.
    Schkolnik, Ilya. Luna Park Theatre, St. Petersburg: 1913. B&W. Rendering. **RST**, 26.
    2 photos.
Die Vogelscheuchen.
    Pirchan, Emil. State Opera, Berlin: B&W. Set. **TCS2**, plate 251.
    Schlemmer, Oskar. Kammertanztheater, Hagen, Westphalia: 1928. B&W. Set. **AST**,
    157. 2 photos.
Voice of the People.
    _____. Provisional Theatre, Los Angeles: B&W. Set. **TCI**, vol. 14, n. 4 (Sep
    1980). 33.
The Voice of the Turtle.
    Chaney, Stewart. Morosco Theatre, NYC: 1943. B&W. Set. **SDA**, 227; B&W. Set.
    TPH, photo 487.
Voices of Spring.
    Simonson, Lee. USA: 1937. B&W. Rendering. **SDA**, 275.
La Voix Humaine.
    Battersby, Martin. Glyndebourne Festival Opera, England: B&W. Set. **TCI**, vol. 13, n.
    3 (May/Jun 1979). 21. 2 photos.
Volpone.
    Alkazi, Ebrahim. Theatre Unit, Meghdoot Terrace Theatre, Bombay: 1958. Color.
    Model. **SDW2**, 115.
    Barsacq, André. Théâtre de l'Atelier, Paris: 1929. B&W. Rendering. **RSD**, illus. 398;
    B&W. Rendering. **SDW1**, 84; B&W. Rendering. **TAT**, plate 270; B&W. Render-
    ing. **TPH**, photo 357.
    Bauer-Ecsy, Leni. Württembergische Staatstheater, Stuttgart: 1960. Color. Rendering.
    SDW2, 61.
    Beaton, Cecil. Cambridge: 1923. Color. Rendering. **CBS**, 17.
    Bury, John. National Theatre (Olivier), London: 1977. B&W. Set. **TCI**, vol. 11, n. 5
    (Oct 1977). 32; B&W. Set. **TDT**, vol. XIX, n. 3 (Fall 1983). 6.
    Damonte, Marcelo. Histrión-Teatro de Arte, Lima: 1961. B&W. Set. **SDW2**, 164.

Dorsey, Kent. Berkeley Repertory Theatre, California: 1993. Color. Set. **TCI**, vol. 27, n. 5 (May 1993). 6.

Dullin, Charles. Théâtre de l'Atelier, Paris: B&W. Set. **SCM**, 40. 2 photos.

Francini, Mauro. Teatro Brasileiro de Comédia, Rio de Janeiro: 1955. B&W. Rendering. **SDW2**, 35.

Graham, Steven. Carnegie-Mellon University, Pittsburgh: 1970. B&W. Set. **TCI**, vol. 7, n. 5 (Oct 1973). 25; B&W. Set. **CSD**, 50.

Krohg, Per. Oslo, Norway: 1929. B&W. Rendering. **TPH**, photo 394.

Lee, Ming Cho. Mark Taper Forum, Los Angeles: 1972. B&W. Set. **TCI**, vol. 14, n. 4 (Sep 1980). 48.

Lovejoy, Robin. Arrow Theatre, Melbourne: 1952. B&W. Rendering. **SDW1**, 40.

Simonson, Lee. Guild Theatre, NYC: 1928. B&W. Set. **TAS**, 145. 2 photos.

Wittstein, Ed. Playhouse in the Park, Cincinnati: B&W. Set. **TCI**, vol. 5, n. 1 (Jan/Feb 1971). 17, 20.

_____. Actor's Laboratory, Hollywood, California: 1951. B&W. Set. **WTP**, 78, 79. 4 photos.

_____ Theatre in the Square, Atlanta: Color. Set. **TCI**, vol. 22, n. 3 (Mar 1988) 56.

_____. University of Virginia: 1973. B&W. Set. **TCI**, vol. 8, n. 3 (May/Jun 1974). 16, 17.

The Vortex.

Prowse, Philip. NYC: 1991. B&W. Set. **TCI**, vol. 25, n. 3 (Mar 1991). 18.

The Vow.

Calvo, Aldo. Quirino, Rome: 1947. B&W. Rendering. **SDW1**, 120.

Vulcani.

Prampolini, Enrico. Teatro Argentina, Rome: 1924. B&W. Rendering. **AST**, 72; B&W. Rendering. **TCS2**, plate 157.

-W-

Waiting for Godot.

Boruzescu, Radu. The Acting Company tour: 1980. B&W. Set. **TCI**, vol. 15, n. 5 (May 1981). 24.

Giacometti, Alberto. Odeon Theatre, Paris: 1961. B&W. Set. **RSD**, illus. 457.

Hendrickson, Stephen. Antioch Area Theatre, Yellow Springs, Ohio: 1966. B&W. Set. **SDW3**, 120.

Howard, Pamela. Power Center for the Arts, University of Michigan, Ann Arbor: 1987. B&W and color. Model & set. **TDT**, vol. XXIV, n. 2 (Summer 1988). front cover, 7. 3 photos.

Howarth, Donald. Long Wharf Theatre, New Haven, Connecticut: B&W. Set. **DSL**, figure 30.15(a).

Lee, Ming Cho. Arena Stage, Washington, DC: 1976. B&W. Set. **ASD1**, 102.

Olson, Stephan. (project): 1986. B&W. Rendering. **DDT**, 184.

Svoboda, Josef. Landestheater, Salzburg: 1970. B&W. Set. **SDW3**, 219; B&W. Set. **SDW4**, illus. 258; B&W. Set. **SJS**, 158; B&W. Set. **STS**, 9; B&W. Set. **TDT**, n. 23 (Dec 1970). front cover.

Tumarkin, Igael. Ha' Teatron Haleumi Habimah, Tel-Aviv: 1968. B&W. Set. **SDW3**, 121. 3 photos.

Walton, Tony. Lincoln Center, NYC: 1989. Color. Set. **TCI**, vol. 24, n. 8 (Oct 1990). 38.

The Waiting Room.

> Wendland, Mark. Mark Taper Forum, Los Angeles: 1994. Color. Set. **TCI**, vol. 28, n. 9 (Nov 1994). 10.

The Wakefield Cycle.

> Gianini, A. Christina. North Carolina School of the Arts, Winston-Salem: B&W. Set. **TCI**, vol. 12, n. 6 (Oct 1978). 36.

Walk a Little Faster.

> Aronson, Boris. St. James Theatre, NYC: 1932. Color. Show curtain. **TAB**, 48; B&W. Model & set. **TAB**, 50-52, 294. 12 photos.

A Walk in the Woods.

> Lucas, Greg. Arizona Theatre Company, Tucson: 1989. Color. Set. **TCI**, vol. 23, n. 8 (Oct 1989). 20.
>
> Marzolff, Serge. Companyia Flotats, Barcelona: 1992. Color. Set. **TCI**, vol. 26, n. 4 (Apr 1992). 37.
>
> McCarry, Charles E. Zellerbach Theatre, Philadelphia: 1990. B&W. Model. **DDT**, 152; B&W. Set. **TDT**, vol. XXVIII, n. 2 (Spring 1992). 7 of insert.

Walkaround Time.

> Johns, Jasper. Odeon Theatre, Paris: 1970. B&W. Set. **RSD**, illus. 486.

Die Walküre.

> Appia, Adolphe. Theater Municipal, Basel: 1924/1925. B&W. Sketch. **JSS**, 15; B&W. Set. **RSD**, illus. 65; B&W. Rendering & set. **TCS2**, plates 35, 39; B&W. Rendering. **WLA**, 101-103. 4 photos.
>
> Björnson, Maria. English National Opera, London: 1983. B&W. Set. **BTD**, 110.
>
> Conklin, John. San Francisco Opera: 1983. B&W. Set. **ASD1**, 17; Color. Set. **TCI**, vol. 20, n. 2 (Feb 1986). 27; Chicago Lyric Opera: 1993. Color. Set. **TCI**, vol. 28, n. 3 (Mar 1994). 10.
>
> Dudley, William. Beyreuth Festival Theatre: 1983. B&W. Set. **TCI**, vol. 18, n. 3 (Mar 1984). 16, 17; B&W. Set. **TDT**, vol. XXV, n. 3 (Fall 1989). 17.
>
> Israel, Robert. Seattle Opera: 1990. Color. Set. **TCI**, vol. 24, n. 9 (Nov 1990). 38.
>
> Koltai, Ralph. English National Opera, London: 1970. B&W. Model. **TDT**, vol. XIX, n. 3 (Fall 1983). 11.
>
> Peduzzi, Richard. Beyreuth Festival Theatre: 1976. B&W. Set. **TCI**, vol. 11, n. 2 (Mar/Apr 1977). 17.
>
> Preetorius, Emil. Beyreuth Festival Theatre: 1936. B&W. Set. **JSS**, 17. Act III.
>
> Schneider-Siemssen, Günther. Salzburg Festival & Metropolitan Opera, NYC: 1967-1972. B&W. Set. **TCI**, vol. 10, n. 5 (Oct 1976). 18; B&W. Set. **TCI**, vol. 12, n. 6 (Oct 1978). 31; B&W. Set. **TCI**, vol. 4, n. 1 (Jan/Feb 1970). 10; B&W. Rendering. **TCI**, vol. 4, n. 4 (Sep 1970). 21; Metropolitan Opera, NYC: 1992. Color. Set. **TCI**, vol. 27, n. 3 (Mar 1993). 24-26. 3 photos.
>
> Simonson, Lee. Metropolitan Opera, NYC: 1948. B&W. Set. **RSD**, illus. 434; B&W. Set. **SDA**, 268; B&W. Set. **TAS**, 156. 2 photos; B&W. Set. **TDT**, vol. XXII, n. 3 (Fall 1986). 51.
>
> Sirlin, Jerome. Artpark, Lewiston, New York: 1986. Color. Model. **TCI**, vol. 22, n. 1 (Jan 1988). 34.
>
> Svoboda, Josef. Covent Garden, London: 1974. B&W. Set. **CGA**, 191; B&W. Set. **JSS**, 65. Sc. 1; B&W. Set. **JSS**, 66. Act II; Color. Set. **JSS**, between 54 & 55. Act III; B&W. Set. **STS**, 85; B&W. Set. **TDT**, vol. XII, n. 2 (Summer 1976). 29. 3 photos; Grand Theater, Geneva: 1976. B&W. Set. **JSS**, 82; B&W. Set. **JSS**, 86. Act III; B&W. Set. **JSS**, 86. Sc. 1; Color. Set. **JSS**, between 54 & 55. Act I.
>
> Wagner, Wieland. Beyreuth Festival Theatre: 1951/1952. B&W. Set. **RSD**, illus. 549; B&W. Set. **TPH**, photo 316; 1965. B&W. Set. **TDT**, n. 29 (May 1972). 17. Act I;

B&W. Set. **TCI**, vol. 3, n. 4 (Sep 1969). 33.

Wagner, Wolfgang. Beyreuth Festival Theatre: 1960. B&W. Set. **RSD**, illus. 551; 1970. Color. Set. **SDW4**, illus. 137.

_____. Beyreuth Festival Theatre: 1906. B&W. Set. **TPH**, photo 314.

_____. Beyreuth Festival Theatre: 1928. B&W. Set. **TPH**, photo 315.

The Wall.

Bay, Howard. Billy Rose Theatre, NYC: 1960. B&W. Set. **SDW2**, 233; B&W. **TCI**, vol. 17, n. 2 (Feb 1983). 55.

Hallegger, Kurt. Residenz Theater, Munich: 1961. B&W. Rendering. **SDW2**, 60.

Longhofer, John. B&W. Rendering. **BSE2**, 42.

The Waltz of the Toreadors.

Bloodgood, William. Berkeley Repertory Theatre, California: B&W. Set. **TCI**, vol. 14, n. 4 (Sep 1980). 30.

Edwards, Ben. Coronet Theatre (Eugene O'Neill Theatre), NYC: 1957. B&W. Rendering. **DPT**, 180; B&W. Rendering & set. **TCI**, vol. 23, n. 7 (Aug/Sep 1989). 53, 54.

Pecktal, Lynn. Barter Theatre, Abington, Virginia: 1962. B&W. Set. **DPT**, 98.

Waltzes from Vienna.

Johnson, Albert R. Alhambra Theatre, London: 1931. B&W. Set. **MCD**, plate 168.

The Wandering Jew.

Dart, Paul. National Theatre (Olivier), London: 1987. B&W. Sketch & set. **BTD**, 76.

Die Wandlung.

Baumeister, Willi. Deutsches Theater, Stuttgart: 1920. B&W. Rendering. **AST**, 158. 4 photos.

Gudurian, P.G. B&W. Rendering. **DIT**, plate 104.

War and Peace.

Conklin, John. Seattle Opera: 1990. Color. Model. **TCI**, vol. 24, n. 7 (Aug/Sep 1990). 36.

Lenneweit, H.W. Schiller Theatre, Berlin: 1955. B&W. Set. **SDW2**, 64.

Owen, Paul. Alley Theatre, Houston: B&W. Set. **TCI**, vol. 7, n. 3 (May/Jun 1973). 6.

Piscator, Erwin. B&W. Set. **SIP**, 311.

Ryndine, Vadim. Bolshoi Theatre, Moscow: 1959. Color. Rendering. **SDW2**, 185.

Sciltian, Gregorio. Maggio Musicale Fiorentino, Florence: 1953. B&W. Rendering. **SDE**, 150.

Svoboda, Josef. National Theatre, Prague: 1975. B&W. Set. **TDT**, vol. XII, n. 2 (Summer 1976). 32.

Wexler, Peter. Phoenix-APA, NYC: 1964. B&W. Model. **DMS**, plate 57; B&W. Model. **SDB**, 100; B&W. Model. **TDT**, n. 5 (May 1966). inside back cover.

Zmrzly, Karel. Czechoslovakia: 1985. B&W. Model. **TDT**, vol. XXIII, n. 4 (Winter 1988). 49.

War for War.

Daszewski, Wladyslaw. Polski Theater, Warsaw: 1927. B&W and color. Rendering & set. **RSD**, illus. 268, 269.

The Warrant.

Meyerhold, Vsevelod, plan, Ilya Shlepyanov, execution. Meyerhold Theatre, Moscow: 1925. B&W. Set. **MOT**, between 200 & 201. 2 photos; B&W. Set. **MOT**, between 200 & 201. 2 photos; B&W. Model & set. **RSD**, illus. 203, 204; B&W. Set. **RST**, 183. 2 photos; B&W. Set. **TCS2**, plate 185 .

The Warrior Ant Part 1.

_____. Spoleto Festival, Charleston, South Carolina: 1988. B&W. Set. **TCI**, vol. 22, n. 7 (Aug/Sep 1988). 25.

The Wars of the Roses.
  Bury, John. Royal Shakespeare Company, Stratford-upon-Avon: 1963. B&W. Set.
    SDW3, 35; B&W. Set. **TDT**, vol. XIX, n. 3 (Fall 1983). 6.
  Minks, Wilfried. Stuttgart: 1967. B&W. Set. **TCI**, vol. 12, n. 1 (Jan/Feb 1978). 29.
Washington Crossing the Delaware.
  Katz, Alex. Maidman Theatre, NYC: 1962. B&W. Set. **ASC**, 33.
Wasted.
  McClennahan, Charles. WPA Theatre, NYC: 1986. B&W. Set. **ASD2**, 118.
Wastrals in Paradise.
  Svoboda, Josef. National Theatre Studio, Prague: 1946. B&W. Rendering. **SJS**, 133;
    B&W. Rendering. **STS**, 50.
Watch It Come Down.
  Griffin, Hayden. Lyttleton, Theatre, London: B&W. Set. **TCI**, vol. 11, n. 5 (Oct 1977).
    32.
The Water Engine.
  Beatty, John Lee. New York Shakespeare Festival, NYC: 1978. B&W. Set. **TCI**, vol.
    12, n. 6 (Oct 1978). 20. 3 photos.
  Emmons, David. St. Nicholas Theatre, Chicago: 1977. B&W. Rendering. **TCI**, vol. 12,
    n. 1 (Jan/Feb 1978). 8.
  Larsen, Lawrence. University of Washington, Seattle: 1984. B&W. Rendering. **BSE4**,
    29.
The Water Hen.
  Kantor, Tadeusz. Cricot Theater, Cracow: 1967. B&W. Set. **RSD**, illus. 635, 636;
    B&W. Set. **SDW3**, 100. 2 photos.
Waters of the Moon.
  Pemberton, Reece. Theatre Royal, Haymarket, London: 1951. B&W. Rendering. **TOP**,
    55-57. 4 photos.
The Way of Kings.
  Faure, Raymond. Théâtre du Vieux-Columbier, Paris: 1947. B&W. Model. **SDW1**, 96.
The Way of the World.
  Beatty, John Lee. (project): 1972/1973. B&W. Rendering. **CSD**, 62; B&W. Rendering.
    DPT, 43. Acts I & III.
  Wurtzel, Stuart. Carnegie-Mellon University, Pittsburgh: 1972. B&W. Set. **TCI**, vol. 7,
    n. 5 (Oct 1973). 25. 2 photos.
  _____. Chichester/London: 1985. Color. Set. **TCI**, vol. 23, n. 2 (Feb 1989). 37.
Way Upstream.
  Tagg, Alan. National Theatre (Lyttleton), London: 1982. B&W. Set. **BTD**, 61.
We Come to the River.
  Henze, Jürgen. Royal Opera House, Covent Garden, London: 1976. B&W. Set. **CGA**,
    189; B&W. Set. **TCI**, vol. 10, n. 6 (Nov/Dec 1976). 4.
We Comrades Three.
  Tilton, James. Lyceum Theatre, NYC: 1966. B&W. Set. **TCI**, vol. 1, n. 1 (Mar/Apr
    1967). 23.
We Won't Pay.
  _____. Horizon Theatre Company, Atlanta: Color. Set. **TCI**, vol. 22, n. 3 (Mar
    1988). 55.
Weapons of Happiness.
  Griffin, Hayden. Lyttleton, Theatre, London: B&W. Set. **TCI**, vol. 11, n. 5 (Oct 1977).
    33.
The Weaver of Bagdad.
  Gamlin, Yngve. Marsyas Teatern, Stockholm: 1955. B&W. Set. **SDW2**, 209.

The Weavers.
>Heller, Vladimir. Divadlo J.K. Tyla, Pilsen, Czechoslovakia: 1961. B&W. Set. **SDW2**, 42.

>_____. Freie Bühne, Berlin: B&W. Set. **SCM**, 64; B&W. Set. **TCR**, 61.

The Wedding.
>Akakia-Viala. Art and Action, Paris: 1923. B&W. Set. **RSD**, illus. 387.

>Akimov, Nikolai. Theatre of Comedy, Leningrad: 1936. B&W. Rendering. **SOW**, plates 69, 70.

>Chifrine, Nisson. Tsentralnyi Teatr Sovietskoï Armii, Moscow: 1959. B&W. Rendering. **SDW2**, 179.

>Kilian, Adam. Teatr Narodowy, Poland: B&W. Set. **TCI**, vol. 15, n. 4 (Apr 1981). 13.

>Seyffer, Robert. Centrum voor Theaterstudio, Brugge, Belgium: 1971. B&W. Set. **SDW4**, illus. 229, 230.

>Svoboda, Josef. Schiller Theatre, Berlin: 1968. B&W. Set. **SJS**, 45; B&W. Set. **STS**, 28.

>_____. Seattle Repertory Theatre: 1985. Color. Set. **TCI**, vol. 20, n. 9 (Nov 1986). 21.

Weekends Like Other People.
>_____. Actors Theatre of Louisville: 1980. B&W. Set. **TCI**, vol. 15, n. 4 (Apr 1981). 16.

Weep for the Virgins.
>Aronson, Boris. 46th Street Theatre, NYC: 1935. B&W. Set. **TAB**, 295.

Welcome to the Club.
>Jenkins, David. Music Box Theatre, NYC: 1989. B&W. Set. **MBM**, 143.

Well-Hung.
>_____. Trinity Square Theatre, Providence, Rhode Island: B&W. Set. **TCI**, vol. 9, n. 6 (Nov/Dec 1975). 24.

Werther.
>Conklin, John. Houston Opera: 1979. B&W. Rendering. **ASD1**, 23.

>Heinrich, Rudolf. Metropolitan Opera, NYC: B&W. Set. **TCI**, vol. 10, n. 6 (Nov/Dec 1976). 15.

West Memphis Mojo.
>McClennahan, Charles. Negro Ensemble Company: 1988. B&W. Set. **ASD2**, 120.

West Side Story.
>Smith, Oliver. Winter Garden Theatre, NYC: 1957. B&W. Set. **BMF**, title page, 61; B&W. Set. **BWM**, 104-107. 3 photos; B&W. Set. **HPA**, 77; B&W and color. Set. **SON**, 42, 43, 45, 47; B&W Rendering & set. **TCI**, vol. 16, n. 4 (Apr 1982). 15, 62; B&W. Set. **TCI**, vol. 23, n. 7 (Aug/Sep 1989). 56; B&W. Set. **TMT**, 188; B&W. Set. **WMC**, 232, 234; Her Majesty's Theatre, London: 1958. B&W. Set. **MCD**, plate 210.

Western Waters.
>Aronson, Boris. Hudson Theatre, NYC: 1937. B&W. Set. **TAB**, 296.

What Every Woman Knows.
>_____. 1946. B&W. Set. **WTP**, 158, 159. 4 photos.

What the Butler Saw.
>Dancy, Virginia & Elmon Webb. Syracuse Stage, New York: 1977. B&W. Set. **DDT**, 268.

>Head, Eric. Carnegie-Mellon University, Pittsburgh: 1971. B&W. Set. **TCI**, vol. 7, n. 5 (Oct 1973). 24.

>Jampolis, Neil Peter. Playhouse in the Park, Cincinnati: 1976. B&W. Set. **DDT**, 269.

What the Storm Left.
   Salas, José. Teatro Nacional, Caracas: 1961. B&W. Set. **SDW2**, 244.
What's New Haruspice?
   Renard, Raymond. Théâtre du Rideau de Bruxelles: 1970. B&W. Set. **SDW3**, 138.
What's Up.
   Aronson, Boris. Nederlander Theatre, NYC: 1943. B&W and color. Renderings & set.
      TAB, 81, 298. 4 photos.
When We are Married.
   Landwehr, Hugh. Long Wharf Theatre, New Haven, Connecticut: B&W. Set. **TCI**,
      vol. 23, n. 4 (Apr 1989). 14.
When We Dead Awaken.
   Alsaker, John-Kristian. National Theatre, Norway: 1994. Color. Set. **TCI**, vol. 28, n. 9
      (Nov 1994). 36.
   Conklin, John & Robert Wilson. American Repertory Theatre, Cambridge, Massachu-
      setts: 1991. B&W. Rendering & set. **TDT**, vol. XXVII, n. 2 (Spring 1991). 16. 4
      photos.
   Scott, Henry III. Circle Theatre, NYC: B&W. Set. **TCI**, vol. 8, n. 2 (Mar/Apr 1974). 8.
   Simov, Victor Andréiévich. Moscow Art Theatre: 1900. B&W. Set. **RSD**, illus. 17.
   Täuber, Harry. Akademietheater, Vienna: B&W. Set. **TCS2**, plates 134, 135.
      _____. Yale Repertory Theatre, New Haven: B&W. Set. **TCI**, vol. 6, n. 3 (May/
      Jun 1972). 27.
When You Comin' Back Red Ryder?
   Eigsti, Karl. Playhouse in the Park, Cincinnati: 1976. B&W. Rendering. **DDT**, 67.
   Stabile, Bill. Circle Theatre, NYC: 1973. B&W. Set. **TCI**, vol. 8, n. 2 (Mar/Apr 1974).
      9.
   Stapleton, Christopher. B&W. Rendering. **BSE3**, 89.
Where Death Fastens Its Flags.
   Benavente, Saulo. Teatro Nacional Cervantes, Buenos Aires: 1959. B&W. Set. **SDW2**,
      25.
Where's Charley?
   Ffolkes, David. St. James Theatre, NYC: 1948. B&W. Set. **BWM**, 265. 5 photos;
      B&W. Set. **WTP**, 152, 153.
Whereabouts Unknown.
   Owen, Paul. Actors Theatre of Louisville: 1988. Color. Set. **TCI**, vol. 22, n. 5 (May
      1988). 16; B&W. Set. **TCI**, vol. 23, n. 3 (Mar 1989). 36.
The Whip.
   Smith, Bruce. Drury Lane Theatre, London: 1909. B&W. Set. **SDG**, 140.
A Whistle in the Dark.
   Dancy, Virginia & Elmon Webb. Long Wharf Theatre, New Haven, Connecticut:
      B&W. Model. **TCI**, vol. 7, n. 5 (Oct 1973). 8.
The White Black.
   Popov, Vladimir. Teatrul Tineretului, Piatra Neamt, Romania: 1970. B&W. Set.
      SDW4, illus. 179.
The White Desease.
   Vychodil, Ladislav. Bratislava: 1958. B&W. Rendering. **SDB**, 86; B&W. Set. **TDT**,
      vol. XV, n. 2 (Summer 1979). 11.
The White Guard.
   Viliams, Piotr. Moscow Art Theatre: 1943. Color. Rendering. **SDW2**, 195.
White Horse Inn.
   Stern, Ernst. Coliseum, London: 1931. B&W. Set. **MCD**, plate 166; Center Theatre,
      NYC: 1936. B&W. Set. **MCN**, 131; B&W. Set. **RBS**, 131.

The White Plague.

> Hoffman, Vlastislav. National Theatre, Prague: 1937. B&W. Model. **TPH**, photo 387. 3 photos.

The White Rose.

> Schultz, Rudolf. Landestheater, Hanover: 1952. Color. Rendering. **SDW1**, 75.

A Whitman Portrait.

> Elder, Eldon. Gramercy Arts Theatre, NYC: 1966-1967. B&W. Rendering. **EED**, (pages not numbered).

Who They Are and How It Is With Them.

> Landwehr, Hugh. Center Stage, Baltimore: 1985. B&W. Set. **ASD2**, 84, 86; Color. Set. **TCI**, vol. 20, n. 2 (Feb 1986). 19; B&W. Set. **TCI**, vol. 20, n. 9 (Nov 1986). 21.

Who's Afraid of Virginia Woolf?

> Scheffler, John. Playhouse in the Park, Cincinnati: 1974. B&W. Set. **DPT**, 342.
> Vychodil, Ladislav. Konigliches Dramatisches Theatre, Stockholm: B&W. Sketches & set. **TDT**, vol. XXVI, n. 2 (Summer 1990). 35, 36. 3 photos.
> Wareing, John. Playbox Community Theatre, Tuscon: B&W. Set. **SDT**, 280.

The Who's Tommy (see Tommy).

Whoopee.

> Beatty, John Lee. Goodspeed Opera House, East Haddam, Connecticut: 1978. B&W. Set. **TCI**, vol. 12, n. 6 (Oct 1978). 23.

Wielopole-Wielopole.

> Kantor, Tadeusz. Florence: 1979. B&W. Sketch. **TDT**, vol. XXIII, n. 3 (Fall 1987). 15.

Wild Birds.

> Mullen, Joseph. Cherry Lane Playhouse, NYC: 1925. B&W. Set. **MCN**, 70.

The Wild Duck.

> Hein, Peter. Volksbühne, Berlin: 1973. B&W. Set. **SDW4**, illus. 174-176.
> Tilton, James. Lyceum Theatre, NYC: 1966. B&W. Set. **TCI**, vol. 1, n. 1 (Mar/Apr 1967). 22.
> Vos, Marik. Dramatiska Teatern, Stockholm: 1972. B&W. Set. **SDW4**, illus. 169-173.
> Yeargan, Michael. Yale Repertory Theatre, New Haven: 1978. B&W. Set. **TCI**, vol. 16, n. 5 (May 1982). 27.
> _____. Théâtre Antoine, Paris: 1906. B&W. Set. **RSD**, illus. 12.

Wild Honey.

> Gunter, John. Virginia Theatre, NYC: 1986. Color. Set. **TCI**, vol. 21, n. 1 (Jan 1987). 26.

Wild Oats.

> Devine, Michael. Fourth Step Theatre (South Coast Repertory), Costa Mesa, California: 1979. B&W. Set. **TCI**, vol. 14, n. 4 (Sep 1980). 36.
> Koltai, Ralph. Aldwych Theatre, London: 1977. B&W. Set. **TCI**, vol. 12, n. 3 (Mar/Apr 1978). 10.

Wild Violets.

> Hammond, Aubrey. Drury Lane Theatre, London: 1932. B&W. Set. **SCM**, 22.

Wildcat.

> Larkin, Peter. Alvin Theatre, NYC: 1960. B&W. Rendering. **TCI**, vol. 23, n. 1 (Jan 1989). 42.

The Wilderness.

> Chang, Li. China: B&W. Model. **TDT** vol. XXXI, n. 2 (Spring 1995). 11.

Wildflower.

> Gates, Frank E. & E.A. Morange. Casino Theatre, NYC: 1923. B&W. Set. **WMC**, 103.

Der Wildschütz.

> Reinking, Wilhelm. State Theatre, Wiesbaden: 1952. B&W. Set. **SDE**, 145.

The Will Rogers Follies.
>   .Walton, Tony. Palace Theatre, NYC: 1991. B&W and color. Set & paint elevation.
>   **DDT**, VIII, 24c; Color. Set. **MBM**, 153, 156, 157; Color. Set. **TCI**, vol. 25, n. 6
>   (Aug/Sep 1991). 45-47. 5 photos.

William Tell.
>   Fiume, Salvatore. La Scala, Milan: 1964-1965. B&W. Rendering. **SIO**, 147. 2 photos.
>   Pirchan, Emil. State Theatre, Berlin: 1919. B&W. Rendering. **RSD**, illus. 130.
>   Pizzi, Pier Luigi. 1972. B&W. Rendering. **SIO**, 110. 2 photos.
>   _____. Zurich Municipal Theater: 1903. B&W. Rendering. **TPH**, photo 397.

The Wind in the Willows.
>   Ezell, John: Repertory Theatre of St. Louis: Color. Model. **TCI**, vol. 26, n. 5 (May
>   1992). 13.

The Window Man.
>   Chepulis, Kyle. NYC: Color. Set. **TCI**, vol. 29, n. 4 (Apr 1995). 41.

A Window on a Nether Sea.
>   Clay, Paul & Lora Nelson. Downtown Art Co., NYC: 1990. B&W. Set. **TCI**, vol. 25,
>   n. 4 (Apr 1991). 25.

Windy City.
>   Anania, Michael. Paper Mill Playhouse, Milburn, New Jersey: 1985. B&W. Set.
>   **BSE4**, 9; B&W. Model & rendering. **TCI**, vol. 21, n. 5 (May 1987). 33; Color. Set.
>   **TCI**, vol. 24, n. 2 (Feb 1990). 66.

Winesburg, Ohio.
>   Smith, Oliver. Nederlander Theatre, NYC: 1958. Color. Backdrop. **DPT**, between 316
>   & 317; B&W. Rendering. **SDW2**, 239.

Wings Over Europe.
>   Sovey, Raymond. Theatre Guild, NYC: 1928. B&W. Set. **SCM**, 108.

Wings.
>   Eigsti, Karl. Eastside Playhouse, NYC: 1975. B&W. Sketch. **DPT**, 115.
>   Goetz, Kent. Illinois Wesleyan University, Bloomington: Color. Set. **TDT**, vol. XXVI,
>   n. 1 (Spring 1990). 9 of insert.
>   Moyer, Allen. Pittsburgh Public Theatre: 1994. Color. Set. **TCI**, vol. 28, n. 5 (May
>   1994). 7.

The Winslow Boy.
>   Gillette, A.S. University of Iowa, Iowa City: 1951. B&W. Rendering. **TDP**, 76.

The Winter Dancers.
>   Funicello, Ralph. Mark Taper Forum, Los Angeles: 1977. B&W. Set. **TCI**, vol. 14, n. 4
>   (Sep 1980). 41.

The Winter's Tale.
>   Cairns, Tom. Crucible Theatre, Sheffield, England: 1987. B&W. Set. **BTD**, 48.
>   Conklin, John. Goodman Theatre, Chicago: 1990. B&W. Set. **TCI**, vol. 24, n. 8 (Oct
>   1990). 43.
>   Eckart, William. Southern Methodist University, Dallas: B&W. Rendering. **BSE1**, 23.
>   3 photos.
>   Motley (Margaret Harris, Sophia Harris, & Elizabeth Montgomery). Shakespeare
>   Memorial Theatre, Stratford-upon-Avon: 1948. B&W. Set. **PST**, 79.
>   Moulaert, René. Comédie Française, Paris: 1950. B&W. Set. **SDW1**, 102.
>   Oenslager, Donald. Yale School of Drama, New Haven, Connecticut: 1927. B&W. Set.
>   **SDA**, 82, 83. 3 photos.
>   Orlik, Emil. Deutsches Theater, Berlin: 1906. B&W and color. Rendering. **MRH**,
>   facing 50, 136. 2 photos; B&W. Rendering. **MRT**, 32; Color. Rendering. **RSD**,
>   illus. 99; B&W. Rendering. **SDC**, plate 46; B&W. Rendering. **SOW**, plate 46;

B&W. Set. **TCS2**, plate 14; B&W. Sketch. **TPH**, photo 332.

Ristic, Dusan. Narodno Pozoriste, Beograd: 1969. B&W. Set. **SDW3**, 63. 2 photos.

Seger, Richard. American Conservatory Theatre, Geary Theatre, San Francisco: 1978. B&W. Set. **TCI**, vol. 14, n. 4 (Sep 1980). 20; B&W. Set. **TCI**, vol. 13, n. 3 (May/Jun 1979). 50.

Straiges, Tony. Arena Stage, Washington, DC: 1979. B&W. Set. **TCI**, vol. 16, n. 2 (Feb 1982). 17; B&W. Set. **TCI**, vol. 16, n. 9 (Nov/Dec 1982). 27; B&W. Set. **TCI**, vol. 14, n. 6 (Nov/Dec 1980). 34. 2 photos.

Ward, Anthony. Royal Shakespeare Company, Stratford-upon-Avon: 1993. Color. Set. **TCI**, vol. 29, n. 2 (Feb 1995). 33; Color. Set. **TCI**, vol. 27, n. 4 (Apr 1993). 44.

_____. Centenary College, Louisiana: 1962. Color. Set. **MOR**, 11.

Die Winterkönigin.

Teschner, Richard. Austria: 1926. B&W. Rendering. **SCM**, 70.

Winterset.

Mielziner, Jo. Martin Beck Theatre, NYC: 1935. B&W. Rendering. **CSD**, 13; B&W. Rendering. **DOT**, 225; B&W. Rendering. **DTT**, 89; B&W. Rendering. **FCS**, plate 213; B&W. Set. **MCN**, 124; B&W. Rendering. **RSD**, illus. 450; B&W. Rendering & set. **SDA**, 118. 2 photos; B&W. Rendering. **SDO**, 246, 247; B&W. Rendering. **SDW1**, 203; B&W. Rendering. **SOW**, plate 82; B&W. Rendering. **TPH**, photo 480.

Ratto, Gianni. Odeon, Milan: B&W. Set. **SDW1**, 130.

Zimmerman, Remo. State Theatre, Chur, Switzerland: 1950. B&W. Rendering. **SDW1**, 119.

Wipe-Out Games.

Loquasto, Santo. Kreeger Theatre, Arena Stage, Washington, DC: 1971. B&W. Model. **CSD**, 100; B&W. Set. **DPT**, 39; B&W. Set. **TCI**, vol. 7, n. 5 (Oct 1973). 16, 18.

Wise Child.

Larkin, Peter. Helen Hayes Theatre, NYC: 1972. B&W. Rendering. **DPT**, 37.

A Wise Man.

Eisenstein, Sergei M. Proletkult Theatre, Moscow: 1923. B&W. Set. **RSD**, illus. 172.

Wish You Were Here.

Mielziner, Jo. Imperial Theatre, NYC: 1952. B&W. Set. **WMC**, 193.

The Witch of Endor.

Lee, Ming Cho. Martha Graham Dance Company: 1965. B&W. Model. **ASD1**, 101.

The Witch of Konotop.

Cecik, Anatoly. USSR: B&W. Model. **TDT**, vol. XX, n. 1 (Spring 1984). 15.

The Witching Hour.

_____. Hackett Theatre, NYC: 1907. B&W. Set. **MCN**, 31.

The Witty Students.

Fülöp, Zoltán. Allami Operház, Budapest: 1948. B&W. Set. **SDW2**, 140.

The Wiz.

John, Tom H. Majestic Theatre, NYC: 1975. Color. Set. **BWM**, 335. 2 photos; B&W. Set. **DSL**, figure 2.6(a); B&W. Set. **TCI**, vol. 9, n. 3 (May/Jun 1975). 9; B&W. Set. **WMC**, 368.

The Wizard of Oz.

Anania, Michael. Paper Mill Playhouse, Milburn, New Jersey: 1992. Color. Set. **TCI**, vol. 27, n. 1 (Jan 1993). 5.

Shortt, Paul. Playhouse in the Park, Cincinnati: 1982. B&W. Model. **TCI**, vol. 17, n. 2 (Feb 1983). 4.

Thompson, Mark. Royal Shakespeare Company, GB: 1987. B&W. Set. **BTD**, 164.

Woe from Wit.
> Shestakov, Victor. Meyerhold Theatre, Moscow: 1928. B&W. Set. **RST**, 26. 2 photos.
> Lansere, Evgheni. Maly Theatre, Moscow: 1938. B&W. Rendering. **SDW2**, 189.

The Wolf.
> Carzou, Jean. Théâtre Marigny, Paris: 1953. B&W. Rendering. **SDW1**, 89.

The Wolves.
> Kroschel, Michael. The Magic Theatre, San Francisco: 1977. B&W. Set. **TCI**, vol. 14, n. 4 (Sep 1980). 22.
> Vychodil, Ladislav. Theatre d'Etat, Brno: 1963. B&W. Rendering. **RSD**, illus. 462.

The Woman.
> Griffin, Hayden. National Theatre (Olivier), London: 1978. B&W. Set. **TCI**, vol. 13, n. 1 (Jan/Feb 1979). 8; B&W. Set. **TDT**, vol. XIX, n. 1 (Spring 1983). 7.

Woman is Fickle.
> Rognoni, Franco. La Scala, Milan: 1957. B&W. Rendering. **SDW2**, 130.

A Woman Killed With Kindness.
> Herbert, Jocelyn. Old Vic Theatre, London: 1971. B&W. Set. **TDT**, vol. XXX, n. 5 (Fall 1994). 17.
> Jourdain, Francis. Théâtre du Vieux-Columbier, Paris: 1913. B&W. Set. **RSD**, illus. 102.

A Woman of No Importance.
> Sainthill, Loudon. Savoy Theatre, London: 1953. B&W. Rendering. **LST**, 36.

Woman of the Year.
> Walton, Tony. Palace Theatre, NYC: 1981. Color. Set. **MBM**, 161.

The Woman Warrior.
> Lee, Ming Cho. James Doolittle Theatre, University of California, Los Angeles: 1995. Color. Set. **TCI**, vol. 29, n. 6 (Jun/Jul 1995). 16.

The Women.
> Voytek. Yvonne Arnaud Theatre, Guildford: 1986. Color. Set. **BTD**, 79.

Women Beware Women.
> Straiges, Tony. Yale School of Drama, New Haven, Connecticut: 1973. B&W. Set. **TCI**, vol. 16, n. 2 (Feb 1982). 18.
> _____. X Drama Workshop, Juilliard School, Lincoln Center, NYC: B&W. Set. **TCI**, vol. 8, n. 4 (Sep 1974). 18.

Women from Shanghai.
> Egemar, Christian. Den Nationale Scene, Bergen, Norway: 1968. B&W. Set. **SDW3**, 131.

Women in Parliament.
> Capek, Josef. Vinohrady Theatre, Prague: 1923. B&W. Rendering. **TDT**, n. 42 (Fall 1975). 24.

The Women of Trachis.
> Lenneweit, H.W. Schiller Theatre, Berlin: 1959. B&W. Rendering. **SDW2**, 64.
> Meyer, Hans. Landestheater, Darmstadt: 1959. B&W. Set. **SDW2**, 65.

The Wonder Bar.
> Barratt, Watson. Bayes Theatre, NYC: 1931. B&W. Set. **MCN**, 103.

The Wonder Hat.
> Hume, Samuel J. Arts and Crafts Theatre, Detroit: 1916. B&W. Set. **TDT**, vol. XX, n. 2 (Summer 1984). 13.

Wonderful Tennessee.
> Vanek, Joe. Abbey Theatre, Dublin: 1993. Color. Set. **TCI**, vol. 28, n. 1 (Jan 1994). 38.

Wonderful Town.
> Du Bois, Raoul Pène. Winter Garden Theatre, NYC: 1953. B&W. Set. **BWM**, 289, 290.

The Wood Demon.
> Schindler, Otaker. National Theatre, Prague: 1974. B&W. Set. **SDW4**, illus. 183.
> Vassiliev, Alexandre. Teatr Mossovieta, Moscow: 1960. B&W. Rendering. **SDW2**, 199.

Working.
> _____. Northwestern University, Boston: 1988-1989. B&W. Set. **TCI**, vol. 23, n. 9 (Nov 1989). 53.

The World of Paul Slickey.
> Casson, Hugh. Palace Theatre, London: 1959. B&W. Rendering. **SDW2**, 215.

The World We Make.
> Horner, Harry. Guild Theatre, NYC: 1939. B&W. Set. **WTP**, 206. 3 photos.

The Worship of Nati.
> Tagore, Rabindranath. Calcutta: 1930. B&W. Set. **SDW2**, 114.

The Would-be Gentleman.
> Dvigoubskij, Nikolaj. Teatr imeni Vakhtangova, Moscow: 1969. B&W. Rendering. **SDW3**, 72.
> _____. B&W. Set. **WTP**, 92. 4 photos.

Wozzeck.
> Colciaghi, Ebe, Virginio Puecher, & Ugo Mulas. Teatro Communale, Bologna: 1969. B&W. Set. **SDW3**, 191. 3 photos.
> Freyer, Achim. Cologne Opera: 1975. B&W. Set. **TCI**, vol. 13, n. 5 (Oct 1979). 20.
> Hill, Hainer. Deutsches Staatsoper, Berlin: 1955. B&W. Set. **SDW2**, 54.
> Hoffman, Vlastislav. National Theatre, Prague: B&W. Set. **TCS2**, plate 362.
> Masson, André. Opéra de Paris: 1963. B&W. Rendering. **AST**, 203.
> Neher, Caspar. Teatro San Carlo, Naples: 1953. B&W. Rendering. **SDE**, 126; Metropolitan Opera, NYC: 1958. B&W. Rendering. **MOM**, 12.
> Reinking, Wilhelm. State Theatre, Wiesbaden: 1952. B&W. Set. **SDE**, 145.
> Schenk von Trapp, Lothar. Landestheater, Darmstadt: 1930-1931. B&W. Set. **RSD**, illus. 248.
> Svoboda, Josef. La Scala, Milan: 1971. B&W. Set. **SDW4**, illus. 216-219; B&W. Set. **STS**, 79; Teatro Stabile, Turin: 1971. B&W. Set. **SJS**, 169.
> _____. Yale Repertory Theatre, New Haven: B&W. Set. **TCI**, vol. 6, n. 3 (May/Jun 1972). 26, 27.

The Wrath of Achilles.
> Stern, Ernst. Deutsches Theater, Berlin: 1912. Color. Rendering. **MRH**, facing 52.

A Wrathful God.
> _____. B&W. Set. **WTP**, 88, 89.

Written in Stone.
> _____. Green Thumb Theatre for Young People, Canada: B&W. Set. **TDT** vol. XXXI, n. 2 (Spring 1995). 22.

Die Wupper.
> Stern, Ernst. Berlin: 1919. B&W. Set. **DOT**, 216; B&W. Set. **MRH**, facing 139. 2 photos.

-X-

Xerxes.
> Fielding, David. English National Opera, London: 1985. Color. Set. **BTD**, 106.

XSR: Die! ("Cross stage right, then drop dead").
> _____. Pegasus Theatre, Dallas: 1991. Color. Set. **TCI**, vol. 25, n. 5 (May 1991). 14.

-Y-

Yabuhara Kengyo.
> Asakura, Setsu. Gogatsu-sha. Seibu Gekijo, Tokyo: 1973. Color. Set. **SDW4**, illus.
> 357-362. 6 photos.

Yankee Dawg You Die.
> Dorsey, Kent. Berkeley Repertory Theatre, California: Color. Set. **TCI**, vol. 25, n. 8
> (Oct 1991). 49.

The Year of Grace.
> _____. NYC: 1928. B&W. Set. **TMT**, 111.

Years of the Locust.
> _____. Trinity Square Theatre, Providence, Rhode Island: B&W. Set. **TCI**, vol.
> 13, n. 3 (May/Jun 1979). 15.

Yegor Bulichov.
> Dancy, Virginia & Elmon Webb. Long Wharf Theatre, New Haven, Connecticut: 1970.
> B&W. Model & set. **DPT**, 99; B&W. Model & set. **TCI**, vol. 7, n. 5 (Oct 1973). 8.
> 2 photos.

Yellow Jack.
> Mielziner, Jo. Martin Beck Theatre, NYC: 1934. B&W. Rendering. **DTT**, 107. Burial
> of fever victims; B&W. Rendering. **DTT**, 108. Basic set; B&W. Rendering. **DTT**,
> 109. First fever inoculations; B&W. Set. **MCN**, 117; B&W. Rendering. **RSD**, illus.
> 451; B&W. Rendering. **SDA**, 226; B&W. Rendering. **SDW1**, 201; B&W. Render-
> ing. **TAT**, plate 584.
> _____. Yale Dramatic Association, New Haven, Connecticut: B&W. Set. **SFT**,
> 287.

The Yellow Jacket.
> _____. Kammerspiele, Munich: 1914. B&W. Set. **MRH**, facing 21.

Yentl.
> Eigsti, Karl. Eugene O'Neill Theatre, NYC: 1975. B&W. Rendering. **DDT**, 102. 2
> photos.

Yerma.
> Alkazi, Ebrahim. Theatre Unit, Bombay: 1960. B&W. Set. **SDW2**, 114.
> Caballero, José. Teatro Eslava, Madrid: 1960. B&W. Set. **SDW2**, 77.
> Garcia, Victor. Thêátre de la Ville, Paris: 1973. B&W. Set. **SDW4**, illus. 248, 249.
> Ivaneanu-Damaschin, Andrei. Nederlands Toneel Gent, Belgium: 1973. B&W. Set.
> **SDW4**, illus. 250, 251.
> Lechtveld, Noni. Koninklijken Schouwburg, The Hague: 1952. B&W. Set. **SDW1**,
> 138.

Yes, My Darling Daughter.
> Sovey, Raymond. Playhouse Theatre, NYC: 1937. B&W. Set. **MCN**, 138.

Yolanda of Cyprus.
> Jones, Robert Edmond. Charles Hopkins Theatre, NYC: 1929. B&W. Rendering. **REJ**,
> 71.

Yolanta.
> Svoboda, Josef. Chemnitz: 1993. Color. Set. **TDT**, vol. XXX, n. 5 (Fall 1994). 38.

You Can't Take It With You.
> Lee, Eugene. Trinity Square Theatre, Providence, Rhode Island: 1970. B&W. Set.
> **TDT**, vol. XVIII, n. 2 (Summer 1982). 9.
> Oenslager, Donald. Music Box Theatre, NYC: 1936. B&W. Set. **MCN**, 134; B&W.
> Set. **SDA**, 202; B&W. Set. **TDO**, 73.

Wolf, Craig. B&W. Set. **SDL**, 367.

_____. B&W. Sketch. **SDL**, 127.

You Never Can Tell.

Chaney, Stewart. Martin Beck Theatre, NYC: 1948. B&W. Rendering. **SDW1**, 193.

Clarke, Bill. Playmakers Repertory Company, Paul Green Theatre, Chapel Hill, North Carolina: Color. Set. **TCI**, vol. 25, n. 3 (Mar 1991). 49.

Dancy, Virginia & Elmon Webb. Pittsburgh Public Theatre: 1978. B&W and color. Set. **DDT**, 248, 440d.

Porteous, Cameron. Shaw Festival Theatre, Niagara-on-the-Lake, Canada: 1988. B&W. Set. **TCI**, vol. 22, n. 7 (Aug/Sep 1988). 64; B&W. Model. **TDT**, vol. XXVII, n. 4 (Fall 1991). 24.

You Never Know.

Pecktal, Lynn. Ogunquit Playhouse, Ogunquit, Maine: 1963. B&W. Set. **DPT**, 331.

You Should Be So Lucky.

Whitehill, Brian T. Primary Stages, NYC: 1994. Color. Set. **TCI**, vol. 29, n. 3 (Mar 1995). 9.

You Touched Me.

Motley (Margaret Harris, Sophia Harris, & Elizabeth Montgomery). Booth Theatre, NYC: 1945. B&W. Set. **SDA**, 227.

You Won't Always Be on Top.

Bury, John. Theatre Royal, Stratford East, London: 1956. B&W. Set. **DMS**, plate 52.

You're a Good Man, Charlie Brown.

Kimmel, Alan. Theatre 80 St. Marks, NYC: 1971. B&W. Rendering. **TCI**, vol. 1, n. 4 (Sep/Oct 1967). 28-30.

The Young Lord.

Kleiber, Eleonore & Reinhart Zimmerman. Komische Oper, Berlin: 1968. B&W. Set. **SDW3**, 210.

Young Mark Twain.

_____. Performing Arts Repertory Theatre: B&W. Set. **TCI**, vol. 5, n. 2 (Mar/Apr 1971). 11.

Yours, Anne.

Colavecchia, Franco. Playhouse 91, NYC: 1985. B&W. Rendering. **DDT**, 76.

Yvone.

Svoboda, Josef. Schiller Theatre, Berlin: 1970. B&W. Model. **SJS**, 51.

-Z-

Zanguesi.

Tatlin, Vladimir. Academy of Plastic Arts and Geological Institute, Leningrad: 1923. B&W. Model. **AST**, 133; B&W. model & rendering. **RSD**, illus. 166, 167.

Zem (The Earth).

Ciller, Josef. Dubova, Czechoslovakia: 1973. B&W. Rendering. **TDT**, vol. XXVIII, n. 2 (Spring 1992). 34.

Serroni, J.C. Municipal de São Paulo, Brazil: B&W. Model. **TCI**, vol. 28, n. 4 (Apr 1994). 37.

The Ziegfeld Follies of 1923.

Erté (Romain de Tirtoff). New Amsterdam Theatre, NYC: 1923. B&W. Rendering. **FCS**, plate 199.

Der Zigeunerbaron (The Gypsy Baron).

Halmen, Pet. Gärtnerplatz Theatre, Munich: 1993. B&W. Set. **TCI**, vol. 27, n. 9 (Nov 1993). 18.

Zizka.
> Hoffman, Vlastislav. National Theatre, Prague: 1925. B&W. Set. **TCS2**, plate 240.

Zoditch's Room.
> Lundell, Kurt. American Place Theatre, NYC: 1966. B&W. Rendering. **TCI**, vol. 1, n.
> 1 (Mar/Apr 1967). 28.

Zoika's Apartment.
> Isakov, Sergei. Vakhtangov Theatre, Moscow: 1926. B&W. Set. **RST**, 248.

Zoot Suit.
> Morales, Roberto & Thomas A. Walsh. Mark Taper Forum, Los Angeles: 1978. B&W.
> Set. **TCI**, vol. 14, n. 4 (Sep 1980). 45. 2 photos; B&W. Set. **TCI**, vol. 13, n. 1 (Jan/
> Feb 1979). 6.

Zorba.
> Aronson, Boris. Imperial Theatre, NYC: 1968. B&W. Model. **CSD**, 35; B&W and
> color. Rendering, model, & set. **TAB**, 201, 202, 204-206, 308. 10 photos.

Zum Grossen Wurstel.
> Heinrich, Rudolf. Salzburg Festival: 1970. B&W. Set. **TCI**, vol. 10, n. 6 (Nov/Dec
> 1976). 16.

Zuzana Vojírová.
> Vychodil, Ladislav. Bratislava: 1959. B&W. Set. **TDT**, vol. XV, n. 2 (Summer 1979).
> 12.

DESIGNERS

-A-

Aaes, Eric.
   Jeppe on the Hill. **SDW1**, 55.
   Macbeth. **SDW1**, 55.
Abril, Jean Philippe. *Macbeth.* **SDW3**, 96.
Ackerman, P. Dodd. *Five Star Final.* **MCN**, 100; **SDA**, 226.
Acquart, André.
   The Blacks. **RSD**, illus. 498; **SDW2**, 83.
   The Last Ones. **SDW3**, 55.
   Macbeth. **SDW3**, 55.
   The Narrow Road to the Deep North. **SDW3**, 163.
   Ondine. **TDT**, vol. XX, n. 1 (Spring 1984). 6.
   Penny Pantomime. **SDW2**, 83.
   The Resistible Rise of Arturo Ui. **RSD**, illus. 540.
   Romeo and Juliet. **SDW3**, 36.
   The Screens. **RSD**, illus. 538; **SDW3**, 127.
   The Story of Tobias and Sara. **SDW2**, 83.
   Troilus and Cressida. **RSD**, illus. 537, 539; **SDW3**, 49.
   Turcaret. **SDW3**, 74.
Acquart, Claude. *Lucifer and the Lord.* **SDW3**, 119.
Adam, H.G. *The Flies.* **RSD**, illus. 399.
Adams, Ken. *The Girl of the Golden West.* **TCI**, vol. 19, n. 9 (Nov 1985). 16.
Adar, Arnon.
   Grand Hotel. **SDL**, 84.
   A View from the Bridge. **SDW2**, 117.
Adducci, Alexander F. *The Tempest.* **SCT**, 83.
Adshead, Mary. *The King of the Castle.* **SCM**, 26.
Aeberli, Hans. *Altona.* **SDW2**, 57.
Ahlbom, Martin. *A Dream Play.* **SDW1**, 160.
Ahmed, Samir. *The Song of the Lusitanian Bogey.* **SDW3**, 136.
Akakia-Viala. *The Wedding.* **RSD**, illus. 387.
Akalaitis, Joanne. *Dressed Like an Egg.* **TCI**, vol. 13, n. 1 (Jan/Feb 1979). 33.
Akhvlediana, Elena. *Hoppla, Wir Leben!* **RST**, 133.
Akimov, Nicolai.
   Armoured Train No. 14-69. **RST**, 218; **TAT**, plate 637.
   The Affair. **SDW2**, 177.

Evgraf. **RST**, 228, 229.
Hamlet. **RSC**, 9; **RST**, 1932; **SCM**, 90; **SOS**, 222.
The Inspector General. **SDW2**, 177.
Mister Magridge Junior. **RSD**, illus. 190.
Now for Hamlet. **FCS**, plate 183; **SDO**, 209.
The Shadow. **SDW2**, 177.
Tartuffe. **RSD**, illus. 191; **RST**, 294, 295.
The Wedding. **SOW**, plates 69, 70.
Alarcon, Enrique & Victor Garcia. *The Maids.* **SDW3**, 124.
Albert, Ernest (from drawings by Jules Guerin). *Antony and Cleopatra.* **MCN**, 34.
Albert, Ernest & John A. Young. *George Washington, Jr.* **MCN**, 29.
Albert, Ernest & Joseph Physioc. *The Climbers.* **MCN**, 14.
Ali, Sakina Mohamed. *The Good Woman of Setzuan.* **SDW3**, 115.
Alkazi, Ebrahim.
    Macbeth. **SDW2**, 115.
    The Merchant of Venice. **SDW2**, 115.
    Volpone. **SDW2**, 115.
    Yerma. **SDW2**, 114.
Alley Friends, Architects. *Don't Walk on the Clouds.* **ASC**, 35.
Allinson, Adrian. *Tristan and Isolde.* **DIT**, plate 40.
Allio, René.
    The Anabaptists. **SDW3**, 143.
    Bérénice. **SDW3**, 73, 219.
    Dead Souls. **RSD**, illus. 573; **SDB**, 87; **SDW2**, 84.
    Edward II. **SDW2**, 84.
    Henry IV. **RSD**, illus. 571; **SOS**, 188.
    The Merchant of Venice. **SDW4**, illus. 22.
    Tartuffe. **RSD**, illus. 574; **SDW2**, 84.
Alma-Tadema, Laurence. *Coriolanus.* **SDG**, 136.
Alme, Gunnar. *The Insect Comedy.* **SDW2**, 151.
Alsaker, John-Kristian. *When We Dead Awaken.* **TCI**, vol. 28, n. 9 (Nov 1994). 36.
Alswang, Ralph. *Sunrise at Campobello.* **SDT**, 42.
Altandag, Seza. *A Clinical Case.* **SDW2**, 213.
Altman, Günther. *Hamlet.* **TDT**, vol. XII, n. 3 (Fall 1976). 36.
Altman, Nathan.
    The Dybbuk. **RSD**, illus. 217; **SCM**, 92; **TPH**, photo 413.
    Hamlet. **SDW2**, 178.
    King Lear. **SDW2**, 178.
    Uriel Acosta. **RST**, 72, 73; **TCS2**, plates 170-173.
Amable, A. Petit. *Chantecler.* **RSD**, illus. 4.
Amenós, Montse & Isidre Prunés.
    Mar I Cel. **TCI**, vol. 27, n. 1 (Jan 1993). 3, 43.
    Night Flowers. **TCI**, vol. 27, n. 1 (Jan 1993). 42.
Anania, Michael.
    The Desert Song. **BSE5**, 10; **TCI**, vol. 24, n. 2 (Feb 1990). 67.
    The Pajama Game. **TCI**, vol. 23, n. 5 (May 1989). 26-27; **TCI**, vol. 24, n. 2 (Feb 1990). 63.
    Phantom. **TCI**, vol. 27, n. 8 (Oct 1993). 8.
    Rhythm Ranch. **TCI**, vol. 24, n. 2 (Feb 1990). 64.
    Romeo and Juliet. **TCI**, vol. 20, n. 8 (Oct 1986). 25.
    Sayonara. **TCI**, vol. 21, n. 10 (Dec 1987). 24.

Orpheus and Euridice. **BSE4**, 47; **DOT**, 209; **RSD**, illus. 61; **RSD**, illus. 67; **TCS2**, plate 38; **TPH**, photo 312; **WLA**, 111.

Parsifal. **RSD**, illus. 62; **SOW**, plate 55; **TCR**, 74; **WLA**, 93.

Prometheus. **WLA**, 105, 107.

Das Rheingold. **SDB**, 17; **WLA**, 99.

The Tidings Brought to Mary. **SDC**, plate 111.

Tristan and Isolde. **JSS**, 15; **TAS**, 96, 97; **TCS2**, plate 34;. **TDT**, n. 38 (Oct 1974). 20, 21; **TSS**, 506, 507; **WLA**, 97.

Die Walküre. **JSS**, 15; **RSD**, illus. 65; **TCS2**, plates 35, 39; **WLA**, 101-103.

Arapov, Anatoly. *The Bridge of Fire.* **RST**, 281.

Aravantinos, P. *Carmen.* **DIT**, plate 105.

Arcenas, Loy.

Blue Window. **SDL**, 9.

The Day Room. **ASD2**, 14.

Day Trips. **ASD2**, 6; **DDT**, 34.

Fences. **ASD2**, 13.

Gilette. **TCI**, vol. 25, n. 3 (Mar 1991). 39.

The Glass Menagerie. **ASD2**, 11, 12, and between 108 & 109; **DDT**, 61.

The Good Woman of Setzuan. **TCI**, vol. 25, n. 3 (Mar 1991). 38.

Italian-American Reconciliation. **ASD2**, 8.

Life is a Dream. **ASD2**, 14; **TCI**, vol. 25, n. 3 (Mar 1991). 39.

Love! Valour! Compassion! **TCI**, vol. 29, n. 1 (Jan 1995). 6.

Major Barbara. **TCI**, vol. 25, n. 3 (Mar 1991). 38.

Once in a Lifetime. **TCI**, vol. 25, n. 3 (Mar 1991). 36, 37.

Once On This Island. **ASD2**, 2; **DDT**, 178; **TCI**, vol. 24, n. 8 (Oct 1990). 35.

Prelude to a Kiss. **ASD2**, 10; **ASD2**, 9.

Spring's Awakening. **DDT**, 586.

Three Postcards. **ASD2**, 5; **DDT**, 35.

Archer, Julie. *Hajj.* **BSE4**, 65.

Arent, Benno von. *Major Barbara.* **TPH**, photo 427.

Arle, Asmund & Yngve Larson. *Modell Beatrice.* **SDW2**, 208.

Armistead, Horace.

Carmen. **SDW2**, 229.

The Consul. **WTP**, 214, 215.

The Medium. **SDW1**, 189; **TPH**, photo 486; **WTP**, 212, 213.

The Misanthrope. **SFT**, 13.

I Pagliacci. **MOM**, 14.

Punch and the Child. **SDW1**, 189.

Armstrong, Will Steven.

Carnival. **BWM**, 297.

Misalliance. **SDW2**, 229.

The Taming of the Shrew. **TCI**, vol. 1, n. 1 (Mar/Apr 1967). 17, 18.

Arnold, Richard.

Close Ties. **SCT**, 18, 26.

The Mikado. **SST**, plate XII.

Misalliance. **SCT**, between 152 & 153.

Arnone, John.

American Notes. **ASD2**, 22.

As You Like It. **TCI**, vol. 21, n. 8 (Oct 1987). 27.

The Cave. **TCI**, vol. 27, n. 9 (Nov 1993). 9.

Frankenstein: Playing With Fire. **ASD2**, 24; **DDT**, 205.

Happy End. **ASD2**, 24, 28.
How To Succeed in Business Without Really Trying. **TCI**, vol. 29, n. 5 (May 1995). cover, 46, 47.
K: Impressions of Kafka's THE TRIAL. **ASD2**, 30; **TCI**, vol. 15, n. 6 (Jun/Jul 1981). 27.
Lulu. **ASD2**, between 108 & 109.
Made in Bangkok. **ASD2**, 16.
The Miser. **ASD2**, 26.
Music Hall Sidelights. **TCI**, vol. 13, n. 4 (Sep 1979). 53; **TCI**, vol. 15, n. 6 (Jun/Jul 1981). 28.
New Jerusalem. **TCI**, vol. 15, n. 6 (Jun/Jul 1981). 28.
On the Verge or The Geography of Yearning. **ASD2**, 21; **DDT**, 174.
Patio/Porch. **TCI**, vol. 15, n. 6 (Jun/Jul 1981). 29.
Red and Blue. **ASD2**, 19; **DDT**, 157.
The School for Wives. **TCI**, vol. 25, n. 9 (Nov 1991). 43.
The Seagull. **ASD2**, 21; **TCI**, vol. 21, n. 8 (Oct 1987). 29.
Shout Up a Morning. **TCI**, vol. 21, n. 8 (Oct 1987). 27
The Tempest. **ASD2**, 21.
Tommy. **TCI**, vol. 26, n. 9 (Nov 1992). 7; **TCI**, vol. 27, n. 7 (Aug/Sep 1993). cover, 7, 26-30.
Vanities. **TCI**, vol. 15, n. 6 (Jun/Jul 1981). 29.
Aronson, Boris.
Andorra. **TAB**, 307.
Angels on Earth. **TAB**, 34 , 294.
Anthony and Cleopatra. **PST**, 211.
Arthur Adamov. **PST**, 440.
The Assassin. **TAB**, 299.
Awake and Sing. **MCN**, 123; **TAB**, 54, 55.
Ballade. **TAB**, 18, 302.
Barefoot in Athens. **TAB**, 302.
Battleship Gertie. **TAB**, 295.
The Big People. **TAB**, 300.
The Bird Cage. **TAB**, 99.
The Body Beautiful. **TAB**, 14, 295.
The Bronx Express. **BAT**, plates 1, 12; **TAB**, 36, 37, 293; **TCS2**, plate 180; **TDT**, vol. XXV, n. 3 (Fall 1989). 14.
Bus Stop. **TAB**, 112, 113, 303.
Cabaret. **BMF**, 174; **BWM**, 127; **CSD**, 35; **DDT**, 24c; **HPA**, 42, 63; **SST**, plate VII; **TAB**, 19, 189, 190-197, 307; **TCI**, vol. 21, n. 5 (May 1987). 11; **WMC**, 332.
Cabin in the Sky. **TAB**, 75-78, 297.
Café Crown. **TAB**, 297.
The Changeling. **TAB**, 300.
Clash by Night. **TAB**, 17, 297.
The Cold Wind and the Warm. **TAB**, 305.
Company. **BMF**, 83, 191; **BWM**, 320, 321; **CSD**, 36; **DPT**, 60; **HPA**, 92; **HPR**, 173; **SDB**, 64; **SDW3**, 212; **SON**, 82; **TAB**, 20, 220, 222-227, 229, 308; **TCI**, vol. 4, n. 5 (Oct 1970). 15; **TCI**, vol. 14, n. 1 (Jan/Feb 1980). 20; **TCI**, vol. 18, n. 8 (Oct 1984). 15; **TDT**, vol. XXV, n. 3 (Fall 1989). 11.
Coriolanus. **TAB**, 132-134, 305.
The Country Girl. **TAB**, 100, 101, 301; **WTP**, 180.
The Creation of the World and Other Business. **TAB**, 167-169, 308.

The Crucible. **TAB**, 105, 303.
Dancing in the Chequered Shade. **TAB**, 304.
Danton. **PST**, 410; **TPH**, photo 337.
Day and Night. **BAT**, 15, 31; TAB, 33, 293.
The Desert Song. **TAB**, 299.
Detective Story. **TAB**, 96.
The Diary of Anne Frank. **TAB**, 122, 123, 125-128, 304.
Do Re Mi. **TAB**, 148-155, 306; **TDT**, vol. XXV, n. 3 (Fall 1989). 12; **WMC**, 257.
Dreyfus in Rehearsal. **TAB**, 309.
Ernani. **PST**, 333.
The Family. **TAB**, 298.
Les Fausses Confidences. **PST**, 279.
Fiddler on the Roof. **DPT**, 59; **CSD**, 34; **HPR**, 103; **MAM**, 48, 49, 133, 136, 143, 150,
    151; **TAB**, 19, 172-186, 307; **TCI**, vol. 4, n. 3 (May/Jun 1970). 32; **TCI**, vol. 20,
    n. 5 (May 1986). 28; **TCI**, vol. 23, n. 7 (Aug/Sep 1989). 59; **TCI**, vol. 28, n. 3
    (Mar 1994). 32; **TMI**, 252.
Fidelio. **FCS**, plate 214; **MOM**, 80-87; **SDB**, 78, 79; **SDO**, 249; **TAB**, 216, 308.
The Final Balance. **BAT**, 3, 18; **TAB**, 35, 293.
The Firstborn. **TDT**, vol. XXV, n. 3 (Fall 1989). 11; **TAB**, 130, 305; **TCI**, vol. 23, n. 8
    (Oct 1989). 10.
Flowering Cherry. **TAB**, 306.
Follies. **CSD**, 36, 59, 126; **DDT**, 15; **DPT**, 8; **HPA**, 99, 100, 102; **SON**, 91, 93, 98,
    99; **TAB**, 20, 235, 236, 238-242, 247, 249, 250, 253, 308; **TCI**, vol. 14, n. 1 (Jan/
    Feb 1980). 21; **TDT**, vol. XXIV, n. 3 (Fall 1988). 17; **TDT**, vol. XXV, n. 3 (Fall
    1989). 12.
The Fortune Teller. **TAB**, 300.
The Frogs of Spring. **TAB**, 303.
From Morn to Midnight. **PST**, 389.
The Garden of Sweets. **TAB**, 306.
The Gentle People. **DDT**, 24a; **SDB**, 36; **SDW1**, 190; **SOW**, plate 101; **TAB**, 64, 65,
    67, 296.
A Gift of Time. **TAB**, 158-160.
Gilles de Rais. **PST**, 443.
Girls of Summer. **TAB**, 304.
The Golden Door. **TAB**, 300.
The Golem. **TAB**, 294.
The Good Woman of Setzuan. **PST**, 414.
The Great American Goof. **TAB**, 16, 70-72, 296.
The Great God Brown. **TAB**, 170, 309.
Heavenly Express. **TAB**, 297.
L'Histoire du Soldat. **TAB**, 307.
A Hole in the Head. **TAB**, 114, 115, 304.
I Am a Camera. **SDW1**, 195; **TAB**, 104, 302.
I've Got Sixpence. **TAB**, 302.
Incident at Vichy. **TAB**, 161, 162, 307.
J.B. **DPT**, 387; **RSD**, illus. 456; **SDR**, 56; **SDW2**, 230; **TAB**, 18, 141-144, 305; **TCI**,
    vol. 23, n. 8 (Oct 1989). 10.
Jew Süss. **TAB**, 294.
Jim Cooperkop. **TAB**, 294.
Judith. **TAB**, 137, 306.
Ladies and Gentlemen. **TAB**, 296.

The Tenth Commandment. **BAT**, 8, 23, 24, 26, 27, 29; **SDB**, 21; **SDC**, plate 121; **TAB**, 39, 42-46; **TDT**, vol. XXV, n. 3 (Fall 1989). 13.

This is Goggle. **TAB**, 305.

Three Men on a Horse. **TAB**, 58-59.

The Time of Your Life. **SOW**, plate 102; **TAB**, 61.

Titus Andronicus. **PST**, 80.

The Tragedy of Nothing. **BAT**, 21; **TAB**, 293.

Truckline Café. **TAB**, 300.

20,000. **TAB**, 6; **TPH**, photo 414.

2x2=5. **BAT**, 6; **TAB**, 11, 293.

The Tzaddik. **TAB**, 309.

The Unconquered. **TAB**, 296.

A View from the Bridge. **SDW2**, 230; **TAB**, 18, 107.

Walk a Little Faster. **TAB**, 48, 50-52, 294.

Weep for the Virgins. **TAB**, 295.

Western Waters. **TAB**, 296.

What's Up. **TAB**, 81, 298.

Zorba. **CSD**, 35; **TAB**, 201, 202, 204-206, 308.

Arquitectonica. *In Closed Time.* **TDT**, vol. XXII, n. 1 (Spring 1986). 9.

Arrighi, Luciana. *I and Albert.* **SST**, 97, 543.

Arrocha, Eduardo. *Entreacto Barroco.* **SDW2**, 48.

Arroyo, Eduardo.

　From the House of the Dead. **TCI**, vol. 27, n. 1 (Jan 1993). 25.

　Splendid's. **TCI**, vol. 29, n. 3 (Mar 1995). 12.

Artaud, Antonin. *Life is a Dream.* **RSD**, illus. 394.

Arzadun, Nestor de & J. Monod. *The Tempest.* **RSD**, illus. 638.

Asakura, Setsu.

　Breaking the Code. **TDT**, vol. XXVII, n. 4 (Fall 1991). 25.

　Echizen Bamboo Doll. **SDW4**, illus. 282-285.

　In Search of Hakamadare. **SDW3**, 152.

　Vietnam Discourse. **SDW3**, 137.

　Yabuhara Kengyo. **SDW4**, illus. 357-362.

Asplin, Wilfred. Peter and the Wolf. **SDW1**, 39.

Assman, Jost. *The Life of Galileo.* **SDW3**, 112.

Aston, Tom A. & James Hayes.

　Delightful Gardens of Existence. **TCI**, vol. 4, n. 1 (Jan/Feb 1970). 34.

Aston, Tom A. *The Medium.* **TCI**, vol. 3, n. 2 (Mar/Apr 1969). 17.

Atkinson, Patrick.

　The Best Little Whorehouse in Texas. **BSE4**, 68.

　The Misanthrope. **BSE2**, 6.

Atlakson, Phil. *The Empire Builders.* **TCI**, vol. 19, n. 4 (Apr 1985). 115.

Autant, Edouard. *The Temptation of Saint Anthony.* **RSD**, illus. 386.

Avellana, Lamberto V. *Unwounded.* **SDW4**, illus. 186.

Averyt, Bennett. *Let's Get a Divorce.* **TCI**, vol. 13, n. 5 (Oct 1979). 36.

Avetissian, Minas. *Boléro.* **SDW3**, 188.

Axer, Otto.

　Iphigenia in Taurus. **SDW2**, 165.

　The Key to the Precipice. **SDW2**, 165.

　Macbeth. **SDW3**, 53.

Axtell, Barry. *A Touch of the Poet.* **BSE1**, 13.

Ayers, Lemuel.
    Angel Street. **SDA**, 204.
    Bloomer Girl. **SDA**, 248; **SDB**, 56; **SDW1**, 191; **TMT**, 157; **WMC**, 181.
    Cyrano de Bergerac. **SDT**, 40.
    Inside U.S.A. **WMC**, 169.
    Kismet. **BMF**, 35; **MCD**, plate 208.
    Kiss Me Kate. **BMF**, 70; **BWM**, 213-215; **MCD**, plate 201; **TMT**, 173; **WMC**, 155; **WTP**, 244, 245.
    Oklahoma! **BMF**, 44; **BWM**, 14, 15, 186, 187; **CSD**, 14; **HOB**, 77; **MCD**, plate 194; **TCI**, vol. 20, n. 5 (May 1986). 36; **TMI**, 135, 175, 236; **TMT**, 152, plate 8; **WMC**, 210, 211; **WTP**, 228, 229.
    Out of This World. **BWM**, 217; **SDA**, 156; **SDW1**, 191; **WTP**, 48.
    The Pajama Game. **BWM**, 94; **HPA**, 28; **HPR**, 19; **SDW1**, 191.
    The Pirate. **SDA**, 260, 261; **SDB**, 37; **SOW**, plate 105.
    St. Louis Woman. **BWM**, 253, 254.

B

Babberger, Ludwig. *Ein Geschlecht.* **TPH**, photo 419.
Babic, Ljubo.
    Diogenes. **TCS2**, plate 264.
    Richard III. **TCS2**, plate 119.
    Twelfth Night. **SDC**, plate 87; **TCS2**, plate 112.
Bailey, James.
    As You Like It. **SDW1**, 169.
    A Midsummer Night's Dream. **DMS**, plate 27.
    The Millionairess. **WTP**, 140.
    The Nutcracker. **SDW2**, 215.
Bainbridge, Martyn. *Shadow of a Gunman.* **BTD**, 77.
Baird, Campbell.
    Candide. **TCI**, vol. 23, n. 9 (Nov 1989). 51.
    The Nutcracker. **TCI**, vol. 27, n. 9 (Nov 1993). 70.
Bakkom, James. *Oklahoma.* **TCI**, vol. 20, n. 5 (May 1986). 36.
Bakst, Leon.
    L'Apres-midi d'un Faune. **DOT**, 217.
    Aladin ou la Lampe Merveilleuse. **LBT**, 196, 198, 199.
    Boris Godounov. **TPH**, photo 348.
    Le Dieu Blue. **RSC**, 16.
    Hélène de Sparte. **LBT**, 130.
    Hippolytus. **LBT**, 41, 42.
    Lâcheté. **DIT**, plate 72; **TCS2**, plate 230.
    Le Martyre de Saint Sébastien. **DIT**, plate 71; **LBT**, 122, 123; **TCS2**, plate 231.
    Oedipus at Colonus. **LBT**, 45.
    Phaedra. **LBT**, 226, 227.
    La Pisanella. **LBT**, 163-165; **TCS2**, color plate 5.
    Salomé. **LBT**, 158.
    Schéhérazade. **CSD**, 44; **LBT**, 94, 95; **RSD**, illus. 37; **SDC**, plate 63; **SDG**, 169.
Baldasso, Carl A. *She Loves Me.* **TCI**, vol. 20, n. 5 (May 1986). 27.
Baldessari, Luciano.
    Six Characters in Search of an Author. **SCM**, 79; **SDE**, 29; **TPH**, photo 380.
Baldwin, Phillip. *Lady in the Dark.* **TCI**, vol. 26, n. 1 (Jan 1992). 14.

Ball, Delbert & Marvin Carpentier. *Cyrano de Bergerac*. **TCI**, vol. 24, n. 3 (Mar 1990). 20.
Balla, Giacomo.
   Fireworks. **RSD**, illus. 351-354.
   Fuochi d'Artificio. **AST**, 70.
   Typografica. **RSD**, illus. 350.
Ballif, Ariel. *Beethoven*. **SFT**, 118.
Ballou, Bill. *The Comedy of Errors*. **TCI**, vol. 18, n. 5 (May 1984). 12.
Balo, Maurizio.
   The Damnation of Faust. **TDT**, vol. XX, n. 1 (Spring 1984). 7.
   The Flying Dutchman. **TCI**, vol. 27, n. 10 (Dec 1993). 16.
Balthes, Heinz. *The Deputy*. **RSD**, illus. 577.
Baltus. *State of Siege*. **SDW1**, 84.
Baral, Vicki & Gerry Hariton.
   Mail. **TCI**, vol. 22, n. 2 (Feb 1988). 51.
   South Pacific. **TCI**, vol. 22, n. 2 (Feb 1988). 51.
Barba, Eugenio & Bernt Nyberg.
   Kaspariana. **RSD**, illus. 633, 634; Kaspariana. **SDW3**, 142.
Barba, Eugenio, Iben Nagel Rasmussen, & Jacob Jensen. *Ferai*. **SDW3**, 146.
Barber, David M. *Anna Christie*. **TDT**, vol. XXVI, n. 1 (Spring 1990). 18 of insert.
Barbey, Valdo. *Sept Chansons*. **DIT**, plate 103.
Barburini, Gilberto.
   Ardelio e la Margherita. **SDE**, 30.
   Il Trovatore. **SDE**, 29.
Barcelo, Randy. *Blood Wedding*. **DDT**, 440a.
Barch, Ruddi. *Iphigenia in Taurus*. **SDL**, 33.
Bardo, Dagmar. *Ain't Misbehavin'*. **BSE4**, 71.
Bardon, Henry.
   Cendrillion. **TCI**, vol. 18, n. 1 (Jan 1984). 8.
   Ride a Cock Horse. **DMS**, plates 59, 60.
Bardon, Henry & David Walker.
   La Bohème. **TCI**, vol. 13, n. 3 (May/Jun 1979). 20.
   Così fan tutte. **CGA**, 178.
Barendse, Ferry. *Medea*. **SDW3**, 29.
Barker, Rochelle. *Othello*. **TDT**, vol. XXV, n. 3 (Fall 1989). 37.
Barkhin, Sergei.
   Dostoevsky House. **TDT**, vol. XIX, n. 1 (Spring 1983). 21.
   Romeo and Juliet. **TDT**, vol. XIX, n. 1 (Spring 1983). front cover, 20.
   Tartuffe. **SDW3**, 68.
Barkla, Jack.
   The Country Wife. **TCI**, vol. 16, n. 8 (Oct 1982). 24; **TCI**, vol. 18, n. 4 (Apr 1984). 10.
   The 500 Hats of Bartholomew Cubbins. **TCI**, vol. 17, n. 7 (Aug/Sep 1983). 31.
   Frankenstein. **TCI**, vol. 22, n. 5 (May 1988). 45.
   Hamlet. **TDT**, vol. XXII, n. 4 (Winter 1987). 9.
   Mr. Pickwick's Christmas. **TCI**, vol. 17, n. 7 (Aug/Sep 1983). 29.
   Requiem for a Nun. **TCI**, vol. 17, n. 7 (Aug/Sep 1983). 23; **TCI**, vol. 18, n. 7 (Aug/Sep 1984). 41.
   Room Service. **TCI**, vol. 17, n. 7 (Aug/Sep 1983). 29.
Barlach, Ernst. *Der Blaue Boll*. **AST**, 209.
Barlow, Alan. *Norma*. **CGA**, 142.
Barnes, Robert. *Peter Pan*. **TDP**, 119.

Barratt, Watson.
  The Rivals. **WTP**, 130, 131.
  Three Waltzes. **RBS**, 157.
  The Time of Your Life. **TAB**, 61; **WTP**, 181.
  The Wonder Bar. **MCN**, 103.
Barreca, Christopher.
  Captains Courageous. **TCI**, vol. 27, n. 1 (Jan 1993). 5.
  The Heliotrope Bouquet by Scott Joplin and Louis Chauvin. **TCI**, vol. 25, n. 5 (May 1991). 10.
  Our Country's Good. **TCI**, vol. 25, n. 3 (Mar 1991). 5, 41.
Barreiro, Manuel. *The Crucible.* **SDW3**, 131.
Barsacq, Alberte. *Lady Macbeth from Minsk.* **TCI**, vol. 27, n. 5 (May 1993). 11.
Barsacq, André.
  Colombe. **SDW1**, 84.
  Ring Around the Moon. **SDW1**, 84.
  Savonarola. **RSD**, illus. 108.
  Volpone. **RSD**, illus. 398; **SDW1**, 84; **TAT**, plate 270; **TPH**, photo 357.
Bartau. *Rebecca.* **SDW1**, 84.
Barth, Ruodi.
  Blood Wedding. **SDW2**, 109.
  Carmina Burana. **TCI**, vol. 11, n. 2 (Mar/Apr 1977). 19.
  Don Carlos. **OPE**, 150, 154, 156, 159, 160, 162.
  The Liar. **SDW1**, 113.
Bartz, Axel & Bill Passmore. *Pericole.* **TCI**, vol. 27, n. 5 (May 1993). 12.
Baruch & Co. *The Girl in the Taxi.* **MCD**, plate 94.
Basing, Charles & Hewlett. *Beyond the Horizon.* **MCN**, 49.
Basing, Charles, Ernest Gros, J.M. Hewlett, & A.T. Hewlett. *Chantecler.* **MCN**, 36.
Battersby, Martin. *La Voix Humaine.* **TCI**, vol. 13, n. 3 (May/Jun 1979). 21.
Baty, Gaston.
  Cri des coeurs. **RSD**, illus. 416.
  The Dybbuk. **RSD**, illus. 415.
  Madame Bovary. **SOW**, plate 65; **TPH**, photo 359.
  Maya. **RSD**, illus. 413; **SCM**, 48.
  Tetes de rechange. **RSD**, illus. 414.
Bauchau, B., R. Moscoso, J. N. Cordier, A. Ferreira, Cl. Forget, G. Cl. Francois, L. de Grandmaison, & A. Salomon.
  The Revolutionary City Belongs to this World. **SDW4**, illus. 385-390.
Bauer-Ecsy, Leni.
  Don Pasquale. **OPE**, 137, 142, 145, 146.
  Die Frau ohne Schatten. **OPE**, 234, 240, 242, 248.
  The House of Bernarda Alba. **SDW1**, 62.
  Der Mond. **SIP**, 298.
  Phaedra. **SDW1**, 62.
  Under Milkwood. **SDW2**, 57.
  Volpone. **SDW2**, 61.
Baumeister, Willi.
  Ariodante. **SCM**, 65.
  Kasperlespiele. **AST**, 160.
  Das Klagelied. **AST**, 158.
  Liberty. **RSD**, illus. 243.
  Macbeth. **AST**, 158.

Monte Cassino. **AST**, 159.

Transfiguration. **RSD**, illus. 244, 245.

Die Wandlung. **AST**, 158.

Bay, Howard.

The Autumn Garden. **TCI**, vol. 17, n. 2 (Feb 1983). 14.

Brooklyn, USA. **SDB**, 47; **TCI**, vol. 17, n. 2 (Feb 1983). 54.

Carmen. **SDB**, 71, 108; **SDL**, plates 8-14a; **SDT**, 44; **SDW2**, 231; **TDT**, n. 3 (Dec 1965). inside back cover.

Carmen Jones. **BWM**, 332; **TCI**, vol. 17, n. 2 (Feb 1983). 12, 55; **TDT**, n. 19 (Dec 1969). 22; **TMT**, 153.

Casey Jones. **SDB**, 110.

A Certain Joy. **SDB**, 116.

The Children's Hour. **TCI**, vol. 17, n. 2 (Feb 1983). 15.

Come Back Little Sheba. **SDA**, 228; **TCI**, vol. 17, n. 2 (Feb 1983). 15; **TDT**, n. 19 (Dec 1969). 21; **WTP**, 205.

Deep Are the Roots. **SDB**, 42; **TCI**, vol. 17, n. 2 (Feb 1983). 14.

The Desperate Hours. **SDA**, 229; **TCI**, vol. 17, n. 2 (Feb 1983). 15.

Dog Beneath the Skin. **SDB**, 189; **TCI**, vol. 17, n. 2 (Feb 1983). 10.

Follow the Girls. **SDB**, 59; **TCI**, vol. 17, n. 2 (Feb 1983). 12, 54.

Halloween. **CSD**, 65; **SDB**, 193; **TCI**, vol. 17, n. 2 (Feb 1983). 17.

Interlock. **SDA**, 206.

Life and Death of an American. **NTO**, facing 300; **SDB**, 190; **SOW**, plate 87; **TCI**, vol. 17, n. 2 (Feb 1983). 11.

The Little Foxes. **MCN**, 144; **SDA**, 203; **TCI**, vol. 17, n. 2 (Feb 1983). 19; **TCI**, vol. 17, n. 2 (Feb 1983). 19; **TDT**, n. 19 (Dec 1969). 20; **TDT**, n. 19 (Dec 1969). 21; **WTP**, 177.

The Love for Three Oranges. **SDB**, 192; **TCI**, vol. 17, n. 2 (Feb 1983). 11.

Magdalena. **SDB**, 72; **TDT**, n. 19 (Dec 1969). 23.

Man of La Mancha. **CSD**, 61; **DPT**, 325; **SFT**, 6; **TCI**, vol. 17, n. 2 (Feb 1983). 17; **TDT**, n. 5 (May 1966). 25.

Marching Song. **DPT**, 329; **SOW**, plate 85; **TCI**, vol. 17, n. 2 (Feb 1983). 11.

Marinka. **SDW1**, 192.

Midsummer. **SDB**, 98.

Milk and Honey. **BWM**, 305.

The Music Man. **BWM**, 298, 299; **SDA**, 252; **SDB**, 57, 109; **TCI**, vol. 17, n. 2 (Feb 1983). 16; **TCI**, vol. 20, n. 5 (May 1986). 20.

My Mother, My Father and Me. **SDB**, 196.

Night of the Auk. **SDB**, 112; **TCI**, vol. 17, n. 2 (Feb 1983). 16; **TDT**, n. 19 (Dec 1969). 23.

One Third of a Nation. **DPT**, 324; **SDA**, 125; **SDB**, 188; **SDB**, 89; **SIP**, 310; **TCI**, vol. 17, n. 2 (Feb 1983). 9; **TCI**, vol. 17, n. 2 (Feb 1983). 9; **TPH**, photo 479.

One Touch of Venus. **WMC**, 203.

I Pagliacci. **TCI**, vol. 17, n. 2 (Feb 1983). 13.

Peer Gynt. **SDB**, 50.

Red Roses for Me. **TCI**, vol. 17, n. 2 (Feb 1983). 55.

Show Boat. **DPT**, 327; **SDB**, 111; **SDB**, 58; **TCI**, vol. 17, n. 2 (Feb 1983). 18; **TCI**, vol. 17, n. 2 (Feb 1983). 18; **TMI**, 127; **WTP**, 220, 221.

Something for the Boys. **DPT**, 41; **SDA**, 252; **TCI**, vol. 17, n. 2 (Feb 1983). 12.

Til Eulenspiegel. **SDB**, 96; **SDW1**, 192.

Toys in the Attic. **SDB**, 43; **TCI**, vol. 17, n. 2 (Feb 1983). 14.

Trojan Incident. **TCI**, vol. 17, n. 2 (Feb 1983). 10.

Uncle Harry. **TCI**, vol. 17, n. 2 (Feb 1983). 54.

Up in Central Park. **CSD**, 18; **DPT**, 328; **SDA**, 252; **SDB**, 56; **SDL**, 54; **SDW1**, 192; **TCI**, vol. 17, n. 2 (Feb 1983). 13; **TDT**, n. 19 (Dec 1969). 22; **WMC**, 48.

The Utter Glory of Morrissey Hale. **TCI**, vol. 17, n. 2 (Feb 1983). 55.

The Wall. **SDW2**, 233; **TCI**, vol. 17, n. 2 (Feb 1983). 55.

Bazaine, Jean. *In His Garden Don Perlimplin Loves Belisa*. **AST**, 241.

Beard, Mark. *Big Hotel*. **TCI**, vol. 24, n. 1 (Jan 1990). 23.

Beaton, Cecil.

Apparitions. **CBS**, 53; **SDW1**, 170.

Coco. **TCI**, vol. 14, n. 1 (Jan/Feb 1980). 20; **TMT**, plate 12.

Crisis in Heaven. **CBS**, 33.

The Cry of the Peacock. **CBS**, 44, 45.

The Duchess of Malfi. **CBS**, 19.

A Family and a Fortune. **CBS**, 61.

First Class Passengers Only. **CBS**, 26.

The Gainsborough Girls. **CBS**, 51; **SDW1**, 169.

The Gyp's Princess. **CBS**, 19.

Henry IV. **CBS**, 21.

Lady Windermere's Fan. **BTD**, 18; **CBS**, 18, 34, 36, 37, 59; **SOW**, plate 73; **WTP**, 132, 133.

Look After Lulu. **CBS**, 35.

Love's Labor's Lost. **CBS**, 49.

Quadrille. **SDW1**, 170; **WTP**, 162.

The Return of the Prodigal. **CBS**, 39.

Saratoga. **CBS**, 36; **WMC**, 183.

The School for Scandal. **CBS**, 40, 41.

Streamline. **CBS**, 17.

Tenderloin. **BWM**, 294; **WMC**, 299.

Turandot. **CBS**, 76; **MOM**, 12.

Vanessa. **CBS**, 74.

Volpone. **CBS**, 17.

Beatty, John Lee.

Ain't Misbehavin'. **BWM**, 338; **TCI**, vol. 12, n. 6 (Oct 1978). 15.

Alice in Wonderland. **TCI**, vol. 17, n. 4 (Apr 1983). 16, 17.

The Amorous Flea. **DPT**, between 124 & 125.

Angels Fall. **DDT**, 544.

Anna Christie. **TCI**, vol. 27, n. 4 (Apr 1993). 7.

Ashes. **ASD1**, 6; **TDT**, vol. XVIII, n. 4 (Winter 1982). 8.

Baby. **MBM**, 164; **TCI**, vol. 19, n. 5 (May 1985). 23.

Battle of Angels. **DPT**, 15.

The Bed Before Yesterday. **TDT**, vol. XVIII, n. 4 (Winter 1982). 7.

Black Comedy. **TCI**, vol. 27, n. 9 (Nov 1993). 8.

Broadway. **TCI**, vol. 15, n. 5 (May 1981). 22.

Burn This. **DDT**, 540; **TCI**, vol. 21, n. 5 (May 1987). 37.

Candide. **BSE4**, 97.

Come Back Little Sheba. **DPT**, 121.

Crimes of the Heart. **DDT**, 301; **TCI**, vol. 16, n. 9 (Nov/Dec 1982). 26; **TDT**, vol. XVIII, n. 4 (Winter 1982). 6.

The Destiny of Me. **TCI**, vol. 27, n. 1 (Jan 1993). 7.

The Diviners. **DDT**, 546.

Duet for One. **DDT**, 382; **DSL**, figure 2.7(a).

5th of July. **ASD1**, 10; **DDT**, 440d; **TDT**, vol. XVIII, n. 4 (Winter 1982). 10, 11.

Fools. **ASD1**, between 70 & 71; **TDT**, vol. XVIII, n. 4 (Winter 1982). 7.

Hit the Deck. **TCI**, vol. 11, n. 6 (Nov/Dec 1977). 10; **TCI**, vol. 12, n. 6 (Oct 1978). 23.

The House of Bernarda Alba. **ASD1**, 9; **TCI**, vol. 12, n. 6 (Oct 1978). 21.

Johnny On a Spot. **ASD1**, 5, **TDT**, vol. XVIII, n. 4 (Winter 1982). 6.

Knock Knock. **TCI**, vol. 10, n. 3 (May/Jun 1976). 24; **TCI**, vol. 12, n. 6 (Oct 1978).
    18, 19; **TCI**, vol. 16, n. 5 (May 1982). 28.

A Life in the Theatre. **DDT**, 548; **TCI**, vol. 12, n. 6 (Oct 1978). 18.

Lips Together, Teeth Apart. **DDT**, 30.

Little Johnny Jones. **TCI**, vol. 15, n. 8 (Oct 1981). 29; **TCI**, vol. 21, n. 9 (Nov 1987).
    37.

Livin' Dolls. **ASD1**, 11.

Look Homeward Angel. **ASD1**, between 70 & 71.

The Miss Firecracker Contest. **DDT**, 543.

The Most Happy Fella. **TCI**, vol. 25, n. 6 (Aug/Sep 1991). 14.

The Mound Builders. **DPT**, 23; **TCI**, vol. 12, n. 6 (Oct 1978). 20; **TCI**, vol. 9, n. 3
    (May/Jun 1975). 2.

Mr. Gogol and Mr. Preen. **DDT**, 545.

Mrs. Murray's Farm. **TCI**, vol. 12, n. 6 (Oct 1978). 21.

The Octette Bridge Club. **TDT**, vol. XXII, n. 4 (Winter 1987). 18.

Oh, Hell. **DDT**, 11.

Philadelphia, Here I Come! **DPT**, 333.

Rebel Women. **ASD1**, 2; **TCI**, vol. 12, n. 6 (Oct 1978). 21.

Redwood Curtain. **TCI**, vol. 27, n. 4 (Apr 1993). 8; **DDT**, 469.

The Rover. **TCI**, vol. 23, n. 7 (Aug/Sep 1989). 20.

The Sisters Rosensweig. **DDT**, 350.

Song of Singapore. **TCI**, vol. 25, n. 6 (Aug/Sep 1991). 32.

A Tale Told. **ASD1**, 5; **TDT**, vol. XVIII, n. 4 (Winter 1982). 7.

Talley's Folly. **ASD1**, 13; **DDT**, 152a; **TCI**, vol. 16, n. 5 (May 1982). 29; **TDT**, vol.
    XVIII, n. 4 (Winter 1982). 5.

Three Men on a Horse. **DDT**, 547.

Tip-Toes. **TCI**, vol. 12, n. 6 (Oct 1978). 22, 23.

Tomorrow's Monday. **DDT**, 542.

A Tribute to Lili Lamont. **TCI**, vol. 12, n. 6 (Oct 1978). 21.

The Water Engine. **TCI**, vol. 12, n. 6 (Oct 1978). 20.

The Way of the World. **CSD**, 62; **DPT**, 43.

Whoopee. **TCI**, vol. 12, n. 6 (Oct 1978). 23.

Beavan, Jenny. *Carmen.* **CGA**, 187.

Bechtler, Hildegard.
    Electra. **BTD**, 74.
    The Tourist Guide. **BTD**, 74.
    Coriolanus. **TCI**, vol. 27, n. 8 (Oct 1993). 11.

Beck, Julian.
    Frankenstein. **RSD**, illus. 623, 624; **SDW3**, 171.
    Oedipus Tyrannos. **SDW3**, 24.

Beck, Peter Dean. *Tosca.* **TCI**, vol. 20, n. 8 (Oct 1986). 21.

Becker, Victor.
    The Italian Straw Hat. **TCI**, vol. 29, n. 3 (Mar 1995). 62.
    Southern Cross. **TCI**, vol. 23, n. 10 (Dec 1989). 10.

Begovich, Patrice. *Feast of Youth.* **TCI**, vol. 20, n. 8 (Oct 1986). 16.

Beisker, Heinz. *Measure for Measure.* **SDW1**, 63.

Bel Geddes, Norman.
  Dante. **SDC**, plate 103.
  Dead End. **MCN**, 126; **SDA**, 103; **SOW**, plate 80.
  The Divine Comedy. **CSD**, 11; **DIT**, plates 118.1-119.2; **NTO**, facing 276; **RSD**, illus.
    440-442; **SDA**, 69; **SIP**, 6; **SOW**, plate 79; **TCM**, xvii; **TCS2**, plates 220, 221;
    TDT, vol. XVI, n. 1 (Spring 1980). 13.
  The Eternal Road. **RSD**, illus. 439; **TPH**, photo 466.
  Fifty Million Frenchmen. **BMF**, 38.
  Flying Colors. **RBS**, 69; **SCM**, 107.
  Hamlet. **SDA**, 213; **SOS**, 173; **SOW**, facing frontispiece, plate 49;
    TAS, 166, 167; **TPH**, photo 475.
  Jeanne d'Arc. **TCS2**, plate 70; **TDT**, n. 18 (Oct 1969). 4-11.
  King Lear. **DOT**, 227; **SCM**, 104, 105; **SDC**, plate 102; **SOW**, plate 47; **TAT**, plates
    505, 506; **TCS2**, plate 94.
  Lazarus Laughed. **SDC**, plate 101; **TCS2**, plate 69.
  Lysistrata. **SCM**, 103; **SDA**, 213.
  The Miracle. **MCN**, 66; **MRH**, between 6 & 7, between 248 & 249, facing 314; **SDD**,
    between 210 & 211.
  The Mother of Christ. **SDC**, plate 101.
  The Patriot. **SDB**, 40; **SDT**, 37.
  St. Joan. **RSD**, illus. 438.
  The Singing Globe. **TCS2**, plate 386.
Belcher, Richard. *Strider*. **TCI**, vol. 16, n. 7 (Aug/Sep 1982). 34.
Belden, Ursula.
  K2. **TCI**, vol. 19, n. 5 (May 1985). 26.
  Night of the Iguana. **TDT**, vol. XXX, n. 3 (Summer 1994). 4.
  Room Service. **TCI**, vol. 21, n. 7 (Aug/Sep 1987). 35.
  Serenading Louie. **TCI**, vol. 21, n. 7 (Aug/Sep 1987). 36.
  Tom Jones. **BSE4**, 73.
Belli, Keith. *The Mystery of Edwin Drood*. **TCI**, vol. 23, n. 4 (Apr 1989). 55.
Bellman, Willard F. *The Rake's Progress*. **DSL**, plate VIII; **SST**, plate XVI.
Belojanski, Stacha. *Eros from the Other World*. **SDW1**, 133.
Benavente, Saulo.
  Amphitryon 38. **SDW1**, 33.
  Azouk. **SDW1**, 35.
  Facundo in the Citadel. **SDW2**, 25.
  Santos Vega. **SDW1**, 33.
  Where Death Fastens Its Flags. **SDW2**, 25.
Benedek, Kata. *Faust*. **SCM**, 71.
Benois, Alexander.
  Andrea Chenier. **SDE**, 33.
  Armida's Pavilion. **RSD**, illus. 42; **SDE**, 31.
  Camille. **SCM**, 42.
  Fée de Sagasse. **FCS**, plate 173, color plate 18; **SDO**, plate 18.
  The Idiot. **RSC**, 20.
  The Imaginary Invalid. **FCS**, plate 172; **SDO**, 194.
  La Locandiera. **TCS2**, plates 9, 10.
  Parsifal. **RSC**, 20.
  Petrouchka. **RSC**, 22; **RSD**, illus. 41, 43; **SDE**, 32; **SDR**, 26.
  The Stone Guest. **RSC**, 23.
  Les Sylphides. **RSD**, illus. 44.

Benois, Nicola.
  Ann Boleyn. **SDW2**, 121.
  La Bohème. **SDE**, 34.
  Boris Godounov. **SDE**, 35; **TCS2**, plate 232.
  Jeanne au Bucher. **SDE**, 39.
  Khovanschina. **SDE**, 33.
  Nabucco. **TCI**, vol. 16, n. 8 (Oct 1982). 22.
  Les Noces. **SDE**, 38.
  Rigoletto. **SDW2**, 121.
  The Siege of Corinth. **TCI**, vol. 10, n. 5 (Oct 1976). 17.
  Siegfried. **SDE**, 34.
  I Vespri Siciliani. **SDE**, 35.
Benson, Gary. *I'm Not Rappaport.* **TDT**, vol. XXVIII, n. 2 (Spring 1992). 11 of insert.
Benson, Susan. *The Tempest.* **TCI**, vol. 26, n. 9 (Nov 1992). 29.
Benson, Tom.
  Cabaret. **SDT**, 300; **SDT**, between 152 & 153; **TDP**, 108-110.
  The Life and Adventures of Nicholas Nickleby. **TDP**, 24, 26.
  Richard III. **SDT**, 280.
Bérard, Christian.
  Amphitryon. **WTP**, 45.
  Clock Symphony. **SDW1**, 82.
  Don Juan. **RSD**, illus. 410, 411; **SDW1**, 83.
  Les Forains. **SDW1**, 85.
  Les Fourberies de Scapin. **SDR**, 31.
  The Madwoman of Chaillot. **SDB**, 66; **SDW1**, 83; **WTP**, 118, 119.
  Scapin the Trickster. **SDW1**, 82.
  The School for Wives. **RSD**, illus. 406-409; **SDW1**, 82, 83; **SOW**, plate 38.
Berg, Yngye. *Himlens Hemlighet.* **TCS2**, plate 139.
Bergallo, Armando & Hector Vilche.
  The Transparent City. **TDT**, vol. XX, n. 1 (Spring 1984). front cover.
Berger, Genia. *Mihal, Daughter of Saul.* **SDW2**, 117.
Bergling, Birger. *The Rake's Progress.* **SDR**, 52.
Bergner, Yossl. *Six Wings for Everybody.* **SDW2**, 118.
Berka, Tomás.
  Candide. **TCI**, vol. 18, n. 1 (Jan 1984). 10; **TDT**, vol. XX, n. 1 (Spring 1984). 8.
  The Cherry Orchard. **TDT**, vol. XXIII, n. 4 (Winter 1988). 28; **TDT**, vol. XXVII, n. 4
      (Fall 1991). 47.
Berliner, Charles.
  A Christmas Carol. **TCI**, vol. 21, n. 8 (Oct 1987). 40.
  To Die for Grenada. **BSE5**, 14; **TCI**, vol. 21, n. 8 (Oct 1987). 45.
Berman, Eugene.
  Danses Concertantes. **SDR**, 32.
  Don Giovanni. **MOM**, 13.
  La Forza del Destino. **DPT**, 120; **SDA**, 262, 263.
  Giselle. **SDE**, 44, 45.
  The Island God. **SDE**, 41.
  Rigoletto. **SDB**, 66; **SDE**, 46, 47; **SDW1**, 193; **TCM**, xxi.
  Symphonie Italienne. **FCS**, plate 208.
  Twelfth Night. **TPH**, photo 483.
Bernard, Roger & Joelle Roustan. *I Trionfi del Petrarca.* **SDW4**, illus. 289-294.
Bernedo, Mario. *El Desden, con el Desden.* **TCI**, vol. 26, n. 4 (Apr 1992). 35.

The Phantom of the Opera. **ALW**, 186-188, 190, 191; **BTD**, 156, 157; **DDT**, 24c;
    HPR, 351, 357; **MBM**, 6, 68, 70; **TCI**, vol. 21, n. 1 (Jan 1987). 10; **TCI**, vol. 22,
    n. 2 (Feb 1988). 32-35; **TCI**, vol. 22, n. 2 (Feb 1988). 36; **TCI**, vol. 23, n. 2 (Feb
    1989). 16.
Toussaint. **TDT**, vol. XIX, n. 1 (Spring 1983). 6; **TCI**, vol. 15, n. 5 (May 1981). 15.
Die Walküre. **BTD**, 110.
Black, F. Scott. *The Sound of Music.* **TCI**, vol. 20, n. 5 (May 1986). 23.
Blackman, Robert.
    The Cherry Orchard. **TSY**, 164.
    Cyrano de Bergerac. **SST**, 377.
    Dandy Dick. **TCI**, vol. 6, n. 5 (Oct 1972). 16, 17.
    The Importance of Being Earnest. **TCI**, vol. 14, n. 4 (Sep 1980). 35.
    The Mikado. **TCI**, vol. 14, n. 4 (Sep 1980). 35.
    Much Ado About Nothing. **TCI**, vol. 14, n. 4 (Sep 1980). 35.
    Richard III. **SST**, 446; **TCI**, vol. 14, n. 4 (Sep 1980). 18, 19.
    Valentine and Valentina. **TCI**, vol. 14, n. 4 (Sep 1980). 35.
Blake, Kathleen. *Tintypes.* **TCI**, vol. 20, n. 5 (May 1986). 25.
Blake, Warner.
    Brain. **CSD**, 63.
    Situation Comedy. **CSD**, 51; **TCI**, vol. 7, n. 5 (Oct 1973). 22.
Blanch, Lesley. *The Merchant of Venice.* **TAT**, plate 208.
Blane, Sue.
    Christmas Eve. **BTD**, 108, 109.
    Fear and Misery in the Third Reich. **TCI**, vol. 15, n. 7 (Aug/Sep 1981). 26.
    The Marriage of Figaro. **BTD**, 108, 109.
    Pygmalion. **TCI**, vol. 15, n. 7 (Aug/Sep 1981). 26.
Bleynie, Claude. *Suspense.* **SDW2**, 85.
Bliese, Thomas H.
    The Cherry Orchard. **BSE2**, 7.
    Exit the King. **TCI**, vol. 6, n. 6 (Nov/Dec 1972). 12, 13.
    Sour Angelica. **BSE1**, 14.
Bloodgood, William.
    Measure for Measure. **TCI**, vol. 15, n. 8 (Oct 1981). 8.
    A Streetcar Named Desire. **TCI**, vol. 11, n. 6 (Nov/Dec 1977). 8.
    The Waltz of the Toreadors. **TCI**, vol. 14, n. 4 (Sep 1980). 30.
Bloumberg, Ilmar. *Joan of Arc.* **SDW4**, illus. 210.
Boehlke, Bain. *Macbeth.* **TCI**, vol. 17, n. 7 (Aug/Sep 1983). 21.
Boehm, Herta.
    Macbeth. **SDE**, 48; **SDW1**, 62.
    The Mayor of Zalamea. **SDW2**, 57.
Boerner, Edward. *Hamlet.* **TCI**, vol. 14, n. 4 (Sep 1980). 15.
Bogaerts, John. *King John.* **SDW3**, 43.
Bohanetzky, Polly Scranton & Tanya Moiseiwitsch.
    The Inspector General. **TCI**, vol. 20, n. 7 (Aug/Sep 1986). 17.
Bohrer, Robert. *Ophelia and the Words.* **SDW4**, illus. 332, 333.
Boland, Bridgette. *The Prisoner.* **MOR**, 4.
Boley, James. *Mattress.* **TCI**, vol. 12, n. 1 (Jan/Feb 1978). 8.
Boll, André.
    Coriolanus. **SDW2**, 85.
    Oedipus. **SDW1**, 87.
Bondt, Werner de. *Lucifer and the Lord.* **TCI**, vol. 13, n. 6 (Nov/Dec 1979). 24.

Bonnat, Yves (Yves-Bonnat).
  Carmen. **SDW2**, 97.
  Joan at the Stake. **SDW1**, 87.
  Monsieur Beaucaire. **SDW1**, 85.
  Oedipus Rex. **SDW3**, 200.
  Siegfried. **SDW1**, 87.
  The Snow Knight. **SDW2**, 86.
  Star Turns Red. **SDW3**, 98.
Borges, Jacobo.
  Blood Wedding. **SDW2**, 243.
  The Glass Menagerie. **SDW2**, 243.
  The Inkpot. **SDW3**, 148.
Borisch, Frank. *The Hall.* **SDW3**, 148.
Boros, Frank. *Life With Father.* **TCI**, vol. 21, n. 7 (Aug/Sep 1987). 32.
Borovsky, David.
  The Convoy. **TDT**, vol. XII, n. 3 (Fall 1976). 41.
  Crime and Punishment. **TCI**, vol. 21, n. 4 (Apr 1987). 14.
  The Dawns are Quiet Here. **SDW4**, illus. 288; **TCI**, vol. 12, n. 7 (Nov/Dec 1978). 36,
    37.
  Hamlet. **SDW4**, illus. 26-30; **TCI**, vol. 12, n. 7 (Nov/Dec 1978). 32.
  Ivanov. **TDT**, vol. XVI, n. 1 (Spring 1980). 24; **TDT**, vol. XXIII, n. 4 (Winter 1988). 6,
    25.
  Lady Macbeth from Minsk. **SDW3**, 200.
  The Mother. **SDW3**, 96; **TCI**, vol. 12, n. 7 (Nov/Dec 1978). 35.
  The Rush Hour. **SDW3**, 140.
  Valentine and Valentina. **TCI**, vol. 12, n. 7 (Nov/Dec 1978). 35.
Boruzescu, Radu.
  Il Campanello. **TCI**, vol. 15, n. 5 (May 1981). 24.
  Waiting for Godot. **TCI**, vol. 15, n. 5 (May 1981). 24.
Borzik, Rolf.
  Arien. **TCI**, vol. 20, n. 2 (Feb 1986). 14; **TDT**, vol. XXII, n. 1 (Spring 1986). 10.
Bosquet, Thierry.
  Der Rosenkavalier. **SDW2**, 27.
  La Traviata. **SDW4**, illus. 140-142.
Bosserdet, Jean. *South Africa Amen.* **SDW3**, 161.
Bossoulaev, Anatoli. *The Optimistic Tragedy.* **SDW2**, 179.
Bottari, Michael & Ronald Case.
  The Mystery of Edwin Drood. **TCI**, vol. 23, n. 4 (Apr 1989). 53.
Bouchène, Dimitri.
  Pelléas and Mélisande. **SDE**, 50.
  Snow White. **SDW1**, 88.
Bourne, Mel. *The Male Animal.* **WTP**, 208.
Boutté, Jean-Luc. *Don Juan.* **DSL**, figure 2.8(d).
Boyce, Raymond.
  The Lady's Not for Burning. **SDW1**, 141.
  Ned Kelly. **SDW1**, 141.
Boylen, Daniel P. *Count Dracula.* **TCI**, vol. 11, n. 5 (Oct 1977). 36, 37.
Brade, Helmut & Ezio Toffolutti. *Margarete in Aix.* **SDW4**, illus. 319-323.
Bradley, Scott.
  The Lost Boys. **TCI**, vol. 25, n. 1 (Jan 1991). 34.
  The Notebooks of Leonardo Da Vinci. **TCI**, vol. 28, n. 1 (Jan 1994). 6.

Bradshaw, Laurence. *Macbeth*. **DIT**, plate 61.
Bragaglia, Anton Giulia.
    Oedipus Rex. **SCM**, 76.
    Pelléas and Mélisande. **TPH**, photo 381.
    Pierrot Funeste. **SCM**, 76.
    Samson. **SCM**, 76.
    La Torre Rossa. **TCS2**, plate 156.
Bragdon, Claude.
    Cyrano de Bergerac. **SDA**, 218, 219; **TCS2**, plate 136.
    The Glittering Gate. **TAT**, plate 489.
    Hamlet. **SDC**, plate 52.
    Othello. **FCS**, plate 197; **SDO**, 225.
Braque, Georges.
    Les Facheux. **AST**, 86; **AST**, 88; **RSD**, illus. 310.
    Tartuffe. **AST**, 86; **RSD**, illus. 412.
Brayer, Yves.
    Dolores or the Miracle of the Plain Woman. **SDW2**, 86.
    Love the Sorcerer. **SDW1**, 88.
Brazda, Jan.
    Götterdämmerung. **OPE**, 190, 192, 194, 196.
    Parsifal. **SDR**, 20.
    Siegfried. **SDW3**, 180.
Bregni, Paolo.
    Cin-Ci-La. **SIO**, 15.
    The Cloak. **SIO**, 16.
    The Condemnation of Lucullus (Brecht). **SIO**, 20-23.
    Julius Caesar. **SIO**, 17.
    Madame Butterfly. **SIO**, 17.
    I Pagliacci. **SIO**, 18, 19.
Breyer, Gaston. *Trip to the Coast*. **SDW2**, 25.
Brianchon, Maurice. *False Confidences*. **SDW1**, 88.
Brill, Robert.
    Fortinbras. **TCI**, vol. 25, n. 8 (Oct 1991). 22.
    The Good Woman of Setzuan. **TCI**, vol. 28, n. 9 (Nov 1994). 8.
    Pravda. **TCI**, vol. 29, n. 5 (May 1995). 8.
    Pre-Paradise Sorry Now. **TCI**, vol. 26, n. 1 (Jan 1992). 36.
    The Revenger's Tragedy. **TDT** vol. XXXI, n. 2 (Spring 1995). 16.
Brockman, C. Lance.
    Charley's Aunt. **BSE3**, 12.
    The Girl of the Golden West. **BSE4**, 16.
    Man of La Mancha. **TDT**, n. 36 (Feb 1974). 29.
Broë, Roger. *Fidelio*. **SDW2**, 27.
Bromberg, Louis. *The Field God*. **MCN**, 84.
Brook, Peter.
    King Lear. **SDW3**, 52.
    The Mahabharata. **TCI**, vol. 21, n. 9 (Nov 1987). 7, 27-30.
    Titus Andronicus. **DMS**, plates 48, 49; **SDW2**, 216.
Brotherston, Lez.
    Princess Ivona. **BTD**, 88.
    Silverlake. **BTD**, 138.
Brown, Bado. *Red Noses*. **TCI**, vol. 26, n. 3 (Mar 1992). 39.

Brown, Lewis. *Becket.* **TCI**, vol. 9, n. 1 (Jan/Feb 1975). 11.

Brown, Louis & Stuart Wurzel. *A Flea in Her Ear.* **TCI**, vol. 6, n. 5 (Oct 1972). 17.

Brown, Michael. *A Cola Day in Hell.* **TDT**, vol. XXX, n. 5 (Fall 1994). 61.

Brown, Paul. *Lady Macbeth from Minsk.* **TCI**, vol. 29, n. 2 (Feb 1995). 6.

Brown, Penny. *Rutherford and Son.* **BTD**, 66.

Brown, Zack.

    The Abduction from the Seraglio. **TDT**, vol. XXVII, n. 3 (Summer 1991). 11.

    Candide. **TCI**, vol. 18, n. 3 (Mar 1984). 28.

    The Consul. **DDT**, 249.

    Gaité Parisienne. **DDT**, 152d.

    La Gioconda. **TCI**, vol. 17, n. 9 (Nov/Dec 1983). 20.

    The Magic Flute. **TDT**, vol. XXVII, n. 2 (Spring 1991). 36; **TDT**, vol. XXVII, n. 3
        (Summer 1991). 11.

    Manon. **DDT**, 152a, 267.

    The Marriage of Figaro. **TDT**, vol. XXVII, n. 2 (Spring 1991). 37; **TDT**, vol. XXVII,
        n. 3 (Summer 1991). 10.

    The Merry Widow. **DDT**, 312a.

    On Your Toes. **DDT**, 154.

    Otello. **TCI**, vol. 27, n. 3 (Mar 1993). 6.

    Rigoletto. **DDT**, 161.

    La Sonnambula. **DDT**, 301.

    Spring's Awakening. **DDT**, 9.

Bruland, Arne. *The Man Outside.* **SDW1**, 152.

Brulin, Tone. *Macbeth.* **SDW1**, 43.

Brumley, Keith. *Sleuth.* **TCI**, vol. 22, n. 5 (May 1988). 31.

Bubeník, Kvetoslav.

    Don Carlos. **SDW2**, 41.

    Electra. **SDR**, 58, 83.

Buchholz, Gerhard T.

    Electra. **TCS2**, plate 215.

    Salomé. (Strauss). **TCS2**, plate 214.

Buchmuller, Eva.

    Dreamland Burns. **TCI**, vol. 20, n. 7 (Aug/Sep 1986). 10.

    L-Train to Eldorado. **TCI**, vol. 22, n. 9 (Nov 1988). 12.

Buck, Gene Davis. *The Red Shoes.* **TCI**, vol. 17, n. 7 (Aug/Sep 1983). 31.

Buckingham, William.

    The Lower Depths. **BSE1**, 32; **TCI**, vol. 13, n. 3 (May/Jun 1979). 38.

Buderwitz, Tom. *Great Expectations.* **SDT**, 297.

Buffet, Bernard. *Carmen.* **SDW2**, 86.

Burbridge, Edward.

    Chemin de Fer. **TCI**, vol. 8, n. 6 (Nov/Dec 1974). 17.

    The Dream on Monkey Mountain. **SDL**, 7; **SDW3**, 151; **TCI**, vol. 8, n. 1 (Jan/Feb
        1974). 17.

    The Song of the Lusitanian Bogey. **TCI**, vol. 8, n. 2 (Mar/Apr 1974). 11.

    Status Quo Vadis. **TCI**, vol. 7, n. 3 (May/Jun 1973). 23.

    The Visit. **TCI**, vol. 8, n. 6 (Nov/Dec 1974). 17.

Burchette, Ginger Mae. *Escurial.* **BSE2**, 41.

Burgos, Emilio.

    A Dreamer for the People. **SDW2**, 75.

    The Thrust. **SDW2**, 76.

    Today is a Holiday. **SDW2**, 79.

Burman, Sigfrido. *The Dolphins*. **SDW3**, 147.
Burra, Edward.
   Don Quixote. **SDW1**, 173.
   Miracle in the Gorbals. **SDW1**, 170.
Burri, Alberto. *The Adventures of a Poor Christian*. **SDW3**, 118.
Burridge, Walter. *The Prince of Pilsen*. **MCD**, plate 50.
Burroughs, Robert C.
   Arsenic and Old Lace. **SDT**, 64.
   Dinny and the Witches. **SDT**, 295.
   The Guardsman. **SDT**, 117.
   Misalliance. **SDT**, 292.
   Peer Gynt. **SDT**, 278, and between 152 & 153.
   The Royal Family. **SDT**, 281.
   The School for Husbands. **SDT**, 284.
   Under Two Flags. **SDT**, 288.
Bury, John.
   Amadeus. **TCI**, vol. 15, n. 3 (Mar 1981). 10, 11; **TCI**, vol. 26, n. 1 (Jan 1992). 47.
   Betrayal. **BTD**, 62; **TCI**, vol. 14, n. 3 (May/Jun 1980). 6.
   La Calisto. **TCI**, vol. 26, n. 1 (Jan 1992). 48.
   Coriolanus. **BTD**, 15, 63.
   Così fan Tutti. **BTD**, 114; **TCI**, vol. 13, n. 3 (May/Jun 1979). 21.
   Don Giovanni. **TCI**, vol. 13, n. 3 (May/Jun 1979). 21.
   Electra. **TCI**, vol. 26, n. 1 (Jan 1992). 46.
   Hamlet. **RSD**, illus. 520; **TCI**, vol. 11, n. 5 (Oct 1977). 33.
   Happy Days. **TCI**, vol. 11, n. 5 (Oct 1977). 32.
   The Homecoming. **SDR**, 7; **TCI**, vol. 26, n. 1 (Jan 1992). 45.
   Landscape-Silence. **SDW3**, 153; **TDT**, vol. XII, n. 3 (Fall 1976). 36.
   A Midsummer Night's Dream. **BTD**, 114, 115; **TCI**, vol. 26, n. 1 (Jan 1992). 47.
   Moses and Aaron. **RSD**, illus. 594; **SDB**, 77; **SDR**, 49; **TCI**, vol. 26, n. 1 (Jan 1992).
      49; **CGA**, 163; **CGA**, 163.
   L'Orione. **TCI**, vol. 26, n. 1 (Jan 1992). 48.
   The Other Animals. **DMS**, plate 51.
   The Physicists. **SIP**, 65.
   Richard II. **SDG**, 194.
   The Rothschilds. **TCI**, vol. 26, n. 1 (Jan 1992). 49; **TCI**, vol. 4, n. 6 (Nov/Dec 1970).
      22-26.
   Salomé. **BTD**, 115.
   Silence. **TDT**, vol. XIX, n. 3 (Fall 1983). 7.
   Strife. **TCI**, vol. 13, n. 6 (Nov/Dec 1979). 25; **TDT**, vol. XVI, n. 1 (Spring 1980). 24.
   Tamburlaine the Great. **TCI**, vol. 11, n. 5 (Oct 1977). 32.
   Tristan and Isolde. **TDT**, vol. XIX, n. 3 (Fall 1983). 7.
   Volpone. **TCI**, vol. 11, n. 5 (Oct 1977). 32; **TDT**, vol. XIX, n. 3 (Fall 1983). 6.
   The Wars of the Roses. **SDW3**, 35; **TDT**, vol. XIX, n. 3 (Fall 1983). 6.
   You Won't Always Be on Top. **DMS**, plate 52.
Butlin, Roger.
   Alceste. **TCI**, vol. 17, n. 4 (Apr 1983). 8.
   The Barber of Seville. **OPE**, 130, 133, 134.
   Eugene Onegin. **TCI**, vol. 15, n. 5 (May 1981). 11, 14, 15.
Butsch, Tom.
   Carousel. **TCI**, vol. 14, n. 5 (Oct 1980). 24, 25.
   Fiddler on the Roof. **TCI**, vol. 14, n. 5 (Oct 1980). 24.

-C-

Clavé, Antoni.
   Carmen. **RSD**, illus. 493; Carmen. **SDW1**, 90.
   Devil en 24 Heures. **SDR**, 33.
   The Love of Don Perlimplin and Belisa in the Garden. **SDW1**, 90.
Clay, Paul & Lora Nelson. *A Window on a Nether Sea*. **TCI**, vol. 25, n. 4 (Apr 1991). 25.
Clayburg, Jim.
   LSD-Just the High Points. **TCI**, vol. 23, n. 5 (May 1989). 47.
   Oedipus (Seneca). **TDT**, vol. XIV, n. 2 (Summer 1978). 29.
Clerici, Fabrizio.
   Armida. **SDE**, 65; Armida. **SDW1**, 121.
   Poppea's Coronation. **SDW1**, 121.
   Turandot. **SIO**, 144, 145.
Clifton, Randy.
   From the Journal of Hazard McCauley. **TCI**, vol. 19, n. 7 (Aug/Sep 1985). 41.
Cloffe. *The Pretenders*. **SDR**, 66.
Clonis, Cl. *Oedipus Rex* **SDW1**, 109.
Coble, McKay.
   For Lease or Sale. **TCI**, vol. 25, n. 3 (Mar 1991). 49.
   The Rivals. **TCI**, vol. 25, n. 3 (Mar 1991). 46.
Coburg, Wally. *Gyubal Wahazar*. **TCI**, vol. 8, n. 4 (Sep 1974). 4.
Cochran, Randel R. *Mother Hicks*. **BSE4**, 76.
Cochren, Felix E.
   And the World Laughs With You. **TCI**, vol. 28, n. 4 (Apr 1994). 6.
   Home. **DDT**, 250.
Cocteau, Jean.
   Antigone. **SDE**, 65.
   Les Chevaliers de la Table Ronde. **TPH**, photo 363.
   Oedipus Rex. **SDW1**, 93.
   Phaedra. **AST**, 121.
Colasanti, Veniero.
   The Marriage of Figaro. **SDE**, 66.
   Mary Stuart. **SDW1**, 122.
   The Obedient Daughter. **SDE**, 66, 67; **SDW1**, 122.
   Turandot. **SDW1**, 122.
Colasanti, Veniero & John Moore. *La Traviata*. **SDW2**, 123.
Colavecchia, Franco.
   Casanova. **DDT**, 179, 312d.
   Cavalleria Rusticana. **DDT**, 151.
   The Magic Flute. **DDT**, 211.
   Rasputin. **DDT**, 171.
   Terra Nova. **DDT**, 468.
   Yours, Anne. **DDT**, 76.
Colciaghi, Ebe, Virginio Puecher, & Ugo Mulas. *Wozzeck*. **SDW3**, 191.
Colin, Paul.
   Factory Work. **SDW1**, 93.
   The Stuff We Are Made Of. **SDW1**, 93.
Colonello, Attilio. *The Taming of the Shrew*. **SDW2**, 124.
Coltellacci, Giulio.
   Amahl and the Night Visitors. **SDE**, 69; **SDW2**, 124.
   Anne of the Thousand Days. **SDW1**, 125.

The Beggars. **SDW1**, 125.
Julius Caesar. **SDE**, 69.
Conklin, John.
   Ardéle. **ASD1**, 24.
   Ariodante. **TCI**, vol. 21, n. 8 (Oct 1987). 19.
   The Au Pair Man. **TCI**, vol. 14, n. 3 (May/Jun 1980). 22.
   Un Ballo in Maschera. **TCI**, vol. 14, n. 3 (May/Jun 1980). 23.
   Beatrix Cenci. **DPT**, 310.
   Camino Real. **ASD1**, between 70 & 71; **DDT**, 486; **TCI**, vol. 14, n. 3 (May/Jun 1980).
      16.
   Dalliance. **SDL**, 70.
   Don Giovanni. **TDT**, vol. XXVII, n. 3 (Summer 1991). 13.
   Don Quichotte. **ASD1**, 20.
   A Dybbuk. **TCI**, vol. 29, n. 6 (Jun/Jul 1995). 7.
   Galileo. **TCI**, vol. 14, n. 3 (May/Jun 1980). 20.
   The Good Woman of Setzuan. **TCI**, vol. 14, n. 3 (May/Jun 1980). 19.
   Götterdämmerung. **DDT**, 480; **TCI**, vol. 20, n. 2 (Feb 1986). 27.
   Hamlet. **DDT**, 478; **TCI**, vol. 25, n. 9 (Nov 1991). 42.
   Henry IV, parts 1 & 2. **TCI**, vol. 28, n. 3 (Mar 1994). 9.
   The Hostage. **CSD**, 69.
   Idomeneo. **TDT**, vol. XXVII, n. 3 (Summer 1991). 12.
   The Illusion. **TCI**, vol. 24, n. 4 (Apr 1990). 12; **TCI**, vol. 25, n. 9 (Nov 1991). 40.
   Journey's End. **TCI**, vol. 14, n. 3 (May/Jun 1980). 23.
   The Magic Flute. **TDT**, vol. XXVII, n. 2 (Spring 1991). 36.
   Marat/Sade. **TCI**, vol. 14, n. 3 (May/Jun 1980). 19.
   The Marriage of Figaro. **TDT**, vol. XXVII, n. 3 (Summer 1991). 13.
   Miss Havisham's Fire. **ASD1**, 19; **DDT**, 483; **TCI**, vol. 14, n. 3 (May/Jun 1980). 23.
   A Month in the Country. **TCI**, vol. 14, n. 3 (May/Jun 1980). 17.
   Peer Gynt. **TCI**, vol. 25, n. 9 (Nov 1991). 42; **TDT**, n. 9 (May 1967). front cover.
   Pericles. **DDT**, 485; **SDL**, 35, 74; **TCI**, vol. 25, n. 9 (Nov 1991). 38, 39.
   Peter Pan. **TCI**, vol. 23, n. 3 (Mar 1989). 39.
   Picnic. **TCI**, vol. 27, n. 4 (Apr 1993). 11.
   Pygmalion. **TCI**, vol. 25, n. 5 (May 1991). 12.
   Rain. **ASD1**, 27; **DDT**, 484.
   The Resistible Rise of Arturo Ui. **ASD1**, 15; **BSE4**, 79; **DDT**, 482; **TCI**, vol. 14, n. 3
      (May/Jun 1980). 18.
   Rex. **DDT**, 152b; **TCI**, vol. 11, n. 3 (May/Jun 1977). 11.
   Das Rheingold. **DDT**, 125, 481; **TCI**, vol. 20, n. 2 (Feb 1986). 26.
   Der Ring des Nibelungen. **TCI**, vol. 21, n. 5 (May 1987). 28.
   Romeo and Juliet. **ASD1**, between 70 & 71, back cover.
   The Shepherd King. **TDT**, vol. XXVII, n. 3 (Summer 1991). 13.
   The Skin of Our Teeth. **TCI**, vol. 14, n. 3 (May/Jun 1980). 22; **TCI**, vol. 7, n. 5 (Oct
      1973). 8.
   Skinflint Out West. **ASD1**, 21.
   The Taming of the Shrew. **TCI**, vol. 14, n. 4 (Sep 1980). 38.
   The Tempest. **TCI**, vol. 26, n. 2 (Feb 1992). 11.
   The Threepenny Opera. **TCI**, vol. 14, n. 3 (May/Jun 1980). 18; **TCI**, vol. 26, n. 8 (Oct
      1992). 8.
   The Tooth of Crime. **TCI**, vol. 20, n. 5 (May 1986). 8.
   The Turk in Italy. **TCI**, vol. 14, n. 3 (May/Jun 1980). 23.
   Ubu Roi. **TCI**, vol. 14, n. 3 (May/Jun 1980). 23.

Die Walküre. **ASD1**, 17; **TCI**, vol. 20, n. 2 (Feb 1986). 27; **TCI**, vol. 28, n. 3 (Mar 1994). 10.

War and Peace. **TCI**, vol. 24, n. 7 (Aug/Sep 1990). 36.

Werther. **ASD1**, 23.

The Winter's Tale. **TCI**, vol. 24, n. 8 (Oct 1990). 43.

Conklin, John & Robert Wilson.

When We Dead Awaken. **TDT**, vol. XXVII, n. 2 (Spring 1991). 16.

Constable, William.

Les Amants Éternels. **SDW1**, 39.

The Black Swan. **SDW1**, 41.

Corroboree. **SDW1**, 40.

Conti, Primo. *Olympia*. **SDE**, 70.

Copeau, Jacques. *The Brothers Karamazov*. **SDC**, plate 98.

Cordier, J. N., B. Bauchau, R. Moscoso, A. Ferreira, Cl. Forget, G. Cl. Francois, L. de Grandmaison, & A. Salomon.

The Revolutionary City Belongs to this World. **SDW4**, illus. 385-390.

Corey, Irene. *The Book of Job*. **TCI**, vol. 6, n. 3 (May/Jun 1972). 15.

Corinth, Lovis. *Faust*. **AST**, 32, 33.

Cornell, Allen. *The Show-Off*. **TCI**, vol. 21, n. 7 (Aug/Sep 1987). 37.

Cornwell, Bruce. *Vanities*. **TCI**, vol. 15, n. 2 (Feb 1981). 67.

Corrigan, Robert. *The Recruiting Officer*. **TDT**, n. 19 (Dec 1969). 32.

Corrodi, Annelies.

Lucia di Lammermoor. **DSL**, figure 39.11 & pg. 428; **SST**, 558.

Macbeth. **DSL**, figure 39.1(b) & plate III; **SST**, 543.

Corso, Arturo. *Mistero Buffo*. **SDW4**, illus. 306.

Cortezo, Victor. *The Sheep-Well*. **SDW2**, 77.

Cory, Lauren. *The Skin of Our Teeth*. **TCI**, vol. 14, n. 4 (Sep 1980). 30.

Cosler, Charles.

Coming Through the Rye. **TCI**, vol. 20, n. 5 (May 1986). 12.

K2. **TCI**, vol. 19, n. 5 (May 1985). 27.

Costa, Valeria. *Venice Preserved*. **SDW2**, 124.

Cousins, Derek. *Canterbury Tales*. **MCD**, plate 228.

Coutaud, Lucien.

As You Like It. **SOS**, 187.

Medea. **SDE**, 74.

Proteus. **SDW2**, 87.

The Satin Slipper. **SDW1**, 94.

Covarrubias, M. *Androcles and the Lion*. **TSS**, 517.

Crabb, Sally. *The Risen People*. **TCI**, vol. 29, n. 2 (Feb 1995). 7.

Craig, Edward Gordon.

Acis and Galatea. **EGC**, plates 3a, 3b; **SDG**, 149.

Bethlehem. **EGC**, plates 4, 5.

Caesar and Cleopatra. **FCS**, plate 167, color plate 16; **SDO**, 189 & plate 16; **TNT**, facing 51, 53, 55.

Cinderella. **TNT**, facing 25.

Dido and Aeneas. **TNT**, facing 57.

Electra. **EGC**, plates 10-11a; **OAT**, xiv; **RSD**, illus. 79, 84; **TNT**, facing 35; **TPH**, photo 321.

Hamlet. **COT**, 144, 151; **DMS**, plates 19-21; **EGC**, plates 14a, 14b, 15-18, 20b; **OAT**, 136; **RSD**, illus. 92; **SDC**, plate 67; **SDG**, 151; **SDR**, 18, 19; **SOS**, 140; **TDT**, n. 29 (May 1972). 15, 16; **TNT**, II, facing 21, 33, 81, 83.

Hour Glass. **SDG**, 151.

Hunger. **OAT**, 104, 112, 262.

Julius Caesar. **OAT**, 48; **SDC**, plate 68; **TNT**, facing 37; **TPH**, photo 322.

King Lear. **EGC**, 95; **TDT**, n. 29 (May 1972). 12.

The Lights of London. **TNT**, facing 17.

Macbeth. **COT**, 149, 150; **FCS**, plate 169, **OAT**, 118, 280; **RSD**, illus. 80-82, **SDC**, plates 69, 70; **SDO**, 191; **TDT**, n. 29 (May 1972). 11, **TNT**, facing 64, 69, 71, 73, 75, 77, 79; **TPH**, photo 320.

The Masque of London. **OAT**, frontispiece; **TNT**, facing 19, 27.

The Merchant of Venice. **COT**, 147.

The Pretenders. **COT**, 145, 146; **DOT**, 208; **TPH**, photo 323.

Psyche. **OAT**, 176; **RSD**, illus. 83.

Romeo and Juliet. **FCS**, plate 168; **OAT**, 224; **SDO**, 190.

Rosmersholm. **TNT**, facing 64.

The Taming of the Shrew. **COT**, 148.

Venice Preserved. **EGC**, plate 7; **OAT**, 148; **TNT**, facing 29, 30.

The Vikings at Helgeland. **EGC**, plates 6a, 6b; **RSD**, illus. 55, 74, 75; **TDT**, n. 29 (May 1972). 4, 11.

Craig, Russell.

Così fan Tutti. **TDT**, vol. XX, n. 1 (Spring 1984). 18.

The Magic Flute. **BTD**, 124.

Craven, Hawes.

A Midsummer Night's Dream. **SDT**, 260.

Olivia. **SDT**, 270.

The Orchid. **MCD**, plate 49.

Quo Vadis. **SDT**, 261.

Twelfth Night. **SDG**, 138.

Craven, Hawes, T.E. Ryan, Alfred Terraine, & Joseph Hunter.

The Girl from Utah. **MCD**, plate 96.

Crayon.

Bauer als Millionär. **TCS2**, plate 275.

Die Jüdische Wittwe. **TCS2**, plate 89.

Manon Lescaut. **CSD**, 38; **MOM**, 11.

Der Revolutionär. **TPH**, photo 422.

Crespi, Maria Grazia. *The Siege of Corinth*. **SDE**, 71.

Creuz, Serge.

Hamlet. **SDW4**, illus. 25.

Juliet or the Key to Her Dreams. **SDW1**, 43.

Proteus. **SDW3**, 94.

The Servant of Two Masters. **SDW2**, 28.

Cristini, Cesare M.

Misery and Nobless. **SDE**, 73.

Il Trovatore. **SDE**, 72.

Crome, Sara. *Mother Hicks*. **TDT**, vol. XXVI, n. 2 (Summer 1990). 63.

Crowley, Bob.

As You Like It. **BTD**, 54; **SDT**, 274.

Carousel. **TCI**, vol. 27, n. 4 (Apr 1993). 38, 39.

The Comedy of Errors. **SDT**, 274.

Hamlet. **TCI**, vol. 27, n. 4 (Apr 1993). 40, 41.

Henry V. **BTD**, 55.

The King Goes Forth to France. **BTD**, 144.

King Lear. **BTD**, 54.
Les Liaisons Dangereuses. **TCI**, vol. 21, n. 7 (Aug/Sep 1987). 26, 27, 31.
The Magic Flute. **BTD**, 144.
The Plantagenets. **BTD**, 55; **TCI**, vol. 23, n. 4 (Apr 1989). 112.
Csányi, Arpád.
Faust, part 1. **TDT**, vol. XVI, n. 1 (Spring 1980). 7.
Ivanov. **SDW3**, 91.
Culbert, John. *The Triumph of Love*. **TCI**, vol. 28, n. 2 (Feb 1994). 9.
Culshaw, Bernard. *Fidelio*. **TCI**, vol. 19, n. 4 (Apr 1985). 18.
Curiel, Nicolas. *Twelfth Night*. **SDW2**, 243.
Curreri, Alan. *Marathon '33*. **TCI**, vol. 14, n. 4 (Sep 1980). 24.
Curtis, Ann & Christopher Morley. *Die Fledermaus*. **CGA**, 196.
Cytrynowski, Carlos. *Carmen*. **TCI**, vol. 28, n. 1 (Jan 1994). 12.
Czelényi, Jósef.
Biedermann and the Firebugs. **SDW2**, 139.
A Midsummer Night's Dream. **SDW**~~²~~ ~~¹²²~~
~~Czerniawski, Jerzy~~ *The Silver Dream* ,   13
Czeschka, Carl O.
King Lear. **RSD**, illus. 93; **DOT**, 2   , 18.

Da Costa, Liz.
Breaking the Code. **BTD**, 64; **TCI**, vol. 23, n. 9 (Nov 1989). 59.
Kiss Me Kate. **BTD**, 161.
Dahlstrom, Robert A.
Ah, Wilderness. **BSE2**, 8.
Così fan Tutti. **TDT**, vol. XXVII, n. 3 (Summer 1991). 5.
Don Giovanni. **TDT**, vol. XXVII, n. 3 (Summer 1991). 7.
A Midsummer Night's Dream. **TCI**, vol. 22, n. 1 (Jan 1988). 36.
Man and Superman. **TCI**, vol. 14, n. 4 (Sep 1980). 18, 19; **SCT**, between 152 & 153.
Dali, Salvador.
Don Juan Tenorio. **AST**, 198; **SDW2**, 78, 79.
Mad Tristan. **RSD**, illus. 483, 484.
Salomé. **AST**, 199; **CGA**, 136.
Dam, Jan Van. *Hamlet*. **DIT**, plate 114.
Damiana, Luciano.
Our Milan. **SDW2**, 125.
Le Baruffe Chiozzotte. **SIO**, 41-45.
The Black Pig. **SDW4**, illus. 339-342.
Cavalleria Rusticana. **SDW3**, 185.
The Emperor Jones. **SDE**, 76.
The Life of Galileo. **RSD**, illus. 578-581; **SIO**, 38-40.
The Magic Flute. **SDW4**, illus. 106-112.
Schweik in the Second World War. **SIO**, 35-37.
Sergeant Musgrave's Dance. **SIO**, 46.
Skutarewshy. **SDE**, 77.
Damonte, Marcelo.
An Inspector Calls. **SDW2**, 163.
Volpone. **SDW2**, 164.

Dancy, Virginia & Elmon Webb.
    Peter Pan. **BSE3**, 17; **DDT**, 42, 337.
    The Plough and the Stars. **DDT**, 210, 211.
    What the Butler Saw. **DDT**, 268.
    You Never Can Tell. **DDT**, 248, 440d.
    The Contractor. **TCI**, vol. 7, n. 5 (Oct 1973). 10.
    The Iceman Cometh. **CSD**, 140; **DPT**, 100; **TCI**, vol. 7, n. 5 (Oct 1973). 6.
    Long Day's Journey into Night. **DPT**, 85.
    A Whistle in the Dark. **TCI**, vol. 7, n. 5 (Oct 1973). 8.
    Yegor Bulichov. **DPT**, 99; **TCI**, vol. 7, n. 5 (Oct 1973). 8.
    A Streetcar Named Desire. **TCI**, vol. 7, n. 5 (Oct 1973). 8.
Daniel, Heinz.
    Brunhild. **TCS2**, plate 191.
    Faust. **TAT**, plate 327.
Dar, Ruth. *The Spotted Tiger*. **SDW4**, illus. 350.
Dardenne, James. *Hauptmann*. **TCI**, vol. 26, n. 7 (Aug/Sep 1992). 12.
Dare, Daphne.
    Macbeth. **TCI**, vol. 22, n. 7 (Aug/Sep 1988). 112.
    Richard III. **TCI**, vol. 12, n. 4 (May/Jun 1978). 22.
Darling, Jonathan. *The Danton Case*. **TDT**, vol. XXVIII, n. 2 (Spring 1992). 5 of insert.
Darling, Robert Edward.
    Fashion. **SFT**, 115.
    Marat/Sade. **TCI**, vol. 24, n. 8 (Oct 1990). 17; **TCR**, 112.
    The Seagull. **TCI**, vol. 14, n. 3 (May/Jun 1980). 18.
    Tannhäuser. **TCI**, vol. 20, n. 8 (Oct 1986). 25.
    The Visit of the Old Lady. **CSD**, 73.
Dart, Paul.
    The Marriage. **BTD**, 28.
    The Wandering Jew. **BTD**, 76.
Daszewski, Wladislaw.
    Cracovians and Mountaineers. **SDW1**, 156.
    The Tempest. **SDW1**, 156.
    War for War. **RSD**, illus. 268, 269.
Davis, Ashley Martin. *Translations*. **TCI**, vol. 29, n. 5 (May 1995). 62.
Davis, Collis & David Mitchell. *A Photograph*. **TCI**, vol. 13, n. 1 (Jan/Feb 1979). 33.
Davis, Janice. *The Lower Depths*. **TCI**, vol. 16, n. 2 (Feb 1982). 27.
Davis, Peter. *Purlie*. **TCI**, vol. 14, n. 4 (Sep 1980). 34.
Davison, Peter J.
    Medea. **TCI**, vol. 28, n. 7 (Aug/Sep 1994). 10.
    The School for Wives. **TCI**, vol. 28, n. 4 (Apr 1994). 13.
Daydé, Bernard.
    The Miraculous Mandarin. **SDW3**, 188.
    Orpheus in the Underworld. **SDW2**, 88.
    The School for Wives. **SDW3**, 67.
de Chirico, Georgio.
    Bacchus et Ariane. **AST**, 182.
    Le Bal. **AST**, 181; **RSD**, illus. 311, 312.
    The Daughter of Jorio. **TPH**, photo 366.
    Don Quixote. **SDE**, 63, 64; **SDW1**, 126.
    L'Estasi. **SIO**, 146.
    La Jarre. **AST**, 185.

Diss, Eileen.
   Close at Play. **TCI**, vol. 15, n. 5 (May 1981). 12.
   Old Heads and Young Hearts. **TCI**, vol. 15, n. 5 (May 1981). 13.
   Translations. **BTD**, 61.
Dmitriev, Vladimir
   Moscow! **RST**, 200.
   The Dawn. **MOT**, between 144 & 145; **RSD**, illus. 168, 169; **RST**, 86, 87; **TCT**, plates
      15, 16.
   Egor Bulychov and Others. **RST**, 300, 301.
   Eugene the Unlucky. **RST**, 132.
   The Humble and the Offended. **SDW2**, 182.
   The Poor Bride. **SDW2**, 182.
   The Queen of Spades. **SDW2**, 181.
   The Three Sisters. **DMS**, plate 24; **SDW2**, 181.
   Uncle Vanya. **DMS**, plate 25; **SDW2**, 182.
Doboujinsky, Mstislav.
   Un Ballo in Maschera. **MOM**, 10.
   Boris Godounov. **RSC**, 28.
   Macbeth. **RST**, 111.
   A Month in the Country. **DOT**, 206; **FCS**, plate 176,color plate 19; **RSC**, 28; **SDO**,
      199, plate 19; **TCS2**, plates 7, 8.
   Petrouchka. **RSD**, illus. 26.
   Le Régiment qui passe. **SDC**, plate 94; **TCS2**, color plate 3.
Dobrev, Rumen. *January*. **TDT**, vol. XXIII, n. 4 (Winter 1988). 12.
Dobujinsky, Rostislav. *L'Enlevement du Serail*. **TCS2**, plate 268.
Docherty, Peter.
   The Adventures of Mr. Broucek. **TCI**, vol. 15, n. 5 (May 1981). 15.
   Side By Side By Sondheim. **SON**, 2, 3.
Dodd, Joseph D. *The Halloween Tree*. **BSE2**, 9.
Dodge, D. Frank. *Mrs. Bumpstead-Leigh*. **MCN**, 38.
Dodge, D. Frank & Ernest Gros. *Salvation Nell*. **MCN**, 32.
Döepp, John.
   K2. **TCI**, vol. 19, n. 5 (May 1985). 27.
   Misalliance. **TDP**, 116.
   Troilus and Cressida. **CSD**, 74.
Doeve, J.F. *Time Remembered*. **SDW1**, 137.
Domergue, J.G. *Arlechino*. **DIT**, plate 88.
Don, Robin.
   L'Elisir D'Amore. **BTD**, 123.
   The Midsummer Marriage. **BTD**, 123.
   More Light. **BTD**, 40.
   Someone Who'll Watch Over Me. **TCI**, vol. 27, n. 2 (Feb 1993). 11.
   Tamerlano. **BTD**, 123.
Donnelly, Mark.
   Billy Bishop Goes to War. **SDT**, 105.
   Cyrano de Bergerac. **SDT**, 279.
   A Delicate Balance. **SDT**, 104.
   Love's Labor's Lost. **SDT**, 293.
   My Fair Lady. **SDT**, 282.
   Picnic. **SDT**, 287.
   The Playboy of the Western World. **BSE5**, 35.

Dornes, Roger. *Britannicus*. **SDW1**, 95.
Dorrer, Valeri.
   Iphigenia. **TDT**, vol. XII, n. 3 (Fall 1976). 41.
   The Path of Thunder. **SDW2**, 183.
Dorsey, Kent.
   And a Nightingale Sang. **TCI**, vol. 25, n. 8 (Oct 1991). 49.
   Blue Window. **TCI**, vol. 21, n. 7 (Aug/Sep 1987). 14.
   Breakfast with Les and Bess. **TCI**, vol. 19, n. 5 (May 1985). 19.
   A Christmas Carol. **SDL**, 373.
   The Last Love. **TCI**, vol. 25, n. 8 (Oct 1991). 49.
   The Marriage of Figaro. **TCI**, vol. 25, n. 8 (Oct 1991). 46.
   Serious Money. **TCI**, vol. 25, n. 8 (Oct 1991). 47.
   Steel Magnolias. **TCI**, vol. 24, n. 2 (Feb 1990). 58.
   The Tempest. **TCI**, vol. 25, n. 8 (Oct 1991). 48.
   The Tooth of Crime. **TCI**, vol. 25, n. 8 (Oct 1991). 49.
   Volpone. **TCI**, vol. 27, n. 5 (May 1993). 6.
   Yankae Dawg You Die. **TCI**, vol. 25, n. 8 (Oct 1991). 49.
Douking, Georges.
   Journey into Hell. **SDW1**, 95.
   Night Flight. **SDW2**, 89.
   This Evening at Samarcande. **SDW1**, 95.
Downing, Desmonde. *Dark of the Moon*. **SDW1**, 39.
Drabik, Vincent.
   As You Like It. **RSD**, illus. 144.
   The Last Pierrot. **SCM**, 84.
   Le Songe Argenté de Salonica. **TCS2**, plate 239.
   The Undivine Comedy. **RSD**, illus. 263.
Draghici, Marina. *Mad Forest*. **TCI**, vol. 27, n. 3 (Mar 1993). 7.
Drake, Jim. *Noises Off*. **TDT**, vol. XXIX, n. 5 (Fall 1993). 36.
Dreier, Jurgen.
   Káta Kabanová. **TDT**, vol. XX, n. 1 (Spring 1984). 6.
   The Tales of Hoffmann. **OPE**, 203, 206, 209, 211, 213.
Dresa. *Aimer*. **DIT**, plate 85.
Dreyfuss, Henry.
   The Cat and the Fiddle. **BWM**, 170; **MCN**, 106; **RBS**, 55; **SCM**, 118; **SDA**, 245.
Drury, Walter. *Much Ado About Nothing*. **SDG**, 178, 179.
Dryden, Dan
   Blood Wedding. **TCI**, vol. 8, n. 6 (Nov/Dec 1974). 2.
   K2. **TCI**, vol. 19, n. 5 (May 1985). 27.
Du Bois, Raoul Pène.
   Bells Are Ringing. **BWM**, 104.
   Call Me Madam. **BWM**, 246.
   Doctor Jazz. **DPT**, 288; **DSL**, 206.
   DuBarry Was a Lady. **BWM**, 210; **MCN**, 148; **RBS**, 188, 190.
   Irene. **DPT**, 286; **TCI**, vol. 7, n. 4 (Sep 1973). 25.
   John Murray Anderson's Almanac. **DPT**, 290; **SDA**, 253.
   No, No Nanette. **TCI**, vol. 14, n. 1 (Jan/Feb 1980). 20; **TCI**, vol. 7, n. 4 (Sep 1973).
      25; **BWM**, 250; No, No, Nanette. **DPT**, 289; **TCI**, vol. 5, n. 6 (Nov/Dec 1971). 10.
   Panama Hattie. **BWM**, 211.
   Sugar Babies. **TCI**, vol. 14, n. 1 (Jan/Feb 1980). 8.
   Wonderful Town. **BWM**, 289, 290.

Duckwall, Ralph. *The Country Wife*. **SST**, plate VI.
Dudley, William.
  Bartholomew Fair. **BTD**, 43; **TDT**, vol. XXV, n. 3 (Fall 1989). 20.
  Billy Budd. **TCI**, vol. 16, n. 9 (Nov/Dec 1982). 30.
  Candleford. **TCI**, vol. 18, n. 1 (Jan 1984). 36.
  Cat on a Hot Tin Roof. **TCI**, vol. 24, n. 5 (May 1990). 47.
  The Changeling. **BTD**, 42, 43; **TDT**, vol. XXV, n. 3 (Fall 1989). 20.
  Dispatches. **TCI**, vol. 18, n. 1 (Jan 1984). 36.
  Don Quixote. **TDT**, vol. XIX, n. 1 (Spring 1983). 12.
  Futurists. **BTD**, 42.
  Götterdämmerung. **TCI**, vol. 18, n. 3 (Mar 1984). 16.
  Kiss Me Kate. **TDT**, vol. XXV, n. 3 (Fall 1989). 23.
  Lark Rise. **TCI**, vol. 18, n. 1 (Jan 1984). 36; **TDT**, vol. XIX, n. 1 (Spring 1983). 12.
  A Midsummer Night's Dream. **TDT**, vol. XXV, n. 3 (Fall 1989). 19.
  Mutiny! **TCI**, vol. 20, n. 2 (Feb 1986). 33.
  The Mysteries. **BTD**, 44, 45.
  Das Rheingold. **BTD**, 119; **TCI**, vol. 18, n. 3 (Mar 1984). 17.
  Richard III. **TDT**, vol. XXV, n. 3 (Fall 1989). 24.
  Der Ring des Nibelungen. **BTD**, 118.
  Schweik in the Second World War. **BTD**, 56.
  The Shaughraun. **TCI**, vol. 23, n. 1 (Jan 1989). 10; **TDT**, vol. XXV, n. 3 (Fall 1989).
    22.
  The Tales of Hoffmann. **TDT**, vol. XIX, n. 1 (Spring 1983). 11.
  Die Walküre. **TCI**, vol. 18, n. 3 (Mar 1984). 16, 17; **TDT**, vol. XXV, n. 3 (Fall 1989).
    17.
Duer, Fred. *A Midsummer Night's Dream*. **TCI**, vol. 19, n. 4 (Apr 1985). 10.
Dufy, Raoul.
  Le Boeuf sur le Toit. **AST**, 110; **TBB**, 128.
  The Fiancés of Harve. **AST**, 111; **SDW1**, 95.
Dulberg, Ewald.
  Fidelio. **RSD**, illus. 71.
  Oedipus Rex. **RSD**, illus. 70.
Dullin, Charles. *Volpone*. **SCM**, 40.
Dunham, Clarke.
  The Apprenticeship of Duddy Kravitz. **DDT**, 163.
  Candide. **HPA**, 155; **MBM**, 89; **TCI**, vol. 18, n. 8 (Oct 1984). 18.
  End of the World. **TCI**, vol. 18, n. 8 (Oct 1984). 19; **TCI**, vol. 19, n. 8 (Oct 1985). 19.
  Grind. **HPA**, 139; **MBM**, 80, 81, 85; **TCI**, vol. 19, n. 7 (Aug/Sep 1985). 42, 43.
  Hansel und Gretel. **DDT**, 84.
  Madame Butterfly. **DDT**, 395, 587; **TCI**, vol. 18, n. 8 (Oct 1984). 16.
  More Fun Than Bowling. **DDT**, 476.
  A Phantasmagoria Historia of D. Johan Fausten Magister, PhD, MD, DD, DL, etc.
    DDT, 85.
  Play Memory. **DDT**, 312c.
  The Tales of Hoffmann. **DDT**, 23.
Dunkel, Eugene.
  Legend of the Invisible City of Kitezh and the Maiden of Sevronia. **RSC**, 29.
  Naughty-Naught. **RBS**, 141.
Dunn, Henry. *The Green Bird*. **TCI**, vol. 28, n. 2 (Feb 1994). 6.
Dupont, Jacques.
  Castle in Sweden. **SDW2**, 89.

Faust. **MOM**, 15.

God is Not Guilty. **SDW1**, 96.

Durfee, Duke.

Metamorphosis (scenic supervisor). **TCI**, vol. 23, n. 5 (May 1989). 24.

Ten Little Indians. **TCI**, vol. 22, n. 5 (May 1988). 7, 41.

Dusek, Jan.

The Brothers Karamazov. **TDT**, vol. XXIII, n. 1 (Spring 1987). 13.

Danton's Death. **TDT**, vol. XXVII, n. 4 (Fall 1991). 47.

Duck Hunting. **TDT**, vol. XXVI, n. 4 (Fall 1990). 26.

King Lear. **TDT**, vol. XXVI, n. 2 (Summer 1990). 38.

Long Day's Journey Into Night. **TDT**, vol. XXIII, n. 4 (Winter 1988). 49; **TDT**, vol. XXVI, n. 4 (Fall 1990). 25, 26.

Duthie, Diane. *Mud.* **BSE4**, 90.

Dvigoubskij, Nikolaj. *The Would-be Gentleman.* **SDW3**, 72.

Dyer, Chris.

Billy Budd. **BTD**, 125.

King Lear. **BTD**, 67.

Macbeth. **SDT**, 272.

Montag aus Licht. **BTD**, 125.

The Roaring Girl. **BTD**, 67; **TDT**, vol. XX, n. 1 (Spring 1984). 19.

The Taming of the Shrew. **TDT**, vol. XIX, n. 1 (Spring 1983). 5.

Timon of Athens. **TDT**, vol. XIX, n. 1 (Spring 1983). 5.

-E-

Eagan, Michael. *Brighton Beach Memoirs.* **TCI**, vol. 21, n. 2 (Feb 1987). 24, 25.

Easley, Holmes.

The Father. **TCI**, vol. 8, n. 2 (Mar/Apr 1974). 12.

The Play's the Thing. **TCI**, vol. 8, n. 2 (Mar/Apr 1974). 13.

Eastman, Donald.

The Gang on the Roof. **TCI**, vol. 28, n. 1 (Jan 1994). 10.

On the Open Road. **TCI**, vol. 27, n. 5 (May 1993). 7.

Echarri, Isabel.

Antigone. **TDT**, vol. XX, n. 1 (Spring 1984). 9.

Don Juan or The Love of Geometry. **SDW3**, 203.

Echave, José.

The Dance of Death. **SDW2**, 241

My Four Angels. **SDW2**, 241.

Eck, Marsha Louis.

All's Well that Ends Well. **TCI**, vol. 7, n. 2 (Mar/Apr 1973). 10.

Manon. **DPT**, 36.

Eckart, William. *The Winter's Tale.* **BSE1**, 23.

Eckart, William & Jean.

Anyone Can Whistle. **HPA**, 82; **SON**, 67-70.

Damn Yankees. **BWM**, 293; **SDW2**, 233; **TMT**, 189.

The Education of H*Y*M*A*N K*A*P*L*A*N. **CSD**, 123; **DDT**, 312c.

Fiorello! **BWM**, 97; **DDT**, 312b; **HPA**, 30; **SDD**, between 210 & 211.

Flora, The Red Menace. **DDT**, 24b.

The Golden Apple. **DDT**, 394, 438, 439; **SDA**, 253; **SDB**, 61.

Mame. **CSD**, 76; **SDB**, 61; **TMT**, 212.

Mister Johnson. **DDT**, 264, 324; **SDW2**, 233.

The Mother of Us All. **DDT**, 152d.

Once Upon a Mattress. **DDT**, 363; **TCI**, vol. 20, n. 5 (May 1986). 30.

Reuben, Reuben. **DDT**, 153, 312d; **SDT**, 43.

She Loves Me. **BWM**, 295; **HPA**, 34; **HPR**, 87; **TCI**, vol. 20, n. 5 (May 1986). 26.

Edlund, Michael. *The Glass Menagerie.* **BSE2**, 46.

Edmunds, Kate.

    Fuente Ovejuna. **TCI**, vol. 25, n. 8 (Oct 1991). 50.

    Guys and Dolls. **TCI**, vol. 20, n. 5 (May 1986). 18, 19.

    True West. **TCI**, vol. 16, n. 8 (Oct 1982). 14.

Edwards, Ben.

    The Aspern Papers. **DDT**, 367.

    Dark at the Top of the Stairs. **TCI**, vol. 23, n. 7 (Aug/Sep 1989). 50.

    Death of a Salesman. **DDT**, 586.

    Finishing Touches. **DPT**, 127.

    Heartbreak House. **TCI**, vol. 23, n. 7 (Aug/Sep 1989). 51.

    The Iceman Cometh. **TCI**, vol. 23, n. 4 (Apr 1989). 50.

    Jane Eyre. **DDT**, 285.

    Lilian. **TCI**, vol. 23, n. 4 (Apr 1989). 51.

    Long Day's Journey Into Night. **TCI**, vol. 23, n. 7 (Aug/Sep 1989). 49.

    Master of Thornfield. **SFT**, 111.

    A Matter of Gravity. **DDT**, 125; **TCI**, vol. 23, n. 7 (Aug/Sep 1989). 53.

    Medea. **DDT**, 178; **TCI**, vol. 23, n. 7 (Aug/Sep 1989). 54.

    A Moon for the Misbegotten. **DPT**, 177; **DSL**, frontispiece; **TCI**, vol. 23, n. 7 (Aug/Sep 1989). 53.

    More Stately Mansions. **DDT**, 27, 404; **DPT**, 24.

    Purlie. **BWM**, 334; **DPT**, 181, 182; **TCI**, vol. 23, n. 7 (Aug/Sep 1989). 50; **TCI**, vol. 7, n. 3 (May/Jun 1973). 20.

    Purlie Victorious. **DDT**, 152b; **SDD**, between 210, 211.

    The Remarkable Mr. Pennypacker. **DDT**, 163.

    The Tempest. **TCI**, vol. 7, n. 2 (Mar/Apr 1973). 11.

    The Time of the Cuckoo. **DDT**, 404; **TCI**, vol. 23, n. 7 (Aug/Sep 1989). 55.

    A Touch of the Poet. **DPT**, 179; **TCI**, vol. 1, n. 3 (Jul/Aug 1967). 24-27; **TCI**, vol. 23, n. 7 (Aug/Sep 1989). 3, 53.

    The Waltz of the Toreadors. **DPT**, 180; **TCI**, vol. 23, n. 7 (Aug/Sep 1989). 53, 54.

Edwards, Jack. *'night Mother.* **TCI**, vol. 19, n. 5 (May 1985). 22.

Edwards, Norman.

    The Marriage of Figaro. **SDC**, plate 124.

    Oedipus Rex. **TCS2**, plates 376, 377.

Efimenko, Sergei. *Roar China.* **RST**, 234; **SCM**, 86.

Egemar, Christian.

    The Assassins. **SDW3**, 154.

    Brand. **SDW3**, 85.

    The Merchant of Venice. **SDW3**, 43.

    Marat/Sade. **SDW3**, 135.

    Uncle Vanya. **SDW4**, illus. 185.

    Women from Shanghai. **SDW3**, 131.

Egg, Lois.

    Parisian Comedy. **SDW2**, 155.

    Torquato Tasso. **SDW2**, 155.

Egorov, V.E.

    The Blue Bird. **RSD**, illus. 31; **SDC**, plates 65, 66.

The Drama of Life. **RSD**, illus. 30.

The Life of Man. **MOT**, between 48 & 49; **RSD**, illus. 32, 33.

Eich, Harry. *Shackles.* **SDW4**, illus. 193.

Eichbauer, Helio.

Antigone. **SDW3**, 22.

The Assassins. **SDW3**, 154.

The Balcony. **SDW3**, 125.

Family Album. **SDW3**, 118.

The King of the Candle. **SDW3**, 104.

The Trojan Women. **SDW3**, 29.

Eigsti, Karl.

The Accidental Death of an Anarchist. **ASD1**, 32; **DDT**, 167.

Amen Corner. **DDT**, 395.

Baba Goya. **TCI**, vol. 8, n. 4 (Sep 1974). 21.

Boesman and Lena. **ASD1**, 35; **DPT**, 121.

The Curse of the Starving Class. **ASD1**, 40.

Death of a Salesman. **ASD1**, 28.

Duck Hunting. **ASD1**, 33.

Eubie! **DDT**, 317.

Horatio. **DPT**, 3.

The House of Blue Leaves. **DPT**, 331; **ASD1**, 39.

Inquest. **DPT**, 121.

Joseph and the Amazing Technicolor Dreamcoat. **ALW**, 41-44; **ASD1**, 34; **DDT**, 440a.

Julius Caesar. **ASD1**, 36.

The Karl Marx Play. **CSD**, 77, 124; **DPT**, 33.

Knockout. **ASD1**, between 70 & 71.

The Last Meeting of the Knights of the White Magnolia. **ASD1**, 31; **DPT**, 97.

Murder at the Howard Johnson's. **ASD1**, 35.

Orphans. **DDT**, 188; **TCI**, vol. 21, n. 7 (Aug/Sep 1987). 35.

The Resistible Rise of Arturo Ui. **TCI**, vol. 8, n. 3 (May/Jun 1974). 2.

Screenplay. **DDT**, 157; **TCI**, vol. 18, n. 3 (Mar 1984). 28.

Speed-the-Plow. **TCI**, vol. 25, n. 4 (Apr 1991). 14.

Twelfth Night. **ASD1**, 38.

When You Comin' Back Red Ryder? **DDT**, 67.

Wings. **DPT**, 115.

Yentl. **DDT**, 102.

Eisenstein, Sergei M.

Heartbreak House. **RSD**, illus. 184.

The Mexican. **RST**, 129.

A Wise Man. **RSD**, illus. 172.

Eisenstein, Sergei & Sergei Yutkevich. *Macbeth.* **RST**, 112.

Elder, Eldon.

Amazing Grace. **CSD**, 95; **DDT**, 296; **EED**, (pages not numbered); **TCI**, vol. 21, n. 5 (May 1987). 11.

The Beaux' Stratagem. **EED**, (pages not numbered); **TCI**, vol. 7, n. 3 (May/Jun 1973). 15.

The Child Buyer. **EED**, (pages not numbered).

Cyrano de Bergerac. **BSE4**, 74; **EED**, (pages not numbered); **TCI**, vol. 9, n. 6 (Nov/ Dec 1975). 14.

The End of the Beginning. **EED**, (pages not numbered).

A Family and a Fortune. **DDT**, 214; **EED**, (pages not numbered).

Fidelio. **EED**, (pages not numbered).
Henry V. **EED**, (pages not numbered); **SDW2**, 234.
Hizzoner! **DDT**, 329.
Legend of Lovers. **EED**, (pages not numbered).
Love Letters on Blue Paper. **EED**, (pages not numbered).
The Lower Depths. **EED**, (pages not numbered).
The Oresteia. **EED**, (pages not numbered).
Pantagleize. **CSD**, 78; **EED**, (pages not numbered).
Pygmalion. **EED**, (pages not numbered).
A Whitman Portrait. **EED**, (pages not numbered).
Elson, Charles.
  Don Giovanni. **SDW2**, 234.
  Lohengrin. **SDL**, 34; **SDW1**, 197.
  Norma. **SDW1**, 197.
  Private Lives. **WTP**, 161.
Emens, Homer. *Mlle. Modiste.* **TMI**, 98; **WMC**, 15.
Emmons, David. *The Water Engine.* **TCI**, vol. 12, n. 1 (Jan/Feb 1978). 8.
Engelbach, Claude.
  The Maids. **SDW3**, 124.
  The Misanthrope. **SDW3**, 71.
English, Gary.
  The Roar of the Greasepaint, The Smell of the Crowd. **SDT**, 66.
  Sunday in the Park With George. **TCI**, vol. 21, n. 9 (Nov 1987). 51.
Ensor, A.C. *The Merry Wives of Windsor.* **DIT**, plate 56.
Eren, Refik.
  Oedipus Rex. **SDW2**, 214.
  Sultana Hürrem. **SDW2**, 213.
Ericson, Sven.
  Aniara. **SDR**, 58; **SDW2**, 208.
  Richard III. **SDW1**, 163.
  Romeo and Juliet. **SDW1**, 163.
Erler, Fritz.
  Faust. **SDC**, plate 55; **TCS2**, plates 57, 58, 60.
  Hamlet. **MRH**, facing 48; **TCS2**, plate 59; **TPH**, photo 333.
Erni, Hans. *Titus.* **SDW1**, 114.
Ernst, Max.
  Romeo and Juliet. **AST**, 117; **RSD**, illus. 302, 303.
  Turangalila. **AST**, 119.
  Ubu Enchainé. **AST**, 118.
Erté (Romain de Tirtoff). *The Ziegfeld Follies of 1923.* **FCS**, plate 199.
Erven, Charles E. *Love's Labor's Lost.* **BSE2**, 10.
Esbjornson, David. *The Maids.* **TCI**, vol. 27, n. 10 (Dec 1993). 8.
Essman, Manuel. *The Tower.* **TAT**, plate 501.
Ettinger, Daniel H. *The Man of Mode.* **BSE1**, 6.
Evancho, Mark. *Noises Off.* **TCI**, vol. 22, n. 1 (Jan 1988). 41.
Evans, Bill. *Hamlet.* **TCI**, vol. 7, n. 2 (Mar/Apr 1973). 8.
Evans, Lloyd.
  L'Incoronazione de Poppea. **DPT**, 131.
  Pelléas and Mélisande. **DPT**, 292; **TCI**, vol. 7, n. 1 (Jan/Feb 1973). 12, 13.
Exter, Alexandra.
  La Dama Duende. **DOT**, 215.

-F-

The Balcony. **BTD**, 66.

Henry V. **TDT**, vol. XIX, n. 3 (Fall 1983). 12.

Oedipus Rex. **SDW2**, 90.

1000 Franks Reward. **SDW2**, 89.

Tiny Alice. **SDW3**, 150.

Faucheur, Yves. *Harlequin's Family*. **SDW2**, 90.

Faulkner, Cliff.

Before I Got My Eye Put Out. **TCI**, vol. 20, n. 9 (Nov 1986). 25.

Blue Window. **BSE4**, 75; **TCI**, vol. 20, n. 4 (Apr 1986). 16.

The Comedy of Errors. **TCI**, vol. 14, n. 4 (Sep 1980). 38.

The Importance of Being Earnest. **TCI**, vol. 20, n. 9 (Nov 1986). 25.

Julius Caesar. **TCI**, vol. 14, n. 4 (Sep 1980). 38.

The Last Meeting of the Knights of the White Magnolia. **TCI**, vol. 14, n. 4 (Sep 1980). 36.

Peg O' My Heart. **TCI**, vol. 14, n. 4 (Sep 1980). 36.

The Seagull. **TCI**, vol. 20, n. 9 (Nov 1986). 29.

Faure, Raymond. *The Way of Kings*. **SDW1**, 96.

Faust, Vince. *Ain't Misbehavin*. **TCI**, vol. 20, n. 5 (May 1986). 25.

Favorski, Vladimir. *Twelfth Night*. **SDW2**, 183; **RSD**, illus. 220.

Fedorovitch, Sophie.

Madame Butterfly. **SDW1**, 175.

Orfeo. **CGA**, 141.

Fedorovsky, Feodor.

Lohengrin. **AST**, 134.

Prince Igor. **SDW2**, 184

Feher, Miklos. *The Silence of the Dead*. **SDW4**, illus. 276.

Feiner, Harry.

Becoming Memories. **BSE4**, 20.

The Dresser. **BSE3**, 22.

The Family. **BSE3**, 20.

The Good Person of Szechuan. **BSE2**, 11.

The Italian Girl in Algiers. **BSE4**, 19.

The Marriage of Figaro. **TDT**, vol. XXVII, n. 3 (Summer 1991). 6.

The Plough and the Stars. **BSE2**, 12.

Terra Nova. **BSE3**, 21.

Twelfth Night. **BSE2**, 13.

Feitscher, Vicki.

The Rise and Fall of the City of Mahagonny. **TDT**, vol. XX, n. 1 (Spring 1984). 10.

Fenes, Romulus. *The Cherry Orchard*. **TDT**, vol. XXIII, n. 4 (Winter 1988). 29.

Fenneker, Josef. *The Patience of the Poor*. **SDW1**, 63.

Ferbus, Jean-Pol & Frédéric Flamand. *Real Reel*. **SDW3**, 168.

Fercioni, Gian Maurizio. *L'Ambleto*. **SDW4**, illus. 287.

Feres, Sarah. *The Lover's Tears on the Tomb of the Beloved*. **SDW3**, 175.

Ferguson, John. *The Tempest*. **TCI**, vol. 12, n. 4 (May/Jun 1978). 22.

Fernandez, Salvador & Raúl Oliva. *Saint Joan of America*. **SDW2**, 48.

Ferreira, A., B. Bauchau, R. Moscoso, J. N. Cordier, Cl. Forget, G. Cl. Francois, L. de Grandmaison, & A. Salomon.

The Revolutionary City Belongs to this World. **SDW4**, illus. 385-390.

Feuerstein, Bedrich.

Ass and Shadow. **TDT**, n. 41 (Summer 1975). 21.

Edward II. **RSD**, illus. 272, 273; **TCS2**, plates 202, 203; **TDT**, n. 41 (Summer 1975). 20.

The Imaginary Invalid. **TCS2**, plates 244, 245; **TDT**, n. 41 (Summer 1975). 20.

Love and Death. **TDT**, n. 41 (Summer 1975). 20.

Lovers from the Kiosk. **TDT**, n. 41 (Summer 1975). 21.

Master Pathelin. **TDT**, n. 41 (Summer 1975). 20.

R.U.R. **TDT**, n. 41 (Summer 1975). 19.

Ffolkes, David.

Richard II. **MCN**, 137.

Where's Charley? **BWM**, 265; **WTP**, 152, 153.

Fiala, Jeffrey A. *Rosmersholm*. **CSD**, 79.

Fielding, David.

The Abduction from the Seraglio. **TCI**, vol. 15, n. 5 (May 1981). 15.

Simon Boccanegra. **BTD**, 106.

The Tempest. **BTD**, 87.

Xerxes. **BTD**, 106.

Fielding, Eric.

Lamp at Midnight. **BSE2**, 14.

The Marriage of Figaro. **TDT**, vol. XXVII, n. 3 (Summer 1991). 6.

Tango. **BSE4**, 21; **TCI**, vol. 21, n. 5 (May 1987). 41.

Fievez, Jean-Marie.

Pericles. **SDW4**, illus. 53.

Seven Ways to Cross a River. **SDW4**, illus. 370-373.

Total Eclipse. **SDW4**, illus. 407.

Fini, Léonor. *The Man of Honor*. **SDW2**, 91.

Finke, Jochen.

Faust. **TDT**, vol. XIX, n. 1 (Spring 1983). 20, 21.

Love and Intrigue. **SDW4**, illus. 115-117.

Torquato Tasso. **TDT**, vol. XVI, n. 1 (Spring 1980). 16.

Fioroni, Giosetta & Vittorio Gregotti. *Carmen*. **SDW3**, 183.

Firth, Tazeena. *Il Seraglio*. **BTD**, 104.

Firth, Tazeena & Timothy O'Brien.

The Bassarids. **TDT**, vol. XII, n. 3 (Fall 1976). 35.

A Doll's Life. **HPA**, 137; **MBM**, 84, 85; **TCI**, vol. 16, n. 9 (Nov/Dec 1982). 22, 23.

Evita. **ALW**, 89, 93-95; **BTD**, 152, 153; **HPA**, 160, 161, 164, 168; **HPR**, 273, 277; **MBM**, 57, 59, 60, 61, 82; **TCI**, vol. 12, n. 6 (Oct 1978). 6; **TCI**, vol. 13, n. 6 (Nov/Dec 1979). 14-19; **TCI**, vol. 18, n. 8 (Oct 1984). 15; **TCI**, vol. 19, n. 5 (May 1985). 20; **TDT**, vol. XIX, n. 3 (Fall 1983). 16; **TMT**, 229.

The Man of Mode. **TDT**, vol. XIX, n. 3 (Fall 1983). 9.

A Midsummer Night's Dream. **BTD**, 102.

Pericles. **SDW3**, 62.

Peter Grimes. **BTD**, 101.

The Rake's Progress. **BTD**, 101; **TDT**, vol. XIX, n. 3 (Fall 1983). 8.

Richard II. **TCI**, vol. 8, n. 2 (Mar/Apr 1974). 2.

Turandot. **BTD**, 102, 103.

Fischer, Hans. *Orpheus in the Underworld*. **SDW1**, 115.

Fischer-Dieskau, Mathias. *Der Rosenkavalier*. **TCI**, vol. 27, n. 10 (Dec 1993). 14.

Fisher, Randi & Lennart Mörk. *The Jewels of the Queen*. **SDW2**, 210.

Fiume, Salvatore.

Medea. **SDE**, 84, 85.

Nabucco. **SDW2**, 126.

La Vida Breve. **SDE**, 81.

William Tell. **SIO**, 147.

Fjell, Kai. *The Lady from the Sea*. **SDW2**, 151.

Flamand, Frédéric & Jean-Pol Ferbus. *Real Reel*. **SDW3**, 168.

Fletcher, Robert.

    Hadrian VII. **TCI**, vol. 6, n. 5 (Oct 1972). 14.

    Oedipus Rex. **TSY**, 41.

    The Tempest. **TCI**, vol. 6, n. 5 (Oct 1972). 14.

Flood, Marty. *Hiawatha*. **BTD**, 47.

Flores, Leonida. *Diana e la Tuda*. **SDE**, 86.

Florez, Modesto. *The Automobile Graveyard*. **SDW3**, 158.

Floriet, Bernard.

    The Devotion of the Cross. **SDW3**, 65.

    Le Menteur. **SDW3**, 67.

Flournoy, Sue. *Of Mice and Men*. **BSE4**, 81.

Fo, Dario. *Death and Resurrection of a Puppet*. **SDW4**, illus. 307.

Fontaine, Joel C. *Guys and Dolls*. **BSE1**, 36.

Fontanels, Manuel. *The Tempest*. **TCS2**, plate 199.

Ford, Rodney. *Return to the Forbidden Planet*. **TCI**, vol. 25, n. 8 (Oct 1991). 11.

Foreman, Richard.

    Book of Splendors: Part II. **TCI**, vol. 12, n. 4 (May/Jun 1978). 33.

    Blvd de Paris (I've got the shakes). **TCI**, vol. 12, n. 4 (May/Jun 1978). 30, 32.

    Don Juan. **TCI**, vol. 18, n. 7 (Aug/Sep 1984). 41.

Foreman, Richard & Heidi Landesman.

    Penguin Touquet. **TCI**, vol. 15, n. 5 (May 1981). 6.

Forget, Cl., B. Bauchau, R. Moscoso, J. N. Cordier, A. Ferreira, G. Cl. Francois, L. de
      Grandmaison, & A. Salomon.

    The Revolutionary City Belongs to this World. **SDW4**, illus. 385-390.

Forray, Gabor.

    Bánk Bán. **TDT**, n. 38 (Oct 1974). 13.

    Don Carlos. **TDT**, n. 38 (Oct 1974). 15.

    Duke Bluebeard's Castle. **TDT**, n. 38 (Oct 1974). 10.

    Samson. **TDT**, n. 38 (Oct 1974). 14.

Forrester, Bill. *Brighton Beach Memoirs*. **TCI**, vol. 21, n. 2 (Feb 1987). 24.

Fortunato, Franz. *Il Trovatore*. **SDE**, 88.

Fortuny, Mariano. *Tristan and Isolde*. **MOM**, 7.

Foser, Bill. *Phantom*. **TCI**, vol. 26, n. 7 (Aug/Sep 1992). 12.

Fost-Moulene. *Les Indes Galantes*. **SDW1**, 97.

Foujita, Tajakawa. *Madame Butterfly*. **SDE**, 87.

Foy, Kenneth.

    Gypsy. **SON**, 31, 56, 57, 59.

    Oh, Kay! **DDT**, 152c; **MBM**, 28, 29.

    Rags. **DDT**, 103.

Franceschi, Edgar. *Salammbo*. **TCI**, vol. 20, n. 3 (Mar 1986). 34, 35.

Francini, Mauro.

    The Queen and the Rebels. **SDW2**, 35.

    Volpone. **SDW2**, 35.

Francois, André. *Pas de Deux*. **SDW2**, 91.

Francois, Guy-Claude. *The Awful Yet Unfinished Story of Norodom Sihanouk*. **TCI**, vol.
      20, n. 3 (Mar 1986). 31.

Francois, Guy-Claude, B. Bauchau, R. Moscoso, J. N. Cordier, A. Ferreira, Cl. Forget, L. de Grandmaison, & A. Salomon.
    The Revolutionary City Belongs to this World. **SDW4**, illus. 385-390.
Frankish, Leslie. *Misalliance.* **TCI**, vol. 24, n. 7 (Aug/Sep 1990). 10.
Franko, Rodolfo. *The Tidings Brought to Mary.* **SDW1**, 34.
Franz, Ernest. *Romeo and Juliet.* **SDW1**, 134.
Fraser, Claude Lovat.
    As You Like It. **TOP**, 137.
    The Beggar's Opera. **SDG**, 176.
    Henry IV. **TCS2**, color plate 1.
Frazer, Anne.
    A Day in the Life of Joe Egg. **SDW3**, 149.
    The Taming of the Shrew. **SDW4**, illus. 24.
Fredrikson, Kristian & Richard Prins. *Henry IV.* **SDW3**, 44.
Freibergs, A. *The Legend of Kaupo.* **TDT**, vol. XII, n. 3 (Fall 1976). 35.
Freudenberger, Daniel. *Serjeant Musgrave's Dance.* **SFT**, 15.
Frey, Maxim. *St. Jacobs Fahrt.* **DIT**, plate 101.
Freyer, Achim.
    The Barber of Seville. **SDW3**, 177.
    Clavigo. **TCI**, vol. 13, n. 5 (Oct 1979). 19; **TCI**, vol. 13, n. 5 (Oct 1979). 19.
    Fidelio. **TCI**, vol. 13, n. 5 (Oct 1979). 20.
    The Good Woman of Setzuan. **SDW4**, illus. 241, 242; **TCI**, vol. 13, n. 5 (Oct 1979). 21.
    Das Käthchen von Heilbronn. **TCI**, vol. 13, n. 5 (Oct 1979). 16.
    Lear. **SDW4**, illus. 355, 356; **TCI**, vol. 13, n. 5 (Oct 1979). 18.
    Maulwerke. **TCI**, vol. 13, n. 5 (Oct 1979). 18.
    Monument to Kleist. **TCI**, vol. 13, n. 5 (Oct 1979). 16.
    Moses and Aaron. **TCI**, vol. 24, n. 9 (Nov 1990). 13.
    Pelléas and Mélisande. **DSL**, figure 2.7(c&d); **OPE**, 218, 220, 224, 226; **SST**, 46, 47.
    Wozzeck. **TCI**, vol. 13, n. 5 (Oct 1979). 20.
Freyer, Ilona. *Uncle Vanya.* **TCI**, vol. 11, n. 2 (Mar/Apr 1977). 26.
Frigerio, Ezio.
    I Capuleti e i Montecchi. **SIO**, 62.
    Fidelio. **OPE**, 114, 123, 124, 127; **SIO**, 56, 57.
    Francesca da Rimini. **MOM**, 88-99.
    The Giants of the Mountain. **SIO**, 55.
    King Lear. **SDW4**, illus. 42-45; **SIO**, 64, 65.
    St. Joan of the Stockyards. **SIO**, 58-61.
    The Servant of Two Masters. **SDW2**, 125; **SIO**, 66, 67.
    Simon Boccanegra. **SIO**, 63.
    The Threepenny Opera. **SDW4**, illus. 231, 232; **SIO**, 66.
Fritzsche, Max.
    Biedermann and the Firebugs. **SDW2**, 110.
    The Petrified Forest. **SDW1**, 64.
    The Threepenny Opera. **SDW2**, 58.
Frycz, Karol. *Julius Caesar.* **RSD**, illus. 264; **SCM**, 85.
Fuerst, Walter René.
    Le Bourgeois Gentilhomme. **TCS2**, plate 266.
    Candide. **TCS2**, plate 265.
    The Emperor Jones. **TCS2**, plate 219.
    Faust. **TCS2**, plate 223.

L'Homme et ses Fantomes. **TCS2**, plate 208.
The Marriage of Figaro. **TCS2**, plate 110; **TCS2**, plate 111.
Simoun. **TCS2**, plate 218.
The Taming of the Shrew. **TCS2**, plate 267; **TPH**, photo 356.
Tristan and Isolde. **TCS1**, plates 43, 44.
Fülöp, Zoltán.
    Salomé. **SDW2**, 140.
    The Witty Students. **SDW2**, 140.
Fulton, Larry.
    The Cat and the Canary. **TCI**, vol. 14, n. 3 (May/Jun 1980). 43.
    Dark Ages. **TCI**, vol. 14, n. 3 (May/Jun 1980). 43.
Funicello, Ralph.
    The Alcestiad. **TCI**, vol. 13, n. 3 (May/Jun 1979). 37.
    Another Part of the Forest. **ASD1**, 52.
    Candide. **CSD**, 81.
    The Caucasian Chalk Circle. **TCI**, vol. 22, n. 1 (Jan 1988). 51.
    Dear Antoine. **ASD1**, 49.
    Division Street. **ASD1**, 42; **ASD1**, 46; **TCI**, vol. 14, n. 4 (Sep 1980). 40.
    The Front Page. **ASD1**, between 70 & 71.
    General Gorgeous. **TCI**, vol. 14, n. 4 (Sep 1980). 21.
    Hamlet. **TDT** vol. XXXI, n. 2 (Spring 1995). 16.
    Hay Fever. **TCI**, vol. 14, n. 4 (Sep 1980). 21.
    The Learned Ladies. **ASD1**, 51.
    Marco Millions. **TCI**, vol. 23, n. 1 (Jan 1989). 15.
    Master Harold...and the Boys. **ASD1**, 44.
    Measure for Measure. **DDT**, 83.
    Misalliance. **DDT**, 170; **TCI**, vol. 22, n. 7 (Aug/Sep 1988). 13.
    The Miser. **TDT** vol. XXXI, n. 2 (Spring 1995). 16.
    Noises Off. **TCI**, vol. 22, n. 1 (Jan 1988). 40.
    Peer Gynt. **ASD1**, 47.
    Pillars of the Community. **ASD1**, 51.
    Savages. **ASD1**, 46.
    A Streetcar Named Desire. **DDT**, 152c.
    The Taming of the Shrew. **ASD1**, 48.
    Tartuffe. **DDT**, 374.
    The Tempest. **TCI**, vol. 25, n. 9 (Nov 1991). 14.
    Twelfth Night. **TCI**, vol. 29, n. 2 (Feb 1995). 32.
    The Winter Dancers. **TCI**, vol. 14, n. 4 (Sep 1980). 41.
Furse, Roger.
    Caesar and Cleopatra. **SDW1**, 175; **WTP**, 144.
    The Duchess of Malfi. **TPH**, photo 436; **WTP**, 80, 81.
    The Skin of Our Teeth. **TOP**, 77.
    Twelfth Night. **SDW1**, 175.

-G-

Gabo, Naum & Antoine Pevsner. *La Chatte.* **AST**, 136; **RSD**, illus. 200; **TCS2**, plate 165.
Gade, Svend.
    Scherz, Satire, Ironie und tiefere Bedeutung. **TPH**, photo 418.
    Traumspiel. **TCS2**, plates 210, 211.
Galitzine, Prince, Joseph Harker & Phil Harker. *Funny Face.* **MCD**, plates 157, 158.

Galliard-Risler, Francine. *St. Joan.* **SDW1**, 97.

Gallis, Paul. Cyrano: *The Musical.* **TCI**, vol. 28, n. 2 (Feb 1994). 42, 43.

Gallo, David. *The Triumph of Love.* **TCI**, vol. 28, n. 6 (Jun/Jul 1994). 10.

Galup, Mario.
  The Lower Depths. **SDW2**, 241.
  Moon on a Rainbow Shawl. **SDW2**, 242.

Gamlin, Yngve.
  Antigone. **SDW1**, 164.
  The Sleeping Beauty. **SDW1**, 164.
  The Weaver of Bagdad. **SDW2**, 209.

Gamrekeli, Irakly.
  Anzor. **RSD**, illus. 159; **RST**, 288, 289.
  The Business Man. **TAT**, plate 709.
  Hamlet. **RST**, 115, 172, 173.
  Die Räuber. **RST**, 269, 290, 291; **SDW2**, 184
  Tetnould. **TAT**, plate 711.

Ganeau, François.
  The Birds. **SDW3**, 32.
  The Double Inconstancy. **SDW1**, 97.
  Il Matrimonio Segreto. **SDW1**, 103.
  The Shoemaker's Wife. **SDW2**, 92.
  The Telephone. **SDE**, 89.

Gansonskaya, Liona.
  Looking for the Wind in the Field. **TDT**, vol. XX, n. 1 (Spring 1984). 17.

Garbuglia, Mario. *A View from the Bridge.* **SDW2**, 126.

Garcia, Victor.
  The Automobile Graveyard. **SDW3**, 159.
  Yerma. **SDW4**, illus. 248, 249.

Garcia, Victor & Enrique Alarcon. *The Maids.* **SDW3**, 124.

Garcia, Victor & W. Pereira Cardoso.
  The Balcony. **RSD**, illus. 622; **SDB**, 200; **SDW4**, illus. 262-264.

Gardiner, Robert. *Jack and the Beanstalk.* **TCI**, vol. 28, n. 3 (Mar 1994). 11.

Gardner, John. *Crimes of the Heart.* **BSE4**, 54.

Gariano, Eliane. *Electra.* **SDW4**, illus. 11.

Gates, Frank E. & E.A. Morange.
  Rose Marie. **TMT**, 62.
  Leah Kleschna. **MCN**, 24.
  Wildflower. **WMC**, 103.

Gauchat, Pierre. *Carmen.* **SCM**, 80.

Gauer, Glenn. *Under the Gas Lights.* **SDL**, 242.

Gauguin, Paul René.
  Caesar and Cleopatra. **SDW1**, 152.
  Clochemerle. **SDW2**, 152.

Geddes, Tony. *The Merchant of Venice.* **TDT**, vol. XXVII, n. 4 (Fall 1991). 21.

Geenens, Robert. *Sire Halewijn.* **SDW2**, 29.

Gelpi, Germén.
  The Man With the Flower in His Mouth. **SDW1**, 34.
  The Raid of the Ranquels. **SDW1**, 34.

Georgiadis, Nicholas.
  As You Desire Me. **BTD**, 75.
  La Clemenza di Tito. **BTD**, 132, 133.

Love's Triumph. **SDW2**, 92.

Marie Tudor. **RSD**, illus. 532.

Thomas More, A Man for All Seasons. **RSD**, illus. 535.

Le Triomphe de l'Amour. **RSD**, illus. 536.

Gjelsteen, Karen.

The Importance of Being Earnest. **TCI**, vol. 11, n. 6 (Nov/Dec 1977). 96.

Glenn, David.

Ah, Wilderness. **TCI**, vol. 13, n. 3 (May/Jun 1979). 31.

Still Life. **TCI**, vol. 18, n. 3 (Mar 1984). 28.

Gliese, Rochus. *Love's Labor's Lost.* **SOS**, 213.

Gliese, Rochus & Knut Ström. *Macbeth.* **DIT**, plate 106; **SDC**, plate 56.

Glossop, Roger. *'Tis Pity She's a Whore.* **BTD**, 52.

Godefroid, Charlie. *Everyman.* **SDW1**, 44.

Godfrey, Peter. *All God's Chillun Got Wings.* **SCM**, 23.

Goetz, Kent. *Wings.* **TDT**, vol. XXVI, n. 1 (Spring 1990). 9 of insert.

Goffin, Peter. *In Time to Come.* **DOT**, 246.

Goheen, Douglas-Scott. *Arms and the Man.* **SFT**, 350.

Golovin, Aleksandr.

Orpheus. **MOT**, between 64 & 65.

Boris Godounov. **TPH**, photo 349.

Don Juan. **MOT**, between 64 & 65.

Le Marriage of Figaro. **RST**, 221, 222.

Masquerade. **MOT**, between 96 & 97; **RSD**, illus. 27; **RST**, 34, 36, 37.

Gonçalves, Martin.

Blood Wedding. **SDW1**, 49.

Desire Under the Elms. **SDW1**, 49.

Oedipus Rex. **SDW1**, 49.

Goncharova, Natalia.

Le Coq D'Or. **DIT**, plate 70; **RSD**, illus. 286, 287; **SDC**, plate 95; **TCT**, plate 12.

The Firebird. **AST**, 54; **DOT**, 219.

Foire Espagnole. **TCS2**, plate 258.

Les Noces. **AST**, 55.

Sorochinsky Fair. **SDR**, 15.

Thamar. **FCS**, plate 178, color plate 21.

Gondolf, Walter. *Blood Wedding.* **SDW2**, 59.

Goodwin, Richard R. *Division Street.* **TCI**, vol. 20, n. 2 (Feb 1986). 20.

Gordon, Pip. *Catch My Brother's Eye.* **TDT**, vol. XXV, n. 3 (Fall 1989). 37.

Gorelik, Mordecai.

All My Sons. **TPH**, photo 469.

Casey Jones. **NTO**, facing 68; **SOW**, plate 90.

Dead End. **NTO**, facing 68.

Desire Under the Elms. **SDA**, 228; **SDW1**, 194; **WTP**, 172, 173.

Golden Boy. **SDA**, 175.

Men In White. **MCN**, 112; **SDA**, 240, 241.

Processional. **TPH**, photo 468.

R.U.R. **SDC**, plate 90.

They Shall Not Die. **NTO**, facing 428; **RSD**, illus. 446.

Thunder Rock. **RSD**, illus. 447; **SDA**, 175, 289; **SDW1**, 195.

King Hunger. **SDB**, 28.

Gorey, David. *The Mikado.* **TCI**, vol. 18, n. 4 (Apr 1984). 43.

Gorey, Edward.
    Amphigorey: The Musical. **DDT**, 20, 187.
    Dracula. **DDT**, 222, 223, 420; **DDT**, 438; **DSL**, figures 2.8(c), 16.4; **TCI**, vol. 13, n. 1
       (Jan/Feb 1979). 32; **TCI**, vol. 22, n. 5 (May 1988). 39.
Gough, Philip. *A Midsummer Night's Dream.* **SCM**, 35.
Gould, Peter David. *A Musical Nightmare.* **TCI**, vol. 22, n. 5 (May 1988). 39.
Gould, Richard. *End of the World.* **TCI**, vol. 19, n. 8 (Oct 1985). 19.
Goyette, Claude. *Nelligan.* **TDT**, vol. XXVII, n. 4 (Fall 1991). 21.
Graham, Colin. *Death in Venice.* **TCI**, vol. 28, n. 4 (Apr 1994). 6.
Graham, Steven. *Volpone.* **CSD**, 50; **TCI**, vol. 7, n. 5 (Oct 1973). 25.
Grandmaison, L. de, B. Bauchau, R. Moscoso, J. N. Cordier, A. Ferreira, Cl. Forget, G. Cl.
    Francois, & A. Salomon.
    The Revolutionary City Belongs to this World. **SDW4**, illus. 385-390.
Granval, Charles. *Les Fourberies de Scapin.* **TCS2**, plate 250.
Grate, Eric. *The Flies.* **SDW1**, 165.
Graves, Lynn. *Fen.* **TCI**, vol. 20, n. 3 (Mar 1986). 18.
Greco, Ricardo. *Eternal Husband.* **SDW2**, 164.
Greenleaf, Jamie. *K2.* **TCI**, vol. 19, n. 5 (May 1985). 27.
Greer, Howard. *Greenwich Village Follies of 1922.* **MCN**, 60.
Gregotti, Vittorio & Giosetta Fioroni. *Carmen.* **SDW3**, 183.
Greter, Johan.
    The Killer. **SDW2**, 143.
    The Story of Vasco. **SDW2**, 144.
Grey, Terence. *Oedipus.* **SDG**, 184.
Griffeth, Michael J. *In Contempt.* **TDT**, vol. XIX, n. 3 (Fall 1983). 17.
Griffin, Hayden.
    The Admirable Crichton. **TCI**, vol. 23, n. 2 (Feb 1989). 36.
    As You Like It. **TCI**, vol. 19, n. 9 (Nov 1985). 25.
    The Broken Jug. **TCI**, vol. 19, n. 9 (Nov 1985). 21.
    Così fan Tutti. **BTD**, 107; **TDT**, vol. XIX, n. 1 (Spring 1983). 7.
    Duck Song. **TCI**, vol. 19, n. 9 (Nov 1985). 25.
    A Fleet Street Comedy. **TCI**, vol. 19, n. 9 (Nov 1985). 24.
    Glengarry Glen Ross. **BTD**, 89.
    Golden Boy. **TCI**, vol. 19, n. 9 (Nov 1985). 20, 24.
    Henry VIII. **TCI**, vol. 19, n. 9 (Nov 1985). 23, 25.
    The Iceman Cometh. **TCI**, vol. 19, n. 9 (Nov 1985). 24.
    King Lear. **BTD**, 88.
    A Map of the World. **TCI**, vol. 19, n. 9 (Nov 1985). 19, 25.
    Mayor of Zalamea. **TCI**, vol. 19, n. 9 (Nov 1985). 22, 23.
    Parsifal. **BTD**, 107.
    Pericles. **TCI**, vol. 19, n. 9 (Nov 1985). 20.
    Plenty. **TCI**, vol. 19, n. 9 (Nov 1985). 25.
    Pravda. **BTD**, 89.
    Rosmersholm. **TCI**, vol. 19, n. 9 (Nov 1985). 21.
    Total Eclipse. **TCI**, vol. 19, n. 9 (Nov 1985). 20.
    Watch It Come Down. **TCI**, vol. 11, n. 5 (Oct 1977). 32.
    Weapons of Happiness. **TCI**, vol. 11, n. 5 (Oct 1977). 33.
    The Woman. **TCI**, vol. 13, n. 1 (Jan/Feb 1979). 8; **TDT**, vol. XIX, n. 1 (Spring 1983).
       7.
Gris, Juan. *Les Tentations de la Bergere ou l'amour vainqueur.* **AST**, 85.
Griswold, Mary. *The Heidi Chronicles.* **TCI**, vol. 27, n. 3 (Mar 1993). 43.

Griswold, Mary & John Paoletti.
  The Good Soldier Schweik. **TCI**, vol. 18, n. 3 (Mar 1984). 24.
Groff, Robert A. *The Blue Bird*. **TDT**, vol. XXVIII, n. 2 (Spring 1992). 6 of insert.
Gröning, Karl.
  Don Carlos. **SDW1**, 65.
  Ondine. **SDW1**, 65.
Gronovsky, Tadeusz. *The Tower of Babel*. **RSD**, illus. 270, 271.
Grooms, Red.
  City Junket. **TCI**, vol. 18, n. 4 (Apr 1984). 29.
  The Death of the Kangaroo. **ASC**, 22.
Gropman, David.
  Bingo. **ASD2**, 35.
  Come Back to the Five and Dime, Jimmy Dean, Jimmy Dean. **ASD2**, 32; **DDT**, 40.
  Death and the King's Horseman. **ASD2**, 37.
  Mister Puntila and His Chauffer Matti. **ASD2**, 40, 41; **DDT**, 170.
  The 1940's Radio Hour. **TCI**, vol. 23, n. 8 (Oct 1989). 47.
  A Quiet Place. **ASD2**, 44-46.
Gros, Ernest.
  The Bird of Paradise. **MCN**, 39.
  The Concert. **SDA**, 22.
  The Darling of the Gods. **MCN**, 21.
  The Easiest Way. **MCN**, 33; **SDA**, 23.
  The Girl of the Golden West. **MCN**, 26, 27.
  The Gold Diggers. **MCN**, 48.
  The Governor's Lady. **SDA**, 23.
  Kiki. **MCN**, 55.
  Peter Pan. **MCN**, 25.
  The Rose of the Rancho. **MCN**, 30.
  Under Two Flags. **MCN**, 16.
Gros, Ernest & Frank D. Dodge. *Salvation Nell*. **MCN**, 32.
Gros, Ernest, J.M. Hewlett, A.T. Hewlett, & Charles Basing. *Chantecler*. **MCN**, 36.
Grosz, George. *Caesar and Cleopatra*. **AST**, 176.
Grosz, George & Edward Suhr.
  The Drunken Ship. **AST**, 176; **RSD**, illus. 242; **TPH**, photo 375.
Grosz, George & Erwin Piscator. *The Good Soldier Schweik*. **NTO**, facing 420; **RSD**,
  illus. 241; **TBB**, 109; **TPH**, photo 377.
Grotowski, Jerzy. *Acropolis*. **SDW3**, 97.
Grübler, Ekkehard.
  Idomeneo. **TCI**, vol. 11, n. 2 (Mar/Apr 1977). 10; **TDT**, vol. XII, n. 1 (Spring 1976).
  28.
  Oedipus Rex. **OPE**, 68.
  Picnic in the Field. **SDW2**, 60.
  Romulus the Great. **TDT**, n. 14 (Oct 1968). 23.
  The Sicilian Vespers. **TCI**, vol. 11, n. 2 (Mar/Apr 1977). 18.
Grund, Françoise. *Danton's Death*. **SDW4**, illus. 127-129.
Grund, Manfred. *V for Vietnam*. **SDW3**, 220.
Grünewald, Isaac.
  Fiesco. **TAT**, plate 442.
  Sakuntala. **TPH**, photo 389.
  Samson et Dalila. **CSC**, facing 120, 122; **TCS2**, plate 222; **TPH**, photo 390; **RSD**,
  illus. 141.

-H-

Haferung, Paul.
    Karl V. **SDW1**, 66.
    Die Meistersinger von Nürnberg. **SDW1**, 66.
    Mister Puntila and His Man Matti. **SDW2**, 61.
    Moses and Aaron. **RSD**, illus. 455; **SDW2**, 60.
    Otello. **SDW1**, 66.
    The Satin Slipper. **SDW1**, 66.
    Troilus and Cressida. **SDW1**, 75.
    Venus Observed. **SDW1**, 66.
Hajdu, Etienne. *Cantate Profane*. **RSD**, illus. 491.
Hajek, Otto Herbert. *The Tempest*. **AST**, 235.
Hall, Peter J. & Franco Zeffirelli. *Romeo and Juliet*. **SDW2**, 133; **SOS**, 262.
Hall, Stafford, Conrad Tritschler, R.C. McCleery, & W. Holmes.
    The Arcadians. **MCD**, plate 80.
Hallegger, Kurt. *The Wall*. **SDW2**, 60.
Halmen, Pet.
    La Straniera. **TCI**, vol. 23, n. 7 (Aug/Sep 1989). 9; **TCI**, vol. 24, n. 5 (May 1990). 29,
      30.
    Der Zigeunerbaron (The Gypsy Baron). **TCI**, vol. 27, n. 9 (Nov 1993). 18.
Halty, Adolpho. *The Bonds of Interest*. **SDW2**, 242.
Hamel, Niels. *The Good Woman of Setzuan*. **SDW3**, 114.
Hamilton, Rob. *Hair*. **TDT**, vol. XXVI, n. 1 (Spring 1990). 10 of insert.
Hammond, Aubrey.
    Acropolis. **DOT**, 222.
    The Pilgrim of Love. **DIT**, plate 7.
    The Rose and the Ring. **DIT**, plate 7; **TCS2**, plate 227.
    Wild Violets. **SCM**, 22.
Hampton, Michael. *The Insect Comedy*. **DIT**, plate 57; **TPH**, photo 434.
Hanák, Ján. *The Gods of Amsterdam*. **SDW2**, 41.
Hancock, Carolyn.
    The Garrick Gaieties. **MCN**, 75
    The Taming of the Shrew. **WTP**, 77.
Hann, Walter & Philip Howden. *The Chinese Honeymoon*. **MCD**, plate 35.
Hann, Walter, R.C. McCleery, & Conrad Tritschler. *Oh! Oh!! Delphine!!!* **MCD**, plate 95.
Hanson, Debra. *Romeo and Juliet*. **TCI**, vol. 26, n. 9 (Nov 1992). 29.
Hardie, Peter. *Something's Afoot*. **TCI**, vol. 22, n. 5 (May 1988). 35.
Harford, W. *The Bell of Mayfair*. **MCD**, plate 61.
Hariton, Gerry & Vicki Baral.
    Mail. **TCI**, vol. 22, n. 2 (Feb 1988). 51.
    South Pacific. **TCI**, vol. 22, n. 2 (Feb 1988). 51.
Harker, Joseph.
    Captain Kidd. **MCD**, plate 84.
    Henry VIII. **SDG**, 139.
    Our Miss Gibbs. **MCD**, plate 78.
    Peggy. **MCD**, plate 87.
Harker, Joseph & Alfred Terraine. *The Dollar Princess*. **MCD**, plate 82.
Harker, Joseph & Phil Harker.
    Betty in Mayfair. **MCD**, plate 130.
    Chu Chin Chow. **MCD**, plate 108.
    Heads Up! **MCD**, plate 162.
    Lady, be Good! **MCD**, plate 142.

Hastings. *The Greeks*. **TCI**, vol. 24, n. 10 (Dec 1990). 78.

Hausner, Xenia. *Fiesko of Genoa*. **TCI**, vol. 22, n. 2 (Feb 1988). 8.

Havemann, Franz. *Hamlet*. **SDW2**, 50.

Hay, Richard L.
   Antony and Cleopatra. **TCI**, vol. 11, n. 6 (Nov/Dec 1977). 8.
   The Alchemist. **SDL**, 75.
   Brand. **SDL**, 60.
   Camino Real. **BSE3**, 28.
   The Cherry Orchard. **PST**, 362.
   An Enemy of the People. **BSE5**, 11; **SCT**, between 152 & 153.
   King Lear. **BSE4**, 69.
   Macbeth. **TCI**, vol. 13, n. 4 (Sep 1979). 31.
   A Moon for the Misbegotten. **SDL**, 75.
   Pericles. **TDT**, vol. XXVI, n. 1 (Spring 1990). 10 of insert.

Hayes, Dermot, Neil Peter Jampolis, & John Napier. *The Life and Adventures of Nicholas Nickleby*. **TCI**, vol. 15, n. 9 (Nov/Dec 1981). 12-15.

Hayes, Dermot. *The Last Supper*. **BTD**, 77.

Hayes, James & Tom Aston.
   Delightful Gardens of Existence. **TCI**, vol. 4, n. 1 (Jan/Feb 1970). 34.

Haymann, Henry. *Two Gentlemen of Verona*. **SDL**, 71.

Hays, David.
   All the Way Home. **SDR**, 57; **SDW2**, 235.
   Cyrano de Bergerac. **TCI**, vol. 2, n. 6 (Nov/Dec 1968). 31.
   Electronics. **SDW2**, 235.
   Gideon. **SDR**, 57.
   Long Day's Journey Into Night. **TCI**, vol. 23, n. 8 (Oct 1989). 43.
   No Strings. **BWM**, 198; **WMC**, 226.
   St. Joan. **TCI**, vol. 2, n. 6 (Nov/Dec 1968). 33.
   Tiger at the Gates. **TCI**, vol. 2, n. 6 (Nov/Dec 1968). 33.
   Two by Two. **BWM**, 199; **TCI**, vol. 5, n. 1 (Jan/Feb 1971). 7.

Head, Eric. *What the Butler Saw*. **TCI**, vol. 7, n. 5 (Oct 1973). 24.

Hecht, Torsten. *Gyges und sein Ring*. **TCS2**, plate 132.

Heckroth, Heinrich.
   Alexander Balus. **TCS2**, plate 217.
   The Green Table. **RSD**, illus. 138, 139.
   Radamisto. **RSD**, illus. 249.
   Royal Palace. **RSD**, illus. 252.
   Salomé. **TCS2**, plate 148.
   The Seven Deadly Sins. **SDW2**, 63.
   Theodora. **RSD**, illus. 143; **TCS2**, plates 120, 121.

Hedeby - Pawlo, Kerstin. *Alcino*. **SDW2**, 209.

Heeley, Desmond.
   The Barber of Seville. **TCI**, vol. 22, n. 8 (Oct 1988). 58.
   The Circle. **SDD**, between 210 & 211.
   Don Pasquale. **TCI**, vol. 22, n. 8 (Oct 1988). 60.
   Henry V. **RSD**, illus. 618.
   Manon Lescaut. **DDT**, 155; **MOM**, 147-150; **TCI**, vol. 14, n. 6 (Nov/Dec 1980). 15.
   The Merchant of Venice. **TCI**, vol. 7, n. 2 (Mar/Apr 1973). 10.
   Oedipus Rex. **TCI**, vol. 22, n. 8 (Oct 1988). 61; **TSY**, 35.
   Pelléas and Mélisande. **OPE**, 216, 223, 224.
   Solitaire. **SDW2**, 216.

Suor Angelica. **DDT**, 477.
La Traviata. **TCI**, vol. 27, n. 10 (Dec 1993). 12.
Hegle, Kaare.
    Castle in Sweden. **SDW2**, 152.
    A Jade for Don Juan. **SDW1**, 153.
    Lysistrata. **SDW1**, 153.
Heiliger, Bernhard. *Faust, part II*. **SDW3**, 80.
Hein, Keith.
    Long Day's Journey Into Night. **TCI**, vol. 14, n. 4 (Sep 1980). 47.
    Morning's at Seven. **TCI**, vol. 14, n. 4 (Sep 1980). 47.
Hein, Peter.
    Die Bauren (The Peasants). **TDT**, vol. XVI, n. 1 (Spring 1980). 16.
    Die Räuber. **SDW4**, illus. 118-123.
    The Wild Duck. **SDW4**, illus. 174-176.
Heinrich, Reinhard. *La Traviata*. **TCI**, vol. 21, n. 10 (Dec 1987). 16.
Heinrich, Rudolf.
    Antigone. **TCI**, vol. 10, n. 6 (Nov/Dec 1976). 17; **TDT**, vol. XII, n. 1 (Spring 1976).
        27.
    Ariadne auf Naxos. **TCI**, vol. 10, n. 6 (Nov/Dec 1976). 15.
    The Clever Little Vixen. **SDW2**, 50.
    Don Carlos. **SCT**, 188; **TCI**, vol. 10, n. 6 (Nov/Dec 1976). 16; **TDT**, vol. XII, n. 1
        (Spring 1976). 27.
    Electra. **TCI**, vol. 10, n. 6 (Nov/Dec 1976). 15.
    Fidelio. **OPE**, 113, 122, 125, 127; **OPE**, 121, 122, 124, 126; **TCI**, vol. 10, n. 6 (Nov/
        Dec 1976). 12.
    The Good Soldier Schweik. **SDW2**, 53.
    Götterdämmerung. **OPE**, 184, 192, 194, 196, 198.
    Káta Kabanová. **TCI**, vol. 15, n. 1 (Jan 1981). 37.
    Macbeth. **SDW3**, 181.
    The Magic Flute. **OPE**, 98, 100, 104, 108, 110; **SDB**, 74; **TCI**, vol. 15, n. 1 (Jan
        1981). 36.
    The Marriage of Figaro. **TCI**, vol. 10, n. 6 (Nov/Dec 1976). 15, 16
    Die Meistersinger von Nürnberg. **SDW2**, 53.
    A Midsummer Night's Dream. **TCI**, vol. 15, n. 1 (Jan 1981). 36.
    Moses and Aaron. **SDW4**, illus. 205-208.
    The Old Ones. **SDW4**, illus. 348.
    Parsifal. **SDB**, 76.
    Der Ring des Nibelungen. **TCI**, vol. 10, n. 6 (Nov/Dec 1976). 17.
    Salomé. **MOM**, 15; **TCI**, vol. 10, n. 5 (Oct 1976). 15; **TCI**, vol. 10, n. 6 (Nov/Dec
        1976). 14.
    Werther. **TCI**, vol. 10, n. 6 (Nov/Dec 1976). 15.
    Zum Grossen Wurstel. **TCI**, vol. 10, n. 6 (Nov/Dec 1976). 16.
Heising, Ulrich & Karl Kneidl. *Stallerhof*. **SDW4**, illus. 408.
Heiskanen, Pekka. *Endgame* **SDW2**, 203.
Heller, Vladimir. *The Weavers*. **SDW2**, 42.
Helmuth, Suzanne. *Hospital*. **TCI**, vol. 14, n. 4 (Sep 1980). 22.
Hembrow, Victor. *Macbeth*. **DIT**, plate 19; **TPH**, photo 431.
Hendrickson, Stephen. *Waiting for Godot*. **SDW3**, 120.
Henze, Jürgen. *We Come to the River*. **CGA**, 189; **TCI**, vol. 10, n. 6 (Nov/Dec 1976). 4.
Hepworth, Barbara.
    Electra. **AST**, 220.

L'Autre Messie. **TCS2**, plate 102.

Cirkus Dandin. **RSD**, illus. 279.

Desire under the Elms. **RSD**, illus. 281, 282; **TAT**, plate 169; **TDT**, n. 41 (Summer 1975). 22.

The Fateful Play of Love. **TDT**, n. 41 (Summer 1975). 23.

The Great God Brown. **TAS**, 98; **TAT**, plates 170, 171.

Mannequin's Ball. **TDT**, n. 41 (Summer 1975). 23.

The Merchant of Venice. **TAT**, plate 172; **TDT**, n. 41 (Summer 1975). 23.

The Millionairess. **SOW**, plates 60, 61.

The Silent Canary. **RSD**, illus. 280.

Thesmophoriazusae. **RSD**, illus. 278; **TDT**, n. 41 (Summer 1975). 22.

Hicks, Grant.

American Buffalo. **BTD**, 83.

California Dog Fight. **BTD**, 29.

The Slab Boys. **BTD**, 83.

Hicks, Julian. *The Girl Behind the Counter*. **MCD**, plate 59.

Higgins, Douglas.

Love for Love. **TCI**, vol. 8, n. 6 (Nov/Dec 1974). 14.

Mercy Street. **TCI**, vol. 6, n. 3 (May/Jun 1972). 21.

Hill, Hainer.

Electra. **SDW2**, 54.

The Visit. **TDT**, vol. XII, n. 3 (Fall 1976). 33.

Wozzeck. **SDW2**, 54.

Hines, Thomas G. *The Crucible*. **SCT**, 4.

Hird, Thomas C.

Cabaret. **BSE1**, 15.

Fiddler on the Roof. **BSE1**, 8.

The Ice Wolf. **BSE1**, 15.

The Philadelphia Story. **BSE1**, 32.

Seascape. **BSE2**, 16.

Hlawa, Stefan.

Don Carlos. **SDW2**, 156.

Fairy Lady. **SDW2**, 156.

Hockney, David.

L'Enfant et les Sortilèges. **HPS**, 150-155, 169, 170, 172, 174, 175, 177.

The Magic Flute. **HPS**, 62, 66, 67, 106-111, 116, 118, 120; **TCI**, vol. 13, n. 3 (May/Jun 1979). 21; **TDT**, vol. XXVII, n. 2 (Spring 1991). 36; **TDT**, vol. XXVII, n. 3 (Summer 1991). 8.

Les Mamelles de Tirésias. **HPS**, 126, 146-159, 164-166; **TCI**, vol. 18, n. 4 (Apr 1984). 42.

Parade. **MOM**, 167-175; **TCI**, vol. 15, n. 6 (Jun/Jul 1981). 10; **TCI**, vol. 16, n. 9 (Nov/Dec 1982). 31.

The Rake's Progress. **HPS**, 60, 70, 71, 74, 79, 80, 82-84, 90-97, 103.

Le Rossignol. **BTD**, 112; **TCI**, vol. 16, n. 9 (Nov/Dec 1982). 31.

Tristan and Isolde. **BTD**, 112; **TCI**, vol. 22, n. 3 (Mar 1988). 22.

Ubu Roi. **SDR**, 42.

Hoffer, Hans. *The English Cat*. **TCI**, vol. 22, n. 3 (Mar 1988). 64, 65, 67.

Hoffman, Vlastislav.

Adam the Creator . **TCS2**, plate 243.

Armoured Train No. 14-69. **SDW1**, 51.

The Bacchantes. **TCS2**, plate 144.

Campaign Against Death. **TDT**, n. 41 (Summer 1975). 17.

Columbus. **TCS2**, plate 145.

The Dictator. **TAT**, plate 188.

L'Echange. **TCS2**, plate 272.

Elizabeth of England. **TDT**, n. 41 (Summer 1975). 18.

Les Esclaves. **TCS2**, plate 241.

Falkensteyn. **TCS2**, plate 98.

Hamlet. **SCM**, 82; **SDC**, plate 120; **SOW**, plate 43; **TAS**, 164; **TAT**, plates
    184-187; **TDT**, n. 41 (Summer 1975). 17, back cover.

Hedy. **TCS2**, plate 270.

Herakles. **RSD**, illus. 145.

The Hussites. **TDT**, n. 41 (Summer 1975). 16.

The Hydra. **RSD**, illus. 128.

Jeu de l'Amour et de la Mort. **TCS2**, plate 271.

The Man Who Was Thursday. **RSD**, illus. 276; **TDT**, n. 41 (Summer 1975). 17.

Mourning Becomes Electra. **TDT**, n. 41 (Summer 1975). 18.

Oedipus. **TDT**, n. 41 (Summer 1975). 18.

R.U.R. **RSD**, illus. 277; **TAT**, plate 193.

Tristan and Isolde. **TDT**, n. 41 (Summer 1975). 17.

Une Affaire de Famille. **TCS2**, plate 99.

The White Plague. **TPH**, photo 387.

Wozzeck. **TCS2**, plate 362.

Zizka. **TCS2**, plate 240.

Hoffmann, Ludwig von. *Aglavaine et Sélysette.* **TCS2**, plates 15, 16.

Hoflehner, Rudolf.

Ein Indisches Märchenspiel. **AST**, 232.

Iphigenia in Taurus. **AST**, 233.

Lass wehen die Zeit. **AST**, 232.

Hofmann, Hans. *Country Fete.* **SDW1**, 111.

Hogland, Roy. *Approaching Zanzabar.* **TDT**, vol. XXX, n. 3 (Summer 1994). 6.

Holamon, Ken. *Something's Afoot.* **TCI**, vol. 12, n. 5 (Sep 1978). 40, 41.

Holland, Anthony.

The Mousetrap. **TCI**, vol. 22, n. 5 (May 1988). 41.

The Three Sisters. **SDW1**, 176.

Holmes, W., Conrad Tritschler, R.C. McCleery, & Stafford Hall.

The Arcadians. **MCD**, plate 80.

Holzmeister, Clemens.

Don Juan. **SDE**, 89.

Faust. **MRT**, 77.

Fidelio. **DIT**, plate 109.

Hordijk, Gérard. *Manon.* **SDW1**, 137.

Horner, Harry.

Lady in the Dark. **BWM**, 263; **SDA**, 236, 237; **SOW**, plates 103, 104.

The Magic Flute. **MOM**, 14.

Me and Molly. **TPH**, photo 485.

Star and Garter. **SDB**, 59.

The World We Make. **WTP**, 206.

Hotopp, Michael J.

Brigadoon. **TCI**, vol. 15, n. 1 (Jan 1981). 30-33.

The Passion of Dracula. **TCI**, vol. 15, n. 8 (Oct 1981). 19.

Hotopp, Michael J. & James Leonard Joy. *Peter Pan.* **TCI**, vol. 25, n. 3 (Mar 1991). 26.

Hotopp, Michael J. & Paul DePass. *The Tap Dance Kid*. **MBM**, 1, 168, 169.
Houseman, Laurence. *Bethlehem*. **DMS**, plate 23.
Howard, Pamela.
   As You Like It. **SDW3**, 46.
   Border Warfare. **BTD**, 199.
   Happy Days. **TDT**, vol. XXX, n. 1 (Winter 1994). 18.
   John Brown's Body. **TDT**, vol. XXVII, n. 4 (Fall 1991). 36.
   The Madras House. **TDT**, vol. XXX, n. 1 (Winter 1994). 20.
   The Merchant of Venice. **TDT**, vol. XXIV, n. 2 (Summer 1988). 50.
   The Revenger's Tragedy. **TDT**, vol. XXX, n. 1 (Winter 1994). 19.
   The School for Wives. **TDT**, vol. XXIV, n. 2 (Summer 1988). 48.
   The Taming of the Shrew. **TDT**, vol. XXIV, n. 2 (Summer 1988). 5.
   Waiting for Godot. **TDT**, vol. XXIV, n. 2 (Summer 1988). front cover, 7.
Howarth, Donald. *Waiting for Godot*. **DSL**, figure 30.15(a).
Howden, Philip & Walter Hann. *The Chinese Honeymoon*. **MCD**, plate 35.
Howden, Philip, Alfred Terraine, Conrad Tritschler, & R.C. McCleery.
   The Boy. **MCD**, plate 113.
Howland, Gerald.
   L'Elisir D'Amore. **BTD**, 116.
   Scenes from a Marriage. **BTD**, 46.
   La Bohème. **TCI**, vol. 27, n. 9 (Nov 1993). 9.
   The Dangerous Liaisons. **TCI**, vol. 29, n. 3 (Mar 1995). 33, 36.
   Herodiade. **TCI**, vol. 29, n. 3 (Mar 1995). 33.
   Lucia di Lammermoor. **TCI**, vol. 29, n. 3 (Mar 1995). 33.
   Macbeth. **TCI**, vol. 29, n. 3 (Mar 1995). 33, 34, 36.
   Otello. **TCI**, vol. 29, n. 3 (Mar 1995). cover, 33, 35, 36.
   Tannhäuser. **TCI**, vol. 29, n. 3 (Mar 1995). 32, 33.
   Il Trovatore. **TCI**, vol. 29, n. 3 (Mar 1995). 33.
Hrska, Alexander Vladimir.
   As You Like It. **TCS2**, plate 91.
   Der Kreidekreis. **TCS2**, plate 246.
Hruska, Olimpio & Emilio Carcano.
   The Marriage of Figaro. **TCI**, vol. 24, n. 5 (May 1990). 29.
Hruza, Lubos. *The Inspector General*. **SDW3**, 82.
Hubert, René. *Going Greek*. **MCD**, plate 182.
Hudak, Stefan. *Dr. Burke's Strange Afternoon*. **SDW3**, 161.
Hudson, Richard.
   La Bête: A Comedy of Manners. **TCI**, vol. 25, n. 4 (Apr 1991). 46-49.
   Candide. **TCI**, vol. 23, n. 4 (Apr 1989). 20.
   A Clockwork Orange. **TDT**, vol. XXVII, n. 4 (Fall 1991). 7; **TDT**, vol. XXVIII, n. 2
     (Spring 1992). 21.
   Manon. **BTD**, 147.
   The Marriage of Figaro. **TDT**, vol. XXVIII, n. 2 (Spring 1992). 21.
   The Master Builder. **TDT**, vol. XXVIII, n. 2 (Spring 1992). 23.
   Die Meistersinger von Nurnburg. **TCI**, vol. 28, n. 1 (Jan 1994). 12.
   A Night at the Chinese Opera. **BTD**, 146, 147.
   The Rake's Progress. **TCI**, vol. 29, n. 3 (Mar 1995). 55.
   The Tempest. **BTD**, 59.
   Too Clever By Half. **BTD**, 59; **TDT**, vol. XXVIII, n. 2 (Spring 1992). 21.
   Twelfth Night. **TDT**, vol. XXVIII, n. 2 (Spring 1992). front cover, 19, 22.
Hughes, Allen Lee. *Strange Interlude*. **TCI**, vol. 20, n. 2 (Feb 1986). 13.

Hugo, Jean.
　　Olive chez les Negres. **TCS2**, plate 113.
　　Roméo et Juliette (Shakespeare-Cocteau). **TCS2**, plates 256, 257.
　　Ruy Blas. **SDW1**, 98.
　　The Silent Woman. **TCS2**, color plate 4.
Hugo, Valentine. *Pelléas and Mélisande.* **SDW1**, 98.
Hugoké. *One-Way Pendulum.* **SDW3**, 139.
Hume, Samuel J.
　　Doctor Faustus. **TCS2**, plate 63; **TDT**, vol. XX, n. 2 (Summer 1984). 15.
　　The Doorway. **TCS2**, plate 64.
　　The Golden Doom. **TCS2**, plate 62.
　　Helena's Husband. **TDT**, vol. XX, n. 2 (Summer 1984). 14.
　　The Intruder. **TDT**, vol. XX, n. 2 (Summer 1984). 14.
　　The Romance of the Rose. **TDT**, vol. XX, n. 2 (Summer 1984). 15.
　　The Tents of the Arabs. **TPH**, photo 454; **SDC**, plate 88; **TDT**, vol. XX, n. 2 (Summer
　　　1984). 13.
　　The Wonder Hat. **TDT**, vol. XX, n. 2 (Summer 1984). 13.
Humm, Ambrosius.
　　Everyone Goes Toward the Castle. **SDW4**, illus. 203.
　　The Garden of Delights. **SDW4**, illus. 344.
　　The Ride Across Lake Constance. **SDW4**, illus. 396.
　　The Sunken Town. **SDW1**, 115.
　　The Tinker's Wedding. **SDW4**, illus. 202.
Hunt, Jeff. *Actual Sho.* **TDT**, vol. XXVIII, n. 2 (Spring 1992). 6 of insert.
Hunter, Joseph, T.E. Ryan, Alfred Terraine, & Hawes Craven.
　　The Girl from Utah. **MCD**, plate 96.
Hurry, Leslie.
　　Becket. **SDW2**, 216.
　　The Cenci. **TOP**, 23.
　　Cymbeline. **SDW1**, 176.
　　Hamlet. **SDG**, 190; **SDW1**, 177.
　　Swan Lake. **BTD**, 20.
　　Tamburlaine the Great. **SDW1**, 171.
Hurwitz, Albert. *The School for Scandal.* **TCI**, vol. 18, n. 3 (Mar 1984). 30.
Huszti, Douglas A. *The Visit.* **TDT**, vol. XXVIII, n. 2 (Spring 1992). 12 of insert.

-I-

Iacovelli, John.
　　A Burning Beach. **TDT**, vol. XXVI, n. 1 (Spring 1990). 11 of insert.
　　The Caretaker. **TDT**, vol. XXVI, n. 1 (Spring 1990). 11 of insert.
Iacovleff, Alexandre. *Semiramis.* **RSC**, 43.
Ichijô, Tatsuo. *The Man Who Did Not Come Back.* **SDW2**, 147.
Idoine, Chris. *One Flew Over the Cuckoo's Nest.* **TCI**, vol. 13, n. 3 (May/Jun 1979). 36.
Iliprandi, Gian Carlo.
　　The Barber of Seville. **SDE**, 92.
　　Expropriete Propriety. **SDE**, 92.
　　La Fable du Fils Changé. **SDE**, 90.
　　Rigoletto. **SDE**, 91.
Imero Fiorentino Associates.
　　Orlando Furioso. **TCI**, vol. 5, n. 4 (Sep 1971). 7, 9, 10, 24, 25.

Indiana, Robert. *The Mother of Us All*. **ASC**, 14.
Inglessi, Marion. *Twelfth Night*. **TCI**, vol. 23, n. 9 (Nov 1989). 54.
Ingrand, Max. *Christopher Columbus*. **SDW1**, 99.
Ironside, Robin. *Der Rosenkavalier*. **CGA**, 133.
Isackes, Richard M.
    Chipita Rodreguez. **TDT**, vol. XXX, n. 3 (Summer 1994). 6.
    Così fan Tutti. **TDT**, vol. XXVII, n. 3 (Summer 1991). 5 of insert.
    Postcard from Morocco. **BSE5**, 14; **SCT**, between 152 & 153.
    The Seagull. **TDT**, vol. XXVI, n. 1 (Spring 1990). 2, 12 of insert.
Isakov, Sergei. *Zoika's Apartment*. **RST**, 248.
Ishioka, Eiko.
    M. Butterfly. **TCI**, vol. 22, n. 5 (May 1988). 9; **TCI**, vol. 22, n. 8 (Oct 1988). 54.
Isler, Albert. *Arlechino*. **TCS2**, plate 88.
Israel, Robert.
    Endangered Species. **ASD2**, 59.
    The Fiery Angel. **ASD2**, 60; **TCI**, vol. 22, n. 1 (Jan 1988). 10; **TCI**, vol. 24, n. 9 (Nov 1990). 35.
    Götterdämmerung. **ASD2**, between 108 & 109; **TCI**, vol. 22, n. 5 (May 1988). 22.
    The Hunger Artist. **ASD2**, 54, 55.
    A Midsummer Night's Dream. **TCI**, vol. 4, n. 5 (Oct 1970). 23.
    Miracolo d'Amore. **ASD2**, 48; **TCI**, vol. 22, n. 7 (Aug/Sep 1988). 24; **TCI**, vol. 24, n. 5 (May 1990). 30; **TCI**, vol. 24, n. 9 (Nov 1990). 39.
    Orphée. **TCI**, vol. 27, n. 8 (Oct 1993). 10.
    Das Rheingold. **ASD2**, 56; **TCI**, vol. 24, n. 9 (Nov 1990). 38.
    The Rise and Fall of the City of Mahagonny. **TCI**, vol. 24, n. 9 (Nov 1990). 36.
    Satyagraha. **ASD2**, between 108 & 109; **TCI**, vol. 24, n. 9 (Nov 1990). 37; **TDT**, vol. XVII, n. 2 (Summer 1981). 10, 11.
    Siegfried. **ASD2**, 52; **TCI**, vol. 24, n. 9 (Nov 1990). 38.
    The Turn of the Screw. **ASD2**, 51.
    Vienna: Lusthaus. **TCI**, vol. 21, n. 4 (Apr 1987). 37.
    Die Walküre. **TCI**, vol. 24, n. 9 (Nov 1990). 38.
Itô, Juichi.
    Rashomon. **SDW2**, 147.
    Taira no Masakado. **SDW1**, 144, 145.
Itô, Kisaku.
    Before the Dawn. **SDW1**, 148, 149.
    Lysistrata. **SDW1**, 149.
    The Simpleton. **SDW2**, 150.
    The Thousand Cranes. **SDW1**, 144, 145.
Ivaneanu-Damaschin, Andrei. *Yerma*. **SDW4**, illus. 250, 251.
Ivanov, Kalina. *Don Juan*. **BSE3**, 90.
Ivo, Lode.
    Lady Godiva. **SDW1**, 45.
    The Second-hand Dealer. **SDW2**, 28.

-J-

Jackness, Andrew.
    An American Comedy. **DDT**, 83.
    Beyond Therapy. **TCI**, vol. 21, n. 4 (Apr 1987). 35.
    The Bundle. **TCI**, vol. 13, n. 4 (Sep 1979). 8.

Frida. **TCI**, vol. 27, n. 2 (Feb 1993). 52.

Geniuses. **DDT**, 587.

Intermezzo. **TCI**, vol. 24, n. 7 (Aug/Sep 1990). 34.

The Little Foxes. **DDT**, 354; **DSL**, figure 16.2(a).

Little Murders. **BSE5**, 37.

Our Country's Good. **TCI**, vol. 25, n. 3 (Mar 1991). 43.

The Seagull. **TCI**, vol. 13, n. 4 (Sep 1979). 8.

South Pacific. **DDT**, 164, 165.

Spoils of War. **TCI**, vol. 22, n. 10 (Dec 1988). 14.

Jackson, Bruce, Jr. *Dracula.* **BSE4**, 28.

Jacobs, Sally.

Endgame. **TCI**, vol. 19, n. 5 (May 1985). 21.

Fidelio. **BTD**, 121.

Gethsemane Springs. **TCI**, vol. 14, n. 4 (Sep 1980). 45.

Marat/Sade. **SIP**, 221, 231; **TDT**, n. 5 (May 1966). 23, back cover.

A Midsummer Night's Dream. **SDT**, 273; **SIP**, 248; **SOS**, 280; **TCI**, vol. 5, n. 3
    (May/Jun 1971). 23; **TCI**, vol. 5, n. 4 (Sep 1971). 23; **TCR**, 117; **TSY**, 217.

Romeo and Juliet. **SDW3**, 39-41.

Three Birds Alighting on a Field. **TCI**, vol. 28, n. 4 (Apr 1994). 8.

Turandot. **BTD**, 121.

Jacoulov, Georges.

Giroflé-Girofla. **RSD**, illus. 192; **RST**, 148, 149; **SCM**, 92; **TCS2**, plate 166; **AST**,
    134.

Pas d'Acier. **RSD**, illus. 201; **TCS2**, plate 164.

Princess Brambilla. **RSD**, illus. 176; **RST**, 144, 145, 147.

Jakab, William. *Romeo and Juliet.* **TDT**, vol. XXX, n. 3 (Summer 1994). 15.

Jambon and Bailly. *Patrie.* **TPH**, photo 252.

Jampolis, Neil Peter.

La Bohème. **DPT**, 42.

The Devil and Kate. **TCI**, vol. 24, n. 7 (Aug/Sep 1990). 34.

Eugene Onegin. **DDT**, 152a, 497.

Fidelio. **DDT**, 454.

First Night. **TCI**, vol. 28, n. 10 (Dec 1994). 11.

The Flying Dutchman. **DDT**, 455.

La Forza del Destino. **DPT**, 292.

L'Incoronazione di Poppea. **DPT**, title page.

Jacob's Ladder. **SDW3**, 187.

A Midsummer Night's Dream. **DDT**, 477.

Salomé. **DPT**, between 124 & 125.

The Threepenny Opera. **DDT**, 370.

What the Butler Saw. **DDT**, 269.

Jampolis, Neil Peter, John Napier, & Dermot Hayes. *The Life and Adventures of Nicholas
    Nickleby.* **TCI**, vol. 15, n. 9 (Nov/Dec 1981). 12-15.

Jampolis, Neil Peter/Maurice Sendak. *The Cunning Little Vixen.* **DDT**, 189.

Janco, Marcel. *Street Scene.* **SDW2**, 107.

Jankowska, Liliana & Antoni Tosta. *Caligula.* **SDW2**, 171.

Jankus, Yozak.

Frank Kruk. **SDW2**, 187.

Porgy and Bess. **FCS**, plate 184, color plate 24; **SDO**, 210, plate 24.

Janoir, Jean. *Pelléas and Mélisande.* **SDW2**, 92.

Janosa, Lajos. *The Mirror.* **SDW3**, 219.

John, Tom H.
> *George M!* **TCI**, vol. 2, n. 6 (Nov/Dec 1968). 36; **WMC**, 28.
> *The Wiz.* **BWM**, 335; **DSL**, figure 2.6(a); **TCI**, vol. 9, n. 3 (May/Jun 1975). 9; **WMC**, 368.

Johns, Jasper. *Walkaround Time*. **RSD**, illus. 486.

Johns, Martin. *Me and My Girl*. **BTD**, 158; **MBM**, 27.

Johnson, Albert R.
> *As Thousands Cheer.* **BWM**, 238, 239; **RBS**, 83-88; **SDB**, 55.
> *The Band Wagon.* **BWM**, 63, 251, 252; **MCN**, 104; **RBS**, 47, 48; **SCM**, 126; **SOW**, plate 95; **WMC**, 165.
> *Face the Music.* **RBS**, 61; **SCM**, 126, 127; **WMC**, 75.
> *The Great Waltz.* **MCN**, 119; **RBS**, 103; **SDA**, 92, 93.
> *Jumbo.* **BWM**, 88; **WMC**, 121.
> *Leave It to Me!* **RBS**, 171; **WMC**, 152.
> *Let 'Em Eat Cake.* **BWM**, 228.
> *The Skin of Our Teeth.* **WTP**, 186, 187.
> *Three's a Crowd.* **MCN**, 99; **RBS**, 34.
> *Waltzes from Vienna.* **MCD**, plate 168.

Johnson, Carlos. *Too Funny for Words*. **SDW1**, 54.

Johnson, Doug & Christopher Nowak.
> *Pump Boys and Dinettes.* **TCI**, vol. 16, n. 9 (Nov/Dec 1982). 26.

Johnson, Gilbert V. *Escurial*. **BSE2**, 42.

Johnstone, Alick:
> *Careless Rapture.* **MCD**, plate 181.
> *The Land of Smiles.* **MCD**, plate 169.

Jon-And, John. *On Board*. **NTO**, facing 292.

Jones, Arne & Pierre Olofsson. *The Coronation*. **SDW2**, 209.

Jones, Christine. *Iolanthe.* **TCI**, vol. 28, n. 9 (Nov 1994). 9.

Jones, Robert Edmond.
> *Ah, Wilderness.* **MCN**, 113.
> *The Ancient Mariner.* **DFT**, plate 33; **SDL**, 55; **TDT**, vol. XXIV, n. 4 (Winter 1988). 10.
> *At the Gateway.* **DFT**, plate 34; **REJ**, 53.
> *The Barber of Seville.* **REJ**, 99.
> *Beyond.* **DFT**, plate 18; **TCS2**, plates 96, 97.
> *The Birthday of the Infanta.* **DFT**, plates 10, 11; **DIT**, plate 117.1; **REJ**, 35; **SDA**, 272.
> *The Buccaneer.* **SDC**, plate 126.
> *Caliban.* **DFT**, plate 2.
> *Camille.* **REJ**, 87, 89; **SCM**, 101; **SDB**, 40.
> *Carmen.* **SDA**, 282, 283.
> *The Cenci.* **DFT**, plates 29-32; **REJ**, 29; **RSD**, illus. 428; **TPH**, photo 459.
> *The Children of Darkness (Gaoler's Wench).* **SCM**, 102.
> *Desire Under the Elms.* **DFT**, plate 26; **MCN**, 69; **REJ**, 55; **TPH**, photos 460, 461.
> *The Devil's Garden.* **SDC**, plate 48.
> *Faust.* **REJ**, 67.
> *The Fountain.* **DFT**, plate 27; **REJ**, 57.
> *La Gioconda.* **REJ**, 65; **SCM**, 100.
> *Die Glückliche Hand.* **FCS**, plate 205; **SDO**, 235.
> *Good Gracious Annabelle.* **SDA**, 198.
> *The Great God Brown.* **MCN**, 73.
> *The Green Pastures.* **MCN**, 96; **REJ**, 73, 75, 77; **WTP**, 174, 175.

Medea. SDC, plate 83.
Jordan, Dale and Leslie Taylor. *Sea Marks*. TCI, vol. 16, n. 7 (Aug/Sep 1982). 27.
Jordan, Hanna. *The Cherry Orchard*. TCI, vol. 5, n. 3 (May/Jun 1971). 26, 28.
Jordanov, Ljubomir. *The Seagull*. TDT, vol. XXIII, n. 4 (Winter 1988). 37.
Jorgulesco, Jonel.
    Caesar and Cleopatra. TCS2, plates 212, 213.
    Macbeth. TCS2, plate 361.
    Too True to Be Good. SCM, 132.
Joseph, Larry. *The Sound of Music*. TCI, vol. 20, n. 5 (May 1986). 22.
Joukovski, Arik & Elisabeth de Wée. *Phaedra*. SDW4, illus. 80-85.
Jourdain, Francis. *A Woman Killed with Kindness*. RSD, illus. 102.
Jouvet, Louis.
    The Brothers Karamazov. CSC, facing 174; RSD, illus. 106; SOW, plate 62.
    La Carosse du Saint-Sacrement. CSC, facing 180; SDC, plate 98; SOW, plate 63;
        TPH, photo 355.
    Knock. RSD, illus. 404; SDC, plate 122.
    Malbrouck s'en va-t-en guerre. RSD, illus. 403; SCM, 48.
    La Mort de Sparta. RSD, illus. 107.
    Pelléas and Mélisande. RSD, illus. 103.
    La Surprise de l'Amour. RSD, illus. 105; TCS2, plate 48.
    Twelfth Night. TCS2, plate 49.
Joy, James Leonard.
    Carnival. TCI, vol. 21, n. 9 (Nov 1987). 33.
    The Gay Divorce. TCI, vol. 21, n. 9 (Nov 1987). 33.
    High Button Shoes. TCI, vol. 21, n. 9 (Nov 1987). 37.
Joy, James Leonard & Michael J. Hotopp. *Peter Pan*. TCI, vol. 25, n. 3 (Mar 1991). 26.
Joy, Michael. *Majority of Two*. TCI, vol. 18, n. 9 (Nov/Dec 1984). 39.
Jozwick, Tim. *Richard III*. TCI, vol. 15, n. 9 (Nov/Dec 1981). 20.
Juillac, Jean. *Hamlet*. SDW3, 47.
Jürgens, Helmut.
    The Clever One. SDW1, 67.
    The Dead City. SDW1, 69.
    Electra. FCS, plate 195; SDO, 223.
    Faust. SDW1, 69.
    Idomeneo. SDW2, 63.
    Die Meistersinger von Nürnberg. OPE, 165, 172, 175, 176, 179.
    Peer Gynt. SDW1, 69.
    Der Rosenkavalier. TCI, vol. 11, n. 2 (Mar/Apr 1977). 11.
    Die schweigsame Frau. OPE, 67.
Jurkowitsch, Peter H. *The Beard*. SDW3, 152.
Justin, David. *Adrift*. TCI, vol. 25, n. 8 (Oct 1991). 19.

-K-

Kalinauskas, Vytautas. *Merry-go-round*. SDW4, illus. 278.
Kallapos, John. *The Incredible Rocky*. DSL, figure 4.3(b); SST, 93.
Kamm, Tom & Robert Wilson.
    Alcestis. TCI, vol. 20, n. 9 (Nov 1986). 30, 31; TCI, vol. 24, n. 8 (Oct 1990). 41.
Kanamori, Kaoru.
    The Crow. SDW4, illus. 330.
    Farewell Tokyo! SDW3, 214.

Jesus Christ Superstar. **SDW4**, illus. 409-421; **TDT**, vol. XII, n. 3 (Fall 1976). 38.

Luminous Moss. **SDW4**, illus. 277.

Romeo and Juliet. **SDW3**, 37.

Tiger at the Gates. **SDW3**, 99.

Kandinsky, Vassily. *Pictures at an Exhibition.* **AST**, 141; **RSD**, illus. 330-332.

Kantor, Tadeusz.

The Coot. **AST**, 244.

The Fool and the Nun. **AST**, 244.

Happening by the Sea. **RSD**, illus. 615.

The Lovelies and the Dowdies. **RSD**, illus. 637.

The Madman and the Nun. **SDW3**, 101.

Rhinocéros. **RSD**, illus. 477.

St. Joan. **SDW2**, 166.

The Water Hen. **RSD**, illus. 635, 636; **SDW3**, 100.

Wielopole-Wielopole. **TDT**, vol. XXIII, n. 3 (Fall 1987). 15.

Kapezinskas, Augis. *The Emigrant from Briskane.* **TDT**, vol. XX, n. 1 (Spring 1984). 16.

Kaplevich, Pasha. *N (Nijinsky).* **TDT**, vol. XXX, n. 5 (Fall 1994). 35, 36.

Karakachev, Gueorgui.

A Civilization Misunderstood. **SDW2**, 37.

Liubov Yarovaya. **SDW2**, 37.

Karavan, Dani.

Electra. **RSD**, illus. 474.

Mary Stuart. **SDW2**, 119.

The Seven Deadly Sins. **SDW4**, illus. 238.

Karlin, Robert Lewis. *Catch Me If You Can.* **TCI**, vol. 3, n. 4 (Sep 1969). 27.

Karson, Nat.

The Color Box. **TAT**, plate 576.

Hot Mikado. **BWM**, 331; **RBS**, 180; **TMI**, 228.

Macbeth. **SOS**, 179; **SOW**, plate 42.

Katsioula, Elina. *Little Eyolf.* **TCI**, vol. 20, n. 3 (Mar 1986). 8.

Katz, Alex.*Washington Crossing the Delaware.* **ASC**, 33.

Kauffer, E. McKnight. *Henry IV.* **DIT**, plates 24, 25.

Kautskj, Robert.

Don Juan. **SDE**, 110.

The Knight of the Rose. **SDE**, 111.

Take the Fool Away. **SDW2**, 157.

Kavelin, John.

As You Like It. **SDL**, 172.

Bike Inquest. **TCI**, vol. 14, n. 4 (Sep 1980). 46.

Maude Gonne Says No to the Poet. **TCI**, vol. 14, n. 4 (Sep 1980). 46.

Kay, Barry. *Anastasia.* **CGA**, 176.

Keegan, Shelagh. *The Iron Man.* **TCI**, vol. 28, n. 2 (Feb 1994). 12.

Kegler, Kathrin. *La Chulapona.* **TCI**, vol. 26, n. 4 (Apr 1992). 36.

Keienberg, Eberhard. *The Magic Flute.* **TDT**, vol. XVI, n. 1 (Spring 1980). 17.

Keleher, Kate. *La Bohème.* **SST**, plate IV.

Keller, Ronald E.

Anything Goes. **TCI**, vol. 21, n. 3 (Mar 1987). 22.

The Merry Widow. **TDT**, vol. XXVI, n. 1 (Spring 1990). 12 of insert.

Kellner, Peggy J.

Nobody Loves an Albatross. **SDT**, 291.

The Petrified Forest. **SDT**, 286; **TDP**, 13.

Garrick. **EIF**, photo 47.
Helen Retires. **EIF**, photo 13.
Henry IV. **EIF**, photo 45.
In the Pasha's Garden. **EIF**, photo 15.
Iphigenia in Tauris. **EIF**, photo 23.
The Magic Flute. **EIF**, photos 22, 38.
Maria Malibran. **EIF**, photos 16-19.
The Mother of Us All. **EIF**, photos 48, 49.
The Mother. **EIF**, photo 24.
No Exit. **EIF**, photos 29-34.
Oedipus Rex. **EIF**, photo 36.
Orpheus and Euridice. **EIF**, photo 26.
The Play of Robin and Marion. **EIF**, photo 42.
The Poor Sailor. **EIF**, photo 35.
The Prisoner. **EIF**, photo 41; **SDE**, 111.
R.U.R. **EIF**, photo plate 1; **RSD**, illus. 382; **TCS2**, plates 158, 159.
Santa Claus. **EIF**, photo 46.
Sodom and Gomorrah. **EIF**, photo 40.
Solomon and Balkis. **EIF**, photo 25.
The Tales of Hoffmann. **EIF**, photo 20.
The Tempest. **EIF**, photo 44.
The Triumph of St. Joan. **EIF**, photo 43.
Kilger, Heinrich.
    King Lear. **SDW2**, 55.
    Minna von Barnhelm. **SDW2**, 55.
    Nathan the Wise. **SDW3**, 77.
Kilian, Adam. *The Wedding.* **TCI**, vol. 15, n. 4 (Apr 1981). 13.
Kim, Jakyoung. *Deungsinbul (A Life Size Buddha).* **TCI**, vol. 27, n. 1 (Jan 1993). 7.
Kimmel, Alan.
    Heartbreak House. **BSE4**, 58.
    The King and I. **TCI**, vol. 2, n. 5 (Sep/Oct 1968). 19.
    My Fair Lady. **TCI**, vol. 2, n. 5 (Sep/Oct 1968). 20.
    Show Boat. **TCI**, vol. 2, n. 5 (Sep/Oct 1968). 19.
    You're a Good Man, Charlie Brown. **TCI**, vol. 1, n. 4 (Sep/Oct 1967). 28-30.
King, Edith. *Nala and Damayanti.* **SOW**, plate 35.
King, Lawrence. *Lincoln.* **TCI**, vol. 11, n. 5 (Oct 1977). 12, 13.
Kinmonth, Patrick. *Káta Kabanová.* **TCI**, vol. 28, n. 3 (Mar 1994). 14.
Kirby, Michael. *Double Gothic.* **TDT**, vol. XV, n. 4 (Winter 1979). 21.
Kirkpatrick, Sam. *Nefertiti.* **TCI**, vol. 11, n. 6 (Nov/Dec 1977). 16-19.
Kiselev, Viktor. *Mystery Bouffe.* **MOT**, between 144 & 145.
Kissel, David. *Side By Side By Sondheim.* **TCI**, vol. 20, n. 5 (May 1986). 24.
Kissuer. *As You Like It.* **SST**, 258, 376.
Kitaïev, Mark.
    The Adventures of Chichikov. **TDT**, vol. XII, n. 3 (Fall 1976). 35.
    The Brothers Karamazov. **SDW4**, illus. 146, 147.
    The Cherry Orchard. **TDT**, vol. XXIII, n. 4 (Winter 1988). 27; **TDT**, vol. XXIII, n. 4 (Winter 1988). front cover.
    Ivanov. **TDT**, vol. XXIII, n. 4 (Winter 1988). 27.
    Legend of the Invisible City of Kitezh and the Maiden of Sevronia. **TCI**, vol. 29, n. 5 (May 1995). 10.
    The Town at Dawn. **SDW4**, illus. 259, 260.

Kleiber, Eleonore & Reinhart Zimmerman. *The Young Lord.* **SDW3**, 210.
Klein, Allen Charles.
   Great American Backstage Musical. **TCI**, vol. 11, n. 6 (Nov/Dec 1977). 10.
   Lulu. **DDT**, 8.
   Manon. **DPT**, 120, 187, 348.
   Tosca. **TCI**, vol. 20, n. 8 (Oct 1986). 21.
Klein, César.
   Caligula. **SDW1**, 70.
   Don Carlos. **SDW1**, 70.
   Faust. **TCS2**, plate 92.
   From Morn to Midnight. **RSD**, illus. 122.
   Holle, Weg, Erde. **RSD**, illus. 142; **TPH**, photo 421.
   Napoleon. **CSC**, facing 126; **RSD**, illus. 132, 133; **TCS2**, plate 93.
   Othello. **TCS2**, plate 252.
   Pelléas and Mélisande. **TCS2**, plate 253.
Klein, Julius V. *Julius Caesar.* **TPH**, photo 344.
Klicius, Galius. *Ionas and Edinc.* **TDT**, vol. XX, n. 1 (Spring 1981). 17.
Klingeelhoefer. *Love's Labor's Lost.* **BSE5**, 15.
Klingelhoffer, Robert. *Cambodia Agonistes.* **TCI**, vol. 27, n. 1 (Jan 1993). 6.
Kneidl, Karl. *Hölderlin.* **SDW4**, illus. 281.
Kneidl, Karl & Ulrich Heising. *Stallerhof.* **SDW4**, illus. 408.
Knight, Michael. *The Tempest.* **TCI**, vol. 12, n. 6 (Oct 1978). 57.
Knoblock, Boris.
   The Aristocrats. **RSD**, illus. 225, 226.
   My Friend Kolka. **SDW2**, 187.
   Ramayana. **SDW2**, 187.
Kochergin, Edward Stepanovich.
   Boris Godounov. **SDW4**, illus. 126; **TCI**, vol. 11, n. 5 (Oct 1977). 40; **TDT**, vol. XII,
      n. 3 (Fall 1976). 26.
   Coming Back to the Very Start. **TCI**, vol. 13, n. 6 (Nov/Dec 1979). 25; **TDT**, vol. XVI,
      n. 1 (Spring 1980). 24.
   Hamlet. **TCI**, vol. 11, n. 5 (Oct 1977). 41.
   Man and Superman. **TCI**, vol. 23, n. 8 (Oct 1989). 15.
   Monologue about Marriage. **SDW4**, illus. 368; **TCI**, vol. 11, n. 5 (Oct 1977). 38.
   My Mocking Happiness. **SDW3**, 122.
   Notes of a Madman. **TCI**, vol. 11, n. 5 (Oct 1977). 41.
   Tale of a Horse. **TCI**, vol. 11, n. 5 (Oct 1977). 40.
   Uncle Vanya. **TDT**, vol. XXIII, n. 4 (Winter 1988). 25.
Koenig, John.
   Charley's Aunt. **WTP**, 152.
   This Is the Army. **BWM**, 240, 241.
Kohno, Kunio. *The Rise of a Frog.* **SDW1**, 150.
Kokkos, Yannis.
   Don't Be In Too Late. **SDW3**, 149.
   Electra. **SDW4**, illus. 8-10; **TCI**, vol. 21, n. 8 (Oct 1987). 33; **TDT**, vol. XXIII, n. 3
      (Fall 1987). front cover; **TDT**, vol. XXIII, n. 4 (Winter 1988). 22.
   La Guerre de Troie. **SDB**, 187.
   Hamlet. **TDT**, vol. XXIII, n. 4 (Winter 1988). 20.
   Hernani. **TDT**, vol. XXIII, n. 4 (Winter 1988). 22.
   The Seagull. **TDT**, vol. XXIII, n. 4 (Winter 1988). 6.

Kokoschka, Oskar.
   The Cursed Crown. **AST**, 210; **SDW2**, 158, 159.
   A Midsummer Night's Dream. **AST**, 211.
   Moisasur's Magic Curse. **SDW2**, 157.
Kolar, Zbynek.
   Krakatit. **TDT**, vol. XX, n. 1 (Spring 1984). 9.
   Resurrection. **TDT**, vol. XX, n. 1 (Spring 1984). 11.
Kollenborn, Greg. *The Trial: A Funhouse*. **TCI**, vol. 13, n. 5 (Oct 1979). 32.
Kolodziej, Marian.
   The Anonymous Work. **SDW3**, 102.
   Kordian. **SDW3**, 82.
   The Mother. **SDW3**, 102.
   The Seagull. **TCI**, vol. 15, n. 4 (Apr 1981). 15.
Kolouch, Fred. *A Letter for Queen Victoria*. **SDW4**, illus. 405.
Koltai, Ralph.
   Anna Karenina. **TDT**, vol. XIX, n. 3 (Fall 1983). 10.
   As You Like It. **RSD**, illus. 519; **SDG**, 196; **SDW3**, 44; **TCI**, vol. 11, n. 1 (Jan/Feb 1977). 15.
   Baal. **BTD**, 30.
   Back to Methuselah. **RSD**, illus. 518; **SDB**, 46; **SDW3**, 88, 89; **TCI**, vol. 11, n. 1 (Jan/Feb 1977). 14, 15.
   Bluebeard's Castle. **TCI**, vol. 11, n. 1 (Jan/Feb 1977). 12.
   Cul de Sac. **SDR**, 25.
   Cyrano de Bergerac. **TCI**, vol. 19, n. 1 (Jan 1985). 39, 40.
   Don Giovanni. **DMS**, plates 42, 43.
   Götterdämmerung. **TCI**, vol. 11, n. 1 (Jan/Feb 1977). 13.
   The Jew of Malta. **SDR**, 40.
   Man and Superman. **TDT**, vol. XIX, n. 3 (Fall 1983). 10.
   Metropolis. **BTD**, 168; **TDT**, vol. XXVII, n. 4 (Fall 1991). 37.
   Much Ado About Nothing. **SDT**, 275; **TDT**, vol. XIX, n. 3 (Fall 1983). front cover.
   Murder in the Cathedral. **DMS**, plate 41.
   Resurrection. **SDB**, 88.
   Das Rheingold. **TCI**, vol. 11, n. 1 (Jan/Feb 1977). 13.
   Richard III. **SDL**, 42.
   The Rise and Fall of the City of Mahagonny. **DMS**, plate 53; **SDW3**, 197.
   Romeo and Juliet. **TCI**, vol. 15, n. 5 (May,1981). 12.
   The Soldiers. **BTD**, 126, 127.
   Taverner. **CGA**, 181; **TCI**, vol. 11, n. 1 (Jan/Feb 1977). 10, 11; **TDT**, vol. XII, n. 3 (Fall 1976). 26.
   Terra Nova. **TDT**, vol. XIX, n. 3 (Fall 1983). 9.
   Troilus and Cressida. **BTD**, 31.
   Die Walküre. **TDT**, vol. XIX, n. 3 (Fall 1983). 11.
   Wild Oats. **TCI**, vol. 12, n. 3 (Mar/Apr 1978). 10.
Komisarjevsky, Theodore.
   La Foire de Sorotchin. **SCM**, 46.
   The Hatter's Castle. **SCM**, 28.
   The Inspector General. **SOW**, plate 68.
   King Lear. **SDG**, 181; **SOS**, 160.
   Lohengrin. **SCM**, 29.
   Macbeth. **SCM**, 29; **SOS**, 161; **TPH**, photo 437.

Koniarsky, Helmut.
    The Inspector General. **SDW2**, 63.
    The Thyme and Dragon's Death. **SDW1**, 70.
    Troilus and Cressida. **SDW1**, 70.
Kôno, Kunio.
    Far Away Songs of Triumph. **SDW2**, 150.
    The Stream. **SDW2**, 149.
Kooning, Willem de. *Labyrinth.* **ASC**, 26.
Köpeczi-Bócz, István.
    Too True To Be Good. **SDW3**, 87.
    The Tricks of Scapin. **SDW2**, 139.
Korovin, Konstantin.
    La Belle au Bois Dormant. **FCS**, plate 171, color plate 17.
    The Living Corpse. **TPH**, photo 300.
Kosinski, Jan.
    The Dossier. **RSD**, illus. 502.
    Lucifer and the Lord. **SDW2**, 167.
    Oedipus Rex. **RSD**, illus. 509.
    The Police. **SDW2**, 167.
    Revenge. **SDW1**, 157.
Kouril, Miroslav.
    The Barber of Seville. **RSD**, illus. 283.
    John B. Conquers the World. **RSD**, illus. 284.
    Spring's Awakening. **RSD**, illus. 285; **TDT**, n. 42 (Fall 1975). 31.
    The Suffering of Young Werther. **TDT**, n. 42 (Fall 1975). 31.
Kourilko, Mikhäil. *The Red Poppy.* **SDW2**, 188.
Kovalenko, Evgheni & Valentina Krivocheina. *Spring Violins.* **SDW2**, 188.
Krakowski, Wojciech. *The Old Woman Broods.* **SDB**, 202; **SDW3**, 141.
Kralj, Matthias. *Summer Folk.* **TCI**, vol. 14, n. 6 (Nov/Dec 1980). 38.
Kramer, Simon. *They Handcuffed the Flowers.* **SDW4**, illus. 343.
Kravjansky, Mikulás.
    The House of Bernarda Alba. **SDW2**, 42.
    Il Trovatore. **SDW3**, 182.
Krehan, Hermann (see Crayon).
Krem, Fritz. *Die Glückliche Hand.* **SCM**, 66.
Kritzler, Ilse. *Cabaret.* **CSD**, 90.
Krivocheina, Valentina & Evgheni Kovalenko. *Spring Violins.* **SDW2**, 188.
Kroder, Olghert. *The Legend of Kaupo.* **SDW4**, illus. 367.
Krohg, Guy.
    The Comedy of Errors. **DOT**, 244; **SDW1**, 154.
    The Defeat. **SDW2**, 152.
    The Madwoman of Chaillot. **SDW1**, 154.
Krohg, Per. *Volpone.* **TPH**, photo 394.
Kroschel, Michael.
    Buried Child. **TCI**, vol. 14, n. 4 (Sep 1980). 22.
    The Wolves. **TCI**, vol. 14, n. 4 (Sep 1980). 22.
Kruger, Halina. *Too Good to be True.* **SCM**, 84; **TPH**, photo 395.
Kruschenick, Nicholas. *The Man in the Moon.* **ASC**, 13.
Kruse, Max. *Salomé.* **MRT**, 16; **TPH**, photo 324.
Krymov, Nikolai. *The Passionate Heart.* **RST**, 180.
Kubik, Boris. *Hello, Dolly!* **TDT**, vol. XII, n. 3 (Fall 1976). 33.

Kula, Marie Liis. *Around the World in 80 Days*. **SDW3**, 149.
Kumankov, J. *Tsar Feodor Ivanovitch*. **TDT**, vol. XII, n. 3 (Fall 1976). 26.
Kunishima, Yoshiko. *Rusalka*. **TDT**, vol. XXIII, n. 4 (Winter 1988). 7.
Kuper, Yuri. *Sophisticated Ladies*. **TCI**, vol. 23, n. 5 (May 1989). 37.
Kurtz, Kenneth.
    5th of July. **TCI**, vol. 17, n. 3 (Mar 1983). 19.
    Juno and the Paycock. **TCI**, vol. 7, n. 6 (Nov/Dec 1973). 18.
    Philadelphia, Here I Come. **TCI**, vol. 7, n. 6 (Nov/Dec 1973). 21.
Kustodiev, Boris. *The Flea*. **RST**, 233.
Kysela, Frantisek. *The Schooling of Don Quixote*. **TDT**, n. 41 (Summer 1975). 15.

-L-

La Ferla, Sandro.
    Le Coq D'Or. **DPT**, between 284 & 285.
    The Great Divide. **DPT**, between 284 & 285.
    The Knack. **DPT**, 119.
    The Medium. **DPT**, 331.
    Marat/Sade. **DPT**, 349.
    The Ruling Class. **CSD**, 84; **DPT**, 355.
    Saturday, Sunday, Monday. **TCI**, vol. 13, n. 5 (Oct 1979). 36.
    Sebastian. **CSD**, 91; **DPT**, 311.
Labenz, Craig.
    *Catherine: Concerning the Fateful Origins of Her Grandeur with Diverse Musical
        Interludes, 3 Elephants, and No Ballet*. **TCI**, vol. 26, n. 8 (Oct 1992). 6.
    A Midsummer Night's Dream. **TCI**, vol. 26, n. 3 (Mar 1992). 36.
Labisse, Félix.
    The Day's Dividing. **SDW1**, 99.
    Lucifer and the Lord. **SDW1**, 103.
    Nights of Wrath. **RSD**, illus. 496.
    The Oresteia. **SDW2**, 93.
    The Trial. **RSD**, illus. 495; **SDW1**, 99.
Labò, Savino.
    Carmen. **SDE**, 94.
    La Forza del Destino. **SDE**, 93, 94.
    Il Trovatore. **SDE**, 93.
Lacy, Robin. *Sweet Charity*. **TDT**, n. 35 (Dec 1973). 14.
Lagrange, Jacques. *The Shoemaker's Holiday*. **SDW2**, 93.
Lagut, Irene. *Les Mariés de la Tour Eiffel*. **TCS2**, plate 259.
Laing, Stewart. *All's Well That Ends Well*. **TCI**, vol. 27, n. 8 (Oct 1993). 6.
Lalique, Susanne. *Le Bourgeois Gentilhomme*. **SIP**, 228; **SDW1**, 99.
Lambert, Isabel. *Jabez and the Devils*. **SDW2**, 219.
Lanc, Émile.
    The Duenna. **SDW1**, 45.
    Eel Beach. **SDW2**, 29.
    Pamela's Bag. **SDW2**, 29.
Lancaster, Osbert.
    La Fille mal gardée. **CGA**, 170.
    The Rake's Progress. **SDW2**, 220.
    Tirésias. **SDW2**, 219; **TOP**, 31.

Landesman, Heidi.
>   *Approaching Zanzibar.* **ASD2**, 74.
>   *Big River.* **ASD2**, 72; **BSE4**, 88; **DDT**, 171; **MBM**, 24; **TCI**, vol. 19, n. 7 (Aug/Sep
>   1985). 31-36; **TCI**, vol. 20, n. 9 (Nov 1986). 21; Big River. **TCI**, vol. 21, n. 8 (Oct
>   1987). 28; **TDT**, vol. XXI, n. 2 (Summer 1985). 6, 7.
>   *The Cherry Orchard.* **ASD2**, 62, 65, 66, 67, 73.
>   *Elmer Gantry.* **TCI**, vol. 26, n. 1 (Jan 1992). 11.
>   *Holeville.* **DDT**, 314.
>   *A Midsummer Night's Dream.* **ASD2**, 68; **DDT**, 166, 167; **TCI**, vol. 15, n. 5 (May
>   1981). 24.
>   *'night Mother.* **TCI**, vol. 19, n. 5 (May 1985). 22.
>   *Painting Churches.* **TCI**, vol. 19, n. 5 (May 1985). 18; **ASD2**, 70, 71; **DDT**, 259.
>   *The Red Shoes.* **TCI**, vol. 28, n. 3 (Mar 1994). 13.
>   *The Secret Garden.* **ASD2**, between 108 & 109; **TCI**, vol. 25, n. 4 (Apr 1991). 12;
>   **TCI**, vol. 25, n. 8 (Oct 1991). 7, 42-44.
>   *Smoky Joe's Cafe.* **TCI**, vol. 29, n. 5 (May 1995). 48, 49.

Landesman, Heidi & Richard Foreman.
>   *Penguin Touquet.* **TCI**, vol. 15, n. 5 (May 1981). w6.

Landi, Angelo Maria.
>   *Cavalleria Rusticana.* **SDE**, 95.
>   *Master Pathelin.* **SDE**, 95.

Landwehr, Hugh.
>   *Buried Child.* **ASD2**, 79; **TCI**, vol. 20, n. 9 (Nov 1986). 19.
>   *Candide.* **TCI**, vol. 26, n. 7 (Aug/Sep 1992). 9.
>   *Children of the Sun.* **TCI**, vol. 14, n. 3 (May/Jun 1980). 16, 17.
>   *Danton's Death.* **TCI**, vol. 20, n. 2 (Feb 1986). 16.
>   *Execution of Justice.* **TCI**, vol. 20, n. 2 (Feb 1986). 20.
>   *Glengarry Glen Ross.* **ASD2**, 90, 92; **DDT**, 586.
>   *John Brown's Body.* **DDT**, 511.
>   *Les Liaisons Dangereuses.* **TCI**, vol. 23, n. 2 (Feb 1989). 48.
>   *Major Barbara.* **ASD2**, 83.
>   *Measure for Measure.* **ASD2**, 80, 81; **DDT**, 488.
>   *The Miser.* **ASD2**, between 108 & 109.
>   *Painting Churches.* **TCI**, vol. 20, n. 2 (Feb 1986). 16.
>   *Past Tense.* **ASD2**, 88.
>   *The Philanthropist.* **TCI**, vol. 26, n. 3 (Mar 1992). 19.
>   *The Rose Tattoo.* **ASD2**, 76.
>   *She Loves Me.* **TCI**, vol. 20, n. 5 (May 1986). 26.
>   *Uncle Vanya.* **ASD2**, 87.
>   *A View from the Bridge.* **TCI**, vol. 21, n. 5 (May 1987). 16.
>   *When We are Married.* **TCI**, vol. 23, n. 4 (Apr 1989). 14.
>   *Who They Are and How It Is With Them.* **ASD2**, 84, 86; **TCI**, vol. 20, n. 2 (Feb 1986).
>   19; **TCI**, vol. 20, n. 9 (Nov 1986). 21.

Langhoff, Matthias. *Lieber Georg.* **TCI**, vol. 14, n. 6 (Nov/Dec 1980). 39.
Lanphier, Dawn. *The Kitchen.* **TDT**, vol. XXVIII, n. 2 (Spring 1992). 13 of insert.
Lansere, Evgheni. *Woe from Wit.* **SDW2**, 189.
Lara, Carlos. *Don Juan Tenorio.* **SDW2**, 81.
Larionov, Michel.
>   *Le Chout.* **AST**, 49; **RSD**, illus. 292.
>   *La Petite Catherine.* **SCM**, 45.
>   *Renard.* **RSD**, illus. 295.

Lazaridis, Stefanos & Michael Stennett. *The Marriage of Figaro*. **CGA**, 180.

Leach, Wilford & Bob Shaw. *The Pirates of Penzance*. **MBM**, 26; **TCI**, vol. 15, n. 6 (Jun/Jul 1981). 12, 13; **TCI**, vol. 20, n. 1 (Jan 1986). 23.

Leahy, Gerry.

    Cabaret. **TCI**, vol. 26, n. 3 (Mar 1992). 40.

    The Seagull. **TCI**, vol. 26, n. 3 (Mar 1992). 41.

Lebois, Michel & Patrick Chauveau. *Good Bye Mister Freud*. **SDW4**, illus. 374, 375.

Lebois, Michel, Patrick Chauveau, Charles Marty, & Sabine.

    From Moses to Mao. **SDW4**, illus. 397-404.

Lechtveld, Noni. *Yerma*. **SDW1**, 138.

Ledesma, A. L. *Doctor Faustus*. **SDB**, 176.

Lee, Eugene.

    Agnes of God. **TDT**, vol. XXII, n. 4 (Winter 1987). 11.

    The Ballad of Soapy Smith. **ASD1**, 72.

    Billy Budd. **TCI**, vol. 4, n. 2 (Mar/Apr 1970). 13; **TDT**, vol. XVIII, n. 2 (Summer 1982). 9.

    Brother to Dragons. **DPT**, 151; **TDT**, vol. XVIII, n. 2 (Summer 1982). 9.

    Camino Real. **TCI**, vol. 22, n. 9 (Nov 1988). 58.

    Endgame. **TDT**, vol. XVIII, n. 2 (Summer 1982). 9.

    The Girl of the Golden West. **ASD1**, 75; **TCI**, vol. 18, n. 8 (Oct 1984). 16.

    House of Breath. **TCI**, vol. 5, n. 4 (Sep 1971). 13; **TDT**, vol. XVIII, n. 2 (Summer 1982). 5.

    King Lear. **ASD1**, 82.

    Les Liaisons Dangereuses. **TCI**, vol. 23, n. 2 (Feb 1989). 51; **TCI**, vol. 23, n. 9 (Nov 1989). 59.

    Macbeth. **SDW3**, 58.

    A Man for All Seasons. **DPT**, 35; **TDT**, vol. XVIII, n. 2 (Summer 1982). 9.

    Merrily We Roll Along. **MBM**, 42, 45, 86; **SON**, 40, 147-151; **TCI**, vol. 19, n. 8 (Oct 1985). 18; **TCI**, vol. 18, n. 8 (Oct 1984). 19.

    Of Mice and Men. **ASD1**, 83.

    Peer Gynt. **TDT**, vol. XVIII, n. 2 (Summer 1982). 5.

    Rosmersholm. **ASD1**, 73; **TDT**, vol. XVIII, n. 2 (Summer 1982). 9.

    Seven Keys to Baldpate. **ASD1**, 78, 79.

    Show Boat. **TCI**, vol. 28, n. 2 (Feb 1994). 5, 26-28.

    Slave Ship. **ASD1**, 76; **DPT**, 91; **SDB**, 198; **SDW3**, 162; **TCI**, vol. 5, n. 4 (Sep 1971). 12.

    Son of Man and the Family. **ASD1**, 71; **TDT**, vol. XVIII, n. 2 (Summer 1982). 6.

    Sweeney Todd. **ASD1**, 81, 84; **BWM**, 327; **HPA**, 121, 122; **HPR**, 290; **MBM**, 36; **SON**, 124, 126, 129, 133, 144; **TCI**, vol. 14, n. 1 (Jan/Feb 1980). 18; **TCI**, vol. 15, n. 2 (Feb 1981). 12, 13; **TCI**, vol. 18, n. 8 (Oct 1984). 17; **TCI**, vol. 22, n. 5 (May 1988). 35; **TDT**, vol. XVIII, n. 2 (Summer 1982). 7; Sweeney Todd. **WMC**, 293.

    Tom Jones. **ASD1**, 68.

    The Visit. **TCI**, vol. 22, n. 9 (Nov 1988). 59, 62.

    You Can't Take It With You. **TDT**, vol. XVIII, n. 2 (Summer 1982). 9.

Lee, Eugene & Franne.

    Candide. **BWM**, 291; **CSD**, 23; **DPT**, 57; **HPA**, 152, 153; **HPR**, 219.

Lee, Eugene, Franne Lee, & Jean Monod. *Orghast*. **SDW4**, illus. 295, 296.

Lee, Ming Cho.

    Ann Boleyn. **TCI**, vol. 18, n. 2 (Feb 1984). 21.

    Antony and Cleopatra. **DMS**, plate 36.

    Ascent of Mt. Fuji. **TCI**, vol. 18, n. 2 (Feb 1984). 18.

Attila. **DDT**, 24b; **TCI**, vol. 18, n. 2 (Feb 1984). 20.

The Barber of Seville. **TDT**, n. 24 (Feb 1971). 8.

Bomarzo. **TCI**, vol. 18, n. 2 (Feb 1984). 21; **TCI**, vol. 7, n. 1 (Jan/Feb 1973). 15;
    TDT, n. 24 (Feb 1971). 9.

Boris Godounov. **ASD1**, 94; **CSD**, 93; **DPT**, 32, 240; **DPT**, between 124 & 125;
    MOM, 28-39; **TCI**, vol. 10, n. 5 (Oct 1976). 16.

Camille. **SDL**, 60.

The Comedy of Errors. **TDT**, n. 24 (Feb 1971). 6.

Death of a Salesman. **DDT**, 190.

Desire Under the Elms. **TCI**, vol. 18, n. 2 (Feb 1984). 19.

Dog Lady. **ASD1**, 99.

Don Juan. **ASD1**, 90, 91; **TCI**, vol. 20, n. 4 (Apr 1986). 21.

Don Rodrigo. **CSD**, 42; **DPT**, 245; **TCI**, vol. 7, n. 1 (Jan/Feb 1973). 19.

Electra. **ASD1**, 97; **DDT**, 197; **RSD**, illus. 542; **SDW3**, 28; **TDT**, n. 1 (May 1965).
    back cover; **TDT**, n. 24 (Feb 1971). 4.

The Entertainer. **ASD1**, front cover; **TCI**, vol. 18, n. 2 (Feb 1984). 14.

Ergo. **FCS**, plate 217; **SDO**, 253.

Execution of Justice. **TCI**, vol. 20, n. 2 (Feb 1986). 12.

Faust. **SDB**, 65.

La Favorita. **DPT**, 244.

The Glass Menagerie. **TCI**, vol. 18, n. 2 (Feb 1984). 15; **TCI**, vol. 18, n. 2 (Feb 1984).
    19; **TCI**, vol. 25, n. 4 (Apr 1991). 17.

Die Gnadiges Fraulein. **ASD1**, 98; **DPT**, 242; **TDT**, n. 24 (Feb 1971). 8; **SDB**, 38.

Hair. **ASD1**, between 70 & 71; **SDW3**, 213.

Hamlet. **ASD1**, 93.

Henry IV, part 1. **DPT**, 137; **TCI**, vol. 8, n. 1 (Jan/Feb 1974). 12.

Jack MacGowran in the Works of Samuel Beckett. **ASD1**, 103.

Julius Caesar. **TCI**, vol. 18, n. 2 (Feb 1984). 21.

K2. **ASD1**, 89; **TCI**, vol. 16, n. 8 (Oct 1982). 16; **TCI**, vol. 18, n. 2 (Feb 1984). 15;
    TCI, vol. 19, n. 5 (May 1985). 27.

Khovanschina. **DDT**, 192, 193.

King Lear. **TCI**, vol. 11, n. 1 (Jan/Feb 1977). 6.

Love's Labor's Lost. **DMS**, plate 54.

Montezuma. **TCI**, vol. 20, n. 3 (Mar 1986). 25.

Mother Courage and Her Children. **TCI**, vol. 15, n. 5 (May 1981). 23.

Much Ado About Nothing. **CSD**, 92; **SDB**, 60; **TCI**, vol. 29, n. 3 (Mar 1995). 7; **TCI**,
    vol. 7, n. 2 (Mar/Apr 1973). 9.

Peer Gynt. **RSD**, illus. 543; **SDB**, 49; **TDT**, n. 24 (Feb 1971). 7; **TDT**, n. 24 (Feb
    1971). front cover.

Prince Igor. **TCI**, vol. 7, n. 1 (Jan/Feb 1973). 18.

I Puritani. **MOM**, 203-210.

Richard III. **SDB**, 45; **TCI**, vol. 18, n. 2 (Feb 1984). 16.

Roberto Devereaux. **SDT**, 278, and between 152 & 153; **TCI**, vol. 18, n. 2 (Feb 1984).
    21; **ASD1**, 95; **DPT**, 243; **TCI**, vol. 7, n. 1 (Jan/Feb 1973). 14.

Romeo and Juliet. **DDT**, 198.

St. Joan. **TCI**, vol. 18, n. 2 (Feb 1984). 18.

St. Matthew Passion. **DPT**, 7.

The Tempest. **ASD1**, between 70 & 71; **TCI**, vol. 14, n. 4 (Sep 1980). 41; **TCI**, vol. 18,
    n. 2 (Feb 1984). 19.

Traveler in the Dark. **DDT**, 194, 195; **TCI**, vol. 19, n. 7 (Aug/Sep 1985). 38.

The Sunshine Boys. **DPT**, 331.

Zoditch's Room. **TCI**, vol. 1, n. 1 (Mar/Apr 1967). 28.

Lutze, V.V. *Bread*. **TAS**, 80; **TAT**, plate 692.

Luzzati, Emanuele.

Allez-Hop! **SDW3**, 210.

The Barber of Seville. **SDE**, 102.

La Celestina. **SDE**, 99.

Colombe. **SDE**, 107.

Così fan Tutti. **TCI**, vol. 11, n. 2 (Mar/Apr 1977). 19.

La Diavolessa. **SDE**, 100.

Ettore Fieramosca. **SIO**, 95.

Filottete. **SIO**, 92.

The Golem. **RSD**, illus. 575, 576; **SIO**, 90, 91.

The Imaginary Invalid. **SDE**, 99.

Macbeth. **SIO**, 94.

The Magic Flute. **SDR**, 77.

The Man from Cordova. **SDW2**, 129.

Méphistophélès. **SDE**, 105.

A Midsummer Night's Dream. **SIO**, 94.

Il Mio Carso. **SIO**, 89.

The Miser. **SDE**, 106.

La Moscheta. **SIO**, 93.

The Shoemaker's Wife. **SDW2**, 127.

Tieste. **SDE**, 103, 104.

Titus Andronicus. **SIO**, 88.

Luzzatti, Lele. *Thyestes*. **SDW1**, 127.

Lynch, Thomas.

The Abduction from the Seraglio. **TDT**, vol. XXVII, n. 3 (Summer 1991). 9.

Candide. **TCI**, vol. 18, n. 3 (Mar 1984). 26.

Don Juan Comes Back From the Wars. **DDT**, 171.

Lohengrin. **TCI**, vol. 28, n. 8 (Oct 1994). 9.

My Favorite Year. **TCI**, vol. 27, n. 3 (Mar 1993). 5, 30, 31.

Orpheus and Euridice. **DDT**, 587.

Pal Joey. **DDT**, 9.

A Quiet Place. **DDT**, 158.

The Time of Your Life. **BSE4**, 89.

Lyndhurst, F.L. & Phil Harker. *The Girl Friend*. **MCD**, plate 148.

-M-

MacArthur, Molly. *Love's Labor's Lost*. **TPH**, photo 441.

Maccari, Mino. *Gli Esami non Finiscono Mai*. **SDW4**, illus. 252, 253.

Macdermott, Norman.

Arms and the Man. **TCS2**, plate 78.

Romeo and Juliet. **TCS2**, plate 77.

MacDonald, Kim. *Mr. BURT his MEMORY of Mr. WHITE his FANTASY of Mr. DUNSTABLE his MUSICK/PAGODE*. **ASC**, 32.

Macewen, Molly. *The Three Estates*. **DMS**, plate 38.

Macie, Tom.

Appear and Show Cause. **SDT**, 277.

Joseph and the Amazing Technicolor Dreamcoat. **TCI**, vol. 25, n. 4 (Apr 1991). 74.

The Liar. **SDT**, 127-129.

Macke, August. *Macbeth.* **AST**, 36.

MacKichan, Robert. *As Mortal Men.* **SFT**, 76.

MacLiammoir, Michael. *Not for Children.* **SOW**, plate 58.

MacNamara, Brooks. *The Brig.* **SFT**, 129.

MacNeil, Ian.

    Ariodante. **TCI**, vol. 28, n. 4 (Apr 1994). 31.

    An Inspector Calls. **TCI**, vol. 28, n. 4 (Apr 1994). 5, 28, 29.

    Machinal. **TCI**, vol. 28, n. 4 (Apr 1994). 30, 31.

    The Picture of Dorian Gray. **TCI**, vol. 29, n. 2 (Feb 1995). 7.

Madau Diaz, Antonello. *The Lighted Factory.* **SDW3**, 207.

Mahnke, Adolf.

    Anarchie auf Silian. **TCS2**, plate 160.

    Dame Kobold. **TCS2**, plate 346.

    All's Well That Ends Well. **SOS**, 266.

Mai, Wolfgang. *Light o' Love.* **SDW4**, illus. 187, 188.

Maillart, Jean Dénia.

    Camille. **SDE**, 112.

    The Fourposter. **SDE**, 113.

Majewski, Andrej.

    The Artful Widow. **SDW2**, 168.

    Macbeth. **DSL**, plate II; **SST**, 5, plate III.

    The Magic Flute. **SST**, plate II.

    Orphée. **DSL**, figure 16.3(b); **SST**, 263.

Mäkinen, Veikko. *Electra.* **SDW2**, 205.

Makkonen, Tina. *A Midsummer Night's Dream.* **TDT**, vol. XXVII, n. 4 (Fall 1991). 53.

Malclés, Jean Dénis.

    Adrienne Lecouvreur. **SDE**, 114.

    Ardéle. **SDW1**, 100.

    The Baker, the Baker's Wife and the Baker's Errand Boy. **SDW3**, 123.

    Becket or the Honour of God. **SDW2**, 94.

    The Count of Clérambard. **SDW1**, 101.

    The Lark. **RSD**, illus. 494.

    Rehearsal for Love. **SDW1**, 101.

    Richard III. **SDW3**, 35.

Malevich, Kasimir.

    Mystery Bouffe **TCT**, plate 14

    Victory Over the Sun. **AST**, 129; **RSD**, illus. 152-54; **RST**, 28; **TDT**, vol. XXVI, n. 4
        (Fall 1990). 10.

Malina, Jaroslav.

    Antigone. **TDT**, vol. XXIV, n. 2 (Summer 1988). 8-13, 18.

    Carmen. **TDT**, vol. XXX, n. 2 (Spring 1994). 23-25.

    The Claw. **TDT**, vol. XXVII, n. 2 (Spring 1991). 30, 34; **TDT**, vol. XXX, n. 2 (Spring
        1994). 19, 21, 22.

    Manon Lescaut. **TDT**, vol. XXVI, n. 2 (Summer 1990). 36, 37.

    Merlin. **TDT**, vol. XXVI, n. 2 (Summer 1990). 37.

    A Midsummer Night's Dream. **TDT**, vol. XXIII, n. 1 (Spring 1987). 6, 7, 12, 13.

    Love's Labor's Lost. **TDT**, vol. XXVII, n. 3 (Summer 1991). 23.

Malinaouskaïte, Janina. *The Bolsheviks.* **SDW3**, 160.

Malolepsy, John F.

    The Adding Machine. **BSE5**, 20.

City of Voices. **BSE1**, 17.
Cloud Nine. **BSE5**, 16.
The Coronation of Poppea. **BSE4**, 31.
The Normal Heart. **TDT**, vol. XXVI, n. 1 (Spring 1990). 13 of insert.
The Rimers of Eldritch. **BSE1**, 16.
Malureanu, F. *Elisabeth.* **TDT**, vol. XII, n. 3 (Fall 1976). 39.
Mamposo, Manuel. *Don Juan Tenorio.* **SDW2**, 81.
Mancera, Antonio. *Life is a Dream.* **DMS**, plate 37.
Manninen, Tanu. *The Burning Flame.* **SDW1**, 158.
Manthey, Axel. *Der Ring des Nibelungen.* **TCI**, vol. 21, n. 10 (Dec 1987). 18.
Manzu, Giacomo. *L'Histoire du Soldat.* **AST**, 222.
Marc-Henri & London Laverdet. *Peggy Ann.* **DIT**, plate 66.
Marchi, Mario Vellani .
    L'Elisir D'Amore. **SIO**, 155.
    The Barber of Seville. **SDE**, 118.
    Regina Uliva. **SDE**, 117.
    Sheherazade. **SDE**, 118.
Marenic, Vladimir.
    Don Juan. **SDW3**, 69.
    The Heavenly Squadron. **SDW2**, 135.
    The Merry Wives of Windsor. **SDW3**, 48.
Maret, Jean-Claude. *Baal.* **SDW4**, illus. 228.
Marillier, Jacques.
    Antony and Cleopatra. **SDW3**, 60.
    Penthesilea. **SDW2**, 95.
Marini, Marino. *La Sagra della Primavera.* **SIO**, 149-151.
Maronek, James E.
    Alice in Wonder. **BSE1**, 9.
    A Dream Play. **TCI**, vol. 1, n. 2 (May/Jun 1967). 34, 36-38.
    The Good Woman of Setzuan. **SDW2**, 236.
    House of Agamemnon. **BSE4**, 32.
    The Rivals. **BSE3**, 31.
    The Threepenny Opera. **CSD**, 103.
Marosin, Mircea.
    Ovidiu. **SDW2**, 174.
    Twelfth Night. **SDW2**, 174.
Marr, Scott.
    The Caucasian Chalk Circle. **TDT**, vol. XXVI, n. 1 (Spring 1990). 20 of insert.
Marron, Bill & Catherine Martin.
    A Midsummer Night's Dream. **TCI**, vol. 29, n. 1 (Jan 1995). 9.
Marstboom, Antoon. *The Deceiver.* **SDW1**, 47.
Martin, Brian. *The Curse of the Starving Class.* **TCI**, vol. 20, n. 3 (Mar 1986). 10.
Martin, Catherine & Bill Marron.
    A Midsummer Night's Dream. **TCI**, vol. 29, n. 1 (Jan 1995). 9.
Martin, Denis.
    Barabbas. **SDW2**, 30.
    Bear Skin. **SDW2**, 33.
    Le Bourgeois Gentilhomme. **SDW1**, 46.
    The Skin of our Teeth. **SDW1**, 46.
    La Vie Parisienne. **SDW1**, 46.
Martin, Harald. *Ghosts.* **SDW2**, 153.

Martin, Karlheinz.
    Antigone. **TCS2**, plate 374.
    Europa. **TCS2**, plate 375.
    Franziska. **TCS2**, plate 176.
    Razzia. **TCS2**, plate 281.
Martin, Tyr. *Master Pathelin*. **SDW2**, 210.
Martin-Davies, Ashley. *Measure for Measure*. **TCI**, vol. 29, n. 6 (Jun/Jul 1995). 12.
Marty, André.
    Chandelier. **SOW**, plate 66.
    Nuit des Quatre-Temps. **TPH**, photo 399.
Marty, Charles, Patrick Chauveau, Michel Lebois, & Sabine.
    From Moses to Mao. **SDW4**, illus. 397-404.
Marussig, Guido.
    Götterdämmerung. **SDE**, 120.
    Die Meistersinger von Nürnberg. **SDE**, 120.
    Nabucco. **SDE**, 121.
    Otello. **SDE**, 119.
    Samson et Dalila. **SDE**, 121.
    The Ship. **TPH**, photo 379.
Marzolff, Serge. *A Walk in the Woods*. **TCI**, vol. 26, n. 4 (Apr 1992). 37.
Masereel, Frans.
    Die Bluthochzeit. **AST**, 212.
    Liluli. **RSD**, illus. 389.
Masic, Slobodan. *The Brothers Karamazov*. **SDW4**, illus. 148-154.
Masson, André.
    The Earth is Round. **SDW1**, 101.
    The Golden Head. **RSD**, illus. 497; **SDW2**, 95.
    Iphigenia in Taurus. **AST**, 202.
    Medea. **AST**, 201.
    Morts sans Sépulture. **AST**, 202.
    Numance. **AST**, 200.
    Les Présages. **SDR**, 28.
    Tete d'or. **AST**, 204.
    Wozzeck. **AST**, 203.
Mataré, Ewald.
    Oedipus Rex. **AST**, 234.
    The Trojan Women. **AST**, 234.
Matcaboji, Mircea. *Hamlet*. **SDW2**, 175.
Matisse, Henri. *Le Chant du Rossignol*. **AST**, 80.
Matsoukis, Theophanes. *L'Histoire du Soldat*. **SDE**, 122.
Matteis, Maria de. *Le Compt Ory*. **SDE**, 122.
Matthews, William. *Right You Are If You Think You Are*. **SDL**, 69.
Mau, Waltraut, Ilse Träbing, & Klaus Weiffenbach.
    The Song of the Lusitanian Bogey. **SDW3**, 136.
Maximowna, Ita.
    The Coronation of Poppea. **PST**, 212.
    Death in Venice. **OPE**, 68.
    Lucifer and the Lord. **SDW1**, 71.
    The Masked Ball. **SDW2**, 65.
    Peer Gynt. **SDW1**, 71.
Maxwell, George. *Cabaret*. **TCI**, vol. 28, n. 1 (Jan 1994). 6.

May, Henry.
   Machinal. **TCI**, vol. 15, n. 8 (Oct 1981). 10.
   Peer Gynt. **CSD**, 104.
Mayakovsky, Vladimir. *Mystery Bouffe*. **RST**, 65.
McCallin, Tanya. *Hard Shoulder*. **BTD**, 52.
McCarry, Charles E.
   The Comedy of Errors. **DDT**, 24a.
   The Debutante Ball. **TDT**, vol. XXVIII, n. 2 (Spring 1992). 7 of insert.
   The Girl of the Golden West. **DDT**, 298.
   Hooters. **DDT**, 103; **TCI**, vol. 13, n. 3 (May/Jun 1979). 30.
   The Importance of Being Earnest. **TDT**, vol. XXVI, n. 1 (Spring 1990). 14 of insert.
   The Jack the Ripper Revue. **TDT**, vol. XXVIII, n. 2 (Spring 1992). 7 of insert.
   A Kiss Is Just a Kiss. **DDT**, 102.
   Merrily We Roll Along. **DDT**, 477.
   L'Ormindo. **DDT**, 476.
   Painting Churches. **DDT**, 259; **TDT**, vol. XXVIII, n. 2 (Spring 1992). 7 of insert.
   The Road to Mecca. **TDT**, vol. XXVIII, n. 2 (Spring 1992). 7 of insert.
   A Walk in the Woods. **DDT**, 152; **TDT**, vol. XXVIII, n. 2 (Spring 1992). 7 of insert.
McCarthy, Dessis. *The Song of the Lusitanian Bogey*. **SDL**, 211.
McCleery, R.C. *The Gay Gordons*. **MCD**, plate 63.
McCleery, R.C. & Conrad Tritschler. *The Dairymaids*. **MCD**, plate 57.
McCleery, R.C., Alfred Terraine, Conrad Tritschler, & Philip Howden.
   The Boy. **MCD**, plate 113.
McCleery, R.C., Conrad Tritschler, Stafford Hall, & W. Holmes.
   The Arcadians. **MCD**, plate 80.
McCleery, R.C., Walter Hann, & Conrad Tritschler. *Oh! Oh!! Delphine!!!* **MCD**, plate 95.
McClennahan, Charles.
   Ceremonies in Dark Old Men. **ASD2**, 114.
   Fences. **ASD2**, 122.
   Long Time Since Yesterday. **ASD2**, 120.
   Ma Rainey's Black Bottom. **ASD2**, 110, 116.
   Moonchildren. **ASD2**, between 108 & 109.
   That Serious He-Man Ball. **ASD2**, 120.
   Wasted. **ASD2**, 118.
   West Memphis Mojo. **ASD2**, 120.
McDonald, Anthony.
   Black Snow. **TCI**, vol. 27, n. 3 (Mar 1993). 9.
   Hamlet. **TCI**, vol. 25, n. 9 (Nov 1991). 17; **TDT**, vol. XXVII, n. 4 (Fall 1991). 37.
   Mary Stuart. **BTD**, 40.
   Orlando. **BTD**, 131.
   The Seagull. **TCI**, vol. 26, n. 5 (May 1992). 12.
McDonald, Anthony & Tom Cairns.
   Billy Budd. **BTD**, 145.
   The Midsummer Marriage. **BTD**, 145.
McDonald, P.J. *The Stickiness of Gelatine*. **MCN**, 19.
McGarity, Michael. *Measure for Measure*. **TCI**, vol. 28, n. 5 (May 1994). 6.
McGillivray, Steven R.
   Kabuki/Bacchae. **TDT**, vol. XXVIII, n. 2 (Spring 1992). 14 of insert.
McGowan, Julian. *Heart-throb*. **BTD**, 84, 85.
McGreevy, David. *DADADADADADA*. **TCI**, vol. 18, n. 7 (Aug/Sep 1984). 16.

McLane, Derek.
    Early Girl. **TCI**, vol. 21, n. 10 (Dec 1987). 10.
    Figaro/Figaro. **TCI**, vol. 29, n. 3 (Mar 1995). 6.
    Henry VI. **TCI**, vol. 29, n. 5 (May 1995). 7.
    Misalliance. **TCI**, vol. 26, n. 4 (Apr 1992). 14.
    Titus Andronicus. **TCI**, vol. 28, n. 5 (May 1994). 6.
McLeish, Iona. *Savannah Bay.* **BTD**, 68.
McNamara, Brooks.
    The Brig. **TCI**, vol. 2, n. 6 (Nov/Dec 1968). 16, 17, 19, 20.
    Doctor Faustus. **TCI**, vol. 2, n. 6 (Nov/Dec 1968). 15, 18.
McPhillips, Tom. *Uptown Its Hot.* **MBM**, 185.
Meczies, Aliute & Günther Schneider-Siemssen. *Der Freischütz.* **CGA**, 197.
Mednikov, Vera. *Clarence Darrow.* **TCI**, vol. 17, n. 7 (Aug/Sep 1983). 28.
Medunetsky, K. & V.A. Stenberg. *The Thunderstorm.* **RSD**, illus. 195.
Mélat, Maurice. *King David.* **SDW2**, 95.
Melena, Miroslav.
    The Birds. **TDT**, vol. XXVII, n. 2 (Spring 1991). 30.
    The Crocodile. **TDT**, vol. XXVII, n. 2 (Spring 1991). 29, 30.
    The Good Soldier Schweik. **TDT**, vol. XXIII, n. 4 (Winter 1988). 49.
    Matthew the Honest. **TDT**, vol. XXVII, n. 2 (Spring 1991). 30.
    The Suicide. **TDT**, vol. XXVI, n. 2 (Summer 1990). 38.
Meller, Vadim. *The People's Malakhy.* **RST**, 235.
Menconi, Lee. *The House of Bernarda Alba.* **BSE1**, 36.
Menessier. *Earth.* **RSD**, illus. 14.
Menshutin, Nikolai. *Liubov Yarovaya.* **RST**, 212, 213.
Mercer, G.W. *Frankenstein.* **TCI**, vol. 22, n. 5 (May 1988). 44.
Mercer, Thomas Travix. *Tango.* **CSD**, 49.
Merritt, Michael.
    American Buffalo. **ASD2**, between 108 & 109.
    The Curse of the Starving Class. **ASD2**, 133.
    Glengarry Glen Ross. **ASD2**, 138.
    Hail Scrawdyke! or Little Malcolm and His Struggle Against the Eunuchs. **ASD2**, 131.
    Hamlet. **ASD2**, 128; **BSE5**, 39.
    The Inspector General. **ASD2**, 124, 127; **TCI**, vol. 21, n. 2 (Feb 1987). 29.
    Lakeboat. **ASD2**, 129.
    Mother Courage and Her Children. **ASD2**, 130.
    Oleanna. **TCI**, vol. 27, n. 3 (Mar 1993). 8.
    Romeo and Juliet. **ASD2**, 134.
Mertz, Franz.
    Oedipus Rex. **DSL**, 282; **RSD**, illus. 516; **SDW1**, 73; **TSY**, 42.
    Penthesilea. **SDW2**, 66.
Messel, Oliver.
    The Abduction from the Seraglio. **OMB**, 201.
    Ariadne auf Naxos. **OMB**, 149.
    Le Compt Ory. **MEM**, 28, 29.
    Comus. **MEM**, 105.
    The Country Wife. **MEM**, 92, 93; **OMB**, 91; **SOW**, plate 39; **TPH**, photo 440.
    Die Entführung Aus Dem Serail (The Elopement from the Harem). **MEM**, 118.
    Francesca da Rimini. **MEM**, 95-97.
    Glamorous Night. **MCD**, plates 177, 178; **MEM**, 91; **OMB**, 95.
    Helen! **MEM**, 35, 86, 87; **OMB**, 57, 59, 66; **SCM**, 17, 18.

House of Flowers. **OMB**, 172, 173, 181; **WMC**, 182.

Idomeneo. **DMS**, plate 26; **OMB**, 154; **SDG**, 188; **SDW1**, 178.

The Lady's Not for Burning. **OMB**, 136, 137; **WTP**, 166, 167.

The Magic Flute. **CGA**, 132; **MEM**, 115; **OMB**, 133.

The Marriage of Figaro. **MEM**, 156; **OMB**, 182, 183, 190, 191.

A Midsummer Night's Dream. **MEM**, 98, 99; **OMB**, 108, 109; **TPH**, photo 443.

Mother of Pearl. **MEM**, 90.

The Play's the Thing. **WTP**, 125.

The Queen of Spades. **OMB**, 152; **SDW1**, 178.

Ring Around the Moon. **MEM**, 26, 120, 121; **OMB**, 141; **SDW1**, 178; **TDT**, vol.
    XXIII, n. 3 (Fall 1987). 28.

The Rivals. **MEM**, 107; **OMB**, 70, 120, 121.

Romeo and Juliet. **MEM**, 127-129; **OMB**, 152.

Samson. **OMB**, 185.

The Sleeping Princess. **DOT**, 242.

The Tempest. **MEM**, 101; **OMB**, 111.

Traveller Without Luggage. **OMB**, 223.

Twang!! **OMB**, 225.

Messerer, Boris. *Carmen.* **SDW3**, 183.

Metheny, Russell. *The Bright and Bold Design.* **TCI**, vol. 27, n. 1 (Jan 1993). 7.

Meyer, Eloise. *The Student Prince.* **TCI**, vol. 10, n. 5 (Oct 1976). 4.

Meyer, Hans.

A Dream Play. **SDW2**, 110.

The Women of Trachis. **SDW2**, 65.

Meyer, Stan. *Beauty and the Beast.* **TCI**, vol. 28, n. 7 (Aug/Sep 1994). 43.

Meyerhold, Vsevelod, plan, Ilya Shlepyanov, execution.

Bubus, the Teacher. **MOT**, between 200 & 201.

D.E. (Give Us Europe). **RST**, 140, 141; **TBB**, 111; **TCS2**, plate 184.

The Warrant. **MOT**, between 200 & 201; **RSD**, illus. 203, 204; **RST**, 183; **TCS2**, plate
    185.

Meyerhold, Vsevelod, plan; Alexander Rodchenko, execution.

The Bed-bug, part 2. **RST**, 258, 259.

Meyerhold, Vsevelod, plan; Ivan Leistikov, execution.

Camille. **MOT**, between 304 & 305.

Meyerhold, Vsevelod, plan; Sergei Vakhtangov, execution.

The Bathhouse. **MOT**, between 272 & 273; **RST**, 260, 261.

Commander of the Second Army. **MOT**, between 256 & 257.

Meyerhold, Vsevelod, plan; The. Kukriniksky, execution.

The Bed-bug, part 1. **RST**, 256, 257.

Meyerhold, Vsevelod, plan; Vasilii Federov, execution.

The Forest. **DOT**, 216; **MOT**, between 184 & 185; **RSD**, illus. 180, 181; **RST**, 178,
    179; **SCM**, 92; **TCT**, plate 21.

Meyerhold, Vsevelod, plan; Victor Kisselev, execution. *The Inspector General.* **MOT**,
    between 224 & 225 and between 240 & 241; **NTO**, facing 324; **RSD**, illus. 205-
    207; **RST**, 191 and 224, 225; **TPH**, photo 412; **TSS**, 523.

Mickley, William. *The Devils.* **SDB**, 46.

Micunis, Gordon Jules. *The Venetian Twins.* **CSD**, 107; **DPT**, 99.

Mielziner, Jo.

·Abe Lincoln in Illinois. **DTT**, 112; **MCN**, 141; **SDA**, 121.

After the Fall. **DPT**, 48; **DTT**, 219; **SDW3**, 131.

Allegro. **BWM**, 191; **DTT**, 137; ·HOB, 79.

Miller, Bruce. *Candide*. **TCI**, vol. 12, n. 3 (Mar/Apr 1978). 28.

Miller, Kenny. *The Machine Wreckers*. **BTD**, 64.

Miller, Lawrence. *Nine*. **MBM**, 96, 97, 104; **TCI**, vol. 16, n. 7 (Aug/Sep 1982). 16-19;
    TCI, vol. 19, n. 5 (May 1985). 17; **TCI**, vol. 21, n. 7 (Aug/Sep 1987). 22.

Miller, Michael. *As You Like It*. **TCI**, vol. 25, n. 3 (Mar 1991). 23.

Minelli, Vincent.
    At Home Abroad. **SDA**, 248.
    The Show is On. **RBS**, 137.

Minks, Wilfried.
    Antigone. **TCI**, vol. 12, n. 1 (Jan/Feb 1978). 29.
    Bremer Frieheit. **SDW4**, illus. 406; **TCI**, vol. 12, n. 1 (Jan/Feb 1978). 28.
    Captain Bada. **SDW2**, 66.
    Castle Wetterstein. **SDW4**, illus. 192.
    The Coffee House. **SDW3**, 75.
    Frühlings Erwachen. **SDB**, 197.
    Hamlet. **RSD**, illus. 584; **TCI**, vol. 12, n. 1 (Jan/Feb 1978). 28.
    Macbeth. **TCI**, vol. 12, n. 1 (Jan/Feb 1978). 28.
    Maid of Orleans. **TCI**, vol. 12, n. 1 (Jan/Feb 1978). 31.
    Measure for Measure. **SDW3**, 50; **TCI**, vol. 12, n. 1 (Jan/Feb 1978). 28.
    The Miser. **SDW3**, 72.
    Peer Gynt. **TCI**, vol. 12, n. 1 (Jan/Feb 1978). 29.
    Die Räuber. **RSD**, illus. 583; **SDW3**, 81; **TCI**, vol. 12, n. 1 (Jan/Feb 1978). 30.
    Revenger's Tragedy. **TCI**, vol. 12, n. 1 (Jan/Feb 1978). 28.
    Schweik in the Second World War. **RSD**, illus. 582.
    The Soldiers. **SDW3**, 157.
    Spring's Awakening. **TCI**, vol. 12, n. 1 (Jan/Feb 1978). 30.
    The Tempest. **SDW3**, 64; **TCI**, vol. 12, n. 1 (Jan/Feb 1978). 31.
    Toller. **TCI**, vol. 12, n. 1 (Jan/Feb 1978). 30.
    Torquato Tasso. **SDW3**, 78; **TCI**, vol. 12, n. 1 (Jan/Feb 1978). 28.
    Wars of the Roses. **TCI**, vol. 12, n. 1 (Jan/Feb 1978). 29.

Minshall, Peter. *Man Better Man*. **TCI**, vol. 9, n. 5 (Oct 1975). 12, 13.

Miró, Joán. *Jeux d'Enfants*. **SDR**, 28.

Mitchell, David.
    Annie. **ASD1**, 132; **BWM**, 152, 153, 156, 158, 159; **DDT**, 101; **TCI**, vol. 11, n. 6
        (Nov/Dec 1977). 28-31; **TCI**, vol. 14, n. 1 (Jan/Feb 1980). 20; **WMC**, 310.
    Barnum. **ASD1**, 133; **DDT**, 309, 312, 331; **DSL**, plate V; **MBM**, 140, 141; **TCI**, vol.
        14, n. 5 (Oct 1980). 16, 17; **TCI**, vol. 21, n. 1 (Jan 1987). 30, 32; **TDT**, vol. XVII,
        n. 1 (Spring 1981). 12, 13; **WMC**, 7.
    The Basic Training of Pavlo Hummel. **ASD1**, 134.
    The Big Love. **TCI**, vol. 25, n. 2 (Feb 1991). 10.
    The Boys of Winter. **DDT**, 114, 115.
    Brighton Beach Memoirs. **TCI**, vol. 21, n. 2 (Feb 1987). 22.
    Bring Back Birdie. **TCI**, vol. 17, n. 8 (Oct 1983). 29.
    Cabal of Hypocrites. **ASD1**, 127.
    Can-Can. **DDT**, 304.
    Dance a Little Closer. **MBM**, 210.
    Foxfire. **DDT**, 24a.
    The Gin Game. **ASD1**, 124; **TCI**, vol. 12, n. 3 (Mar/Apr 1978). 12.
    Hamlet **DPT**, 89.
    Harrigan and Hart. **TCI**, vol. 19, n. 4 (Apr 1985). 24.
    Henry V. **ASD1**, 129; **DDT**, 310.

I Remember Mama. **DDT**, 219, 403; **MBM**, 192.

In the Boom Boom Room. **DSL**, plate VI.

La Cage aux Folles. **ASD1**, between 70 & 71, 121; **MBM**, 23, 154; **TCI**, vol. 17, n. 9 (Nov/Dec 1983). 17-19.

Legs Diamond. **DDT**, 311.

Mefistofele. **DPT**, 22; **TCI**, vol. 4, n. 1 (Jan/Feb 1970). 18; **TCI**, vol. 7, n. 1 (Jan/Feb 1973). 16.

Mrs. Warren's Profession. **TCI**, vol. 10, n. 3 (May/Jun 1976). 24.

Naked Hamlet. **ASD1**, 131.

On the Waterfront. **ASD1**, 125; **DDT**, 308.

The Price. **TCI**, vol. 13, n. 4 (Sep 1979). 50.

Short Eyes. **ASD1**, 126; **CSD**, 110.

The Steadfast Tin Soldier. **ASD1**, 135.

Steambath. **ASD1**, 123; **DPT**, 84.

Il Trovatore. **DPT**, 118.

Mitchell, David & Collis Davis. *A Photograph.* **TCI**, vol. 13, n. 1 (Jan/Feb 1979). 33.

Mitchell, Poppy. *Amabel.* **BTD**, 86.

Mitchell, Robert D.

Cantique des Cantiques. **DPT**, 184

Medea. **DDT**, 81.

Oedipus Rex. **DDT**, 75.

La Peri. **DPT**, 29.

The Screens. **TCI**, vol. 8, n. 2 (Mar/Apr 1974). 16.

Mnouchkine, Ariane. *Mephisto.* **TCI**, vol. 14, n. 6 (Nov/Dec 1980). 36, 38.

Mohirta, T. *Ripa Albastra.* **TDT**, vol. XII, n. 3 (Fall 1976). 43.

Moholy-Nagy, Lászlo.

Hin und Zurück. **SCM**, 57.

Der Kaufmann von Berlin. **SCM**, 56; **AST**, 147.

Madame Butterfly. **RSD**, illus. 260; **SCM**, 58.

Menschen. **AST**, 146.

The Tales of Hoffmann. **AST**, 144, 145; **NTO**, facing 396; **RSD**, illus. 253-259; **SCM**, 57.

Moiseiwitsch, Tanya.

All's Well That Ends Well. **DMS**, plate 40; **TCI**, vol. 20, n. 7 (Aug/Sep 1986). 22.

Bless the Bride. **MCD**, plate 193.

Henry V. **DOT**, 239.

Henry VIII. **SDG**, 182.

Kidnapped in London. **TCI**, vol. 20, n. 7 (Aug/Sep 1986). 22.

The Misanthrope. **SDW4**, illus. 79.

Much Ado About Nothing. **SDW2**, 39, 220.

Peter Grimes. **CGA**, 134; **MOM**, 176-186; **SDW1**, 179; **TOP**, 139.

Rigoletto. **TCI**, vol. 20, n. 7 (Aug/Sep 1986). 19.

St. Joan. **TCI**, vol. 20, n. 7 (Aug/Sep 1986). 23.

The Three Sisters. **TCI**, vol. 20, n. 7 (Aug/Sep 1986). 23.

Moiseiwitsch, Tanya & Polly Scranton Bohanetzky.

The Inspector General. **TCI**, vol. 20, n. 7 (Aug/Sep 1986). 17.

Molander, Olav & Sven-Eric Skawonius. *Master Olof.* **TAT**, plate 469.

Molka, Viktor. *Scandal in the Valley of St. Florian.* **SDW1**, 134.

Mondrian, Piet. *The Ephemeral is Eternal.* **AST**, 148; **RSD**, illus. 333-335.

Monin, Guilliaume. *Electra.* **SDW1**, 102.

Moniz Freire, Napoleão. *Cross Purpose.* **SDW2**, 36.

Monloup, Hubert.
  A Dream Play. **SDW3**, 86.
  Public Chant Before Two Electric Chairs. **RSD**, illus. 511-513.
  Tartuffe. **SDW4**, illus. 71-78.
  Thirteen Suns of the Rue Saint Blaise. **SDW3**, 145.
Monod, Jean. *Metaphysics of the Two-headed Calf*. **SDW4**, illus. 215.
Monod, Jean & Nestor de Arzadun. *The Tempest*. **RSD**, illus. 638.
Monod, Jean, Eugene Lee, & Franne Lee. *Orghast*. **SDW4**, illus. 295, 296.
Montelius, Olle. *Gustav III*. **SDW4**, illus. 181.
Montgomery, Richard.
  The Exception and the Rule. **SDW3**, 111; **SDW4**, illus. 239.
  In a Fine Castle. **SDW4**, illus. 334.
Montonati, Bruno.
  La Bohème. **SDE**, 124.
  Orfeo. **SDE**, 124.
Montresor, Beni.
  Aïda **TCI**, vol. 16, n. 5 (May 1982). 14
  L'Amore dei Tre Re. **TCI**, vol. 16, n. 5 (May 1982). 17.
  Benvenuto Cellini. **CGA**, 189.
  Do I Hear a Waltz? **BWM**, 199.
  L'Elisir d'Amore. **CGA**, 192.
  Esclarmonde. **TCI**, vol. 16, n. 5 (May 1982). 16.
  La Gioconda. **TCI**, vol. 10, n. 5 (Oct 1976). 16, 17; **TCI**, vol. 16, n. 5 (May 1982). 16.
  The Last Savage. **MOM**, 15; **TCI**, vol. 16, n. 5 (May 1982). 17.
  The Magic Flute. **TCI**, vol. 16, n. 5 (May 1982). 16; **TCI**, vol. 4, n. 1 (Jan/Feb 1970).
        17; **TCI**, vol. 7, n. 1 (Jan/Feb 1973). 16.
  The Marriage of Figaro. **TCI**, vol. 17, n. 7 (Aug/Sep 1983). 21; **TCI**, vol. 18, n. 7
        (Aug/Sep 1984). 40.
  A Midsummer Night's Dream. **TCI**, vol. 20, n. 1 (Jan 1986). 16.
  L'Ormindo. **TCI**, vol. 18, n. 3 (Mar 1984). 27.
  Platée. **TCI**, vol. 16, n. 5 (May 1982). 16.
  Rags. **MBM**, 223.
  Reynard. **TCI**, vol. 20, n. 9 (Nov 1986). 12.
  Turandot. **TCI**, vol. 16, n. 5 (May 1982). 16.
Moon, Jill. *The Three Cuckolds*. **TCI**, vol. 21, n. 8 (Oct 1987). 26.
Moore, Henry. *Don Giovanni*. **AST**, 221.
Moore, John & Veniero Colasanti. *La Traviata*. **SDW2**, 123.
Morales, Roberto & Thomas A. Walsh.
  Zoot Suit. **TCI**, vol. 13, n. 1 (Jan/Feb 1979). 6; **TCI**, vol. 14, n. 4 (Sep 1980). 45.
Moralis, Yannis.
  Plutus. **SDW2**, 104.
  The Shoemaker's Wife. **SDW2**, 104.
Moran, Jim. *To Kill a Mockingbird*. **TDT**, vol. XXVIII, n. 2 (Spring 1992). 8 of insert.
Morange, E.A. & Frank E. Gates.
  Leah Kleschna. **MCN**, 24.
  Wildflower. **WMC**, 103.
Morcom, James Stewart.
  Five Kings. **DDT**, 416.
  Native Son. **DDT**, 170; **WTP**, 184, 185.
Morgan, James.
  Anna Karenina. **TCI**, vol. 26, n. 9 (Nov 1992). 8.

Pacific Overtures. **TCI**, vol. 19, n. 5 (May 1985). 25.
Morgan, Roger. *Bonus March*. **TCI**, vol. 7, n. 3 (May/Jun 1973). 14.
Mork, Lennart. *Jeanne d'Arc*. **TDT**, vol. XXIII, n. 4 (Winter 1988). 7.
Mörk, Lennart & Randi Fisher. *The Jewels of the Queen*. **SDW2**, 210.
Morley, Christopher & Ann Curtis. *Die Fledermaus*. **CGA**, 196.
Mörner, Stellan.
    The Apollo of Bellac. **SDW1**, 167.
    Erik XIV. **DSL**, 4, 5; **SDW1**, 161; **SDW2**, 221.
    A Midsummer Night's Dream. **SDW2**, 210.
    Salomé. **SDW1**, 167.
    Twelfth Night. **SDW1**, 167.
Morton, Mark W.
    Guys and Dolls. **TCI**, vol. 20, n. 5 (May 1986). 18.
    She Loves Me. **TCI**, vol. 20, n. 5 (May 1986). 26.
Morton, Ree. *Dressed Like an Egg*. **ASC**, 30.
Moscoso, Roberto, B. Bauchau, J. N. Cordier, A. Ferreira, Cl. Forget, G. Cl. Francois, L.
        de Grandmaison, & A. Salomon.
    The Revolutionary City Belongs to this World. **SDW4**, illus. 385-390.
Moscoso, Roberto.
    The Revolution Must End With the Perfection of Happiness. **SDW4**, illus. 379-384.
    1789. **RSD**, illus. 642-644.
Mostafa, Ramzi.
    The Playboy of the Western World. **SFT**, 14.
    Seat of Justice. **SDW3**, 108.
Motley (Margaret Harris, Sophia Harris, & Elizabeth Montgomery).
    The Cherry Orchard. **WTP**, 98, 99.
    Hamlet. **SDG**, 191; **TDT**, vol. XXIX, n. 3 (Summer 1993). 26, 28; **TDT**, vol. XXIX, n.
        3 (Summer 1993). 26, 28.
    Henry V. **TPH**, photo 442.
    The Importance of Being Earnest. **WTP**, 134, 135.
    A Man for All Seasons. **SDW2**, 221.
    The Merry Wives of Windsor. **DMS**, plates 30-32.
    A Midsummer Night's Dream. **DDT**, 312a.
    Richard of Bordeaux. **SCM**, 21.
    Romeo and Juliet. **PST**, 155.
    The Tempest. **SOW**, plate 106; **WTP**, 66, 67.
    The Three Sisters. **TCR**, 67; **WTP**, 100-103.
    The Winter's Tale. **PST**, 79.
    You Touched Me. **SDA**, 227.
Moukosseeva, Margarita. *The Promise*. **SDW3**, 122.
Moulaert, René.
    A quoi revent les jeunes filles. **TCS2**, plate 50.
    L'Amour Médicin. **TCS2**, plate 52.
    Aniara. **SDW2**, 30.
    Tyl. **TCS2**, plate 179.
    The Winter's Tale. **SDW1**, 102.
Moyer, Allen.
    On the Bum. **TCI**, vol. 27, n. 2 (Feb 1993). 10.
    Wings. **TCI**, vol. 28, n. 5 (May 1994). 7.
Mozuras, Vitalijus. *An Ordinary Woman*. **SDW4**, illus. 318.
Mrkvicka, Teige & Zelenka. *Prsy Tiresiovy*. **SDB**, 186.

Mulas, Ugo, Virginio Puecher, & Ebe Colciaghi. *Wozzeck*. **SDW3**, 191.

Mullen, Joseph. *Wild Birds*. **MCN**, 70.

Müller, Traugott.

  Gewitter über Gothland. **TCS2**, plate 358.

  Segel am Horizont. **TCS2**, plate 125.

Müller-Brockman, Josef. *Caligula*. **SDW1**, 116.

Mumcu, Hüseyin. *Love and Peace*. **SDW2**, 214.

Mumford, Peter.

  Fidelio. **BTD**, 117.

  Hamletmachine. **BTD**, 46.

Munch, Edvard. *Ghosts*. **AST**, 22, 23; **MRH**, facing 16; **MRT**, 63; **RSD**, illus. 34-36.

Muñoz, Gori.

  Don Friolera's Horns. **SDW1**, 37.

  Fenisa's Bait. **SDW2**, 26.

  The Jealous Old Man. **SDW1**, 37.

  Sinfonia Argentina. **SDW1**, 37.

  Sister Josephine. **SDW2**, 33.

Muntner. *Ghosts*. **SST**, 265.

Muraoka, Alan E. *Marat/Sade*. **BSE3**, 33.

Musatescu, Sanda. *Master Builder Manole*. **SDW3**, 105.

Musika, Frantisek.

  The Alchemist. **TDT**, n. 42 (Fall 1975). 25.

  Androcles and the Lion. **TDT**, n. 42 (Fall 1975). 25.

  Hadrian of Rome. **TDT**, n. 42 (Fall 1975). 25.

  Hamlet. **TDT**, n. 42 (Fall 1975). 25.

  Julieta. **TDT**, n. 42 (Fall 1975). 25.

-N-

Naccarato, John. *Manon Lescaut*. **TCI**, vol. 20, n. 8 (Oct 1986). 21.

Nagasaka, Motohiro. *Madame Butterfly*. **MOM**, 14.

Nagy, Elemer.

  Boris Godounov. **TCI**, vol. 4, n. 1 (Jan/Feb 1970). 28.

  Falstaff. **SFT**, 123.

Nakamori, Kaoru. *Elephant Man*. **TDT**, vol. XX, n. 1 (Spring 1984). 12.

Nannini, Elena. *Orlando Furioso*. **SDW3**, 33.

Napier, John.

  Cats. **ALW**, 129-131, 134, 135, 136-141; **BTD**, 148; **DDT**, 3, 591; **MBM**, 2, 3, 64;
    SDL, 1, 134, 135; **TCI**, vol. 17, n. 1 (Jan 1983). 18-21; **TDT**, vol. XIX, n. 1
    (Spring 1983). 10; Cats. **TDP**, 46.

  Henry IV, part 1. **TDT**, vol. XIX, n. 1 (Spring 1983). 10; Henry VI, part 1. **BTD**, 37.

  Iphigenia in Tauris. **TDT**, vol. XIX, n. 1 (Spring 1983). 10.

  A Midsummer Night's Dream. **TDT**, vol. XVI, n. 1 (Spring 1980). 22.

  Les Misérables. **BTD**, 150; **DDT**, 596; **MBM**, 129, 132, 133; **TCI**, vol. 20, n. 9 (Nov
    1986). 32, 33, 35.

  Miss Saigon. **DDT**, 7, 595; **MBM**, 136, 137; **TCI**, vol. 24, n. 1 (Jan 1990). 22; **TCI**,
    vol. 25, n. 4 (Apr 1991). 35, 38; **TCI**, vol. 25, n. 8 (Oct 1991). 24.

  Once in a Lifetime. **BTD**, 37.

  Starlight Express. **ALW**, 143, 146-151; **BTD**, 154; **DDT**, 588; **MBM**, 65, 66; **TCI**,
    vol. 21, n. 5 (May 1987). 8; **TCI**, vol. 24, n. 8 (Oct 1990). 44, 47.

Each Man Helps His Country. **SDW2**, 43.
The Sword of Damocles. **SDW2**, 43.

-O-

O'Brien, Timothy.
    The American Clock. **BTD**, 35.
    The Flying Dutchman. **SDW2**, 223.
    La Grand Macabre. **BTD**, 105.
    The Knot Garden. **SDW3**, 199; **TDT**, vol. XIX, n. 3 (Fall 1983). 8.
    Love's Labor's Lost. **TDT**, vol. XXVII, n. 4 (Fall 1991). 37.
    Old Times. **BTD**, 35.
    Samson. **BTD**, 105.
    The Three Sisters. **BTD**, 36.
    Twelfth Night. **TDT**, vol. XXVII, n. 4 (Fall 1991). 37.
O'Brien, Timothy & Tazeena Firth.
    The Bassarids. **TDT**, vol. XII, n. 3 (Fall 1976). 35.
    A Doll's Life. **HPA**, 137; **MBM**, 84, 85; **TCI**, vol. 16, n. 9 (Nov/Dec 1982). 22, 23.
    Evita. **ALW**, 89, 93-95; **BTD**, 152, 153; **HPA**, 160, 161, 164, 168; **HPR**, 273, 277;
        MBM, 57, 59, 60, 61, 82; **TCI**, vol. 12, n. 6 (Oct 1978). 6; **TCI**, vol. 13, n. 6
        (Nov/Dec 1979). 14-19; **TCI**, vol. 18, n. 8 (Oct 1984). 15; **TCI**, vol. 19, n. 5 (May
        1985). 20; **TDT**, vol. XIX, n. 3 (Fall 1983). 16; **TMT**, 229.
    The Man of Mode. **TDT**, vol. XIX, n. 3 (Fall 1983). 9.
    A Midsummer Night's Dream. **BTD**, 102.
    Pericles. **SDW3**, 62.
    Peter Grimes. **BTD**, 101.
    The Rake's Progress. **BTD**, 101; **TDT**, vol. XIX, n. 3 (Fall 1983). 8.
    Richard II. **TCI**, vol. 8, n. 2 (Mar/Apr 1974). 2.
    Turandot. **BTD**, 102, 103.
O'Connor, Charles.
    Fabriola. **SDT**, 298.
    The Greeks. **SDT**, 291.
O'Hearn, Robert.
    Annie Get Your Gun. **DDT**, 395.
    La Bohème. **DDT**, 96.
    L'Elisir D'Amore. **DPT**, 34; **MOM**, 15; **SDA**, 264.
    Die Frau Ohne Schatten. **CSD**, 113; **DPT**, 72, 73, 365; **MOM**, 100-111; **OPE**, 233,
        240, 242, 247, 248; **SDB**, 80, 81; **SDR**, 61; **TCI**, vol. 10, n. 5 (Oct 1976). 16.
    Idomeneo. **DDT**, 98.
    Macbeth. **DDT**, 299.
    Die Meistersinger von Nürnberg. **DDT**, 92; **DPT**, between 124 & 125.
    Parsifal. **DDT**, 95.
    The Pearl Fishers. **TCI**, vol. 15, n. 4 (Apr 1981). 38.
    Porgy and Bess. **MOM**, 188-199; **TCI**, vol. 11, n. 2 (Mar/Apr 1977). 22.
    Der Rosenkavalier. **DPT**, 9.
Öberg, Barbara W.
    Kristina. **SDW2**, 211.
    Lysistrata. **SDW2**, 211.
    Richard II. **SDW2**, 211.
Oberle, Karl Friedrich. *Don Giovanni.* **TDT**, vol. XXVII, n. 3 (Summer 1991). 7.
Obolensky, Chloë. *The Cherry Orchard.* **TCI**, vol. 22, n. 4 (Apr 1988). 23.

Ockel, Reinhold. *Bauernzorn*. **TCS2**, plate 137.

Oda, Otoya. *At the South-East of Tokyo*. **SDW2**, 148.

Odorisio, Rob. *Tales of the Lost Formicans*. **TCI**, vol. 26, n. 1 (Jan 1992). 40.

Oechslin, Ary.

> *Adam and Eve*. **SDW4**, illus. 316.
>
> *The Caucasian Chalk Circle*. **SDW3**, 117.
>
> *The Fisherwomen*. **SDW4**, illus. 101.
>
> *Intrigue and Love*. **SDW2**, 112.
>
> *Penthesilea*. **SDW3**, 81.
>
> *Rosencrantz and Guildenstern are Dead*. **SDW3**, 167.

Oenslager, Donald.

> *The Abduction from the Seraglio*. **BSE2**, 54; **TDO**, 115.
>
> *Amelia Goes to the Ball*. **BSE2**, 52, 55.
>
> *The American Way*. **TDO**, 89-91.
>
> *Antigone*. **CSD**, 83; **DPT**, 362; **SDW3**, 123; **TDO**, 139.
>
> *Anything Goes*. **BWM**, 56, 207; **SDA**, 247; **TDO**, 59; **TMT**, 127.
>
> *As You Like It*. **TDO**, 109
>
> *The Ballad of Baby Doe*. **CSD**, 40; **DDT**, 334; **DPT**, 123; **SDA**, 267; **SDB**, 70; **TDO**, 128, 129.
>
> *The Beautiful Galatea*. **TDO**, 125.
>
> *The Birds*. **SCM**, 129; **STN**, 57-67.
>
> *La Bohème*. **BSE2**, 53.
>
> *Born Yesterday*. **SDA**, 204; **SDW1**, 204; **TDO**, 113; **WTP**, 192, 193.
>
> *Le Bourgeois Gentilhomme*. **STN**, 141.
>
> *Brand*. **RSD**, illus. 443; **STN**, 233-241; **TDO**, 33.
>
> *A Call on Kuprin*. **TDO**, 135.
>
> *Casina*. **STN**, 79.
>
> *Le Cid*. **STN**, 135.
>
> *Coriolanus*. **SDA**, 216; **TDO**, 127.
>
> *Dance With Your Gods*. **TDO**, 53.
>
> *Dido and Aeneas*. **DPT**, 359; **FCS**, plate 215, color plate 31; **FCT**, plate 14; **SDA**, 267, 291; **SDL**, plates 8-14b; **SDO**, 250, plate 31; **TDT**, n. 39 (Dec 1974). 15; **TDO**, 126, facing 16.
>
> *The Doctor's Dilemma*. **TDO**, 99, 100.
>
> *Don Carlos*. **CSD**, 112; **DDT**, 26, 326; **DPT**, 363; **TDO**, 140.
>
> *Egmont*. **STN**, 189-197; **TDO**, 142-145.
>
> *The Emperor Jones*. **DOT**, 224; **RSD**, illus. 444, 445; **SCM**, 128; **SFT**, 121; **STN**, 257-263; **TCI**, vol. 4, n. 4 (Sep 1970). 22; **TDO**, 44, 45.
>
> *The Fabulous Invalid*. **SDA**, 110-113, 288; **SDB**, 34, 35; **TDO**, 84-86, facing 152.
>
> *The Father*. **WTP**, 97.
>
> *Fidelio*. **SDL**, 54; **SDW1**, 204.
>
> *First Lady*. **SFT**, 34, 41.
>
> *First Love*. **TDO**, 136 and facing 136.
>
> *The Flying Dutchman*. **SCM**, 128; **TDO**, 48, 49.
>
> *Girl Crazy*. **BWM**, 224; **TDO**, facing 40.
>
> *Gold Eagle Guy*. **MCN**, 121.
>
> *Good News*. **WMC**, 135.
>
> *Hamlet*. **STN**, frontispiece, 109-117; **TAS**, 174; **TAT**, plate 593.
>
> *L'Histoire du Soldat*. **TDO**, 36.
>
> *I'd Rather Be Right*. **BWM**, 180; **RBS**, 149; **SDA**, 246; **TDO**, 77; **TMI**, 241.
>
> *J.B.* **SDL**, 56; **TDO**, 133; **SDW2**, 237.

Job. **TDO**, 103-107.
Johnny Johnson. **WMC**, 198; **SOW**, plate 84; **TDO**, 70, 71.
King Lear. **TDO**, 23.
The Lady from the Sea. **TDO**, 51.
Land's End. **TDO**, 117.
The Leading Lady. **DPT**, 361; **SDB**, 43; **TDO**, 119.
Life With Mother. **DPT**, 21; **TDO**, 121-123.
The Love for Three Oranges. **STN**, 167-177.
Major Barbara. **DPT**, 360; **TDO**, 130, 131.
A Majority of One. **SDA**, 192-195.
The Man Who Came to Dinner. **MCN**, 146; **WTP**, 182, 183.
Mary Stuart. **DMS**, plate 28; **TDO**, 132.
A Masked Ball. **TDO**, 138.
The Merchant. **WTP**, 44.
Of Mice and Men. **SOW**, plates 92, 93; **TDO**, 79.
The Old Foolishness. **TDO**, facing 96.
Orfeo. **SDW2**, 237; **TDO**, facing 8 and 134.
Le Pauvre Matelot. **SDA**, 266; **SOW**, plate 83; **TDO**, 75.
Pinwheel. **SDA**, 274; **SDB**, 23; **TCS2**, plate 181; **TDO**, 31.
Present Laughter. **SDA**, 205.
Prometheus Bound. **SDL**, 38; **STN**, 31-41; **TDO**, 94, 95.
Pygmalion. **TDO**, 111.
Red Hot and Blue! **BWM**, 203; **SDA**, 246; **TDO**, 67; **WMC**, 150.
Der Ring des Nibelungen. **SDC**, plate 104; **TCS2**, plate 381; **TDO**, 25, 26.
Salomé. **MOM**, 10.
The Searcher. **TDO**, 39, 40.
Stage Door. **MCN**, 133.
Sweet River. **TDO**, facing 64.
Tapestry in Gray. **SDA**, 216; **TDO**, 61.
The Temporary Mrs. Smith. **TDO**, 124.
Ten Million Ghosts. **TDO**, 63.
Tosca. **DPT**, 358; **SDB**, 120; **TDO**, 137.
Tristan and Isolde. **CSD**, 13; **SDA**, 266; **STN**, 221-225; **TDO**, xv, 56, 57; **TPH**, photo
    467.
Uncle Tom's Cabin. **SDT**, 39; **STN**, 207, 209.
Venice Preserved. **STN**, 149-151.
The Winter's Tale. **SDA**, 82, 83.
You Can't Take It With You. **MCN**, 134; **SDA**, 202; **TDO**, 73.
Oeschger, Suzanne. *The Happiness Cage*. **TDT**, n. 37 (May 1974). 21.
Oháh, Gustave. *Coppélia*. **SCM**, 72, 73.
Ohasi, Jasuhiro. *My Miracle*. **TDT**, vol. XX, n. 1 (Spring 1984). 42.
Okajima, Sigeo. *A Man's a Man*. **TDT**, vol. XX, n. 1 (Spring 1984). 7.
Okun, Alexander.
    Aladdin. **TCI**, vol. 21, n. 9 (Nov 1987). 47.
    The Cherry Orchard. **TCI**, vol. 21, n. 9 (Nov 1987). 45.
    Roza. **HPA**, 52;. **MBM**, 89; **TCI**, vol. 21, n. 9 (Nov 1987). 46.
    Transposed Heads. **TCI**, vol. 21, n. 9 (Nov 1987). 46.
Olich, Michael.
    The Kentucky Cycle. **TCI**, vol. 25, n. 8 (Oct 1991). 14; **TCI**, vol. 28, n. 1 (Jan 1994).
        62.
    The Marriage of Figaro. **TDT**, vol. XXVII, n. 3 (Summer 1991). 6.

Our Country's Good. **TCI**, vol. 26, n. 3 (Mar 1992). 37.

Oliva, Raúl & Salvador Fernandez. *Saint Joan of America*. **SDW2**, 48.

Olivastro, John J. *Lysistrata*. **BSE2**, 24, 39.

Olko, Wieslaw. *The Gates of Paradise*. **TCI**, vol. 22, n. 9 (Nov 1988). 23.

Olmstead, Richard. *Antigone*. **TDT**, vol. XXVIII, n. 2 (Spring 1992). 14 of insert.

Olofsson, Pierre & Arne Jones. *The Coronation*. **SDW2**, 209.

Olsen, Stephan. *On the Town*. **TCI**, vol. 27, n. 8 (Oct 1993). 70.

Olson, Erik. *Barabbas*. **SDW1**, 168.

Olson, Stephan. *Waiting for Godot*. **DDT**, 184.

Oman, Julia Trevelyan. *A Man for All Seasons*. **BTD**, 80.

Oosthoek, Peter & Roger Chailloux. *That Boy Pete*. **SDW4**, illus. 376, 377.

Orezzoli, Hector & Claudio Segovia.

    Black and Blue. **MBM**, 180, 181.

    Tango Argentina. **MBM**, 184

Orlik, Emil.

    The Merchant of Venice. **MRH**, facing 212, 213; **TCS2**, plates 11, 12.

    Oedipus Rex. **MRH**, facing 32, 119; **TPH**, photo 336

    Die Räuber. **FCS**, plate 189; **SDO**, 215; **TCS2**, plate 13.

    The Winter's Tale. **MRH**, facing 50, 136; **MRT**, 32; **RSD**, illus. 99; **SDC**, plate 46;
        SOW, plate 46; **TCS2**, plate 14; **TPH**, photo 332.

Ormerod, Nick.

    Fuente Ovejuna. **BTD**, 41.

    Pericles. **BTD**, 41.

Orphanidis, Stelios. *Our Town*. **SDW1**, 110.

Orsini, Humberto. *The Other History of Hamlet*. **SDW3**, 47.

Orubo, Robert. *I and Albert*. **DSL**, figure 39.1(c).

Osorovitz, Camillo. *Così fan Tutti*. **SDW3**, 176.

Ostoja-Kotkowski, J.S. *The Balcony*. **SDW3**, 125.

Ostroff, Boyd. *Il Trovatore*. **TCI**, vol. 20, n. 8 (Oct 1986). 24.

Othuse, James. *The Creation & Other Mysteries*. **TCI**, vol. 24, n. 3 (Mar 1990). 33.

Otskheli, Petr. *Othello*. **RST**, 293.

Ott, Paul. *King Lear*. **TCS2**, plates 194, 195.

Otto, Teo.

    Aïda. **SDR**, 51.

    Andorra. **SDW2**, 111.

    Carmen. **TDT**, n. 27 (Dec 1971). 14.

    Faust, part II. **TCI**, vol. 11, n. 2 (Mar/Apr 1977). 20; **RSD**, illus. 453.

    Galileo. **TBB**, 46, 80.

    The Giants of the Mountain. **SDW1**, 117.

    Henry V. **SOS**, 261.

    The Magic Flute. **OPE**, 94, 100, 103, 104, 107, 108, 110.

    Mother Courage and Her Children. **RSD**, illus. 558, 559; **TBB**, 122.

    Propaganda plays. **RSD**, illus. 228, 229.

    Requiem for a Nun. **SDW2**, 111.

    St. Joan of the Stockyards. **SDR**, 46.

    The Skin of Our Teeth. **TPH**, photo 401.

    The Threepenny Opera. **SDR**, 67.

    Tiger at the Gates. **SDW1**, 117.

    Die Verlobung in San Domingo. **TDT**, n. 2 (Oct 1965). 8.

    The Visions of Simone Machard. **TBB**, 54.

Oudot, Roland. *Queen after Death*. **SDW1**, 105.

Ounz, Aïmi. *How the Steel Was Tempered.* **SDW3**, 119.
Oustinov, Alexandre. *The Cherry Orchard.* **SDW2**, 189.
Owen, Paul.
    All the Way Home. **TCI**, vol. 7, n. 3 (May/Jun 1973). 9.
    Caprices of Marianne. **TCI**, vol. 23, n. 3 (Mar 1989). 39.
    Engaged. **TCI**, vol. 23, n. 3 (Mar 1989). 39.
    Food From Trash. **TCI**, vol. 17, n. 7 (Aug/Sep 1983). 10; **TCI**, vol. 23, n. 3 (Mar
        1989). 37.
    The Heidi Chronicles. **TCI**, vol. 27, n. 3 (Mar 1993). 42.
    K2. **TCI**, vol. 23, n. 3 (Mar 1989). 34.
    Matrimonium. **TCI**, vol. 14, n. 6 (Nov/Dec 1980). 43.
    One Flew Over the Cuckoo's Nest. **TCI**, vol. 23, n. 3 (Mar 1989). 34.
    Six Characters in Search of an Author. **TCI**, vol. 23, n. 3 (Mar 1989). 38.
    A Streetcar Named Desire. **TCI**, vol. 23, n. 3 (Mar 1989). 35.
    Third & Oak. **TCI**, vol. 23, n. 3 (Mar 1989). 35.
    War and Peace. **TCI**, vol. 7, n. 3 (May/Jun 1973). 6.
    Whereabouts Unknown. **TCI**, vol. 22, n. 5 (May 1988). 16; **TCI**, vol. 23, n. 3 (Mar
        1989). 36.

-P-

Pace.
    The Death of Agrippina. **SDW2**, 99.
    The Parachutists. **SDW2**, 97.
    Rodogune. **SDW2**, 96.
Packard, Stephen.
    A Streetcar Named Desire. **TDT**, vol. XXVI, n. 1 (Spring 1990). 14 of insert.
Padovani, Gianfranco.
    The Boors. **SIO**, 99.
    L'Erba della Stella dell'Alba. **SIO**, 101.
    Julius Caesar. **SIO**, 102.
    Mother Courage and Her Children. **SIO**, 100.
    September 8. **SIO**, 101.
    Tartuffe, or rather the Life, Loves, Self-censorship and Death on Stage of Seigneur
        Molière, our Contemporary. **SDW4**, illus. 222, 223.
    Tonight We Improvise. **SIO**, 102.
    Una delle Utime Domeniche di Carnovale. **SIO**, 98.
    The Venetian Twins. **SIO**, 97.
Paes Leme, Bellá. *Electra in the Circus.* **SDW2**, 36.
Paladini, Vinicio. *Goldoni E Le Sue 16 Commedie Nuove.* **SCM**, 78.
Palencia, Benjamín. *Don Juan Tenorio.* **SDW2**, 81.
Palitzsch, Hans Heinrich. *A Modern Dream.* **RSD**, illus. 595.
Palkovic, Tim.
    Cyrano de Bergerac. **TDT**, vol. XX, n. 3 (Fall 1984). 11; **TDT**, vol. XXX, n. 3
        (Summer 1994). 45.
    The Dining Room. **TDT**, vol. XX, n. 3 (Fall 1984). 11; **TDT**, vol. XXX, n. 3 (Summer
        1994). 45.
    The Playboy of the Western World. **TDT**, vol. XX, n. 3 (Fall 1984). 7; **TDT**, vol. XXX,
        n. 3 (Summer 1994). 41.
Palmstierna-Weiss, Gunilla.
    Auschwitz, The Investigation. **TCI**, vol. 12, n. 7 (Nov/Dec 1978). 43.

The Dance of Death. **SDW3**, 86.

The Investigation. **SDW3**, 134.

Marat/Sade. **RSD**, illus. 592; **SDW3**, 135; **TCI**, vol. 12, n. 7 (Nov/Dec 1978). 40;
   TCI, vol. 12, n. 7 (Nov/Dec 1978). 41.

St. Joan of the Stockyards. **RSD**, illus. 593; **TCI**, vol. 12, n. 7 (Nov/Dec 1978). 42, 43.

The Song of the Lusitanian Bogey. **RSD**, illus. 589; **TCI**, vol. 12, n. 7 (Nov/Dec 1978).
   40.

Twelfth Night. **TCI**, vol. 12, n. 7 (Nov/Dec 1978). 40.

Vietnam Discourse. **RSD**, illus. 590; **SDW3**, 137; **TCI**, vol. 12, n. 7 (Nov/Dec 1978).
   38, 39.

Pán, Jozef. *Uncle Vanya.* **SDW2**, 141.

Paoletti, John. *She Always Said, Pablo.* **BSE5**, 35; **BSE5**, back cover.

Paoletti, John & Mary Griswold.
   The Good Soldier Schweik. **TCI**, vol. 18, n. 3 (Mar 1984). 24.

Pardess, Yael. *Gilligan's Island.* **TCI**, vol. 27, n. 2 (Feb 1993). 9.

Parker, W. Oren.
   Don Juan, Or the Love of Geometry. **TDT**, n. 3 (Dec 1965). 2.
   The Visit. **SFT**, 119.

Parkman, Russell.
   Arms and the Man. **TCI**, vol. 27, n. 5 (May 1993). 6.
   True Blue and Trembling. **TCI**, vol. 25, n. 1 (Jan 1991). 39.

Parr, Mme. *L'Homme et son Désir.* **TCS2**, plate 122.

Parra, Carmen. *Donna Giovanni.* **TCI**, vol. 21, n. 8 (Oct 1987). 20.

Parravicini, Angelo. *Aïda.* **MOM**, 6.

Pascoe, John. *Don Giovanni.* **TCI**, vol. 24, n. 5 (May 1990). 15.

Pasetti, Leo. *The Tales of Hoffmann.* **SCM**, 59.

Pasetti & Adolphe Linnebach. *Das Rheingold.* **CSC**, facing 64, 76.

Pass, Paul de. *She Loves Me.* **TCI**, vol. 7, n. 5 (Oct 1973). 27.

Passmore, Bill & Axel Bartz. *Pericole.* **TCI**, vol. 27, n. 5 (May 1993). 12.

Paston, Doria.
   The Inspector General. **SDG**, 173.
   The Makropoulos Secret. **SCM**, 30.
   The Merchant of Venice. **SCM**, 31.

Pate, Catherine. *Scapino.* **TCI**, vol. 13, n. 3 (May/Jun 1979). 38.

Pátek, J. *The Taming of the Shrew.* **TDT**, vol. XVI, n. 1 (Spring 1980). 27.

Patel, Neil.
   The Adding Machine. **TCI**, vol. 29, n. 4 (Apr 1995). 6.
   The Inspector General. **TCI**, vol. 25, n. 1 (Jan 1991). 40.
   Scarlet Letter. **TCI**, vol. 29, n. 1 (Jan 1995). 7.
   Slavs! (Thinking About the Longstanding Problems of Virtue and Happiness). **TCI**,
      vol. 29, n. 3 (Mar 1995). 7.
   T Bone N Weasel. **TCI**, vol. 27, n. 2 (Feb 1993). 7.

Payne, Darwin Reid.
   Aïda. **SIP**, 12; **TCM**, 133.
   Antigone. **SIP**, 167; **TCM**, 105, 106.
   Arsenic and Old Lace. **TCM**, 15.
   As You Like It. **TCM**, 38, 134, 136; **TDP**, 124.
   La Bohème. **SIP**, 9; **TCM**, 19, 42, 49, 65, 66.
   The Caretaker. **SIP**, 42, 43, 69, 306, 307.
   Cat on a Hot Tin Roof. **SIP**, 175; **TCM**, 29.
   A Christmas Carol. **SIP**, 17.

Die Walküre. **TCI**, vol. 11, n. 2 (Mar/Apr 1977). 17.
Peetermans, Mimi.
  Don Gil with the Green Trousers. **SDW2**, 31.
  The Double Inconstancy. **SDW3**, 74.
Peiran, Teng. *Fidelio.* **TDT**, vol. XXVIII, n. 2 (Spring 1992). 14 of insert.
Pelletier, Jacques. *The Miser.* **SDW2**, 40.
Pember, Clifford. *Healthy, Wealthy and Wise.* **SCM**, 36.
Pemberton, Reece.
  The Old Ladies. **TOP**, 75.
  Peer Gynt. **SDW1**, 180.
  Summer and Smoke. **SDW1**, 183.
  Waters of the Moon. **TOP**, 55-57.
Perahim, Jules. *It Happened in Irkutsk.* **SDW2**, 175.
Perdziola, Robert.
  Cherubin. **DDT**, 19.
  La Fedelta Premiata. **DDT**, 152d, 399.
  The Nose. **DDT**, 170; **TCI**, vol. 21, n. 8 (Oct 1987). 19.
  Tartuffe. **TCI**, vol. 23, n. 2 (Feb 1989). 14.
Perina, Peter. *The Three Sisters.* **TDT**, vol. XXIII, n. 4 (Winter 1988). 29.
Perrottet-von Laban, André.
  Alcestis. **SDW1**, 118.
  The Count of Clérambard. **SDW1**, 118.
Peters, Philip. *Much Ado About Nothing.* **BSE2**, 21.
Peters, Rollo.
  John Ferguson. **MCN**, 47.
  Mme. Sand. **SDC**, plate 45.
  The Streets of New York. **SCM**, 102.
Petritzki, Anatoli. *The Guelder Rose Grove.* **SDW2**, 190.
Pevsner, Antoine & Naum Gabo. *La Chatte.* **AST**, 136; **RSD**, illus. 200; **TCS2**, plate 165.
Pfahnl, William. *Born Yesterday.* **BSE2**, 25.
Pfeiffenberger, Heinz. *The Clever One.* **SDW1**, 73.
Phillips, Jason.
  Long Day's Journey Into Night. **TCI**, vol. 7, n. 3 (May/Jun 1973). 12.
  Park. **TCI**, vol. 7, n. 3 (May/Jun 1973). 14.
  The Tempest. **TCI**, vol. 7, n. 3 (May/Jun 1973). 12.
Phillips, Van.
  Light Up the Sky. **SST**, 18.
  Long Day's Journey into Night. **SST**, 262.
  Morowitz Hamlet. **SST**, 446.
  Remembrances in a Louisville Harem. **BSE1**, 18.
Physioc, Joseph A.
  The Climbers. **SDA**, 27.
  The Lion and the Mouse. **MCN**, 28.
  The Stubbornness of Geraldine. **MCN**, 18.
Physioc, Joseph & Ernest Albert. *The Climbers.* **MCN**, 14.
Picabia, Francis. *Relache.* **RSD**, illus. 328; **TCS2**, plate 155.
Picasso, Pablo.
  Oedipus Rex. **SDW1**, 105.
  Oedipus Tyrranos. **AST**, 79.
Pignon, Edouard. *Platonov.* **SDW2**, 99.

Pillartz, T.C.
  Der Befreite Don Quichote. **TCS2**, plate 138.
  Hassan. **TCS2**, plate 228.
  Louis Ferdinand. **SDC**, plate 123.
  Oedipus Rex. **DIT**, plate 99; **RSD**, illus. 72; **SDC**, plate 106; **TPH**, photo 426.
  Sirocco. **SDC**, plate 123.
Pimenov, Youri.
  New Year's Eve. **SDW2**, 190.
  The Spring Torrent. **SDW2**, 190.
Piot, René.
  Le Chagrin dans le palais de Han. **RSD**, illus. 50.
  Idomeneo. **RSD**, illus. 49.
Piper, John.
  Billy Budd. **CGA**, 140; **SDW1**, 183.
  Don Giovanni. **SDE**, 132; **SDR**, 44; **SDW1**, 171; **TOP**, 207-209.
  Gloriana. **CGA**, 144; **FCS**, plate 212, color plate 29; **SDO**, 245, plate 29.
  A Midsummer Night's Dream. **SDW2**, 224.
  The Quest. **BTD**, 20.
  The Rape of Lucrece. **SDG**, 189.
  The Turn of the Screw. **SDB**, 67; **SDR**, 44; **SDW1**, 184.
  The Broken Heart. **TCI**, vol. 29, n. 3 (Mar 1995). 10.
Piplits, Erwin. *The Exception and the Rule*. **SDW3**, 111.
Pira, John. *Barabbas*. **SDW1**, 47.
Pirchan, Emil.
  Boris Godounov. **TCS2**, plates 90, 107.
  Empörung des Lucius. **TCS2**, plate 124.
  Marquis von Keith. **RSD**, illus. 134, 137; **SDC**, plate 125; **TCS2**, plate 106; **TPH**, photo 423.
  Othello. **CSC**, facing 128, 130, 132, 134; **DIT**, plate 90; **RSD**, illus. 129, 131; **SDC**, plate 109; **SOS**, 214, 215; **SOW**, plate 41; **TCS2**, plates 126-129.
  Richard III. **CSC**, facing 136, 138, 140, 142, 144, , 146; **RSD**, illus. 135, 136; **SOS**, 209; **TCS2**, plate 123.
  Der Schatzgräber. **CSC**, facing 60.
  Die Vogelscheuchen. **TCS2**, plate 251.
  William Tell. **RSD**, illus. 130.
Piscator, Erwin. *War and Peace*. **SIP**, 311.
Piscator, Erwin & George Grosz. *The Good Soldier Schweik*. **NTO**, facing 420; **RSD**, illus. 241; **TBB**, 109; **TPH**, photo 377.
Pisoni, Edward. *A Streetcar Named Desire*. **SDL**, 376, 377.
Pitoëff, Georges.
  Brand. **RSD**, illus. 420.
  Camille. **RSD**, illus. 421.
  The Hairy Ape. **RSD**, illus. 422; **SCM**, 54; **TPH**, photo 361.
  Hamlet. **RSD**, illus. 423.
  Hunger and Thirst. **CSD**, 114.
  Le Juif du Pape. **SCM**, 54; **TCS2**, plate 216.
  Le Lache. **TCS2**, plate 200.
  Liliom. **RSD**, illus. 384, 418, 419; **TSS**, 524.
  Macbeth. **RSD**, illus. 424, 425; **TCS2**, plate 117.
  Romeo and Juliet. **RSD**, illus. 426, 427; **TPH**, photo 362.
  Uncle Vanya. **CSC**, facing 124.

Pizzi, Pier Luigi.
>   *Aïda*. **SIO**, 108.
>   *La Calandria*. **SIO**, 106.
>   *Castor et Pollux*. **TCI**, vol. 26, n. 4 (Apr 1992). 38.
>   *The Good-Humoured Ladies*. **SDW2**, 127.
>   *Metti, Una Sera a Cena*. **SIO**, 107.
>   *Oedipus Rex*. **SIO**, 107.
>   *Right You Are-If You Think You Are*. **SDW4**, illus. 195-198.
>   *The Rules of the Game*. **SIO**, 105.
>   *Il Signor Bruschino*. **SIO**, 104.
>   *The Three Sisters*. **SIO**, 104.
>   *Twelfth Night*. **SDW2**, 130.
>   *I Vespri Siciliani* (Verdi). **SIO**, 108, 109.
>   *William Tell*. **SIO**, 110.

Placido, Stephen, Jr. *Mass Appeal*. **TCI**, vol. 21, n. 3 (Mar 1987). 23.
Plate, Roberto. *The Tempest*. **TCI**, vol. 24, n. 5 (May 1990). 33.
Platt, Livingston
>   *Dinner at Eight*. **SCM**, 115.
>   *Grand Hotel*. **SDA**, 232.

Pogany, Willy. *The Italian Girl in Algiers*. **MOM**, 7.
Poklman, Donald. *A Circle in the Sun*. **TCI**, vol. 17, n. 7 (Aug/Sep 1983). 31.
Polakov, Lester.
>   *The Bartered Bride*. **DPT**, 113, between 124 & 125.
>   *Call Me Mister*. **DDT**, 404.
>   *Cock-a-Doodle-Dandy*. **DDT**, 169.
>   *The Life and Times of Joseph Stalin*. **CSD**, 115; **TCI**, vol. 9, n. 3 (May/Jun 1975). 16-
>   19.
>   *The Member of the Wedding*. **DDT**, 37; **TPH**, photo 489; **WTP**, 203.
>   *Mrs. McThing*. **DDT**, 183, 284.
>   *The Purple Dust*. **DPT**, 187.

Polidori, Gianni.
>   *The Bacchae*. **SIO**, 118.
>   *Battaglia Navale*. **SIO**, 113.
>   *Le Bourgeois Gentilhomme*. **SDE**, 134.
>   *Caligula*. **SIO**, 120.
>   *The Dance of Death*. **SIO**, 113.
>   *Don Carlos*. **SIO**, 119.
>   *Emmeti*. **SDW3**, 144.
>   *Il Fattaccio del Giugno*. **SIO**, 117.
>   *La Figlia di Lorio*. **SIO**, 120.
>   *The Golden Coach*. **SDE**, 133.
>   *Lucifer and the Lord*. **SIO**, 112.
>   *Oreste*. **SDW1**, 128.
>   *Il Prigioniero*. **SIO**, 116.
>   *The Queen of Spades*. **SDW1**, 128.
>   *Se Questo è un Uomo*. **SIO**, 117.
>   *Le Troiane* (Euripides/Sartre). **SIO**, 116.
>   *Troilus and Cressida*. **SIO**, 114, 115.

Poncy, Eric. *Antony and Cleopatra*. **SDW1**, 118.
Pond, Helen & Herbert Senn.
>   *Ariadne auf Naxos*. **DPT**, 132.

The Jocky Club Stakes. **DPT**, 332.
Summer and Smoke. **DPT**, 93.
The Trojans. **DPT**, 365.
Ponnelle, Jean-Pierre.
 The Barber of Seville. **OPE**, 128, 132, 135; **TCI**, vol. 12, n. 3 (Mar/Apr 1978). 19.
 La Bohème. **TCI**, vol. 13, n. 3 (May/Jun 1979). 50.
 Carmen. **TCI**, vol. 17, n. 9 (Nov/Dec 1983). 20.
 La Clemenza di Tito. **TCI**, vol. 12, n. 3 (Mar/Apr 1978). 16; **TCI**, vol. 12, n. 3 (Mar/
   Apr 1978). 19.
 Le Compt Ory. **SDW2**, 67.
 Così fan Tutti. **TCI**, vol. 12, n. 3 (Mar/Apr 1978). 19.
 Don Carlos. **OPE**, 149, 154, 156, 158, 161, 163.
 Don Giovanni. **OPE**, 75, 82, 86, 89, 90; **SST**, 379; **TCI**, vol. 12, n. 3 (Mar/Apr 1978).
   19.
 Falstaff. **TCI**, vol. 10, n. 6 (Nov/Dec 1976). 4; **TCI**, vol. 13, n. 3 (May/Jun 1979). 18.
 Idomeneo. **DDT**, 29; **DSL**, figure 27.1(d); **MOM**, frontispiece, 112-123; **SST**, 379,
   445; **TCI**, vol. 17, n. 4 (Apr 1983). 8.
 The Italian Girl in Algiers. **MOM**, 124-131.
 Lear. **TDT**, vol. XVII, n. 3 (Fall 1981). 4, 5.
 Liebestrank. **TCI**, vol. 12, n. 3 (Mar/Apr 1978). 16.
 The Magic Flute. **OPE**, 96, 101, 103, 104, 106, 109, 110.
 The Marriage of Figaro. **TCI**, vol. 12, n. 3 (Mar/Apr 1978). 19.
 Orfeo. **TCI**, vol. 12, n. 7 (Nov/Dec 1978). 4.
 Pelléas and Mélisande. **OPE**, 217, 221, 222, 225, 227, 228; **TCI**, vol. 12, n. 3 (Mar/
   Apr 1978). 16.
 Sant'Alessio. **TCI**, vol. 12, n. 3 (Mar/Apr 1978). 17.
 Tosca. **TCI**, vol. 12, n. 3 (Mar/Apr 1978). 14, 16.
Popov, Assen. *King Lear.* **SDW2**, 38.
Popov, Dimitri. *Left-Handed.* **SDW2**, 185.
Popov, Vladimir. *The White Black.* SDW4, illus. 179.
Popova, Lyubov.
 The Earth in Turmoil. **MOT**, between 184 & 185; **RST**, 138, 139.
 The Magnanimous Cuckold. **AST**, 135; **DIT**, plate 110; **MOT**, between 160 & 161;
   PST, 411; **RSD**, illus. 173-175; **SDC**, plate 118; **TAB**, 7; **TCR**, 85; **TCS2**, plate
   174; **TCT**, plates 17-19; **TPH**, photo 409; **TSY**, 198.
Poppe, Catherine. *Oedipus Rex.* **TCI**, vol. 16, n. 7 (Aug/Sep 1982). 10.
Porteous, Cameron.
 Cavalcade. **TCI**, vol. 22, n. 7 (Aug/Sep 1988). 62.
 The Crucible. **TDT**, vol. XVI, n. 1 (Spring 1980). 12.
 Cyrano de Bergerac. **TCI**, vol. 18, n. 9 (Nov/Dec 1984). 40.
 The Madwoman of Chaillot. **SDL**, 4, plates 8-17.
 Major Barbara. **TCI**, vol. 22, n. 7 (Aug/Sep 1988). 61.
 Peter Pan. **TCI**, vol. 22, n. 7 (Aug/Sep 1988). 62, 63.
 You Never Can Tell. **TCI**, vol. 22, n. 7 (Aug/Sep 1988). 64; **TDT**, vol. XXVII, n. 4
   (Fall 1991). 24.
Potts, David.
 Childe Byron. **TCI**, vol. 15, n. 6 (Jun/Jul 1981). 16, 17.
 The Musical Comedy Murders of 1940. **TCI**, vol. 22, n. 5 (May 1988). 33, 37.
 On the Waterfront. **TCI**, vol. 23, n. 1 (Jan 1989). 96.
Prabhavalkar, Nigel. *The Magic Flute.* **BTD**, 116.

Puecher, Virginio. *The Investigation*. **RSD**, illus. 609, 610.
Puecher, Virginio, Ugo Mulas & Ebe Colciaghi. *Wozzeck*. **SDW3**, 191.
Puigserver, Fabia.
    The Good Woman of Setzuan. **TCI**, vol. 26, n. 4 (Apr 1992). 34.
    Peace. **SDW3**, 32; **TDT**, vol. XII, n. 3 (Fall 1976). 39.
Puncan, John & Malloy Chichester. *Bonjour La Bonjour*. **BSE3**, 91.
pupils of Pavel Filonov. *The Inspector General*. **RST**, 251.
Puumalainen, Kaj. *The Seven Brothers*. **SDW4**, illus. 177, 178.

-Q-

Quay, Stephen & Timothy.
    Le Bourgeois Gentilhomme. **TCI**, vol. 27, n. 1 (Jan 1993). 45.
    A Flea in Her Ear. **TCI**, vol. 27, n. 1 (Jan 1993). 44.
Quinn, Jeff. *Dialogues of the Carmelites*. **BSE5**, 19.

-R-

Raban, Josef. *Croquignole*. **SDW1**, 51.
Rabinovitch, Isaac.
    Don Carlos. **TCS2**, plate 168.
    The Embezzlers. **RST**, 254, 255.
    Great Cyril. **SDW2**, 191.
    The Inspector General. **TCS2**, plate 183.
    Lysistrata. **RSD**, illus. 197; **SDC**, plate 119; **TCS2**, plate 169.
    The Sorceress. **RSD**, illus. 212, 213; **RST**, 161; **TCS2**, plate 178.
Radice, Ronald. *The Hot l Baltimore*. **TCI**, vol. 8, n. 2 (Mar/Apr 1974). 9.
Raffaëlli, Michel.
    Amerika. **RSD**, illus. 544; **SDW3**, 206.
    The Black Feast. **SDW2**, 100.
    The Dragon. **SDW3**, 105.
    Medea. **RSD**, illus. 545.
    Moses and Aaron. **SDW2**, 100.
    Passion of General Franco. **SDW3**, 145.
    Urfaust. **SDW3**, 78.
Rager, John. *The Mystery of Edwin Drood*. **TCI**, vol. 23, n. 4 (Apr 1989). 53.
Ragey, Joe.
    Tartuffe. **BSE4**, 78.
    Value of Names. **BSE4**, 72.
Raheng, Rahé. *Peer Gynt*. **TPH**, photos 287, 288.
Rajkai, György.
    The Aristocrats. **SDW2**, 140.
    Prometheus. **SDW2**, 142.
Randolph, Robert.
    Applause. **DPT**, 144; **TCI**, vol. 4, n. 3 (May/Jun 1970). 9-12.
    Bye Bye Birdie. **DPT**, 209; **BMF**, 62; **BWM**, 141.
    Golden Rainbow. **DPT**, 207.
    Gypsy. **DPT**, 205; **SON**, 33, 59.
    How to Succeed in Business Without Really Trying. **BWM**, 269, 270; **DPT**, 208.
    Little Me. **BWM**, 118, 119; **MBM**, 208.

Vetsera does not Bloom for Everybody. **SDW1**, 57.
Reigbert, Otto.
    Drums in the Night. **CBM**, 42; **RSD**, illus. 124-127; **TBB**, 23.
    Nachfolge Christi-spiel. **TAT**, plate 384.
    Der Sohn. **TPH**, photo 420.
    Spiel des Lebens. **TCS2**, plates 254, 255.
Reiman, Walter. *Macbeth.* **TCS2**, plates 130, 131.
Reimer, Tom. *The Two Gentlemen of Verona.* **SDW4**, illus. 329.
Reimer, Treva. *The Father.* **BSE3**, 34.
Reinhardt, Andreas.
    The Barber of Seville. **SDW4**, illus. 124; **TCI**, vol. 11, n. 2 (Mar/Apr 1977). 10; **TDT**,
        vol. XII, n. 1 (Spring 1976). 26.
    Cement. **SDW4**, illus. 324-328.
    Einstein. **SDW4**, illus. 225-227.
    Faust, part 1. **SDW3**, 79.
    Omphale. **SDW4**, illus. 313-315.
    Squire Puntila and His Servant Matti. **SDR**, 71; **SDW3**, 194.
    The Threepenny Opera. **TCI**, vol. 22, n. 1 (Jan 1988). 14.
Reinhardt, Andreas & Johanna Kieling. *Richard III.* **SDW4**, illus. 19.
Reinhardt, Max. *Jedermann.* **TCS2**, plate 373.
Reinking Wilhelm.
    Aïda. **SDB**, 19.
    Alkmene. **SDW2**, 68.
    Don Juan. **SDE**, 143, 144.
    Fidelio. **SDE**, 144.
    Love and Intrigue. **SDW1**, 80.
    News of the Day. **RSD**, illus. 251.
    Orpheus. **SDW2**, 69.
    Der Wildschütz. **SDE**, 145.
    Wozzeck. **SDE**, 145.
Remisoff, Nicolai.
    Faust. **MRT**, 77.
    The Lovers. **RSC**, 49.
Remson, Ira. *The Long Voyage Home.* **MCN**, 44.
Renard, Raymond.
    Captain Bada. **SDW2**, 31.
    The Servant of Two Masters. **SDW2**, 31.
    What's New Haruspice? **SDW3**, 138.
Reppa, David. *Dialogues of the Carmelites.* **TCI**, vol. 16, n. 9 (Nov/Dec 1982). 28.
Reufersward, Carl Frederik.
    Faust. **SDB**, 142.
    Herr von Haucken. **SDR**, 66.
Reymond, Suzanne. *Cinna.* **SDW1**, 106.
Reynolds, James.
    The Last Night of Don Juan. **SDC**, plate 59.
    The Royal Family. **MCN**, 87.
    The Vagabond King. **MCD**, plate 147.
Rice, Peter.
    Ariadne auf Naxos. **DMS**, plate 50; **SDB**, 91; **SDW2**, 225.
    Die Fledermaus. **BTD**, 108.
Richter, Gerd. *The Fish with the Golden Sword.* **SDW2**, 69.

Richter, Kurt. *Die Räuber*. **MRH**, between 156 & 157.
Richter-Forgach, Thomas.
    King Lear. **RSD**, illus. 541.
    Götterdämmerung. **OPE**, 182, 192, 194, 196, 198, 199.
Rickabaugh, Clive. *The Swing Mikado*. **RBS**, 180.
Ricketts, Charles.
    Agamemnon. **DIT**, plate 12; **TPH**, photo 354.
    The Betrothal. **TDC**, 143.
    The Death of Tintagiles. **TDC**, 45.
    The Eumenides. **SDT**, 33.
    King Lear. **DIT**, plate 11; **SDG**, 163.
    St. Joan. **TDC**, 120-129.
    Salomé. **SDT**, 271; **TDC**, 24; **TPH**, photo 353.
Riddell, Richard.
    Agamemnon. **TCI**, vol. 11, n. 3 (May/Jun 1977). 24.
    The Eumenides. **TCI**, vol. 11, n. 3 (May/Jun 1977). 24.
    The Libation Bearers. **TCI**, vol. 11, n. 3 (May/Jun 1977). 24.
Riechetoff, Nina. *The Boors*. **SDW2**, 101.
Rigdon, Kevin.
    Balm in Gilead. **TCI**, vol. 21, n. 2 (Feb 1987). 30.
    Bang! **TCI**, vol. 21, n. 2 (Feb 1987). 30.
    Coyote Ugly. **TCI**, vol. 21, n. 2 (Feb 1987). 31.
    Frank's Wild Years. **TCI**, vol. 21, n. 2 (Feb 1987). 31.
    Glengarry Glen Ross. **TCI**, vol. 21, n. 2 (Feb 1987). 31.
    The Grapes of Wrath. **TCI**, vol. 23, n. 1 (Jan 1989). 96; **TCI**, vol. 24, n. 9 (Nov 1990).
        19.
    Heart's Desire. **TCI**, vol. 24, n. 10 (Dec 1990). 19.
    Lydie Breeze. **TCI**, vol. 21, n. 2 (Feb 1987). 29.
Rindin, V. *The Unknown Soldiers*. **TAT**, plate 729.
Rinfret, Jean-Claude. *The Litigants*. **SDW2**, 40.
Ringbom, Jon. *Poppie Nongena*. **TCI**, vol. 17, n. 4 (Apr 1983). 10.
Ristic, Dusan.
    Hérakales: **SDW2**, 137.
    Mandragola. **SDW4**, illus. 15-17.
    Oedipus Rex. **SDW3**, 190.
    The Quarrels in Chioggia. **SDW4**, illus. 98.
    Sweet Orthodoxy. **SDW4**, illus. 261.
    The Winter's Tale. **SDW3**, 63.
Ritman, William.
    Deathtrap. **TCI**, vol. 12, n. 6 (Oct 1978). 4; **TCI**, vol. 22, n. 5 (May 1988). 32.
    A Delicate Balance. **TDT**, n. 6 (Oct 1966). 50.
Robbins, Kathleen M. & W.M. Schenk.
    From Morn to Midnight. **TCI**, vol. 12, n. 5 (Sep 1978). 48, 49.
Roberts, Thom. *Revolution of the Heavenly Orbs*. **TCI**, vol. 17, n. 7 (Aug/Sep 1983). 20.
Robertson, Patrick.
    Boots with Strawberry Jam. **SFT**, 122.
    The Cunning Little Vixen. **TCI**, vol. 13, n. 3 (May/Jun 1979). 20.
    Danton's Death. **TDT**, vol. XIX, n. 3 (Fall 1983). 5.
    Pelléas and Mélisande. **TDT**, vol. XIX, n. 3 (Fall 1983). 4.
    Salad Days. **MCD**, plate 206.

Fools. **TCI**, vol. 17, n. 4 (Apr 1983). 25.

The Merry Wives of Windsor, Texas. **TCI**, vol. 24, n. 3 (Mar 1990). 22.

Rupprecht, Martin. *The Sinking of the Titanic.* **TCI**, vol. 14, n. 1 (Jan/Feb 1980). 17.

Russel, James. *Heartbreak House.* **SDL**, 62.

Rutherston, Albert.

    Androcles and the Lion. **TCS2**, plate 142.

    Cymbeline. **DIT**, plate 54; **SDC**, plate 81; **SOW**, plate 44.

    Le Mariage Forcé. **DIT**, plate 55; **SDG**, 161; **TPH**, photo 429.

Ryan, E.H. *Lilac Time.* **MCD**, plate 122.

Ryan, E.H. & Alfred Terraine.

    Betty. **MCD**, plate 106.

    The Marriage Market. **MCD**, plates 100, 101.

Ryan, T.E., Alfred Terraine, Hawes Craven, & Joseph Hunter.

    The Girl from Utah. **MCD**, plate 96.

Ryan, Thomas M.

    Fallen Angels. **BSE4**, 95.

    Sylvia's Real Good Advice. **TCI**, vol. 25, n. 9 (Nov 1991). 22.

Rychtarik, Richard. *The Magic Flute.* **MOM**, 11.

Ryndine, Vadim.

    Hamlet. **SDW2**, 192; **SDW2**, 195.

    The Mother. **SDW2**, 192.

    Much Ado About Nothing. **SDW2**, 191.

    The Optimistic Tragedy. **RSD**, illus. 218; **RST**, 286, 287; **SDW2**, 191.

    War and Peace. **SDW2**, 185.

-S-

Sabine, Patrick Chauveau, Michel Lebois, & Charles Marty.

    From Moses to Mao. **SDW4**, illus. 397-404.

Sabo, Jonathan. *A Streetcar Named Desire.* **SDT**, 277.

Sadowski, Andrzej.

    The Birds. **SDW2**, 169.

    Card Index. **TCI**, vol. 15, n. 4 (Apr 1981). 14.

Sagert, Horst.

    The Dragon. **RSD**, illus. 587; **SDW3**, 106, 107.

    King Bamba. **TDT**, vol. XVI, n. 1 (Spring 1980). 17.

    Medea. **TDT**, vol. XVI, n. 1 (Spring 1980). 15.

    Oedipus Tyrranos. **SDW3**, 26, 27.

    Turandot or The Congress of Washerwomen. **RSD**, illus. 588.

Saint-Phalle, Niki de. *Lysistrata.* **RSD**, illus. 487.

Sainthill, Loudon.

    Aladdin. **LST**, 46, 47.

    Cinderella. **LST**, 49.

    Le Coq d'Or. **LST**, 28-31.

    Pericles. **SDW2**, 226.

    The Tempest. **LST**, 19, 23.

    Tiger at the Gates. **LST**, 41.

    A Woman of No Importance. **LST**, 36.

Salas, José. *What the Storm Left.* **SDW2**, 244.

Salle, David. *The Birth of a Poet.* **TCI**, vol. 19, n. 9 (Nov 1985). 36; **TDT**, vol. XXII, n. 1
    (Spring 1986). 14, 15.

Frankenstein. **ASD1**, 140, 141; **DDT**, 142, 312c; **DSL**, plate IV; **SDD**, between 210 & 211; **TCI**, vol. 15, n. 6 (Jun/Jul 1981). 30, 31; **TCI**, vol. 27, n. 8 (Oct 1993). 5, 35; **TDT**, vol. XVII, n. 2 (Summer 1981). 21, 22.

The Good Woman of Setzuan. **SDW3**, 115; **TDT**, vol. XVII, n. 2 (Summer 1981). 17.

Grease. **ASD1**, 147; **BMF**, 79; **BWM**, 313; **DPT**, 64; **TCI**, vol. 20, n. 5 (May 1986). 34; **TDT**, vol. XVII, n. 2 (Summer 1981). 16.

Holy Blood and Crescent Moon. **TCI**, vol. 23, n. 9 (Nov 1989). 18.

Huui-Huui. **TDT**, vol. XVII, n. 2 (Summer 1981). 17.

King John. **ASD1**, 151.

Macbeth. **ASD1**, 142.

Macbeth. **CSD**, 127.

The Mines of Sulfer. **DPT**, 114.

Nick and Nora. **TCI**, vol. 24, n. 8 (Oct 1990). 37.

Over Here! **ASD1**, 137; **DPT**, 62, 63; **SDT**, 281, and between 152 & 153; **TCI**, vol. 8, n. 3 (May/Jun 1974). 6-8; **TDT**, vol. XVII, n. 2 (Summer 1981). 19.

Porgy and Bess. **ASD1**, frontis; **DDT**, 145, 160; **TCI**, vol. 17, n. 7 (Aug/Sep 1983). 12.

The Robber Bridegroom. **TCI**, vol. 10, n. 6 (Nov/Dec 1976). 10.

Samson et Dalila. **ASD1**, between 70 & 71; **DDT**, 140, 141; **TCI**, vol. 17, n. 9 (Nov/Dec 1983). 21; **TDT**, vol. XXII, n. 4 (Winter 1987). 13.

Scapino. **TDT** vol. XXXI, n. 2 (Spring 1995). 16.

The School for Scandal. **BSE4**, 55.

The Skin of Our Teeth. **ASD1**, 149.

Smile. **TCI**, vol. 21, n. 1 (Jan 1987). 19, 21-23.

The Snow Ball. **TCI**, vol. 25, n. 9 (Nov 1991). 25.

A Streetcar Named Desire. **DPT**, 19; **TCI**, vol. 27, n. 4 (Apr 1993). 33; **TDT**, vol. XVII, n. 2 (Summer 1981). 18.

The Tempest. **DDT**, 146.

They're Playing Our Song. **ASD1**, 139; **TDT**, vol. XVII, n. 2 (Summer 1981). 21.

Truffles in the Soup. **DDT**, 138.

Twelfth Night. **BSE4**, 57.

Veronica's Room. **DPT**, between 124 & 125; **TDT**, vol. XVII, n. 2 (Summer 1981). 18.

Schmidt, Emile O. *Inherit the Wind.* **TCI**, vol. 3, n. 2 (Mar/Apr 1969). 18.

Schmidt, Robert N.

Billy Bishop Goes to War. **TDT**, vol. XXX, n. 3 (Summer 1994). 11.

Julius Caesar. **TDT**, vol. XXVIII, n. 2 (Spring 1992). 8 of insert.

Schmidt, Saladin. *Henry V.* **SOS**, 210.

Schmidt, Willi.

Six Characters in Search of an Author. **SDW2**, 70.

The Trial. **SDW1**, 74.

Schmückle, Hans-Ulrich.

Don Giovanni. **OPE**, 77, 82, 85, 86, 88, 90.

The Investigation. **SDW3**, 130, 134.

The Officer's Revolt. **RSD**, illus. 510.

Robespierre. **RSD**, illus. 500; **SDB**, 89.

Schneider-Manns-Au, Rudolf. *Andorra.* **SDW3**, 128.

Schneider-Siemssen, Günther.

Boris Godounov. **TDT**, n. 27 (Dec 1971). 15.

Comedy of the End of Time. **TCI**, vol. 11, n. 2 (Mar/Apr 1977). 21; **TCI**, vol. 12, n. 6 (Oct 1978). 32; **TCI**, vol. 27, n. 3 (Mar 1993). 28.

De temporum fine comoedia. **OPE**, 54.

Don Carlos. **OPE**, 152, 155, 157, 158, 161, 163; **TCI**, vol. 12, n. 6 (Oct 1978). 33;
    TCI, vol. 27, n. 3 (Mar 1993). 29; **TDT**, vol. XII, n. 1 (Spring 1976). 28.
Don Giovanni. **OPE**, 75, 83, 85, 86, 89, 91; **TCI**, vol. 12, n. 6 (Oct 1978). 33; **TDT**, n.
    27 (Dec 1971). 14.
Erwartung. **OPE**, 53.
Falstaff. **TCI**, vol. 27, n. 3 (Mar 1993). 28.
Fidelio. **OPE**, 115, 122, 125, 126.
Die Frau ohne Schatten. **OPE**, 237, 241, 242, 245, 246, 249; **OPE**, 53; **TCI**, vol. 12,
    n. 6 (Oct 1978). 32; **TDT**, vol. XII, n. 1 (Spring 1976). 26.
Götterdämmerung. **OPE**, 182, 192, 195, 197; **TCI**, vol. 10, n. 5 (Oct 1976). 18; **TCI**,
    vol. 12, n. 6 (Oct 1978). 31; **TCI**, vol. 27, n. 3 (Mar 1993). 24.
The Harmony of the World. **OPE**, 39; **SDW2**, 70.
Káta Kabanová. **TCI**, vol. 12, n. 6 (Oct 1978). 32.
Mathis der Maler. **OPE**, 53.
Die Meistersinger von Nürnberg. **OPE**, 168, 173, 174, 177, 179; **TCI**, vol. 27, n. 3
    (Mar 1993). 27.
Otello. **TCI**, vol. 27, n. 3 (Mar 1993). 28.
Othello. **TDT**, n. 27 (Dec 1971). 15.
Parsifal. **SCT**, 30; **TCI**, vol. 11, n. 2 (Mar/Apr 1977). 18.
The Passion of Jonathan Wade. **TCI**, vol. 27, n. 3 (Mar 1993). 27.
Pelléas and Mélisande. **OPE**, 215, 221, 222, 225, 227, 229.
Das Rheingold **TCI**, vol. 10, n. 5 (Oct 1976). 18; **TCI**, vol. 27, n. 3 (Mar 1993). 24.
Rusalka. **TCI**, vol. 27, n. 3 (Mar 1993). 26.
Siegfried. **TCI**, vol. 10, n. 5 (Oct 1976). 18; **TCI**, vol. 12, n. 6 (Oct 1978). 31.
The Tales of Hoffmann. **MOM**, 56-67; **TCI**, vol. 17, n. 5 (May 1983). 8.
Tannhäuser. **MOM**, 212-221; **TCI**, vol. 12, n. 6 (Oct 1978). 28, 30.
Tod eines Jägers. **TCI**, vol. 12, n. 6 (Oct 1978). 33.
Tristan and Isolde. **MOM**, 228-235; **OPE**, 40.
Die Walküre. **TCI**, vol. 10, n. 5 (Oct 1976). 18; **TCI**, vol. 12, n. 6 (Oct 1978). 31; **TCI**,
    vol. 27, n. 3 (Mar 1993). 24-26; **TCI**, vol. 4, n. 1 (Jan/Feb 1970). 10; **TCI**, vol. 4,
    n. 4 (Sep 1970). 21.
Schneider-Siemssen, Günther & Aliute Meczies. *Der Freischütz*. **CGA**, 197.
Schöffer, Nicolas. *Kyldex 1*. **SDW4**, illus. 308-312; **RSD**, illus. 472.
Schönberg, Lars-Henrik. *Strontium*. **SDW3**, 220.
Schoukhaeff, Vassily.
    La Pastourelle. **TCS2**, plate 234.
    La Traviata. **TCS2**, plate 235.
Schuette, James. *The Treatment*. **TCI**, vol. 28, n. 1 (Jan 1994). 9.
Schultz, Johannes. *Machandel*. **TCI**, vol. 23, n. 9 (Nov 1989). 11.
Schultz, Karen.
    The Foreigner. **DDT**, 124; **TDP**, 116.
    Hedda Gabler. **DDT**, 152c.
    The Inspector General. **DDT**, 112.
    Red River. **DDT**, 170.
Schultz, Rudolf.
    Antigone. **SDW1**, 77.
    Ostend Masks. **SDW2**, 71.
    The Trial. **SDW1**, 77.
    The White Rose. **SDW1**, 75.
Schultz, Werner. *Don Pasquale*. **OPE**, 140, 142, 144, 146.
Schumacher, Fritz. *Macbeth*. **DIT**, plate 91.

The Jocky Club Stakes. **DPT**, 332.

Summer and Smoke. **DPT**, 93.

Les Troyens. **DPT**, 365.

Serban, Milenko.

   Macbeth. **SDW2**, 136.

   Uncle Maroje. **SDW2**, 135.

Serebrovskij, Vladimir. *A Pound of Flesh.* **SDW3**, 139.

Serroni, J.C.

   The Coffe Trade Foxes. **TCI**, vol. 28, n. 4 (Apr 1994). 36, 37.

   A Midsummer Night's Dream. **TCI**, vol. 28, n. 4 (Apr 1994). 38.

   Paradise North Side. **TCI**, vol. 28, n. 4 (Apr 1994). 39.

   Vereda da Salvação. **TCI**, vol. 28, n. 4 (Apr 1994). 37.

   Zero. **TCI**, vol. 28, n. 4 (Apr 1994). 37.

Sestina, L. *Four Rough Fellows.* **TDT**, vol. XVI, n. 1 (Spring 1980). 29.

Severini, Gino.

   Amphiparnassus. **SDW1**, 131.

   L'Anfiparnaso. **AST**, 189.

Seyffer, Robert. *The Wedding.* **SDW4**, illus. 229, 230.

Seymour, Di. *As You Like It.* **BTD**, 52.

Sharir, David.

   The Dove of Arden. **SDW4**, illus. 346.

   Peer Gynt. **SDW3**, 84.

   Pendulum. **SDW4**, illus. 351, 352.

Sharpe, Robert Redington.

   Joseph. **TDT**, vol. XXVII, n. 1 (Winter 1991). 19.

   Major Barbara. **TCR**, 62.

   The Makropoulos Secret. **SDC**, plate 91.

   Pelléas and Mélisande. **TDT**, vol. XXVII, n. 1 (Winter 1991). 19.

   Tobacco Road. **TDT**, vol. XXVII, n. 1 (Winter 1991). 16.

Shaw, Bob. *The Mystery of Edwin Drood.* **MBM**, 172; **TCI**, vol. 20, n. 1 (Jan 1986). 23.

Shaw, Bob & Wilford Leach.

   The Pirates of Penzance. **MBM**, 26; **TCI**, vol. 15, n. 6 (Jun/Jul 1981). 12, 13; **TCI**,
       vol. 15, n. 6 (Jun/Jul 1981). 12; **TCI**, vol. 20, n. 1 (Jan 1986). 23.

Shchuko, Vladimir.

   Antony and Cleopatra. **RST**, 167; **SOS**, 221.

   Don Carlos. **RST**, 75.

Sheffield, Ann.

   Laughing in the Sea Wind. **TCI**, vol. 17, n. 7 (Aug/Sep 1983). 8.

   The Rivals. **TCI**, vol. 25, n. 1 (Jan 1991). 42.

Sheintsis, Oleg. *Juno and Avas.* **TDT**, vol. XX, n. 1 (Spring 1984). 16.

Sheklashviki, Shmagi. *Beautiful Aklunersta.* **TDT**, vol. XX, n. 1 (Spring 1984). 15.

Shelley, John.

   Desire Under the Elms. **SCM**, 30.

   Peer Gynt. **SCM**, 31.

Shelving, Paul.

   Back to Methuselah. **DIT**, plates 29, 30.

   Gas. **SDG**, 172.

   The Immortal Hour. **TCS2**, plate 226.

   The Interlude of Youth. **DOT**, 221.

Sheppard, Guy. *The Hanging Judge.* **SDW1**, 185.

Sheriff, Paul. *Crime and Punishment.* **SDW1**, 185.

Sheringham, George.
> *The Duenna.* **DIT**, plate 16; **TPH**, photo 430.
> *The Tempest.* **SCM**, 37.
> *Twelfth Night.* **SCM**, 37; **SDG**, 177; **TPH**, photo 438.

Sherman, Loren.
> *Assassins.* **SON**, 182, 186; **TCI**, vol. 25, n. 3 (Mar 1991). 45.
> *Chekov in Yalta.* **BSE4**, 98.
> *The Critic.* **DDT**, 321.
> *The Dining Room.* **DDT**, 257.
> *The Forest.* **TCI**, vol. 20, n. 4 (Apr 1986). 12.
> *Marat/Sade.* **DDT**, 258.
> *The Marriage of Bette and Boo.* **DDT**, 201; **TCI**, vol. 21, n. 4 (Apr 1987). 35.
> *Merrily We Roll Along.* **TCI**, vol. 19, n. 8 (Oct 1985). 18; **TCI**, vol. 21, n. 8 (Oct 1987). 30.
> *The Nest of the Woodgrouse.* **DDT**, 61.
> *Privates on Parade.* **TCI**, vol. 23, n. 8 (Oct 1989). 11.
> *Shogun: The Musical.* **DDT**, 24a, 31, 587; **TCI**, vol. 24, n. 10 (Dec 1990). 11; **TCI**, vol. 24, n. 8 (Oct 1990). 36; **TCI**, vol. 28, n. 3 (Mar 1994). 33.
> *Sleight of Hand.* **DDT**, 550, 551.
> *That's It, Folks.* **TCI**, vol. 17, n. 8 (Oct 1983). 10.

Sherriff, Paul. *Crime and Punishment.* **WTP**, 104, 105.

Shervashidze, Alexander.
> *A Month in the Country.* **TCS2**, plate 51.
> *Tristan and Isolde.* **MOT**, between 64 & 65.

Shestakov, Victor.
> *Echo.* **RST**, 134.
> *Lake Lyul.* **RSD**, illus. 182; **RST**, 102, 136.
> *Man and the Masses.* **RSD**, illus. 183.
> *A Profitable Post.* **RST**, 176, 177.
> *Woe from Wit.* **RST**, 26.

Shigeoka, Kan-ichi. *Aoi-No-Ue.* **SDW1**, 146.

Shimizu, Kesatoshi. *Romeo and Juliet.* **SDW3**, 37.

Shipulin, M.N. *Maria Stuart.* **TDT**, n. 33 (May 1973). 17.

Shlepyanov, Ilya.
> *Give Us Europe.* **MOT**, between 184 & 185; **RSD**, illus. 202; **TCT**, plates 22, 23.
> *My Friend.* **RST**, 278, 279.
> *The Poem of the Axe.* **RST**, 276, 277.

Shoakang, Wang. *Beyond the Horizon.* **TDT**, vol. XXV, n. 1 (Spring 1989). 11, 12.

Shock, Amy. *Der Ring des Nibelungen.* **TCI**, vol. 28, n. 3 (Mar 1994). 62.

Shortt, Paul. *The Wizard of Oz.* **TCI**, vol. 17, n. 2 (Feb 1983). 4.

Shtoffer, Jacob.
> *The Mother.* **NTO**, facing 364; **RSD**, illus. 223, 224; **RST**, 285; **SCM**, 93; **TPH**, photo 408; **TSE**, 7.
> *The Start.* **NTO**, facing 364; **RSD**, illus. 221, 222.

Sibbald, George. *The Music Man.* **TCI**, vol. 20, n. 5 (May 1986). 21.

Sicangco, Eduardo.
> *Babes in Toyland.* **DDT**, 152d.
> *Das Barbecü.* **TCI**, vol. 29, n. 2 (Feb 1995). 35.
> *The Barber of Seville.* **BSE3**, 36, 37.
> *Gentlemen Prefer Blondes.* **TCI**, vol. 29, n. 2 (Feb 1995). 36, 37.
> *Lady Be Good!* **TCI**, vol. 21, n. 9 (Nov 1987). 37.

The Most Happy Fella. **BSE4**, 40.

The Nutcracker. **DDT**, 366; **TCI**, vol. 27, n. 2 (Feb 1993). 6.

Siercke, Alfred.

Cardillac. **SDW2**, 72.

Fidelio. **SDW1**, 79.

The Italian Girl in Algiers. **SDW1**, 78.

The Magic Flute. **SDW1**, 78.

The Moon. **SDW1**, 79.

Pallas Athene Weeps. **SDW2**, 72.

The School for Wives. **SDW2**, 72.

Sievert, Ludwig.

The Broad Highway. **RSD**, illus. 120; **TAS**, 73; **TAT**, plate 396.

Cain. **RSD**, illus. 140.

Don Juan. **TCS2**, plate 205.

Judith. **DIT**, plate 97.

Maria Stuart. **CSC**, facing 112, 114.

Murderer, Hope of Women. **CSC**, facing 32; **FCS**, plate 194; **SDO**, 222; **TCS2**, plate 207.

Parsifal. **FCS**, plate 193; **SDO**, 221.

Penthesilea. **TCS2**, plate 118.

Das Rheingold. **RSD**, illus. 69.

Salomé. **TAT**, plate 397.

The Son. **RSD**, illus. 118.

Trommeln in der Nacht (Drums in the Night). **RSD**, illus. 119; **TCS2**, plate 206.

Siki, Emil. *Hamlet.* **SDB**, 44; **SDW2**, 141.

Silberstein, Frank. *How the Other Half Loves.* **TDT**, vol. XVI, n. 4 (Winter 1980). 5.

Silitch, Lioubiv. *The Cherry Orchard.* **SDW2**, 193.

Sima, Joseph. *The Executioner of Peru.* **RSD**, illus. 390.

Simond, Anne-Marie & Pierre. *Der Ring des Nibelungen.* **SDW3**, 180.

Simonini, Pierre. *Andromaque.* **SDW2**, 101.

Simonson, Lee.

The Adding Machine. **TPH**, photo 463.

Amphytrion 38. **PLT**, illus. 54-56; **SOW**, plate 36; **TAS**, 153; **TPH**, photo 464; **WTP**, 46, 47.

The Apple Cart. **PLT**, illus. 25; **SCM**, 114.

As You Like It. **SDC**, plate 82; **TAS**, 128, 129; **TCS2**, plates 75, 76.

Back to Methuselah. **MCN**, 57; **PLT**, illus. 22-24; **TAS**, 124, 125; **TCS2**, plate 363; **TPH**, photo 369.

Bockegesang. **TCS2**, plates 100, 101.

The Cat Bird. **PLT**, illus. 2, 3.

Days Without End. **PLT**, illus. 53.

Don Juan. **PLT**, illus. 19.

Dynamo. **CSD**, 12; **MCN**, 94, 95; **PLT**, illus. 52; **RSD**, illus. 436, 437; **SCM**, 110, 111; **SDT**, 36; **TDT**, n. 8 (Feb 1967). 35; **TSS**, 521.

Elizabeth the Queen. **PLT**, illus. 47.

The Failures. **PLT**, illus. 20; **SDC**, plate 115; **TSS**, 515, 516.

The Faithful. **PLT**, illus. 6-9, 60; **SDC**, plate 84; **TAS**, 118, 119; **TCS2**, plate 108; **TSS**, 514.

Faust. **PLT**, illus. 38; **SCM**, 109, 110; **TAS**, 146, 147; **TSS**, 527.

The Goat Song. **BSE4**, 50; **PLT**, illus. 36, 37, 62; **SDC**, plate 127; **TDT**, vol. XXII, n. 3 (Fall 1986). front cover, 7, 8.

Sirlin, Jerome.
>   *The Architecture of Catastrophic Change.* **TCI**, vol. 25, n. 4 (Apr 1991). 21.
>   *Kiss of the Spider Woman.* **TCI**, vol. 27, n. 5 (May 1993). 5, 36, 37.
>   *1,000 Airplanes on the Roof.* **TCI**, vol. 22, n. 10 (Dec 1988). 10.
>   *Rare Area.* **TCI**, vol. 22, n. 1 (Jan 1988). 34.
>   *See Hear.* **TCI**, vol. 22, n. 1 (Jan 1988). 34.
>   *Die Walküre.* **TCI**, vol. 22, n. 1 (Jan 1988). 34.

Sironi, Mario.
>   *Doctor Faustus.* **AST**, 192.
>   *Don Carlos.* **AST**, 192; **SDE**, 152.
>   *I Lombardi alla prima Crociata.* **AST**, 192; **SDE**, 153.

Sissons, Narelle. *Iphigenia and Other Daughters.* **TCI**, vol. 29, n. 4 (Apr 1995). 7.
Sitter, Inger & Carl Nesjar. *Don Juan.* **SDW2**, 153.
Sjöberg, Alf. *The Holy Family.* **SOW**, plate 59.
Skalicki, William. *Otello.* **TCI**, vol. 20, n. 8 (Oct 1986). 22.
Skalicki, Wolfram. *The Magic Flute.* **SDW2**, 162.
Skalicky, Jan & Reinhart Zimmerman. *Jenufa.* **SDW3**, 185.
Skawonius, Sven Erik.
>   *The Masked Ball.* **SDR**, 54.
>   *The Saga of the Folkungs.* **DSL**, 84.

Skawonius, Sven-Eric & Olav Molander. *Master Olof.* **TAT**, plate 469.
Sköld, Otte. *Medea.* **SOW**, plate 33.
Sladek, Jan. *Dalibor.* **SDW1**, 52.
Slayton, Kati. *The Playboy of the Western World.* **TCI**, vol. 9, n. 1 (Jan/Feb 1975). 15.
Slevogt, Max.
>   *Don Giovanni.* **AST**, 34.
>   *Florian Geyer.* **AST**, 34.
>   *The Magic Flute.* **AST**, 35.
>   *The Merry Wives of Windsor.* **TPH**, photo 325.

Sliwinski, Stanislas.
>   *L'Echange.* **TCS2**, plate 238.
>   *La Malédiction.* **TCS2**, plate 209.

Smith, Bruce. *The Whip.* **SDG**, 140.
Smith, Gary. *Six Characters in Search of an Author.* **SDW2**, 238.
Smith, Jerrard & Diane. *Ra.* **TCI**, vol. 18, n. 3 (Mar 1984). 26.
Smith, Oliver.
>   *Baker Street.* **TCI**, vol. 16, n. 4 (Apr 1982). 63.
>   *Barefoot in the Park.* **TCI**, vol. 16, n. 4 (Apr 1982). 16.
>   *Beggar's Holiday.* **TCI**, vol. 16, n. 4 (Apr 1982). 13, 62.
>   *Brigadoon.* **BWM**, 280; **CSD**, 17; **HOB**, 78; **SDT**, 41; **SOW**, plate 107; **TCI**, vol. 16, n. 4 (Apr 1982). 13; **TMT**, 167; **WMC**, 240.
>   *Camelot.* **BWM**, 285, 286; **DPT**, 155; **SDA**, 256; **TCI**, vol. 16, n. 4 (Apr 1982). 16; **TMI**, 246; **TMT**, plate 10.
>   *Candide.* **TCI**, vol. 16, n. 4 (Apr 1982). 62.
>   *A Clearing in the Woods.* **SDA**, 156.
>   *Destry Rides Again.* **WMC**, 195.
>   *Don Giovanni.* **TCI**, vol. 16, n. 4 (Apr 1982). 63.
>   *Fall River Legend.* **DOT**, 243; **SDA**, 276; **SDW1**, 205.
>   *Fancy Free.* **SDA**, 276; **TPH**, photo 368.
>   *Flower Drum Song.* **HOB**, 177; **TCI**, vol. 16, n. 4 (Apr 1982). 14; **TMI**, 136, 170; **WMC**, 222.

Sonrel, Pierre.
    Cinna. **SDW1**, 106.
    King Lear. **SOS**, 187.
Soto, Jésus-Raphaël. *Violostries*. **RSD**, illus. 492.
Soudeikine, Serge.
    Chauve Souris. **FCS**, plate 177; **SDO**, 200.
    Petrouchka. **TCS2**, plate 237.
    Porgy and Bess. **BMF**, 40; **BWM**, 231; **RBS**, 116, 117; **TMT**, 132, 134;
        WMC, 97, 98.
    Le Rossignol. **MOM**, 8.
Soule, Robert D.
    Glengarry Glen Ross. **TCI**, vol. 22, n. 9 (Nov 1988). 62.
    The House of Blue Leaves. **TCI**, vol. 22, n. 9 (Nov 1988). 61.
    Ma Rainey's Black Bottom. **TCI**, vol. 22, n. 9 (Nov 1988). 63.
    Sherlock's Last Case. **TCI**, vol. 22, n. 9 (Nov 1988). 60.
Soumbatashvili, Iossif.
    The Death of Ivan the Terrible. **RSD**, illus. 503; **SDW3**, 99.
    Squire Puntila and His Servant Matti. **SDW3**, 116.
    The Steel Workers. **SDW4**, illus. 353, 354.
    Theresa's Birthday. **SDW3**, 120.
Sousa, Larry. *Scapino*. **TDT**, vol. XXVI, n. 1 (Spring 1990). 24 of insert.
Sovey, Raymond.
    Babes in Arms. **BWM**, 181.
    The Front Page. **MCN**, 91.
    Green Grow the Lilacs. **MCN**, 101; **SCM**, 125; **SDA**, 239.
    Libel! **SOW**, plate 88.
    Our Town. **MCN**, 140; **NTO**, facing 436; **SDA**, 120; **SOW**, plate 100; **WTP**, 178, 179.
    Saint Joan. **MCN**, 64.
    Tovarich. **MCN**, 132.
    Twelfth Night. **SCM**, 124; **SDA**, 238.
    Wings Over Europe. **SCM**, 108.
    Yes, My Darling Daughter. **MCN**, 138.
Soyinka, Wole. *Kongi's Harvest*. **SDW3**, 162.
Spatz-Rabinowitz, Elaine.
    Orchids in the Moonlight. **TCI**, vol. 16, n. 8 (Oct 1982). 14.
    Orlando. **TCI**, vol. 16, n. 8 (Oct 1982). 15.
Sporre, Dennis J.
    The Amorous Flea. **SDT**, 85.
    The Bacchae. **SDT**, 63, 102.
    King John. **SDT**, 83.
    Love for Love. **TCI**, vol. 5, n. 6 (Nov/Dec 1971). 18, 19, 21.
Sprott, Eoin. *A Man's a Man*. **TCI**, vol. 9, n. 1 (Jan/Feb 1975). 10.
Stabile, Bill.
    Spookhouse. **BSE4**, 99.
    States of Shock. **TCI**, vol. 25, n. 6 (Aug/Sep 1991). 19.
    When You Comin' Back Red Ryder? **TCI**, vol. 8, n. 2 (Mar/Apr 1974). 9.
Stacklin, Andy. *Fool for Love*. **TCI**, vol. 17, n. 8 (Oct 1983). 12.
Staheli, Paul.
    The Architect and the Emperor of Assyria. **TCI**, vol. 6, n. 5 (Oct 1972). 17.
    The Three Sisters. **TCI**, vol. 6, n. 5 (Oct 1972). 14.

Stapleton, Christopher.
    Olympus on My Mind. **BSE5**, 23.
    When You Comin' Back Red Ryder? **BSE3**, 89.
Starowieyska, Eva. *Uncle Vanya*. **SDW4**, illus. 184.
Stegars, Rolf.
    A Dream Play. **SDW2**, 206.
    The Judge. **SDW3**, 108.
    Lea. **SDW1**, 159.
    Macbeth. **SDW3**, 54.
    The School for Wives. **SDW2**, 206.
Steger, Rod. *The Firebird*. **BSE3**, 38.
Stein, Douglas O.
    American Vaudeville. **TCI**, vol. 26, n. 7 (Aug/Sep 1992). 11.
    The Cherry Orchard. **DDT**, 240, 241.
    Endgame. **TCI**, vol. 19, n. 5 (May 1985). 21; **TDP**, 114.
    Fantasio. **TCI**, vol. 26, n. 2 (Feb 1992). 11.
    A Man's a Man. **TCI**, vol. 21, n. 8 (Oct 1987). 27, 28
    The Molière Comedies. **TCI**, vol. 29, n. 3 (Mar 1995). 6.
    The Skin of Our Teeth. **TCI**, vol. 24, n. 10 (Dec 1990). 22.
    Through the Leaves. **BSE4**, 100; **TCI**, vol. 24, n. 9 (Nov 1990). 27.
Steinberg, Paul.
    The Beggar's Opera. **TCI**, vol. 29, n. 4 (Apr 1995). 32.
    Cavalleria Rusticana. **TCI**, vol. 29, n. 4 (Apr 1995). 32.
    L'Etoile. **TCI**, vol. 29, n. 4 (Apr 1995). 30.
    Harvey Milk. **TCI**, vol. 29, n. 4 (Apr 1995). 31.
    Idomeneo. **TCI**, vol. 29, n. 4 (Apr 1995). 32, 33; **TDT** vol. XXXI, n. 2 (Spring 1995).
       15.
    Lohengrin. **TCI**, vol. 29, n. 4 (Apr 1995). 5; **TDT** vol. XXXI, n. 2 (Spring 1995). 16.
    Madame Butterfly. **TCI**, vol. 29, n. 4 (Apr 1995). 30.
    The Sailor Who Fell from Grace with the Sea. **TCI**, vol. 29, n. 4 (Apr 1995). 34.
    Turandot. **TCI**, vol. 29, n. 4 (Apr 1995). cover, 33.
    The Visit. **TCI**, vol. 25, n. 6 (Aug/Sep 1991). 31.
Steiof, Adolf. *Hölderlin*. **SDW4**, illus. 279, 280.
Stell, W. Joseph.
    Cabaret. **TDT**, vol. XIX, n. 3 (Fall 1983). 15, 17.
    Camelot. **TDT**, vol. XXX, n. 3 (Summer 1994). 11 of insert.
    The Caucasian Chalk Circle. **TCI**, vol. 3, n. 1 (Jan/Feb 1969). 32-36.
    Once Upon a Mattress. **TCI**, vol. 1, n. 5 (Nov/Dec 1967). 13, 15-17.
Stelletsky, Dimitri. *Tsar Feodor Ivanovitch*. **RSC**, 55.
Stenberg, Enar. G.
    Galileo. **SDW3**, 113; **TDT**, n. 33 (May 1973). 16.
    Man of La Mancha. **TDT**, vol. XII, n. 3 (Fall 1976). 42.
Stenberg, Georgiy A. *October*. **RAG**, 58.
Stenberg, Vladimir & K. Medunetsky. *The Thunderstorm*. **RSD**, illus. 195.
Stenberg, Vladimir & Georgiy A.
    Kukirol. **TCI**, vol. 24, n. 7 (Aug/Sep 1990). 8.
    All God's Chillun Got Wings. **RST**, 196; **TAT**, plate 700.
    Day and Night. **RST**, 238, 239.
    Desire Under the Elms. **RST**, 237; **SCM**, 88.
    The Hairy Ape. **AST**, 135; **RSD**, illus. 194; The Hairy Ape. **RST**, 236; **SCM**, 88; **TSS**,
       522.

Stevens, John Wright.
  La Bohème. **SDT**, 296 and between 152 & 153.
  The Duchess of Gerolstein. **SDT**, 293.
  A Grave Undertaking. **TCI**, vol. 9, n. 6 (Nov/Dec 1975). 14.
  Life With Father. **TCI**, vol. 9, n. 6 (Nov/Dec 1975). 14.
  Norma. **SDT**, 279.
Stewart, Anita C.
  The House of Bernarda Alba. **TCI**, vol. 25, n. 1 (Jan 1991). 44.
  The Illusion. **TCI**, vol. 25, n. 8 (Oct 1991). 20.
  Love's Labor's Lost. **TCI**, vol. 25, n. 3 (Mar 1991). 47.
Stockemer, Richard. *Titus Andronicus.* **BSE2**, 41.
Stohl, Phyllis. *The Forest.* **SFT**, 75.
Stone, Alex. *The Taming of the Shrew.* **SDW2**, 227.
Stone, James Merrill. *Faust.* **TCI**, vol. 20, n. 8 (Oct 1986). 23.
Stopka, Andrzej. *The Story of the Glorius Ressurection of Our Lord.* **RSD**, illus. 504.
Stover, Frederick. *Man and Superman.* **WTP**, 148, 149.
Stowe, Laura. *The Visit.* **BSE2**, 22.
Strachan, Kathy. *Frankenstein.* **BTD**, 68.
Straiges, Tony.
  Artist Descending a Staircase. **TCI**, vol. 24, n. 3 (Mar 1990). 23.
  The Beggar's Opera. **ASD2**, 147; **DDT**, 235; **TCI**, vol. 16, n. 2 (Feb 1982). 15, 19; **TCI**, vol. 17, n. 4 (Apr 1983). 23.
  Buried Child. **DDT**, 234; **TCI**, vol. 18, n. 3 (Mar 1984). 28.
  Coppélia. **ASD2**, 140; **TCI**, vol. 25, n. 3 (Mar 1991). 10.
  Copperfield. **DDT**, 314; **TCI**, vol. 16, n. 2 (Feb 1982). 16.
  Diamonds. **TCI**, vol. 19, n. 2 (Feb 1985). 10.
  Galileo. **TCI**, vol. 16, n. 2 (Feb 1982). 17.
  Geniuses. **DDT**, 152, 312d; **TCI**, vol. 18, n. 3 (Mar 1984). 29.
  The Great Magoo. **DDT**, 171.
  Harold and Maude. **DDT**, 333.
  A History of the American Film. **TCI**, vol. 16, n. 2 (Feb 1982). 17.
  The Importance of Being Earnest. **DDT**, 236; **TCI**, vol. 18, n. 3 (Mar 1984). 29.
  Into the Woods. **ASD2**, 156 and between 108 & 109; **DDT**, 173, 397; **MBM**, 40, 41; **SON**, 169, 173, 176; **TCI**, vol. 22, n. 1 (Jan 1988). 29, 32, 33.
  Jake's Women. **DDT**, 356.
  Julius Caesar. **ASD2**, 153; **DDT**, 237; **TCI**, vol. 16, n. 2 (Feb 1982). 19.
  A Lesson from Aloes. **ASD2**, 144; **DDT**, 586; **TCI**, vol. 16, n. 2 (Feb 1982). 14; **TCI**, vol. 20, n. 2 (Feb 1986). 20.
  Major Barbara. **TCI**, vol. 16, n. 2 (Feb 1982). 15.
  A Midsummer Night's Dream. **DDT**, 238; **TCI**, vol. 10, n. 1 (Jan/Feb 1976). 72.
  On the Razzle. **ASD2**, 149.
  On the Verge or the Geography of Yearning. **ASD2**, 155; **TCI**, vol. 20, n. 9 (Nov 1986). 18.
  Our Town. **ASD2**, 152.
  The Physicists. **TCI**, vol. 16, n. 2 (Feb 1982). 18.
  The Rise and Fall of the City of Mahagonny. **CSD**, 130; **TCI**, vol. 16, n. 2 (Feb 1982). 19.
  Romeo and Juliet. **TCI**, vol. 16, n. 2 (Feb 1982). 18.
  Rumors. **ASD2**, 148.
  Savages. **ASD2**, 143; **TCI**, vol. 16, n. 8 (Oct 1982). 25.
  Summer. **ASD2**, 150; **DDT**, 291.

Sunday in the Park with George. **ASD2**, 157; **BSE4**, 92; **DDT**, 24a, 232; **MBM**, 48-
    50; **SON**, 154, 157, 159, 163, 165; **TCI**, vol. 18, n. 7 (Aug/Sep 1984). 24-27; **TCI**,
    vol. 27, n. 8 (Oct 1993). 35; **TCI**, vol. 28, n. 3 (Mar 1994). 33; **TMT**, plate 14.
The Three Sisters. **ASD2**, 155; **TCI**, vol. 14, n. 3 (May/Jun 1980). 18.
Timbuktu. **ASD2**, 150; **TCI**, vol. 12, n. 4 (May/Jun 1978). 14, 15; **TCI**, vol. 16, n. 2
    (Feb 1982). 18.
Troilus and Cressida. **TCI**, vol. 16, n. 2 (Feb 1982). 15.
The Winter's Tale. **TCI**, vol. 14, n. 6 (Nov/Dec 1980). 34; **TCI**, vol. 16, n. 2 (Feb
    1982). 17; **TCI**, vol. 16, n. 9 (Nov/Dec 1982). 27.
Women Beware Women. **TCI**, vol. 16, n. 2 (Feb 1982). 18.
Strebelle, Olivier. *I.* **SDW4**, illus. 391-393.
Strenger, Friedhelm.
    The Naval Battle. **DSL**, figure 27.1(a).
    The Story of Vasco. **SDW2**, 71.
Strike, Maurice.
    Misalliance. **TCI**, vol. 22, n. 7 (Aug/Sep 1988). 64.
    Thark. **TCI**, vol. 12, n. 4 (May/Jun 1978). 23.
Strnad, Oskar.
    Danton. **TCS2**, plate 192.
    Danton's Death. **DIT**, plate 108; **MRT**, 81; **TAT**, plate 150.
    Hamlet. **RSD**, illus. 94; **TCS2**, plates 71, 72.
    King Lear. **TAT**, plate 145; **TCS2**, plate 197.
    The Merchant of Venice. **TCS2**, plates 32, 33.
    The Miracle. **MEM**, 81; **OMB**, 74, 75; **TCS2**, plates 371, 371.
    Oesterreichische Komödie. **TCS2**, plate 30.
Stroem, Carl Johan. *Tristan and Isolde.* **SDR**, 53.
Strohbach, Hans.
    Masse Mensch. **CSC**, facing 148, 150, 152, 154, 156; **NTO**, facing 276.
    Der Traum, ein Leben. **CSC**, facing 44.
Ström, Carl-Johan.
    Doña Rosita. **SDW1**, 168.
    A Dream Play. **SDW1**, 168.
Ström, Knut & Rochus Gliese. *Macbeth.* **DIT**, plate 106; **SDC**, plate 56.
Stromberg, Christine. *Faust, part 1.* **SDW3**, 79.
Stros, Ladislav.
    Don Pasquale. **OPE**, 136, 143, 147.
    The Tales of Hoffmann. **OPE**, 202, 207, 208, 213.
Strosser, Pierre. *Pelléas and Mélisande.* **TCI**, vol. 20, n. 3 (Mar 1986). 12.
Strzelecki, Zenobiusz.
    Agamemnon. **RSD**, illus. 505.
    The Seagull. **SDW2**, 169.
Sturm, Eduard.
    Kaiser und Galiläer. **TCS2**, plate 347.
    Manfred. **TCS2**, plate 348.
    Maria Stuart. **TCS2**, plate 190.
    Prince of Homburg. **TCS2**, plate 133.
Suchánek, Vladimír. *Don Pasquale.* **OPE**, 138, 143, 145, 147.
Suhr, Edward.
    The Lower Depths. **TCS2**, plate 104.
    Sturmflut (Storm Flood or Tidal Wave). **RSD**, illus. 232; **TBB**, 108; **TCS2**, plate 280;
        TPH, photo 376.

Suhr, Edward & George Grosz. *The Drunken Ship*. **RSD**, illus. 242.
Sujan. *The Threepenny Opera*. **SDB**, 76.
Sullivan, Gary. *Oklahoma*. **TCI**, vol. 20, n. 5 (May 1986). 37.
Sulzbachner, Max. *Romulus the Great*. **SDW1**, 116.
Suominen, Paul. *Prince Igor*. **SDW2**, 205.
Surrey, Kit. *Twelfth Night*. **BTD**, 46.
Survage, Leopold. *The School for Wives*. **SDE**, 153.
Sutcliffe, Berkeley. *Love from Judy*. **MCD**, plate 202.
Svoboda, Josef.
  Abis's Action. **SJS**, 134.
  The Amorous Devil. **TDT**, vol. XXX, n. 5 (Fall 1994). 42.
  The Anabaptists. **SDW3**, 143; **SJS**, 128-130; **STS**, 8.
  Antigone. **TCI**, vol. 21, n. 8 (Oct 1987). 34.
  Antony and Cleopatra. **STS**, 93.
  Ariadne auf Naxos. **SJS**, 154; **STS**, 68, 69.
  As You Like It. **SJS**, 156, 157; **STS**, 7.
  Astray. **STS**, 32; **TDT**, vol. XXVIII, n. 5 (Fall 1992). 10.
  Atomic Death. **SDW3**, 215.
  The August Sunday. **TDT**, n. 7 (Dec 1966). 25.
  The Bartered Bride. **STS**, 42, 43; **TDT**, vol. XXX, n. 5 (Fall 1994). 38, 41.
  Biedermann and the Firebugs. **TDT**, vol. XXX, n. 5 (Fall 1994). 41.
  Boris Godounov. **SDW1**, 53; **STS**, 98; **TDT**, vol. XII, n. 2 (Summer 1976). 13.
  Break of Noon. **TCI**, vol. 21, n. 8 (Oct 1987). 35.
  Cardillac. **SJS**, 152.
  Carmen. **SJS**, 153; **STS**, 72-74; **TCI**, vol. 10, n. 5 (Oct 1976). 17; **TDT**, vol. XII, n. 2
    (Summer 1976). 23.
  Children of the Sun. **SDW4**, illus. 199; **STS**, 16; **TDT**, vol. XII, n. 2 (Summer 1976).
    31.
  Clavigo. **TDT**, vol. XXX, n. 5 (Fall 1994). 41.
  Coriolanus. **TDT**, vol. XII, n. 2 (Summer 1976). 24.
  The Crown Bride. **STS**, 35.
  Cyrano de Bergerac. **SDW4**, illus. 200; **STS**, 24; **TDT**, vol. XII, n. 2 (Summer 1976).
    21.
  Dalibor. **SJS**, 58; Dalibor. **STS**, 45; **TDT**, n. 7 (Dec 1966). 25.
  The Devil's Wall. **TDT**, vol. XII, n. 2 (Summer 1976). 14.
  Don Carlos. **SJS**, 149; **SST**, 45; **TDT**, vol. XII, n. 2 (Summer 1976). 26.
  Don Giovanni. **SJS**, 47, 76, 77, 140-142; **TDT**, n. 20 (Feb 1970). 18, 19.
  Don Juan. **TDT**, vol. XII, n. 2 (Summer 1976). 14.
  Drahomíra. **SJS**, 64; **STS**, 60.
  A Dream of Reason. **TDT**, vol. XII, n. 2 (Summer 1976). 15.
  A Dream Play. **STS**, 68, 69; **TDT**, vol. XVI, n. 4 (Winter 1980). 23.
  The Effect of Gamma Rays on Man-in-the-Moon Marigolds. **TDT**, vol. XII, n. 2
    (Summer 1976). 26.
  Electra. **SJS**, 13, 54.
  The Eleventh Commandment. **SJS**, 52.
  Empedokles. **SJS**, 148; **STS**, 35; **TDT**, vol. XXVIII, n. 5 (Fall 1992). 10.
  The Entertainer. **SJS**, 122; **STS**, 65.
  Eugene Onegin. **TDT**, vol. XII, n. 2 (Summer 1976). 12.
  Faust. **STS**, 102; **TDT**, vol. XXVIII, n. 5 (Fall 1992). 18; **TDT**, vol. XXX, n. 5 (Fall
    1994). 41.
  Feedback. **STS**, 90.

The Fiery Angel. **SJS**, 120; **TDT**, n. 20 (Feb 1970). 11.
The Firebird. **STS**, 91; **TDT**, vol. XII, n. 2 (Summer 1976). 16.
The Firebugs. **TDT**, vol. XXVIII, n. 2 (Spring 1992). 40.
The Flying Dutchman. **JSS**, 24-26, 28, 29, and between 54 & 55; **STS**, 76, 82, 94;
    TCI, vol. 14, n. 1 (Jan/Feb 1980). 22; **TCI**, vol. 5, n. 1 (Jan/Feb 1971). 31; **TDT**,
    n. 29 (May 1972). 11, 13.
La Forza del Destino. **TDT**, vol. XXX, n. 5 (Fall 1994). 41.
Die Frau ohne Schatten. **CGA**, 171; **SDW3**, 186; **SJS**, 69-71; **STS**, 29, 30; **TDT**, n.
    20 (Feb 1970). 8.
From the House of the Dead. **TDT**, vol. XXVI, n. 2 (Summer 1990). 35.
Ghetto. **TCI**, vol. 21, n. 8 (Oct 1987). 35; **TDT**, vol. XXIII, n. 4 (Winter 1988). 49.
Götterdämmerung. **JSS**, 72, 74, 77, 92, and between 54 & 55; **OPE**, 186, 192, 195,
    196, 198; **STS**, 85.
Hamlet. **RSD**, illus. 95, 546; **SDR**, 22; **SDW2**, 45; **SJS**, 125-127; **STS**, 56, 57; **TDT**,
    n. 7 (Dec 1966). 23; **TDT**, vol. XXIII, n. 1 (Spring 1987). 9, 11.
Henry V. **SJS**, 164; **STS**, 62.
The House of Bernarda Alba. **STS**, 26.
Idomeneo. **SJS**, 165; **STS**, 22, 78, 79.
The Insect Comedy. **SDB**, 143; **SJS**, 116, 118; **STS**, 51; **TDT**, n. 20 (Feb 1970). 4.
The Inspector General. **SJS**, 134; **STS**, 52.
Intolerance. **SDW3**, 208; **SJS**, 104.
The Italian Girl in Algiers. **SJS**, 151.
Ivanov. **SDW3**, 90; **SJS**, 42.
Jan Hus. **SDW1**, 52.
The Journey. **SDL**, 478; **SJS**, 96; **TDT**, n. 20 (Feb 1970). 9.
Julieta. **SJS**, 151.
Kanala's Eyes. **SJS**, 40; **STS**, 39.
Káta Kabanová. **SJS**, 40; **STS**, 46; **TDT**, vol. XII, n. 2 (Summer 1976). 12; **TDT**, vol.
    XXVIII, n. 5 (Fall 1992). 10.
King Lear. **SJS**, 153.
Krutnava. **TDT**, vol. XII, n. 2 (Summer 1976). 10.
The Labyrinth of the World and the Paradise of the Heart. **SJS**, 20.
Lady From the Sea. **TDT**, vol. XXX, n. 5 (Fall 1994). 38.
The Last Ones. **DSL**, figure 1.1(b); **SJS**, 100-102; **STS**, 67, 70; **TDT**, n. 20 (Feb
    1970). 5; **TDT**, n. 7 (Dec 1966). 24; **TDT**, vol. XIX, n. 3 (Fall 1983). 15.
The Little Foxes. **STS**, 64.
Loneliness. **DSL**, figure 1.1(c).
The Lost Fairy Tale. **STS**, 118.
The Love for Three Oranges. **SJS**, 136; **STS**, 66; **TDT**, n. 20 (Feb 1970). 12, 13.
Lucia di Lammermoor. **TDT**, vol. XXX, n. 5 (Fall 1994). 41.
Macbeth. **SJS**, 41; **TCI**, vol. 21, n. 8 (Oct 1987). 35.
The Magic Flute. **OPE**, 95, 100, 102, 104, 106, 108, 110; **SDW2**, 45; **SJS**, 43; **STS**,
    44; **TDT**, n. 7 (Dec 1966). 24, 25; **TDT**, vol. XXX, n. 5 (Fall 1994). 41.
The Makropoulos Secret. **SDR**, 65; **SJS**, 137; **TDT**, n. 20 (Feb 1970). 14.
Mary Stuart. **TCI**, vol. 21, n. 8 (Oct 1987). 34.
Die Meistersinger von Nurnburg. **JSS**, 95.
A Midsummer Night's Dream. **SJS**, 68.
The Mill. **SJS**, 46.
Mother Courage and Her Children. **SJS**, 160, 162; **STS**, 63.
Nabucco. **STS**, 101; **TCI**, vol. 21, n. 8 (Oct 1987). 36; **TDT**, vol. XII, n. 2 (Summer
    1976). 22; **TDT**, vol. XXIII, n. 4 (Winter 1988). 50.

No More Heroes in Thebes. SJS, 54.

Oberon. DSL, figure 27.1(c); SJS, 68, 69; SST, 378; TCI, vol. 5, n. 1 (Jan/Feb 1971). 30.

Odysseus. STS, 18, 101, 120; TDT, vol. XXIII, n. 4 (Winter 1988). 49; TDT, vol. XXIV, n. 4 (Winter 1988). front cover, 17-27.

Oedipus Rex. RSD, illus. 73; SJS, 56, 57; STS, 61; TDT, vol. XXIII, n. 4 (Winter 1988). 50.

Oedipus Tyrannos-Antigone. SDW3, 25.

Oedipus, Oedipus at Colonus, Antigone. SDW3, 20, 21; SJS, 164; STS, 20.

Die Operetta. STS, 92; TDT, vol. XII, n. 2 (Summer 1976). 31.

The Optimistic Tragedy. SJS, 59; STS, 24; TDT, vol. XII, n. 2 (Summer 1976). 32.

Orpheus in the Underworld. STS, 89.

Osamene. SDR, 65.

Otello. STS, 93, 101; TDT, vol. XXVIII, n. 5 (Fall 1992). 9.

Othello. SJS, 149.

Otto Dix. TDT, vol. XXX, n. 5 (Fall 1994). 38.

Our Hotheads. STS, 66.

The Outburst at Chiozza. STS, 53.

The Owners of the Keys. RSD, illus. 598; SJS, 114, 115; STS, 17.

The Pelican. TDT, vol. XXX, n. 5 (Fall 1994). 42.

Pelléas and Mélisande. RSD, illus. 601; SJS, 73, 74; TDT, n. 20 (Feb 1970). 10.

Prometheus. RSD, illus. 608; SDW3, 196; SJS, 107; STS, 2, 75; TCI, vol. 4, n. 1 (Jan/Feb 1970). 35; TCI, vol. 5, n. 1 (Jan/Feb 1971). 28, 29; TDT, n. 20 (Feb 1970). 8; TDT, vol. XII, n. 2 (Summer 1976). 16; TDT, vol. XXIV, n. 4 (Winter 1988). 12.

The Queen of Spades. STS, 48.

Raduz znd Mahulena. SJS, 72.

The Rake's Progress. TDT, vol. XII, n. 2 (Summer 1976). 22.

Das Rheingold. CGA, 190; JSS, 60, 62, 63, 82, 84, and between 54 & 55; STS, 84, 86; TDT, vol. XII, n. 2 (Summer 1976). 27, 28; TDT, vol. XXVIII, n. 5 (Fall 1992). 18.

Rigoletto. SJS, 138, 139; STS, 23; TDT, n. 20 (Feb 1970). 15-17; TDT, vol. XXVIII, n. 5 (Fall 1992). 12; TDT, vol. XXX, n. 5 (Fall 1994). 38.

Der Ring des Nibelungen. TDT, vol. XXX, n. 5 (Fall 1994). 41.

Rites of Spring. TDT, vol. XII, n. 2 (Summer 1976). 15.

Romeo and Juliet. SDW3, 38; SJS, 109-112; STS, 63; TDT, n. 7 (Dec 1966). 24.

Romeo, Juliet, and the Darkness. SJS, 96

Rusalka. SJS, 150; STS, 41; TDT, vol. XXX, n. 5 (Fall 1994). 37, 41.

St. Joan. SJS, 150; TDT, vol. XXIII, n. 4 (Winter 1988). 50.

St. Joan at the Stake. TCI, vol. 21, n. 8 (Oct 1987). 34.

Salomé. TDT, vol. XXIII, n. 4 (Winter 1988). 50; TDT, vol. XXVIII, n. 5 (Fall 1992). 16; TDT, vol. XXX, n. 5 (Fall 1994). 38.

The School for Scandal. TDT, vol. XII, n. 2 (Summer 1976). 14.

The Seagull. SDW2, 44; SJS, 62; STS, 25, 58; TDT, vol. XII, n. 2 (Summer 1976). 31; TDT, vol. XXVIII, n. 5 (Fall 1992). 12; TDT, vol. XXX, n. 5 (Fall 1994). 38.

The Secret. TDT, vol. XII, n. 2 (Summer 1976). 14.

The Seven Deadly Sins. TDT, vol. XXX, n. 5 (Fall 1994). 42.

The Sicilian Vespers. SJS, 66; STS, 97; TDT, n. 20 (Feb 1970). 10.

Siegfried. JSS, 68, 70, 88, 90, and between 54 & 55; STS, 83; TDT, vol. XII, n. 2 (Summer 1976). 30; TDT, vol. XV, n. 1 (Spring 1979). 8; TDT, vol. XVI, n. 1 (Spring 1980). 29; TDT, vol. XXVIII, n. 5 (Fall 1992). 9.

Simon Boccanagra. **TDT**, vol. XII, n. 2 (Summer 1976). 21.

Six Characters in Search of an Author. **STS**, 96, 101.

The Snow Queen. **STS**, 119, 120.

The Soldiers. **RSD**, illus. 603, 604; **SDW3**, 205; **SJS**, 98, 99; **STS**, 80, 81; **TCI**, vol. 11, n. 2 (Mar/Apr 1977). 19; **TCI**, vol. 5, n. 1 (Jan/Feb 1971). 26, 27.

The Story of a Real Man. **SDW2**, 44; **SJS**, 50.

Straying. **SJS**, 52.

A Sunday in August. **SJS**, 61, 62; **STS**, 54; **TDT**, vol. XXVIII, n. 5 (Fall 1992). 12.

The Suzanna Play. **SJS**, 96.

Svanda the Bagpiper. **SJS**, 152.

Svätopluk. **SJS**, 62; **TDT**, n. 7 (Dec 1966). 24.

Symphonie Fantastique. **TDT**, vol. XII, n. 2 (Summer 1976). 15.

The Tales of Hoffmann. **SJS**, 131, 132; **STS**, 14, 15, 21, 40, 41, 117.

Tannhäuser. **JSS**, 33, 34, 38, and between 54 & 55; **RSD**, illus. 602; **SJS**, 75, 76; **TDT**, vol. XII, n. 2 (Summer 1976). 19.

Their Day. **RSD**, illus. 607; **SJS**, 94; **STS**, 55; **TDT**, n. 7 (Dec 1966). 25.

The Three Sisters. **SJS**, 48, 49; **STS**, 99.

The Threepenny Opera. **TDT**, vol. XII, n. 2 (Summer 1976). 20.

Today the Sun Still Sets on Atlantida. **STS**, 19.

Tosca. **SJS**, 52; **STS**, 47.

Il Trovatore. **SJS**, 58, 148.

La Traviata. **TDT**, vol. XXX, n. 5 (Fall 1994). 38, 42.

Tristan and Isolde. **JSS**, 41, 42, 44, 47, 50, 51, and between 54 & 55; **SDL**, 470; **SJS**, 66; **STS**, 23, 59, 82, 95; **TCI**, vol. 14, n. 1 (Jan/Feb 1980). 22; **TDT**, vol. XII, n. 2 (Summer 1976). 17, 18; **TDT**, vol. XXVIII, n. 5 (Fall 1992). 9, 16.

The Trojans. **STS**, 88; **TDT**, vol. XII, n. 2 (Summer 1976). 25.

Turandot. **STS**, 73.

Twelfth Night. **TDT**, vol. XXX, n. 5 (Fall 1994). 41.

I Vespri Siciliani. **TCI**, vol. 16, n. 9 (Nov/Dec 1982). 30.

Vivisection. **STS**, 119; **TDT**, vol. XXIV, n. 4 (Winter 1988). 19, 20.

Waiting for Godot. **SDW3**, 219; **SDW4**, illus. 258; **SJS**, 158; **STS**, 9; **TDT**, n. 23 (Dec 1970). front cover.

Die Walküre. **CGA**, 191; **JSS**, 65, 66, 82, 86, and between 54 & 55; **STS**, 85; **TDT**, vol. XII, n. 2 (Summer 1976). 29.

War and Peace. **TDT**, vol. XII, n. 2 (Summer 1976). 32.

Wastrals in Paradise. **SJS**, 133; **STS**, 50.

The Wedding. **SJS**, 45; **STS**, 28.

Wozzeck. **SDW4**, illus. 216-219; **SJS**, 169; **STS**, 79.

Yolanta. **TDT**, vol. XXX, n. 5 (Fall 1994). 38.

Yvone. **SJS**, 51.

Sykora, Peter.

Andre Chenier. **TDT** vol. XXXI, n. 2 (Spring 1995). 13, 14.

The Flying Dutchman. **TCI**, vol. 14, n. 1 (Jan/Feb 1980). 22.

Sylbert, Paul.

Oedipus Rex. **TCI**, vol. 15, n. 7 (Aug/Sep 1981). 31.

Street Scene. **TCI**, vol. 15, n. 7 (Aug/Sep 1981). 31.

Susannah. **TCI**, vol. 15, n. 7 (Aug/Sep 1981). 31.

Synek, Vladimir. *Simple Takes a Wife.* **SDW2**, 46.

Syrjala, Sointu.

Pins and Needles. **RBS**, 152, 153.

Stevedore. **MCN**, 118.

Syrjala, Sointu & Aline Bernstein. *The Children's Hour*. **MCN**, 120.
Syrkus, Szymon. *Boston*. **RSD**, illus. 262.
Szajna, Josef.
    Acropolis. **SDW3**, 97.
    Antigone. **SDW3**, 23.
    The Bathhouse. **SDW3**, 221.
    Dante. **SDW4**, illus. 13, 14; **TCI**, vol. 15, n. 4 (Apr 1981). 12.
    Death in a Pear Tree. **TCI**, vol. 15, n. 4 (Apr 1981). 15.
    Deserted Field. **SDW3**, 132, 133.
    Exit the Actor. **SDW2**, 170.
    Faust. **RSD**, illus. 482; **SDW4**, illus. 103-105.
    The Names of Powers. **SDW2**, 170.
    November Dictum. **SDB**, 184
    Regarding November. **RSD**, illus. 556.
    Smierc na Gruszy. **SDB**, 184
    They (Oni). **RSD**, illus. 553.
Szekely, Laszlo. *The Imaginary Invalid*. **SDW3**, 72.
Szinte, Gabor. *The Barrels*. **SDW3**, 156.

-T-

Tagg, Alan.
    The Entertainer. **SDW2**, 227.
    Way Upstream. **BTD**, 61.
Tagore, Rabindranath. *The Worship of Nati*. **SDW2**, 114.
Tahara, Eiji. *Richard III*. **SDW3**, 36.
Taivassalo, Reino. *The Last Temptations*. **SDW2**, 207.
Takada, Ichiro.
    Hamlet. **SDW3**, 47.
    Romeo and Juliet. **SDW3**, 38.
    Summer Play, White Comedy. **SDW3**, 80.
    The Servant of Two Masters. **SDW2**, 150.
Tanaka, Béatrice.
    M. Monsieur's Theatre (The Box Office). **SDW2**, 36.
    A Strange Escapade at the Basile Circus. **SDW3**, 160.
Tannenberg, Winkler. *The Magic Flute*. **DIT**, plate 89.
Tarassov, Alexandr. *Ten Days That Shook the World*. **SDW3**, 102.
Tatlin, Vladimir.
    Ivan Sussanin (or) The Life of the Tsar. **RSD**, illus. 165.
    Zanguesi. **AST**, 133; **RSD**, illus. 166, 167.
Täuber, Harry.
    Gas. **TCS2**, plate 161.
    When We Dead Awaken. **TCS2**, plates 134, 135.
Taylor, Leslie and Dale Jordan. *Sea Marks*. **TCI**, vol. 16, n. 7 (Aug/Sep 1982). 27.
Taylor, Michael. *Mountain Language*. **BTD**, 80.
Taylor, Robert U.
    The Beggar's Opera. **CSD**, 133; **TCI**, vol. 11, n. 1 (Jan/Feb 1977). 25.
    The Caucasian Chalk Circle. **TCI**, vol. 11, n. 1 (Jan/Feb 1977). 25.
    Coriolanus. **DPT**, 101.
    Enrico IV. **TDT**, vol. XVI, n. 1 (Spring 1980). 13.
    Happy End. **TCI**, vol. 11, n. 5 (Oct 1977). 14.

The Judas Applause. **DPT**, 90.
A Month in the Country. **TCI**, vol. 11, n. 1 (Jan/Feb 1977). 24.
Polly. **TCI**, vol. 11, n. 1 (Jan/Feb 1977). 24, 25.
Raisin. **CSD**, 105; **DPT**, 129.
The Seagull. **TCI**, vol. 11, n. 1 (Jan/Feb 1977). 24.
The Tempest. **DPT**, between 124 & 125.
Taymor, Julie. *The Haggadah.* **TCI**, vol. 16, n. 8 (Oct 1982). 25.
Tchekhonine, Serge. *Hamlet* (?). **RAG**, 65.
Tchelitchew, Pavel.
    Concerto. **FCS**, plate 210; **FCT**, plate 13.
    Ode. **RSD**, illus. 329.
    Ondine. **FCS**, plate 209, color plate 30; **RSD**, illus. 405; **SDO**, 240, plate 30; **TPH**,
       photo 365.
    Orpheus and Eurydice. **MOM**, 10.
Tchemodourov, Evgheni. *Takhir i Zoukhra.* **SDW2**, 194.
TenEyck, Karen. *The Illusion.* **TCI**, vol. 28, n. 3 (Mar 1994). 11.
Teodoroff. *Hamlet.* **TPH**, photo 396.
Ter-Arutunian, Rouben.
    All Over. **CSD**, 135; **TCI**, vol. 5, n. 5 (Oct 1971). 6.
    The Bassarids. **DPT**, 110.
    Coppélia. **DPT**, 109.
    The Devils of Louden. **TCI**, vol. 4, n. 5 (Oct 1970). 11.
    Four Saints in Three Acts. **TCI**, vol. 21, n. 5 (May 1987). 14.
    Goodtime Charley. **DPT**, 104.
    Hot Spot. **BWM**, 347.
    Light o' Love. **SDW4**, illus. 189, 190.
    Maria Golovin. **CSD**, 39; **SDW2**, 231.
    The Nutcracker. **DPT**, 294.
    Orpheus and Eurydice. **DPT**, 106; **DPT**, 107.
    Pelléas and Mélisande. **OPE**, 215, 220, 223, 226, 228; **SDB**, 69; **SDR**, 76; **TCI**, vol.
       5, n. 5 (Oct 1971). 11.
    Ricercare. **CSD**, 47.
    The Seven Deadly Sins. **SDB**, 24.
    Swan Lake. **SDB**, 68.
    The Taming of the Shrew. **SDB**, 165.
    Twelfth Night. **SDW2**, 240.
Terraine, Alfred, Conrad Tritschler, Philip Howden, & R.C. McCleery.
    The Boy. **MCD**, plate 113.
Terraine, Alfred, & E.H. Ryan.
    Betty. **MCD**, plate 106.
    The Marriage Market. **MCD**, plates 100, 101.
Terraine, Alfred, & Joseph Harker. *The Dollar Princess.* **MCD**, plate 82.
Terraine, Alfred, Joseph Harker & Phil Harker. *Madame Pompadour.* **MCD**, plate 125.
Terraine, Alfred, T.E. Ryan, Hawes Craven, & Joseph Hunter.
    The Girl from Utah. **MCD**, plate 96.
Teschner, Richard.
    Eisdom. **SCM**, 69.
    Die Winterkönigin. **SCM**, 70.
Thee, Christian. *Countess Dracula!* **TCI**, vol. 22, n. 5 (May 1988). 38.
Themerson, Francizka. *Ubu Roi.* **SDW3**, 220; **RSD**, illus. 459, 460.
Thiersch, Paul. *Kabale und Liebe.* **TCS2**, plates 276, 277.

Right You Are. **TCI**, vol. 1, n. 1 (Mar/Apr 1967). 23.
Seascape. **DPT**, Facing 28.
Sweet of You To Say So. **TCI**, vol. 1, n. 1 (Mar/Apr 1967). 22.
We Comrades Three. **TCI**, vol. 1, n. 1 (Mar/Apr 1967). 23.
The Wild Duck. **TCI**, vol. 1, n. 1 (Mar/Apr 1967). 22.
Tiné, Hal.
A Christmas Carol. **SDT**, 294.
The Gin Game. **SDT**, 282.
Jerry's Girls. **SDT**, 299 and between 152 & 153.
Tiramani, Jenny. *Steaming.* **BTD**, 77.
Tischler, Alexander.
King Lear. **NTO**, facing 324; **SDW2**, 197; **TPH**, photo 416.
Mystery Bouffe. **SDW2**, 198.
Richard III. **RSD**, illus. 219; **SDW2**, 197; **SOS**, 220; **TPH**, photo 407.
South of the 38th Parallel. **SDW2**, 198.
Tofan, Mihai. *The Calamity.* **SDW2**, 176.
Toffolutti, Ezio.
The Last Paradise. **SDW4**, illus. 297.
Der Seidene Schuh (The Silk Shoe). **TCI**, vol. 20, n. 4 (Apr 1986). 8.
Toffolutti, Ezio & Helmut Brade. *Margarete in Aix.* **SDW4**, illus. 319-323.
Tománek, A. *The Creation of the Sun.* **TDT**, vol. XVI, n. 1 (Spring 1980). 27.
Tomek, Milos. *The Insect Comedy.* **SDW2**, 46.
Tomlinson, Charles D. *The Tempest.* **TCI**, vol. 1, n. 4 (Sep/Oct 1967). 37.
Toms, Carl.
The Browning Version. **TCI**, vol. 15, n. 5 (May 1981). 13.
Caesar and Cleopatra. **TCI**, vol. 6, n. 1 (Jan/Feb 1972). 17.
Love's Labor Lost. **TCI**, vol. 6, n. 1 (Jan/Feb 1972). 17.
The Magistrate. **TCI**, vol. 6, n. 1 (Jan/Feb 1972). 16.
New Cranks. **SDW2**, 228.
Night and Day. **TCI**, vol. 14, n. 2 (Mar/Apr 1980). 6.
Norma. **TCI**, vol. 13, n. 3 (May/Jun 1979). 28.
On the Razzle. **BTD**, 78.
La Reja. **SDW2**, 228.
Reunion in Vienna. **TCI**, vol. 6, n. 1 (Jan/Feb 1972). 17.
The Rivals. **TCI**, vol. 6, n. 1 (Jan/Feb 1972). 15.
Rough Crossing. **BTD**, 78.
Sherlock Holmes. **TCI**, vol. 14, n. 1 (Jan/Feb 1980). 18; **TCI**, vol. 9, n. 1 (Jan/Feb 1975). 21.
Sleuth. **TCI**, vol. 6, n. 1 (Jan/Feb 1972). 14.
Vivat! Vivat Regina! **TCI**, vol. 6, n. 1 (Jan/Feb 1972). 12, 13.
Toren, Roni. *Tannhäuser.* **TCI**, vol. 29, n. 2 (Feb 1995). 8.
Toronczyk, Jerzy. *Sacrifice to the Wind.* **SDW2**, 171.
Tortora, Michael. *The Swan.* **TDT**, vol. XXX, n. 3 (Summer 1994). 12.
Tosa, Yoshi. *Rosencrantz and Guildenstern are Dead.* **SDW3**, 167.
Tosar, Beatriz & Aida Rodriguez. *To Die, Perchance to Dream.* **SDW2**, 242.
Tosi, Piero. *Uncle Vanya.* **SDW2**, 132.
Tosta, Antoni & Liliana Jankowska. *Caligula.* **SDW2**, 171.
Touchagues. *The Fraud.* **SDW1**, 107.
Touhy, Susan. *The Sorrows of Frederick.* **TCI**, vol. 14, n. 4 (Sep 1980). 37.
Tovaglieri, Enrico.
The Glad Death. **SDE**, 155.

Luisa Miller. **SDE**, 157.

St. Joan of the Stockyards. **SDE**, 156.

Träbing, Ilse, Klaus Weiffenbach, & Waltraut Mau.

The Song of the Lusitanian Bogey. **SDW3**, 136.

Trapp, S. Von. *Aïda*. **TAS**, 92, 93.

Traugott, Muller.

Hurrah, We Live! **RSD**, illus. 233-237.

Rasputin. **RSD**, illus. 239, 240.

Storm over Gothland. **RSD**, illus. 231.

Trautvetter, Paul. *The Italian Straw Hat*. **SDW2**, 238.

Travis, Warren. *Teddy*. **TCI**, vol. 14, n. 4 (Sep 1980). 27.

Tréhard, Jo. *The Disguised Prince*. **SDW3**, 74.

Tréhard, Jo & A. Chevalier.

A Chronicle of Hitler's Life and Death. **SDW3**, 163; **SDW4**, illus. 363.

Tribouilloy, Brigitte.

The Devotion of the Cross. **SDW3**, 65.

La Montour. **SDW3**, 67.

Trimble, David. *Sleuth*. **TCI**, vol. 22, n. 5 (May 1988). 37.

Tripp, Tony.

High Society. **TCI**, vol. 27, n. 3 (Mar 1993). 5, 10, 11.

Hotspur. **TCI**, vol. 28, n. 10 (Dec 1994). 16.

Tritschler, Conrad. *Princess Charming*. **MCD**, plate 143.

Tritschler, Conrad & R.C. McCleery. *The Dairymaids*. **MCD**, plate 57.

Tritschler, Conrad, Alfred Terraine, Philip Howden, & R.C. McCleery.

The Boy. **MCD**, plate 113.

Tritschler, Conrad, R.C. McCleery, & Walter Hann. *Oh! Oh!! Delphine!!!* **MCD**, plate 95.

Tritschler, Conrad, R.C. McCleery, Stafford Hall, & W. Holmes.

The Arcadians. **MCD**, plate 80.

Troike, Gero. *Leonce and Lena*. **TDT**, vol. XVI, n. 1 (Spring 1980). 16.

Tröster, Frantisek.

A Charmed Life. **TDT**, n. 42 (Fall 1975). 29.

The Cherry Orchard. **TDT**, vol. XXVII, n. 4 (Fall 1991). 46.

Don Juan. **SDW2**, 47.

Fidelio. **RSD**, illus. 275.

Fuente Ovejuna. **SOW**, plate 32; **TDT**, n. 42 (Fall 1975). 28.

The Inspector General. **TDT**, n. 42 (Fall 1975). 29.

Julius Caesar. **TDT**, n. 42 (Fall 1975). 28.

The Mischief of Being Clever. **SDW1**, 53.

Public Enemy. **TDT**, n. 42 (Fall 1975). 28.

Svätopluk. **RSD**, illus. 274; **TDT**, n. 42 (Fall 1975). 28.

Truscott, John. *Camelot*. **MCD**, plate 220.

Tsarouchis, John. *Uncle Vanya*. **SDW2**, 106.

Tschetter, Dean. *Breakfast with Les and Bess*. **TCI**, vol. 19, n. 5 (May 1985). 19.

Tsypin, George.

Ajax. **ASD2**, 173; **TCI**, vol. 20, n. 9 (Nov 1986). 20; **TCI**, vol. 24, n. 5 (May 1990).

41; **TCI**, vol. 25, n. 2 (Feb 1991). 35; **TDT**, vol. XXVII, n. 3 (Summer 1991). 12.

The Cherry Orchard. **TCI**, vol. 28, n. 4 (Apr 1994). 9.

Cymbeline. **ASD2**, 164; **TCI**, vol. 25, n. 2 (Feb 1991). 38.

Death in Venice. **ASD2**, between 108 & 109; **DDT**, 43; **TCI**, vol. 25, n. 2 (Feb 1991).

36; **TDT**, vol. XXVII, n. 3 (Summer 1991). 11.

The Death of Klinghoffer. **TCI**, vol. 25, n. 2 (Feb 1991). 34; **TDT**, vol. XXVII, n. 3 (Summer 1991). front cover, 10; **DDT**, 312d.

Don Giovanni. **ASD2**, 166, 167; **TCI**, vol. 25, n. 2 (Feb 1991). 37; **TDT**, vol. XXVII, n. 3 (Summer 1991). 15.

The Electrification of the Soviet Union. **DDT**, 168; **TDT**, vol. XXVII, n. 3 (Summer 1991). 13.

Henry IV, part 1. **TDT**, vol. XXVII, n. 3 (Summer 1991). 14.

Idiot's Delight. **ASD2**, 169; **DDT**, 159.

In the Summer House. **TCI**, vol. 27, n. 8 (Oct 1993). 6.

Landscape of the Body. **DDT**, 405.

Leon and Lena and Lenz. **ASD2**, 172; **DDT**, 440d; **TCI**, vol. 25, n. 2 (Feb 1991). 37.

McTeague: A Tale of San Francisco. **TCI**, vol. 26, n. 4 (Apr 1992). 11.

The Misanthrope. **ASD2**, 170, 171.

Oedipus Rex. **TDT** vol. XXXI, n. 2 (Spring 1995). 16.

Saint François d'Assise. **TCI**, vol. 26, n. 8 (Oct 1992). 9.

The Screens. **ASD2**, 159, 168; **DDT**, 24; **TCI**, vol. 24, n. 1 (Jan 1990). 15; **TCI**, vol. 24, n. 8 (Oct 1990). 42; **TCI**, vol. 25, n. 2 (Feb 1991). 39; **TDT**, vol. XXVII, n. 3 (Summer 1991). 11.

The Seagull (renamed *A Seagull*). **ASD2**, 163; **DDT**, 410.

Tannhäuser. **ASD2**, 161; **DDT**, 171; **TCI**, vol. 23, n. 2 (Feb 1989). 10; **TDT**, vol. XXVII, n. 3 (Summer 1991). 18.

Tumarkin, Igael. *Waiting for Godot.* **SDW3**, 121.

Turina, Drago.
Arden of Faversham. **SDW3**, 34.
The Croatian Faustus. **TCI**, vol. 18, n. 1 (Jan 1984). 11; **TDT**, vol. XX, n. 1 (Spring 1984). 7.
Macbeth. **SDW4**, illus. 47-52.
Philoctetes. **SDW4**, illus. 12.
Timon of Athens. **SDW4**, illus. 54-56.

Tvadze, D.M. *Macbeth.* **TDT**, n. 33 (May 1973). 15.

-U-

Uecker, Gunther.
Fidelio. **OPE**, 118, 119, 123, 126.
Lohengrin. **TCI**, vol. 14, n. 1 (Jan/Feb 1980). 23.

Ueno, Watoku. *Deshima.* **TCI**, vol. 27, n. 4 (Apr 1993). 9.

Ultz.
The Art of Success. **BTD**, 64.
Good. **TCI**, vol. 17, n. 7 (Aug/Sep 1983). 37.
A Night in Old Peking. **TCI**, vol. 17, n. 7 (Aug/Sep 1983). 38.
Our Friends of the North. **TCI**, vol. 17, n. 7 (Aug/Sep 1983). 39.
The Servant of Two Masters. **TCI**, vol. 17, n. 7 (Aug/Sep 1983). 38.
The Twin Rivals. **TCI**, vol. 17, n. 7 (Aug/Sep 1983). 38.

Ulyanov, Nikolai.
Carmen. **SDW2**, 192.
The Days of the Turbins. **SOW**, plate 71; **RST**, 214-217.
Schluck and Jau. **MOT**, between 48 & 49; **RSD**, illus. 24.

Underdown, William.
The Devotion of the Cross. **SDW3**, 65.
Measure for Measure. **SDW3**, 50.

Unitt, Edward G.
  Captain Jinks of the Horse Marines. **MCN**, 15.
  If I Were King. **MCN**, 17.
Unitt, Edward G. & Joseph Wickes.
  The Blue Bird. **MCN**, 35.
  A Good Little Devil. **MCN**, 41.
Unruh, Del & Ione. *Macbeth.* **TDT**, vol. XVII, n. 1 (Spring 1981). 11; **BSE1**, 34.
Upor, Tibor.
  Lysistrata. **SDW2**, 142.
  Macbeth. **SCM**, 75.
Urban, Joseph.
  Don Quixote. **DIT**, plate 120.
  Electra. **SCM**, 100.
  Faust. **MOM**, 9.
  The Garden of Paradise. **SDA**, 56; **SDB**, 51, 52.
  La Juive. **MOM**, 9.
  The Love of the Three Kings. **SDC**, plate 57.
  Monna Vanna. **TPH**, photo 450.
  Music in the Air. **BWM**, 171; **RBS**, 71; **WMC**, 63.
  Parsifal. **FCS**, plate 200; **SDC**, plate 47; **SDO**, 229; **SOW**, plate 57; **TPH**, photo 319.
  Pelléas and Mélisande. **TCS2**, plates 224, 225.
  Le Prophète. **TCS2**, plate 189.
  Show Boat. **BMF**, 32; **BWM**, 166, 167; **HPA**, 11; **SDA**, 244; **TMI**, 116; **WMC**, 61.
  The Three Musketeers. **MCN**, 90; **WMC**, 39.
  Twelfth Night. **TPH**, photo 470.
Utrillo, Maurice.
  Barabau. **SCM**, 47.
  Louise. **AST**, 109.

-V-

Vagnetti, Gianni.
  Aroldo. **SDE**, 160, 161.
  Il Maestro di Cappella. **SDE**, 157.
Vakalo, Georges.
  Caesar and Cleopatra. **SDW1**, 110.
  Richard III. **SDE**, 161.
  Thieves' Carnival. **SDW1**, 111.
Van Dalsum, Albert. *Twelfth Night.* **SDW1**, 136.
Van Eyck, Aldo. *Labyrinth.* **SDW3**, 216.
Van Hellem, Huib. *The Farce of the Harmless Murderer.* **SDW1**, 44.
Van Lint, Louis. *The Playboy of the Western World.* **SDW1**, 48.
Van Nerom, Jacques.
  Don Juan. **SDW3**, 70.
  Hamlet. **SDW2**, 32.
  The Morning Bride. **SDW2**, 32.
  The Spaniard of Brabant. **DMS**, plate 39.
Van Norden, Hans. *Don Pasquale.* **SDW1**, 138.
Vanarelli, Mario. *Proserpine and the Stranger.* **SDW2**, 26.
Vancura, Jan.
  The Flying Dutchman. **TDT**, vol. XXIX, n. 1 (Winter 1993). 23.

Der Freischütz. **TDT**, vol. XXIX, n. 1 (Winter 1993). 19.

Indians. **TDT**, vol. XXVII, n. 3 (Summer 1991). 26.

The Magic Flute. **TDT**, vol. XXIX, n. 1 (Winter 1993). 18, 22; **TDT**, vol. XXVII, n. 4 (Fall 1991). 46.

The Marriage of Figaro. **TDT**, vol. XXIX, n. 1 (Winter 1993). 18; **TDT**, vol. XXVII, n. 4 (Fall 1991). 6.

An Opera for Three Butts. **TDT**, vol. XX, n. 1 (Spring 1984). 8.

Rodelinda. **TDT**, vol. XXVII, n. 3 (Summer 1991). 27.

Vanek, Joe.

Ariane and Bluebeard. **TCI**, vol. 28, n. 1 (Jan 1994). 39.

Dancing at Lughnasa. **TCI**, vol. 25, n. 9 (Nov 1991). 12; **TCI**, vol. 28, n. 1 (Jan 1994). 39; **TDT**, vol. XXVII, n. 4 (Fall 1991). 36.

Desire Under the Elms. **BTD**, 51.

Don Pasquale. **TCI**, vol. 28, n. 1 (Jan 1994). 41.

The Duenna. **TCI**, vol. 28, n. 1 (Jan 1994). 40.

Peer Gynt. **TCI**, vol. 28, n. 1 (Jan 1994). 39.

Same Old Moon. **TCI**, vol. 28, n. 1 (Jan 1994). 39.

Wonderful Tennessee. **TCI**, vol. 28, n. 1 (Jan 1994). 38.

Vanek, Marian. *On the High Seas*. **SDW3**, 151.

Vanerelli, Mario.

The Calendar that Lost Seven Days. **SDW1**, 38.

The Furies. **SDW1**, 38.

The Garden of Ashes. **SDW1**, 35.

The Manure Cart. **SDW1**, 38.

Vardaunis, Edgars. *Rigonda*. **SDW2**, 199.

Varga, Joseph A. *Macbeth*. **BSE3**, 39.

Varga, Matyas. *The Tragedy of Man*. **SDW2**, 142.

Varona, José.

Attila. **DPT**, 18, 46; **TCI**, vol. 14, n. 5 (Oct 1980). 30.

Cinderella. **DDT**, 28.

Coppélia. **DDT**, 245; **TCI**, vol. 14, n. 5 (Oct 1980). 28.

Don Quixote. **DDT**, 337.

Giulio Cesare. **TCI**, vol. 14, n. 5 (Oct 1980). 31.

Lucrezia Borgia. **DPT**, between 124 & 125; **TCI**, vol. 14, n. 5 (Oct 1980). 33.

The Merry Widow. **DDT**, 281; **TCI**, vol. 14, n. 5 (Oct 1980). 30.

Rodelinda. **CSD**, 66; **TCI**, vol. 14, n. 5 (Oct 1980). 31.

The Sleeping Beauty. **DDT**, 152a; **DPT**, 4.

The Tales of Hoffmann. **OPE**, 204, 207, 209, 211, 212.

La Traviata. **DPT**, 117.

Vasara, Eero. *Daniel Hjort*. **SDW1**, 159.

Vaselesco, Valer. *The Saga of Soimaresti*. **SDW2**, 176.

Vassiliev, Alexandre.

St. Petersburg Dreams (Crime and Punishment). **SDW3**, 83.

The Wood Demon. **SDW2**, 199.

Vassiliou, Spyros. *Don Juan*. **SDW1**, 110.

Vedova, Emilio. *Intolleranza 1960*. **AST**, 243.

Venza, Jac. *The Turn of the Screw*. **TCI**, vol. 7, n. 1 (Jan/Feb 1973). 19.

Vera, Gerardo. *Azabache*. **TCI**, vol. 26, n. 9 (Nov 1992). 10.

Vercoe, Rosemary & Patrick Robertson.

Rigoletto. **BTD**, 100; **TCI**, vol. 19, n. 4 (Apr 1985). 20, 21.

The Turn of the Screw. **BTD**, 92; **SDL**, 80, 472, 473.

Vychodil, Ladislav.
    Atlantida. **TDT**, n. 38 (Oct 1974). front cover; **TDT**, vol. XV, n. 2 (Summer 1979). 13;
        TDT, n. 20 (Feb 1970). 20.
    Ave Eva. **TDT**, vol. XV, n. 2 (Summer 1979). 10.
    Balladyna. **TDT**, vol. XV, n. 2 (Summer 1979). 13.
    The Comedy of Errors. **TCI**, vol. 21, n. 8 (Oct 1987). 37.
    Crime and Punishment. **TCI**, vol. 21, n. 8 (Oct 1987). 36; **TDT**, vol. XXIII, n. 4
        (Winter 1988). 49.
    Dalibor. **TDT**, vol. XXIII, n. 4 (Winter 1988). 49.
    The Dance of Death. **TDT**, vol. XVI, n. 4 (Winter 1980). 23.
    Dido and Aeneas. **TDT**, n. 38 (Oct 1974). 25.
    Fuente Ovejuna. **TDT**, vol. XV, n. 2 (Summer 1979). 11.
    Galileo. **TDT**, vol. XV, n. 2 (Summer 1979). 11.
    Hamlet. **TDT**, vol. XXVI, n. 2 (Summer 1990). 36.
    Ivan the Terrible. **TDT**, vol. XV, n. 2 (Summer 1979). 10.
    Jenufa. **TCI**, vol. 21, n. 8 (Oct 1987). 38.
    Káta Kabanová. **TDT**, vol. XV, n. 2 (Summer 1979). 16.
    Lady Thief. **TDT**, vol. XV, n. 2 (Summer 1979). 15.
    Les Liaisons Dangereuses. **TDT**, vol. XXVII, n. 3 (Summer 1991). 26.
    Libuse. **TDT**, vol. XV, n. 2 (Summer 1979). 15.
    The Magic Flute. **TCI**, vol. 21, n. 8 (Oct 1987). 36.
    Marriage. **TDT**, vol. XV, n. 2 (Summer 1979). 15.
    Optimistic Tragedy. **TDT**, vol. XV, n. 2 (Summer 1979). 11.
    Platonov. **TDT**, vol. XXIII, n. 4 (Winter 1988). 28.
    The Play of Love and Death. **TDT**, vol. XV, n. 2 (Summer 1979). 15, 16.
    Romeo and Juliet. **TCI**, vol. 21, n. 8 (Oct 1987). 38.
    The Strange Case of Dr. Jekyll and Mr. Hyde. **TCI**, vol. 21, n. 2 (Feb 1987). 12; **TCI**,
        vol. 21, n. 8 (Oct 1987). 38.
    Svätopluk. **TDT**, vol. XV, n. 2 (Summer 1979). 16.
    Tartuffe. **TDT**, vol. XV, n. 2 (Summer 1979). 10.
    Thief-woman from London. **SDB**, 77.
    Tragedia Cloveka. **TDT**, n. 38 (Oct 1974). back cover.
    The Trial. **TDT**, vol. XV, n. 2 (Summer 1979). 16.
    Twelfth Night. **TDT**, vol. XV, n. 2 (Summer 1979). 14.
    A View From the Bridge. **TDT**, n. 38 (Oct 1974). 26; **TDT**, vol. XV, n. 2 (Summer
        1979). 12.
    The White Desease. **SDB**, 86; **TDT**, vol. XV, n. 2 (Summer 1979). 11.
    Who's Afraid of Virginia Woolf? **TDT**, vol. XXVI, n. 2 (Summer 1990). 35, 36.
    The Wolves. **RSD**, illus. 462.
    Zuzana Vojírová. **TDT**, vol. XV, n. 2 (Summer 1979). 12.
Vyzga, Bernard. *The Hairy Ape.* **BSE1**, 10.

-W-

Wade, John. *The Greeks.* **SDT**, 64.
Wagner, Robin.
    And the Wind Blows. **ASD1**, 157.
    Angels in America, Perestroika. **TCI**, vol. 28, n. 7 (Aug/Sep 1994). 44.
    Ballroom. **BWM**, 135; **TCI**, vol. 13, n. 2 (Mar/Apr 1979). 14; **TCI**, vol. 23, n. 8 (Oct
        1989). 46.
    The Barber of Seville. **ASD1**, 167; **TDT**, vol. XIX, n. 4 (Winter 1983). 10.

Chess. **ALW**, 197; **DDT**, 344; **MBM**, 75, 211; **TCI**, vol. 22, n. 8 (Oct 1988). 3, 70-73;
  TCI, vol. 22, n. 8 (Oct 1988). 74.
A Chorus Line. **BMF**, 74, 75; **BWM**, 34, 136; **TCI**, vol. 14, n. 1 (Jan/Feb 1980). 21;
  TCI, vol. 9, n. 6 (Nov/Dec 1975). 6, 11; **TDT**, vol. XIX, n. 4 (Winter 1983). 5.
City of Angels. **DDT**, 16, 17, 340, 348; **MBM**, 144-146, 149-151; **TCI**, vol. 24, n. 5
  (May 1990). 46; **TCI**, vol. 24, n. 7 (Aug/Sep 1990). 14.
The Condemned of Altoona. **TDT**, n. 5 (May 1966). 24.
Crazy For You. **TCI**, vol. 26, n. 4 (Apr 1992). 28, 29.
Dark of the Moon. **ASD1**, 159.
Dreamgirls. **ASD1**, 152; **DDT**, 343; **SCT**, 246; **TCI**, vol. 16, n. 5 (May 1982). 12, 13.
42nd Street. **ASD1**, 155 and between 70 & 71; **MBM**, 20, 21; **TCI**, vol. 14, n. 6 (Nov/
  Dec 1980). 28-30; **TDT**, vol. XIX, n. 4 (Winter 1983). 7; **WMC**, II.
The Great White Hope. **TCI**, vol. 4, n. 3 (May/Jun 1970). 32.
Hair. **ASD1**, 161; **WMC**, 349.
Inner City. **TCI**, vol. 7, n. 6 (Nov/Dec 1973). 8.
Jerome Robbin's Broadway. **DDT**, 152d, 347; **MBM**, 32, 33; **TCI**, vol. 23, n. 7 (Aug/
  Sep 1989). 57-59.
Jesus Christ Superstar. **ALW**, 46-49; **DPT**, 388, 389, 394; **TCI**, vol. 5, n. 6 (Nov/Dec
  1971). 9; **TCI**, vol. 6, n. 3 (May/Jun 1972). 10, 11; **TCI**, vol. 7, n. 6 (Nov/Dec
  1973). 9; **TCI**, vol. 8, n. 1 (Jan/Feb 1974). 18.
Kicks. **ASD1**, 160.
Lenny. **ASD1**, 163; **DPT**, 390, 391; **DSL**, figures 1.1(a), 2.7(e); **SDB**, 195; **TCI**, vol. 5,
  n. 6 (Nov/Dec 1971). 7.
Macbeth. **TCI**, vol. 5, n. 6 (Nov/Dec 1971). 13.
Mack and Mabel. **TCI**, vol. 8, n. 6 (Nov/Dec 1974). 6.
Mary C. Brown and the Hollywood Sign. **DPT**, 393; **TCI**, vol. 7, n. 6 (Nov/Dec 1973).
  8.
Merlin. **TDT**, vol. XIX, n. 4 (Winter 1983). 8, 9.
On the Twentieth Century. **ASD1**, 164, 165; **BWM**, 72-81; **DSL**, figure 2.7(b); **HPR**,
  255; **TCI**, vol. 12, n. 4 (May/Jun 1978). 12, 13; **TCI**, vol. 14, n. 1 (Jan/Feb 1980).
  18; **TCI**, vol. 18, n. 8 (Oct 1984). 15.
Promises, Promises. **BWM**, 312; **TCI**, vol. 3, n. 3 (May/Jun 1969). cover, 7-9; **WMC**,
  352.
Seesaw. **BWM**, 137; **DPT**, 124; **TCI**, vol. 7, n. 4 (Sep 1973). 25.
Song and Dance. **MBM**, 73.
Swing. **TCI**, vol. 18, n. 4 (Apr 1984). 54.
Teddy and Alice. **DDT**, 345.
The Trojans. **ASD1**, 156.
Wagner, Wieland.
Aïda. **SDW3**, 182.
Götterdämmerung. **OPE**, 181, 192, 197, 199; **TCI**, vol. 3, n. 4 (Sep 1969). 29, 33.
Lohengrin. **SDW2**, 73.
Die Meistersinger von Nürnberg. **OPE**, 166, 167, 172-174, 176-178; **SDW2**, 73.
Parsifal. **RSD**, illus. 550; **SDB**, 39; **SDW1**, 81.
Das Rheingold. **JSS**, 18; **TCI**, vol. 14, n. 1 (Jan/Feb 1980). 22; **TCI**, vol. 3, n. 4 (Sep
  1969). 33.
Siegfried. **RSD**, illus. 548.
Tannhäuser. **RSD**, illus. 547; **SDW1**, 81; **SDW3**, 179; **TDT**, n. 29 (May 1972). 12.
Tristan and Isolde. **JSS**, 19; **RSD**, illus. 552; **TCI**, vol. 3, n. 4 (Sep 1969). 30.
Die Walküre. **RSD**, illus. 549; **TCI**, vol. 3, n. 4 (Sep 1969). 33; **TDT**, n. 29 (May
  1972). 17; **TPH**, photo 316.

Wagner, Wolfgang.
  Götterdämmerung. **SDW4**, illus. 138, 139.
  Parsifal. **TDT**, n. 29 (May 1972). 7.
  Das Rheingold. **SDW4**, illus. 131, 135, 136; **TDT**, n. 29 (May 1972). 14.
  Der Ring des Nibelungen. **SDW4**, illus. 132-134.
  Siegfried. **JSS**, 20; **TDT**, n. 29 (May 1972). 10.
  Die Walküre. **RSD**, illus. 551; **SDW4**, illus. 137.
Wahkévitch, Georges.
  L'Aventure. **SDE**, 168.
  The Carmelites. **SDW2**, 102.
  Hamlet. **TOP**, 25.
  Le Jeune Homme et la Mort. **SDE**, 164.
  The Little Hut. **SDW1**, 107.
  Mad Joan. **SDW1**, 108.
  Le Rayon des Jouets. **SDE**, 167.
  South. **SDB**, 48; **SDW1**, 108.
Wajda, Andrej.
  November Night. **TCI**, vol. 15, n. 4 (Apr 1981). 12.
  The Possessed. **SDW4**, illus. 145.
Walentin, Arne.
  Lost in the Stars. **SDW2**, 154.
  Midsummer Dream in the Workhouse. **DOT**, 241; **SDW1**, 155.
  The Tempest. **SDW2**, 154.
Walker, David & Henry Bardon.
  La Bohème. **TCI**, vol. 13, n. 3 (May/Jun 1979). 20.
  Così fan tutte. **CGA**, 178.
Wallace, Bill. *Sunday in the Park With George.* **TCI**, vol. 21, n. 9 (Nov 1987). 48.
Wallbaum, Walter. *The Dog's Will.* **SDW3**, 139.
Walmsley, Andy. *Buddy.* **TCI**, vol. 24, n. 8 (Oct 1990). 34, 35.
Walser, Karl.
  Alpenkönig und Menschenfeind. **AST**, 30.
  The Awakening of Spring. **MRH**, facing 77.
  Caesar and Cleopatra. **TPH**, photo 331.
  The Call of Life. **TPH**, photo 293.
  Leonce and Lena. **AST**, 30.
  A Midsummer Night's Dream. **AST**, 29.
  Romeo and Juliet. **FCS**, plate 188, color plate 20; **MRH**, facing 81-83; **SDO**, 214,
    plate 20.
  So ist das Leben. **AST**, 31.
Walsh, Thomas A. *Children of a Lesser God.* **TCI**, vol. 14, n. 4 (Sep 1980). 45.
Walsh, Thomas A. & Roberto Morales.
  Zoot Suit. **TCI**, vol. 13, n. 1 (Jan/Feb 1979). 6; **TCI**, vol. 14, n. 4 (Sep 1980). 45.
Walter, Paul. *Die Räuber.* **RSD**, illus. 621.
Walton, Tony.
  Anything Goes. **DDT**, 176, 177, 440d; **MBM**, 14, 15; **TCI**, vol. 22, n. 7 (Aug/Sep
    1988). 3.
  The Apple Tree. **BWM**, 296.
  Chicago. **BWM**, 121; **DDT**, 285; **TCI**, vol. 28, n. 3 (Mar 1994). 33; **TCI**, vol. 9, n. 5
    (Oct 1975). 8.
  A Christmas Carol. **TCI**, vol. 29, n. 1 (Jan 1995). 66.
  Conversations With My Father. **DDT**, 14.

A Day in Hollywood/A Night in the Ukraine. **MBM**, 99; **TCI**, vol. 14, n. 5 (Oct 1980).
    18, 19; **TCI**, vol. 24, n. 8 (Oct 1990). 53.
Death and the Maiden. **DDT**, 331.
Four Baboons Adoring the Sun. **DDT**, 2, 440a.
The Front Page. **TCI**, vol. 21, n. 3 (Mar 1987). 16, 17, 20.
A Funny Thing Happened on the Way to the Forum. **BMF**, 71; **DDT**, 46; **HPA**, 81;
    HPR, 77; **SON**, 61, 64; **WMC**, 287.
Golden Boy. **BWM**, 302.
Grand Hotel. **DDT**, 44; **MBM**, 13, 108, 113, 123; **SDD**, between 210 & 211; **TCI**, vol.
    24, n. 1 (Jan 1990). 42, 44; **TCI**, vol. 25, n. 3 (Mar 1991). 14.
Guys and Dolls. **DDT**, 24c; **TCI**, vol. 26, n. 7 (Aug/Sep 1992). 5, 40-43.
The House of Blue Leaves. **BSE5**, 2; **TCI**, vol. 21, n. 3 (Mar 1987). 20.
Hurlyburly. **DDT**, 166.
I'm Not Rappaport. **DDT**, 148.
Laughter on the 23rd Floor. **TCI**, vol. 28, n. 2 (Feb 1994). 7.
Lend Me a Tenor. **SDL**, 61.
Macbeth. **TCI**, vol. 22, n. 7 (Aug/Sep 1988). 112.
Pippin. **BWM**, 315; **CSD**, 139; **DDT**, 55; **DPT**, 65; **TCI**, vol. 11, n. 3 (May/Jun 1977).
    9; **TCI**, vol. 14, n. 1 (Jan/Feb 1980). 18; **TCI**, vol. 28, n. 3 (Mar 1994). 33; **TCI**,
    vol. 7, n. 4 (Sep 1973). 25.
The Real Thing. **DDT**, 373; **TCI**, vol. 18, n. 5 (May 1984). 20.
She Loves Me. **TCI**, vol. 27, n. 7 (Aug/Sep 1993). 70.
Shelter. **DDT**, 58.
Six Degrees of Separation. **TCI**, vol. 24, n. 8 (Oct 1990). 22.
Sophisticated Ladies. **DDT**, 316, 397; **MBM**, 188, 189.
Valmouth. **BMF**, 102; **DDT**, 106, 107, 394; **MCD**, plate 211.
Waiting for Godot. **TCI**, vol. 24, n. 8 (Oct 1990). 38.
The Will Rogers Follies. **DDT**, VIII, 24c; **MBM**, 153, 156, 157; **TCI**, vol. 25, n. 6
    (Aug/Sep 1991). 45-47.
Woman of the Year. **MBM**, 161.
Wang, Ru Jun. *Life is a Dream.* **TDT**, vol. XXVIII, n. 2 (Spring 1992). 15 of insert.
Warburton, Jeffrey L. *The Rimers of Eldritch.* **SDT**, 290.
Ward, Anthony.
Alice in Wonderland. **BTD**, 161.
Artists and Admirers. **TCI**, vol. 27, n. 4 (Apr 1993). 44.
Assassins. **TCI**, vol. 27, n. 4 (Apr 1993). 42.
Medea. **TCI**, vol. 27, n. 4 (Apr 1993). 44.
A Midsummer Night's Dream. **TCI**, vol. 29, n. 2 (Feb 1995). 32.
Napoli Milionaria. **TCI**, vol. 27, n. 4 (Apr 1993). 44.
Oliver! **TCI**, vol. 29, n. 4 (Apr 1995). 38, 39.
The Rehearsal. **TCI**, vol. 27, n. 4 (Apr 1993). 43.
The Tempest. **BTD**, 50.
Troilus and Cressida. **TCI**, vol. 27, n. 4 (Apr 1993). 45.
The Winter's Tale. **TCI**, vol. 27, n. 4 (Apr 1993). 44; **TCI**, vol. 29, n. 2 (Feb 1995). 33.
Ward, Randy. *Museum.* **TCI**, vol. 21, n. 3 (Mar 1987). 25.
Wareing, John.
Aïda. **SDT**, 297.
Butterflies Are Free. **SDT**, 292.
Merlin. **SDT**, 283.
Le Roman de Fauvel. **SDT**, 284.
Romeo and Juliet. **SDT**, 285.

The Merchant of Venice. **DIT**, plate 113.

Wijnberg, Nicolaas.

    The Comedy of Errors. **SDW2**, 146.

    Het Moortje. **SDW2**, 146.

    L'Heure Espagnole. **SDW1**, 140.

    The Masked Ball. **SDW1**, 140.

    A Midsummer Night's Dream. **SDW3**, 42.

Wilcox, Richard. *The Flowering Peach.* **SDW2**, 240.

Wildermann, Hans. *Parsifal.* **TCS2**, plate 187.

Wiley, William. *Ubu Roi.* **ASC**, 24.

Wilke, Ralph A., Jr. *The Homecoming.* **BSE4**, 77.

Wilkinson, Norman.

    The Faithful Shepherdess. **DIT**, plate 18.

    A Midsummer Night's Dream. **SCM**, 21; **SDC**, plate 80; **SDG**, 160; **TCS2**, plates 140, 141.

    Twelfth Night. **SDC**, plate 60; **TPH**, photo 352.

Williams, Christopher. *The First Distiller.* **SCM**, 35.

Williams, F. Elaine. *Mother Courage and Her Children.* **BSE3**, 42.

Williams, Jerry.

    The Andersonville Trial. **TCI**, vol. 7, n. 3 (May/Jun 1973). 9.

    Camino Real. **TCI**, vol. 7, n. 3 (May/Jun 1973). 9.

    Child's Play. **TCI**, vol. 7, n. 3 (May/Jun 1973). 9.

    Fiddler on the Roof. **TCI**, vol. 20, n. 5 (May 1986). 28.

    A Flea in Her Ear. **TCI**, vol. 7, n. 3 (May/Jun 1973). 9, 10.

    Hadrian VII. **TCI**, vol. 7, n. 3 (May/Jun 1973). 9.

    Tartuffe. **TCI**, vol. 7, n. 3 (May/Jun 1973). 7.

Wilson, Robert.

    The Black Rider. **TCI**, vol. 28, n. 2 (Feb 1994). 8; **TCI**, vol. 25, n. 5 (May 1991). 20.

    the CIVIL warS. **RWT**, 97, 110-112, 115-118; **TCI**, vol. 19, n. 7 (Aug/Sep 1985). 45; **TCI**, vol. 19, n. 8 (Oct 1985). 24, 25; **TCI**, vol. 20, n. 3 (Mar 1986). 27; **TCI**, vol. 24, n. 8 (Oct 1990). 41; **TDT**, vol. XXVII, n. 2 (Spring 1991). 14.

    Deafman Glance. **RWT**, 16-19; **TCI**, vol. 19, n. 8 (Oct 1985). 23.

    Death Destruction and Detroit. **RWT**, 65, 66, 69-73, 151; **TDT**, vol. XVI, n. 2 (Summer 1980). 11.

    DIA LOG/Curious. **RWT**, 62, 63.

    DIA LOG/Network. **RWT**, 61.

    $ Value of Man. **RWT**, 42, 43.

    Edison. **RWT**, 74-76, 78, 79.

    The Forest. **TCI**, vol. 23, n. 1 (Jan 1989). 46, 47.

    The Golden Windows. **RWT**, 90, 91; **TDT**, vol. XXII, n. 1 (Spring 1986). front cover, 6, 12, 13.

    Great Day in the Morning. **RWT**, 92, 93.

    I Was Sitting On My Patio This Guy Appeared I Thought I Was Hallucinating. **RWT**, 55-58, 138, 149, 150; **TCI**, vol. 19, n. 8 (Oct 1985). 22.

    The King of Spain. **RWT**, 11.

    A Letter for Queen Victoria. **RWT**, 33-36, 38-41.

    The Life and Times of Joseph Stalin. **RWT**, 28-31.

    The Life and Times of Sigmund Freud. **RWT**, 12-14.

    The Man in the Raincoat. **RWT**, 86.

    Medea. **RWT**, 89.

    Overture. **RWT**, 24-27.

Wulp, John.
>   *Bosoms and Neglect.* **DDT**, 383.
>   *The Crucifer of Blood.* **DDT**, 162, 220; **TCI**, vol. 13, n. 1 (Jan/Feb 1979). 20-23; **TCI**,
>   vol. 22, n. 5 (May 1988). 42; **TCI**, vol. 27, n. 8 (Oct 1993). 35.
>   *Endecott and the Red Cross.* **TCI**, vol. 13, n. 1 (Jan/Feb 1979). 25.
>   *Landscape of the Body.* **TCI**, vol. 13, n. 1 (Jan/Feb 1979). 24.
>   *The Master Builder.* **TCI**, vol. 13, n. 1 (Jan/Feb 1979). 25.
>   *My Kinsman, Major Molyneaux.* **TCI**, vol. 13, n. 1 (Jan/Feb 1979). 25.
Wurtzel, Stuart.
>   *Glory! Hallelujah!* **TCI**, vol. 14, n. 1 (Jan/Feb 1980). 39; **TCI**, vol. 6, n. 5 (Oct 1972).
>   16.
>   *Hamlet.* **TCI**, vol. 6, n. 5 (Oct 1972). 14.
>   *Tartuffe.* **TSY**, 5.
>   *Tiny Alice.* **TCI**, vol. 6, n. 5 (Oct 1972). 12; **TCI**, vol. 14, n. 1 (Jan/Feb 1980). 38.
>   *The Way of the World.* **TCI**, vol. 7, n. 5 (Oct 1973). 25.
Wurzel, Stuart & Louis Brown. *A Flea in Her Ear.* **TCI**, vol. 6, n. 5 (Oct 1972). 17.
Wyspianski, Stanislaw.
>   *Akropolis.* **RSD**, illus. 629, 630.
>   *The Legend.* **RSD**, illus. 96.

-X-

Xenakis, Iannis. *Polytope de Cluny.* **RSD**, illus. 600.
Xinglin, Liu. *Return.* **TDT** vol. XXXI, n. 2 (Spring 1995). 11.

-Y-

Yabara, Yoshio. *ATLAS: an opera in three parts.* **TCI**, vol. 25, n. 3 (Mar 1991). 13.
Yamada, Shinkichi. *Carmen.* **SDW1**, 151.
Yamazaki, Junnosuke. *The Fishing Port.* **SDW1**, 150.
Yanik, Don. *Jungalbook.* **TDT**, vol. XXVIII, n. 2 (Spring 1992). 9 of insert.
Yasuda, Yukihiko. *The Tale of Genji.* **SDW1**, 151.
Yeargan, Michael.
>   *Ah, Wilderness.* **ASD2**, between 108 & 109.
>   *An Attempt at Flying.* **ASD2**, 177; **DSL**, figure 2.6(b); **TCI**, vol. 16, n. 5 (May 1982).
>   27.
>   *The Changeling.* **ASD2**, 187.
>   *Cyrano de Bergerac.* **TCI**, vol. 27, n. 4 (Apr 1993). 12.
>   *Eugene Onegin.* **ASD2**, 190, 191; **TCI**, vol. 16, n. 5 (May 1982). 22.
>   *The Frogs.* **ASD2**, 178.
>   *The Ghost Sonata.* **TCI**, vol. 16, n. 5 (May 1982). 26.
>   *Happy Days.* **TCI**, vol. 16, n. 5 (May 1982). 25; **TCI**, vol. 17, n. 4 (Apr 1983). 17.
>   *Julius Caesar.* **TCI**, vol. 25, n. 9 (Nov 1991). 43.
>   *The King Stag.* **TCI**, vol. 22, n. 3 (Mar 1988). 51; **TCI**, vol. 24, n. 8 (Oct 1990). 42.
>   *A Lesson from Aloes.* **TCI**, vol. 14, n. 5 (Oct 1980). 79.
>   *Macbeth.* **TCI**, vol. 22, n. 5 (May 1988). 50.
>   *The Magic Flute.* **TCI**, vol. 16, n. 5 (May 1982). 26.
>   *Martin Guerre.* **TCI**, vol. 27, n. 4 (Apr 1993). 8.
>   *The Matchmaker.* **TCI**, vol. 21, n. 8 (Oct 1987). 25.
>   *The Merry Widow.* **ASD2**, 189.

A Midsummer Night's Dream. **ASD2**, 174; **SDL**, 367; **TCI**, vol. 23, n. 7 (Aug/Sep
    1989). 14; **TCI**, vol. 25, n. 9 (Nov 1991). 40, 41.

Morocco. **ASD2**, 18; **SDL**, 72.

Regina. **ASD2**, 181; **TCI**, vol. 22, n. 7 (Aug/Sep 1988). 29.

The Rise and Fall of the City of Mahagonny. **TCI**, vol. 13, n. 3 (May/Jun 1979). 46.

Rodelinda. **TCI**, vol. 16, n. 5 (May 1982). 26.

The Seagull. **TCI**, vol. 16, n. 5 (May 1982). 24; **TCI**, vol. 17, n. 4 (Apr 1983). 16.

Sganarelle. **TCI**, vol. 12, n. 5 (Sep 1978). 26-29; **TCI**, vol. 16, n. 5 (May 1982). 25.

Six Characters in Search of an Author. **ASD2**, 188; **BSE4**, 102.

The Stick Wife. **ASD2**, 180.

The Tempest. **TCI**, vol. 19, n. 10 (Dec 1985). 8; **TCI**, vol. 20, n. 4 (Apr 1986). 23.

Timon of Athens. **TCI**, vol. 14, n. 5 (Oct 1980). 80.

Tobacco Road. **ASD2**, 183.

Il Trovatore. **ASD2**, 189.

The Umbrellas of Cherbourg. **TCI**, vol. 16, n. 5 (May 1982). 25; **TDT**, vol. XV, n. 4
    (Winter 1979). 25, 26.

Uncle Vanya. **TCI**, vol. 24, n. 1 (Jan 1990). 48.

The Wild Duck. **TCI**, vol. 16, n. 5 (May 1982). 27.

Yodice, Robert.

Ariadne auf Naxos. **TCI**, vol. 10, n. 3 (May/Jun 1976). 11.

Don Pasquale. **TCI**, vol. 10, n. 3 (May/Jun 1976). 10.

Macbeth. **CSD**, 145.

Rich and Famous. **TCI**, vol. 19, n. 7 (Aug/Sep 1985). 40.

La Traviata. **TCI**, vol. 10, n. 3 (May/Jun 1976). 11.

Yoshida, Kenkishi.

The River Mouth. **SDW1**, 151.

Romeo and Juliet. **SDW1**, 150.

Yoshimura, Akita. *Catch 22.* **TCI**, vol. 10, n. 4 (Sep 1976). 6.

You Beijing Wen Hua Gong Zuozhe, Gong Ren, Nong Min, Xue Sheng Jiti Bian.

The Red Orient. **SDW3**, 174.

Youens, Frederic. *The Measures Taken.* **SDL**, 80, 366.

Youmans, James.

Soda Jerk at HOME. **TCI**, vol. 25, n. 1 (Jan 1991). 46.

The Swan. **TCI**, vol. 28, n. 2 (Feb 1994). 8.

Young, John. *Babes in Toyland.* **WMC**, 13.

Young, John A. & Ernest Albert. *George Washington, Jr.* **MCN**, 29.

Younovitch, Sophia.

The Dead End. **SDW2**, 201.

Sadko. **SDW2**, 202.

Yunker, Don. *The Clown of God.* **TCI**, vol. 17, n. 7 (Aug/Sep 1983). 16.

Yutkevich, Sergei. *The Mysteries of the Canary Islands.* **RST**, 100.

Yutkevich, Sergei & Sergei Eisenstein. *Macbeth.* **RST**, 112.

-Z-

Zachwatowicz, Krystyna.

Forefather's Eve. **SDW4**, illus. 125.

The Historic Role of Mr. Pigwa. **SDW2**, 172.

Zahorski, Lech. *The Little Donkey Porfirion.* **SDW2**, 172.

Zak, Leon. *La Patisserie Enchantée.* **RSC**, 59.

Zaki, Samir. *Man and the Shadow.* **SDW3**, 140.

Zalon, Paul. *Guys and Dolls*. **TCI**, vol. 20, n. 5 (May 1986). 17, 19.
Zboril, M. *The Seagull*. **TDT**, vol. XII, n. 3 (Fall 1976). 43.
Zborilová, Jana. *Ivanov*. **TDT**, vol. XXVI, n. 4 (Fall 1990). 27.
Zdravkovic, Margo. *The Rivals*. **TCI**, vol. 23, n. 9 (Nov 1989). 54.
Zeffirelli, Franco.
    Antony and Cleopatra. **TDT**, n. 7 (Dec 1966). 26, 27.
    La Bohème. **MOM**, 16-27; **SIO**, 138.
    Cavalleria Rusticana. **MOM**, 40-55; **TCI**, vol. 10, n. 5 (Oct 1976). 16.
    La Cecchina o la Buona Figliola. **SIO**, 137.
    Don Giovanni. **OPE**, 76, 83, 84, 87, 88, 90; **SDW4**, illus. 113, 114.
    Don Pasquale. **SIO**, 138.
    L'Elisir D'Amore. **SIO**, 134, 135.
    Falstaff. **MOM**, 69-79.
    The Italian Girl in Algiers. **SIO**, 134.
    Otello. **MOM**, 154-163.
    I Pagliacci. **MOM**, 40-55.
    Rigoletto. **SDW2**, 133.
    The Three Sisters. **SDE**, 168, 169; **SDW1**, 132.
    Troilus and Cressida. **DOT**, 245; **SDW1**, 132.
    The Turk in Italy. **SIO**, 136; **TCI**, vol. 13, n. 3 (May/Jun 1979). 16.
Zeffirelli, Franco & Peter J. Hall. *Romeo and Juliet*. **SDW2**, 133; **SOS**, 262.
Zelenka, Frantisek.
    The Barber of Seville. **TDT**, n. 42 (Fall 1975). 26.
    Bassoon and Flute. **TDT**, n. 42 (Fall 1975). 26.
    Faust. **TDT**, n. 42 (Fall 1975). 26.
    The Firebrand. **TDT**, n. 42 (Fall 1975). 26.
    The Giant. **TDT** vol. XXXI, n. 2 (Spring 1995). 41.
    The Third Sound of the Bells. **TDT** vol. XXXI, n. 2 (Spring 1995). 42.
    The Three Musketeers. **TDT**, n. 42 (Fall 1975). 26.
Zelinske, Stephen. *Così fan Tutti*. **TCI**, vol. 12, n. 6 (Oct 1978). 37.
Zentis, Robert. *On the Air*. **TCI**, vol. 14, n. 4 (Sep 1980). 43.
Zhenguang, Wang. *The Emperor Jones*. **TDT**, vol. XXV, n. 1 (Spring 1989). 9-12, 18.
Zhongguo Wujutuan Jiti Gaibian. *The Red Women's Detachment*. **SDW3**, 174.
Zídek, Ivo.
    Don Juan. **TDT**, vol. XXVIII, n. 2 (Spring 1992). 37.
    Largo Desolato. **TDT**, vol. XXVIII, n. 2 (Spring 1992). 37, 41.
    Marketa Lazarová. **TDT**, vol. XXVIII, n. 2 (Spring 1992). 37.
    The Neapolitan Desease. **TDT**, vol. XXVIII, n. 2 (Spring 1992). 36.
    Period Dances. **TDT**, vol. XXVIII, n. 2 (Spring 1992). 36.
    The Talisman. **TDT**, vol. XXVIII, n. 2 (Spring 1992). 36.
    The Tartar's Fair. **TDT**, vol. XXVIII, n. 2 (Spring 1992). 36.
    Uncle Vanya. **TDT**, vol. XXVIII, n. 2 (Spring 1992). 36.
Zimelli, Umberto. *L'Osteria della Pergola*. **SCM**, 77.
Zimmerer, Frank J. *The Gods of the Mountain*. **MCN**, 45.
Zimmerman, Reinhart.
    The Beggar's Opera. **SDB**, 75.
    Boom-Boom Land. **TCI**, vol. 15, n. 1 (Jan 1981). 37.
    Madame Butterfly. **TCI**, vol. 15, n. 1 (Jan 1981). 37; **TDT**, vol. XVI, n. 1 (Spring 1980). 17.
    Return of Ulysses. **SDB**, 140.
    The Rise and Fall of the City of Mahagonny. **TCI**, vol. 15, n. 1 (Jan 1981). 36.

About the Compiler

W. PATRICK ATKINSON is Professor of Theatre at the University of Missouri-Columbia. He has been a scenic and lighting designer for over twenty-five years and has shown his work in regional, national, and international exhibitions. He has served as managing director of the Missouri Summer Repertory Theatre and as its resident scenic designer for the last seventeen years.

Southern Virginia University

Theatrical design in the twentieth century :
PN 2091 .S8 T47 1996   255744

Von Canor

Southern Virginia University